Asian American
Studies

Edited by
Jean Yu-wen Shen Wu
and Min Song

RUTGERS UNIVERSITY PRESS

NEW BRUNSWICK, NEW JERSEY,

AND LONDON

sian
American
Studies:
A Reader

Library of Congress Cataloging-in-Publication Data

Asian American studies : a reader / edited by Jean Wu and Min Song.
    p.   cm.
    Includes bibliographical references and index.
    ISBN 0-8135-2725-2 (cloth : alk. paper). — ISBN 0-8135-2726-0
(paper : alk. paper)
    1. Asian Americans—History.   2. Asian Americans—Social
conditions.   3. American literature—Asian American authors.
I. Wu, Jean, 1948–   2. II. Song, Min, 1970–
E184.06A8417   2000   99-24625
973′.0495—dc21   CIP

British Cataloging-in-Publication data for this book is available from the British Library

Manufactured in the United States of America

Contents

Acknowledgments

We thank our students, whose commitment to learning as much as they can about Asian America spurred us to envision and embark on this project, and kept us from abandoning it in the moments where our energies flagged. We thank Elizabeth Ammons, whose guidance at the very start of this project was instrumental, and Eric Reyes, whose comments on the introduction were essential. We also thank the following people who gave us support, advice, aid, and (much needed) criticism: Robert Chang, the East of California Faculty Group, Rhonda Frederick, Juliana Koo, Sunyoung Lee, Russell Leong, Lynn Lu, Thea Marston, Yuko Matsukawa, Susette Min, Mae Ngai, Jane Singh, Rajini Srikanth, Dana Takagi, Emma Jinhua Teng, Linda Võ, Leti Volpp, Scott Wong, and May Wu. Finally, Leslie Mitchner at Rutgers University Press was the best editor we could have asked for. The blame for all errors, misjudgments, or gaps in this book belongs, of course, entirely to the editors.

Introduction

We began this project almost three years ago. It was late in the evening, we were sitting in a cramped office around a small conference table, the room smelled of ink, and our mistakes overflowed the blue recycling bin. We were in the process of organizing stacks of photocopies, still warm to the touch, into neat packets. The packets would be distributed, the next day, to Jean Wu's Introduction to Asian American Studies class. As we collated, we began to talk about how nice it would be if this task had already been done for us—by someone else.

"Wouldn't it be nice," Jean asked, "if these materials were collected into one book? We use many of the same articles every year, and the topics remain consistent." We decided to test this assertion by listing a number of articles that might fit into such a book. We blocked these articles into broad categories and, in the ensuing months, began calling the whole thing a table of contents. By this time, the list had grown to seven pages, single spaced. We cut the list in half, and then in half again. We threw away the list and started all over. We cut, added, and threw away in a tango of list making. We argued about what topics were important. We debated how these articles should be taught in classrooms.

What do curious readers need to learn about Asian American Studies in order to sustain their interest? What would students find most illuminating? What did we mean by Asian American Studies? Clearly, the project we had stumbled upon that evening was not as simple as it first seemed. What is Asian American Studies? We can begin to address this question with a number of observations.

Asian American Studies as an interdisciplinary field of academic study is a recent invention, probably originating in the late 1960s in California. It concerns itself with the lives of people in the United States, and perhaps other parts of the Americas, who trace their ancestry to Asia. Often, this means people of Chinese, Japanese, and Korean ancestry. People of Filipino, Vietnamese, and Indian ancestry are also included here, though their inclusion often seems an afterthought and raises concerns about proper representation. Other Asian countries that can claim to have given birth to an Asian American ethnic group include Bangladesh, Burma (also known as Myanmar), Cambodia (also known as Kampuchea), East Timor, Indonesia, Laos, Malaysia, Pakistan, Singapore, Sri Lanka (once known as Ceylon), Taiwan (formerly Formosa), Thailand, and Tibet. Asian American Studies of native Hawai'ians and Pacific Islanders go by the name of Asian Pacific American Studies, as at New York University. If there is debate about who should be included under the category of Asian America, and in what ways, almost everyone seems to agree that people of West Asian, Arab, and North African descent should be excluded— though, if we consider this for a moment, there is no particularly good reason why this should be so.

The first general claim we can make about Asian American Studies, then, is that it has difficulty defining what its object of study is. Even if we try to split up the notion of Asian American into smaller subgroups, this problem persists. For example, as Vijay Prashad helpfully enumerates, the regionally defined category of South Asian American is shot through with contradictory differences: "first, by religion, which is often but not always synonymous with nation (India/Hindu, Pakistan/Muslim, etc.); second, by language, which is often but not always synonymous with region and class (Tamil/Tamil Nadu, Hindi/Gangetic Plains, Gujarati/Gujarat, English/elites, etc.); and third, by class (professionals, taxi drivers, storekeepers, etc.)."[1] Why stop here? For the sake of completion, we could also add that this category is divided by sexual orientation (homosexual/heterosexual, gay/lesbian) and sex (male/female, gendered/transgendered). There may be other ways of counting differences that we have excluded here.

The question remains, however: do these differences invalidate a field of study whose object is admittedly imaginary and constructed? Another way to put this question is: does Asian American Studies foreground, in its difficulty defining an object of study, the imaginary and constructed nature of most, if not all, identities?[2] One way to think about this problem is to compare Asian American Studies with another field of inquiry, namely literary criticism, that has had similar difficulties defining an object of study. Literary criticism begins with the assumption that there is something called literature that can be treated critically. But what are the criteria for differentiating between literature and mere works of fiction, poetry, drama, philosophy, and so forth? Why should, for instance, Toni Morrison's *Beloved* and Maxine Hong Kingston's *Woman Warrior* be considered literature, if indeed such a consensus exists, and Stephen King's *The Shining* and Michael Crighton's *Rising Sun* not? As Terry Eagleton writes,

> Any belief that the study of literature is the study of a stable, well-definable entity, as entomology is the study of insects, can be abandoned as a chimera.

Some kinds of fiction are literature and some are not; some literature is fictional and some is not; some literature is verbally self-regarding, while some highly wrought rhetoric is not literature. Literature, in the sense of a set of works of assured and unalterable value, distinguished by certain shared inherent properties, does not exist.[3]

This particular way of thinking about literature, which has become increasingly popular in English departments during the past two decades, has led to many fierce debates among literary critics as to what this uncertainty might mean to their discipline. This problem has not, however, led to the demise of literary criticism, or even to the demise of literature itself; rather, it has led to innovative scholarship that has had to begin with the assumption that their object of study is irrevocably constructed and imaginary. In many ways, the acknowledgment of this problem has enlivened literary criticism and made its existence more relevant to the rest of the world. The same, we suggest, can and, in all likelihood, will happen to Asian American Studies.

The second observation we wish to make about Asian American Studies is that it began to be institutionalized because of community activism, as Glenn Omatsu's piece in this volume persuasively recounts. Many academics who consider themselves engaged in Asian American Studies continue to trace their work's origin to this history and point proudly to the ways in which their work fits within this tradition. The introduction to the inaugural issue of the *Journal of Asian American Studies,* the official publication of the Association for Asian American Studies, indicates in both content and tone the truth of this claim. The journal's founding, we are told by coeditors John Liu and Gary Okihiro, "is a testament to the power of the original vision of Asian American studies and represents a fruition of decades of struggle for a more inclusive and equitable present and future."[4]

The sense of mission the coeditors evoke here is not uncommon to other Asian American Studies scholars. Yen Le Espiritu, for instance, writes in her introduction to *Asian American Women and Men,* "This book . . . explores how racist and gendered labor conditions and immigration laws have affected relations between Asian American men and women. The first goal is to document how the historical and contemporary oppression of Asian Americans has (re)structured the balance of power between Asian American men and women and shaped their struggles to create and maintain social institutions and systems of meaning."[5] Similarly, Lisa Lowe begins her influential *Immigrant Acts: Essays on Asian American Cultural Politics* this way:

Understanding Asian immigration to the United States is fundamental to understanding the racialized foundations of both the emergence of the United States as a nation and the development of American capitalism. This is far from claiming that Asians are the only group to have been racialized in the founding of the United States but rather to suggest that the history of the nation's attempt to resolve the contradictions between its economic and political imperatives through laws that exclude Asians from citizenship—from 1790 until the 1940s—contributes to our general understanding of race as a contradictory site of struggle for cultural, economic, as well as political membership in the United States.[6]

Both Espiritu and Lowe (whose works are excerpted in this volume) are typical of self-identified Asian American Studies scholars in their centralization of race in thinking about Americans of Asian ancestry. This emphasis on race compels them to foreground, from the beginning of their studies, how Asian Americans in the United States throughout its national history were racialized as foreigners no matter how much they might have assimilated into mainstream white culture, how they were subsequently subordinated by laws designed to equate citizenship with whiteness, and how their images were insultingly distorted by newspapers and fiction to rationalize such mistreatment. This emphasis also compels Espiritu and Lowe to think about how this tradition of nativism—or the separation of Asians (along with other racial minorities) from whites as foreigners from citizens—informs the current treatment of Asian Americans as explicitly a racial minority in a country obsessed with racial classification and hierarchy. In their works, they envision Asian American Studies as a scholarly enterprise with a manifest political objective: the imagination of Asian Americans as a racial minority, crucial to the understanding of the United States as a nation, whose past subordination leaves them at once vulnerable and resistant to state-sponsored coercion.

Their argument is strong. Anti-Asian American violence, for instance, has been on the rise in tandem with the rise of violence against other racial minorities and marginalized groups. California in particular has been the site of numerous high-profile hate crimes directed at such groups during the first half of the 1990s, and Asian Americans have been targets in a large proportion of these crimes. As Angelo Ancheta points out, during a ten-month period between 1995 and 1996, the following occurred:

- A Chinese American high school student was physically attacked in the parking lot of a fast-food restaurant in the Northern California suburb of Novato by several other students, who shouted "Go back to China where you belong" and "chink, gook, chinaman."
- While walking her dog in a San Francisco park, a Japanese American woman was assaulted by a white woman who grabbed her by the arm, threw dog feces at her, and cried out "Go home! Go home!" and "Hiroshima!"
- A Chinese American man was stabbed repeatedly in the parking lot of a Northern California supermarket by a white male assailant who later admitted to the police that he wanted to kill a "chinaman" because they "got all the good jobs."
- A Vietnamese man was killed while he was skating on a high school tennis court in the South California city of Tustin.[7]

The last incident has been especially eye-opening. Not only was the murder of Thien Minh Ly extremely violent, but the attitude of the killer was horrifyingly indifferent. It was as if, because Ly was Vietnamese American and not white, he ceased to be a person. "I stabbed him in the side about seven or eight times," the killer wrote to a prison pen pal in ungrammatical English, he rolled over a little so I stabbed his back out eighteen to nineteen times then he layed flat and I slit one side of his through on his jugular vain. Oh, the sounds the guy was making were like Uhhh.

Then Dominic said "do it again" and I said "he's already Dead" Dominic Said "Stab him in the heart" So I stabbed him about twenty or twenty-one times in the heart.[8]

This violence against Asian Americans in California should be understood in the context of heightened anti-immigrant sentiments that have targeted all minority groups. Or, to put this another way, Asian Americans are vulnerable to the same kind of violence directed at other racial minorities and at gays and lesbians. Just before the ten-month rash of violence Ancheta identifies, voters in California considered and approved Proposition 187, which dramatically curtailed the rights of undocumented workers. Fliers were stuffed into mailboxes during the days leading up to the vote that read: "WE NEED A REAL BORDER. FIRST WE GOT THE SPICS, THEN THE GOOKS, AND AT LAST WE GET THE NIGGERS. DEPORTATION. THEY'RE ALL GOING HOME."[9] The reference to "a real border" suggests that the exclusion of Asians in the past, and the continued equation of Asian with foreigner (as expressed in racist messages like this one), is one pivotal way in which the United States has defined, and persists in defining, itself as a nation with a clear inside and out. In classic Freudian terms, self-proclaimed defenders of the nation project onto those they determine to be outsiders characteristics they, as consummate insiders, wish to disavow, and it is through such disavowals that the nation as a whole maintains its integrity as a stable self. Ruth Hsu explains: "Who 'Americans' think they are has always been measured in terms of who they supposedly are not. Or, phrased slightly differently, the dominant culture defines itself by excluding others, but in the same sense that the center can only know itself by saying what it is not, by objectifying the other as those dark, inner impulses that are actually within the center itself and that it fears the most."[10] Just like these other Others, then, Asian Americans are a racial minority, whose visibility as such leaves them vulnerable to violence, subordination, and, not least of all, verbal insult. Such vulnerability, in turn, can be seen as connected to the nation-state and how it seeks to define its sense of boundaried selfhood along racial lines.

This national process of disavowal and repudiation was made concrete for us during the writing of this introduction. At Tufts University, where Jean Wu makes her institutional home, a young Asian American student was referred to at a fraternity party as a "Chinese Ho Chi Minh bitch." Two weeks later, at Boston College, where Min Song makes his institutional home, student leaders of AHANA (acronym for African American, Hispanic, Asian American, Native American) received email from an anonymous source that read, "Hey Monkeys and Apes, You all need to go back to where you came from. BC is for white men, not any chinks, spics, niggers or fags." Notice how similar this last message is to the fliers stuffed into Californian mailboxes. Clearly, the rhetorical move of defining an inside as white that must be defended against outsiders, who are racially made visible and simultaneously lumped together by a series of obnoxious epithets, is not peculiar to Boston College or to California. This rhetoric is grounded in a widely accessible national discourse. This discourse defines insiders, of any kind of U.S. national space, as white and outsiders as racial Others, who in turn threaten the purity of such spaces by virtue of the fact that they are not white.[11]

Asian Americans, regardless of class position or educational attainment, are contained by the binary logic of this kind of nationalism. This logic plays itself out not only in the form of hate crimes and verbal assaults but also at the economic and institutional level. Though Asian American families have average median incomes that are higher than white, black, Latino, and Native American families, they are also concentrated in three states—California, Hawai'i, and New York—where incomes are generally higher than in the rest of the country and where the cost of living is equally high. In addition, Asian American families as a whole have more wage earners than their white counterparts and thus their aggregate median incomes reflect the sum total of lesser-paid employees than their white counterparts.[12] These figures are misleading in another way. When we account for ethnicity in tracking socioeconomic status, we find that while Japanese, Chinese, Filipinos, and Asian Indians have high levels of educational attainment and income, other groups like Southeast Asians and Pacific Islanders suffer rates of poverty, income, and educational attainment far below the national average. While there are many Asian American professionals, there are also many Asian Americans working in the service sector performing the lowest-paid labor in the national economy. Professionals tend to be disproportionately made up of Japanese, Chinese, and Asian Indians, and service-sector workers tend to be made up of Filipinos, Koreans, and Chinese Pacific Islanders; Southeast Asians tend to work at even lower-paying jobs.[13] Even when we look at just one ethnic group, however, we find similarly large economic disparities. Even among Asian Indians, for example, who seem to occupy high rungs on the economic and educational ladder, a large subgroup exists with low levels of educational attainment and income; Asian Indian taxi drivers in New York City come immediately to mind here.

In addition, professional Asian Americans are not guaranteed positions and incomes commensurate with their educational attainment. A federal commission reported in March 1995 that "despite their high qualifications, the bulk of Asians [in the United States] found that they were being held in technocratic rather than managerial positions."[14] This split between education and professional advancement holds true, of course, for universities as well as corporations, where the majority of tenured faculty and administrators—the academic equivalent of managerial positions—are overwhelmingly white and where Asian American representation continues to lag behind other racial groups. The lack of Asian Americans at these levels becomes even more pronounced when we consider the large number of Asian Americans in the student population.

Though universities and colleges do a good job of keeping track of student admittance by race, they do less well at keeping an eye on what happens to Asian Americans once they get into higher education. Do they have special needs that go unmet and therefore leave them at a disadvantage in relationship to other students? What kind of employment do they find when they graduate? How well do they fare in the job market, and in career advancement, in comparison to their white peers? These questions, of course, do not do justice to the many Asian Americans who are not lucky enough to go to college, and who face even greater obstacles than economically disadvantaged members of other minorities because of their relative obscurity in national debates about Affirmative Action and economic polarization.

These questions also do not do justice to the experiences of racial, and other identity-based, subordination. This subordination is often characterized by a daily low-intensity assault of discriminatory speech and acts, made even more maddening by their lack of definition. Our minority students, especially our Asian American students, often talk about the frustration of everyday life, punctuated as it is by slights, insults, and coded remarks—some of which may not be racial in content, and others inescapably so. These frustrations build over time but have no outlets. When incidents are pointed out to other students or to faculty, they are waved away as insubstantial, insupportable, or lacking in malicious intent. Students begin to question their own judgment, blame themselves for being overly sensitive, or, conversely, decide that everything is racial and begin to brood with suspicion. Hence, when an event like the email incident at Boston College, which is undeniably racial in content, does take place, students can act with great vigor to call attention to it and to demand an appropriate response. Often, these demands are not for a mere remedy of the single event, but for greater change at the institutional level. Boston College students followed this pattern. On the morning of the email incident, students—many of whom were Asian American—passed out bright orange fliers in the university's main thoroughfares and made announcements in class-rooms about a meeting to be held that evening. The demands that came out of this meeting were concrete and eloquent: they wanted the culprit exposed and punished, they wanted counseling for victims of all discriminatory acts that take place at the university, they wanted greater attention for gays and lesbians who were also targeted by the email, and most of all they wanted a uniform administrative policy that would guide official school responses to similar discriminatory acts in the future.

These demands convey a deeper meaning than their surface might suggest. First, students want the administration to expose, expel, and criminally prosecute the person responsible for sending the email as a sign of the administration's commit-ment to creating a diverse environment. The more severe the punishment, the more serious the administration's commitment. The actual severity of the punish-ment called for by the students thus suggests how much they perceive the adminis-tration's commitment to institutional change as lacking seriousness. Second, the demand for counseling suggests that the students do not feel their needs are being acknowledged by the administration. In other words, students want recognition that an oppressive discriminatory environment exists. The *Boston Globe* quotes Kohtaro Takeuchi, a student spokesperson for the Asian Caucus: "The president of the university said we're not a perfect community. . . . But I also believe we're not even a community, because we can't accept our differences."[15] These words speak suggestively about a deepening divide between administrative and student perceptions. Third, the students' call for greater recognition of gay and lesbian rights demonstrates a laudable sensitivity to the vulnerability of all of its marginal-ized groups. This may be the fruit of coalition-building between AHANA, women, and gay and lesbian student groups. Such coalition-building has been a centerpiece of many minority discourses (including, and especially, Asian American Studies).[16] Finally, the demand for a uniform administrative policy suggests the lack of a coherent administrative response to the concerns expressed in the first three demands. Out of a specific incident, then, the students have fashioned a wide-ranging and coherent list of demands that call attention to how their needs are not being addressed by the current policies of the university.

Student anger at the administration, however, should also be tempered by awareness that this incident does not take place in a vacuum. Administrators' hands are tied by existing laws that make racist acts difficult to prosecute and by a general climate of racial reaction. This climate, for example, enables the media to caricature the maturity of the student response to a threatening racist incident as political correctness. Harvey Silverglate, a Boston attorney, and Alan Kors, a University of Pennsylvania historian, write for the *Boston Globe*, "Hate speech or other such offensive communication that does not directly threaten the recipient with violence or other illegal action would be, in the world outside the college gates, indisputably protected by the First Amendment from official censorship or punishment, though not from censure or moral witness. Why and how, one must ask, should college administrators assume that they have the power to punish such bigoted speech on campus?"[17] This editorial does not mention the fact that the email was delivered illegally through another student's account, and therefore violates school rules governing the use of its computer networks. In doing this, the perpetrator may have violated state laws as well. The editorial also fails to discuss the demands made by the students that say nothing about prohibiting speech but constitute, rather, a particularly powerful example of students exercising their right to "censure" and bear "moral witness."

In raising the fear of restricted free speech with their inflated rhetoric, Silverglate and Kors insult student intelligence, demonize efforts to combat racism, and obfuscate the kind of racial inequalities that are the preconditions for racially motivated verbal assaults. By performing such a neoconservative task, they remind us why an Asian American Studies attentive to racial difference is relevant to the current political climate. Asian American student leaders, who were at the forefront of student responses to the email incident at Boston College, could not have existed if they did not also understand that their interests are intertwined with the well-being of other racial minorities and marginalized groups. Because of their visibility, vulnerability, and lack of enfranchisement within the main socioeconomic controls of the nation-state, Asian Americans have been and continue to be a racial minority alongside other racial minorities. The active recognition of this fact, in turn, underscores how struggles for alternative social formations and new forms of political activism have an immediate impact upon Asian American experiences.

Asian American Studies, insofar as it remains true to its origins, has an essential role to play in fostering such recognition, which is often blurred by mainstream and self-sustained portrayals of Asian Americans as members of a model minority. Because of the complexity of its subject matter and its political objectives, Asian American Studies is interdisciplinary in nature. Historians track the ways in which Asian immigrants and settlers were treated by dominant powers in the United States. Sociologists tally the ways in which this history continues to shape the structure of Asian American experiences. Anthropologists examine the cultural innovations of various Asian American communities that help make such societal structures inhabitable. Artists and writers imagine new possibilities for cultural expression. Art historians and film and literary critics explore the connection between cultural expression and cultural constraints. Psychologists study the mental processes of identity formation. Political scientists test the possibilities for direct political engagement and/or greater political enfranchisement. And legal scholars consider the ways in which these various disciplinary interests impinge upon the process of law making.

This is, of course, only a partial list of the myriad ways we can think about the activities Asian American Studies scholars engage in. But by enumerating their activities in this way, we get a sense of how individual disciplinary approaches can work together to create a common form of study. The complementary nature of these activities suggests the need for continued interdisciplinary dialogue, research, and pedagogy.

This reader is divided into two parts. The first provides a historical survey of Asian America leading up to the 1960s. This was a period of intense and for the most part state-sponsored discrimination against Asians living in the United States. The second part is organized around contemporary issues, though all the sections in this part, if only implicitly, focus on the category of race and its interpenetration by gender, class, sexual orientation, nationalism, and ethnicity. So, the first part of the reader is organized along a temporal axis while the second is organized along topical concerns. This two-principled approach endows the wide range of concerns Asian American Studies scholars profess with historical depth.

The organization of the reader also reflects a desire to retrain our eyes on groups that have existed at the margins of Asian American Studies. As Stephen Sumida asks, "What happens to the category, 'Asian American,' when we include in the field the points of origin and routes of peoples of Asian diasporas who have made their way to the United States via the Atlantic, the Caribbean, the mid-Pacific, and Latin America?"[18] We also wish to add: What happens to this category when we centralize peoples from places like South Asia, Southeast Asia, the Philippines, and the Pacific Islands? What happens when we centralize people of differing sexual orientations? This reader offers no definitive answers to these questions. Rather, it collects primary and secondary materials that help foreground these issues. For this reason, we believe these materials should be used often in introductory Asian American Studies courses that pay special attention to these concerns. Because the reader is a first attempt at such a synthesis, the intellectual terrain it represents is often difficult to navigate. Those who are already somewhat familiar with this terrain probably make the best guides for the rest of us.

Section one, "Early Immigration Patterns," offers a historiographic overview of Asian American community development, starting from an era when the United States was a newly "discovered" land mass yet to be colonized and reshaped as a modern nation-state. This section contains essays by some of the best-known and established historians in the field: Gary Okihiro writes about the time before Asians began immigrating to the United States in large numbers; Ronald Takaki writes about life on the sugar plantations of Hawai'i; and Jane Singh writes about the

Gadar Party, militant anti-British Indians living in the early twentieth-century United States.

Section two, "Treatment," looks at the kinds of subordination Asian Americans had to endure during the period in which Sui Sin Far, Yamamoto, and Santos were at their most creative. Sucheng Chan paints, with broad strokes, a history of nativism that directed its anger against Chinese, and later Japanese and Filipino, immigrant workers. Scott Wong writes about a particular example from this history, as it affected the Boston Chinatown community. The historical document "The Curtis Munson Report," a report commissioned by the United States government at the start of the Second World War, cleared Japanese Americans of any potential wrongdoing and was, as a result, suppressed. Executive Order 9066 is the presidential edict that officially forced west coast Japanese Americans to wartime internment camps.

Section three, "Representations," contains examples of later nineteenth-and early twentieth-century Asian Americans writing creatively about their experiences of a time defined by intense hostility and extreme isolation. Emma Teng supplies a historical and cultural context for thinking about the significance of early Asian American literary interventions. Sui Sin Far, widely considered the first Chinese American to write fiction in English, provides a fable of interracial romance. Hisaye Yamamoto and Bienvenido Santos provide further examples of writings that speak powerfully from a specific time and place in Asian American history.

Section four, "Watershed Years," rounds out the first part of the reader by examining how the long years of federally endorsed discrimination against Asian Americans gave way to an opening up of national borders. Yen Le Espiritu writes about the profound changes affecting Asian Americans during the deep freeze of the Eisenhower-to-Kennedy era. The *U.S. News and World Report* article "Success Story of One Minority Group in U.S.," first published in 1966, signals the virtual start of model minority stereotypes about Asian Americans. These stereotypes were propagated as a way to embarrass other minorities, especially blacks and Latinos. Glenn Omatsu presents a very different picture of Asian Americans during this period—as a politically activated racial minority struggling to gain a sense of self-hood in a persistently hostile society.

Opening Part 2 of the reader, section five, "Racial Formations and the Question of Class," explores the racialization of Asian Americans in the context of capitalism and its voracious need for cheap labor. Michael Omi and Howard Winant argue that race is constitutive of deep social and economic structures rather than secondary to, or separate from, them. Masao Miyoshi complicates this argument by contextualizing the notion of nationhood in a global history of imperialism and increased capital mobility. Peter Kwong calls attention to how these concerns play themselves out concretely in the way racial differences lead American labor unions away from protecting the rights of their Chinese immigrant laborers.

Section six, "Panethnicity," asks how the different groups represented in these essays fit into the binary definitions of race now extant in the United States. Nazli Kibria writes a very personal account of her own racialization, as a South Asian American Bangladeshi woman, in her classrooms. Paul Spickard looks at how Asian American Studies fails to examine the slippery racial classification attending representations of multiracial peoples. Elaine Kim points at the ideological fault lines surrounding representations of the Korean American community after the Los Angeles riots. Linda Võ provides a sociological snapshot of various Vietnamese American communities as they have developed in the wake of another major national emergency, the Vietnam War.

Section seven, "Gender," explores one of the most contentious debates within Asian American studies. King-Kok Cheung asks: in trying to combat the historical feminization of Asian American men, do we inadvertently uphold patriarchal restrictions on Asian American women? Shamita Das Dasgupta and Sayantani Das-Gupta write about this question as it relates to a South Asian American feminist discourse. From a different vantage point, Richard Fung looks at the "desexualization" of Asian male bodies in American culture and its relationship to gay male sexuality. Dana Takagi writes about how an attention to lesbian sexuality might further enrich these debates.

Section eight, "Critical Race Theory," addresses an exciting new development in Asian American studies—its entrance into legal scholarship. Robert Chang introduces this topic with his essay on the possibilities and difficulties of an Asian American jurisprudence. Neil Gotanda further marks the trail by critiquing a judge's decision, on the eve of the Rodney King verdict, to free Soon Ju Da after her brutal killing of Latasha Harlins. Leti Volpp provocatively explores the use of cultural defenses in cases involving immigrants and domestic violence.

Section nine, "Theorizing Asian American Literature," contains essays about the limitations and possibilities of defining a group of writings with a racial category like Asian American. Lisa Lowe argues that what makes literature Asian American is an inescapable "heterogeneity, hybridity, and multiplicity." E. San Juan Jr. interrogates the failure of Asian American Studies to recognize the historical uniqueness of Filipinos writing in the United States. Susan Koshy also explores the weakness inherent in the idea of an Asian American literature, but insists that the idea remains essential to Asian American Studies.

The last section, "Representations and Identities," gives space to experimental, exploratory, and contemporary creative voices that are in the process of redefining what it means to write Asian American literature. Ginu Kamani writes about the unexpected efflorescence of sensuality in a culturally restrictive context. Minh Duc Nguyen eloquently expresses the pain of migration and loss. R. Zamora Linmark explores the importance of having sexual possibilities in an oppressive social setting. Sigrid Nuñez tries to bring to life an "inscrutable" father who made a very long voyage—lasting two generations—to the United States from China, via Panama.

Notes

1. Vijay Prashad, "Crafting Solidarities," in *A Part, Yet Apart,* ed. Lavina Shankar and Rajini Srikanth (Philadelphia: Temple University Press), 115–116.
2. These questions are addressed by a number of writers in the reader, including Michael Omi and Howard Winant, Lisa Lowe, E. San Juan Jr., and Susan Koshy, as well as by the writers in the section titled "Panethnicity." Koshy, in particular, is adamant about the need for more theoretical work on these issues.

3. Terry Eagleton, *Literary Theory: An Introduction* (Minneapolis: University of Minnesota Press, 1983), 11.

4. John Liu and Gary Okihiro, "Introduction," *Journal of Asian American Studies* 1, no. 1 (February 1998): 3.

5. Yen Le Espiritu, *Asian American Women and Men* (Thousand Oaks, Calif.: Sage, 1997), 1.

6. Lisa Lowe, *Immigrant Acts*: *On Asian American Cultural Politics* (Durham, N.C.: Duke University Press, 1996), ix.

7. Angelo Ancheta, *Race, Rights, and the Asian American Experience* (New Brunswick, N.J.: Rutgers University Press, 1998), 8–9.

8. Quoted in Mike Davis, *The Ecology of Fear: Los Angeles and the Imagination of Fear* (New York: Metropolitan, 1998), 408.

9. Ancheta, *Race, Rights, and the Asian American Experience,* 9.

10. Ruth Hsu, "'Will the Model Minority Please Identify Itself?' American Ethnic Identity and Its Discontents," *Diaspora* 5, no. 1 (1996): 39.

11. This discourse also implies that being homosexual is coeval with being nonwhite. This happened in the Boston College email as well, where "fags" are explicitly defined as incompatible with white masculinity.

12. Ronald Takaki, *Strangers from a Different Shore*: *A History of Asian America* (New York: Penguin, 1989), 475.

13. Ancheta, *Race, Rights, and the Asian American Experience,* 132–133.

14. Vijay Prashad, "Crafting Solidarities," 115.

15. Jordana Hart and Thomas Farragher, "Hate-filled e-mail message sparks anger, action at BC," *Boston Globe,* 3 October 1998, A1, A18.

16. Perhaps one of the most intellectually promising developments in Asian American Studies is the realignment of its interests, by some of its scholars, with those of Queer Studies. The best example of this intellectual maneuver is *Q&A: Queer in Asian America,* ed. David Eng and Alice Hom (Philadelphia: Temple University Press, 1998).

17. Harvey Silverglate and Alan Kors, "At area colleges, a disturbing trend on hate speech," *Boston Globe,* 12 October 1998, A17.

18. Stephen Sumida, "East of California: Points of Origin in Asian American Studies," *Journal of Asian American Studies* 1, no. 1 (February 1998): 92.

Legal Chronology of Asian American History

1790   First U.S. nationality act grants naturalized citizenship to "free white persons." (Amended in 1870 to include "persons of African nativity and descent.")

1848   Treaty of Guadalupe Hildago ends Mexican-American War and leads to U.S. possession of California. Gold discovered at Sutter's Mill. Chinese begin to arrive in large numbers (and, circa 1869–1870, Chinese recruited in large numbers to complete the transcontinental railroad).

1850   California becomes a state.

1854   California Supreme Court ruling on *People v Hall* denies Chinese the right to testify in courts, along with "Negroes, mulattos, and Indians."

1878   *In re Ah Yup* court ruling determines Chinese ineligible for citizenship because they are not "white" (first in a series of similar test cases).

1880   Section 69 of California's Civil Code refuses marriage licenses to whites and "Mongolians, Negroes, mulattoes and persons of mixed blood."

1882   Chinese Exclusion Act suspends immigration of Chinese laborers for ten
            years and also declares Chinese ineligible for citizenship.

1886   U.S. Supreme Court rules in *Yick Wo v Hopkins* that the Fourteenth
            Amendment applies to all persons, not just citizens.

1892   Geary Act suspends immigration of Chinese laborers for another ten
            years (renewed in 1902 and made permanent in 1904).

1898   Spanish-American War ends and, after end of the U.S.-Philippine War
            that immediately followed, Philippines becomes U.S. Territory. United
            States also annexes Hawai'i. Supreme Court ruling on *United States v Wong
            Kim Ark* affirms citizenship by nativity, thus protecting the citizenship of
            native-born people of Asian ancestry.

1904   Punjabi Sikhs first enter British Columbia, but are soon forced out. They
            move to Seattle and then California, many settling in Imperial Valley to
            become farmers.

1905   Japanese and Korean Exclusion League established.

1907   Gentleman's Agreement establishes diplomatic protocol, whereby Japan
            agrees to stop issuing passports to laborers.

1908   Japanese and Korean Exclusion League changes name to Asiatic Exclusion
            League, partly in response to increased presence of Punjabi Sikhs along
            the West Coast. President Theodore Roosevelt signs Executive Order
            eliminating entry from U.S. territories to U.S. proper, effectively ending
            immigration from Hawai'i to mainland.

1913   California's Alien Land Law, first in a series, prohibits sale of agricultural
            lands to "aliens ineligible for citizenship" (ownership of residential and
            commercial real estate is allowable under treaty). Because Japanese immi-
            grants are not allowed to naturalize and thus become citizens, this means
            they cannot own land under their own names.

1917   Immigration Act establishes an "Asiatic Barred Zone" (including India).

1920   United States and Japan agree to stop emigration of picture brides.

1922   Supreme Court ruling on *Ozawa v United States* denies Japanese immigrant
            man's request for naturalization because, according to Chief Justice Suth-
            erland, Japanese are not of "that class of persons whom the fathers knew
            as white and denied it to all who could not be so classified."

1923   Supreme Court ruling on *United States v Thind* denies Indian immigrant man's request for naturalization because whiteness is defined by "common" understanding and not, as Thind's lawyers argued, "scientific" understanding. Court ruling in *Thind* applies to all nations of the Asiatic Barred Zone. Supreme Court also upholds legality of alien land laws in *Terrace v Thompson*.

1924   Reed Johnson Immigration Act excludes all immigration of aliens ineligible for citizenship, or virtually all Asian immigrants except from the Philippines (who are not official aliens), thus achieving statutory Japanese exclusion. This is the most restrictive immigration law in U.S. history.

1934   Tydings-McDuffe Act establishes process for creation of a Philippine commonwealth and sets Philippine annual immigration quota at fifty, the lowest in the world. (The Philippines does not become fully independent until 1946.)

1942   President Franklin D. Roosevelt signs Executive Order 9066 leading to internment of Japanese Americans, and Congress passes Public Law 503 authorizing legal penalties for disobeying new executive order.

1943   Chinese exclusion laws repealed, quota of 105 Chinese immigrants from anywhere in the word established, Chinese granted naturalization privileges as a result of wartime alliances between China and the United States.

1944   Supreme Court upholds internment of Japanese Americans in *Korematsu v United States.* and *Hirabayashi v United States*; Hirabayashi is overturned completely on appeal in 1987 after evidence that military officers fabricated claims of military necessity.

1946   Luce-Celler Bill passes through Congress, granting Indian and Filipino immigrants right to naturalize and establishes small quota for these groups.

1952   McCarren-Walter Act eliminates all racial prerequisites for citizenship, thereby permitting all Asians to be naturalized, but continues national origins quotas, including minimal quotas for Asian countries and Asiatic triangle.

1959   Hawai'i attains statehood.

1965   Hart-Celler Immigration and Naturalization Act allows 290,000 total new immigrants each year, with 20,000–person per country preference limit and an exemption for family members. This act also places a quota on Mexican and other Western Hemisphere immigrants for the first time.

1975   United States admits more than 130,000 refugees from Vietnam, Kampu-
        chea (Cambodia), and Laos in the wake of communist government take-
        overs.

1980   Vietnamese begin to emigrate legally to United States through joint pro-
        gram between Vietnamese government and the United Nations High
        Commissioner for Refugees. Refugee Act systematizes flow of refugees
        to the United States.

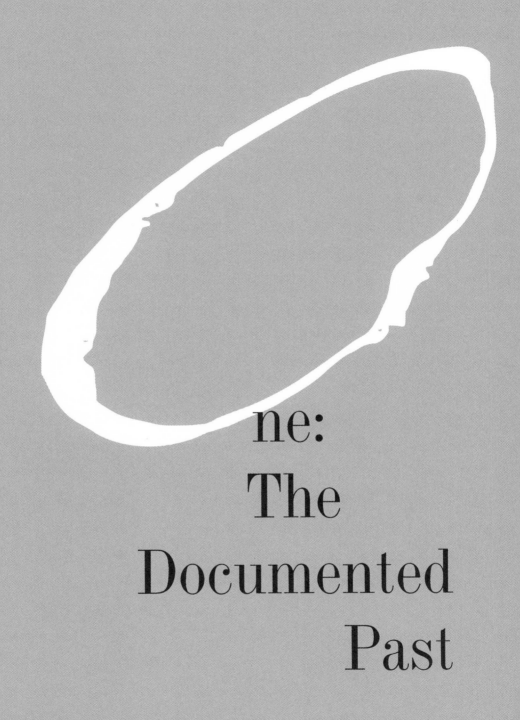

ne:
The
Documented
Past

Early Immigration Patterns

WHEN AND WHERE I ENTER

Gary Okihiro

A solitary figure defies a tank, insofar as a solitary figure can defy a tank. A "goddess of liberty" in the image of the Statue of Liberty arises from the midst of a vast throng gathered in Beijing's Tiananmen Square. The November 1, 1991, issue of *Asiaweek* carries the caption "Welcoming Asians" under a picture of the Statue of Liberty in New York Harbor awash in the light of fireworks.[1] Contained within those images—vivid and memorable—is what Swedish social scientist Gunnar Myrdal called the American creed. Democracy, equality, and liberty form the core of that creed, and the "mighty woman with a torch" has come to symbolize those ideals to, in the words of the poet Emma Lazarus, the tired, the poor, the huddled masses "yearning to breathe free."

On another island, on the other coast, stands not a statue but a wooden barrack. Solitary figures hunch over to carve poems on the walls.[2]

The sea-scape resembles lichen twisting and turning for a thousand li.
There is no shore to land and it is difficult to walk.
With a gentle breeze I arrived at the city thinking all would be so.
At ease, how was one to know he was to live in a wooden building?

In the quiet of night, I heard, faintly, the whistling of wind.
The forms and shadows saddened me; upon seeing the landscape, I composed
  a poem.
The floating clouds, the fog, darken the sky.
The moon shines faintly as the insects chirp.
Grief and bitterness entwined are heaven sent.
The sad person sits alone, leaning by a window.

Angel Island, not Ellis Island, was from 1910 to 1940 the main port of entry for Chinese immigrants "yearning to breathe free."[3] There, separated by cold currents from the golden shore, the migrants were carefully screened by U.S. Immigration officials and held for days, weeks, or months to determine their fitness for America. The 1882 Chinese Exclusion Act had prohibited entry to Chinese workers, indicative of a race- *and* class-based politics, because according to the act, "in the opinion of the Government of the United States, the coming of Chinese laborers to this country endangers the good order of certain localities within the territory thereof."[4]

In New York City, a year after passage of the Chinese Exclusion Act, Emma Lazarus wrote the poem that now graces the base of the Statue of Liberty. But the statue had not been envisioned as a symbol of welcome to the world's "wretched refuse" by its maker, French sculptor Frédéric Auguste Bartholdi, and at its unveiling in 1886, President Grover Cleveland proclaimed that the statue's light would radiate outward into "the darkness of ignorance and man's oppression until Liberty enlightens the world."[5] In other words, the statue commemorated republican stability, and according to the October 29, 1886, *New York World,* it stood forever as a warning against lawlessness and anarchy and as a pledge of friendship with nations that "dare strike for freedom." That meaning was changed by European immigrants, who saw the statue as welcoming them, and by Americanizers, who, in the 1920s and 1930s, after the 1924 Immigration Act restricting mass immigration, sought a symbol to instill within the children of immigrants patriotism and a love for their new country.[6]

The tale of those two islands, separated by the vast interior and lapped by different waters, constitutes a metaphor of America and the Asian American experience. America was not always a nation of immigrants, nor was America unfailingly a land of democracy, equality, and liberty. The romantic sentiment of the American identity, "this new man," expressed by French immigrant J. Hector St. John de Crèvecoeur was probably not the dominant view, nor did it apply to all of America's people. Writing in 1782, Crèvecoeur exclaimed:

What then is the American, this new man? . . . I could point out to you a family whose grandfather was an Englishman, whose wife was Dutch, whose son married a French woman, and whose present four sons have now four wives of different nations. He is an American, who leaving behind him all his ancient prejudices and manners, receives new ones from the new mode of life he has embraced, the new government he obeys, and the new rank he holds. He becomes an American by being received in the broad lap of our great *Alma Mater*. Here individuals of all nations are melted into a new race of men.[7]

Instead, the prevailing view was a narrower construction that distinguished "settler," or original colonist, from "immigrant," and that required a single origin and common culture. Americans, John Jay wrote in the *Federalist* papers, were "one united people—a people descended from the same ancestors, speaking the same language, professing the same religion, attached to the same principles of government, very similar in their manners and customs."[8] That eighteenth-century discrimination between settler and immigrant proved inadequate for the building of a new republic during the nineteenth century. The quest for a unifying national identity, conceived along the lines of Crèvecoeur's notion whereby "individuals of all nations are melted into a new race of men," an idea later called the "melting pot," paralleled the building of networks of roads, railroads, and communications that unified and bound the nation.[9]

Although Asians helped to construct those iron links that connected East to West, they, along with other peoples of color, were excluded from the industrial, masculine, destroying melting pot. Ellis Island was not their port of entry; its statue was not their goddess of liberty. Instead, the square-jawed, androgynous visage of the "Mother of Exiles" turned outward to instruct, to warn, and to repel those who would endanger the good order of America's shores, both at home and abroad. The indigenous inhabitants of Africa, Asia, and the Americas were not members of the community but were more akin to the wilderness, which required penetration and domestication. Three years after the Constitution was ratified, the first Congress met and, through the Naturalization Act of 1790, restricted admission into the American community to "free white persons." Although the act was modified to include "persons of African nativity or descent" in 1870 and Chinese nationals in 1943, the racial criterion for citizenship was eliminated completely only in 1952, 162 years after the original delineation of the Republic's members, or, according to the Naturalization Act, the "worthy part of mankind."

In 1886, African American educator Anna Julia Cooper told a group of African American ministers: "Only the BLACK WOMAN can say 'when and where I enter . . . then and there the whole *Negro race enters with me.*'"[10] Cooper's confident declaration held profound meaning. African American men bore the stigma of race, but African American women bore the stigmata of race and gender. Her liberation, her access to the full promise of America, embraced the admission of the entire race. The matter of "when and where," accordingly, is an engendered, enabling moment. The matter of "when and where," in addition, is a generative, transformative moment. The matter of "when and where," finally, is an extravagant, expansive moment. That entry into the American community, however enfeebled by barriers to full membership, parallels the earlier entry into historical consciousness, and the "when and where" of both moments are engendered/enabling, generative/transformative, extravagant/expansive.

Asians entered into the European American historical consciousness long before the mid-nineteenth-century Chinese migration to "Gold Mountain" and, I believe, even before Yankee traders and American diplomats and missionaries traveled to China in the late eighteenth century. The "when and where" of the Asian American experience can be found within the European imagination and construction of Asians and Asia and within their expansion eastward and westward to Asia for conquest and trade.

Writing in the fifth or fourth century B.C.E., Hippocrates, Greek physician and "father of medicine," offered a "scientific" view of Asia and its people. Asia, Hippocrates held, differed "in every respect" and "very widely" from Europe.[11] He attributed those contrasts to the environment, which shaped the peoples' bodily conformations and their characters. Asia's mild, uniform climate supported lush vegetation and plentiful harvests, but under those conditions "courage, endurance, industry and high spirit could not arise" and "pleasure must be supreme." Asians reflected the seasons in their natures, exhibiting a "monotonous sameness" and "stagnation," and their form of government, led by kings who ruled as "despots," enfeebled them even more. Among Asians, Hippocrates reported, were "Longheads" and "Phasians." The latter had yellowish complexions "as though they suffered from jaundice." Because of the differing environments in which they lived, Hippocrates concluded, Europeans had a wider variety of physical types and were more courageous and energetic than Asians, "for uniformity engenders slackness, while variation fosters endurance in both body and soul; rest and slackness are food for cowardice, endurance and exertion for bravery."[12]

Aristotle mirrored Hippocrates' views of Asia during the fourth century B.C.E. In his *Politics,* Aristotle observed that northern Europeans were "full of spirit, but wanting in intelligence and skill," whereas Asians were "intelligent and inventive," but lacked spirit and were therefore "always in a state of subjection and slavery." The Greeks, in contrast, lived between those two groups and thus were both "high-spirited and also intelligent." Further, argued Aristotle, barbarians were by nature "more servile in character" than Greeks and he reported that some Asians practiced cannibalism.[13] The fourth-century B.C.E. conflict between Persia and Greece, between barbarism and civilization, between inferior and superior, tested the "great chain of being" idea propounded by Plato and Aristotle. Alexander the Great's thrust into India, to "the ends of the world," was a one-sided affair, according to the Roman historian Arrian, a chronicler of the expedition. Using contemporary accounts but writing some four hundred years after Alexander's death in 323 B.C.E., Arrian contrasted Alexander's ingenuity and dauntless spirit—"he could not endure to think of putting an end to the war so long as he could find enemies"—with the cowardice of the barbarian hordes, who fled pell-mell at the sight of the conqueror.[14] As recorded by Arrian, Alexander reminded his officers in a speech that they were "ever conquerors" and their enemies were "always beaten," that the Greeks were "a free people" and the Asians "a nation of slaves." He praised the strength and valor of the Greeks, who were "inured to warlike toils," and he declared that their enemies had been "enervated by long ease and effeminacy" and called them "the wanton, the luxurious, and effeminate Asiatics."[15]

Such accounts of Asia, based upon the belief in a generative relationship between the environment and race and culture, enabled an exotic, alienating construction of Asians, whether witnessed or simply imagined. Literary critics Edward W. Said and Mary B. Campbell have characterized that European conception of Asia and Asians—"the Other"—as "almost a European invention," according to Said, a place of "romance, exotic beings, haunting memories and landscapes, remarkable experiences," and for Campbell, that conception was "the ground for dynamic struggles between the powers of language and the facts of life."[16] Accordingly, the Greek historian Ctesias, writing probably in the fifth century B.C.E., reveled in the accounts of "dog-faced creatures" and "creatures without heads" that supposedly inhabited Africa, and he peopled his Asia with those same monstrous beasts. Likewise, the author of the early medieval account *Wonders of the East* described Asian women "who have boars' tusks and hair down to their heels and oxen's tails growing out of their loins. These women are thirteen feet tall, and their bodies have the whiteness of marble, and they have camels' feet and donkeys' teeth." Alexander the Great, hero of *Wonders of the East,* kills those giant, tusked, and tailed women "because of their obscenity" and thereby eliminates strangeness, making the world sane and safe again. Asia, in *Wonders of the East,* writes Campbell, "stands in opposition to the world we know and the laws that govern it," and is way beyond and outside the realm of order and sensibility.[17]

That otherworldliness, that flight from reality, pervades the earliest Christian European text to define Europe in opposition to Asia, the *Peregrinatio ad terram sanctam* by Egeria, probably written during the late fourth century C.E. Although her account of her journey to the Holy Land contained "moments of awe, reverence, wonder or gratitude," it described an exotic Asia that served to highlight the positive, the real, the substantial Europe. *De locis sanctis,* written during the late seventh century C.E. by Adamnan, abbot at Iona's monastery, recounted a similar Asia from the travels of Bishop Arculf to the Holy Land. Asia, according to *De locis sanctis,* was a strange, even demonic place, where people exhibited grotesque inversions and perversions of human nature, and where a prerational, stagnant configuration existed, "a world stripped of spirit and past."[18]

Asia, according to Campbell and Said, was Europe's Other.[19] Asia was the location of Europe's oldest, greatest, and richest colonies, the source of its civilization and languages, its cultural contestant, and the wellspring of one of its most persistent images of the Other. At the same time, cautions Said, the assumptions of Orientalism were not merely abstractions and figments of the European imagination but composed a system of thought that supported a "Western style for dominating, restructuring, and having authority over" Asia. Within Orientalism's lexicon, Asians were inferior to and deformations of Europeans, and Orientalism's purpose was to stir an inert people, raise them to their former greatness, shape them and give them an identity, and subdue and domesticate them. That colonization, wrote Said, was an engendered subordination, by which European men aroused, penetrated, and possessed a passive, dark, and vacuous "Eastern bride," imposing movement and giving definition to the "inscrutable Orient," full of secrecy and sexual promise.[20] The feminization of Asia was well under way before the colonization of Asia by Europe in the sixteenth century, as evident in the accounts of Hippocrates, Herodotus,[21] Aristotle, Arrian, Egeria, and Adamnan.

Arrian's account of Alexander's effortless victory over "effeminate" Asian men, for example, parallels his discussion of Greek men's easy conquest of erotic Asian women. Indian women, wrote the Roman historian, "who will suffer themselves to be deflowered for no other gift, will easily condescend, when an elephant is promised as the purchase," thinking it "an honour to have their beauty valued at so high a rate."[22] The conqueror took for himself several Asian wives, he "bestowed the daughters of the most illustrious" Persians on his friends, and more than 10,000 of his soldiers married Asian women. Further, commented Arrian, despite being "in the very heat of youth," Alexander curbed his sexual desires and thereby displayed the triumph of mind over body, rationality over sensuality, Greek over Asian. "The daughter of Oxyartes was named Roxana, a virgin, but very marriageable, and, by the general consent of writers, the most beautiful of all the Asiatic women, Darius's wife excepted," wrote Arrian. "Alexander was struck with surprise at the sight of her beauty; nevertheless, being fully resolved not to offer violence to a captive, he forbore to gratify his desires till he took her, afterwards, to wife . . . and herein showed himself no less a pattern of true continency, than he had before done of heroic fortitude." "As to those pleasures which regarded the body," wrote Arrian in eulogizing Alexander, "he shewed himself indifferent; as to the desires of the mind, insatiable."[23]

The Greek representation of Asia yielded not only soft men and erotic women but also hard, cruel men and virile, martial women. Fifth-century B.C.E. polarities of Greek/barbarian, male/female, and human/animal helped to define the citizens of the *polis*—Greek men—as the negation of their Other—barbarian, female, animal—who were linked by analogy such that barbarian was like female was like animal.[24] Athenian patriarchy held that men were the norm, were superior, and brought order, whereas women were abnormal, inferior, and brought chaos. Marriage domesticated women, civilizing their wild, untamed sexuality and disciplining them for admittance into the city. Amazons reversed the gender relations of the *polis* and stood in opposition to its androcentrism by being members of a society of women who refused to marry and become mothers to sons and who assumed the preeminent male characteristics of aggressiveness, leadership, and strength. Although the myth of Amazons originated before the Persian wars, the Greeks considered Asia to be the Amazons' homeland, and they equated Persians with Amazons, in that both Persians and Amazons were barbarians and, according to Isocrates in 380 B.C.E., Amazons "hated the whole Greek race" and sought "to gain mastery over all." Athenians, explained Isocrates, defended themselves against Amazon expansion, defeated them, and destroyed them "just as if they had waged war against all mankind."[25] Besides posing a political threat, Asia served as an object lesson of how, when men ceased to act as men, order and normalcy vanished, resulting in the topsy-turvy world of the Amazons.[26]

The Mongol invasions of the thirteenth century not only breached Alexander's wall but also made palpable a hitherto distant, alien people and culture. "Swarming like locusts over the face of the earth," Friar William of Rubruck wrote in 1255, the Mongols "have brought terrible devastation to the eastern parts [of Europe], laying waste with fire and carnage . . . it seemed that God did not wish them to come out; nevertheless it is written in sacred history that they shall come out toward the end of the world, and shall make a great slaughter of men."[27] The Mongols, of whom the Tatars were the most prominent group, appeared as avenging angels from hell, "Tartarus," and hence the corruption of their name to "Tartars."[28] Although in awe of the Mongols' military prowess and strength, Friar William saw little to admire in their filth and barbarism: "the poor provide for themselves by trading sheep and skins; and the slaves fill their bellies with dirty water and are content with this. They also catch mice, of which many kinds abound there; mice with long tails they do not eat but give to their birds; they eat doormice and all kinds of mice with short tails."[29]

The late-thirteenth-century account of Asia by the Venetian Marco Polo contains both feminine and masculine attributions, chaste women and diabolical men, and grotesque and wondrous objects and people, including unicorns, Amazons, dog-headed creatures, mountain streams flowing with diamonds, and deserts full of ghouls. His narrative is a distillation of the brew that had preceded him. John Masefield, in his introduction to the 1908 edition of Polo's *Travels,* wrote that "his picture of the East is the picture which we all make in our minds when we repeat to ourselves those two strange words, 'the East,' and give ourselves up to the image which that symbol evokes."[30] A prominent part of that image was the exotic and the erotic, highlighted in Polo's ample accounts of prostitutes, sex, and women, leading Henry Hart to speculate: "One may surmise that the numerous references to women—the intimate descriptions of their persons, their various aptitudes in sex relations and many other details not usually related even by hardy travelers of that or a later day . . . were largely, if not entirely, called forth by the frank curiosity and continual questionings of the stay-at-home Westerners for whom his tale was told and written." Polo wrote of the Chinese that "their ladies and wives are also most delicate and angelique things, and raised gently, and with great delicacy, and they clothe themselves with so many ornaments and of silk and of jewels, that the value of them cannot be estimated."[31]

In Europe, *The Travels of Sir John Mandeville* was the most influential book about Asia from its original publication in 1356 to the eighteenth century. "Mandeville" was a pseudonym for perhaps a number of authors, who claimed to have traveled from England to the Holy Land, Egypt, Arabia, and even to the court of the Great Khan in Cathay. Like Polo, Mandeville described the marvels and monsters of the East, from the bounties of gold, silver, precious stones, cloves, nutmeg, and ginger to the horrors of one-eyed and headless beasts, giants, pygmies, and cannibals. In a single passage, Mandeville poses an apparently curious juxtaposition of sexuality and war, but upon reflection, the feminine (sexuality) and masculine (war) so constructed are really two sides of the same coin: the dominance of men over women and territory, achieved through heterosexual sex and war, and, by extension, under imperialism, European men's superiority over Asian women and men and their control of reproduction and the state. On the island of "Calonak" near Java, wrote Mandeville, the king

hath as many wives as he will. For he maketh search all the country to get him the fairest maidens that may be found, and maketh them to be brought before him. And he taketh one one night, and another another night, and so forth continually ensuing;

so that he hath a thousand wives or more. And he lieth never but one night with one of them, and another night with another; but if that one happen to be more lusty to his pleasance than another. And therefore the king getteth full many children, some-time an hundred, some-time a two-hundred, and some-time more.

Without a paragraph break, Mandeville continued: "And he hath also into a 14,000 elephants or more that he maketh for to be brought up amongst his villains by all his towns. For in case that he had any war against any other king about him, then [he] maketh certain men of arms for to go up into the castles of tree made for the war, that craftily be set upon the elephants' backs, for to fight against their enemies."[32]

Christopher Columbus was a great admirer of "Mandeville" and, along with English explorers Martin Frobisher and Walter Raleigh and Flemish cartographer Gerhardus Mercator, read and believed Mandeville's account of Asia and his idea of a circumnavigable and universally inhabited world.[33] The fabulous East, the earthly paradise "discovered" and described by Columbus, was to him and his contemporaries Asia—the "Indies"—and its peoples were Asians—the "Indians." They were just as surely Asian as the lands and peoples in Polo's and Mandeville's travelogues. As Columbus noted in the preface to his ship's daily log, the expedi-tion's purpose was to go "to the regions of India, to see the Princes there and the peoples and the lands, and to learn of their disposition, and of everything, and the measures which could be taken for their conversion to our Holy Faith."[34] Columbus compared the new lands to the virtuous Garden before the Fall, where people were like children, innocent and unselfconscious in their nakedness, and where the feminized land invited conquest. His log entry for October 12, 1492, reported: "At dawn we saw naked people, and I went ashore in the ship's boat, armed. . . . I unfurled the royal banner. . . . After a prayer of thanksgiving I ordered the captains of the Pinta and Nina . . . to bear faith and witness that I was taking possession of this island for the King and Queen."[35] Much of the land was bountiful and laden with fruit, and on his third voyage, Columbus described the mouth of the Orinoco River as shaped "like a woman's nipple," from whence "issued the waters of paradise into the sea."[36]

Some islanders, reported Columbus, were friendly, domestic, tractable, and even cowardly, but others were warlike, monstrous, and evil, even cannibalistic (a word derived from the name "Carib" Indians). "I also understand that, a long distance from here," wrote Columbus on November 4, 1492, "there are men with one eye and others with dogs' snouts who eat men. On taking a man they behead him and drink his blood and cut off his genitals."[37] The timid Indians were eager to submit to Europeans, being "utterly convinced that I and all my people came from Heaven," according to Columbus, whereas the fearless ones required discipline. Both kinds of Indians, "feminine" and "masculine," were fair game for capture, or, in Columbus's euphemism, "I would like to take some of them with me."[38] That, in fact, was what the admiral did, as easily as plucking leaves from the lush, tropical vegetation, intending them to serve as guides, servants, and specimens. Columbus's text and others like it helped to justify a "Christian imperialism" and were the means by which the invaders "communicated—and helped control—a suddenly larger world."[39]

That world grew even larger in about 1510, when a few Europeans questioned Columbus's "India" and proposed the existence of a new continent that stood between Europe and Asia, although cartographers continued to append American discoveries to the Asian coast until the late sixteenth century. Accompanying and justifying their expanded physical world was an ideology, articulated in texts, of a growing racial and cultural distance between Europeans and the peoples of Asia, Africa, and the Americas. The first cracks had appeared, in the perceptions of Asians by Europeans, in the fifth-century B.C.E. works of Hippocrates, who had posited "very wide" differences "in every respect" between Europeans and Asians. The fissures continued to widen thereafter to the degree that Asia, Africa, and the Americas became antipodes of Europe, the habitations of monstrous beasts and perversions of nature itself. That world, it seemed, needed to be appropriated, worked over, and tamed.

The process of colonization and the relationship between colonizer and colonized were incisively described by Albert Memmi, the twentieth-century Tunisian philosopher and author: "The colonialist stresses those things which keep him separate, rather than emphasizing that which might contribute to the foundation of a joint community." That focus on difference is not of itself racist, but it takes on a particular meaning and function within a racist context. According to Memmi: "In those differences, the colonized is always degraded and the colonialist finds justification for rejecting his subject. . . . The colonialist removes the factor [the colonized] from history, time, and therefore possible evolution. What is actually a sociological point becomes labeled as being biological or, preferably, metaphysical. It is attached to the colonized's basic nature."[40] Whether because of race or culture, of biology or behavior, of physical appearance or social construct, Asians appeared immutable, engendered, and inferior. These differences not only served to set Asians apart from the "joint community" but also helped to define the European identity as a negation of its Other.

Reflecting on works published on the five hundredth anniversary of Columbus's "discovery," anthropologist Wilcomb E. Washburn, noted interpreter of American Indian culture and director of the Office of American Studies at the Smithsonian Institution, reminded his readers that the initiative for discovery came from the West and not the East, and thus "Asia was more sharply etched on the European mind than on the Asian mind. . . . Both America and Asia were relatively stagnant," he explained, "being more wedded to their traditions than was the West, which found the novelty of other climes and other cultures stimulating. While the Western mind did not always move in directions that we would now applaud, it moved—indeed, darted here and there—as the Asian mind too often did not."[41]

Following Columbus's "great enterprise" and his "taking possession" of "Asia," the penetration of Asia proper began with the Portuguese, who seized parts of India and Southeast Asia during the early sixteenth century, established a colony at Macao in 1557, and controlled much of the trade with China and Japan. Despite Portugal's presumed sole possession of the hemisphere east of the 1493 papal line of demarcation, Spain, the Netherlands, France, and Britain also participated in the trade with and colonization of Asia. The conquest and colonization of the Americas was, of course, a product of that global expansion of Europeans, and the "when and where" of the Asian American experience must be similarly situated. I do not claim, however, that Orientalism's restructuring and domination of Asia simply migrated with Europeans to the Americas; nor am I arguing a necessary relationship between European and European American perceptions of Asians. My contention is that there is a remarkable familiarity to Orientalism's face on both shores of the Atlantic and that its resemblance extends to European constructions of American Indians and Africans.[42]

Historian Stuart Creighton Miller, in his 1969 book, *The Unwelcome Immigrant: The American Image of the Chinese, 1785–1882,* argued that although it was sensible to assume that American attitudes toward Asians were rooted in the European heritage, he could find no direct connection between those views. Neither the writings nor the libraries of America's leading figures during the colonial period showed any interest in or even curiosity about Asians. Miller characterized that lacuna as indicative of an "innocent, unstructured perception of China in the American mind" and, as proof, pointed to George Washington, who was surprised to learn in 1785 that the Chinese were nonwhites. Further, Miller noted that the English failed to share the Continent's enthusiasm for Chinese government and law and for Confucian philosophy, made popular by Jesuit missionaries and by the iconoclasts of the Age of Reason. In fact, in Britain, Sinophobes such as Daniel Defoe, Samuel Johnson, Jonathan Swift, and Adam Smith launched a vitriolic attack against the Chinese. The American image of Asians, Miller concluded, took shape only after direct American trade with China began with the departure of the *Empress of China* from New York Harbor in 1784.[43]

Miller underestimates the malleability and mobility of racial attitudes and notions of the Other, characteristics that have been amply demonstrated by scholars. Europeans, as noted by historian Dwight W. Hoover, "did not approach new lands and new people devoid of preconceptions. Instead, they brought with them a whole set of ideas concerning both the natural and historical worlds."[44] Some of those preconceptions included the idea of a biological chain of being that evolved from ape to wild man to man and the biblical notion of postdiluvian degeneration and diversification originating with the Tower of Babel.[45] Despite their manifest variety, ideas of race distinguished Europeans from their shadow—non-Europeans—and claimed superiority for the civilized, Christian portion of humankind.

William Shakespeare's *The Tempest,* first performed in 1611, was likely set in Bermuda but might just as well have been an allegory of race relations during the age of European overseas expansion and colonization, or perhaps even an account of the sugar plantation system that was installed along the European Mediterranean coast and on islands like Cyprus and Crete and that by the late fourteenth century was driven mainly by Asian and African slave labor.[46] Prospero, "a prince of power" and lover of books, is set adrift with his daughter, Miranda, and lands on an enchanted island which he takes from Caliban, whom he enslaves and banishes to the island's wasteland. Caliban (anagram of the word "cannibal") is everything Prospero is not: he is dark and physically deformed; he is "poisonous," "lying," "filth," "capable of all ill," and begotten of "the devil himself." He is both African and Indian, his mother was from Algiers and he is descended from Brazilians, Patagonians, and Bermudans, but he is also part fish, part beast. Caliban's mother, Prospero said, was a "damn'd witch," a "hag," who had given birth to Caliban like an animal—"she did litter here" her son, who was "not honour'd with a human shape." Despite being excluded from their company and despite Miranda's abhorrence of him, Caliban is indispensable to Prospero and Miranda, because he "does make our fire, fetch in our wood; and serves in offices that profit us." Prospero pities Caliban, tutors him, and takes "pains to make [him] speak"; Prospero gives meaning to Caliban's "gabble." Instruction, however, proves insufficient. The wild man is driven by savage lust and tries to kill Prospero and rape the virginal Miranda, but he is repulsed by Prospero's magic.[47]

Caliban, the "savage man of Inde," was African and Indian, but he was also Asian insofar as Indians came from Asia, as was contended by Samuel Purchas, scholar and chaplain to the archbishop of Canterbury, in his widely read book *Purchas his Pilgrimage*, published in 1613, and seconded by the astronomer Edward Brerewood in his 1614 book, *Enquiries touching the diversity of languages, and religions through the chiefe parts of the world*, and by Walter Raleigh in his 1614 *History of the World*. The fact that Indians were once Asians accounted for their barbarism, according to these English writers.[48] Thus, although a separate race, Indians were still Asians, both groups having descended from the biblical Shem; and Asians, Indians, and Africans all belonged to the darker races of men, the Calibans of the earth, who were ruled by beastly passions, sought to impregnate white women (to people "this isle with Calibans"), and, although given a language and trained in useful labor, still turned against their benefactors and had to be subdued.[49] Perhaps influenced by those European views, Thomas Jefferson hypothesized the kinship of Asians and America's Indians: "the resemblance between the Indians of America and the eastern inhabitants of Asia would induce us to conjecture that the former are descendants of the latter, or the latter of the former."[50]

Although they arrived in the New World carrying the baggage of the Old World, Americans developed their own projections and invented their own mythologies, peering from their "clearing" into the "wilderness." George Washington may have been reflecting the light of European ideology bent by the prism of American experience when he declared that "being upon good terms with the Indians" was based upon economy and expediency, and instead of driving them "by force of arms out of their Country; which . . . is like driving the wild Beasts of ye forest . . . the gradual extension of our settlements will as certainly cause the savage, as the wolf, to retire; both being beasts of prey, tho' they differ in shape."[51] And Jefferson might have defended Indians as "a degraded yet basically noble brand of white man," but he was also defending the American environment and its quadrupeds, those "other animals of America," against French naturalist Georges Buffon's claim of American inferiority. Having failed to assimilate and civilize the savage and childish Indians, Jefferson argued for their extermination, made "necessary to secure ourselves against the future effects of their savage and ruthless warfare."[52] Jefferson, having reached that conclusion about Indians, linked America's determination to clear the forests with a New World version of British expansion and colonization and predicted that the "confirmed brutalization, if not extermination of this race in our America is . . . to form an additional chapter in the English history of [oppression of] the same colored man in Asia, and of the brethren of their own color in Ireland."[53]

When Yankee traders arrived in China during the late eighteenth century, they saw the Chinese through lenses that had already been ground with the grit of European views of Asia and Asians and the rub of historical and contemporary relations between European Americans and American Indians and Africans. The traders' diaries, journals, and letters were mostly free of racial prejudice, reports Miller, and the negative images of the Chinese that did appear concerned China's government and the officials with whom the traders dealt, whom they saw as despotic, corrupt, barbarous, begging, and cowardly. But traders' accounts also revealed extreme ethnocentrism. According to a trader, the Chinese were "the most vile, the most cowardly and submissive of slaves"; another wrote that whites could bully even Chinese soldiers, whose "silly grunts and menaces mean nothing and are to be disregarded."[54] A prominent theme was the bizarre and peculiar nature of the Chinese in their alleged taste for dogs, cats, and rats; in their music, which was a "mass of detestible discord"; and in their theater, which was "ridiculous or disgracefully obscene." The records, wrote Miller, "portrayed him [the Chinese] as a ludicrous specimen of the human race and [were] not designed to evoke the admiration and respect for Chinese culture." The focus on the exotic, on "strange and curious objects," was complemented by a featuring of vice—gambling and prostitution—and practices showing the "moral debasement" of the people, including idolatry, polygamy, and infanticide. The Chinese, wrote a trader contemptuously, are "grossly superstitious . . . most depraved and vicious: gambling is universal . . . they use pernicious drugs . . . are gross gluttons," and are "a people refined in cruelty, bloodthirsty, and inhuman."[55]

The journey begun in New England and continuing around South America's Cape Horn was just the start of America's masculine thrust westward toward Asia's open shores.[56] Like those Yankee China trade vessels, the Conestoga wagons and prairie schooners pushed their way through "vacant, virgin" land to the Pacific and in the process built a continental empire that stretched "from sea to shining sea." In 1879, Robert Louis Stevenson rode the iron rails that bound the nation together, and his account, "Across the Plains: Leaves from the Notebook of an Emigrant between New York and San Francisco," might be read as the great American epic. America was "a sort of promised land" for Americans like Stevenson, who were immigrants from Europe and who found themselves among a diverse lot of fellow passengers, "a babel of bewildered men, women, and children." As the train carried them westward, Stevenson, like Crèvecoeur, described the beauties of the land, where "all times, races, and languages have brought their contribution." That equality, that melting pot, however, was broken at Chicago, at the frontier of civilization, where the travelers were placed on an "emigrant train" that consisted of segregated coaches: one for white men, another for white women and children, and yet another for Chinese. Stevenson reflected upon the hatreds that had prompted that racial, gender, and age segregation as the train "pushed through this unwatered wilderness and haunt of savage tribes." America, he wrote, was the meeting ground, where "hungry Europe and hungry China, each pouring from their gates in search of provender, had here come face to face," and where Europeans had come with preconceived hatreds of the Chinese that had moved them from one field of conflict to another. "They [Europeans] seemed never to have looked at them [Chinese], listened to them, or thought of them, but hated them a priori," observed Stevenson. "The Mongols were their enemies in that cruel and treacherous battle-field of money."[57]

Despite his contempt for those "stupid," albeit modified, Old World prejudices, prejudices given further license once civilization had been left behind for the "unwatered wilderness" of the frontier, Stevenson was not entirely free of those same perceptions of the Chinese. His fellow Europeans, reported Stevenson, saw the Chinese as physically repulsive, such that the mere sight of them caused "a kind of choking in the throat." "Now, as a matter of fact," admitted the observant Scotsman, "the young Chinese man is so like a large class of European women, that on raising my head and suddenly catching sight of one at a considerable distance, I have for an instant been deceived by the resemblance"—although, he offered, "I do not say it is the most attractive class of our women." And while looking upon the Chinese with "wonder and respect," Stevenson saw them as creatures from "the other" world: "They [the Chinese] walk the earth with us, but it seems they must be of different clay." "They hear the clock strike the same hour, yet surely of a different epoch. They travel by steam conveyance, yet with such a baggage of old Asiatic thoughts and superstitions as might check the locomotive in its course. . . . Heaven knows if we had one common thought or fancy all that way, or whether our eyes, which yet were formed upon the same design, beheld the same world out of the railway windows."[58]

Stevenson's view of the Chinese as "different clay" might have been conditioned by his European origins, but Herman Melville, surely no stranger to the American metaphysics of race relations, cannot be similarly dismissed. His retelling of a story by James Hall, "Indian hating.—Some of the sources of this animosity.—Brief account of Col. Moredock," not only offered a stinging critique of inhumanity masked as morality, embodied in the "confidence-man" and Indian-hater John Moredock, but also foresaw, according to Richard Drinnon, that "when the metaphysics of Indian-hating hit salt water it more clearly became the metaphysics of empire-building." Although believed to be a barbarian, predicted Melville, "the backwoodsman would seem to America what Alexander was to Asia-captain in the vanguard of conquering civilization." Melville, Drinnon points out, correctly saw that the relentless westward advance of the Indian-hater would, after reaching the Pacific Ocean, continue on to Asia, and in Melville's words, his hatreds would ride "upon the advance as the Polynesian upon the comb of the surf."[59] And like Alexander, who had sought to conquer all of India, the "backwoodsman," the "barbarian," "could not endure to think of putting an end to the war so long as he could find enemies."

In truth, America's manifest destiny was "an additional chapter" in the Orientalist text of Europe's "dominating, restructuring, and having authority over" Asia. In July 1853, Commodore Matthew C. Perry pushed into Tokyo Bay carrying a letter from the U.S. president demanding the opening of trade relations. That "opening" of Japan was accomplished, like the "opening" of the American West, with the iron fist of industry and the might of military arms; Perry's "black ships" under full steam power and with matchless guns were complements of the iron horses and Kentucky rifles of the backwoodsmen, who were simultaneously taming the wilderness. Reflecting on the second period of America's manifest destiny, after the annexation of the Philippines and Hawai'i in 1898 and after Secretary of State John Hay's pronouncement of an "Open Door" with China, Theodore Roosevelt declared: "Of course our whole national history has been one of expansion. . . . That the barbarians recede or are conquered, with the attendant fact that peace follows their retrogression or conquest, is due solely to the power of the mighty civilized races which have not lost the fighting instinct, and which by their expansion are gradually bringing peace into the red wastes where the barbarian peoples of the world hold sway."[60]

The filling of those "red wastes," those empty spaces, was, of course, the white man's burden. John Hay, a son of the frontier of sorts, sought "to draw close the bonds" that united "the two Anglo-Saxon peoples" of Britain and America in a common destiny and mission: "All of us who think cannot but see that there is a sanction like that of religion which binds us to a sort of partnership in the beneficent work of the world. Whether we will it or not, we are associated in that work by the very nature of things, and no man and no group of men can prevent it. We are bound by a tie which we did not forge and which we cannot break; we are the joint Ministers of the same sacred mission of liberty and progress, charged with duties which we cannot evade by the imposition of irresistible hands."[61] China's "Open Door" and America's "splendid little war" with Spain, observed Hay, were of that beneficent quality. "We have done the Chinks a great service," wrote Hay of his policy, "which they don't seem inclined to recognize," and he admonished the next generation of backwoodsmen, "as the children of Israel encamping by the sea were bidden, to Go Forward." Indeed, noted Hay, America had gone forward and had charted a "general plan of opening a field of enterprise in those distant regions where the Far West becomes the Far East."[62] In becoming a Pacific power, America had fulfilled a European people's destiny and, like Columbus, had gone ashore, unfurled the royal banner, offered a prayer of thanksgiving, and taken possession of the land. America's Far West had become the Far East, where Indian-fighters became "goo-goo" fighters in the Philippines and Indian savages became Filipino "niggers," and where a war of extermination was pursued with no less determination than the chastising of the Iroquois urged by George Washington in 1779, when he instructed Major General John Sullivan: "but you will, not by any means, listen to any overture of peace before the total ruin of their settlement is effected. . . . Our future security will be in their inability to injure us . . . and in the terror with which the severity of the chastizement they receive will inspire them."[63]

Asians, it must be remembered, did not come to America; Americans went to Asia. Asians, it must be remembered, did not come to take the wealth of America; Americans went to take the wealth of Asia. Asians, it must be remembered, did not come to conquer and colonize America; Americans went to conquer and colonize Asia. And the matter of the "when and where" of Asian American history is located therein, in Europe's eastward and westward thrusts, engendered, transformative, expansive. But another context of the "when and where" is the historical moment in America where Prospero ruled over the hideous, the imperative Caliban. Asia not only provided markets for goods and outposts for military and naval bases, but also supplied pools of cheap labor for the development of America's "plantations" along its southern and western frontiers. In 1848, Aaron H. Palmer, a counselor to the U.S. Supreme Court, anticipated the nation's destiny in the American southwest and Asia when he predicted that San Francisco would become "the great emporium of our commerce on the Pacific; and so soon as it is connected by a railroad with the Atlantic States, will become the most eligible point of departure for steamers to . . . China." To build that rail link and to bring the fertile valleys of California under cultivation, Palmer favored the importation of Chinese workers, explaining that "no people in all the East are so well adapted for clearing wild lands and raising every species of agricultural product . . . as the Chinese."[64]

It was within those American "plantations" that Asians joined Africans, Indians, and Latinos in labor, making Prospero's fire, fetching his wood, and serving in offices that profited him. It was within those "plantations" that Europeans tutored Asians, Africans, Indians, and Latinos and gave meaning to their gabble. And it was within those "plantations" that Asians, Africans, Indians, and Latinos rose up in rebellion against their bondage and struck for their freedom.

In 1885, a Chinese American described his reaction to being solicited for funds for erecting the Statue of Liberty. He felt honored to be counted among "citizens in the cause of liberty," he wrote,

> but the word liberty makes me think of the fact that this country is the land of liberty for men of all nations except the Chinese. I consider it an insult to us Chinese to call on us to contribute toward the building in this land a pedestal for a statue of liberty. That statue represents liberty holding a torch which lights the passage of those of all nations who come into this country. But are the Chinese allowed to come? As for the Chinese who are here, are they allowed to enjoy liberty as men of all other nationalities enjoy it?[65]

For China's prodemocracy students in 1989 and for Asians in America, the "goddess of liberty," featured so prominently by the American news media, situated squarely within the mainstream, and lifting up her torch above the masses in Tiananmen Square, was not a symbol of liberation. Instead, their true symbol, relegated to the background as the camera panned the crowd, situated inconspicuously along the margins, was the declaration emblazoned by the Chinese students on the banners they waved, the shirts they wore, and the fliers they distributed: the words were, "We Shall Overcome."

NOTES

1. I have taken the title of this chapter from a narrative history of African American women by Paula Giddings, *When and Where I Enter: The Impact of Black Women on Race and Sex in America* (New York: William Morrow, 1984).
2. Poems published in Him Mark Lai, Genny Lim, and Judy Yung, *Island: Poetry and History*

of Chinese Immigrants on Angel Island, 1910–1940 (Seattle: University of Washington Press, 1991), 34, 52.

3. A third island, Sullivan's Island, was the point of entry for many African slaves during the eighteenth century. "Sullivan's Island," wrote historian Peter H. Wood, "the sandy spit on the northeast edge of Charlestown harbor where incoming slaves were briefly quarantined, might well be viewed as the Ellis Island of black Americans." Peter H. Wood, *Black Majority: Negroes in Colonial South Carolina from 1670 through the Stono Rebellion* (New York: Alfred A. Knopf, 1975), xiv.

4. The text of the 1882 Chinese Exclusion Act is quoted in Cheng-Tsu Wu, ed., *"Chink!" A Documentary History of Anti-Chinese Prejudice in America* (New York: World Publishing, 1972), 70–75.

5. John Higham, *Send These to Me: Jews and Other Immigrants in Urban America* (New York: Atheneum, 1975), 71–72, 74, 75.

6. Ibid., 75, 77, 79.

7. J. Hector St. John de Crèvecoeur, *Letters from an American Farmer* (New York: Fox, Duffield & Co., 1904), 54–55.

8. Higham, *Send These to Me*, 3.

9. Ibid., 199.

10. Giddings, *When and Where I Enter*, 81–82.

11. For Hippocrates, Asia meant Asia Minor, or the area between the Mediterranean and Black Seas. Depending upon who was writing and when, Asia meant variously Asia Minor (or Anatolia), the Levant, Southwest Asia, Central Asia, or India. Generally, during the fifth and fourth centuries B.C.E. the Greeks called the Persians "Asians."

12. *Hippocrates,* trans. W.H.S. Jones (Cambridge: Harvard University Press, 1923), 1:105–133.

13. *The Politics of Aristotle,* trans. Benjamin Jowett (Oxford: Clarendon Press, 1885), 96, 218, 248. "Barbarians," it should be noted, could refer to Europeans, such as Thracians and Illyrians, as well as to Asians.

14. Arrian's *History of the Expedition of Alexander the Great, and Conquest of Persia,* trans. John Rooke (London: W. McDowall, 1813), 112, 117, 123, 146.

15. Ibid., 42. Arrian was an Asian from Nicomedia in northern Turkey and wrote in Greek, despite serving as a Roman governor. See also Alexander's contrast of intelligent Greeks with Persian and Indian hordes in the influential work of late Greek literature *The Greek Alexander Romance,* trans. Richard Stoneman (London: Penguin Books, 1991), 105, 128, 181; and a similar representation of Persians by Romans during the third century C.E. in Michael H. Dodgeon and Samuel N. C. Lieu, comps. and eds., *The Roman Eastern Frontier and the Persian Wars (A.D. 226–363): A Documentary History* (London: Routledge, 1991), 19, 26.

16. Edward W. Said, *Orientalism* (New York: Random House, 1978), 1; and Mary B. Campbell, *The Witness and the Other World: Exotic European Travel Writing, 400–1600* (Ithaca, N.Y.: Cornell University Press, 1988), 3.

17. Campbell, *Witness,* 51, 63–65, 68–69, 84. See also *Greek Alexander Romance,* 124.

18. Campbell, *Witness,* 7–8, 21, 26, 44–45.

19. Ibid., 3; and Said, *Orientalism,* 1. See also Christopher Miller, *Blank Darkness: Africanist Discourse in French* (Chicago: University of Chicago Press, 1985), who contends that Africa was Europe's Other.

20. Said, *Orientalism,* 1, 59, 62, 72, 74, 86, 207–208, 211, 222. For a cautionary critique of Said, see Lisa Lowe, *Critical Terrains: French and British Orientalisms* (Ithaca, N.Y.: Cornell University Press, 1991).

21. The contest between Greece and Asia was a major theme in ancient Greek literature, as seen in the writings of Homer, Aeschylus, Euripides, Xenophon, and many others. The work of Herodotus, written in the fifth century B.C.E., is perhaps the best known example of this genre. I simply present a selection of the evidence.

22. *Arrian's History,* 220.

23. Ibid., 112–113, 181, 205. Arrian was a Stoic philosopher, accounting for his stress on mind over body.

24. Page duBois, *Centaurs and Amazons: Women and the Pre-history of the Great Chain of Being* (Ann Arbor: University of Michigan Press, 1982), 4–5.

25. Quoted in W. Blake Tyrrell, *Amazons: A Study in Athenian Mythmaking* (Baltimore: Johns Hopkins University Press, 1984), 15–16. For another view of Amazons and their relation to Greek patriarchy, see duBois, *Centaurs and Amazons,* 4–5, 34, 70.

26. On the ambiguities of Greek attributions of male and female and the rhetoric of discourse and reality of practice, see John J. Winkler, *The Constraints of Desire: The Anthropology of Sex and Gender in Ancient Greece* (New York: Routledge, 1990).

27. Campbell, *Witness,* 88–89.

28. David Morgan, *The Mongols* (London: Basil Blackwell, 1986), 56–57.

29. Campbell, *Witness,* 114.

30. *The Travels of Marco Polo the Venetian* (London: J. M. Dent, 1908), xi.

31. Henry H. Hart, *Marco Polo: Venetian Adventurer* (Norman: University of Oklahoma Press, 1967), 117, 135.

32. *The Travels of Sir John Mandeville* (London: Macmillan, 1900), 127–128.

33. Campbell, *Witness,* 10, 161; and *The Log of Christopher Columbus,* trans. Robert H. Fuson (Camden, Maine: International Marine Publishing, 1987), 25.

34. *Log of Christopher Columbus,* 51.

35. Ibid., 75–76.

36. Campbell, *Witness,* 171, 247. Walter Raleigh also believed the Orinoco led to paradise (ibid., 246–247).

37. *Log of Christopher Columbus,* 102.

38. Ibid., 145, 173; and "Letter of Columbus," in *The Four Voyages of Columbus,* ed. and trans. Cecil Jane (New York: Dover Publications, 1988), 10.

30. Campbell, *Witness,* 166.

40. Albert Memmi, *The Colonizer and the Colonized* (Boston: Beacon Press, 1967), 71.

41. Wilcomb E. Washburn, "Columbus: On and off the Reservation," *National Review,* 5 October 1992, 57–58. 42. See chapter 5 for an elaboration of this theme. [Editors' note: This article is an excerpt from Gary Okihiro's *Margins and Mainstreams: Asians in American History and Culture* (University of Washington Press, 1994); this note refers to a chapter in Okihiro's book.]

43. Stuart Creighton Miller, *The Unwelcome Immigrant: The American Image of the Chinese, 1785–1882* (Berkeley and Los Angeles: University of California Press, 1969), 11–14.

44. Dwight W. Hoover, *The Red and the Black* (Chicago: Rand McNally, 1976), 4.

45. I merely allude to the vast literature on the history of racism and racist thought and cite as particularly helpful Arthur O. Lovejoy, *The Great Chain of Being: A Study of the History of an Idea* (Cambridge: Harvard University Press, 1936); and George L. Mosse, *Toward the Final Solution: A History of European Racism* (New York: Howard Fertig, 1978).

46. Hoover, *Red and Black,* 1–2; and David Brion Davis, *Slavery and Human Progress* (New York: Oxford University Press, 1984), 52–57.

47. *The Complete Works of William Shakespeare* (New York: Walter J. Black, 1937), 2–6; Ronald T. Takaki, *Iron Cages: Race and Culture in Nineteenth-Century America* (New York: Alfred A. Knopf, 1979), 11–12; and Leslie A. Fielder, *The Return of the Vanishing American* (New York: Stein & Day, 1968), 42–49. See O. Mannoni, *Prospero and Caliban: The Psychology of Colonization,* trans. Pamela Powesland (London: Methuen, 1956), for a more complex reading of the play, esp. 105–106.

48. Hoover, *Red and Black,* 35–37.

49. See Winthrop Jordan, *White over Black* (Chapel Hill: University of North Carolina Press, 1968), for British and American racial attitudes toward Indians and Africans from 1550 to 1812.

50. Frederick M. Binder, *The Color Problem in Early National America as Viewed by John Adams, Jefferson, and Jackson* (The Hague: Mouton, 1968), 83.

51. Quoted in Richard Drinnon, *Facing West: The Metaphysics of Indian-Hating and Empire-Building* (New York: New American Library, 1980), 65.

52. Ibid., 80–81, 98; and Jordan, *White over Black*, 475–481.

53. Drinnon, *Facing West*, 81.

54. Miller, *Unwelcome Immigrant*, 21, 25–27, 34.

55. Ibid., 27–32, 35.

56. The phrase "masculine thrust toward Asia" is from the title of chapter 11 of Takaki's *Iron Cages*, 253.

57. Robert Louis Stevenson, *Across the Plains, with Other Memories and Essays* (New York: Charles Scribner's Sons, 1900), 1, 11, 26–27, 48, 60, 62; and Drinnon, *Facing West*, 219–221.

58. Stevenson, *Across the Plains*, 62, 65–66.

59. Herman Melville, *The Confidence-Man: His Masquerade*, ed. Elizabeth S. Foster (New York: Hendricks House, 1954), lxv–lxx, 164, 334–341; and Drinnon, *Facing West*, 214–215.

60. Quoted in Drinnon, *Facing West*, 232.

61. Ibid., 267.

62. Ibid., 277, 278.

63. Ibid., 331.

64. Takaki, *Iron Cages*, 229.

65. Renqiu Yu, *To Save China, To Save Ourselves: The Chinese Hand Laundry Alliance of New York* (Philadelphia: Temple University Press, 1992), 199–200.

THE SUGAR KINGDOM

THE MAKING OF PLANTATION HAWAI'I

Ronald Takaki

"AN ENTERING WEDGE"

One day in 1835, the natives of Koloa on the island of Kauai were surprised to see a white man wandering through their village, "a mere hamlet, seldom visited by even a missionary." They had seen white men before: in 1778 many of the natives had traveled to Waimea, sixteen miles away, to get a glimpse of Captain James Cook; or had heard stories about how he had sailed into the bay in two huge ships with billowing white sheets, how his men had carried awesome weapons of fire and destruction, and how they had left a dreadful disease with native women. Many of the natives still possessed souvenirs of Cook's visit—the iron nails they had ripped from his landing boats and the butcher's cleaver one of them had stolen.[1]

As the Koloa natives curiously watched their new visitor, they compared William Hooper of Boston to the other *haoles* "outsiders" living on Kauai: the merchants in Waimea shipping the fragrant sandalwood to China and supplying whaling vessels with water and provisions, and the missionaries building a new church and spreading Christianity among the natives. But the people of Koloa did not realize that Hooper, more than the merchants and the missionaries, represented the beginning of a new era in the history of Hawai'i. Sent to Koloa by Ladd and Company of Honolulu to establish the first sugar cane plantation in the Sandwich Islands, Hooper was there to remake Hawai'i in an American image: to advance the market civilization of the United States beyond Indian lands and Mexican territory to a new Pacific frontier, undermining in the process native Hawai'ian society and the people's traditional relationship with their land.[2]

Though he was only twenty-six years old, Hooper keenly understood the significance of his venture in Koloa. Two years earlier he, Peter Brinsmade, and William Ladd had landed in Honolulu and opened a mercantile trading house they named Ladd and Company. The company had leased from King Kamehameha III 980

acres of land for the cultivation of sugar cane on the east side of the Waihohonu
Stream in Koloa for fifty years at $300 a year. The company had also secured
permission to hire natives to work on the plantation. It had agreed to pay a tax
for each man employed to Kauikeaouli, the king of the Hawai'ian islands, and
Kaikioewa, the governor of Kauai, and to pay the workers satisfactory wages. The
king and governor, in return, would exempt the workers from any taxation, except
the tax paid by their employer.[3]

As Hooper surveyed the newly leased land and the natives to be inducted into
his work force, he certainly thought Koloa was a fitting place for the beginning of
the sugar industry in the islands, for the place name itself means "Great Cane" (*ko*
"cane" and *loa* "great"). Everywhere Hooper looked, wild cane flourished on the
fertile land of Koloa, nourished by rains that fell on towering Kahili Mountain,
almost always shrouded in mist, and then swept southward ten miles toward the
plains of Koloa and finally toward the beaches of Poipu. Far away from American
civilization, initially Hooper lived in a grass hut and was obliged to eat *taro*, a root
which the natives pounded into *poi*; he even jokingly described himself as becoming
a "*real kanaka.*" Anxious to start his operations, Hooper wrote in his diary on
September 11, 1835: "Koloa, Island of Kauai, S. Islands, obtained from Govr.
Kekeiova [Kaikioewal, the use, of 25 kanakas at two dollars each per month." The
next day, he "laid out a piece of land supposed to contain 12 acres to be cultivated
with cane." Two days later, "twenty three of the twenty five kanakas hired from the
Govr. made their appearance on the plantation at sunrise & commenced work after
breakfast"; in the course of the day, they removed the grass from about two acres.[4]

Within one year the young man from Boston had transformed both the land
and native society in Koloa. On September 12, 1836, he proudly listed his accomplishments: twenty-five acres of cane under cultivation, twenty houses for the natives, a house for the superintendent, a carpenter's shop, a blacksmith's shop, a
mill dam, a sugar house, a boiling house, and a sugar mill. Pleased with the progress
of his plantation, Hooper recorded in his diary his thoughts on the meaning of
the Koloa experience:

> Just one year to day since I commenced work on this plantation, during which I have
> had more annoyances from the chiefs and difficulty with the natives (from the fact
> of this land being the first that has ever been cultivated, on the plan of *free* labour,
> at these islands) than I ever tho't it possible for one white man to bear, nevertheless
> I have succeeded in bringing about a place, which if followed up by other foreign
> residents, will eventually emancipate the natives from the miserable system of "chief
> labour" which ever has existed at these Islands, and which if not broken up, will be
> an effectual preventitive to the progress of civilization, industry and national prosper-
> ity. . . . The tract of land in Koloa was [developed] after much pain . . . for the purpose
> of breaking up the system aforesaid or in other words to serve as an entering wedge
> . . . [to] upset the whole system.[5]

A sense of mission lay behind Hooper's energetic enterprise. More than profits
were at stake. In building his plantation, Hooper viewed himself as a white man,
as a pathfinder or vanguard of civilization, introducing the system of free labor in

order to emancipate the natives from the miserable system of "'chief labour.'" For young Hooper, the Koloa Plantation was an "entering wedge" designed to irrevocably split apart traditional Hawai'ian society.

As they watched Hooper begin his enterprise, the natives of Koloa must have felt a profound ambivalence. They undoubtedly were very apprehensive about his new operation, fearful of the negative effects the plantation system would have on their culture and way of life. They also saw him as a haole and identified him with the destruction of the sandalwood forests, with the denuding of the *'aina* "land," and with the sailors who were infecting native women with venereal diseases. But the natives also must have hoped Hooper would offer them an escape from the old Hawai'ian system of exploitation and fear. The king owned all of the lands; and chiefs holding land did so for payment of loyal services and dues. The common people or *makaainana,* in order to have use of small tracts of land, had to labor for the king or local chiefs, the *ah'i. Kapus,* or tabus, strictly enforced by the *ilamuku,* or police, severely restricted their activities and ambitions. The Hawai'ian historian David Mato, educated by missionaries and forty-two years old when Hooper founded the Koloa Plantation, reported that the commoners were subjected to hard labor, heavy taxation, and cruelty. If they were lax in performing labor for their chief, they were expelled from the land or even subject to a death penalty. They held the chiefs in "great dread," and lived in a state of "chronic fear." Theirs was a "life of weariness . . . constantly burdened by one exaction after another."[6]

Seeking to improve their lot, twenty-three natives went to work for Hooper on September 13, 1835. But two days later, they suddenly stopped working. "The kanakas having discovered the chiefs were to pay and not me," Hooper wrote in his diary, "concluded that 'all work and no pay' was poor business, therefore spent most of the forenoon in idleness." Apparently Hooper's workers thought they were to be paid through their chiefs and, doubtful they would be paid at all, refused to work. They were quickly offered an "inducement"—direct payment of "one real," or 12 1/2 cents per day—and "they sprang to it, and at sundown finished their stint." Workers were given food and shelter, in addition to their wages.[7]

But Hooper did not pay his workers in reals or cash. Rather, he issued coupons or scrip, pieces of cardboard on which he wrote amounts for 12 1/2, 25, and 50 cents and which his workers could exchange for goods only at his plantation store. Thus Hooper was able to both pay his workers and make a profit from their purchases. Periodically Hooper ran out of coupons. On November 15, 1837, for example, he wrote to Ladd and Company: "I am excessively annoyed for want of money; had to knock off laying bricks today, to make some." He also found himself looking for new consumer goods for his workers to buy with their coupons. On February 23, 1836 he asked Ladd and Company to send him clothing to sell to the natives: "Their great desire seems to be to get a suit of clothes to show off. In this I intend to gratify them so soon as they shall have earned it. I beg you therefore . . . to purchase say 20 suits of cheap thin clothing, various sizes." But in early 1838 Hooper wrote to his company: "What shall we pay off our men with? Calico, etc., they are tired of. Can't you get up something?" And a year later, he noted how the natives had purchased a sufficient supply of fabric and how the plantation store needed other items to sell to them. In this process, Hooper had created both a wage-earning labor force and a consumer class dependent on a plantation-owned market which had to expand consumer needs constantly.[8]

Native families, reported Hooper's neighbor James Jarvis, readily "volunteered" to have their taxes paid for them and to work for the Koloa Plantation for wages. They were drawn into Hooper's labor force with "the inducement of regular wages, good houses, and plenty of food, when compared with their usual mode of living." Hooper's work force increased from twenty-five in September 1835 to forty in May 1836. In March 1838 Hooper noted that one hundred men, women, and children looked to him for their "daily Poe [poi]."[9]

Among Hooper's workers were native women. Employed to strip the cane and assist in grinding and boiling operations, they proved to be such capable workers that Hooper wrote to Ladd and Company on June 12, 1838: "I am in want of no more Sugar Boys. The women on the plantation now make good ones and it is best that I should keep them constantly at work." They were not only worked constantly but were also paid less than the men: women received only 6 cents per day while the men received 12 1/2 cents. Hooper's justification for this dual-wage system was that it kept the women employed and allowed them to make "more than enough to support their families."[10]

On the plantation, Hooper's laborers found themselves in a new world of modern industrial agriculture. They no longer cultivated their traditionally held small plots of land, sharing their crops with the ali'i. They no longer directed their own labors, making their own decisions regarding what to plant and when to work, rest, or go fishing. As plantation laborers, they found their time controlled by unfamiliar workday sounds, schedules, and rhythms. "At sunrise the laborers are turned out by the ringing of the bell," Jarvis wrote, "and work till sunset, sufficient time being allowed for their meals. At night they are assembled and paid by a sort of bank note, considered as good as money all over the island and redeemable in goods on Saturday." The workers, Hooper reported to Ladd and Company, "meet me in the field at six in the morning, work till 7 1/2—go to breakfast & return to work till 12 1/2—an hour at dinner & then work till sundown at which time I pay them off in paper. . . . Friday is allotted to them to take care of their Tarrow [taro] Patches & Saturday to cook their Grub." Where previously they had planned their time and activities by the movements of the sun, now they awoke by the ringing of the plantation bell, and a clock determined when they would eat, work, rest, and work again. And their days were organized into weeks, with weekdays for working and weekends for tending their gardens.[11]

As plantation workers, they performed a myriad of tasks. Under Hooper's direction, they first cleared grass from tracts of land for cane cultivation and used a plough pulled by oxen to prepare the soil for the planting of cane cuttings. When one of the oxen died from overwork, Hooper replaced it with men. "At one time," Jarvis reported, "in lieu of cattle, he was obliged to employ forty natives, to drag a plough." Hooper filled his diary with descriptions of plantation work tasks. On November 25, 1835 he wrote: "This day the natives finished planting one strip of cane." June 20, 1836: "Men engaged in stripping the dry leaves from cane." August 9, 1836: "Holeing for and Planting cane—clearing land." March 27, 1837: "Commenced the day with 47 natives—Hoeing cane, laying out ground & etc." November

13, 1837: "The natives continued cutting cane." November 16, 1837: "The natives engaged cutting cane." December 2, 1837: "Commenced cutting cane."[12]

In addition to their work in the fields, plantation laborers erected buildings, bridges, and dams, as well as operating the mill. Hooper recorded the construction of a factory in the middle of the cane fields of Koloa in diary entries beginning May 9, 1836: "This Commenced with 40 men to build a dam for a sugar mill to go by water power." May 11: "Continued with our men on Dam. . . . " May 18: "Finished Dam, now employed [men] in setting up Mill." May 28: "Employed 6 men to put up frame for Sugar Mill." May 31: "All hands to work thatching Mill House." August 4: "Natives finished the wall made for new water wheel. . . . " Working with two white carpenters, Manuel and Antoine, the laborers finished building the sugar mill. On November 10, 1836 Hooper proudly wrote to Ladd and Company: "I set the mill in operation on Monday noon. It works admirably taking four men to keep it supplied with cane, or rather to feed it. There is no stop to it. . . . The natives are completely taken 'aback' and consider the Mill as one of the 'seven wonders.'" A month later he was pleased to report that the natives working in the mill were efficiently extracting juice from the cane.[13]

Drawn away from their own lands and traditional homes, Hooper's native workers had entered a new plantation community. They lived on the plantation, in houses allotted to them by Hooper. Assigned plots of land to cultivate crops for their own food and allowed time on weekends to work their gardens, they received from Hooper a barrel of fish every third week. This system in which the workers supplemented their own subsistence needs enabled Hooper to minimize both wages and production costs. On Saturdays, Hooper's workers went to the plantation store to sell vegetables and crafts and to purchase goods with their coupons. Market day on the Koloa Plantation was filled with excitement and noise. According to Jarvis,

> at sunrise the little shops on the plantation are opened, to redeem the paper money, and purchase such articles as the natives bring for sale. Crowds of them in the rudest attire, or no attire at all, early throng the house. One brings vegetables, another fish, fine tapas, mats, curiosities, in short, any thing and every thing which they suppose the *haole* (foreigner), to want. Women leading fat pigs, which . . . they take in their arms and press to their bosoms to still their deafening lamentations, join the throng; while dog and fowl add their voices to the dulcet strain.[14]

Plantation workers not only labored, lived, and shopped on the Koloa Plantation, they also received medical care. Initially Hooper himself attended to the medical needs of his workers. On April 29, 1836 he reported to Ladd and Company: "They are often ailing. . . . They are troubled with sore eyes etc etc which need & ought to have advice & medicine." The next year Hooper contracted the services of a Dr. Lafore. In a letter to the doctor dated October 16, 1837, Ladd and Company wrote: "In reference to your inquiry on Sat. last, as to what amt. might be expected from us, for medical attendance on the natives in our employ, we have only to repeat that it would be exceedingly gratifying to us to have you as a neighbor and for all medical attendance on those in our employ, we should expect to pay you, by the year, the price to be decided by yourself, at its commencement or termination." What Hooper was developing on the Koloa Plantation was a system of capitalist paternalism that would embrace the total needs of plantation workers and set a pattern for planter-worker relationships in Hawai'i.[15]

Though they were dependent on Hooper for their "daily Poe" and other needs, native workers refused to give him the control and loyalty he expected. Time and again Hooper was exasperated because he was unable to exact satisfactory obedience and sustained labor from his workers. Throughout his Koloa diary, he described his workers as undependable, as children, as "dull asses," and as "Indians." His letters to Ladd and Company chronicled the frustrations he felt as the supervisor of recalcitrant laborers. On February 23, 1836, he complained: "It requires the concentrated patience of an hundred Jobs to get along with these natives . . . [their] obedient masks of loyalty . . . [hiding their] dissatisfaction" and disgust for plantation labor. September 21, 1836: "Cane grows rapidly, some of it astonishingly—my natives are on their oars." October 3, 1836: "I would write more on this sheet but my men are, as usual, on their oars in my absence." October 26, 1836: "The natives do but little when my back is turned." December 10, 1836: "The native laborers need to be broken in [but] when that will be I can not tell." May 12, 1838: "A gang of Sandwich Island men are like a gang of School Boys. When their master is with them they mind their lessons, but when he is absent it is 'hurra boys.' They display so little interest for their employment that it makes my *heart ache.*"[16]

Hooper's laborers required constant surveillance or else they would not work. They became skillful pretenders; next-door-neighbor Jarvis often "amusingly" watched them practice their art of deception. While working in the fields, natives were always ready to deceive their employer and escape from work, he reported. If an overseer left for a moment, down they would squat and pull out their pipes. Then the "longest-winded fellow" would begin a story, an improvisation in which he would entertain everyone with "vulgar" humor and often "mimic the haole." As soon as the overseer came within sight, they would seize their spades and quickly "commence laboring with an assiduity" that baffled description and "perhaps all the while not strain a muscle."[17]

But Hooper did not find their behavior amusing. Irritated and impatient, he castigated his native workers for their inefficiency and doubted they would ever become useful as plantation workers. Their habits and customs, handed down to them from their forefathers and preserved tenaciously, would remain "the great obstacle to their employment" as agricultural wage laborers. Centuries, at least, Hooper lamented, would intervene before they would understand that it was a part of their "duty" to serve "their masters faithfully." He conceded that there were many good men among the natives who would take hold and turn themselves into "white kanakas" for one or two years; but he had no confidence that their patience would hold out. As long as the plantation depended on native labor, the superintendent would have to be a *"Slave Driver."*[18]

Hooper employed white overseers to help him supervise his native workers. He discovered that sometimes the overseers themselves needed to be broken in, to be introduced to a system of stern plantation discipline. On one occasion, a recently hired overseer named Titcomb overheard some workers expressing dissatisfaction with their wages. Reporting the incident to Ladd and Company, Hooper wrote:

It seems that he secreted himself long side of his tea stick fence to hear the conversation of some natives in a house nearby—by it, he learned that the natives were on the morrow to demand 25 cts. per day—no mistake—so down he came to find out what was to be done. I very calmly told him that if he would take a whip and undertake to drive off the natives from his land, he would in my opinion have experience enough to last him a month. I have heard nothing more since.[19]

Frustrated because he could not convert the natives into docile and efficient modern agricultural workers, Hooper began employing Chinese laborers. He had first noticed their presence in Waimea: there a few of them were grinding wild cane, brought to them by natives, in a small sugar mill owned by William French. After visiting this mill in the spring of 1835, Hooper wrote to Ladd and Company:

I have seen the Chinese sugar works in successful operations; although extremely crude, yet they are doing well. They have worked 6 days in the week ever since its first establishment, making abt 210 lb sugar per day & molasses by the cord. They could make four times as much by increasing the size of kettles. Mr. F. is much elated with its success and from what I learn from Mr. Whitney you may expect a Host of Chinese. . . . Mr. French's establishment at Waimea is a great eye sore to the natives. They have to work *all* the time—and no regard is paid to their complaints for food, etc., etc. Slavery is nothing to it.

Shortly after the construction of his own mill, Hooper projected the need for Chinese labor. "We may deem it," he advised Ladd and Company, "at a future day, necessary to locate some halfdozen Chinese on the land, if the establishment grows it will require them. The Supt. cannot feed the mill, boil the juice, make the sugar, etc etc, and to trust it to the natives is worse than nothing—they are alas, children, boys, and always will be."[20]

In a letter to Ladd and Company dated December 1, 1838, Hooper insisted that "a colony of Chinese would, probably, put the plantation in order, to be perpetuated, sooner and with less trouble than any other class of husbandmen." By this time, several Chinese were already working for Hooper; they had probably been recruited from French's mill, which had been put out of business due to competition from the Koloa mill. A pattern of ethnic labor segmentation was already evident, for Hooper tended to assign his Chinese laborers to the mill and Hawai'ian laborers to the fields. In Hooper's view, the Chinese had more experience in milling and were more reliable as factory operatives than the Hawai'ians. The Chinese were also placed in separate living quarters. Unlike the native workers, who lived on the plantation with their families in individual houses, the Chinese workers were single men and were housed together in a barrack-type structure. In April 1838 Hooper informed Ladd and Company that a large building had been erected for the "Chinamen." "They are highly pleased," he added, "and by their fixtures on doors I should suppose they intend to spend their days in it." Thus Chinese workers, too, now looked to Hooper for their "daily Poe." Early in 1839 Hooper ordered from Ladd and Company a supply of rice.[21]

But the use of Chinese workers did not mean the end of labor difficulties.

Hooper's workers, Hawai'ian and Chinese, found new ways to resist management and avoid work. Some of the natives shoplifted merchandise from the plantation store. On January 28, 1837 Hooper angrily scribbled into his diary: "[Detected] the natives stealing—therefore paid out no goods today." Three days later he wrote: "5 natives taken before Hukiko [Hukiku, the headman at Koloa]—convicted of stealing and sentenced to work on the roads." But by this time, some of his workers had devised a more ingenious way of acquiring goods from the plantation store. As the natives learned how to read and write from a young schoolmaster in the village, some of them utilized their newly acquired knowledge and skills to make artful reproductions of Hooper's medium of exchange. The counterfeit coupons, according to Jarvis, were "so strikingly like the original, imitating the signatures with scrupulous exactness, that it was some time before the fraud was detected."[22]

But detected it eventually was. On June 11, 1836, Hooper, surprised and dismayed, wrote in his diary: "Some native has attempted to counterfeit the papers which I issued for dollars." Some of the counterfeiters were Chinese. Hooper realized that unless the problem were checked, the counterfeit conspiracy could undermine his entire enterprise. His laborers would have little incentive to work, for they would have their own source of scrip. Determined to outwit his workers, Hooper asked Ladd and Company to have paper bills printed in Boston. In a letter to the printer dated November 15, 1837, Ladd and Company gave instructions to have the currency printed from a copper plate in order to be certain it could not be duplicated: "If the ground work is fine waved lines, or a delicate net work, and the border highly wrought, we doubt if we shall be troubled with counterfeits from the Chinese or any other source." But it took time to order the printed currency from Boston and have it sent to Hawai'i. Meanwhile, on January 5, 1839 Hooper again found counterfeit coupons in circulation and urged Ladd and Company to hurry the order for the printed money: "I send you up a specimen of what I suppose to be *native* ingenuity in shape of counterfeit money. I have six reals of it." Acknowledging its genuine appearance, Hooper confessed: "I would not swear it was not mine." Finally, three months later, Hooper was relieved to receive the bank bills printed in Boston, which he considered "very nicely executed."[23]

The founding of the Koloa Plantation had been a very trying experience for Hooper. The new land did not yield easily. The rainy seasons, with their howling winds and pelting showers, forced him to stay indoors, and the enveloping dampness aggravated his rheumatism. Cut off from family and friends and from the security and comfort of Boston, he suffered from intense isolation, finding his new life in Koloa lonesome and "dull as death." And the people of the new land had not been as pliant as he had hoped: they were difficult to manage and often drove him to despair. They seemed to resist him at almost every point. They were also more intelligent than he had assumed, able to avoid work and to extract extra compensation in creative and devious ways. Physically exhausted from his constant struggle with his workers, Hooper vented his frustrations to Ladd and Company in 1838: "No galley slave looks forward to the day when he is to be made free with half so much satisfaction as I do when I shall bid a *final* adieu to intercourse with Hawai'ians! Gracious Anticipations!"[24]

A year later Hooper was granted his wish, but he left behind him, in Koloa, a place transformed. In a sense Hooper may remind us of William Shakespeare's Prospero (*The Tempest*) and Mark Twain's Connecticut Yankee. Both Prospero and the Yankee, Hank Morgan, viewed themselves as men of civilization involved in a heroic struggle against primitive society. Prospero had settled on an island and inducted a native, Caliban, into his service, his work force; and Hank Morgan had traveled to another island, Arthurian England, where he had imposed a modern industrial order. Reflecting the expansionist culture portrayed in Prospero and Morgan, Hooper had migrated to an island. There, employing native labor, he had cleared the wild grass from the land in order to plant ordered rows of cane and so had altered the very character of the tiny hamlet of Koloa, bringing to it the dark smoke and the loud and dissonant mechanical sounds of a modern factory. Seeking both to earn corporate profits for Ladd and Company and to liberate natives from their traditional society, he had integrated economic and moral motives. He had removed natives from their farms and villages to his plantation and offered them housing, medical care, and a store stocked with consumer goods. More important, Hooper had opened the way for the development of a corporate-dominated sugar economy and a paternalistic racial and class hierarchy in the islands.

Elsewhere in the world—Jamaica, Cuba, Haiti, Puerto Rico—white men had already established plantations for the cultivation of sugar cane. But while they had enslaved both the indigenous and imported populations as agricultural workers, Hooper had employed both natives and Chinese as free or wage-earning laborers in order to produce sugar as a cash crop. His invoices for 1837–1838 showed that he had shipped to Honolulu 30 tons of sugar and 170 barrels of molasses—a small but nonetheless portentous beginning to a new plantation economy that would penetrate traditional Hawai'ian society like an "entering wedge."

"KING SUGAR"

After William Hooper's departure the Koloa Plantation continued to increase its production of sugar and also began to attract widespread attention. On September 30, 1846 the *Sandwich Island News,* reporting the plantation's profitable sugar output, welcomed the introduction of the new sugar industry into the Hawai'ian economy. Four years later the Reverend Daniel Dole visited the Koloa Plantation and was impressed with its success. "The plantation," he reported to a friend, "has been very profitable the past year; the sugar made being worth $20,000 and the expenses being less than 1/2 this sum." In 1857 the Koloa Plantation received international recognition when *De Bow's Review* of New Orleans published an article on the Sandwich Islands, describing the operation and the potential of the Koloa Plantation: "It employs one hundred native and twenty Chinese field laborers, and produces about two hundred tons of sugar per annum; with proper machinery it is capable of yielding five hundred."[25]

As Hooper had hoped, the Koloa Plantation was drawing foreign investors into the sugar business and spawning other plantations in the islands. In 1864, on a windward promontory opposite a small offshore island that would come to be called "Chinaman's Hat" because of its shape, the first sugar plantation on the island of Oahu was founded. In her memoirs, Elizabeth Wilder recalled how her father and husband had moved their families to Koloa, where they erected a stone chimney for the sugar mill: "Fields were fenced and ploughed for the cane, small flumes were put up, Chinese coolies imported as laborers. . . . " The same year, the *Pacific Commercial Advertiser* excitedly described a similar development occurring on the island of Maui: "What a change has taken place in Waikapu within two years! Where there were a few taro-patches . . . a village has sprung up, with its sugar mill and buildings, its waving cane fields and busy laborers, scattering industry, thrift and contentment everywhere. Here, where a few hundred dollar's worth of taro was formerly raised, fifty thousand dollars worth of sugar may now annually be made and sent to market."[26]

The cultivation of cane was spreading rapidly throughout the archipelago, from Kauai to the Big Island. Like Cuba and Puerto Rico, Hawai'i had the essential natural conditions for growing sugar cane: rich soil, warm climate, and an abundance of water. Aware of Hawai'i's agricultural potential, the editor of the *Pacific Commercial Advertiser* predicted in 1864 that sugar would be the "great staple of the islands." On Kauai alone, there were eight plantations by 1877: Koloa, Lihue, Kilauea, Hanalei, Grove Farm, Eleele, Kapaa, and Kawaihau. Surveying the proliferation of plantations and the rise of the new industry, the editor of the *Hawai'ian Gazette* proclaimed: "It is apparent that Sugar is destined most emphatically to be 'King.'"[27]

One of the crucial developments that led to the enthronement of "King Sugar" was the Great Mahele of 1848, which destroyed the traditional system of land ownership in Hawai'i. Previously, all lands were owned by the king, and foreigners were not permitted to purchase or lease land on terms that would justify large capital investments. The lease of land to Ladd and Company for the Koloa Plantation was an exception. During the 1840s American missionaries promoted the idea of private landownership for commoners as a means of encouraging them to become thrifty and industrious; American businessmen meanwhile pressed for changes that would allow them to secure land on a long-term basis. In 1846 American advisers success-fully persuaded the Hawai'ian government to appoint a Board of Land Commission-ers headed by a planter to register land claims and to settle land disputes. The Board revolutionized landownership in the islands when it instituted the 1848 Great Mahele (division), which apportioned the lands of Hawai'i to the crown, government, chiefs, and people. Then in 1850 the government enacted a land law extending to foreign residents the right to acquire and hold land fee simple. Subsequently, lands under private ownership were rapidly transferred from the native population to the haoles: land speculators and sugar growers paid minimal sums for large tracts of land to chiefs eager to get rich quickly, and acquired smaller holdings through the courts from commoners unfamiliar with Western concepts of land and new legal requirements such as applications for land deeds and payment of land taxes. By 1890, three out of four privately held acres were owned by haoles or their corporations. Forty years later the census revealed the continuance of this concentration of land under white ownership. It showed that of the 5,955 farm units, 633 were owned, managed, or leased by haoles, 510 by Hawai'ians, 4,191 by Japanese, and 335 by Chinese. But haole individuals and corporations controlled

2,579,733 acres—according to Lawrence Fuchs, more than 16 times the acreage controlled by Hawai'ians and part-Hawai'ians, more than 45 times Japanese-American holdings, and more than 140 times the acreage held by Chinese.[28]

The availability of land for the expansion of sugar cultivation was timely: in 1848 the discovery of gold in California and the new influx of population on the Pacific coast created a new market for food products shipped from Hawai'i. For example, exports to California from the Port of Koloa from July 1, 1850 to June 30, 1851 included 1 goat, 50 cattle, 130 swine, 542 turkeys, 1,017 fowls, 75 barrels of onions, 360 barrels of sweet potatoes, 1,000 barrels of squashes, 40 barrels of yams, 353 gallons of syrup, 2,851 gallons of molasses, and 26,063 pounds of sugar. Celebrating the bonanza the California gold rush had brought to the islands, the Royal Hawai'ian Agricultural Society depicted the new prosperity: "Our coffee and sugar no longer remain piled in our warehouses. Our fruits and vegetables no longer decay in the spot where they were grown. We are not even compelled to seek for them a market, but clamorous purchasers come to our very doors and carry off our supplies."[29]

The boom quickly subsided after 1851, however, and the demand for Hawai'ian foodstuffs was neither as steady nor as reliable as the Royal Hawai'ian Agricultural Society had so optimistically predicted. Ten years later, however, the Civil War in the United States boosted the price of sugar from 4 cents per pound in 1861 to a high of 25 cents in 1864. Sugar production responded quickly to the new prices, and sugar exports increased from 572 to 8,865 tons. A more important turning point for the profitability of sugar occurred in 1875, when the United States and Hawai'i concluded the Reciprocity Treaty. Under the terms of the treaty, Hawai'i was granted the right to export sugar, duty free, to the United States. The treaty set off an investment hysteria in Hawai'i. "It may be said that the speculation in cane-growing is becoming quite a *furore*, not to say that it is rapidly progressing towards the incipient stage of a regular mania," the *Pacific Commercial Advertiser* reported in 1877. "Thus we hear, upon all sides, of persons heretofore engaged in multifarious businesses, professional men, clerks, employers, in short, individuals representing all classes of the community—talking of making a venture in cane culture."[30]

The "mania" was not economically irrational. Reciprocity returned huge profits to the Hawai'ian sugar planters: it enabled them to sell their duty-free sugar in the tariff-protected American sugar market at the duty-paid price rather than a discounted price, adding two cents per pound duty to their sugar and raising their margin of profit. In 1898 the annexation of Hawai'i to the United States guaranteed Hawai'ian access to the duty-protected American sugar market and the continuation of high profits for the Hawai'ian sugar industry. Consequently the industry paid enormous dividends. Plantations usually averaged more than 10 percent in annual dividends on capitalization, and some of them exceeded this rate of return. The Hawai'ian Commercial and Sugar Company paid annual dividends of 16 percent or more during a nine-year period; the Kekaha Plantation paid a 45 percent dividend in 1911, 40 percent in 1916, and 49 percent in 1920. The Lihue Plantation, incorporated in 1892 at $700,000, doubled the value of its capital stock within six years.

In 1910 it paid a dividend of 100 percent and raised its capitalization to over two million dollars. Six years later the Lihue Plantation paid a 60 percent dividend, and represented a capitalization of three million dollars.[31]

Due to the Great Mahele, the Gold Rush, the American Civil War, and the Reciprocity Treaty, the Hawai'ian sugar industry experienced meteoric success. Sugar production increased from Hooper's 30 tons for 1837–1838 to 375 tons in 1850, 572 tons in 1860, and 9,392 tons in 1870. Ten years later sugar production soared to 31,792 tons and continued to climb to 129,899 tons in 1890, 298,544 tons in 1900, 518,127 tons in 1910, and 556,871 tons in 1920. The value of exported sugar in 1877 was $1,800,248; in 1920 it had risen to $119,490,663. Sugar was Hawai'i's most important export, virtually its only export: in 1897, for example, sugar exports represented $15.4 million out of an export total of $16.2 million. The number of laborers and of acres under sugar cultivation paralleled the expansion of sugar production. Between 1875 and 1910 the plantation work force increased more than thirteen times, from 3,260 to 43,917. Meanwhile, cultivated plantation lands multiplied nearly eighteen times, from 12,000 acres to 214,000 acres, and the number of plantations jumped from 20 to 52.[32]

Corporate consolidation accompanied this tremendous growth of the sugar industry. Five corporations dominated sugar production in Hawai'i: of the total tonnage of sugar produced in 1920, American Factors controlled 29 percent, C. Brewer 26 percent, Alexander and Baldwin 23 percent, Castle and Cooke 10 percent, and T. H. Davies 6 percent. These corporations, known as the "Big Five," also developed extensive control in all other areas of the Hawai'ian economy, including pineapple production, the retail merchandise business, electric power, telephone communication, railroad transportation, steamship lines, banking, and later the tourist industry. The sugar kingdom contained a formidable network of corporations—the California and Hawai'ian Sugar Refinery, Bank of Hawai'i, Inter-Island Steam Navigation Company, Matson Navigation Company, Oahu Railroad and Land Company, Honolulu Rapid Transit Company, Honolulu Gas Company, Hawai'ian Electric Company, and Liberty House.[33]

The pattern of corporate consolidation and control that developed in Hawai'i prompted the United States Commissioner of Labor to report in 1905: "Directly or indirectly all industries in the territory of Hawai'i are dependent upon the sugar industry—the social, the economic, and the political structure of the islands is built upon a foundation of sugar." And six years later, journalist Ray Stannard Baker described the awesome extent of corporate domination of Hawai'i: "Hawai'i has been called . . . the Paradise of the Pacific. But it is a paradise not only of natural beauties and wonders; it is also a paradise of modern industrial combination. In no part of the United States is a single industry so predominant as the sugar industry is in Hawai'i, and nowhere else, perhaps, has the centralized control of property reached a state of greater perfection." But to achieve such perfection, such predominance, the sugar industry required a vast supply of labor. William Hooper had projected such a need and had initiated the development of a multiethnic and transnational plantation labor system. To expand their acreage and production, planters inducted into their work force laborers not only from Hawai'i but also from China, Japan, Portugal, Norway, Germany, Korea, Puerto Rico, the Philippines, and even Russia.[34]

NOTES

1. James J. Jarvis, "Sketches of Kauai," *Hawai'ian Spectator* (January 1838): 66–68; Jarvis, *Scenes and Scenery in the Sandwich Islands* (London: E. Moxon, 1844), 95–102.

2. See William Hooper Diary and William Hooper Correspondence, William Hooper Papers, Hawai'ian Collection, University of Hawai'i, Honolulu.

3. See Frances O. Jackson, "Koloa Plantation under Ladd and Company, 1835–1845," Master's thesis, University of Hawai'i, 1958, 46–47.

4. Hooper, quoted in Arthur C. Alexander, *Koloa Plantation, 1835–1935* (Honolulu: Star Bulletin [hereafter abbreviated *SB*], 1937), 17; Hooper Diary, 11 September 1835, 12 September 1835, and 14 September 1835.

5. Hooper Diary, 12 September 1836.

6. David Malo, *Hawai'ian Antiquities* (Honolulu: Bishop Museum Press, 1951), 56–64.

7. Hooper Diary, 15 September 1835.

8. Ibid., 12 September 1836; Hooper to Ladd and Company, 15 November 1837, 23 February 1836, and 1 January 1839; Hooper, quoted in Alexander, *Koloa Plantation*, 16.

9. Jarvis, *Scenes and Scenery*, 102; Hooper Diary, 29 January 1838; Hooper, quoted in Alexander, *Koloa Plantation*, 16.

10. Hooper Diary, 7 January 1837; Hooper to Ladd and Company, 12 June 1838, 6 March 1839, and 8 March 1839.

11. Jarvis, quoted in Ethel M. Damon, *Koamalu: A Story of Pioneers on Kauai* (Honolulu: *SB*, 1931), 183–184; Hooper to Ladd and Company, 29 April 1836.

12. Hooper Diary, 14 September 1835 and 14 June 1836; Jarvis, *Scenes and Scenery*, 96; Hooper Diary, 25 November 1835, 20 June 1836, 9 August 1836, 27 March 1837, 13 November 1837, 16 November 1837, and 2 December 1837.

13. Hooper Diary, 9 May 1836, 11 May 1836, 28 May 1836, 31 May 1836, 4 August 1836, 10 November 1836, and 10 December 1836.

14. Hooper Diary, 12 September 1836; Hooper to Ladd and Company, 28 April 1836; Hooper Diary, 4 May 1836; Jarvis, *Scenes and Scenery*, 104.

15. Hooper to Ladd and Company, 29 April 1836; Ladd and Company to Dr. Lafore, 16 October 1837, Hooper Papers.

16. Hooper Diary, 15 September 1835, 18 September 1835, and 12 September 1836; Hooper to Ladd and Company, 23 February 1836, 21 September 1836, 3 October 1836, 26 October 1836, 10 December 1836, and 12 May 1838.

17. Jarvis, *Scenes and Scenery*, 102–103.

18. Hooper to Ladd and Company, 1 December 1838.

19. Hooper to Ladd and Company, January 1838.

20. Hooper to Ladd and Company, 28 March 1835 and 16 November 1836.

21. Hooper to Ladd and Company, 1 December 1838 and April 1838.

22. Hooper Diary, 28 January 1837 and 31 January 1837; Jarvis, *Scenes and Scenery*, 97.

23. Ladd and Company to William Henry N. Hooper [printer and brother of William Hooper], 15 November 1837, Hooper Papers; Hooper to Ladd and Company, 5 January 1839 and 7 April 1839.

24. Hooper Diary, 30 September 1835 and 18 October 1835; Hooper to Ladd and Company, 25 June 1838.

25. Daniel Dole to Dwight Baldwin, 10 June 1850, quoted in Alexander, *Koloa Plantation*, 50–51; *De Bow's Commercial Review* 22 (March 1857): 294.

26. Elizabeth Leslie Wright, *The Memoirs of Elizabeth Kinau Wilder* (Honolulu: Honolulu

Paradise of the Pacific Press, 1909), 136; *Pacific Commercial Advertiser* (hereafter abbreviated *PCA*), 9 April 1864.

27. *PCA*, 21 January 1864; *Hawai'ian Gazette*, 27 June 1877, quoted in Ralph S. Kuykendall, *The Hawai'ian Kingdom: The Kalaukaua Dynasty 1874–1893*, vol. 3 (Honolulu: University of Hawai'i Press, 1967), 47.

28. William Henry Taylor, "The Hawai'ian Sugar Industry," unpublished Ph.D. diss., University of California, Berkeley, 1935, 6, 7; Lawrence H. Fuchs, *Hawai'i Pono: A Social History* (New York: Harcourt, Brace and World, 1961), 251, 258.

29. Damon, *Koamalu*, 19; *Royal Hawai'ian Agricultural Society Transactions* 1, no. 1 (February 1852): 6.

30. *PCA*, 9 June 1877.

31. Taylor, "Hawai'ian Sugar Industry," 19–20, 170; Fuchs, *Hawai'i Pono*, 259; Damon, *Koamalu*, 857–858.

32. Taylor, "Hawai'ian Sugar Industry," 66, 166; *Hawai'ian Annual for 1904* (Honolulu: Thrum, 1903), 31; *Hawai'ian Annual for 1921* (Honolulu: Thrum, 1920), 24; J. A. Mollett, *Capital in Hawai'ian Sugar: Its Formation and Relation to Labor Output, 1870–1957* (Honolulu: Hawai'ian Agricultural Experiment Station, 1961), 13, 16, 27, 28.

33. Taylor, "Hawai'ian Sugar Industry," 66; Fuchs, *Hawai'i Pono*, 259; Gavan Daws, *Shoal of Time: A History of the Hawai'ian Islands* (Honolulu: University of Hawai'i Press, 1977), 312.

34. Commissioner of Labor, quoted in Ray Stannard Baker, "How King Sugar Rules," *American Magazine* 73 (November 1911): 28; Baker, ibid.

THE GADAR PARTY

POLITICAL EXPRESSION IN

AN IMMIGRANT COMMUNITY

Jane Singh

First-generation immigrants have typically been intimately involved with the politics of their former homeland. When the homeland happened either to be under colonial domination, or its people subjugated by repressive governments, this involvement often resulted in revolutionary organizational activities. Examples of such organizations include Chinese national organizations, e.g., the Reform Party and the Patriotic Rising Society in San Francisco, the Korean National Association, which sought to plan and finance resistance activities against Japan and even tried to provide military training for participants in the independence movement, and the remarkably similar Gadar (Rebellion) movement among the Asian Indians. The Gadar Party, being very much in the tradition of overseas-based nationalist movements, was dependent on the leadership of particular highly educated individuals for its vitality and impact. When these leaders, often political exiles, left the scene, the rank and file members found it difficult to maintain their political activism. The actual contribution of the Gadar to the Indian nationalist movement, though recognized, has been seen as peripheral, primarily due to their espousal of violence, which was rejected by the mainstream nationalist movement under the leadership of M. K. Gandhi. In the immigrant community, however, particularly among those in the agricultural sectors in California, the Gadar movement is seen as an important part of the Asian Indian heritage, and martyrs of the Gadar uprisings are still commemorated annually.

The first community organizations in North America formed by the Asian Indians were established in 1906 and 1907. These included Gurudwaras in British Columbia in 1906; Sikh centers of worship; ethnic societies such as the United India League in Vancouver, which sought to protect the rights of Indian workers; and nationalist organizations such as the India Independence League, formed in

San Francisco to provide political education for Indian immigrants in the area (Singh 1966: 14; Bose 1971: 48–49). Early in 1907, an Urdu periodical *Circular-i-Azadi* (Circular of Freedom) was published from San Francisco and was openly critical of British rule in India (Ker 1973: 228).

Although a series of similar organizations and periodicals followed that were concerned with immigration rights and the economic and social welfare of the Asian Indian, the anticolonialist sentiment remained an underlying theme in many of these activities. This trend contributed to the development of the Gadar Party in 1913. This militant nationalist movement evolved out of the loosely organized Hindustanee Association, which had branches from Vancouver, British Columbia, to the Imperial Valley on the southern border of California. In 1913, the charismatic Indian expatriate Har Dayal unified the community by clarifying the political objectives of the immigrants and by establishing a central headquarters for the Gadar Party in San Francisco. A printing press was set up and the first issue of the Gadar weekly newspaper was printed in November 1913. By the end of the year, the periodical was being regularly printed in two Indian languages.

In 1915 hundreds of Gadar-inspired immigrants from Canada and the United States returned to India to participate in an attempt to overthrow the British colonial government. In 1917 the U.S. government prosecuted a large number of Gadar leaders on grounds that they had violated American neutrality laws by plotting against the British while in U.S. territory. The intricacy and complexity of the Gadar organization and activities were revealed in a dramatic trial held in San Francisco. Indian, German, and American co-conspirators were tried and sentenced for attempting to smuggle arms, ammunition, and propaganda to revolutionaries inside India. The conviction and sentencing of a number of Gadar participants took the momentum out of the movement, although the Gadar Party continued to receive support from the immigrant community. The Gadar Party continued to print anticolonialist pamphlets and journals, host visiting Indian nationalists, and support revolutionary ventures until 1948, when India gained its independence. Thereafter Asian Indian community support persisted until a memorial hall and library was built on the Gadar premises at 5 Wood Street in San Francisco.

A number of factors led to the politicizing of the Asian Indian community in North America. Three major reasons for the rising political sentiments among the immigrants whose primary goals had been economic were: (1) growing unrest in their home province of Punjab, where widespread disturbances in 1907 over government repression and tax increases resulted in the arrest and deportation of two popular Punjabi leaders, Lajpat Rai and Ajit Singh (Sharma 1971: 48); (2) the presence in North America of expatriate nationalists who though few in number were among the more educated and took charge of ethnic periodicals or became spokesmen for the larger community; and (3) dissatisfaction with the British Indian government for not having supported their challenges to the increasing immigration restrictions being imposed by the United States and Canada. A large number of the Asian Indians in North America who had served their government as soldiers and policemen protested the British imperial government's lack of commitment to its own citizens, and found that they had even fewer rights to immigrate to the United States and Canada than other Asian nationals. The British Indian government refused to negotiate or make any agreement on behalf of those of its citizens who wished to migrate to North America.

It was also a precarious time for the Asian Indian immigrant. In 1907 the Japanese-Korean Exclusion League of San Francisco expanded to become the Asiatic Exclusion League so that Indians could also be targeted in their protests. The League became increasingly active and lobbied successfully for stricter immigration regulations to curb the number of Asians entering the United States (Das 1923: 16). Also in 1907, Canadian and U.S. labor elements were considered responsible for anti-Asiatic riots in Vancouver in which much of the Asian section of the city was destroyed. Indians were assaulted in a series of attacks on their work camps in the towns of Bellingham and Tacoma, Washington, and Astoria, Oregon (Misrow 1971: 30–31). In 1908 a Canadian Order-in-Council also effected a regulation that seriously curtailed Indian immigration: it required that immigrants come directly from their country of origin in a continuous journey (Singh 1966: 12). Most Indians had been coming from East Asian ports, since there were no direct lines operating between India and Canada at that time.

As their presence in North America was being severely challenged, Asian Indians formed a variety of organizations to bolster their position under inhospitable conditions. The Gadar movement grew out of the immigrant community's tendency toward collective activism. Since 1907 Asian Indians had conducted numerous protests and made repeated representations to the Canadian, U.S. and British governments in regard to immigration restrictions that limited their entry to North America. The Hindustanee Association had been formed to present a united front against the oppressive restrictions. This organization regularly dealt with both immigration and nationalist issues (Bose 1971: 53–54). While the immediate concerns of the Indians were their rights to immigrate, to own property, and to gain citizenship and enfranchisement, there was an increasing antipathy toward India's colonial status. Although many of those who migrated to North America had served in the British Indian armed forces, the subservient position of the motherland made a more acute impression on them as they viewed their country from abroad. The seasoned nationalists found willing, if not long-term, support for their anti-British activities among these immigrants.

Har Dayal, a Punjabi Hindu, had come to California with a long career of political activism in India and Europe behind him. He had heard of the rising nationalist consciousness among Indian immigrants on the Pacific west coast (Dharmavira 1970: 145–146). Har Dayal reached California in June 1911, and while he did meet with his fellow Punjabis, he spent most of his time in intellectual circles at the University of California-Berkeley, Stanford University, and San Francisco. He was a lecturer in philosophy at Stanford for several months and actively participated in a number of radical American political groups in the San Francisco bay area. In spite of his diverse activities, Har Dayal was apparently making an impact on the local Indian community. In the summer of 1912, a group of six Indian students arrived at U. C. Berkeley on scholarships sponsored by a successful Sikh farmer, Jawala Singh from Stockton, California. The fellowship program had been designed by Har Dayal to bring dedicated and politically sensitive young men to the United States for higher education. The program came to an abrupt halt when

Jawala Singh's crops failed, but the prospect of politically motivating this new group of students captured Har Dayal's imagination and brought him closer to the Indian student community at Berkeley (Brown 1975: 128). By the end of 1912, Har Dayal was spending more time circulating among the various Indian communities along the Pacific west coast. Indians were concentrated in clusters or groups in major agricultural areas in California such as the Sacramento, San Joaquin, and Imperial Valleys. In Washington, Oregon, and British Columbia the majority worked in major centers of the lumber industry. Har Dayal traveled from community to community with other nationalists, students, and immigrant activists. He and his associates lectured to gatherings of Indians, and when the opportunity arose, he would address American audiences as well, describing India and its condition under British rule. In Astoria, Oregon, where approximately 200 Indians worked in lumber yards, Har Dayal told an American audience that India was being economically drained by the British. In describing the unprecedented poverty in India as a result of colonial rule, he referred to the "British Vampire" instead of the British Empire (quoted in Ker 1973: 235).

In the spring of 1913, a large number of Indians met in Portland, Oregon. Delegates from various communities in the United States and Canada decided to combine the different Hindustanee Associations into one central organization with specific goals and activities. The delegates agreed that funds should be raised to establish a central office and to publish a revolutionary newspaper (Bose 1971: 58; Brown 1975: 140–141). Several Indian leaders were elected officers of the new Hindustanee Association of the Pacific Coast. Har Dayal became the general Secretary. Taking charge, he established the organization's headquarters in San Francisco in November 1913. The Association's name was changed to the Gadar Party (Party of Rebellion), and the first issue of the Gadar weekly was published on November 1.

San Francisco became the center for Gadar activities because Har Dayal had many contacts in the area with local universities and radical political groups. The Indian population in California was growing because immigrants were attracted from northern areas by the state's favorable climate and farming opportunities. Most of the Indian immigrants in North America had come from an agricultural background in Punjab, and many of them were drawn to California's rich farmlands. Finally, San Francisco was a relatively safe place to carry on overt nationalist agitation. Vancouver, Canada had been a center for political activity in earlier days, but critics of the British Empire had to be cautious when speaking out in a commonwealth country.

The initial focus of the Gadar Party was to disseminate the revolutionary message through the weekly newspaper *Gadar*. It was printed in Urdu, a major language in North India, and in Gurumukhi, the script of the Punjabi language. It was sent throughout Indian immigrant communities in North, Central, and South America, Europe, and East and Southeast Asia. The *Gadar* was also sent in large numbers to India, but because it was soon banned by the colonial government, it had to be smuggled into the country. The second major Gadar activity was for representatives to circulate throughout the Indian community presenting political lectures and programs and installing local units of the party which could hold regular meetings and raise funds. The third part of the Gadar program was to develop an international network of individuals and organized units working for the overthrow of the British government in India.

The Gadar Party functioned under a set of rigid rules that emphasized secrecy and confidentiality in all operations (Brown 1975: 143). In the first several months after the Gadar was established, clandestine activities consisted mainly of sending messengers and Gadar publications to immigrant communities and nationalist centers throughout the world. Those privy to secret operations of the organization formed an inner circle of the Gadar structure. These individuals included most of the "full-time" nationalists, such as Taraknath Das and Pandurang Khankhoje, who had been active in the Hindustanee Associations and were committed to the Indian freedom movement. Others were close associates of Har Dayal such as Ram Chandra, Gobind Bihari Lal, and Kartar Singh Sarabha, the latter two students at U. C. Berkeley. Barkatullah and Bhagwan Singh had been politically active in East Asia and became important members of the Gadar organization. The inner circle was made up mainly of educated Indians, many of whom were neither Sikh nor Punjabi. The outer circle of Gadar volunteers comprised mostly average Indian immigrants who gave up their work in lumber mills, farms, and other such enterprises to devote themselves to the cause. The third component of the Gadar structure was the membership, immigrants who paid subscriptions and belonged to local chapters of the Gadar Party. Friction between the educated and the noneducated Indians had arisen in earlier community organizations and was evident in the Gadar Party as well (Singh 1966: 17; Brown 1975: 140–141). Because of the collective enthusiasm for this revolutionary movement, however, these differences did not surface until after the organization was well established.

The Gadar movement quickly gained support among the mainstream of the Asian Indian immigrants on the Pacific west coast. In December 1913 Har Dayal reported to a friend that "they had raised $2,000 among Hindu laborers in California and Canada," which enabled them to establish a center and publication program (quoted in Brown 1975: 143). British intelligence reports noted, with much alarm, that Vancouver was also a center for antigovernment agitation. At a meeting held at a Sikh Gurudwara on December 27, 1913, several militant speeches were delivered and a patriotic poem from the *Gadar* weekly was recited (Ker 1973: 236). A British undercover agent, William Hopkinson, fluent in Indian languages, had kept close watch on the Asian Indian community in Canada for years. On January 8, 1913 he reached San Francisco on special assignment to investigate anti-British activities in California. With the help of the local British consul, Hopkinson was able to enlist the cooperation of U.S. immigration officials and the U.S. Department of Justice to help him make a case against Indian revolutionaries (Brown 1975: 131–132). He focused his attention on several speeches delivered by Har Dayal in 1913, and formulated a case against the Indian. As a result of Hopkinson's presentation, Har Dayal was arrested by U.S. authorities on March 26, 1914 on charges that he, an alien, was a revolutionary who had associations with anarchist organizations (Ker 1973: 237). Released on bail, Har Dayal used the opportunity to present his case in the *Gadar* newspaper as well as the local press. Citing British influence as the cause for his arrest, he stated in his characteristic manner, "It is the despicable pro-British subservience of the U.S. that is responsible for my arrest. The Democratic administration is licking the boots of England" (quoted in Ker 1973: 238; Brown 1975: 162–163). Although lawyers retained by the Gadar Party were preparing his defense, Har Dayal left the country while he was free on bail to avoid the risk of deportation to India.

Gadar headquarters continued to function as usual after Har Dayal's departure. In January he had turned over editorship of the *Gadar* to Ram Chandra, a Punjabi journalist who had accompanied him throughout the 1913 lecture circuit. The press cranked out Urdu and Gurumukhi materials regularly, and added translations in other vernacular Indian languages when volunteers were available to prepare the copy. From the first issues of the *Gadar* printed in November 1913, Gadar publicists wrote of the coming revolution in India and exhorted their readers to be prepared to devote themselves to the cause. At a meeting in Sacramento on December 31, 1913 Har Dayal had said that Germany would soon be at war with Britain and that Indians should be prepared to return home to launch the revolution in such an event (Sed. Com. Report 1918: 146). This rhetoric of preparedness was continued in Gadar publications after Har Dayal left the country, and increased toward the summer of 1914 as war between Germany and Britain appeared imminent. There is no evidence, however, that an actual plan of revolution had been devised by the middle of 1914. There is an account that in November 1914 Indian nationalists were trying to secure a loan from Germany to support a Gadar-directed insurgency in India (Sareen 1979: 121). During the year, Gadarites, as members of the organization have been popularly called, had also made contact with Chinese nationalists in the United States. Many of the tactics discussed and proposed for the prospective Indian revolt were laid out through consultations with Chinese revolutionaries. Gadar activist Pandurang Khankhoje described the jointly devised "plan of action" as follows:

> It was decided to cut communications, by mobbing railway stations and cutting telegraph lines, then destroying the Police Chowkis (police stations), disorganizing the military camps and checkposts, etc. . . . the second step was to establish revolutionary camps in jungles, and border areas, in the hills and valleys, and then to start harassing the English administration and the armies. . . . It was not possible for us to purchase and procure arms and weapons by any other means except by guerrilla raids on army bases of the English. (Quoted in Brown 1975: 151–152)

While Gadar leaders were formulating their revolutionary strategy, two events hastened the departure of immigrants for India. On April 14, 1914 a chartered Japanese ship, the *Komagata Maru*, sailed from Hong Kong with 372 Punjabi passengers on board. The ship, bound for Vancouver, had been chartered by a Sikh contractor from Singapore (Sed. Com. Report 1918: 147). The trip was undertaken to test and challenge the Canadian Order-in-Council that had stipulated that immigrants must purchase their tickets and travel directly from their country of origin. The ordinance was so effective that Indian immigration to Canada dropped from 2,623 in 1908 to 6 in 1909 (Das 1923: 4–5). The *Komagata Maru* reached Vancouver harbor on May 23, 1914. The Canadian government remained firm in its determination to uphold the restrictions, and the passengers were forced to remain on board ship for two months while Asian Indians residing in Vancouver tried to negotiate an arrangement to allow their compatriots to disembark. They made representations to the Dominion government in Ottawa and the British India Office in London, but received no support from either. The immigrant community tried to challenge the legality of the exclusionary regulations, but in a test case the court decision went against them.

The *Komagata Maru* incident generated considerable public debate and excitement. Canadian newspapers covered the developments assiduously and were replete with racist arguments for maintaining a bar against Asian Indians. "Two themes dominated the cries of the nativists: fear of inundation by hordes of Asian immigrants and concern for the unassimilable nature of the Indian" (Ward 1978: 90). Typical press statements included: "The question before the people of Canada is whether the country is to be thrown open to all the people of India or closed to all," and "each race is better off in its own natural environment . . . the unrestrained mixing of the races on this Coast would lead to economic disaster and ethical demoralization" (quoted in Ward 1978: 90–91).

After the court decision the authorities ordered the captain of the *Komagata Maru* to remove the ship from the harbor. When the passengers took over the vessel to prevent the departure, a police unit was sent in by tugboat to enforce the orders. The passengers forced the police to retreat by bombarding them with a hail of coal and any other missile they could find on the ship. The Indians were then given a small concession—an opportunity to meet with a cabinet official, to whom they gave their statement. The passengers agreed to leave and arrangements were made for the return journey. A warship, the HMCS *Rainbow,* was brought in to ensure there were no further incidents as the *Komagata Maru* left Vancouver harbor on July 23, 1914.

The trials of the *Komagata Maru* passengers were not over, however. They were not allowed to return to Hong Kong, nor to disembark at any other port along the way. They reached Budge Budge Harbor near Calcutta on the east coast of India on September 29, 1914 and were received by a police unit that was ordered to escort them back to Punjab by special trains. Concerned about the fate that awaited them once they were returned to Punjab, they resisted; in the ensuing confrontation twenty passengers, two European officers, two Punjabi police officers, and two bystanders were killed (Report of K. M. Com. 1914: 15–17).

The *Komagata Maru* affair had been closely followed by Asian Indians in the United States as well as Canada. Protests expressed through the Gadar reflected the indignation felt by the Indians for the ill treatment of their compatriots. Within a few weeks after the *Komagata Maru* had left Vancouver, war broke out in Europe. Meetings were called throughout the Indian community at which speakers declared that the time had come to return to India to fight in the "Gadar" (rebellion) (Ker 1973: 245). The mood had thus been set by a series of events: Har Dayal's arrest and departure, the *Komagata Maru* incident, and Britain's entry into war with Germany. Britain's distraction by war was of course the long-awaited Gadar opportunity. Hundreds of Indians began returning to India in groups, trying to evade the authorities by entering at different ports. The exodus of Indians from North

America and other parts of the world was well known to the British, and many of the returning immigrants were arrested at ports under the Ingress into India Ordinance (Sed. Com. Report 1918: 148). The Ordinance had been passed in September 1914 to restrict the movements of the *Komagata Maru* passengers once they had landed in India. The regulation conveniently applied to Gadarites who were steadily returning home through the end of 1914 and into 1915.

Most of the prominent Gadar leaders who slipped through the ports and found their way to Punjab were soon tracked down and arrested by British agents (Singh 1966: 37). Those Gadarites who escaped arrest spread the revolutionary message in villages and military cantonments. Gadar pamphlets and newspapers were distributed widely (Sed. Com. Report 1918: 159). Gadarites made contacts with local dissidents and planned a general rebellion of Indian troops on February 21, 1915. The revolt was undermined, however, by the infiltration of a government spy into the Gadar ranks. This led to the immediate arrest of several revolutionaries and their military sympathizers. The imperial government was particularly alarmed by the attempt to subvert the loyalty of the troops, since 40 percent of all Indian army recruits were from Punjab. Since the Gadar movement was a potential threat to the military as well as the political system, the government took every measure to contain the activities of this group. The Imperial Legislative Council passed the Defense of India Act on March 18, 1915 in order to avert the Gadar threat by speeding up the judicial proceedings against those arrested. Special tribunals were appointed to try Gadar cases (Sed. Com. Report 1918: 156). A series of three trials, the Lahore Conspiracy Tribunals, were held during 1915, and 291 persons were prosecuted. As a result of these trials, 42 individuals were sentenced to death and hanged, 114 were sentenced to life imprisonment, and 93 were given prison terms of varying lengths (Singh 1966: 45). The majority of those tried and convicted in these tribunals were Gadarites who had returned from abroad.

Although the failure of the 1915 revolution was a strategic and psychological setback, the Gadar Party continued to be active. By 1915 there were branches of the organization established in China, Malaysia, Bangkok, and South and Central America. There were several Gadar activists in Europe who became members of the India Committee in Berlin. The Berlin Committee, as it was called, was made up of twenty-five expatriates who, with German support, planned and implemented a variety of programs designed to destabilize the colonial government in India. The failure of the February revolt was largely due to a lack of finances, arms, and equipment to organize and launch a substantial attack against government forces. Recognizing this, members of the Berlin Committee arranged to secure a loan from Germany to carry out their activities. The money, given to Indian revolutionaries through German consular offices in different parts of the world, was to be repaid when India regained its freedom (Sareen 1979: 120). With German cooperation and financial assistance, the Berlin Committee and the Gadar Party devised an elaborate plan to purchase and ship arms and ammunition to India. Working with the Germans, Indians in the United States attempted to ship 8,080 Springfield rifles, 2,400 carbines, 410 repeating rifles, 3,759 cases of cartridges, 5,000 cartridge belts and 500 Colt revolvers to India by chartered ships. The plan failed when the two chartered vessels were unable to make contact in the Pacific Ocean. In mid-

1915 the ship carrying these supplies returned to the United States and was seized at Hoquiam Port in the state of Washington (Sareen 1979: 131–132; Bose 1971: 127–130).

The Gadar Party was also involved in a plan to attack India from Southeast Asia. Party members were active in Bangkok, Rangoon, and Singapore. A mutiny among Indian troops in Singapore on February 15, 1915 was inspired by Gadar propagandists. During 1915 many Gadarites were sent from San Francisco to Southeast Asia. In August 1915 several members of the Gadar Party were arrested in Bangkok, and from October 1915 on Indians were not allowed to move about freely in Thailand. Efforts continued, however, in Japan, Korea, and China to secure arms and ship them to India. Gadar emissaries such as Bhagwan Singh spent most of 1915 in East Asia and joined other Indian nationalists in Tokyo in October 1915.[1] They tried to buy arms in Japan, but due to increased British surveillance and lack of accessibility to Thailand, no large shipments were ever smuggled into India (Bose 1971: 152–153). Attempts to deliver necessary equipment to India from East Asia continued in 1916. Taraknath Das went from Germany to China and Japan to explore sources for procuring and shipping arms. Despite several months of trying, Das did not find the means to carry out his mission (Bose 1971: 155–156).

Gadar headquarters in San Francisco remained active during this period. Business continued as usual even though the organization's overall unity had been weakened by its inability to gain a substantial fighting foothold in India. Many Gadar supporters from the Stockton and Sacramento areas were particularly disappointed by the failure of the 1915 revolt, which had sacrificed the lives and freedom of many of their fellow immigrants. They blamed the local leaders for prematurely sending hundreds of their compatriots back to Punjab without adequate preparation and equipment. At a Stockton meeting in August 1915, *Gadar* editor Ras Chandra was turned away without any donations for the Gadar Party (Ker 1973: 257). Bhagwan Singh became the leader of the opposition party when he returned to California from Asia in the middle of 1916. Tension between Singh and Chandra resulted in the two factions setting up different presses and publishing two separate weekly newspapers beginning in February 1917.

The intraparty friction diminished in April 1917 when the United States entered World War I and the local American press began to criticize the Gadar Party for its collusion with Germany against Britain (Ker 1973: 258). Representatives of the Berlin India Committee in New York were arrested in March 1917; a few months later, Gadar Party members on the west coast were taken into custody. They were charged with violating U.S. neutrality by conspiring against the British on American territory. A historic trial was held in San Francisco from November 1917 to April 1918. All but one of the Indian defendants were found guilty, sentenced to prison, and fined (Singh 1966: 52). The internal conflicts within the Gadar Party were dramatically reflected in the courtroom on the last day of the trial when Ram Chandra was shot to death by another Indian, who in turn was killed by a guard.

The abortive revolution in Punjab in 1915 and the trial and conviction of Indian activists in 1918 were the overt manifestations of the Gadar Party's inability to carry out an organized revolt against the British in India. The impact of the movement on the colonial government was nevertheless important. The Gadar Party had gained its momentum from the large numbers of immigrant supporters. The politicizing of a large group of individuals from the Indian mainstream was itself a threat to the colonial government. Even when the organization was weakened from internal conflicts among the leaders, the grassroots membership did not withdraw its support, instead shifting allegiance to different factions. This backing allowed the Gadar activities to continue in one way or another for many years, though many of the leaders and members were periodically dislocated and incarcerated.

Britain's position in India showed signs of destabilization after the Gadar-related disturbances in Punjab. Police officers' firing on a large unarmed crowd in the city of Amritsar in 1919 illustrated that the government had lost its sense of control over the province. The Jallianwala Bagh incident[2] was a political as well as a moral disaster for the government, and won many more converts to the nationalist cause in India and abroad. Revolutionary activities among Punjabi youth increased after the 1915 revolt and the 1919 police firings. The young patriot Bhagat Singh, who was hanged in 1929 with his associates for terrorist activities against the colonial government, stated that he had been inspired by the sacrifices of the Gadarites who returned to India in 1915.

When those convicted in the San Francisco conspiracy case were released, Gadar activities slowly resumed. An English-language monthly, *The Independent Hindustan*, was published by the Gadar Party in 1920–21 with the cooperation of a New York-based society called the Friends of Freedom for India. After serving their respective sentences, Taraknath Das went to New York to establish the latter group while Santokh Singh was one of the individuals who returned to Gadar headquarters to take charge of local operations. Some expatriate activists dropped out of political life after their incarceration in 1918; others, fearing continued persecution in the United States, moved to different parts of the world. This left the control of the Gadar Party largely with immigrant constituents, the Punjabi Sikhs.

In the 1920s many of the Gadarites who had remained in India after 1915 joined the Akali movement, a Sikh insurgency in Punjab against government control over their institutions. The clashes between the Sikhs and the government were well covered in the Gadar periodical ("Who Are the Alkalis?" *U.S. of India,* 1924: 4–7). The Gadar network throughout North America collected funds to support the Akali cause. Another fund established by the Gadar organization was used to get up the Desh Bhagat Parivar Sahayik Committee (Committee to Aid the Families of Patriots) in India, which provided financial assistance to families of Gadarites and Akalis who had been killed or imprisoned. This committee continued to help dissidents' families until after Indian independence in 1948.

In 1918 several members of the Berlin India Committee went to Russia to explore the possibility of getting Soviet support for the Indian freedom movement (Sareen 1979: 220). Since the Russian revolution in 1917 Indian nationalists had become very interested in the newly liberated nation. In 1922 Santokh Singh and Rattan Singh from the San Francisco Gadar office attended the Fourth Congress of the Third International in Moscow. Thereafter a number of Gadar workers were sent to the University for the Toilers of the East in Moscow to learn the theory and practice of revolution. Santokh Singh went to India in 1923 but was put under house arrest and detained in his village in Punjab until 1925. Once freed he went to Amritsar, where he and two other Gadarites established the periodical *Kirti* (Worker) (Josh 1977–78: 223).

The *Kirti* monthly, supported by the Gadar Party, became the official organ for a peasant-worker movement in Punjab. Many of the 76 Gadarites who returned to India via Moscow joined the new movement, as did the majority of the Gadar veterans of the 1915 and Akali revolts. These "Babas" (grandfathers, old men), as they were called because of their advanced age, were released from jails during the 1920s and 1930s after serving their sentences. It was many of these "Babas" who formed the vanguard of the peasant and subsequent socialist movement in Punjab (Singh 1945: 29; Josh 1977–78: 330–332).

Gadar activities in San Francisco after 1920 concentrated mainly on its publications and on financing special movements in India. The *Gadar* was published irregularly and was circulated among the dwindling population of Asian Indian immigrants through the 1930s. Many of the earlier Gadar pamphlets were reprinted during this time. Publications and programs became increasingly irregular during the 1930s, but some level of activity was maintained until 1948. Gadar Party headquarters remained open at 5 Wood Street in San Francisco until 1959 as a meeting place, particularly for old-timers or Indians passing through the city who had no other place to stay. In 1975 the Asian Indian community and the Government of India, in cooperation, built a memorial hall and library where the old Gadar building once stood.

In addition to its political impact in India, the Gadar movement is an important part of the history of the Asian Indian immigrant experience in North America. It illustrates how an immigrant community can unify under adverse circumstances and mobilize itself for action within a relatively short period of time. In 1907, within a year after the first large number of Indians entered the United States and Canada, they established a variety of ethnic organizations that fulfilled various religious, social, and political needs. Six years later the Gadar Party was founded, and within months a revolutionary ideology and organization emerged that was subscribed to by the majority of Indian immigrants in the region. There have been few attempts to understand how and why a complex political network developed in a loosely-knit community at a time when communications, travel, and financial resources were relatively limited. The cultural homogeneity of the early immigrant group, the absence of family life, their tenuous position in North America and therefore their greater vested interest in their homeland, are all factors that may have contributed to the popular support of the Gadar movement. It is remarkable nonetheless to observe the politicizing of the Asian Indian immigrant in America and note the readiness with which the radical Gadar ideology was embraced.

NOTES

1. Herambalal Gupta, Lajpat Rai, Rash Behari Bose.
2. Jallianwala Bagh, an enclosed garden with limited exits, was the site of the police firing.

REFERENCES

Bose, Arun Coomer (1971). *Indian Revolutionaries Abroad, 1905–1922.* Patna: Bharati Bhavan.

Brown, Emily (1975). *Har Dayal: Hindu Revolutionary and Rationalist.* Tucson: University of Arizona Press.

Das, Rajani Kanta (1923). *Hindustani Workers on the Pacific Coast.* Berlin: Walter de Gruyter & Co.

Dharmavira (1970). *Lala Har Dayal and Revolutionary Movements of His Times.* New Delhi: Indian Book Company.

Josh, Sohan Singh (1977–78). *Hindustan Gadar Party: A Short History.* 2 vols. New Delhi: People's Publishing House.

Ker, James Campbell (1973). *Political Trouble in India, 1907–1917.* Reprint. Delhi: Oriental Publishers.

Misrow, Jogesh C. (1971). *East Indian Immigration on the Pacific Coast.* Reprint. San Francisco: R & E Research Associates.

Report of the Komagata Maru *Committee of Inquiry* (1914). Calcutta: Superintendent Government Printing.

Sareen, Tilak Raj (1979). *Indian Revolutionary Movement Abroad (1905–1921).* New Delhi: Sterling Publishers Pvt. Ltd.

Sedition Committee, 1918 Report (1910). Calcutta: Superintendent Government Printing.

Sharma, Sri Ram (1971). *Punjab in Ferment.* New Delhi: S. Chand & Co.(Pvt.) Ltd.

Singh, Khushwant, and Satindra Singh (1966). *Ghadar 1915, India's First Armed Revolution.* New Delhi: R & K Publishing House.

Singh, Randhir (1945). *The Ghadar Heroes: Forgotten History of the Punjab Revolutionaries of 1914–1915.* Bombay: People's Publishing House.

Ward, W. Peter (1978). *White Canada Forever: Popular Attitudes and Public Policy Towards Orientals in British Columbia.* Montreal: McGill-Queen's University Press.

"Who are the Akalis? A Brief Study of Sikhism" (1924). *The United States of India* 1 (March): 8, 4–7.

Treatment

HOSTILITY AND CONFLICT

Sucheng Chan

The presence of Asians on American soil highlighted some fundamental cleavages in American society. This fact makes Asian immigration history more important than the small number of Asians in the United States might otherwise warrant. During the first period of their immigration, vested interests that stood to gain by their labor promoted their influx, while other groups threatened by their coming strove to exclude them. But both those who wanted them and those who did not agreed on one point: like the indigenous populations of Hawai'i, Alaska, and the continental United States pushed aside by Euro-Americans who desired their land, like Africans enslaved and condemned to hard labor in the New World, like Mexicans conquered and subjugated, Asians were deemed members of "inferior races." Negative perceptions of nonwhite peoples have a long history in the Western world. Color prejudice had become such a habit of heart and mind among Euro-Americans by the time Asians started coming that the former had no difficulty justifying hostile actions against the latter—actions that culminated in efforts to expel Asians from some parts of the United States as well as to prevent them from entering the country in the first place.

Hostility against Asian immigrants may be divided into seven categories: prejudice, economic discrimination, political disenfranchisement, physical violence, immigration exclusion, social segregation, and incarceration.[1]

As the Chinese were the first to arrive, prejudice toward them has been most clearly delineated and long-lived. Unfavorable views of the Chinese predated the first landing of Chinese on American soil. Most Americans during the nineteenth century acknowledged that China had once had a magnificent civilization, but they also agreed that the country had reached an advanced state of decay in the several hundred years since its peak. In their eyes, China's people were nothing more than starving masses, beasts of burden, depraved heathens, and opium addicts. As Stuart Creighton Miller has revealed, three groups of Americans who had experienced frustrations in China helped to spread adverse images of the Chinese in the United States: diplomats who resented the elaborate protocols of the Chinese court, merchants who bridled against the limitations placed on their freedom to trade, and missionaries who wrung their hands over the slow rate of Chinese conversion to Christianity. Through private letters and reports, published articles, and public speeches, these men and women disseminated to the American public their negative or at best ambivalent views of the Chinese.[2]

Chinese inferiority soon came to serve in the minds of many as a foil for Euro-American superiority. But interestingly, the fear and loathing that developed over the presence of the Chinese paradoxically became the very "exotica" that titillated many a Euro-American. The exotic image of Chinese was based in part on their unusual appearance. But their looks aroused more than curiosity—they also led to penalties. An ordinance passed in 1870 in San Francisco, for example, authorized prison wardens to cut off the queues worn by Chinese men, even though these pigtails were required by their Manchu rulers and did no one any harm. Fortunately for the Chinese, the ordinance was never implemented because the mayor vetoed it.

Of the other Asian immigrant groups, the Japanese seemed to be most conscious of the controversy their Chinese predecessors' visage had caused, so they tried hard to give an opposite impression. Japanese men walked down gangplanks in Western-style suits; picture brides who arrived wearing kimonos and wooden clogs were upon landing whisked off by their husbands to dressmakers and shoemakers to be outfitted with Victorian clothing and shoes. Unlike Japanese, who could doff their traditional garb without disapproval, Punjabi Sikhs had no alternative except to retain a part of theirs for religious reasons: Sikh men had to wear turbans because not cutting their hair was one of the five requirements of their faith. As a result, they had to endure the opprobrium of being called "ragheads."

Far more serious than such personal harassment were laws that cut into the immigrants' earnings.[3] A Foreign Miners' Tax first passed in 1850 and reenacted in 1852 was enforced primarily against Chinese, even though in theory it applied to all foreigners. More problematic than the tax itself was the manner in which it was collected. Since the collectors received a percentage of the take, they were not above extorting hapless Chinese miners, who were often intimidated into paying more than once for the same piece of ground. Impostors also preyed on them. Worse, once Euro-American miners realized the Chinese had no protection of any sort, they showed no qualms in driving them off good claims. Attacks against and robbery of Chinese became so common that one reporter for the *Placerville American* was moved to declare in 1857, "There ought to be a protection against his having to pay the onerous foreign miners' tax over three or four times; against sham licenses being given out and taken away from him, and his money extorted; and against being gagged, whipped and robbed whenever a worthless white rowdy chooses to abuse him thus, for pleasure or profit."[4]

In urban centers, Chinese laundrymen seemed to have been singled out for discrimination. The San Francisco Board of Supervisors decided in 1870 that every three months, laundries using one horse for their delivery wagons had to pay $2, those using two horses owed $4, while those using no horses were liable for $15. Since it was Chinese who did not use horses, the spirit of the law discriminated against them, even though its letter ostensibly did not. Between 1873 and 1884 the Board of Supervisors passed fourteen separate ordinances to curb the spread of Chinese laundries.

The ability of Chinese, Japanese, Korean, and Asian Indian immigrants to earn a living in agricultural areas was affected by alien land laws, the first of which was passed in California in 1913. Under it, aliens ineligible for citizenship could no longer buy agricultural land or lease it for more than three years. The law had little effect, however, because district attorneys did not try to enforce it strenuously during World War I, given the nation's need for maximum food production. But once the war was over, anti-Japanese groups mounted a new campaign to close the loopholes in the 1913 law. California's voters supported an initiative on the 1920 state ballot that ended the ability of Asian aliens to lease farm land altogether. It also forbade them to purchase land through corporations in which they held more than 50 percent of the stocks or in the names of their American-born (hence citizen) minor children. A 1923 amendment made cropping contracts—agreements between landowners and alien farmers under which the latter planted and harvested crops for wages—illegal, even though such arrangements technically conferred no legal interest in the land itself.[5]

Following California's example, Arizona enacted a similar law in 1917, Washington and Louisiana in 1921, New Mexico in 1922, Idaho, Montana, and Oregon in 1923, and Kansas in 1925, as detailed by Dudley McGovney.[6] (There being few Asians in Kansas, the law in that state very likely was a response to the widespread presence of foreign-born Scottish landlords and creditors in the Great Plains.) Then, during World War II, while most Pacific Coast Japanese were in concentration camps, Utah, Wyoming, and Arkansas also passed alien land laws, probably as preventive measures. The legislatures of those states apparently did not want any Japanese to get the idea they could easily settle there after the war was over.

These various economic sanctions were possible because Asian immigrants, being denied the right of naturalization, could not vote and consequently had no political power. Unlike their European counterparts, who could participate in the electoral process after they acquired citizenship, Asian immigrants were unable to influence politicians to heed their needs. Asians, who could cast neither individual nor bloc votes, had no political voice whatsoever. Denial of the right of naturalization to anyone other than "free, white persons" was first written into the Constitution. Then in 1870, as part of the reforms during Reconstruction, new legislation extended the right to "persons of African nativity or descent." The question of naturalization for Chinese had been debated when a Civil Rights bill was first introduced in 1866. Senator Charles Sumner of Massachusetts had declared that "the right to vote shall not be abridged on account of color,"[7] but the opposition to franchise for the Chinese was so strong that in the end they were not included.

However, since petitions for naturalization during the 1870s were reviewed by local courts, the rule was not applied uniformly across the nation. Fifteen Chinese in New York gained citizenship in 1878, for example, and the newspaper reporter who interviewed them noted that one of their friends had become a citizen as early as 1873 and had "served as a juryman . . . the first Chinaman who ever acted in the capacity in Europe or America."[8] Several dozen others may have been similarly successful before the U.S. circuit court in California declared Chinese ineligible in *In re Ah Yup* (1878). A handful of Japanese and Asian Indian immigrants likewise managed to become naturalized before the U.S. Supreme Court ruled unequivocally in *Ozawa v United States* (1922) and *United States v Bhagat Singh Thind* (1923), respectively, to disqualify them.

An equally severe political handicap to the Chinese was that California, where the vast majority of them lived, during the first dozen years of its statehood disallowed court testimony from blacks, mulattos, and (native American) Indians. The prohibition was originally enunciated in the 1850 Criminal Proceedings Act; it was extended the following year to civil proceedings as well. In late 1853 one George Hall was convicted for the murder of a Chinese, but in 1854 the California Supreme Court reversed his conviction on the grounds that it had been based on evidence given by Chinese witnesses. The chief justice ruled that since native American Indians had originally crossed the Bering Straits from the Asian continent into Alaska, they were in reality "Asiatics"! Hence, the 1850 act that barred Indian testimony applied to "the whole of the Mongolian race." Though the state's Civil Procedure Code was amended in 1863 to permit Negro testimony, the prohibition against Chinese testimony was written into the statute books that same year. Only in 1872 was reference to them quietly dropped from the Civil Procedure Code, as the state legislature revised its statutes to conform to the Fourteenth Amendment. Even after this change, evidence offered by Chinese was virtually never accepted except in cases involving other Chinese, as Hudson Janisch has chronicled.[9]

Deprived of political rights and legal protection, the Chinese were subjected to repeated acts of violence.[10] Violence against Asian immigrants falls into three patterns: the maiming and wanton murder of individuals, spontaneous attacks against and the destruction (usually by fire) of Chinatowns, and organized efforts to drive Asians out of certain towns and cities. (Not all expulsions were violent, though.)

Violence against Asians surfaced in the early 1850s and was directed at Chinese miners. Although there is no accurate record of all the Chinese miners who were injured and killed, in 1862 a committee of the California State Legislature stated that it had received a list of eighty-eight Chinese known to have been murdered by Euro-Americans, eleven of them by collectors of the Foreign Miners' Tax. The committee concluded in its report, "it is a well known fact that there has been a wholesale system of wrong and outrage practised upon the Chinese population of this state, which would disgrace the most barbarous nation upon earth."[11]

The first documented instance of a spontaneous outbreak against a Chinese community took place in Los Angeles in 1871.[12] According to William Locklear, troubles began when two factions within Chinatown, then located in so-called Nigger Alley, fought with each other over possession of a Chinese woman. In the early evening of October 24, a police officer in the vicinity heard shooting and went to investigate. As he neared the Chinese quarters, a shot was fired at him, whereupon he called for help. A large crowd soon gathered. The Chinese, meanwhile, scurried for safety inside their dwellings. One man in the crowd, brandishing a six-shooter and followed by several others, climbed to the roof of an adobe building in which a number of Chinese were hiding. They cut holes through the walls and started firing inside. Chinese attempting to flee were shot down in cold blood. Others were dragged along the street, then hanged. The mob battered down buildings, hauled out the terrified Chinese, beat and kicked each one before lynching him, and looted the Chinese houses in search of gold and other valuables. A number of impatient men cut off the fingers of a Chinese herbalist in order to take the rings he wore. By the time the sheriff arrived with 25 deputized volunteers at 9:30 p.m. to quell the riot, the mob had begun to disperse. The sheriff found fifteen Chinese hanged, four shot, and two wounded. Though eight men were convicted and sent to jail for the crimes, all were released a year later.

In early 1877 there was an outbreak of anti-Chinese violence in Chico, a small town in the Sacramento Valley, and a number of its surrounding communities. First, a soap factory owned by John Bidwell, a pioneer landowner and employer of Chinese, was burned. Next, arsonists set fire to the barn of a widow who had leased part of her farm to Chinese, killing six of her horses. Flames also consumed the shack in which the Chinese tenants lived. Several weeks later, the home of some Chinese in the neighboring town of Nord and a Chinese laundry in Chico Creek were set aflame. Arsonists also attempted unsuccessfully to burn Chico's entire Chinatown. This spate of violence culminated in the murder of four Chinese (whom the Euro-American intruders tied up, doused with kerosene, and set on fire) and the wounding of two others who managed to escape. During the trial of the suspects arrested for the crime it was revealed that the perpetrators were members of a Laborers' Union, an offshoot of the Order of Caucasians, a white supremacist organization. Though the suspects were convicted and sentenced, all were released on parole long before their sentences were up.[13]

Violent outbreaks against the Chinese became more organized in the 1880s. The two best-known incidents—well publicized because they involved the intervention of federal troops—took place at Rock Springs in Wyoming Territory in September 1885 and at Seattle in Washington Territory from October 1885 through February 1886. According to studies by Paul Crane, Alfred Larson, and Shih-shan H. Tsai, in Rock Springs, more than six hundred Chinese employed by a coal mining company worked peaceably side by side with Euro-American laborers for some time.[14] When the Chinese declined to join the latter in their proposed strike for higher wages, however, they became objects of white animosity. On September 2 a mob gathered, marched toward the Chinese workers, blocked all escape routes, and fired at the unarmed and defenseless Chinese. As the latter fled pell-mell, some Euro-Americans shot them down, others searched their persons for valuables before wounding them, while still others put their shacks to the torch. By nightfall the houses owned by the coal company and all seventy-nine huts belonging to the Chinese had been destroyed by fire. Meanwhile, the mob threw the bodies of some dead Chinese as well as those of live but wounded ones into the flames. In all twenty-eight Chinese were killed, and fifteen wounded. Some of the latter eventually died from their wounds.

More than 550 Chinese succeeded in fleeing to safety only because a nearby railroad company telegraphed its conductors to pick up the stragglers making their way to the town of Green River. The survivors had gathered by September 5 in Evanston, where federal troops arrived to protect them. Four days later the soldiers escorted the Chinese back to Rock Springs, where the coal company lent them clothing and provisions, gave them a number of wagons for shelter, and put them back on the payroll.

Chinese suffered losses totalling more than $147,000. Certain that no local justice could be obtained, Chinese diplomats investigated and strenuously protested this outrage, but the U.S. secretary of state denied that the federal government could be held responsible for action that had occurred in a territory. Nevertheless, "solely from a sentiment of generosity and pity," President Grover Cleveland did ask Congress to allocate $150,000 to indemnify the Chinese. Congress complied, but declared that its action should not be construed as a precedent for future compensation.

The anti-Chinese activities in Washington Territory stretched out over a longer period, but caused less bloodshed, as documented by Jules Karlin.[15] In the fall of 1885, in response to the arrest of several men accused of killing some Chinese hop pickers while they were asleep in their tents in Issaquah Valley, an Anti-Chinese Congress convened in Seattle, issued a manifesto demanding that all Chinese leave Tacoma and Seattle by November 1, and formed two committees, whose members visited the Chinese house-to-house to inform them of the impending deadline.

That deadline came, but nothing happened. The Chinese remained in both Tacoma and Seattle. But on November 3, during a heavy rainstorm, about five hundred of Tacoma's residents forcibly expelled six hundred or so Chinese from their town, took them to Lake View, a station on the Northern Pacific Railroad, and dumped them in the open, with no shelter for the night. Two men died from exposure, and one woman eventually went insane as a result of her ordeal. The refugees were rescued by the railroad, which transported them to Portland. Two days later, a fire razed Tacoma's Chinatown.

Meanwhile, certain citizens in Seattle who were concerned about the potential outbreak of violence in their own city formed a Home Guards unit of about eighty men. After being informed of events in the Pacific Northwest, President Cleveland issued a proclamation asking people to respect the treaty rights of the Chinese.

He also sent a part of the Fourteenth Infantry Division to Seattle, but those troops left when no incidents occurred.

It was not until Sunday, February 7, of the following year that an anti-Chinese mob gathered, marched into Chinatown, loaded about 350 Chinese into wagons, and took them to the docks, with the intention of shipping them off on the *Queen*, a steamer that was due to arrive in Seattle from San Francisco that day. The captain of the *Queen*, however, prevented anyone from boarding his ship until fare was paid. The anti-Chinese group thereupon took up a collection among themselves and gathered enough money to pay the passage of about 100 persons. Still the ship could not depart, because a local judge had issued a writ of habeas corpus requiring each Chinese to appear at the courthouse the following morning to be informed of his or her rights and to tell him whether he or she indeed wished to leave.

While all this was happening, Washington's territorial governor issued a proclamation ordering people to desist from violence and to disperse. He also telegraphed the U.S. secretary of war. Throughout that tense Sunday, the Home Guards, aided by small contingents of the Seattle Rifles and the University Cadets, stood off the much larger mob. They succeeded in marching the Chinese (whom they flanked on four sides) back to Chinatown. The next day, after the Chinese were done with their court appearance, the Home Guards escorted those who wished to leave on the *Queen* back to the docks and the rest home to Chinatown. As crowds continued to mill around, the governor declared martial law, imposing a curfew between 7 p.m. and 6 a.m. Federal troops finally arrived on February 10, but the situation remained tense for several months after that, though no further outbreaks of violence occurred.

Though not as well documented, dozens of other anti-Chinese outbreaks occurred in the mid-1880s all over the American West. Incidents outside of California include the murder or expulsion of Chinese at Snake River Canyon in Idaho; Denver, Colorado; Portland, Oregon; and Squaw Valley, Coal Creek, Black Diamond, Tacoma, and Puyallup in Washington. In February 1885, local residents drove the Chinese out of Humboldt County, California, and in November set fire to some buildings and killed thirteen Chinese in San Francisco's Chinatown. Newspaper accounts reveal that the following year Chinese were forcibly removed from the California towns of Redding and Red Bluff in January; Sheridan, Wheatland, Marysville, San Jose, Gold Run, and Arroyo Grande in February; and Sonora, San Pablo, Dutch Flat, Lincoln, and Nicolaus in March. Also in 1886, arsonists set fire to the Chinatowns in Placerville in January; Redding and Chico in February; Yreka, Sawyer's Bar, and Folsom in March; Truckee in June; Red Bluff in August; and Los Angeles and North San Juan in October.[16] A second wave of expulsions took place in 1893, driving the Chinese from Selma, Visalia, Fresno, and Bakersfield in the San Joaquin Valley and from Pasadena, Redlands, Riverside, and San Bernardino in southern California.[17]

Asians who came after the Chinese likewise suffered from violence. Assaults against Japanese began when boys stoned a number of Japanese scientists—including a famous seismologist from Tokyo Imperial University—inspecting the ruins of the 1906 San Francisco earthquake and fire. Later that summer, nineteen Japanese immigrants filed complaints with an investigator sent by President Theodore Roosevelt claiming they had been physically attacked. Then in October, demonstrators smashed the windows of several Japanese restaurants in the city.[18]

Most of the Asian victims of expulsions during the early twentieth century were farm laborers. At the beginning of 1908 in Live Oak, some 30 miles south of Chico, a mob drove approximately one hundred Asian Indian farm workers out of their camp and set it afire. The attackers also robbed the Asian Indians of $2,500. When the local district attorney was asked by California's governor to investigate the incident, he claimed that the fault lay with the Asian Indians because they had allegedly stolen some chickens and had exposed themselves indecently.[19]

Even the very small number of Korean farmworkers on the mainland encountered hostility. Small incidents began in 1909, but one that occurred in 1913 is especially noteworthy. According to Hyung June Moon, in June 1913 an orchard owner in Hemet, some 100 miles southeast of Los Angeles in Riverside County, arranged with a Riverside Korean labor contracting agency to hire fifteen Korean fruit pickers. When the latter disembarked from the train, they were met by several hundred unemployed Euro-Americans, who quickly surrounded them. A spokesperson for the crowd threatened the Koreans with physical harm if they did not leave immediately. Terrified by such an unexpected reception, the Koreans boarded the next train out of town.

This incident was widely reported in the press. When the Japanese ambassador in Washington, D.C. received news of it, he lodged a protest with the U.S. State Department, whereupon the secretary of state asked the Justice Department to investigate the matter. But the Japanese ambassador's action angered the Koreans, who refused to be treated as Japanese subjects, even though their country had been colonized by Japan three years earlier. The Korean National Association wired the State Department, declaring that Koreans were "responsible for" themselves and did not "look to Japan for redress." Not wishing to offend Japan, the secretary of state did not respond directly to the Koreans' message. Instead, he issued a statement to the Associated Press, announcing that the investigation would be "discontinued." He also noted that the Koreans had informed him that they were "not Japanese subjects, . . . [having] left their native land before it was annexed by Japan."[20]

Some years later, Japanese farmworkers themselves became victims of eviction. As Yuji Ichioka has documented, during the summer of 1921 the Chamber of Commerce and the local post of the American Legion in Turlock, a town in the San Joaquin Valley, passed resolutions at the behest of Euro-American workers censuring landowners who employed Japanese. One night, fifty to sixty armed individuals surrounded a Japanese store, forced their way in, and roused the eighteen Japanese farmworkers sleeping inside. They put the men into trucks, drove them to the railroad tracks, and unloaded them in the dark of night. The Japanese were told that should they ever dare to return, they would be lynched. Later that same evening, the mob raided a bunkhouse and three Japanese-operated farms, roused forty more Japanese laborers, and likewise forced them to leave town.

As soon as the Japanese consul general in San Francisco found out about what had happened, he demanded that California's governor investigate the incident.

Meanwhile, he sent two representatives of the Japanese Association of America to carry out an independent inquiry. They discovered that right after the intruders had barged into the store, one of the farm laborers had telephoned the head of the local Japanese Association, who then called the police. However, no one at the police station answered his call, even though two policemen were supposed to be on duty that night. This led the investigators to suspect that the police had been tipped off ahead of time and had deliberately absented themselves at the crucial hour. Six men were eventually arrested, but they did not come to trial until April of the following year. By then, Japanese migrant farm laborers who might have served as witnesses had all left the area. All six defendants were acquitted.[21]

The last major round of violence against Asians was directed against Filipinos-activities that Emory Bogardus and Howard De Witt have studied.[22] The first attempt to drive out Filipinos occurred in the Yakima Valley in Washington in 1928, but the most publicized incident took place in the summer of 1930, when five hundred restless Euro-American youths picketed a new taxi-dance hall in Palm Beach that had just opened to cater to Filipino clients. This facility was located a few miles down the road from Watsonville, an important apple-growing area along the central California coast, where thousands of Filipino and Mexican farm workers gathered every harvest. Several days later, a mob of four hundred attacked the Northern Monterey Filipino Club, beating up dozens of Filipinos and killing one. A second Filipino, a twenty-two-year-old lettuce picker, was shot to death as he hid in a bunkhouse outside of town. The sheriff, along with dozens of deputized citizens, finally ended the rioting. Seven suspects were arrested, but none of them was indicted.

Several factors help to account for the violence Asian immigrants experienced. Quite apart from the racism and nativism that fueled such attacks, the outbreaks were efforts by Euro-American workers to find scapegoats for their problems. It is no coincidence that the incidents tended to occur during years of economic crisis. The string of arson in California in 1877 took place at a time when the effects of the depression of 1873 finally reached California. Likewise, the almost ubiquitous outbreaks between late 1885 and the end of 1886 can be seen as the Western American manifestations of the industrial upheavals that racked the nation in 1886. The 1893 outbursts in southern California also took place during a national economic downturn, and of course the 1930 Watsonville riot occurred during the depths of the Great Depression.

It would be a mistake, however, to assume that these violent episodes were merely spontaneous eruptions. They were, in fact, an integral part of what historian Alexander Saxton has called the "growth sequence" of the anti-Chinese movement—and, by extension, of movements against other Asian groups. First, a seemingly spontaneous attack against the pariah group would occur, followed by the formation of a legal defense committee to support the arrested perpetrators of the violence while they were on trial. After that came mass meetings to protest whatever punishment might be meted out to the criminals. Riding on the crest of the emotions whipped up by the mass meetings would emerge organized political groups to work for the ultimate goal of ridding the country of whichever Asian group was under attack. This pattern first congealed in San Francisco in 1867, but its basic dynamics remained intact thereafter, even though the target of Euro-American hostility changed with the appearance of each new group.[23]

More law-abiding citizens sometimes criticized the violent means used, but they ultimately sympathized with and condoned the actions because they supported the ends espoused by the most vociferous elements. Elaborate "scientific" explanations of nonwhite "inferiority" and the belief that minorities should be kept in their place were widely accepted in the late nineteenth century and provided an ideological justification for treating not only Asians, but other people of color, in a discriminatory and exploitative manner. To preserve Anglo-Saxon purity, it was argued, no interracial mixing should be allowed. The outbreaks of violence, therefore, served two functions: they were at once intimidation tactics to drive out Asians and expressions of frustration over the fact that, even after exclusionary laws had been passed, sizable numbers of the "undesirable" aliens remained.

Attempts to exclude Asians began in 1855 in California, when the state legislature levied a capitation tax of $50 on "the immigration to this state of persons who cannot become citizens thereof." An act passed three years later explicitly named "persons of Chinese or Mongolian races," who would thenceforth be barred. In 1862 another act designed to "protect free white labor against competition with Chinese coolie labor" provided for a $2.50 monthly "Police tax" on every Chinese. Two acts passed in 1870 were directed against the importation of "Mongolian, Chinese, and Japanese females for criminal or demoralizing purposes" and of "coolie slavery." None of these laws had an impact, for they were all declared unconstitutional when tested in the higher courts.

One reason a state such as California could not control immigration was that the U.S. Supreme Court had decided that immigration was a form of international commerce—something only the federal government could regulate. Realizing the handicap states operated under, anti-Chinese forces turned their attention to getting a federal exclusion law enacted. One obstacle in their path was the 1868 Burlingame Treaty, which recognized the right of citizens from the treaty's two signatory nations, China and the United States, to change their domiciles—that is, to emigrate.

But in 1875 Congress passed the Page Law to forbid the entry of Chinese, Japanese, and Mongolian contract laborers, women for the purpose of prostitution, and felons. As George Peffer has argued, this law reduced the influx of Chinese women but not of men.[24] So the United States negotiated a new treaty with China in 1880 that gave it the unilateral right to limit, though not absolutely to prohibit, Chinese immigration. This opened the way for Congress to enact the 1882 Chinese Exclusion Law, which suspended the entry of Chinese laborers for ten years but exempted merchants, students and teachers, diplomats, and travelers from its provisions.[25] The exempted classes could enter either by showing a certificate issued by the Chinese government and countersigned by an American consul in China or on the basis of oral testimony. Parole evidence, however, created innumerable problems, so an 1884 amendment to the 1882 act made certificates the "sole permissible" evidence for all Chinese nonlaborers who wished to land on American soil.

The screws were further tightened in September 1888, when Congress approved an act that allowed Chinese laborers who left the country to return only if they owned at least $1,000 in property or had a wife in the United States. Even this last loophole was closed a scant three weeks later when Congress, acting on a rumor that China would probably not ratify a treaty negotiated earlier that year, passed the Scott Act, under which it became impossible for Chinese laborers to return at all once they left the United States. The Scott Act, which went into effect immediately, abrogated the reentry right of an estimated twenty thousand Chinese laborers with certificates in their possession, including six hundred who were en route across the Pacific. These individuals were denied landing when they reached American shores. Chinese exclusion was extended in 1892 and again in 1902. Finally, in 1904 it was made indefinite. Chinese were also barred from the newly acquired territories of Hawai'i, the Philippines, and Puerto Rico.

Efforts to exclude Japanese took a different form, because the United States was concerned not to antagonize Japan, a rising military power in the Pacific Basin.[26] None of the laws affecting Japanese immigration named them explicitly—a face-saving device. Thus, the Japanese government in 1907 consented to a Gentlemen's Agreement whereby it would stop issuing passports to laborers. Furthermore, it did not protest Executive Order 589, signed by President Theodore Roosevelt to prohibit Japanese laborers holding passports for Hawai'i, Mexico, or Canada from remigrating to the continental United States. Then in 1920 it once again acquiesced by denying passports to picture brides, whose coming had by then become controversial. The Immigration Act of 1924, which barred the entry of "aliens ineligible to citizenship," virtually ended Japanese immigration.

The American government did not have to do anything to exclude Koreans because emigration from Korea had already been curbed by the Japanese colonial administration. Nonetheless, according to Bong-Youn Choy, an estimated five hundred Korean nationalists who had managed to slip out of their country ended up in the United States between 1910 and 1924. Many of them had first gone to Russia, Manchuria, China, or Europe before showing up at American ports where they petitioned to enter as political refugees without passports.[27] The trickle of expatriates ended after 1924, however, as the immigration act passed that year was extremely strict.

An unusual geographic criterion had to be used to exclude Asian Indians because their racial or ethnographic status was unclear. Anthropologists classified some of the inhabitants of the Indian subcontinent as "Aryans," but no one was sure whether Aryans were Caucasians and whether the latter referred only to whites. Between 1910 and 1917, immigration officials tried to minimize the number of Asian Indians coming in by using administrative regulations, but a clause in the 1917 Immigration Act finally enabled them to stop the influx. An imaginary line was drawn from the Red Sea to the Mediterranean, Aegean, and Black Seas, through the Caucasus Mountains and the Caspian Sea, along the Ural River, and then through the Ural Mountains. All people living in areas east of the line—which came to be called the "Barred Zone"—were denied entry from then on. Asian Indians were of course among those excluded.[28]

Restricting Filipino immigration took greater ingenuity. Since Filipinos were "wards" of the United States and were called "nationals," they were neither aliens nor citizens. To exclude them required a change in their status. Accordingly, in the early 1930s, after an unsuccessful attempt to repatriate Filipinos at government expense, those favoring Filipino exclusion joined forces with others who supported independence for the islands. The result was the Tydings-McDuffie Act of 1934. The major clauses of the act spelled out the conditions under which the Philippines would receive its independence, while one small section cut Filipino immigration to fifty persons a year.[29]

Much to the chagrin of the exclusionists, sizable numbers of Chinese, Japanese, and Filipinos, small but visible clusters of Asian Indians, and scattered handfuls of Koreans remained in the country even after the exclusionary laws went into effect. The anti-Asian forces therefore had to find ways to confine those immigrants who doggedly refused to disappear, so that the social "contamination" they represented could be minimized and their presence made invisible. They did so by social segregation of various sorts.

Chinese prostitutes in San Francisco were the first Asians the host society tried to remove to a confined geographic locality outside municipal limits. The city took official notice of their presence in 1854. By the end of that year, a grand jury had indicted and the Court of Sessions had convicted several Chinese madams for keeping Chinese "houses." After imposing a fine of $1,000 on each of the women, however, the judge expressed the hope that "the prisoners might elect the alternative of removing outside certain limits which the Court would hereafter prescribe."[30]

Extant documents do not indicate whether the women chose that option. But the idea of removing Chinese brothels to a less visible location did not die. In 1861 the city's chief of police first arrested and then released fourteen Chinese prostitutes, after giving them a "translated admonition to seek other quarters, which they promised to do . . . in [a] . . . more secluded locality than Washington Alley."[31] This effort succeeded, at least temporarily. But because landlords found renting their property to brothel operators lucrative, the prostitutes soon returned. A new board of health appointed in 1866 once again recommended that Chinese prostitutes be removed outside the city limits. Apparently, the women agreed thereafter to occupy only those buildings and localities approved by the board of health and the police commissioners. Confinement, if not complete removal, had thus been achieved.

The efforts to isolate Chinese prostitutes soon became generalized to a desire to segregate all Chinese persons. A chance to legalize such segregation came in 1879, when the California State Legislature passed a law obligating all incorporated towns and cities to remove Chinese from their territories. Fortunately for the Chinese, the U.S. circuit court in California, while ruling on the constitutionality of another discriminatory law, referred to the one mandating segregation as equally unconstitutional, since it denied Chinese the equal protection guaranteed by the Fourteenth Amendment and violated the terms of the Burlingame Treaty besides. A second attempt, in 1890, to remove San Francisco's Chinatown outside city limits also failed for constitutional reasons.

Constitutional obstacles notwithstanding, San Francisco officials did not give up their efforts to confine or remove the Chinese. An unexpected chance came at the turn of the century when deaths from bubonic plague were reported in the city. As Joan Trauner and Charles McClain have shown, bubonic plague had been found in Canton and Hong Kong in 1894.[32] At the end of 1896 the San Francisco board of health decided that any arriving passengers had to be medically inspected. Chinese and Japanese, however, were singled out for detention in quarantine because the ports of Shanghai, Hong Kong, Yokohama, and Kobe, according to the medical officials in San Francisco, were "infected." Their fears were exacerbated when two cases of the dreaded disease were discovered in Honolulu's Chinatown and the Hawai'ian board of health ordered four thousand five hundred Chinese removed to a quarantine camp and burned Chinatown to the ground. Such drastic measures might not have been taken if not for the strong anti-Chinese sentiments that had existed in Hawai'i for years

In San Francisco, an autopsy of a Chinese corpse in early March 1900 revealed that the deceased had enlarged lymph nodes; the coroner suspected the man had died of plague. City officials immediately cordoned off Chinatown, placed guards to control traffic into and out of the area, and carried out a house-to-house inspection. Chinese and Japanese were forbidden to travel outside of California without certificates issued by the surgeon general of the U.S. Marine Hospital Service, the federal agency responsible for quarantine. Due to the population density of the Chinese quarters and the inability to control any fires that might be set, the solution used in Honolulu could not be applied to San Francisco. Instead, every house in Chinatown was washed from garret to basement with lime, while gutters and sewers were disinfected with sulfur dioxide and mercury bichloride. The cordon around Chinatown was lifted only after a court order declared it discriminatory.

The bubonic plague episode represented the last official attempt to remove Asians from within San Francisco's city limits. However, though residential segregation never became legal, Euro-Americans nevertheless succeeded in confining Asian immigrants by threatening them with violence should they dare to step outside clearly understood (though not visibly demarcated) boundaries. More important, landlords refused to rent any premises outside of the ghetto areas to them, and realtors declined to sell them property anywhere except in the most "undesirable" neighborhoods. This pattern of segregation had become so prevalent that by the time Japanese, Koreans, Asian Indians, and Filipinos arrived in numbers, there was no need for state, county, or municipal officials to pass any laws to specify where they could live.

Those who wished to segregate Asian immigrants and their children socially had more success within the public school system. According to Charlie Wollenberg, black Americans in California, as elsewhere, led the fight against school segregation.[33] A "colored school" was established in San Francisco for forty-five black children in 1854, but in the 1860s black parents decided to challenge school segregation. They took their case to the California Supreme Court, which ruled in 1874 that though Negroes had the right to an education, there was no reason it had to take place in an integrated setting. Black children could attend schools for whites only in those places where no separate facilities were available.

In line with how blacks were treated, as Victor Low has documented, a separate school for Chinese children was opened in the city in 1859, but due to low enrollment, it was made into an evening school a year later. Then in 1871 the school superintendent terminated even the evening classes. Henceforth, the only education available to children of Chinese ancestry, regardless of where they had been born, would be from private tutors hired by their parents or in a few English and Bible classes taught by Protestant missionaries working in Chinatown.

This situation continued until 1884, when Joseph and Mary Tape went to court to challenge the school board's denial of the right of their daughter, Mamie, to a public education. Unwilling to budge, the school superintendent requested funds from the state legislature to build a new "Oriental School," which opened its doors in 1885.[34] San Francisco and the four Sacramento-San Joaquin Delta communities of Rio Vista, Isleton, Walnut Grove, and Courtland kept Chinese children in segregated schools until well into the 1930s.

California was not the only state where the battle for integrated schooling for Chinese children was fought. In the Mississippi Delta, which by the early twentieth century was home to several hundred Chinese, public education for nonwhite children was virtually nonexistent in the rural areas and very poor in the larger urban centers. As James Loewen has found, Chinese children who wished to attend public schools had to go to those set up for black children.[35] In a few small towns, however, where there were only one or two Chinese families, the handful of Chinese children were sometimes allowed to enroll in the schools for whites. In 1924 the school superintendent of Rosedale told Lum Gong, a well-known Chinese merchant in that town, that his elder daughter, Martha, who had been quietly attending the white school, could no longer do so. In response, her father hired white lawyers who argued successfully before the U.S. Circuit Court for the First Judicial District that since no school had been established for Chinese children, she was being denied an equal education. The school officials appealed the decision to the Mississippi Supreme Court, which reversed it. In the opinion of the court, since Chinese were not white, they must be "colored." Martha Lum, the court declared, was not being denied an education because she *could* attend the schools for "colored" children.

Lum's lawyers then took the case to the U.S. Supreme Court, which upheld the Mississippi Supreme Court's ruling and affirmed that "[i]t has been at all times the policy of the lawmakers of Mississippi to preserve the white schools for members of the Caucasian race alone."[36] But perhaps recognizing that such a practice violated the Fourteenth Amendment, the Chief Justice referred to *Plessy v Ferguson* and explained that "[a] child of Chinese blood, born in, and a citizen of, the United States, is not denied the equal protection of the laws by being classed by the State among the colored races who are assigned to public schools separate from those provided for the whites, when equal facilities for education are afforded to both classes."[37] Chinese children were not admitted into white schools in Mississippi until 1950. And of course, a few more years passed before de jure school segregation in the South was ended, although de facto segregation continues in various forms there and elsewhere.

The experience of Japanese students proved to be quite different from that of the Chinese. For one thing, many of the earliest Japanese students were not children but young men. As part of its effort to modernize the country after the Meiji Restoration, the Japanese government sent hundreds of its brightest youth to Europe and the United States on scholarship to study Western science, military technology, business and public administration, and other modern subjects. In the United States, such Japanese government-sponsored students attended some of the most prestigious universities in New England and the middle Atlantic states.

Less fortunate students without government stipends could still hope for an American education: they came as "school boys" to earn their way through school by working, mainly as domestic servants. Most of the poorer students, who ranged in age from fifteen to twenty-five, found their way not to the Atlantic but the Pacific Coast. As early as 1885 an estimated three hundred of them were living in San Francisco, according to Yuji Ichioka.[38] Until the turn of the century, when sugar plantation workers from Hawai'i came to the mainland in large numbers, students composed a majority of the Japanese population in California and Washington, their two favorite destinations on the mainland. Between 1882 and 1890 the Japanese government issued more than one thousand five hundred passports to students—almost 44 percent of the total number of passports issued for travel to the United States.

The presence of Japanese students eventually caught the eye of San Francisco's officials, as Roger Daniels has shown.[39] In 1905 the city's Board of Education ordered Japanese and Korean students in the public schools to transfer to the "Oriental School" serving the Chinese. News of this decision caused a great outcry in Tokyo. Wary of offending Japan, whose new military prowess—as demonstrated during the Russo-Japanese War—had impressed him greatly, President Theodore Roosevelt sent his secretary of commerce and labor to San Francisco to investigate the situation. The secretary discovered that there were only ninety-three students scattered in some two dozen public schools, and fewer of them were over age than the school board had alleged. He tried to persuade the board to rescind its decision, but the latter refused, whereupon Roosevelt asked the U.S. attorney general to initiate court action against the San Francisco Board of Education.

Meanwhile, however, recognizing that what San Franciscans were concerned about was not education per se, but rather immigration, Roosevelt invited some of the city's officials to Washington, D.C., for a conference. Eventually they reached a compromise: in exchange for the school board's willingness to let Japanese students attend public schools reserved for white children, the federal government would persuade Japan to stop issuing passports to laborers.

Compared to the Chinese and Japanese pupils, there were relatively few Korean and Filipino children present in the United States in the period before World War II, so their school attendance never became a political issue. (Or more accurately, no scholar has yet investigated whether it was a problem.) As for Asian Indians, virtually no Asian Indian women immigrated before World War II, so they had few progeny on American soil. The only group of Asian Indian men to form families did so in the Imperial Valley: they wed Mexican women and sired mixed-ancestry children who attended schools set aside for Mexican children.

Regardless of whether they attended integrated or segregated schools, children of Asian ancestry on the mainland were taught by white teachers and learned from textbooks that contained no information about their own cultural heritage. Some teachers of Asian ancestry were employed by the schools in Hawai'i, but there, too, the teachers' main concern was to inculcate Anglo-American values, behavioral patterns, and speech patterns. Students who spoke pidgin English at home and on the playgrounds had to master standard English if they wished to pursue higher education. The message they received everywhere was that their own origins were inferior and their people powerless. Only by "Americanizing" could they hope for a better life.

Another form of social segregation imposed on Asian immigrants was the prohibition against interracial marriage. The colony of Maryland passed the first antimiscegenation law in U.S. history in 1661 to prohibit black-white marriages. In time, thirty-eight states in the union had such laws on their statute books. The question of the legality of Chinese-white marriages came up during California's second constitution convention. A bill to prohibit the "intermarriage of white persons with Chinese, negroes, mulattoes, or persons of mixed blood, descended from a Chinaman or negro from the third generation, inclusive" took final form in 1880 as Section 69 of the Civil Code, which regulated the issuance of marriage licenses, with the word "Mongolian" substituted for the word "Chinese." But Section 60 of the Civil Code, which dealt with antimiscegenation, was not changed to make it applicable to Chinese. These two contradictory sections existed side by side until 1905. In that year, fearful of a new "yellow peril"—the Japanese—California's lawmakers finally amended Section 60 to forbid marriages between whites and "Mongolians."

In those days, Chinese, Japanese, and Koreans were not particularly inclined to marry whites, so while these statutes did pose obstacles, they affected relatively few individuals. The Asian immigrants most inconvenienced by antimiscegenation laws were Filipinos, many of whom were and are of mixed origins—primarily Malayo-Polynesian, Spanish, and Chinese. Concern over a new type of "hybridization" became increasingly hysterical in the late 1920s as anti-Filipino spokespersons called public attention to the tendency of Filipino men to seek the company of white and Mexican women at taxi-dance halls. At these clubs, patrons bought strings of tickets, which the hostesses tore off one at a time as they danced with the men, giving rise to the phrase "ten cents a dance."

Some couples who got acquainted in this way desired to marry. Since the precise racial classification of Filipinos was open to question, some county clerks issued marriage licenses to Filipino men and white women, while others refused to do so. Megumi Dick Osumi has found that Los Angeles recognized such marriages because its county council had decided in 1921 that Filipinos were not Mongolians.[40] Anti-Filipino groups and individuals, including California's attorney general, eventually sued Los Angeles County to compel it to end this practice. In 1930 a superior court judge prohibited the Los Angeles county clerk from issuing a marriage license to Tony Moreno, a Filipino man, and Ruby Robinson, a white woman. Thus chastised, the county clerk thereafter stopped issuing licenses to Filipino-white couples.

But Filipinos refused to abide by this decision. Four cases they filed reached the county superior court in 1931. There the judge decided that Filipino-white marriages did not violate Sections 60 and 69 of the Civil Code because, in his view, Filipinos were not Mongolians. The county, backed by anti-Filipino organizations, appealed one of these cases, *Salvador Roldan v L. A. County.* The majority opinion handed down in 1933 by the appellate court, based on an exhaustive reading of the works of nineteenth-century ethnologists, declared that since the most influential writer of the day divided *homo sapiens* into five racial groups—Caucasian (white), Mongolian (yellow), Ethiopian (black), American (red), and Malay (brown, the category to which Filipinos belonged)—Mongolians and Malays were obviously not synonymous. Thus couples like Salvador Roldan and Marjorie Rogers could wed.

Undaunted by their failure in the courts, the anti-Filipino forces sought remedy through the legislature, which unanimously passed two bills to amend Sections 60 and 69 to allow antimiscegenation laws to include Filipino-white marriages. Only in 1948 were California's antimiscegenation statutes declared unconstitutional, and it was not until 1967 that all such statutes in the United States were removed from the books or lapsed due to disuse.

In terms of their reception by the host society, Asian immigrants shared many experiences with both European immigrants and oppressed racial minority groups. Because ethnocentrism is a worldwide phenomenon, Asian immigrants, as foreigners and newcomers, were looked upon with disdain and curiosity by earlier arrivals. Like most European immigrants, they started at the bottom of the economic ladder. Unlike their European counterparts, however, their upward climb was impeded not only by poor knowledge of the English language, lack of familiarity with the American way of doing things, limited education, and the absence of relevant job skills, but also by laws that severely limited—on racial grounds—the opportunities they could pursue. Like other people of color, they were victims of legally sanctioned color prejudice.

Asian immigrants found it difficult to fight such prejudice because, again like other nonwhite minorities, they lacked political power. They could not vote, because the right of naturalization was denied them. Consequently, they could neither enjoy the rights nor bear the responsibilities of citizenship. Thus the Asian American historical experience has been an ironic one: in a country that prides itself on being a democracy with a government of laws and not of men, those very political and legal structures institutionalized and helped to perpetuate for a century the inferior status of Asian Americans. But despite such institutional racism, a sufficient number of each group remained in the United States to become small but important parts of the American multiethnic mosaic. They were able to do so because almost as soon as each new group arrived, its members set up mechanisms to ensure their own survival.

NOTES

1. Two older works—Mary Roberts Coolidge, *Chinese Immigration* (New York: Holt, 1909), and Elmer Clarence Sandmeyer, *The Anti-Chinese Movement in California* (Urbana: University of Illinois Press, 1939)—still provide the fullest analysis of the anti-Chinese movement. Gunther Barth's *Bitter Strength: A History of the Chinese in the United States, 1850–1870* (Cambridge: Harvard University Press, 1964) has been widely quoted by Euro-American historians but has been severely criticized by Asian American specialists for its blame-the-victim perspective. Alexander Saxton's *The Indispensable Enemy: Labor and the Anti-Chinese Movement in California* (Berkeley and Los Angeles: University of California Press, 1971) shows how the anti-Chinese campaign helped the labor movement to consolidate

itself. Edward C. Lydon (*The Anti-Chinese Movement in the Hawaiian Kingdom, 1852–1886* [San Francisco: R & E Research Associates, 1975]) examines the situation in Hawai'i. The anti-Japanese movement may be divided into three phases: the passage of the alien land acts, the exclusion of Japanese, and the incarceration of persons of Japanese ancestry in so-called relocation camps during World War II. But few scholars have successfully analyzed all three in an integrated manner. One attempt was made, in Jacobus tenBroek et al., *Prejudice, War, and the Constitution: Causes and Consequences of the Evacuation of the Japanese Americans in World War II* (Berkeley and Los Angeles: University of California Press, 1954); another is found in Daniels, *Asian America: Chinese and Japanese in the United States since 1850* (Seattle: University of Washington Press, 1988). Roger Daniels, *The Politics of Prejudice: The Anti-Japanese Movement in California and the Struggle for Japanese Exclusion* (Berkeley and Los Angeles: University of California Press, 1962), remains a standard work, while Yuji Ichioka, *The Issei: The World of the First Generation Japanese Immigrants, 1885–1924* (New York: Free Press, 1988), 176–254, provides the only analysis based on Japanese-language sources. Since there were so few Koreans in the continental United States before World War II, no separate organized anti-Korean movement developed; a few sporadic incidents are briefly described in Choy, *Koreans in America,* 107–110, and Moon, "The Korean Immigrants in America: The Quest for Identity in the Formative Years, 1905–1918" (Ph.D. dissertation, University of Nevada, Reno, 1976), 379–391. The anti-Filipino movement is investigated in the essays in J. M. Saniel, ed., *The Filipino Exclusion Movement, 1927–1935* (Quezon City, Philippines: Institute of Asian Studies, University of the Philippines, 1967). Anti-Asian Indian activities are best covered in Joan Jensen, *Passage from India: Asian Indian Immigrants in North America* (New Haven: Yale University Press, 1988), which stands alone in the entire literature on Asian Americans in its analysis of federal surveillance of dissident Asians in America.

2. Stuart Creighton Miller, *The Unwelcome Immigrant: The American Image of the Chinese, 1785–1882* (Berkeley and Los Angeles: University of California Press, 1969).

3. Hudson N. Janisch's "The Chinese, the Courts, and the Constitution: A Study of the Legal Issues Raised by Chinese Immigration to the United States, 1850–1902" (J.D. diss., University of Chicago, 1971) is an exhaustive study of the legal liabilities imposed on the Chinese. Frank F. Chuman's *The Bamboo People: The Law and Japanese Americans* (Del Mar, Calif.: Publisher's Inc., 1976) is a systematic survey of laws affecting the Japanese.

4. Reprinted in "The Wrongs to Chinamen," *Alta California,* 23 November 1858, as quoted in Janisch, "The Chinese, the Courts, and the Constitution," 60, n. 2.

5. Daniels, *Politics of Prejudice,* 46–64; Chuman, *Bamboo People,* 39–42, 46–51, 76–89.

6. Dudley O. McGovney, "The Anti-Japanese Land Laws of California and Ten Other States," *California Law Review* 35 (1947): 7–54, covers states other than California. Studies of the alien land laws in Washington State include Jack D. Freeman, "The Rights of Japanese and Chinese Aliens in Land in Washington," *Washington Law Review* 6 (1930–31): 127–131; and Theodore Roodner, "Washington's Alien Land Law: Its Constitutionality," *Washington Law Review* 39 (1964): 115–133.

7. U.S. Senate, 40th Cong., 3d sess. (1868–69), *Congressional Globe,* pt. 2, 1030.

8. "A Chinese Citizen," *San Francisco Chronicle,* 28 November 1878, as quoted in Janisch, "The Chinese, the Courts, and the Constitution," 205.

9. Janisch, "The Chinese, the Courts, and the Constitution," 227.

10. Roger Daniels, ed., *Anti-Chinese Violence in North America* (New York: Arno Press, 1978), is a collection of articles recounting violent incidents in various areas.

11. California State Legislature, "Report of the Joint Select Committee Relative to the Chinese Population of the State of California," *Journals of the Senate and Assembly,* Appendix, vol. 3 (Sacramento: State Printing Office, 1862), 7.

12. William R. Locklear, "The Celestials and the Angels: A Study of the Anti-Chinese

Movement in Los Angeles to 1882," *Historical Society of Southern California Quarterly* 42 (1960): 239–256.

13. Sucheng Chan, *This Bittersweet Soil: The Chinese in California Agriculture, 1860–1910* (Berkeley and Los Angeles: University of California Press, 1986), 371–374.

14. Paul Crane and Alfred Larson, "The Chinese Massacre," *Annals of Wyoming* 12 (1940): 47–55; and Shih-shan Henry Tsai, *China and the Overseas Chinese in the United States, 1868–1911* (Fayetteville: University of Arkansas Press, 1983), 72–78, are the sources for the next three paragraphs.

15. Jules Alexander Karlin, "The Anti-Chinese Outbreak in Tacoma, 1885," *Pacific Historical Review* 23 (1954): 271–283; idem, "The Anti-Chinese Outbreaks in Seattle, 1885–1886," *Pacific Northwest Quarterly* 39 (1948): 103–129; and George Kinnear, "Anti-Chinese Riots at Seattle, Washington, February 8th, 1886," in *Twenty-fifth Anniversary of Riots* (Seattle: n.p., 1911), provide information for the next five paragraphs.

16. Sacramento *Daily Record Union*, 4, 11, 26, and 27 January; 1, 2, 6, 12, 16, 19, 20, 23, and 26 February; 2, 5, 6, 8–10, 13, 15–20, 23, 24, 29, and 31 March; 18 June; 10 August; 24, 25, and 28 October 1886.

17. Sacramento *Daily Record Union*, 15, 16, 18–21 August; 2–5, 8, and 11 September 1893.

18. Daniels, *Politics of Prejudice*, 33.

19. Sucheta Mazumdar, "Punjabi Agricultural Workers in California, 1905–1945," in *Labor Immigration under Capitalism: Asian Workers in the United States before World War II*, ed. Lucie Chang and Edna Bonacich (Berkeley and Los Angeles: University of California Press, 1984), 563.

20. The Hemet incident is told in Moon, "Korean Immigrants," 379–391. The telegram from the Koreans was sent on 29 June 1913 by Yi Tae-wi (David Lee), president of the Korean National Association, to Secretary of State William Jennings Bryan. Bryan's reply was sent out by the Associated Press and picked up by the Hemet *News,* 4 July 1913, as cited in Moon, "Korean Immigrants," 390–391.

21. Yuji Ichioka, "The 1921 Turlock Incident: Forceful Expulsion of Japanese Laborers," in *Counterpoint: Perspectives on Asian America,* ed. Emma Gee (Los Angeles: Asian American Studies Center, University of California, Los Angeles, 1976), 195–201. Another incident is described in Stefan Tanaka, "The Toledo Incident: The Deportation of the Nikkei from an Oregon Mill Town," *Pacific Northwest Quarterly* 69 (1978): 116–126.

22. Emory S. Bogardus, *Anti-Filipino Race Riots* (San Diego: Ingram Institute of Social Science, 1930), reprinted in Jesse Quinsaat et al., eds., *Letters in Exile: An Introductory Reader on the History of Pilipinos in America* (Los Angeles: Asian American Studies Center, University of California, Los Angeles, 1976), 51–62, and Howard A. De Witt, *Anti-Filipino Movements in California: A History, Bibliography and Study Guide* (San Francisco: R & E Research Associates, 1976), 46–66.

23. Saxton, *Indispensable Enemy*, 74.

24. George Anthony Peffer, "Forbidden Families: Emigration Experiences of Chinese Women under the Page Law, 1875–1882," *Journal of American Ethnic History* 6 (1986): 28–46.

25. Coolidge, *Chinese Immigration,* has the most detailed account of the political and legislative maneuvers that led to the passage of the various Chinese exclusion laws.

26. Daniels, *Politics of Prejudice*, 92–105; and Ichioka, *The Issei*, 244–254.

27. Choy, *Koreans in America*, 87–88, reveals how a small number of Koreans managed to enter the country after 1910.

28. Jensen, *Passage from India*, 101–120, 139–162.

29. H. Brett Melendy, *Asians in America: Filipinos, Koreans, and East Indians* (Boston: Twayne, 1977), 27–28, 40–44.

30. Sucheng Chan, "The Exclusion of Chinese Women, 1870–1943," in *Entry Denied: Exclusion and the Chinese Community in America, 1882–1943,* ed. Sucheng Chan (Philadelphia: Temple University Press, 1991).

31. *Alta California,* 1 February 1861.

32. Joan B. Trauner, "The Chinese as Medical Scapegoats in San Francisco, 1870–1905," *California History* 57 (1978): 70–87; and Charles J. McClain, "Of Medicine, Race, and American Law: The Bubonic Plague Outbreak of 1900," *Law and Social Inquiry* 13 (1988): 447–513, provide the information for the next two paragraphs.

33. Charles M. Wollenberg, *All Deliberate Speed: Segregation and Exclusion in California Schools, 1855–1975* (Berkeley and Los Angeles: University of California Press, 1976), 8–27.

34. Victor Low, *The Unimpressible Race: A Century of Educational Struggle by the Chinese in San Francisco* (San Francisco: East/West, 1982), 13–71.

35. James W. Loewen, *The Mississippi Chinese: Between Black and White* (Cambridge: Harvard University Press, 1971), 65–69, is the basis for the next two paragraphs.

36. *Rice et al. v Gong Lum et al.,* 139 Mississippi Reports 763 (1925), as quoted in Loewen, *Mississippi Chinese,* 67.

37. *Gong Lum et al. v Rice et al.,* 275 U. S. Reports 78 (1927), as quoted in Loewen, *Mississippi Chinese,* 68.

38. Ichioka, *The Issei,* 7–19, 22–28, describes the lives of the first immigrant students.

39. Daniels, *Politics of Prejudice,* 31–45, documents efforts to segregate Japanese children.

40. The most detailed study of antimiscegenation laws against Asian immigrants is Megumi Dick Osumi, "Asians and California's Anti-Miscegenation Laws," in *Asian and Pacific American Experiences: Women's Perspectives,* ed. Nobuya Tsuchida (Minneapolis: Asian/Pacific American Learning Resources Center, University of Minnesota, 1982), 1–37. This study contains the information used in the next three paragraphs.

"The Eagle Seeks

a Helpless Quarry"

Chinatown, the Police, and the Press:

The 1903 Boston Chinatown Raid Revisited

K. Scott Wong

The combined police and Immigration Bureau raid on Boston Chinatown in 1903 is fairly well known among scholars of Chinese American history. It is often cited as an example of continued police harassment of the community well after the passage of the original Chinese Exclusion Act in 1882 and as one of the incidents that gave rise to the boycott of American goods in China in 1905. At first glance, the raid is indeed a clear example of how American authorities sought to enforce exclusion policy—in this case the 1892 Geary Act, which demanded that Chinese laborers in the country register with the "collector of internal revenue of their respective districts" to obtain a certificate of residence. Failure to register or provide this certificate upon demand could result in imprisonment and deportation.[1]

However, a thorough examination of the events that preceded the raid and its aftermath not only addresses the exclusion policy and its enforcement, but can also offer new insights into Chinese immigrant communities during the late nineteenth and early twentieth centuries. It also provides an opportunity to explore how the enforcement of exclusion affected the residents of Chinatown; Euro-American perceptions of the Chinese community during this period, and how these images were portrayed in the press; and most important, interracial relations between Chinese and the general society in the urban northeast around the turn of the century. Finally, this raid has particular resonance with current concerns with illegal immigration and the call for national identification cards distinguishing "legal" from "illegal" immigrants. By examining these issues, this article contributes to the growing body of scholarship on Asian Americans in areas other than the West Coast while linking the Asian American past to contemporary issues.

The raid took place on the evening of October 11, 1903, but the full story begins more than a week before, on October 2.[2] That evening, Wong Yak Chong, a thirty-year-old laundryman with a business in Roslindale, was shot and killed in Chinatown by two men, later identified as Wong Ching and Charlie Chinn.[3] Two other men, Ning Munn and Yee Shong Teng, were wounded. The victims were identified as belonging to the Hip Sing Tong and the assailants were said to be members of the On Leung Tong, a "rival" association.[4] The two main newspapers of that time, the *Boston Daily Globe* and the *Boston Herald,* maintained coverage of the murder and its aftermath, and it is this press coverage that frames my discussion of the subsequent raid.

The murder was immediately cast in racial and cultural terms rather than simply as a crime of violence. The *Boston Herald* reported that "Boston's Chinatown had its first murder last night, and Boston's police have their first real case of Highbinder tactics on their hands to unravel."[5] At one point, the *Herald* reported that Wong had told some of his "white friends" that he was going to sell his business and then visit his mother in San Francisco. He reportedly said that he "wanted to become an American citizen and that before he discarded his Chinese costume and had his queue cut off, and by such act renounce his allegiance to the 'Son of Heaven,' he must see his mother."[6] Furthermore, the same article claimed, members of the Hip Sing Tong feared that once he renounced his allegiance to China, Wong would "prove a traitor to the secrets of the Highbinders, and they determined to put him out of the way."[7] Curiously, this explanation for the murder was never brought up again in subsequent reports. Instead, both the *Herald* and the *Globe* maintained that the murder was related to a long-standing gambling feud between the two associations and that this incident had been planned well in advance. The *Globe* believed this probable because the On Leung Tong was known to have recently retained a lawyer who appeared at the police station shortly after the two assailants were arrested.[8] The *Herald* even reported that the police were warned "that there was murder in the air, but they had become so sceptical regarding Chinese 'tips' that they refused to credit the warning."[9] The authorities' belief reflected a general attitude toward the Chinese in America that they could not be trusted or taken seriously.[10]

Details of the murder were covered in rather lurid fashion, with descriptions of the wounds suffered and the weapons recovered from the suspects and at the crime scene. Besides the .44 caliber Colt revolver found on one of the suspects and an Iver Johnson gun found at the scene, the police also recovered an elaborate hunting axe, a weapon to which the press devoted considerable space, because of its unusual design and its association with Highbinder or "hatchet men" activities. One of the assailants, Wong Ching, was also found wearing hidden armor, described as a "coat of mail," a vest composed of a large number of pieces of "sheet steel, about two inches square and a sixteenth of an inch thick . . . joined by little bands of copper wire."[11]

For the next few days, the press described the atmosphere of Chinatown as uneasy, tense, and unusually quiet. It appears that a crowd of Euro-Americans had gathered in Chinatown expecting more action, but nothing took place and the police had to keep them in order.[12] By the Tuesday after the murder, however, the press reported that the police had increased their surveillance of Chinatown and that all Chinese new to the area would be investigated in order to determine their business in Boston. Captain Lawrence Cain, head of the police in the Chinatown area, announced that three Chinese from New York had arrived to seek revenge for Wong's murder. The police detained these men and demanded that they leave Boston later that day. Though denying the charges, these men apparently did leave on an afternoon train for New York. Captain Cain justified these actions by stating, "It is the first time that such a bloody feud has broken out among the Chinese in Boston. We must check it. That is the reason we have had to resort to such extreme measures. The community must be protected from such high-handed acts. We intend to take every precaution, even if innocent men are brought to the station."[13] This action, admittedly persecuting people who may have been innocent, was the first sign that the authorities intended to punish the residents of Chinatown for the crime. They would also use the murder as an excuse to verify the legal status of the Chinese in Chinatown even if they had to resort to extralegal means to do so.

That this was the intention of the raid would later become quite evident in statements made immediately afterward. According to the *Globe* during a meeting between Captain Cain and George Billings, the Immigration Commissioner for the port of Boston, it was "agreed that Chinatown should be thoroughly gone through after Shong's [sic] funeral."[14] Billings is reported to have said,

> We have had it in mind for a long time to do something of this sort. We are satisfied that there are many unregistered Chinese in the city and in other places in New England. It required something like the murder of Shong [sic], however, to give us the proper excuse for taking action. I think we have done our job pretty thoroughly tonight. I have no doubt that many of the Chinese we took tonight have their papers. They should have had them in their possession. Those who left them in their homes will have an opportunity tomorrow to produce them. If they have not got their papers, they will be deported.[15]

Cain then commented that it would have a good effect if all unregistered Chinese were deported because he believed they were responsible for most of the crimes committed in Chinatown.[16] Although it was never stated whether the victims or the alleged assailants were registered or not, these statements by Billings and Cain make it very clear that the raid was part of a concerted effort to decrease the Chinese population through harassment and the threat of deportation.[17]

Claiming that Chinatown was on the verge of a "Highbinder war," with "hatchet men" being brought in from out of town, the police increased their presence in the area. They said that they were tipped off about the impending conflict by two informants who are described in significantly different terms than the Chinese who had first warned them of the murder. As mentioned above, the Chinese who initially came to the police were said to be "such liars that we [the police] couldn't believe half they told us."[18] The new informants, however, were seen as more reliable because the first was a "white woman who is much in Chinatown, and has heretofore been of assistance to the police." Soon after, they were given similar information by a "Chinaman who has discarded his queue and wears American clothes" and is not known to be "affiliated with either of the Tongs."[19] Thus, Chinese who were members of the associations, spoke little or no English, and continued to dress in Chinese fashion were in the opinion of the authorities not as reliable as white informants or Chinese who demonstrated signs of assimilation.

By the evening of October 7, the murder case had taken a new twist, one that would have a direct relation to the eventual raid. Captain Cain stated that the friction between the two associations was not a gambling feud, but was the result of the On Leung Tong's anger over the Hip Sing Tong's collecting more than their share of the organized blackmail that was allegedly taking place in Chinatown as a result of the Geary Act of 1892. According to the *Globe,* "It is an open secret that both societies have been bleeding the more ignorant of their countrymen by promising them immunity from police interference. They have also been levying blackmail upon the Chinese who are in the city without having complied with the requirements of the Chinese registration law."[20] An unidentified police official claimed that when the Geary Act was passed, "Some of the more intelligent of the Chinese went to their ignorant compatriots and advised them they had better not be registered."[21] When the time limit for registration expired, those who had advised them not to register are said to have returned demanding a fee in exchange for not turning them in to the authorities. The police thus implied that the Hip Sing Tong was making more money on this system of protection than the On Leung Tong, a situation that precipitated the murder of Wong Yak Chong.

With the murder now framed in the context of illegal immigration and a black-mail scheme designed to profit from it, the raid that took place on October 11 can be firmly linked to the events of the previous week. On October 8, the *Globe* reported that Captain Cain met with authorities of the U.S. Treasury Department who had "a hand in the execution of the Chinese registration law." Cain reportedly sought a means by which unregistered Chinese might be removed from the community." The police believed "that half of the Celestials [in Boston had] no papers [to] authorize them to remain in this country."[22] Government officials, however, are said to have doubted that so many Chinese avoided registration. Captain Cain did not discuss his plans with the press, but the newspaper maintained that it was "safe to say that a pretty careful inspection of the district will be made."[23]

For the next three days, the press reported on the mood of Chinatown, claiming that the upcoming funeral of the slain Wong Yak Chong, which was to be held on Sunday, October 11, might be the occasion for another conflict. The two associations were each scheduled to hold a meeting that day and the Hip Sing Tong was reportedly considering moving their headquarters in order to avoid the threats of the On Leung Tong.[24]

The morning papers of October 11 reported that most Chinese and "others familar with the stealthy and far-reaching plans of the Celestials entangled in the present controversy" doubted that any disruption would take place at such a large public gathering.[25] The reports went on to say that additional police would be on hand to monitor the funeral procession from Chinatown to the Mount Hope Cemetery.[26] One article concluded with a brief warning of events to come: "There were rumors last night that action against the Chinese would be taken on entirely new lines by the police tonight."[27] Given what would take place over the next few days, those rumors were indeed correct.

Sunday, October 11, 1903, was a tumultous day for the residents of Chinatown. Wong Yak Chong was buried in the morning and the Boston police, in collusion with federal and state authorities, made a surprise raid on the neighborhood during the evening. The funeral and burial were carried out in a three-part progression. A Christian service was conducted at the funeral home where Wong's Sunday School teacher, Alice L. Specht, and a number of white male friends belonging to the Roslindale Club were present.[28] After leaving the funeral home, the procession went through Chinatown and out to Mount Hope Cemetery. It was estimated that 2,000 people witnessed the procession,[29] and that another 3,000 gathered at the cemetery but were kept back by the police.[30] Once in the cemetery, the body was interred according to Chinese burial practices, which included the burning of incense and "spirit money," and the offering of ritual foods.[31] All these steps are described in great detail in both newspapers, offering a valuable glimpse into Chinese American burial rituals during the early twentieth century, many of which are still carried out today.

With a large number of Chinese from surrounding areas and an indeterminate number from other cities present in Chinatown, the evening of the funeral proved to be an opportune time to conduct a sweep of the community. A force of about fifty local police and more than twenty federal and state authorities conducted the raid. The police arrived in Chinatown about 8:00 P.M., going in pairs so as not to arouse suspicion.[32] Chinatown was described as "going full blast [with] great merriment in the restaurants, the shops, the clubhouses, and the homes. . . . In rapid succession, and without a hitch, the searching parties tramped into and surrounded the Celestial quarter. Policemen lined up and formed a picket line around the entire quarter so that no Chinaman could escape when the puckering string of the bag was drawn taut."[33] To facilitate the transportation of the anticipated arrestees, patrol wagons from all of the downtown precincts were sent to the scene.[34]

The headquarters of the Hip Sing and On Leung Tongs were raided first, and every person who could not produce registration certificates on demand was taken into custody. About twenty-five arrests were made in each place.[35] The police then took control of a building on Harrison Street and used it as a headquarters where the Chinese were brought before they were taken away. In a fashion similar to the infamous Palmer Raids of 1919–1920, the authorities entered homes and businesses without warrants demanding to see registration certificates and lined the streets waiting for Chinese to appear.[36] Those who had papers were "measured" against their documents, and held if the papers and the person did not match up. Those without papers were not allowed to go get them, but were immediately taken into custody.[37] Even those with valid papers were reported to have been "shoved into a back room so that [they] would not have to be looked over a second time."[38]

The *Boston Herald,* which presented the murder and raid with a rather sensational flair, described the scene of the round-up as follows:

> The officers dragged the frightened Chinamen out from under beds, from behind boxes and doors and from all conceivable places of concealment. They were all driven down the winding stairways to the big marble hallway at the street entrance and huddled together like panting sheep. The jabbering was deafening and bewildering.[39]

The account continued,

> Policemen were stationed at the ends of all the dark passageways and alleyways and
> these men had thrilling experiences with the terrified Chinamen. Chinamen popped
> up as if out of the ground and scampered like rats through the dark alleys, only to
> be nabbed by policemen. Out of the very bowels of the earth they seemed to come,
> for even beneath the cellars deep down in the ground under the long buildings were
> sub-cellars from which came Chinamen, tan and short, lean and fat, old and young.[40]

These two passages paint a picture of fear on the part of the Chinese and a perverse
pleasure on the part of the police. Likened to animals ("panting sheep" and "rats"),
the Chinese are prey of hunters who had "thrilling experiences" with their quarry.
Like subterranean animals, the Chinese were flushed from their underground
hiding places, "the very bowels of the earth," only to be caught in "dark passageways
and alleyways." Using this imagery, the *Herald* contributed to the long-standing
stereotype that "Chinatown" was laced with an underground network of tunnels,
making "Chinatown" generic, as this image applied to "Chinatowns" across the
country, offering grist for the anti-Chinese mill, appearing in print media, the
visual arts, and eventually, motion pictures.[41]

In addition to being seen as foreign and frightening, "Chinatown" was also
considered to have a demoralizing effect on Americans. Here again, the *Boston
Herald* offers a glimpse into this trope. Aside from the Chinese rounded up in the
raid, the newspaper reported,

> Some degenerate young American men, who, by long and constant association with
> the Chinamen have come to look as yellow and to smell as strongly of opium as do
> the Celestials themselves, were caught in the big net and found difficulty in proving
> that they are or were once Americans and did not require registration papers from
> the government.[42]

Apparently, the degenerative effects of opium and contact with Chinese were so
great that it was possible to "become Chinese" merely through association![43]

It appears that there was a kind of voyeurism on the part of some white patrons
of "Chinatown" as well. In the weeks following the mass arrests, several raids were
staged against Chinese businesses suspected of being places where opium was
smoked. A witness for the defense after one such raid testified that he had never
seen opium smoked at the place in question but that he "had on several occasions
taken slumming parties through Chinatown and Yee Wah [the person under arrest]
had shown for their delectation how opium was smoked."[44] In this case, it is obvious
that although a crime might have taken place, it was acceptable for whites to
observe it and thus gain vicarious pleasure from their hours spent in the presence
of the Chinese "guides" they employed to decode their experiences.

There was also a gendered reading of whites who frequented Chinatown. The
Euro-American women encountered during the raid were not viewed with the
same ambiguity afforded American males. Not only were they not confused for
being Chinese, they were definitely depicted as "fallen." The paper reported,

White women, young girls in some instances, who frequent Chinatown and live among and with the Chinamen, came in for a fright which should be a warning to them in the future. Some were found lounging about the dingy dens of the half-civilized and semi-opium-drunk Chinamen. They were ordered to dress themselves properly and to leave the district at once for their homes.[45]

"Chinatown," therefore, was not simply a residential and business community. In the eyes of the press and the critics of the Chinese, "Chinatown" was a site of cultural pollution. In this sense, "Chinatown" was a "borderland" where cultures collided and were often transformed, though usually for the worse. Euro-American men and women, judged with gendered biases, succumbed to the demoralizing effects of the Chinese, adding to the reasons why Chinese should be excluded from American society. The theme of white women being lured into laundries or "opium dens" apppears frequently in anti-Chinese literature. In each of the stories concerning raids on "opium dens" soon after the raid, it was reported that white women or girls, in various stages of undress, were found at each site. In the reporting of these cases, issues of vice, race, gender, and sexuality were all entwined in the cultural mapping of "Chinatown."[46]

Yet, on the other hand, there was obviously "acceptable" contact between the Chinese immigrant community and American society at large, as evidenced by the presence of Wong Yak Chong's Sunday School teacher and friends at his funeral. In fact, as the Chinese were being rounded up, they are reported to have "screamed for their white friends, their American wives, the Sunday school teachers, the missionaries and habituès of Chinatown."[47]

As Shepard Schwartz and, more recently, John Kuo Wei Tchen have uncovered in their research on the history of the Chinese community in New York City, a number of Chinese there were married to Irish women.[48] The same appears to be true for the Chinese in Boston at the turn of the century. In the press coverage of the raid, two interracial couples are mentioned. Both the *Herald* and the *Globe* report that a woman named Kittie O'Connell came to the Federal Building to verify the status of her husband, Charlie Yen Goon (also printed as Yen Koon). Likewise, both papers describe Yen Goon as dressed in "American clothes."[49] The *Herald* also mentioned a couple, a Mr. and Mrs. Wong, who were caught up in the raid. They too appear to have been a Chinese-Irish union. While the *Herald* may have fabricated Mrs. Wong's tirade against the police, it was done in what seems to be stereotypical working-class Irish American dialect, "I'll have the law yese all, though ye be officers of the law itself. Leave Mr. Wong alone, now. He's me husband."[50] Although it is impossible to verify this exchange, it is likely that they were among the Chinese-Irish marriages in Boston. In contrast to the depiction of the women found in the "opium dens," the white spouses of the Chinese were not denigrated in moral terms. Perhaps the institution of marriage gave them a legitimacy and respectability that was not extended to the other women described in the press as having relations with Chinese men.

These marriages point to interracial relations within Boston Chinatown that warrant further investigation. Luckily, an examination of the Federal Census of 1900 offers valuable information concerning the demographics of the Chinese community and some insights into interethnic relations. The Census lists 254 Chinese living in the eight-block area of Chinatown, out of approximately 850 Chinese in the greater Boston area. This figure for Chinatown consists of 243 males and 11 females, 7 of whom are children (all but one having been born in the United States). There are also 12 American-born Chinese males included in this total number. In addition, there are 21 Chinese listed as having laundries in the area south of Chinatown, all operated by one or two males. The occupational distribution was centered around a service industry of waiters, launderers, servants, clerks, butchers, and grocers, as well as some skilled workers such as carpenters and tailors, and a smaller group of merchants, tea agents, druggists, and physicians. Nearly all of these men claimed to be able to read and write, and about half could speak English. Most were married (their wives presumably still in China), some for twenty to forty years, and most had been in the United States since the 1870s.[51]

Of the six married couples, two involved Chinese-Caucasian unions. Aside from the Goons mentioned earlier, Mr. Lee Wee had been married to Alice Maude Blanche Lee for four years, with a two-year-old son. The other marriages were among Chinese, including Charles Doane, an American-born Chinese from California, who was married to a woman, Jengsy, who had been born in China. They had two daughters, one born in China and the other in Vermont. Mr. Doane was employed as an interpreter for the U.S. government. (He may have been involved with the processing of the arrested Chinese in the aftermath of the raid.) It is interesting to note that there are no marriages listed between Chinese men, foreign-born or native, and American-born Chinese women. In fact, the Census does not list any single Chinese women of marriageable age living in the Chinese American community, regardless of nativity. While this might confirm the commonly held belief that there was a miniscule female population in American Chinatowns, it might also mean that women were undercounted in the Census, such as single women who did not speak with the Census taker, prostitutes, and others whose names simply never made it onto the rolls. When one looks at the streets surrounding Chinatown, as well as the non-Chinese residents, one sees a multiethnic population that must have had contact with each other. There were boarding houses employing large numbers of single Irish women who worked as servants, manglers, chambermaids, and pantry girls. The Census indicates that the Chinese population lived among and were surrounded by first- and second-generation German, English, Irish, French, Syrian, and black Americans. Not only did the Chinese live near these other ethnic groups; one address indicates that James Johnston, a white male of Irish immigrant parents, worked as a servant and rented a room in a boarding house that catered mainly to Chinese. In addition, two white women, Mary McDonald and Rebecca Adams, rented rooms to two Chinese men. While it is difficult to determine the nature or depth of most of these relationships, given what the Census reveals in terms of demographics and what took place after the police raided Chinatown, it appears that some Chinese maintained contact with Euro- and African Americans. Most important, the Census data and the press accounts claim that Chinese had frequent contact with non-Chinese. This stands in contrast to the long-held stereotype of Chinatown as an isolated and inpenetrable foreign enclave, forever detached from the rest of American society.

Specific examples of interracial cooperation (as well as racial harassment) can, in fact, be seen in how the incarceration and freeing of the Chinese was handled. Once those arrested were taken to the Federal Building they were crowded into small holding rooms. After those rooms were full, the Chinese were placed in a larger court room and the office of the U.S. Deputy Marshals. In this office, about forty men were confined in a thirty-foot by twelve-foot steel cage.[52] In total, 234 Chinese were arrested and taken into custody.[53] After they were placed in various rooms and offices, the police and immigration officials, with the aid of interpreters, finally tried to ascertain their legal status. Their friends, relatives, associates, and in Charlie Yen Goon's case, his wife, arrived at the Federal Building with their papers to facilitate their release. Once a person was released, he was often beseeched by others to go to the homes or businesses of those still detained in order to procure their papers and return with them so that they could prove their legal status. Of the 234 arrested, 122 were released within twelve to fourteen hours once their papers were seen to be in order.[54] Another 49 were released on bail over the next few days; 5 were immediately tried before a U.S. Commissioner and ordered deported, while another 11 were later released after producing their papers, which, for some reason, they had refused to show before in court.[55] The judge whose courtroom held the overflow of prisoners responded to the overcrowding by ordering the room "thoroughly cleansed and fumigated before the court came in there again."[56]

While being held, the Chinese were questioned about their homes and reasons for being in Chinatown. Many explained that they were laundrymen from outlying areas and usually kept their resident certificates at home or with trusted friends. They also said it was common for them to come to Chinatown on Sunday to visit friends. Some claimed to have had no knowledge of the feud between the two associations, explaining that their own presence in Chinatown that day was simply due to the desire to make social calls.[57]

Bail was set at $500. Of the 24 released on bail, it is interesting to note that while most must have been assisted by fellow Chinese, the press reported a number of cases of whites and blacks posting bond. Bertha Crane, identified as a "colored woman," put up bail for four men. James Stokes, identified as a Negro, bailed out two men, while James Briggs, presumably white since his race was not identified, posted bond for eight men.[58] It was not made clear who these people were, though the *Globe* reported that many of those who posted bail owned property in or near Chinatown, while in some cases "as soon as the parties became aware that their names might be published they declined to supply the necessary bond."[59] As the week progressed, other Americans of varying ethnic backgrounds (based on surnames) posted bail for individual Chinese.[60] It is uncertain why all of these individuals offered their help. Some were indentified as professional bail bondsmen, but others may have been business associates, employers, Sunday School teachers, landlords, or simply friends. In any case, the presence of these non-Chinese and the roles they played indicate that Chinatown was not the isolated and insular community so often depicted. The Chinese evidently had established relationships with people outside their community and had maintained a network of contacts that could be used in time of need.

In fact, the raid also brought a group of Euro-American supporters of the Chinese into the public eye. Stephen W. Nickerson, serving as the Chinese Vice Consul in Boston, immediately protested to the authorities that the raid was illegal since warrants were not issued for the arrests, which therefore violated the standing treaty between the United States and China that provided Chinese citizens in the States "all the legal rights of the most favored nation."[61] Nickerson later revealed that there were one or two warrants issued for the raid, but the remaining warrants were written out the following day to account for those still held.[62]

Furthermore, Nickerson and the press pointed out that American citizens of Chinese ancestry were also arrested during the raid. Nickerson cited the case of Lue Hee Fong, age thirty-two, of San Francisco, who was held for two and a half days before his status was confirmed.[63] Another U.S. citizen who was initially arrested with the others was George Sing, age twenty, of New York. The *Globe* described him as a young man "with a bright face that had unmistakable evidence of Caucasian blood and good breeding. He was well-dressed and spoke English without a flaw."[64] This young man, who said his mother was a white woman, was released and then asked by the arrested Chinese if he could assist them in getting out.[65]

Perhaps more significant than Nickerson's protest was the public demonstration against the raid held at Faneuil Hall on October 16. This gathering was attended by several hundred people including a "goodly sprinkling of women, some of them Sunday school teachers" as well as "15 or 20 prominent merchants from Chinatown, all in American attire."[66] The meeting was called to order by Nickerson, who then turned the proceedings over to a group of "prominent men." William Lloyd Garrison, the son of the well-known social reformer and abolitionist, made the first speech, denouncing the raid as a transgression against basic rights of everyone living in the United States. He declared,

> We are gathered to protest against the recent flagrant outrage upon ourselves and upon the fair fame of the city. It is a menace to constitutional government. A few orientals serve today as a pretext for this encroachment of a power hostile to democratic institutions. Tomorrow the victims may be negroes or Jews.[67]

Garrison addressed the racial and political motives behind the raid:

> The preliminary excuse for the brutality in Chinatown was the fact of a single and exceptional murder of one Chinaman by another, a crime almost of daily occurence in other parts of the city among natives and foreigners.
>
> The pretense of the police cloaked a purpose to round up the Chinese colony and capture the pitiful number who were unable to produce on the instant their certificates—the chattel tag which the great republic, founded by emigrants from oppression, exacts of these later refugees.
>
> Imagine the tables turned and American citizens in China corraled and dragged into confinement on suspicion! The apathetic deadness of Boston would burst into volcanic wrath and the navy yard bristle with activity. Or, suppose a descent upon the Italian quarter were planned by the police, inspired by federal authority. Even let the

Japanese be the intended victims. Strenuous and inflated as is our new "world power," the United States would shrink from the attempt. The eagle seeks a helpless quarry.[68]

Other well-known figures spoke out against the raid. Rev. Dr. John Galbraith spoke of the high moral values exhibited by the Chinese and equated the raid with the "sand lots outrages of the Pacific coast."[69] And the Hon. T. J. Gargan declared that "one of the greatest outrages ever perpetrated upon a people was inflicted upon the Chinese of this city last Sunday night."[70]

Later that week, the *Herald* reported that three local ministers began their Sunday sermons with impassioned denunciations of the raid, one pointing out that the "Chinaman has no friends; has no vote; has no gunboat; so he is an easy victim of the bully and the coward."[71] While such sermons and the mass rally did little to alleviate the plight of those arrested, detained, and eventually deported, the positions taken by these social reformers and ministers points to the impact that Chinese immigration had on American society. By coming to terms with how the Chinese were treated, some Americans addressed American immigration laws, racial preferences, and social mores. Indeed, the Chinese presence forced a number of Bostonians to examine the society they helped create.

Despite these protests, however, the raid apparently achieved its desired effect. The number of Chinese deported soon after the raid was five, and another forty-five were deported later. Thus, about 20 percent of those arrested were declared to be in the country illegally and were deported at the expense of the United States government.[72] Ironically, the *Herald*'s first account of the raid ended with the statement, "If the officials succeed in deporting 50 Boston Celestials out of last night's batch, they will feel that they have done the greatest night's work of their lives."[73] While the total number of people deported was small, the results of the raid can be measured in yet another way. Both papers reported on October 26 that about 150 Chinese had left the city by train the previous evening. Although it was said that Chinese in New England often left the area during autumn, it was also reported that it was "probable" that their leaving was related to the raid and its aftermath, as this was the largest group of Chinese to ever leave the area at one time.[74]

The 1903 raid on Boston Chinatown was thus not an isolated incident of police checking for registration certificates, but part of a larger movement that sought to rid the country of the Chinese who had managed to settle in the United States despite the passage of a series of exclusion acts. Therefore, the raid was successful to the degree that a small number of Chinese were eventually deported, and soon after, another 150 left the city for points west, or perhaps China itself.

Conversely, the raid also had an unintended effect on Sino-American relations as well as on the 1905 Chinese boycott of American goods in China. This can be seen in the case of Feng Hsia-wei (Fung Ah-wai, Fernando Ruiz). After being caught up in the raid, he went to the Philippines and later returned to China. Angered by his experiences in the United States, he wrote a book denouncing American attitudes toward the Chinese. In 1905, he committed suicide by taking poison near the American consulate in Shanghai and thus became a martyr for supporters of the boycott of American goods in China. When his body arrived in Canton for burial, mass demonstrations took place in support of the boycott movement.[75] Although the boycott did little to alleviate the severity of the exclusion policy, it was one of the first concrete expressions of modern Chinese nationalism, a movement that would eventually lead to the fall of the Qing dynasty and the founding of the Republic of China.

Although this raid is generally viewed in terms of American persecution of Chinese immigrants, I have analyzed it here as a vehicle to gain a broader perspective of Boston Chinatown at the turn of the century, and by extension, perhaps other Chinese communities as well.[76] The initial pretext for the raid was a murder, supposedly brought on by competition over money taken in by a rival association in a blackmail scheme designed to protect those who had not registered in accordance with the 1892 Geary Act. If this is true, it offers new information on how some of the Chinese may have dealt with the institutionalization of the exclusion policy. If not true, it can then be seen as a kind of "disinformation" the authorities used to discredit the Chinese community and simultaneously give justification to their own illegal activities.

The coverage of the Chinese in these accounts of the feud, murder, raid, and its aftermath, while often similar to the common imagery that denigrated immigrants in cultural terms, also disclosed an American preference for those who showed signs of assimilation. The newspapers often paid attention to those Chinese who wore American clothes, had cut their queues, and who spoke English, perhaps to say that some had been able to shed their "old ways" and achieve a degree of civilization. By making a distinction between those Chinese who had adopted some habits of the West and those who had not, the press not only revealed a preference for assimilated Chinese immigrants, but more importantly, acknowledged that such assimilation did indeed take place. Much of the anti-Chinese rhetoric of the nineteenth century, especially that originating in the western states, deemed the Chinese unassimilable and perpetually foreign. Here, however, is evidence that a number of Chinese had indeed become part of the American landscape, wearing American clothes, adopting certain social customs, and had learned the benefits of having American allies to come to their defense.

Thus, the central importance of "re-visiting" this murder, funeral, and the subsequent raid is that they provide evidence of close interracial relations between the Chinese and others. White Sunday School teachers, wives, friends, bail bondsmen, and associates of different ethnicities all played roles in this episode of Chinese American history that has heretofore been seen merely as a case of police harassment. From the cases of interracial cooperation and the information found in the Federal Census of 1900, it is evident that the Chinese had established roots in the city and had a broader network of associates and supporters than is often acknowledged. This may not have lessened the intensity of the anti-Chinese movement, but it certainly defies the once commonly held belief that the Chinese were unassimilable, isolated from the rest of society, and without interest in being active members in American society. While this case study is focused on Boston Chinatown, where the absence of antimiscegenation laws prohibiting Chinese-Caucasian marriages would contribute to such interracial mixing, it is possible that scholars researching communities in other regions will, in reevaluating their sources (census data, newspaper accounts, insurance maps, etc.), find similar examples of interracial relations. Such inquiry might thus bring to light a new perspective on the evolution of Asian American community life.

Finally, when placed in a contemporary context, the arrest of hundreds of Chinese on the basis of their failure to produce valid residence certificates upon demand speaks to the dangers of the use of a national identity card. In recent years, a variety of politicians and policy makers have advocated the use of identity cards to distinguish "legal" and "illegal residents." While "legal residents" are told that they will have "nothing to fear," the 1903 raid on Boston Chinatown is an important example of the degree of power such a system of identification would give to the state. The overwhelming majority of the Chinese arrested in the raid were indeed legal residents, or even American citizens, but their presence in the immigrant community made them vulnerable to a mass arrest of questionable legality. The law obviously did not ensure that the "legal residents" "had nothing to fear." With the flood of contemporary images that depict Chinatown and other communities of color as being populated by large numbers of unassimilable "illegal aliens," it is vital that we learn from historical practices in order to better understand, contextualize, and respond to similar pressures on present-day Asian American communities.

Notes

The author wishes to thank Charles Dew, Bob Lee, Peggy Pascoe, and the anonymous readers for their helpful comments on an earlier draft of this piece. This article is dedicated to my friends and colleagues in the East of California caucus with the hope that it will inspire further research on Asian Americans "east of California."

1. *The Statutes at Large of the United States of America,* vol. 27, 1893, 25–26.

2. I first became aware of the intricacies of this event when I noticed that the various secondary sources that cited the raid were inconsistent in stating the year in which it took place. Many of the sources placed the raid in October 1902, while others had it occurring in October 1903. After going through the Boston newspapers for October of both years, I determined that 1903 was the correct year. The confusion appears to have arisen from the most frequently cited article on the raid, which had 1902 as the date—probably a printer's error. Later scholars depending on this source simply repeated the mistake. The article in question is John Foster, "The Chinese Boycott," *Atlantic Monthly* 97 (1906): 118–127. The only other text that links the murder to the raid is a brief passage in Doris C. J. Chu, *Chinese in Massachusetts: Their Experiences and Contributions* (Boston: Chinese Culture Institute, 1987), 52.

3. Throughout the press coverage of this murder and its aftermath, Wong Yak Chong, Wong Ching, and Charlie Chinn are referred to by a variety of names. Wong Yak Chong is usually called Chong, Chung, or Shong. Wong Ching is sometimes called Wong Cheng, Chong, or Jung, and Charlie Chinn is sometimes called Chin Toy.

4. Here, too, spellings change throughout the coverage. The Hip Sing Tong is referred to as the Hep Sing or Hep Sen Tong. The On Leung Tong is sometimes referred to as the On Lion Tong.

5. *Boston Herald,* 3 October 1903, 1. Unless otherwise indicated, all citations of newspapers refer to the morning edition of the paper. The term "Highbinder" was a common term for those belonging to *tongs.* It implies that they were involved in illegal activity and violence. Another common term for these men was "hatchet men," referring to one of

their alleged weapons of choice. For a rather lurid account of the *tongs,* see Richard H. Dillon, *The Hatchet Men* (New York: Coward-McLunn, 1962).

6. *Boston Herald,* 6 October 1903, 11.

7. Ibid.

8. *Boston Daily Globe,* 3 October 1903, 11.

9 *Boston Herald,* 4 October 1903, 28.

10. Similar depictions of the Chinese as untrustworthy can be found in Jacob Riis, *How the Other Half Lives: Studies Among the Tenements of New York* (New York: Dover Publications, 1971; originally published in 1890), 77–83.

11. *Boston Herald,* 4 October 1903, 28. After a speedy trial, Wong and Chinn were found guilty and sentenced to life in prison. For coverage of the trial, see *Boston Daily Globe,* 23–25 November and 1–6 December 1903; and *Boston Herald,* 3–6 December 1903.

12. *Boston Daily Globe,* 5 October 1903, 2.

13. *Boston Daily Globe,* 6 October 1903, 9.

14. *Boston Daily Globe,* 12 October 1903, 8.

15. Ibid.

16. Ibid.

17. This position echoes that of Delber K. McKee's *Chinese Exclusion Versus the Open Door Policy, 1900–1906: Clashes Over China Policy in the Roosevelt Era* (Detroit: Wayne State University Press, 1977), 68.

18. *Boston Herald,* 4 October 1903, 28.

19. *Boston Daily Globe,* 5 October 1903, 2.

20. *Boston Daily Globe,* 7 October 1903, 8. Although it is well known that the Chinese Consolidated Benevolent Association urged Chinese immigrants to resist the registration requirement, this is the only case I have come across of alleged blackmail among the Chinese relating to the Geary Act.

21. Ibid.

22. *Boston Globe,* 8 October 1903, 5. The two previous quoted sentences in this paragraph are from this same article. Later, on November 23, an article on the front page of the evening edition of the *Boston Globe* simply stated, "It was the murder of Chong [*sic*] which led to the raid upon the Chinese."

23. Ibid.

24. *Boston Daily Globe,* 9 October 1903, 7; and 10 October 1903, 1.

25. *Boston Herald,* 11 October 1903, 5.

26. This cemetery was the main burial ground for the Chinese in the Boston area. It is located in Mattapan, about eight miles from Chinatown. The remains of the Chinese there were often disinterred and sent back to China for final burial in ancestral plots. I thank Ting-fun Yeh of the Chinese Historical Society of New England for providing me with information on the cemetery, including news of current efforts to restore the Chinese headstones there.

27. *Boston Daily Globe,* 11 October 1903, 3.

28. *Boston Herald,* 12 October 1903, 5. According to the *Boston Herald* of 6 October (11), Wong was a member of the Roslindale Club, enjoyed bicycle riding, and regularly attended the "Chinese class in the Sunday school of the Bromfield Street Methodist Church."

29. *Boston Herald,* 12 October 1903, 5.

30. *Boston Daily Globe,* 12 October 1903, 8.

31. Ibid. Both papers also report that there was a final viewing of the body at the grave site before the coffin was sealed. This is the only reference of such a practice that I have encountered in the study of Chinese burial rituals. For studies of Chinese burial practices, see Emily Ahern, *The Cult of the Dead in a Chinese Village* (Stanford, Calif.: Stanford University Press, 1983); J.J.M. de Groot, *The Religious System of China,* 6 vols. (Leiden: Brill Publishers, 1894); and *Death Ritual in Late Imperial and Modern China,* ed.

James L. Watson and Evelyn S. Rawski (Berkeley: University of California Press, 1988). The study of the transformation of religious practices among Chinese immigrants in America is one of the areas in Chinese American history that is still underdeveloped.

32. *Boston Daily Globe,* 12 October 1903, 8.

33. *Boston Herald,* 12 October 1903, 2.

34. *Boston Daily Globe,* 12 October 1903, 8.

35. Ibid.

36. At the height of the Red Scare after the First World War, Attorney General A. Mitchell Palmer authorized a series of raids in thirty-three cities with the intention of arresting and deporting political radicals. As in the raid on Boston Chinatown, government agents entered homes and other establishments without warrants, arrested large numbers, and deported relatively few. For a concise synopsis of these raids, see Stanley Coben, *A. Mitchell Palmer: Politician* (New York: Columbia University Press, 1963), 217–245.

37. *Boston Daily Globe,* 12 October 1903, 8.

38. *Boston Herald,* 12 October 1903, 8.

39. Ibid.

40. Ibid.

41. When "Chinatown" appears within quotation marks, I am using it to denote images of "Chinatown" rather than the actual community. The body of literature on the imagery of "Chinatowns" is far too large and commonly known to be cited here. A recent motion picture that depicted "Chinatown" as a crime-ridden community where much of the illicit activity takes place in restaurant basements is Michael Cimino's *Year of the Dragon* (1985). For a study examining the use of "Chinatown" imagery to promote political agendas that have little to do with the residents of Chinatown, see K. Scott Wong, "Chinatown: Conflicting Images, Contested Terrain," *MELUS* 20, no. 1 (spring 1995). The image of "Chinatown" as a district of exotic vice is not confined to North American sensibilities. In Barcelona, the section of the city known as "Barrio Chino" ("Chinatown") became known as the "center of everything conservatives feared, from vice to anarcho-syndicalism." This term for this area was apparently first used by the Republican journalist Francisco Madrid in the early twentieth century. See Temma Kaplan, *Red City, Blue City: Social Movements in Picasso's Barcelona* (Berkeley: University of California Press, 1992), 148. I thank Joel Wolfe for bringing this similarity in images to my attention.

42. *Boston Herald,* 12 October 1903, 8.

43. For a recent study of how opium smoking was used against the Chinese by their detractors, see Gregory Yee Mark, "Opium and the 'Chinese Question,'" in *Bearing Dreams, Shaping Visions,* ed. Linda A. Revilla, Gail M. Nomura, Shawn Wong, and Shirley Hune (Pullman: Washington State University Press, 1993), 5–13.

44. *Boston Herald,* 27 October 1903, 8.

45. *Boston Herald,* 12 October 1903, 8.

46. For cases that appeared in the press soon after the raid of white women being found in "opium dens" or being lured into Chinese residences, see *Boston Daily Globe,* 27 November 1903, 1; *Boston Herald,* 27 November 1903, 1, 8; *Boston Herald,* 24 January 1904, 12; and *Boston Herald,* 27 January 1904, 11. For a different, yet equally manipulative, reading of the relationships between Chinese men and white girls/women, see D. W. Griffith's 1919 film *Broken Blossoms* and John Kuo Wei Tchen's study of the film, "Modernizing White Patriarchy: Re-Viewing D. W. Griffith's *Broken Blossoms,*" in Russell Leong, ed., *Moving the Image: Independent Asian Pacific American Media Arts* (Los Angeles: UCLA Asian American Studies Center, 1991), 133–143.

47. *Boston Herald,* 12 October 1903, 8.

48. See Shepard Schwartz, "Mate-selection Among New York City's Chinese Males, 1931–38," *The American Journal of Sociology* 56, no. 6 (May 1951): 562–568; and John Kuo Wei Tchen, "New York Chinese: The Nineteenth-Century Pre-Chinatown Settlement," in *Chinese America: History and Perspectives, 1990* (San Francisco: Chinese Historical Society

of America, 1990), 157–192. Mary Lui's forthcoming dissertation (Cornell University) on interracial relations, marriage, and family life in turn-of-the-century New York China-town will be a welcome addition to our understanding of these issues.

49. *Boston Herald,* 12 October 1903, 8; and *Boston Daily Globe,* 12 October 1903, 8. The Federal Census of 1900 lists this couple as Ming Yen Goon and Kelly Goon. Mr. Goon was forty-two years old, born in China, and had immigrated to the United States in 1880. Mrs. Goon was twenty-four years old, born in Massachusetts to Irish-immigrant parents. They are both listed as literate and able to speak English. Mr. Goon worked as a janitor; Mrs. Goon had no occupation listed. At the time of the Census, they had been married for four years. *Twelfth Census of the United States of America* (National Archives, microfilm, roll 678), hereafter cited as Federal Census of 1900.

50. *Boston Herald,* 12 October 1903, 8. This couple does not appear in the Federal Census of 1900.

51. All of the specific demographic information found in this and the following two para-graphs are based on the Federal Census of 1900 (roll 678).

52. *Boston Daily Globe,* 12 October 1903, 1 (evening edition).

53. *House Documents* 847, 59th Congress, 1st Session, 1905–1906, 129. The newspapers' figures are inconsistent for the days following the raid. Therefore, I have relied on the 1906 report to the House of Representatives, which was compiled from the records of the Bureau of Immigration, assuming that the figures are more reliable than the inconsistent numbers found in the two newspapers. This number, when compared to the Census figures for the population of Chinatown, indicates that a great many more Chinese were in the area that evening than usual, probably coming from outlying areas and other cities.

54. *House Documents* 847, 129.

55. Ibid.

56. *Boston Daily Globe,* 13 October 1903, 14.

57. *Boston Daily Globe,* 12 October 1903, 1 (evening edition). The custom of laundrymen coming into Chinatown during their day off on the weekends is consistent with that written about in Paul Siu's *The Chinese Laundryman: A Study of Social Isolation* (New York: New York University Press, 1987), 137–155.

58. *Boston Daily Globe,* 12 October 1903, 8 (evening edition).

59. *Boston Daily Globe,* 13 October 1903, 14. This might signify that, like today, some people hired legal or illegal immigrants as inexpensive labor or were otherwise associated with them, but were reluctant to come forward and vouch for them.

60. For examples, see *Boston Daily Globe,* 14 October 1903, 3; and 15 October 1903, 6.

61. *Boston Daily Globe,* 13 October 1903, 1 (evening edition).

62. Stephen W. Nickerson, "Our Chinese Treaties; and Legislation; and their Enforcement," *North American Review* 181 (September 1905): 376.

63. *Boston Daily Globe,* 18 October 1903, 8.

64. *Boston Daily Globe,* 12 October 1903, 8.

65. Ibid.

66. *Boston Daily Globe,* 16 October 1903, 1 (evening edition).

67. Ibid. In December 1901, Garrison presided over a public meeting held at the Methodist Episcopal Church of Boston protesting the continuation of the Geary Act. See McKee, *Chinese Exclusion Versus the Open Door Policy,* 49–50.

68. *Boston Daily Globe,* 16 October 1903, 8 (evening edition).

69. Ibid.

70. Ibid.

71. *Boston Herald,* 19 October 1903, 1.

72. *House Documents* 847, 129.

73. *Boston Herald,* 12 October 1903, 2.

74. *Boston Herald,* 26 October 1903, 1; and *Boston Daily Globe,* 26 October 1903, 14. Both articles also noted that the body of a Chinese woman was on the train being transported

back to China. She was identified as Lee Lou Ping, a victim of tuberculosis. She was also said to have been the first Chinese woman to be taken back to China from Boston for burial. She had originally been interred in Mount Hope Cemetery.

75. For details, see McKee, *Chinese Exclusion Versus the Open Door Policy,* 152 and 164; and Shih-shan Henry Tsai, *China and the Overseas Chinese in the United States, 1868–1911* (Fayetteville: University of Arkansas Press, 1983), 106. For Chinese-language sources on Feng's suicide, see A. Ying, *Fan Mei Huagong jinyue wenxue ji* ("A Collection of Literature Written in Opposition to American Restriction of Chinese Laborers") (Beijing: Zhong hua shu ju, 1962), 696–699; and Zhang Cunwu, *Guangxu sanshiyinian ZhongMei gongyue fengchao* ("The 1905 Sino-American Labor Treaty Crisis") (Taipei: Zhongyang yanjiuyuan xiandaishi yanjiusuo, 1966), 220–221.

76. For a study of a similar raid (though slightly later) on a Chinese American community and the Chinese and Euro-American response, see Shirley Sui-Ling Tam, "Police Round-Up of Chinese in Cleveland in 1925: A Case Study in a Racist Measure and the Chinese Response," M.A. Thesis, Case Western Reserve University, 1988.

JAPANESE ON THE WEST COAST*

C. B. Munson

GROUND COVERED

In reporting on the Japanese 'problem' on the West Coast the facts are, on the whole, fairly clear and opinion toward the problem exceedingly uniform. In reporting, the main difficulty is to know where to leave off and what to leave out. One could gather data for fifteen years with fifteen men and still be in the position of the Walrus and the Carpenter:

> If seven maids with seven mops
> Swept it for half a year—
> Do you suppose, the Walrus said,
> That they could get it clear?

Whisking up the grains of sand is the wrong approach, yet when your reporter declares there is a sea and a shore and some sand, and that he has sampled the general quality of sand in many varying beaches, do not be too hard in your judgment for him if he has stopped far short of sorting out each layer or tint or even each beach. You have to feel this problem—not figure it out with your pencil. We only cite the sand that our reader may never forget the complexities for even a shovel full of sand.

---

*In *Years of Infamy: The Story of America's Concentration Camps* (1976), Michi Weglyn introduced us to the existence of the Munson Report, and the fact that the U.S. government kept it secret until long after the end of World War II and the Japanese American internment. The Japanese American internment has been and continues to be explained in history and political science texts as resulting from military necessity, wartime hysteria, and the government's wish to protect Japanese American citizens. The Munson Report shows these explanations to be false, and thus is critical to a full understanding of the Japanese American internment as one of many anti-Asian actions in this country, beginning in the 1880s, aimed at excluding Asians from permanent settlement in America. The report confirms the major forces fueling the internment in 1942: white America's deep-seated perception of Asians as aliens, ineligible to become "real" Americans, and white America's resentment of both the economic competition Asians posed for white workers and the economic gains that West Coast Japanese Americans had achieved.

Your reporter spent about a week each in the 11th, 12th and 13th Naval Districts with the full cooperation of the Naval and Army intelligences and the F.B.I. Some mention should also be made of the assistance rendered from time to time by the British Intelligence. Our Navy has done by far the most work on this problem, having given it intense consideration for the last ten or fifteen years. Your reporter commenced in the 12th Naval District, which covers Northern California, from thence to the 13th, covering Washington and Oregon, winding up his observations in the 11th Naval District, covering Southern California, where to his mind the whole 'problem' finally focuses. Your reporter also turned the corner into British Columbia through a member of the R.C.M.P. and the corner into Mexico through a conference with our Consul at Tijuana.

Opinions of the various services were obtained, also of business, employees, universities, fellow white workers, students, fish packers, lettuce packers, farmers, religious groups, etc. etc. The opinion expressed with minor differences was uniform. Select Japanese in all groups were sampled. To mix indiscriminately with the Japanese was not considered advisable chiefly because the opinions of many loyal white Americans who had made this their life work for the last fifteen years were available and it was foolish to suppose your reporter could add to the sum of knowledge in three weeks by running through the topmost twigs of a forest.

BACKGROUND

Unless familiar with the religious and family background of the Japanese, this rough background summary should be skimmed over as it has a bearing on the Japanese question. If the reader is familiar with the Japanese background, it may be omitted. An American wit once said, "You cannot tell the truth about Japan without lying." This same witticism might be made with reference to the Japanese people, but, like all generalizations, it needs a corrective explanation. A study of Japan is a study in the category of social fully as much as of political science. The study of the Japanese people is one of absorbing interest.

Who are the Japanese people? From whence did they come and what emotional concepts did they bring with them? While there might not be unanimity of opinion as to the various strains that go to make up the Japanese of today, one leading anthropologist, Dr. Frederick Star of the University of Chicago, a number of years ago said to the writer, "The Japanese are the most mixed race of people that I have ever studied." The Malay strain is pronounced in the Japanese, especially in the Province of Kumamoto. The Mongol is very pronounced in the upper middle as well as in the so-called higher brackets of society. Then there is the Aryan strain still to be seen in its unmixed form in the 17,000 and more Ainu who inhabit portions of Hokkaido and the Kurile Islands. These latter are related-to-the Aryan group in physiognomy and in language. These three strains have produced the Japanese of today.

The Ainu, in so far as we know, was the aboriginal. His social status was changed from time to time as conquering groups drove him farther and farther to the North. These conquering groups came from China via Korea. Japanese history begins with the conqueror Jimnu Tenno, who arrived on 'Floating Bridge of

Heaven'—a poetical expression for his coming to Japan by boat. He found a tribal people with a primitive animistic faith of nature worship. He had a superior religion and he was shrewd. He told the conquered people that their reverence for the tribal chief was a true reverence and that he also revered the head of his clan which was the Sun Goddess, whose beneficent rule was seen in her health-giving rays. Thus began what is known as 'Shinto' ('The Way of the Gods'), as we know it today. From the days of Jimnu (the first Japanese Emperor) to the present, all Japanese have revered the Emperor as a descendant of the Sun Goddess, whose appearance in Japanese mythology is too complicated to be discussed here.

Another cultural element in Japanese life stems from the introduction of Buddhism in Japan in the sixth and seventh centuries. Buddhism is a foreign religion and made little progress in Japan even though it was fostered by the Emperor Prince Shotoku. Buddhism had a very difficult time until some wise propagandist hit upon the idea of incorporating the Shinto Gods into the Buddhist Pantheon. All the Shinto deities were recognized as avatars of Buddha and have continued in Japan until the days of the Restoration what is known as twofold Buddhism—a union of Shinto and Buddhism—a union so intricate that Buddhist God shelves in the home have unmistakable Shinto deities and Shinto God shelves have unmistakable Buddhist deities. Japan can never repay Buddhism for its contribution to the cultural life of the people. Its temples were schools wherein those who wished might be taught. It developed the arts and crafts, and was the developer and preserver of much that is beautiful in the cultural life of the Nation today.

While the Shinto and the Buddhist influence, separate and co-mingled, were moving forward, there developed in Japan a feudal type of society. This society was organized under the rule of a tribal person known as 'The Great Name' (a land baron). He had warriors or knights known as Samurai. They, the Samurai, preserved order and fought battles to maintain the existence of the clan. Besides the Samurai there was the farmer who raised the food, the artisan who fashioned and fabricated the tools, not only of the farmer but also of the warrior, and there was the merchant; below them there was the eta, and lower still the hinin—those who for misconduct or through capture had been reduced in status until they were not considered men, as the term 'hinin' implies.

For nearly 1,000 years, this state of society existed with internecine wars of all too frequent and carnal occurrence until early in the seventeenth century when a great man, Ieyasu, appeared, and became the founder of what is known as the Tokugawa family. The story of this period is interesting, but time and space do not permit the telling of it here, other than to say it was a period of about 250 years of great peace.

During the Tokugawa period, Confucianism had great Vogue. The Samurai children were privileged to attend the few schools which were maintained and where the principles of Confucian ethics were taught, but with one great characteristic change—the Japanese substituted for the chief virtue, loyalty for filial piety. Chugi (loyalty) is loyalty, not to an idea nor an ideal, but to a person. In this feudal society, personal relationships were supreme, and loyalty was the cardinal virtue.

In the feudal state, as well as throughout all Japanese history, the individual as an individual did not exist. He existed only as a member of the family and the family existed as a member of the clan. The family could dispose of individuals at will should occasion merit such action. Even life itself could be taken after the case had been submitted to the family council. In this connection, one should not overlook the tremendous influence of the dead. The living succeed or fail, are happy or sad, through the influence of the dead who live in the tombs of the village or hover over their familiar haunts. It is well to keep this in mind when estimating Japanese activity. The Japanese believe that the dead remain in the World and that all dead become Gods with supernatural powers, and that happiness of the dead depends upon respectful services that are rendered them by the living.

In a feudal society the merchant cuts a very poor figure. He was looked down upon by the Samurai and he was inferior to the farmer and artisan. It is significant that but a very few families of merchants have maintained a good social position. Of these there are the Mitsui, the Iwasaki (this latter being represented by what we know as the Mitsubishi), and also the Sumitomo family.

With the Coming of Commodore Perry in 1853 and 1854, feudalism began to pass away and within 20 years was abolished by Government edict. Although the feudal social system was legally abolished, its influence continues even today.

With the Restoration there appeared a new influence in Japanese life and that was the coming of the Christian missionary with his doctrine of individual responsibility to deity. This was something new to the Japanese system of society. Heretofore religion centered in the family and family culture and family faith were a collective thing and not individual. The success of the missionary movement in Japan is remarkable because it brings this new element into the social picture. Wherever Christianity succeeds, it also succeeds in breaking the old family ties and hangovers of a feudal order. Japan's advance in Government, its development educationally and the vast improvements that we see in society today have been furthered by the application of Western methods of teaching, of Government, etc. But, the Christian influence must not be underestimated nor should one go too far in over stressing its great importance. Christianity is individualistic, and that is one reason why the 'powers that be' in Japan today are endeavoring to regulate its activities, if not to change some of its tenets. The Christian Japanese understand America better than any other group because they have been more and more weaned away from the influence of feudalism.

The Japanese are a perplexing people and their study is a very interesting and very enlightening one. They follow the leader—they have done this throughout all the years of their history. Even today, personal ties are stronger than legal ones.

No estimate of the elements characteristic of the Japanese is complete without a word about 'giri'. There is no accurate English word for 'giri'. The nearest approach to an understanding of the term is our word 'obligation,' which is very inadequate and altogether too weak. Favors of kindnesses done to a Japanese are never forgotten but were stored up in memory and in due time an adequate quid pro quo must be rendered in return. The clever and none-too scrupulous individual often hangs 'giri' upon the unsuspecting, to their hurt and harm. 'Giri' is the great political tool. To understand 'giri' is to understand the Japanese.

Associations

The Japanese is the greatest joiner in the world. To take care of this passion he has furnished himself with ample associations to join. There are around 1,563 of these in the United States. Your reporter has before him a Japanese publication entitled "The Japanese-American Directory of 1941" at least two inches thick listing the Japanese associations in fine print. Your reporter also has before him lists furnished him in the various Naval Districts of some of the leading associations considered the most important, with full descriptions of their activities as far as known. It is endless to clutter up this report with them.

Family Set-up in United States

In the United States there are four divisions of Japanese to be considered:

1. The *ISSEI*—First generation Japanese. Entire cultural background Japanese. Probably loyal romantically to Japan. They must be considered, however, as other races. They have made this their home. They have brought up children here, their wealth accumulated by hard labor is here, and many would have become American citizens had they been allowed to do so. They are for the most part simple people. Their age group is largely 55 to 65, fairly old for a hardworking Japanese.
2. The *NISEI*— Second generation who have received their whole education in the United States and usually, in spite of discrimination against them and a certain amount of insults accumulated through the years from responsible elements, show a pathetic eagerness to be Americans. They are in constant conflict with the orthodox, well disciplined family life of their elders. Age group—1 to 30 years.
3. The *KIBEI*—This is an important division of the NISEI. This is the term used by the Japanese to signify those American born Japanese who received part or all of their education in Japan. In any consideration of the KIBEI—they should be again divided into two classes, i.e. THOSE WHO RECEIVED THEIR EDUCATION IN JAPAN FROM CHILDHOOD TO ABOUT 17 YEARS OF AGE and THOSE WHO RECEIVED THEIR EARLY FORMA-TIVE EDUCATION IN THE UNITED STATES AND RETURNED TO JA-PAN FOR FOUR OR FIVE YEARS OF JAPANESE EDUCATION. The Kibei are considered the most dangerous element and closer to the Issei with especial reference to those who received their early education in Japan. It must be noted, however, that many of those who visited Japan subsequent to their early American education come back with an added loyalty to the United States. In fact it is a saying that all a Nisei needs is a trip to Japan to make a loyal American out of him. The American educated Japanese is a boor in Japan and treated as a foreigner and with a certain amount of contempt there. His trip is usually a painful experience.
4. The *SANSEI*—The third generation Japanese is a baby and may be disregarded for the purposes of our survey.

BACKGROUND

This is tied into the family of which the Issei is the head with more authority and hold over his family than an old New England Bible-thumbing pioneer. Their family life is disciplined and honorable. The children are obedient and the girls virtuous. We must think also of the Associations, some sinister, some emanating from Imperial Japan, some with Japanese Consular contacts. It all weaves up into a sinister pattern on paper. This pattern has been set up in a secret document entitled "Japanese Organizations and Activities in the 11th Naval District," and may be scrutinized with proper authorization in the Navy Department in Washington. We only suggest this to our reader in case our words have not built up the proper Halloween atmosphere. It is like looking at the 'punkin' itself. There is real fire in it, yet in many ways it is hollow and dusty. However, your reporter desires to have you know that all this exists before he goes on to the main body of his report on how the Japanese in the United States are liable to react in case of war with Japan.

THE TOKIO-SUN-GOD-RELIGIOUS-FAMILY-ASSOCIATION PLUS ORIENTAL MIND SET-UP SHOWS SIGNS OF THE HONORABLE PASSAGE OF TIME

There are still Japanese in the United States who will tie dynamite around their waist and make a human bomb out of themselves. We grant this but today they are few. Many things indicate that very many joints in the Japanese set-up show age and many elements are not what they used to be. The weakest from a Japanese standpoint are the Nisei. They are universally estimated from 90 to 98 percent loyal to the United States if the Japanese educated element of the Kibei is excluded. The Nisei are pathetically eager to show this loyalty. They are not Japanese in culture. They are foreigners to Japan. Though American citizens they are not accepted by Americans, largely because they look differently and can be easily recognized. The Japanese American Citizens League should be encouraged, the while an eye is kept open, to see that Tokio does not get its finger in this pie—which it has in a few cases attempted to do. The loyal Nisei hardly know where to turn. Some gesture of protection or wholehearted acceptance of this group would go a long way to swinging them away from any last romantic hankering after old Japan. They are not oriental or mysterious, they are very American and are one of a proud, self-respecting race suffering from a little inferiority complex and a lack of contact with the white boys they went to school with. They are eager for this contact and to work alongside them.

The Issei or first generation is considerably weakened in their loyalty to Japan by the fact that they have chosen to make this their home and have brought up their children here. They expect to die here. They are quite fearful of being put in a concentration camp. Many would take out American citizenship if allowed to do so. The haste of this report does not allow us to go into this more fully. The Issei have to break with their religion, their god and Emperor, their family, their ancestors and their after-life in order to be loyal to the United States. They are also still legally Japanese. Yet they do break, and send their boys off to the Army with pride and tears. They are good neighbors. They are old men fifty-five to sixty-five, for the most part simple and dignified. Roughly they were Japanese lower middle class about analogous to the pilgrim fathers. They were largely farmers and fishermen. Today the Japanese is a farmer, fisherman and businessman. They get very attached to the land they work or own (through the second generation), they like their own business, they do not work at industrial jobs nor for others except as a stepping stone to becoming independent.

The Kibei, educated from childhood to seventeen, are still the element most to be watched.

WHAT WILL THE JAPANESE DO

Sabotage

Now that we have roughly given a background and a description of the Japanese elements in the United States the question naturally arises—what will these people do in case of a war between the United States and Japan? As interview after interview piled up, those bringing in results began to call it the same old tune. Such it was with only minor differences. These contacts ranged all the way from two-day sessions with Intelligence Services through businessmen to Roman Catholic priests who were frankly not interested in the United States and were only interested in making as many Catholics as possible. The story was all the same. There is no Japanese problem on the Coast. There will be no armed uprising of Japanese. There will undoubtedly be some sabotage financed by Japan and executed largely by imported agents or agents already imported. There will be the odd case of fanatical sabotage by some Japanese 'crackpot.' In each Naval District there are about 250 to 300 suspects under surveillance. It is easy to get on the suspect list, merely a speech in favor of Japan at some banquet being sufficient to land one there. The Intelligence Services are generous with the title of suspect and are taking no chances. Privately, they believe that only 50 or 60 in each district can be classed as really dangerous. The Japanese are hampered as saboteurs because of their easily recognized physical appearance. It will be hard for them to get near anything to blow up if it is guarded. There is far more danger from Communists and people of the Bridges type on the Coast than there is from Japanese. The Japanese here is almost exclusively a farmer, a fisherman or a small business man. He has no entree to plants or intricate machinery.

Espionage

The Japanese, if undisturbed and disloyal should be well equipped for obvious physical espionage. A great part of this work was probably completed and forwarded to Tokio years ago, such as soundings and photography of every inch of the Coast. They are probably familiar with the location of every building and garage including Mike O'Flarety's out-house in the Siskiyous with all trails leading thereto. An experienced Captain in Navy Intelligence, who has from time to time and over a period of years intercepted information Tokio bound, said he would certainly hate to be a Japanese coordinator of information in Tokio. He stated that the mass of useless information was unbelievable. This would be fine for a fifth column in

Belgium or Holland with the German army ready to march in over the border, but though the local Japanese could spare a man who intimately knew the country for each Japanese invasion squad, there would at least have to be a terrific American Naval disaster before his brown brothers would need his services. The dangerous part of their espionage is that they would be very effective as far as movement of supplies, movement of troops and movement of ships out of harbor mouths and over railroads is concerned. They occupy only rarely positions where they can get to confidential papers or in plants. They are usually, when rarely so placed, a subject of perpetual watch and suspicion by their fellow workers. They would have to buy most of this type of information from white people.

Propaganda

Their direct propaganda is poor and rather ineffective on the whole. Their indirect is more successful. By indirect we mean propaganda preaching the beauties of Japan and the sweet innocence of the Japanese race to susceptible Americans.

SUMMARY

Japan will commit some sabotage largely depending on imported Japanese as they are afraid of and do not trust the Nesei [*sic*]. There will be no wholehearted response from Japanese in the United States. They may get some helpers from certain Kibei. They will be in a position to pick up information on troop, supply and ship movements from local Japanese.

For the most part the local Japanese are loyal to the United States or, at worst, hope that by remaining quiet they can avoid concentration camps or irresponsible mobs. We do not believe that they would be at least any more disloyal than any other racial group in the United States with whom we went to war. Those being here are on a spot and they *know it*. This is a hurried, preliminary report as our boat sails soon for Honolulu. We have not had a moment even to sort out our voluminous material since we came west. Your reporter is very satisfied he has told you what to expect from the local Japanese, but is horrified to note that dams, bridges, harbors, power stations, etc. are wholly unguarded everywhere. The harbor of San Pedro could be razed by fire completely by four men with hand grenades and a little study in one night. Dams could be blown and half of lower California might actually die of thirst, not to mention the damage to the food supply. One railway bridge at the exit from the mountains in some cases could tie up three or four main railroads. The Navy has to crawl around San Pedro on its marrow bones from oil company to oil company, from lumber yard to harbor board to city fathers, to politicians in lieu of a centralized authority, in order to strive albeit only partially to protect the conglomeration of oil tanks, lumber, gas tanks and heaven knows what else. And this is the second greatest port in the United States. This is the home base of at least the South Pacific Fleet! This is the greatest collection of inflammable material we have ever seen in our lifetime concentrated in a small vulnerable area. We do not suspect the local Japanese above anyone else or as much as the Communists or the Nazis, but before or on the outbreak of war in the South Pacific someone will set fire to this. If they do not they are fools. The

Navy or some unified authority should have complete control of the harbor of Los Angeles, known as San Pedro and Long Beach, from the water's edge in a 25–mile radius inland, before the outbreak of war with Japan. That time is now.

We will re-work this report for final submittal later. We have missed a great deal through haste. We believe we have given the high points to the best of our ability. The Japanese are loyal on the whole, but we are wide open to sabotage on this Coast and as far inland as the mountains, and while this one fact goes unrectified I cannot unqualifiedly state that there is no danger from the Japanese living in the United States which otherwise I would be willing to state.

EXECUTIVE ORDER 9066

Civilian Exclusion Order No. 5
WESTERN DEFENSE COMMAND AND FOURTH ARMY
WARTIME CIVIL CONTROL ADMINISTRATION
Presidio of San Francisco, California
April 1, 1942

INSTRUCTIONS TO ALL PERSONS
OF JAPANESE ANCESTRY LIVING IN
THE FOLLOWING AREA:

All that portion of the City and County of San Francisco, State of California, lying generally west of the north-south line established by Junipero Serra Boulevard, Worchester Avenue, and Nineteenth Avenue, and lying generally north of the east-west line established by California Street, to the intersection of Market Street, and thence on Market Street to San Francisco Bay.

All Japanese persons, both alien and non-alien, will be evacuated from the above designated area by 12:00 o'clock noon, Tuesday, April 7, 1942.

No Japanese persons, both alien and non-alien, will be permitted to enter or leave the above described area after 8:00 a.m., Thursday, April 2, 1942, without obtaining special permission from the Provost Marshal at the Civil Control Station located at:

1701 Van Ness Avenue
San Francisco, California

The Civil Control Station is equipped to assist the Japanese population affected by this evacuation in the following ways:

1. Give advice and instructions on the evacuation.
2. Provide services with respect to the management, leasing, sale, storage or other disposition of most kinds of property including: real estate, business and professional equipment, buildings, household goods, boats, automobiles, livestock, etc.

3. Provide temporary residence elsewhere for all Japanese in family groups.

4. Transport persons and a limited amount of clothing and equipment to their new residence as specified below.

THE FOLLOWING INSTRUCTIONS MUST BE OBSERVED:

1. A responsible member of each family, preferably the head of the family, or the person in whose name most of the property is held, and each individual living alone, will report to the Civil Control Station to receive further instructions. This must be done between 8:00 a.m. and 5:00 p.m., Thursday, April 2, 1942, or between 8:00 a.m. and 5:00 p.m., Friday, April 3, 1942.

2. Evacuees must carry with them on departure for the Reception Center, the following property:
   (a) Bedding and linens (no mattress) for each member of the family;
   (b) Toilet articles for each member of the family;
   (c) Extra clothing for each member of the family;
   (d) Sufficient knives, forks, spoons, plates, bowls and cups for each member of the family;
   (e) Essential personal effects for each member of the family.

   All items carried will be securely packaged, tied and plainly marked with the name of the owner and numbered in accordance with instructions received at the Civil Control Station.

   The size and number of packages is limited to that which can be carried by the individual or family group.

   No contraband items as described in paragraph 6, Public Proclamation No. 3, Headquarters Western Defense Command and Fourth Army, dated March 24, 1942, will be carried.

3. The United States Government through its agencies will provide for the storage at the sole risk of the owner of the more substantial household items, such as iceboxes, washing machines, pianos and other heavy furniture. Cooking utensils and other small items will be accepted if crated, packed and plainly marked with the name and address of the owner. Only one name and address will be used by a given family.

4. Each family, and individual living alone, will be furnished transportation to the Reception Center. Private means of transportation will not be utilized. All instructions pertaining to the movement will be obtained at the Civil Control Station.

Go to the Civil Control Station at 1701 Van Ness Avenue, San Francisco, California, between 8:00 a.m. and 5:00 p.m., Thursday, April 2, 1942, or between 8:00 a.m. and 5:00 p.m., Friday, April 3, 1942, to receive further instructions.

J. L. DeWITT
Lieutenant General, U.S. Army Commanding

Representations

MISCEGENATION AND THE CRITIQUE OF PATRIARCHY IN TURN-OF-THE-CENTURY FICTION

Jinhua Emma Teng

[M]any Chinamen marry Irish, German, or Italian wives, and of half-breed children, or children born of white mothers and Mongolian fathers, there are over a hundred now in New York. Most of these women are poor working girls, who through necessity married well-to-do Chinamen. The Chinamen often make them better husbands than men of their own nation, as quite a number of them who ran away from their former husbands to marry Chinamen have openly declared. The Chinaman never beats his wife, gives her plenty to eat and wear, and generally adopts her mode of life.

WONG CHIN FOO, 1888

Chinese journalist Wong Chin Foo's account of the New York Chinese for the August 1888 issue of New York's *The Cosmopolitan* addressed a subject that was attracting increasing attention in the American press during the late nineteenth century: the intermarriage of "whites" and "Mongolians." Wong's claim for a supposed preference on the part of white working-class women for Chinese husbands can be read in part as a response to the more prevalent sensationalist treatment of white-Chinese relationships in the American media (Wong 1888: 308).

The public concern over "miscegenation" was motivated to a large degree by Yellow Perilist fears. The immigration of Chinese labor was viewed as a threat to both American free labor and the sanctity of white womanhood. Anti-Chinese propagandists proclaimed that Chinese labor would drive down the working wage and force the wives of white working men into prostitution (Takaki 1979: 217). Reflecting (and fueling) such fears, press reports and the popular literature of the time were full of "white slave" narratives, stories of white women coerced into sexual slavery by the Chinese.

At the same time, miscegenation also served as the subject of numerous popular romances, a means of representing cross-cultural contact and/or Utopian visions of racial harmony. Puccini's *Madama Butterfly* (1904) provided the formula for many of these narratives. Since then, the image of the white man and Asian mistress has gradually come to overshadow lovers of the opposite pairing. When we look at fiction from the turn of the century, however, we actually find numerous examples of white women with Chinese lovers. Such stories reflected not only the prevailing fears about miscegenation, but also an aspect of the social reality of the time. Due to laws such as the Page Law of 1875, which banned the immigration of Chinese, Japanese, and "Mongolian" women intended for prostitution, the vast majority of Chinese women were effectively prohibited from entering the United States for most of the early history of Chinese immigration. Interracial marriage or cohabitation was one product of this imbalanced sex ratio. John Tchen (1994) has documented that a significant number of Chinese immigrants in New York city married Irish immigrant women.

The majority of the works on this subject deal with the threatening or debased aspects of miscegenation. Frank Norris's "The Third Circle" is a prime example. Journalist William Norr devoted an entire collection of reportage, *Stories of Chinatown: Sketches from Life in the Chinese Colony of Mott, Pell, and Doyers Streets* (1892), to the subject of "fallen" white women living with Chinese men. There are, nonetheless, a number of noteworthy stories that idealize the relationship between Chinese men and white women as part of a plea for racial tolerance, much as did Wong Chin Foo. The choice of this controversial topic for a work of antiracism seems doubly surprising in light of the fact that relations between white women and men of color have historically been even more taboo than those between white men and women of color.

This theme makes its first appearance in Bret Harte's "Wan Lee the Pagan" (1875), and is taken up by a number of writers at the turn of the century. Katherine Ann Porter's *Mae Franking's My Chinese Marriage* (1921) represents the most extensive treatment of the topic from the period. It is Sui Sin Far and Thomas Burke, however, who perhaps use the theme most effectively to foreground issues of race and gender. Sui Sin Far's "The Story of One White Woman Who Married a Chinese" and "Her Chinese Husband" (1910), and Thomas Burke's "The Chink and the Child" (1916), draw on what appear to be "positive" or "nonthreatening" aspects of the Orientalist stereotype of Chinese men—their gentleness, softness, passivity, and general femininity—to create characters who are morally and spiritually (but never physically) superior to their white counterparts. The authors furthermore ally Chinese men with white women as creatures of sentiment and aestheticism who are pitted against the brutality of Western masculine aggression and patriarchal dominance. The stories thus serve simultaneously as pleas for racial tolerance and critiques of Western patriarchy.

In their fictive imaginings of an idealized Chinese masculinity, defined by its difference from Western patriarchal masculinity, the stories demonstrate links to a crisis of culture growing out of Victorian society—an ambivalence toward masculine striving and aggression. With Sui Sin Far, this response takes the form of Victorian sentimentalism; with Thomas Burke, an Orientalism rooted in one aspect of what Jackson Lears has termed the "antimodernist impulse" of the turn of the century, a turn toward the vitality and spiritualism of the "primitive" East. Both Sui Sin Far and Thomas Burke bring together an idealization of the feminine and the Oriental in mustering their critiques of racial intolerance and patriarchal dominance. Indeed, the nineteenth century was not only a time of rife anti-Chinese sentiment, but also a time of growing interest in Chinoiserie. It was against this background of ambivalent attitudes that the works of Sui Sin Far and Thomas Burke were received.

Sui Sin Far: Physical or Spiritual Manliness

> *"The oily little Chink has won you!" . . . "Yes, honorably and like a man. And what are you that dare sneer at one like him. For all your six feet of grossness, your small soul cannot measure up to his great one."*
>
> Sui Sin Far, 1992

Edith Eaton (1865–1914), a Eurasian raised in America and Canada, became the best-known Chinese American champion of the North American Chinese in her time. Assuming the pen-name Sui Sin Far, she wrote from various locales, including Montreal, San Francisco, and Boston. Her writings were published in serial magazines such as the *Dominion Illustrated*, the *Overland Monthly*, the *Independent, Good Housekeeping*, and the *New England Magazine*. Written from an "insider's" viewpoint, her work went beyond that of previous authors such as Bret Harte in its attempts to create well-rounded, sympathetic portraits of Chinese characters as individuals. In an autobiographical essay, "Leaves from the Mental Portfolio of an Eurasian," Sui Sin Far tells of her pride in her role as champion of the Chinese of North America: "I meet many Chinese persons, and when they get into trouble am often called upon to fight their battles in the papers. This I enjoy. My heart leaps for joy when I read one day an article signed by a New York Chinese in which he declares 'The Chinese in America owe an everlasting debt of gratitude to Sui Sin Far for the bold stand she has taken in their defense'" (Sui Sin Far 1995: 223).

As part of her "defense" of the Chinese man, Sui Sin Far wrote a number of stories extolling the virtues of the Chinese husband. Two such short stories, "The Story of One White Woman Who Married a Chinese" and "Her Chinese Husband," were originally serialized in the *Independent*: the former published in March 1910, and the latter in August 1910 as a sequel. The stories were later reprinted in the collection *Mrs. Spring Fragrance* (1912). The two stories together comprise a narrative of a white working-class woman, Minnie, who escapes an oppressive marriage to a white man and finds domestic happiness with a Chinese husband. It is possible that journalistic reports, such as Wong Chin Foo's *Cosmopolitan* article, could have inspired Sui Sin Far's subject matter. Whether or not Sui Sin Far read this particular account of women who "openly declared" the superiority of their Chinese husbands, it is apparent that she was not writing in a vacuum, but within the cultural context of her time.

Sui Sin Far opens her first story, "Why did I marry Liu Kanghi, a Chinese?" (Sui Sin Far 1912: 111). The narratives that follow aim at justifying this marriage by demonstrating that the Chinese man is, in fact, the better husband. Sui Sin Far asserts the superiority of the Chinese husband as a means of both questioning gender roles and countering the public climate of anti-Chinese sentiment. In a passage where Minnie compares the qualities of her two husbands, she uses personal experience to refute the low popular opinion of Chinese men. Minnie asserts that although "according to American ideas, [James] had been an educated broadminded man; the other, just an ordinary Chinaman" (Sui Sin Far 1912: 134), to her mind, Liu Kanghi is the better husband. It is these so-called American ideas about masculinity and personal worth that Sui Sin Far challenges by turning around conventional notions of the "good catch." The two stories are structured around a series of dichotomies and power struggles between the four central characters: Minnie, a white working-class woman; her first husband, James, a progressive, self-made man; her second husband, Liu Kanghi, a Chinese merchant; and Miss Moran, a white suffragette. Through the use of multiple dichotomies between the four characters, the story of Minnie and James becomes not a simple war of the sexes, but a complex struggle between different models of femininity and masculinity.

In Minnie's marriage to James she is aware that her husband is her "superior" in many senses. He is fifteen years her senior, well educated, and has a salaried office job. He is also an ambitious social progressive who takes woman suffrage as "one of his particular hobbies" (Sui Sin Far 1912: 112). Minnie, by contrast, is a simple, working girl, who gladly gives up stenography for domesticity and finds it a "pleasure to . . . wait upon James, cook him nice little dinners and suppers" (p. 111). She takes no interest in politics or woman suffrage, but attempts to familiarize herself with these topics because she knows that they interest her husband. In turn, her husband silences her when she talks of her own interests. He intimates that he prefers the New Woman to the domestic "angel in the house."

Finally made to feel inferior for her domesticity, Minnie reenters the work world and manages to earn enough money to pay for all household expenses except the rent. Rather than being a measure of independence, however, Minnie's decision to work at an unpleasant job is simply another gesture to please her husband and one which ironically leads to his falling in love with the suffragette, Miss Moran—for the extra income goes to support the production of a book on social reform which James coauthors with Miss Moran. Although Miss Moran rejects James, Minnie is so devastated by the discovery of his extramarital interest that she leaves him.

Minnie is on the verge of committing suicide when she is saved by a Chinese man, Liu Kanghi, and taken to live with a Chinese family. After Minnie recovers from her nervous breakdown, Liu employs her to do piecework embroidery for his shop, enabling her to "gladly give up [her] quest for office work" (p. 125). She eventually marries Liu and gives birth to a son. Before her remarriage, however, James reappears and attempts to coerce Minnie into returning to him. His desire to have Minnie back seems to be motivated in large part by racial competitiveness, and when Minnie refuses him James declares, "So you have sunk! . . . The oily little Chink has won you!" Minnie retorts, "Yes, honorably and like a man" (p. 130). What does it mean, then, to be "like a man"? Minnie consciously redefines the terms of masculinity when she explains: "For all your six feet of grossness, your small soul cannot measure up to his great one" (p. 130). For Minnie, true masculinity depends more on moral than on physical strength.

Indeed, the power struggle between the two men can be read as a struggle between two types of masculinity—of the body and of the soul—types that are racialized within the context of the narrative. James and Liu Kanghi are drawn in clear contrast to one another, just as Minnie's relationship with James is drawn in opposition to her relationship with Liu. Minnie herself establishes a dichotomy between the two men when she declares that she will compare "the differences between the two men as lovers and husbands" (p. 134).

James, while an intellectual, is essentially a man of the body: he is tall, physically imposing, athletic, sexually passionate, and rather brutish in behavior. Ironically, despite being a "progressive" James uses mockery and coercion to compel Minnie to accept new ideas about women's roles. In the end, James is deemed unmanly by Minnie because he is unwilling to protect and care for her, and fails to treat her with the chivalry that she expects is her due as a woman. Liu's masculinity, in contrast, is essentially a masculinity of the soul. Liu lacks both the physique and the sexual passion of James. He is "unlearned" but kind and gentle, and he treats Minnie "as a woman, with reverence and respect" (p. 130). Where James had dismissed Minnie's "trivial" talk, Liu engages Minnie in discussions about needlework and other "things women love to talk about"—religion, life and death. Where James was an indifferent father, Liu is indulgent, nurturing, and adored by children.

Liu's strength comes from steadiness rather than from the exercise of force, and he protects Minnie like a father. Yet Liu's paternal attitude is not one that demands submissiveness from Minnie. Ironically, it is Liu, the less "progressive" of the two men, who enables Minnie to gain true financial independence while engaged in an occupation that allows her to both stay home with her child and express herself artistically. Liu is "manly" in Minnie's eyes because he is protective and has moral strength; at the same time he is preferable to James because he rejects violence, force, and the need to establish intellectual superiority over women. Liu thus becomes representative of a masculinity that is alternative to machismo, a masculinity characterized by tenderness, gentility, and nurturing.

The Cult of Domesticity and the
Victorian Man-Woman

This masculinity of the soul reflects the ideals of the sentimental tradition within which Sui Sin Far was writing, a tradition that valued rarefied emotion over intellect or physicality. Physical prowess is clearly subjected to an ironic undercutting in the stories, for James actually dies while he is exercising at the gymnasium. We can see the sentimental tradition reflected in this passage on the nature of the Chinese man: "the ordinary Chinaman that I would show to you was the sort of man that children, birds, animals, and some women love" (p. 135). Recalling the imagery of St. Francis of Assisi here, Sui Sin Far presents the Chinese man as a man of sensibility. As an anti-authoritarian, maternal father, Liu embodies a masculinity that conforms to the ideals of the cult of domesticity and its attempts to reform nineteenth-century American patriarchy. As Jackson Lears writes, "As early as the 1830s, Tocqueville had noted the intertwining of the achievement ethos and the domestic ideal among American men. . . . Among the bourgeoisie, a number of fathers were trying to cultivate patience and understanding . . . to rule through the orchestration of love rather than through patriarchal command" (1981: 237). It is precisely these qualities that Liu possesses and James lacks. If the split between James and Liu represents the split between rationality and sensitivity, it also represents the split between Philistinism and gentility.

These values of masculine sensitivity and gentility found expression in the Victorian image of the Christian Gentleman that emerged in the writings of authors such as Alfred Lord Tennyson, Coventry Patmore, and John Ruskin. In "Victorian Masculinity and the Angel in the House," Carol Christ demonstrates that the ideal of the domestic True Woman reflected not only anxieties about female roles, but also male ambivalence toward masculine aggressiveness and sexual incontinence. If the nineteenth-century man was defined by a "capacity for action, aggression, and achievement," it was a capacity that was "both frightening and unattractive" (Christ 1977: 149). In turning away from the strivings and Philistinism of the public realm, these writers sought to incorporate what they saw as the higher moral qualities of feminine purity, asexuality, and passivity into themselves. For these writers, "the ideal of the gentleman . . . also represents a more feminine ideal of male behavior" (Christ 1977: 160).

Tennyson, for example, creates an image of the man-woman that tempers masculine faults with superior feminine qualities. In *In Memoriam* he celebrates:

> Manhood fused with female grace
> In such a sort, the child would twine
> A trustful hand, unasked, in thine,
> And find his comfort in thy face.
> (Tennyson 1908: 427)

Tennyson's idealization of feminine identification may have been influential on Sui Sin Far. Biographer Annette White-Parks notes that Tennyson was read in the Eaton household of Sui Sin Far's childhood. Indeed, Sui Sin Far quotes *In Memoriam* in two of her stories (White-Parks 1995: 168). Sui's familiarity with the poem thus suggests that lines such as "manhood fused with female grace" could have formed an important precedent for her efforts to redefine gender identities. Certainly her concerns in the "Chinese husband" stories are much in line with Tennyson's ideas about the feminization of the gentleman: aggression, achievement, Philistinism, and predatory sexuality are criticized; tenderness, nurturing, gentility, and withdrawal from striving are praised.

Tennyson's attempts to move beyond the bounds of fixed gender roles toward an ideal of androgyny are also elaborated in *The Princess*:

> Yet in the long years liker must they grow;
> The man be more of woman, she of man;
> He gain in sweetness and in moral height,
> Nor lose the wrestling thews that throw the world;
> She mental breadth, nor fail in childward care,
> Nor lose the childlike in the larger mind.
> (Tennyson 1908: 135)

Tennyson's rhetoric seems to be reflected in the manner in which Sui Sin Far articulates her ideas of multiple femininities and masculinities. She, too, plays with the idea of the man who is "like" woman, and the woman who is "like" man.

Liu Kanghi represents the man who is "more of woman." Liu is aligned with the feminine in two senses: first, he has physical qualities that would generally be classed as "effeminate"—soft hands and a voice that is "unusually soft for a man's" (Sui 1912: 121); second, he adopts roles that Minnie had played in her marriage with James. While Minnie had attempted to learn about woman suffrage and baseball in order to please James, Liu takes a keen interest in needlework because Minnie enjoys it. While Minnie had loved to cook dinner for James, Liu is eager to take over the cooking from Minnie when she is tired, and enjoys "showing off his skill as a cook" (p. 133). Miss Moran, on the other hand, represents the New Woman who is "more of man," and her description is explicitly masculinized. She is broad-shouldered, masculine-featured, unmotherly, likes baseball, and is strong enough to knock the heavy James flat on his face when he propositions her. The woman-man, however, is not granted the same favor as is the man-woman in the text. Minnie declares that Miss Moran's lack of maternal sentiment makes her "not only not a great woman but, to my mind, no woman at all" (p. 117). A male neighbor too professes to find more "comfort in a woman who was unlike rather than like" himself (p. 115).

The issue of female gender identification in the text is complicated by class issues. The conflict between Minnie and Miss Moran is not simply that between the Cult of Domesticity and New Womanhood, but also between working-class and bourgeois womanhood. Minnie, for her part, continually stresses her class identity as "an ordinary working woman." As Elizabeth Ammons notes, there is a class critique implicit in Sui Sin Far's treatment of the New Woman. "For a working-class woman bound by economics to work outside the home, yet limited by education to boring jobs, staying home had quite a different look than it might to a middle- or upper-middle-class woman forced to stay home but wishing she could leave" (Ammons 1991: 94). Sui Sin Far thus demonstrates a perspicacity about the ways in which social realities such as class (and, as we will see below, race) intercut abstract notions about gender roles.

What Sui Sin Far has done with these characters, then, is to unlink stereotypical gender characteristics from biological sex; that is, gentleness, nurturing, and softness are no longer necessarily womanly traits, and by the same token, aggressiveness, individualism, and physical strength are no longer necessarily manly traits. Minnie's preference for a man who demonstrates affinities with the woman's world may be interpreted as a mark of what critics such as Amy Ling have identified as a possible lesbian subtext in Sui Sin Far's writings (Ling 1990: 48). I read this preference rather as part of the general Victorian idealization of the feminine embodied in the image of the Christian Gentleman.

Racialist ideas about the inherent femininity of Chinese men current during the nineteenth century naturalized Sui Sin Far's choice of a Chinese man for the embodiment of the idealized domestic man. As Dr. Charles Pickering wrote in *The Races of Man; and Their Geographical Distribution:* "One of these peculiarities [of the Mongolian race] consists in the occurrence of a feminine aspect in both sexes. In the absence of any striking difference in stature or dress, I have often seen the stranger at a loss to distinguish men from women" (Pickering 1854: 6).

Orientalist ideas about the gentility of the Chinese race also confirmed this choice. In a passage from "Leaves," Sui Sin Far indicates that she herself subscribed to such notions. She writes:

> I also meet other Chinese men who compare favorably with the white men of my acquaintance in *mind and heart qualities.* Some of them are quite handsome. They have not as *finely cut* noses and as *well-developed chins* as the white men, but they have *smoother* skins and their expression is more *serene;* their *hands are better shaped* and their *voices softer.* (Sui Sin Far 1995: 223, emphasis added)

Here we see the implicit division between a white masculinity of the body and a Chinese masculinity of the soul. The distinction between white men and Chinese men is also gender coded: well-developed chins compared to shapely hands and soft voices. This gender coding serves to effeminize the Chinese man.

Sui Sin Far furthermore demonstrates in the "Chinese husband" stories that the gender role reversals between Minnie and Liu are predicated on the uneven power structure of race relations. While James asserts his proprietorship over Minnie— "once your husband, always your husband" (Sui Sin Far 1912: 130)—Minnie speaks of Liu Kanghi as *her* possession. For example, she explains her determination never to return to China with her husband by declaring that "I look upon you as belonging to me" (p. 140). That the racial hierarchy serves to counteract the expected hierarchy between man and wife is demonstrated explicitly in another passage on the subject of marital proprietorship. "There was also on Liu Kanghi's side an acute consciousness that, though belonging to him as his wife, yet in a sense I was not his, but of the dominant race, which claimed, even while it professed to despise me" (p. 139).

Here we see that the racial hierarchy comes into conflict with the gender hierarchy, making Minnie less than truly Liu's wife; for a Chinese can never have as strong a claim on a white woman as that which the white race exerts upon her. Minnie attempts to compensate for this racial inequity by verbally reaffirming Liu's superior position as a male. She says to him, "Do not talk to me like that. You *are* my superior . . . I would not love you if you were not" (p. 139). Minnie presents the superiority of the male as a requisite for a Victorian heterosexual romantic relationship; she would not love him if he were not superior to her. Thus, by virtue of their marital relationship, the established racial hierarchy between the white woman and the Chinese man should rightly be reversed. Minnie admits, however, that the racial barrier continues to exist between them, and she notes that Liu is pained by "the assumption of the white man that a white woman does not love her Chinese husband" (p. 139). Minnie herself unwittingly reinforces the imbalance of racial superiority by constantly referring to Liu's "boyishness." Minnie's improved status in her second marriage is thus due in part to the privileges of race that enable her to assert a certain measure of superiority as a counterbalance to the gender hierarchy she has internalized as "natural."

Although the creation of Liu Kanghi as an idealized man-woman can be read as an attempt to assimilate masculinity to the ideals of the cult of domesticity—the message being that men would be much improved if only they were more like women—Sui Sin Far ironically reinforces the Chinese man's societal effeminization by making him the representative of this antimachismo masculinity. While characteristics such as softness of voice or hands may make the Chinese man more appealing to Minnie, these are also characteristics generally associated with effeminacy in American society. While Sui Sin Far may challenge American ideals of manliness, she reaffirms the stereotype of the effeminate Chinese houseboy who loves to cook and babysit. We are left to question: is it the kindness of Liu Kanghi or the racial superiority of whiteness that allows Minnie to escape subordination in her second marriage? The effeminization of the Chinese man threatens to slide dangerously into emasculation (the absolute loss of manly power).

Indeed, Liu's emasculation is figured at the end of the second story, where he is carried home at night, shot in the head, with two red balls in his pocket—a clear allusion to lynching. Minnie concludes her narrative by stating: "I can only remember that when they brought my Chinese husband home there were two red balls in his pocket. Such was Liu Kanghi—a man" (p. 143). The em-dash setting off the final two words of the story, "a man," calls our attention again to the question of "what makes a man?" While providing us, on the one hand, with visual proof of the Chinese man's masculinity, Sui Sin Far seems to suggest also that it is Liu's moral strength that makes him a man despite the fact that he has been socially and physically emasculated. By ending with a tragic lynching, however, Sui Sin Far sends an ultimately pessimistic message about both miscegenation and the possibility of creating an alternative masculinity in turn-of-the-century American society.

Thomas Burke's "The Chink and the Child" Purity and Squalor

> "*What makes you so good to me, Chinky?*"
>
> D. W. Griffith, *Broken Blossoms* (1919)

Thomas Burke (1887–1945), an approximate contemporary of Sui Sin Far, was another writer who chose to cast the Chinese man as an exemplar of an antimachismo masculinity. His short story "The Chink and the Child" bears a thematic similarity to Sui Sin Far's "Chinese husband" stories, but also reveals a rather different approach to the material. Where Sui Sin Far emphasizes familiarity, Burke seeks exoticism; where Sui Sin Far focuses on the domestic, Burke's subject is urban life; while Sui Sin Far is a sentimentalist, Burke is a Bohemian romantic. Burke, furthermore, was no champion of the Chinese.

Burke was a native of London whose Orientalist works gained popularity in America in the 1910s along with those of Sax Rohmer. Originally a journalist, and a "slummer" by avocation, Burke wrote both travel sketches and short fiction about various districts of London. The collection in which "The Chink and the Child" appears, *Limehouse Nights* (1916), is a set of lurid tales of the working-class district of London's East End and its Chinatown. Although *Limehouse Nights* is set in London, the collection became immensely popular in the United States, where it was reprinted numerous times. D. W. Griffith's 1919 film adaptation of "The Chink and the Child," *Broken Blossoms,* established the story even more fully as a part of American popular culture.

"The Chink and the Child" is both a romantic story of the power of love to elevate a slum child above the squalor of her life and a lurid and sensationalist story of perversion, pedophilia, sadism, miscegenation, incest, and domestic abuse. The story tells the tale of a sensitive Chinese man, Cheng Huan, who rescues a poor white girl, Lucy, from her brutally abusive father, "Battling Burrows." Burke, like Sui Sin Far, constructs the Chinese man as the negation of the white man, explicitly contrasting Cheng Huan's physique and personality with that of Battling Burrows. Numerous aspects of the Orientalist stereotype of Chinese men inform Cheng Huan's character: he is soft, tender, nurturing, a pacifist, an aesthete, and a "poet-prince." Battling Burrows, on the other hand, is brutal, lustful, violent, and ignorant, a professional boxer and a drunk. Although there are pedophilic overtones to Cheng Huan's relationship with the child Lucy, his love is described as essentially "pure." He gives her a home with safety, material comforts, and affection—all of which Lucy had been denied by her father. Cheng Huan offers Lucy a refuge, where she is able to sleep "weary and trustful . . . knowing that the yellow man was kind and that she might sleep with no fear of a steel hand smashing the delicate structure of her dreams" (Burke 1919: 28). Lucy responds to Cheng Huan's affections, for "he was the first thing that had ever spoken soft words to her; the first thing that had ever laid a hand on her that was not brutal; the first thing that had deferred in manner towards her as though she, too, had a right to live" (p. 24). Therein lies the appeal of the Chinese man for the white girl: his "feminine" qualities of softness and kindness allow her an escape from a dominating and brutalizing father figure.

Tragedy ensues, however, when Lucy's father, outraged at the supposed seduction of his daughter, raids Cheng Huan's rooms and ends up beating his daughter to death. Cheng Huan avenges her death and then commits suicide. Battling's rage takes the form of racial animosity: "the yeller man would go through it. Yeller! It was his supreme condemnation, his final epithet for all conduct of which he disapproved" (p. 30). In this ironic moment, Burke uses a "pot-calling-the-kettle-black" strategy, a technique used also by Bret Harte and Sui Sin Far for pointing out white hypocrisy: for Battling—the drunkard, slacker, lecher, sadist, and perpetrator of incest—is clearly no model himself of moral conduct. Burke uses irony at several other points during the story to distance the reader from Battling's bigotry. It is chiefly through this use of irony and the depiction of the brutish white man as a foil for the Chinese man that the story conveys its plea for racial tolerance.

Yet, Burke declared that he possessed no reformist intent in writing his fiction. Instead, he chose to write about what he called the "dark side" of life, the slums and the opium dens, because he believed it possessed a romantic vitality beyond the stifling grip of bourgeois propriety. Burke's fascination with slumdwellers and Oriental exotica reveal his penchant for a type of naturalism that was embraced by Bohemian writers such as Frank Norris in the United States. Burke's story says less about the working-class or "Orientals" themselves than about Burke's own disaffection from Western bourgeois culture.

"POSITIVE" ORIENTALISM AND AN ANTIMODERNIST TURN TO THE FEMININE

In his discussion of antimodernism in American culture from 1880 to 1920, Jackson Lears demonstrates that the disillusionment with industrial modernization and Victorian bourgeois culture led certain intellectuals to embrace a type of romanticized Orientalism or Medievalism. The trend was quite widespread, according to Lears: "In America (as in Europe), antimodern sentiments affected more than a handful of intellectuals; they pervaded the middle and upper classes" (Lears 1981: xiii). Disenchanted with the ills of an "overcivilized" West and its emphasis on production and achievement, antimodernists romanticized the Orient as the antithesis of the spiritually stunted West. Some sought in the Orient a childlike primitivism, others "the Buddhistic quietude of Nirvana," others a refined aestheticism. Orientalism was a driving force behind the transcendentalism of Emerson, which turned a generation of Americans toward a romantic pastoralism. Numerous turn-of-the-century Bohemians were attracted to Orientalism for a variety of reasons. Lears discusses Orientalism as part of a general critique of the ills of modern Western society:

> Popular Orientalism was unsystematic and diverse; its adherents were often ignorant of the traditions they claimed to embrace. Like the current wave of interest in Oriental mysticism, late-nineteenth-century Orientalism could easily be dismissed as a trivial exercise in exoticism. But it would be a mistake to do so. Then as now, the popularity

of Eastern religion signified more than a fad. . . . Orientalism, like the mind-cure
movement, the fascination with the European folk mind, and the turn toward medieval
mysticism, was a response to the spiritual turmoil of the late nineteenth century.
(Lears 1981: 175)

Out of this disenchantment with modernity grew a critique of liberal individualism, an embracing of "oceanic dependence" with the universe, and a desire for
quietist withdrawal. These related ideals of quietism, inaction, and pacifism were
embodied in Burke's Cheng Huan. As noted before, for the Victorians these were
feminized ideals. Indeed, Lears demonstrates how this antimodern impulse was
gendered.

In the triumphant bourgeois culture of the nineteenth century, to be engaged in
practical affairs was to be in the world of men, where conscious control and autonomous achievement were most highly prized. To withdraw from that realm was to enter
the feminine sphere, which had is own restrictive ideals but which tended to sanction
passive leisure and emotional dependence. (p. 218)

Within the context of the nineteenth century and the capitalist emphasis on
what Weber termed the "Protestant work ethic," the "feminine" mode of Oriental
spiritualism or Catholic Marionism "promised liberation from the systematic morality of the male bourgeoisie" (p. 218). Catholicism in particular embodied the
"feminine" values of the cult of domesticity (p. 242). On many levels, then, there
are suggestive linkages between the rejection of bourgeois patriarchy and antimodernist impulses.

This rejection of patriarchy is played out in various ways in the stories discussed
above. In Sui Sin Far's "Chinese husband" stories we see an oppressive husband,
in "The Chink and the Child" an abusive father. Through the figures of these
fathers and husbands, men such as Battling Burrows and James Carson, white
patriarchy is associated with repression, violence, force, and control. The brutality
of white society leads our heroines to turn to the society of the Chinese. (We
should bear in mind that there was another current stereotype of Chinese men as
extreme patriarchal types. Mae Franking constantly comments on this stereotype
and its inaccuracy in "My Chinese Marriage.") Shunned as a divorcée, Minnie
declares, "I would much rather live with Chinese than Americans" (Sui Sin Far
1912: 122), and "the happiness of the man who loves me is more to me than the
approval or disapproval of those who in my dark days left me to die like a dog"
(p. 131). In "The Chink and the Child," Lucy's receptiveness to Cheng Huan's
tender caresses is a reaction to the abuse she received from her father. Cheng
Huan functions as a type of surrogate father figure for the girl, though his parental
role is described as maternal: "each night he would tend to her, as might mother
to child" (Burke 1919: 29). A dichotomy is established between a hostile society
and the refuge provided by Chinese men with their kindness and sensitivity. Miscegenation could thus be justified not simply as a response to economic necessity,
but as a reaction against the brutality of white society. This provided an important

counterargument to the claim that cheap Chinese labor was stealing American jobs and American wives.

THE KIND CHINAMAN AND THE CRITIQUE OF WHITE PATRIARCHY

"Only 'a dirty Chinaman,' they say, but how few of them have such a heart."
WILLIAM NORR, "THE PEARL OF CHINATOWN" (1892)

Indeed, William Norr adopts this idea of miscegenation as a symptom of the degeneration of white civilization as the premise of his *Stories of Chinatown*. In the preface to his collection he writes:

> The world in general wonders—when it gives the subject a thought—how young and comely white women can cast their lot with the repulsive Chinese. I confess this has also been a puzzle to me. "He's good to me," was the reply of one girl I sounded on the question . . . it speaks ill for a civilized world when a little kindness will drive our women into the arms of heathen. (Norr 1892: 4)

Despite his general condemnation of the immorality of the Chinese quarter, Norr is moved to admit that there are certain Chinese men who are "pretty good fellows." Often, they compare favorably to the white working-class men of New York City. The majority of the stories in Norr's collection depict young white women who escape patriarchal and domestic constraints through common-law marriages with Chinese men, men who are "good to them" and give them the freedom to "do as they like." The final message of Norr's stories is that it is the evils of white society that drive white women to seek refuge with Chinese men. In a story titled "The Pearl of Chinatown," Norr shows Pearl, a white woman, making this declaration on her deathbed:

> "Poor Lee," she again softly murmured, as she kissed him. "You're only a Chinaman, a poor and despised heathen, whom the civilized world shuns. If the Christians, who think you scum beneath their feet, had only treated me one-half as well as you, one-quarter as unselfish, what a different life I would have had. Only 'a dirty Chinaman,' they say, but how few of them have such a heart." (Norr 1892: 83)

This idea that the Chinaman has more heart than the typical white "Christian" serves in Norr's stories to justify the white women's crossing of racial boundaries.
In "A Chinatown Tragedy," Norr more explicitly lays the blame on white patriarchy for driving women away. Abused by their alcoholic, wife-beating father, who squanders their meager wages on drink, the two Cavanagh girls find independence, financial stability, and freedom from abuse living with Chinese men. When Mamie is told by her father, "Go back to your dirty Chineymen an' stay there," she retorts, "So I will . . . for they treat me better than my own folks. . . . Good-by, dear mammy. If I'd got one kind word here tonight, I'd have stayed and worked so hard for you"

(p. 59). The blame for the disreputable state of the women is placed squarely on the white man and his abuse of patriarchal authority. Norr ends his story: "those who know the history of the two handsomest girls in the Chinese colony vaguely wonder whether Tim Cavanagh will contribute any more to the immoral colonization of Chinatown" (pp. 71–72). The disintegration of the moral fiber of the traditional family leaves society open to the sexual encroachment of the yellow peril, colonizing not only American territory but also American [white] women.

If miscegeneration is read as a symptom of the degeneration of Western civilization, it is the excesses of patriarchal masculinity that are to blame. The message of these stories works like this: the Chinese man is kind where her father/husband is cruel. Isn't it these white fathers, then, that are truly deserving of condemnation? Norr implies that reform of masculine power is needed if there are not to be more such "fallen women." An article in *The Overland Monthly,* "The 'Bad Woman's Vote,'" also blamed abusive family situations as the circumstances behind "fallen" white women in Chinatown (Sheldon 1913: 165–169).

The critique of white patriarchy—bourgeois patriarchy in the case of Sui Sin Far, and working-class patriarchy in the cases of Norr and Burke—is tied to the ideals of the cult of domesticity and the antimodernism of the turn of the century, both of which called for a "kinder, gentler" society. The reaction against male aggression and Western "overcivilization" took the forms of a turn toward "feminine" domesticity and the Oriental Other. The "feminine" is elevated, in particular, by Sui Sin Far and Thomas Burke. Sui Sin Far and Burke use white heroines in their narratives, symbolizing purity, virtue, charity, and tolerance, to suggest that racism is primarily a male phenomenon. In their writings it is the white women who represent racial tolerance and who recognize goodness and evil in people without regard to race. The white male characters, on the other hand, represent racial intolerance, violence, and blind bigotry.

The figure of the kind and tender Chinese man plays a central role in the narrative strategies of these turn-of-the-century authors, functioning as a critique of both racism and the Western patriarchal family's suppression of women. The Chinese man is allied with the white woman in these narratives: not only do they share "feminine" sensibilities and characteristics, they are also both victims of the domination of white men. The already effeminized "Oriental" man (given to tenderness, aestheticism, passivity, quietude, and poetic sensitivity) provides a ready model for the creation of an alternative masculinity: the man of sensibility as opposed to the man of machismo. In Sui Sin Far's writing, this alternative masculinity is embodied in the anti-authoritarian father, the domestic gentleman; in Burke's writing it is embodied in the romantic aesthete. Given the intellectual currents outlined above, currents that associated the "feminine" with a rejection of goal-driven, production-oriented, spiritually frigid, capitalist modernity, this type of celebration of the "feminine" qualities of Chinese manhood can be read in a "positive" fashion, rather than as a simple denigration of Chinese masculinity. It is a move that has less to do with the actual nature of Chinese men than with the domestic concerns of the times (as is typical of Orientalism).

The role played by the character of the Chinese male points to a contradiction within the works of Sui Sin Far and Thomas Burke, which, while critiquing racism on one level, have racism built into their very logic. That is, the stories depend upon the reader's assumption of the superiority of the white woman as a key narrative device. White women function as figures of purity, virtue, and spiritual salvation: it is adoration of the white woman that serves to elevate the Chinese man. At the same time, this devoted worship of the white female character also indicates the Chinese man's subordination. In "The Chink and the Child" the adoration is clearly one-way. In Norr's stories, the Chinese men are characterized by their permissiveness toward their white women. It is clear that the Chinese men do not have the same proprietary rights over the white woman's body that the white patriarch has. Sui Sin Far herself makes reference to this contradiction of racism in "My Chinese Husband," when Minnie speaks of whiteness as a mark of superiority over her husband. This racism is portrayed by Sui Sin Far as an external matter, a fact of life in a racist society. Nonetheless, racism is internal to the narrative structure, as it is with our other stories, as both the desirability of the white woman and the Chinese man's willingness to sacrifice himself for her are taken for granted.

Sui Sin Far and Thomas Burke furthermore capitulate to a racist logic in concluding their stories with the deaths of the Chinese male characters. "The Chink and the Child" is perhaps the most tragic, as the attempted lynching of Cheng Huan is thwarted only to result in his suicide. The tragic conclusions of the stories send a double message. They cry out against the injustice of racial intolerance and yet show miscegenation as an act that is punished. The Chinese male is thus finally doubly effeminized: he is effeminized vis-à-vis the white man (and by extension the dominant society), against whom he is powerless to defend himself, and he is disempowered vis-à-vis the white woman, for whom the privilege of race overcomes gender subordination. The death of the Chinese protagonist ultimately reestablishes the racial hierarchy that has been seemingly breached by the taboo act of miscegenation.

EPILOGUE

The stories of Sui Sin Far and Thomas Burke, in their fictional imaginings of the possibilities of miscegenation and of an antimachismo masculinity, provide an interesting contrast against which to read contemporary cultural politics. An understanding of the historical context of these writings should caution us against dismissing *all* images of the effeminized Asian man as "politically incorrect" and derogatory. The stories demonstrate that within a *limited* and *historically particular* framework, the Chinese man can be simultaneously idealized and feminized. This can only be realized if we take a historical view of what the "feminine" signified in various periods. This turn-of-the-century literature should also give us occasion to reflect upon contemporary gendered values. Indeed, what are we saying about femininity and women when we constantly equate "feminization" with degradation and powerlessness?

REFERENCES

Ammons, E. (1991). "The New Woman as Symbol and Reality" [1915], in *The Cultural Moment*, ed. A. Heller and L. Rudnick New Brunswick, N.J.: Rutgers University Press.

Burke, T. (1918). "A Chinese Night: Limehouse," in *Nights in London*. New York: Henry Holt and Co.

―――― (1919). "The Chink and the Child," in *Limehouse Nights*. New York: Robert M. McBride.

Christ, C. (1977). "Victorian Masculinity and the Angel in the House," in *A Widening Sphere: Changing Roles of Victorian Women*, ed. Mardia Vincinus. Bloomington: Indiana University Press.

Fenn, W. P. (1933). *Ah Sin and his Brethren in American Literature*. Peking: College of Chinese Studies.

Harte, B. (1903). "Wan Lee the Pagan," in *Bret Harte's Writings: Tales of the Argonatas and Other Sketches*. Cambridge: Houghton Mifflin.

Lears, T.J.J. (1981). *No Place of Grace: Antimodernism and the Transformation of American Culture, 1880–1920*. Chicago: University of Chicago Press.

Ling, A. (1990). *Between Two Worlds: Women Writers of Chinese Ancestry*. New York: Pergamon Press.

Norr, W. (1892). *Stories of Chinatown: Sketches from Life in the Chinese Colony of Mott, Pell and Doyers Streets*. New York: William Norr.

Overton, G. (1922). *When Winter Comes to Main Street*. New York: George H. Doran Co.

Pickering, C. (1854). *The Races of Man: and Their Geographical Distribution*. London: H. G. Bohn.

Porter, K. A. (1991). *Mae Franking's My Chinese Marriage: An Annotated Edition*. Austin: University of Texas Press.

Sheldon, L. (1913). "The 'Bad Woman's Vote,'" *The Overland Monthly* second series, 61: 165–169.

Sui, Sin Far (1912). "The Story of One White Woman Who Married a Chinese" and "Her Chinese Husband," in *Mrs. Spring Fragrance*. Chicago: A. C. McClurg.

―――― (1995). "Leaves from the Mental Portfolio of an Eurasian," in *Mrs. Spring Fragrance and Other Writings*, ed. A. Ling and A. White-Parks. Chicago: University of Illinois Press.

Takaki, R. (1979). *Iron Cages: Race and Culture in Nineteenth-Century America*. Seattle: University of Washington Press.

Tchen, J.K.W. (1994). "Quimbo Appo's Fear of Fenians: Chinese-Irish-Anglo Relations in New York City," in *The New York Irish, 1625–1990*, ed. R. Bayor and T. Meagher. Baltimore: Johns Hopkins University Press.

Tennyson, A. L. (1908). *The Works of Alfred Lord Tennyson*. Vol. 2. New York: Macmillan Company.

White-Parks, Annette (1995). *Sui Sin Far/Edith Maude Eaton: A Literary Biography*. Chicago: University of Illinois Press.

Wong, C. F. (1888). "The Chinese in New York." *The Cosmopolitan*.

THE STORY OF ONE WHITE WOMAN
WHO MARRIED A CHINESE

Sui Sin Far

I

Why did I marry Liu Kanghi, a Chinese? Well, in the first place, because I loved him; in the second place, because I was weary of working, struggling and fighting with the world; in the third place, because my child needed a home.

My first husband was an American fifteen years older than myself. For a few months I was very happy with him. I had been a working girl—a stenographer. A home of my own filled my heart with joy. It was a pleasure to me to wait upon James, cook him nice little dinners and suppers, read to him little pieces from the papers and magazines, and sing and play to him my little songs and melodies. And for a few months he seemed to be perfectly contented. I suppose I was a novelty to him, he having lived a bachelor existence until he was thirty-four. But it was not long before he left off smiling at my little jokes, grew restive and cross when I teased him, and when I tried to get him to listen to a story in which I was interested and longed to communicate, he would bid me not bother him. I was quick to see the change and realize that there was a gulf of differences between us. Nevertheless, I loved and was proud of him. He was considered a very bright and well-informed man, and although his parents had been uneducated working people he had himself been through the public schools. He was also an omnivorous reader of socialistic and new-thought literature. Woman suffrage was one of his particular hobbies. Whenever I had a magazine around he would pick it up and read aloud to me the columns of advice to women who were ambitious to become comrades to men and walk shoulder to shoulder with their brothers. Once I ventured to remark that much as I admired a column of men keeping step together, yet men and women thus ranked would, to my mind, make a very unbeautiful and disorderly spectacle. He frowned and answered that I did not understand him, and was too frivolous. He would often draw my attention to newspaper reports concerning women of marked business ability and enterprise. Once I told him that I did not admire clever business women, as I had usually found them, and so had other girls of my acquaintance, not nearly so kind-hearted, generous, and helpful as the humble drudges of the world—the ordinary working women. His answer to this was that I was jealous and childish.

But, in spite of his unkind remarks and evident contempt for me, I wished to please him. He was my husband and I loved him. Many an afternoon, when through with my domestic duties, did I spend in trying to acquire a knowledge of labor politics, socialism, woman suffrage, and baseball, the things in which he was most interested.

It was hard work, but I persevered until one day. It was about six months after our marriage. My husband came home a little earlier than usual, and found me engaged in trying to work out problems in subtraction and addition. He laughed sneeringly. "Give it up, Minnie," said he. "You weren't built for anything but taking care of kids. Gee! But there's a woman at our place who has a head for figures that makes her worth over a hundred dollars a month. *Her* husband would have a chance to develop himself."

This speech wounded me. I knew it was James' ambition to write a book on social reform.

The next day, unknown to my husband, I called upon the wife of the man who had employed me as stenographer before I was married, and inquired of her whether she thought I could get back my old position.

"But, my dear," she exclaimed, "your husband is receiving a good salary! Why should you work?"

I told her that my husband had in mind the writing of a book on social reform, and I wished to help him in his ambition by earning some money towards its publication.

"Social reform!" she echoed. "What sort of social reformer is he who would allow his wife to work when he is well able to support her!"

She bade me go home and think no more of an office position. I was disappointed. I said: "Oh! I wish I could earn some money for James. If I were earning money, perhaps he would not think me so stupid."

"Stupid, my dear girl! You are one of the brightest little women I know," kindly comforted Mrs. Rogers.

But I knew differently and went on to tell her of my inability to figure with my husband how much he had made on certain sales, of my lack of interest in politics, labor questions, woman suffrage, and world reformation. "Oh!" I cried, "I am a narrow-minded woman. All I care for is for my husband to love me and be kind to me, for life to be pleasant and easy, and to be able to help a wee bit the poor and sick around me."

Mrs. Rogers looked very serious as she told me that there were differences of opinion as to what was meant by "narrow-mindedness," and that the majority of men had no wish to drag their wives into all their business perplexities, and found more comfort in a woman who was unlike rather than like themselves. Only that morning her husband had said to her: "I hate a woman who tries to get into every kink of a man's mind, and who must be forever at his elbow meddling with all his affairs."

I went home comforted. Perhaps after a while James would feel and see as did Mr. Rogers. Vain hope!

My child was six weeks old when I entered business life again as stenographer for Rutherford & Rutherford. My salary was fifty dollars a month—more than I had ever earned before, and James was well pleased, for he had feared that it would be difficult for me to obtain a paying place after having been out of practise for so long. This fifty dollars paid for all our living expenses, with the exception of rent, so that James would be able to put by his balance against the time when his book would be ready for publication.

He began writing his book, and Miss Moran the young woman bookkeeper at his place collaborated with him. They gave three evenings a week to the work, sometimes four. She came one evening when the baby was sick and James had gone for the doctor. She looked at the child with the curious eyes of one who neither loved nor understood children. "There is no necessity for its being sick," said she. "There must be an error somewhere." I made no answer, so she went on: "Sin, sorrow, and sickness all mean the same thing. We have no disease that we do not deserve, no trouble which we do not bring upon ourselves."

I did not argue with her. I knew that I could not; but as I looked at her standing there in the prime of her life and strength, broad-shouldered, masculine-featured, and, as it seemed to me, heartless, I disliked her more than I had ever disliked anyone before. My own father had died after suffering for many years from a terrible malady, contracted while doing his duty as a physician and surgeon. And my little innocent child! What had sin to do with its measles?

When James came in she discussed with him the baseball game which had been played that afternoon, and also a woman suffrage meeting which she had attended the evening before.

After she had gone he seemed to be quite exhilarated. "That's a great woman!" he remarked.

"I do not think so!" I answered him. "One who would take from the sorrowful and suffering their hope of a happier existence hereafter, and add to their trials on earth by branding them as objects of aversion and contempt, is not only not a great woman but, to my mind, no woman at all."

He picked up a paper and walked into another room.

"What do you think now?" I cried after him.

"What would be the use of my explaining to you?" he returned. "You wouldn't understand."

How my heart yearned over my child those days! I would sit before the typewriter and in fancy hear her crying for her mother. Poor, sick little one, watched over by a strange woman, deprived of her proper nourishment. While I took dictation from my employer I thought only of her. The result, of course, was, that I lost my place. My husband showed his displeasure at this in various ways, and as the weeks went by and I was unsuccessful in obtaining another position, he became colder and more indifferent. He was neither a drinking nor an abusive man; but he could say such cruel and cutting things that I would a hundred times rather have been beaten and ill-used than compelled, as I was, to hear them. He even made me feel it a disgrace to be a woman and a mother. Once he said to me: "If you had had ambition of the right sort you would have perfected yourself in your stenography so that you could have taken cases in court. There's a little fortune in that business."

I was acquainted with a woman stenographer who reported divorce cases and who had described to me the work, so I answered: "I would rather die of hunger, my baby in my arms, then report divorce proceedings under the eyes of men in a court house."

"Other women, as good as you, have done and are doing it," he retorted.

"Other women, perhaps better than I, have done and are doing it," I replied, "but all women are not alike. I am not that kind."

"That's so," said he. "Well, they are the kind who are up to date. You are behind the times."

One evening I left James and Miss Moran engaged with their work and went across the street to see a sick friend. When I returned I let myself into the house very softly for fear of waking the baby whom I had left sleeping. As I stood in the hall I heard my husband's voice in the sitting-room. This is what he was saying:

"I am a lonely man. There is no companionship between me and my wife."

"Nonsense!" answered Miss Moran, as I thought a little impatiently. "Look over this paragraph, please, and tell me if you do not think it would be well to have it follow after the one ending with the words 'ultimate concord,' in place of that beginning with 'These great principles.'"

"I cannot settle my mind upon the work tonight," said James in a sort of thick, tired voice. "I want to talk to you—to win your sympathy—your love."

I heard a chair pushed back. I knew Miss Moran had arisen.

"Good night!" I heard her say. "Much as I would like to see this work accomplished, I shall come no more!"

"But, my God! You cannot throw the thing up at this late date."

"I can and I will. Let me pass, sir."

"If there were no millstone around my neck, you would not say, 'Let me pass, sir,' in that tone of voice."

The next I heard was a heavy fall. Miss Moran had knocked my big husband down.

I pushed open the door. Miss Moran, cool and collected, was pulling on her gloves. James was struggling to his feet.

"Oh, Mrs. Carson!" exclaimed the former. "Your husband fell over the stool. Wasn't it stupid of him!"

* * *

James, of course, got his divorce six months after I deserted him. He did not ask for the child, and I was allowed to keep it.

I I

I was on my way to the waterfront, the baby in my arms. I was walking quickly, for my state of mind was such that I could have borne twice my burden and not have felt it. Just as I turned down a hill which led to the docks, someone touched my arm and I heard a voice say:

"Pardon me, lady; but you have dropped your baby's shoe!"

"Oh, yes!" I answered, taking the shoe mechanically from an outstretched hand, and pushing on.

I could hear the waves lapping against the pier when the voice again fell upon my ear.

"If you go any further, lady, you will fall into the water!"

My answer was a step forward.

A strong hand was laid upon my arm and I was swung around against my will.

"Poor little baby," went on the voice, which was unusually soft for a man's. "Let me hold him!"

I surrendered my child to the voice.

"Better come over where it is light and you can see where to walk!"

I allowed myself to be led into the light.

Thus I met Liu Kanghi, the Chinese who afterwards became my husband. I followed him, obeyed him, trusted him from the very first. It never occurred to me to ask myself what manner of man was succoring me. I only knew that he was a man, and that I was being cared for as no one had ever cared for me since my father died. And my grim determination to leave a world which had been cruel to me, passed away—and in its place I experienced a strange calmness and content.

"I am going to take you to the house of a friend of mine," he said as he preceded me up the hill, the baby in his arms.

"You will not mind living with Chinese people?" he added.

An electric light under which we were passing flashed across his face.

I did not recoil—not even at first. It may have been because he was wearing American clothes, wore his hair cut, and, even to my American eyes, appeared a good-looking young man—and it may have been because of my troubles; but whatever it was I answered him, and I meant it: "I would much rather live with Chinese than Americans."

He did not ask me why, and I did not tell him until long afterwards the story of my unhappy marriage, my desertion of the man who had made it impossible for me to remain under his roof; the shame of the divorce, the averted faces of those who had been my friends; the cruelty of the world; the awful struggle for an existence for myself and child; sickness followed by despair.

The Chinese family with which he placed me were kind, simple folk. The father had been living in America for more than twenty years. The family consisted of his wife, a grown daughter, and several small sons and daughters, all of whom had been born in America. They made me very welcome and adored the baby. Liu Jusong, the father, was a working jeweler; but, because of an accident by which he had lost the use of one hand, was partially incapacitated for work. Therefore, their family depended for maintenance chiefly upon their kinsman, Liu Kanghi, the Chinese who had brought me to them.

"We love much our cousin," said one of the little girls to me one day. "He teaches us so many games and brings us toys and sweets."

As soon as I recovered from the attack of nervous prostration which laid me low for over a month after being received into the Liu home, my mind began to form plans for my own and my child's maintenance. One morning I put on my hat and jacket and told Mrs. Liu I would go downtown and make an application for work as a stenographer at the different typewriting offices. She pleaded with me to wait a week longer—until, as she said, "your limbs are more fortified with strength"; but I assured her that I felt myself well able to begin to do for my-self, and that I was anxious to repay some little part of the expense I had been to them.

"For all we have done for you," she answered, "our cousin has paid us doublefold."

"No money can recompense your kindness to myself and child," I replied; "but if it is your cousin to whom I am indebted for board and lodging, all the greater is my anxiety to repay what I owe."

When I returned to the house that evening, tired out with my quest for work, I found Liu Kanghi tossing ball with little Fong in the front porch.

Mrs. Liu bustled out to meet me and began scolding in motherly fashion.

"Oh, why you go downtown before you strong enough? See! You look all sick again!" said she.

She turned to Liu Kanghi and said something in Chinese. He threw the ball back to the boy and came toward me, his face grave and concerned.

"Please be so good as to take my cousin's advice," he urged.

"I am well enough to work now," I replied, "and I cannot sink deeper into your debt."

"You need not," said he. "I know a way by which you can quickly pay me off and earn a good living without wearing yourself out and leaving the baby all day. My cousin tells me that you can create most beautiful flowers on silk, velvet, and linen. Why not then you do some of that work for my store? I will buy all you can make."

"Oh!" I exclaimed, "I should be only too glad to do such work! But do you really think I can earn a living in that way?"

"You certainly can," was his reply. "I am requiring an embroiderer, and if you will do the work for me I will try to pay you what it is worth."

So I gladly gave up my quest for office work. I lived in the Liu Jusong house and worked for Liu Kanghi. The days, weeks, and months passed peacefully and happily. Artistic needlework had always been my favorite occupation, and when it became a source both of remuneration and pleasure, I began to feel that life was worth living, after all. I watched with complacency my child grow amongst the little Chinese children. My life's experience had taught me that the virtues do not all belong to the whites. I was interested in all that concerned the Liu household, became acquainted with all their friends, and lost altogether the prejudice against the foreigner in which I had been reared.

I had been living thus more than a year when, one afternoon as I was walking home from Liu Kanghi's store on Kearney Street, a parcel of silks and floss under my arm, and my little girl trudging by my side, I came face to face with James Carson.

"Well, now," said he, planting himself in front of me, "You are looking pretty well. How are you making out?"

I caught up my child and pushed past him without a word. When I reached the Liu house I was trembling in every limb, so great was my dislike and fear of the man who had been my husband.

About a week later a letter came to the house addressed to me. It read:

204 BUCHANAN STREET

DEAR MINNIE,—If you are willing to forget the past and make up, I am, too. I was surprised to see you the other day, prettier than ever and much more of a woman. Let me know your mind at an early date.

Your affectionate husband,

JAMES

I ignored this letter, but a heavy fear oppressed me. Liu Kanghi, who called the evening of the day I received it, remarked as he arose to greet me that I was looking troubled, and hoped that it was not the embroidery flowers.

"It is the shadow from my big hat," I answered lightly. I was dressed for going downtown with Mrs. Liu who was preparing her eldest daughter's trousseau.

"Some day," said Liu Kanghi earnestly, "I hope that you will tell to me all that is in your heart and mind."

I found comfort in his kind face.

"If you will wait until I return, I will tell you all tonight," I answered.

Strange as it may seem, although I had known Liu Kanghi now for more than a year, I had had little talk alone with him, and all he knew about me was what he had learned from Mrs. Liu; namely, that I was a divorced woman who, when saved from self-destruction, was homeless and starving.

That night, however, after hearing my story, he asked me to be his wife. He said: "I love you and would protect you from all trouble. Your child shall be as my own."

I replied: "I appreciate your love and kindness, but I cannot answer you just yet. Be my friend for a little while longer."

"Do you have for me the love feeling?" he asked.

"I do not know," I answered truthfully.

Another letter came. It was written in a different spirit from the first and contained a threat about the child.

There seemed but one course open to me. That was to leave my Chinese friends. I did. With much sorrow and regret I bade them goodbye, and took lodgings in a part of the city far removed from the outskirts of Chinatown where my home had been with the Lius. My little girl pined for her Chinese playmates, and I myself felt strange and lonely; but I knew that if I wished to keep my child I could no longer remain with my friends.

I still continued working for Liu Kanghi, and carried my embroidery to his store in the evening after the little one had been put to sleep. He usually escorted me back; but never asked to be allowed, and I never invited him, to visit me, or even enter the house. I was a young woman, and alone, and what I had suffered from scandal since I had left James Carson had made me wise.

It was a cold, wet evening in November when he accosted me once again. I had run over to a delicatessen store at the corner of the block where I lived. As I stepped out, his burly figure loomed up in the gloom before me. I started back with a little cry, but he grasped my arm and held it.

"Walk beside me quietly if you do not wish to attract attention," said he, "and by God, if you do, I will take the kid tonight!"

"You dare not!" I answered. "You have no right to her whatever. She is my child and I have supported her for the last two years alone."

"Alone! What will the judges say when I tell them about the Chinaman?"

"What will the judges say!" I echoed. "What can they say? Is there any disgrace in working for a Chinese merchant and receiving pay for my labor?"

"And walking in the evening with him, and living for over a year in a house for which he paid the rent. Ha! ha! ha! Ha! ha! ha!"

His laugh was low and sneering. He had evidently been making enquiries concerning the Liu family, and also watching me for some time. How a woman can loathe and hate the man she has once loved!

We were nearing my lodgings. Perhaps the child had awakened and was crying for me. I would not, however, have entered the house, had he not stopped at the door and pushed it open.

"Lead the way upstairs!" said he. "I want to see the kid."

"You shall not," I cried. In my desperation I wrenched myself from his grasp and faced him, blocking the stairs.

"If you use violence," I declared, "the lodgers will come to my assistance. They know me!"

He released my arm.

"Bah!" said he. "I've no use for the kid. It is you I'm after getting reconciled to. Don't you know, Minnie, that once your husband, always your husband? Since I saw you the other day on the street, I have been more in love with you than ever before. Suppose we forget all and begin over again!"

Though the tone of his voice had softened, my fear of him grew greater. I would have fled up the stairs had he not again laid his hand on my arm.

"Answer me, girl," said he.

And in spite of my fear, I shook off his hand and answered him: "No husband of mine are you, either legally or morally. And I have no feeling whatever for you other than contempt."

"Ah! So you have sunk!"—his expression was evil—"The oily little Chink has won you!"

I was no longer afraid of him.

"Won me!" I cried, unheeding who heard me. "Yes, honorably and like a man. And what are you that dare sneer at one like him. For all your six feet of grossness, your small soul cannot measure up to his great one. You were unwilling to protect and care for the woman who was your wife or the little child you caused to come into this world; but he succored and saved the stranger woman, treated her as a woman, with reverence and respect; gave her child a home, and made them both independent, not only of others but of himself. Now, hearing you insult him behind his back, I know, what I did not know before—that I love him, and all I have to say to you is, Go!"

And James Carson went. I heard of him again but once. That was when the papers reported his death of apoplexy while exercising at a public gymnasium.

Loving Liu Kanghi, I became his wife, and though it is true that there are many Americans who look down upon me for so becoming, I have never regretted it. No, not even when men cast upon me the glances they cast upon sporting women. I accept the lot of the American wife of an humble Chinaman in America. The happiness of the man who loves me is more to me than the approval or disapproval of those who in my dark days left me to die like a dog. My Chinese husband has his faults. He is hot-tempered and, at times, arbitrary; but he is always a man, and has never sought to take away from me the privilege of being but a woman. I can lean upon and trust in him. I feel him behind me, protecting and caring for me, and that, to an ordinary woman like myself, means more than anything else.

Only when the son of Liu Kanghi lays his little head upon my bosom do I question whether I have done wisely. For my boy, the son of the Chinese man, is possessed of a childish wisdom which brings the tears to my eyes; and as he stands between his father and myself, like yet unlike us both, so will he stand in after years between his father's and his mother's people. And if there is no kindliness nor understanding between them, what will my boy's fate be?

HER CHINESE HUSBAND: SEQUEL TO THE STORY OF THE WHITE WOMAN WHO MARRIED A CHINESE

Now that Liu Kanghi is no longer with me, I feel that it will ease my heart to record some memories of him—if I can. The task, though calling to me, is not an easy one, so throng to my mind the invincible proofs of his love for me, the things he has said and done. My memories of him are so vivid and pertinacious, my thoughts of him so tender.

To my Chinese husband I could go with all my little troubles and perplexities; to him I could talk as women love to do at times of the past and the future, the mysteries of religion, of life and death. He was not above discussing such things with me. With him I was never strange or embarrassed. My Chinese husband was simple in his tastes. He liked to hear a good story, and though unlearned in a sense, could discriminate between the good and bad in literature. This came of his Chinese education. He told me one day that he thought the stories in the Bible were more like Chinese than American stories, and added: "If you had not told me what you have about it, I should say that it was composed by the Chinese." Music had a soothing though not a deep influence over him. It could not sway his mind, but he enjoyed it just as he did a beautiful picture. Because I was interested in fancy work, so also was he. I can see his face, looking so grave and concerned, because one day by accident I spilt some ink on a piece of embroidery I was working. If he came home in the evenings and found me tired and out of sorts, he would cook the dinner himself, and go about it in such a way that I felt that he rather enjoyed showing off his skill as a cook. The next evening, if he found everything ready, he would humorously declare himself much disappointed that I was so exceedingly well.

At such times a gray memory of James Carson would arise. How his cold anger and contempt, as exhibited on like occasions, had shrivelled me up in the long ago. And then I would fall to musing on the difference between the two men as lovers and husbands.

James Carson had been much more of an ardent lover than ever had been Liu Kanghi. Indeed it was his passion, real or feigned, which had carried me off my feet. When wooing he had constantly reproached me with being cold, unfeeling, a marble statue, and so forth; and I poor, ignorant little girl, would wonder how it was I appeared so when I felt so differently. For I had given James Carson my first love. Upon him my life had been concentrated as it has never been concentrated upon any other. Yet—!

There was nothing feigned about my Chinese husband. Simple and sincere as he was before marriage, so was he afterwards. As my union with James Carson had meant misery, bitterness, and narrowness, so my union with Liu Kanghi meant, on the whole, happiness, health, and development. Yet the former, according to American ideas, had been an educated broad-minded man; the other, just an ordinary Chinaman.

But the ordinary Chinaman that I would show to you was the sort of man that children, birds, animals, and some women love. Every morning he would go to the window and call to his pigeons, and they would flock around him, hearing and responding to his whistling and cooing. The rooms we lived in had been his rooms ever since he had come to America. They were above his store, and large and cool. The furniture had been brought from China, but there was nothing of tinsel about it. Dark wood, almost black, carved and antique, some of the pieces set with mother-of-pearl. On one side of the inner room stood a case of books and an ancestral tablet. I have seen Liu Kanghi touch the tablet with reverence, but the faith of his fathers was not strong enough to cause him to bow before it. The elegant simplicity of these rooms had surprised me much when I was first taken to them. I looked at him then, standing for a moment by the window, a solitary pigeon peeking in at him, perhaps wondering who had come to divert from her her friend's attention. So had he lived since he had come to this country—quietly and undisturbed—from twenty years of age to twenty-five. I felt myself an intruder. A feeling of pity for the boy—for such he seemed in his enthusiasm—arose in my breast. Why had I come to confuse his calm? Was it ordained, as he declared?

My little girl loved him better than she loved me. He took great pleasure in playing with her, curling her hair over his fingers, tying her sash, and all the simple tasks from which so many men turn aside.

Once the baby got hold of a set rat trap, and was holding it in such a way that the slightest move would have released the spring and plunged the cruel steel into her tender arms. Kanghi's eyes and mine beheld her thus at the same moment. I stood transfixed with horror. Kanghi quietly went up to the child and took from her the trap. Then he asked me to release his hand. I almost fainted when I saw it. "It was the only way," said he. We had to send for the doctor, and even as it was, came very near having a case of blood poisoning.

I have heard people say that he was a keen business man, this Liu Kanghi, and I imagine that he was. I did not, however, discuss his business with him. All I was interested in were the pretty things and the women who would come in and jest with him. He could jest too. Of course, the women did not know that I was his wife. Once a woman in rich clothes gave him her card and asked him to call upon her. After she had left he passed the card to me. I tore it up. He took those things as a matter of course, and was not affected by them. "They are a part of Chinatown life," he explained.

He was a member of the Reform Club, a Chinese social club, and the Chinese Board of Trade. He liked to discuss business affairs and Chinese and American politics with his countrymen, and occasionally enjoyed an evening away from me. But I never needed to worry over him.

He had his littlenesses as well as his bignesses, had Liu Kanghi. For instance, he thought he knew better about what was good for my health and other things, purely personal, than I did myself, and if my ideas opposed or did not tally with his, he would very vigorously denounce what he called "the foolishness of women." If he admired a certain dress, he would have me wear it on every occasion possible, and did not seem to be able to understand that it was not always suitable.

"Wear the dress with the silver lines," he said to me one day somewhat authoritatively. I was attired for going out, but not as he wished to see me. I answered that the dress with the silver lines was unsuitable for a long and dusty ride on an open car.

"Never mind," said he, "whether it is unsuitable or not. I wish you to wear it."

"All right," I said. "I will wear it, but I will stay at home."

I stayed at home, and so did he.

At another time, he reproved me for certain opinions I had expressed in the presence of some of his countrymen. "You should not talk like that," said he. "They will think you are a bad woman."

My white blood rose at that, and I answered him in a way which grieves me to remember. For Kanghi had never meant to insult or hurt me. Imperious by nature, he often spoke before he thought—and he was so boyishly anxious for me to appear in the best light possible before his own people.

There were other things too: a sort of childish jealousy and suspicion which it was difficult to allay. But a woman can forgive much to a man, the sincerity and strength of whose love makes her own, though true, seem slight and mean.

Yes, life with Liu Kanghi was not without its trials and tribulations. There was the continual uncertainty about his own life here in America, the constant irritation caused by the assumption of the white men that a white woman does not love her Chinese husband, and their actions accordingly; also sneers and offensive remarks. There was also on Liu Kanghi's side an acute consciousness that, though belonging to him as his wife, yet in a sense I was not his, but of the dominant race, which claimed, even while it professed to despise me. This consciousness betrayed itself in words and ways which filled me with a passion of pain and humiliation. "Kanghi," I would sharply say, for I had to cloak my tenderness, "do not talk to me like that. You *are* my superior. . . . I would not love you if you were not."

But in spite of all I could do or say, it was there between us: that strange, invisible—what? Was it the barrier of race—that consciousness?

Sometimes he would talk about returning to China. The thought filled me with horror. I had heard rumors of secondary wives. One afternoon the cousin of Liu Kanghi, with whom I had lived, came to see me, and showed me a letter which she had received from a little Chinese girl who had been born and brought up in America until the age of ten. The last paragraph in the letter read: "Emma and I are very sad and wish we were back in America." Kanghi's cousin explained that the father of the little girls, having no sons, had taken to himself another wife, and the new wife lived with the little girls and their mother.

That was before my little boy was born. That evening I told Kanghi that he need never expect me to go to China with him.

"You see," I began, "I look upon you as belonging to me."

He would not let me say more. After a while he said: "It is true that in China a man may and occasionally does take a secondary wife, but that custom is custom, not only because sons are denied to the first wife, but because the first wife is selected by parents and guardians before a man is hardly a man. If a Chinese marries for love, his life is a filled-up cup, and he wants no secondary wife. No, not even for sake of a son. Take, for example, me, your great husband."

I sometimes commented upon his boyish ways and appearance, which was the reason why, when he was in high spirits, he would call himself my "great husband." He was not boyish always. I have seen him, when shouldering the troubles of kinfolk, the quarrels of his clan, and other responsibilities, acting and looking like a man of twice his years.

But for all the strange marriage customs of my husband's people I considered them far more moral in their lives than the majority of Americans. I expressed myself thus to Liu Kanghi, and he replied: "The American people think higher. If only more of them lived up to what they thought, the Chinese would not be so confused in trying to follow their leadership."

If ever a man rejoiced over the birth of his child, it was Liu Kanghi. The boy was born with a veil over his face. "A prophet!" cried the old mulatto Jewess who nursed me. "A prophet has come into the world."

She told this to his father when he came to look upon him, and he replied: "He is my son; that is all I care about." But he was so glad, and there was feasting and rejoicing with his Chinese friends for over two weeks. He came in one evening and found me weeping over my poor little boy. I shall never forget the expression on his face.

"Oh, shame!" he murmured, drawing my head down to his shoulder. "What is there to weep about? The child is beautiful! The feeling heart, the understanding mind is his. And we will bring him up to be proud that he is of Chinese blood; he will fear none and, after him, the name of half-breed will no longer be one of contempt."

Kanghi as a youth had attended a school in Hong Kong, and while there had made the acquaintance of several half Chinese half English lads. "They were the brightest of all," he told me, "but they lowered themselves in the eyes of the Chinese by being ashamed of their Chinese blood and ignoring it."

His theory, therefore, was that if his own son was brought up to be proud instead of ashamed of his Chinese half, the boy would become a great man.

Perhaps he was right, but he could not see as could I, an American woman, the conflict before our boy.

After the little Kanghi had passed his first month, and we had found a reliable woman to look after him, his father began to take me around with him much more than formerly, and life became very enjoyable.

We dined often at a Chinese restaurant kept by a friend of his, and afterwards attended theatres, concerts, and other places of entertainment. We frequently met Americans with whom he had become acquainted through business, and he would introduce them with great pride in me shining in his eyes. The little jealousies and suspicions of the first year seemed no longer to irritate him, and though I had still cause to shrink from the gaze of strangers, I know that my Chinese husband was for several years a very happy man.

* * *

Now, I have come to the end. He left home one morning, followed to the gate by the little girl and boy (we had moved to a cottage in the suburbs).

"Bring me a red ball," pleaded the little girl.

"And me too," cried the boy.

"All right, chickens," he responded, waving his hand to them.

He was brought home at night, shot through the head. There are some Chinese, just as there are some Americans, who are opposed to all progress, and who hate with a bitter hatred all who would enlighten or be enlightened.

But that I have not the heart to dwell upon. I can only remember that when they brought my Chinese husband home there were two red balls in his pocket. Such was Liu Kanghi—a man.

THE LEGEND OF MISS SASAGAWARA

Hisaye Yamamoto

Even in that unlikely place of wind, sand, and heat, it was easy to imagine Miss Sasagawara a decorative ingredient of some ballet. Her daily costume, brief and fitting closely to her trifling waist, generously billowing below, and bringing together arrestingly rich colors like mustard yellow and forest green, appeared to have been cut from a coarse-textured homespun; her shining hair was so long it wound twice about her head to form a coronet; her face was delicate and pale, with a fine nose, pouting bright mouth, and glittering eyes; and her measured walk said, "Look, I'm *walking!*" as though walking were not a common but a rather special thing to be doing. I first saw her so one evening after mess, as she was coming out of the women's latrine going toward her barracks, and after I thought she was out of hearing, I imitated the young men of the Block (No. 33), and gasped, "Wow! How much does *she* weigh?"

"Oh, haven't you heard?" said my friend Elsie Kubo, knowing very well I had not. "That's Miss Sasagawara."

It turned out Elsie knew all about Miss Sasagawara, who with her father was new to Block 33. Where had she accumulated all her items? Probably a morsel here and a morsel there, and, anyway, I forgot to ask her sources, because the picture she painted was so distracting: Miss Sasagawara's father was a Buddhist minister, and the two had gotten permission to come to this Japanese evacuation camp in Arizona from one further north, after the death there of Mrs. Sasagawara. They had come here to join the Rev. Sasagawara's brother's family, who lived in a neighboring Block, but there had been some trouble between them, and just this week the immigrant pair had gotten leave to move over to Block 33. They were occupying one end of the Block's lone empty barracks, which had not been chopped up yet into the customary four apartments. The other end had been taken over by a young couple, also newcomers to the Block, who had moved in the same day.

"And do you know what, Kiku?" Elsie continued. "Oooh, that gal is really temperamental. I guess it's because she was a ballet dancer before she got stuck in camp, I hear people like that are temperamental. Anyway, the Sasakis, the new couple at the other end of the barracks, think she's crazy. The day they all moved in, the barracks was really dirty, all covered with dust from the dust storms and everything, so Mr. Sasaki was going to wash the whole barracks down with a hose, and he thought he'd be nice and do the Sasagawaras' side first. You know, do them a favor. But do you know what? Mr. Sasaki got the hose attached to the faucet outside and started to go in the door, and he said all the Sasagawaras' suitcases and things were on top of the Army cots and Miss Sasagawara was trying to clean the place out with a pail of water and a broom. He said, 'Here let me flush the place out with a hose for you; it'll be faster.' And she turned right around and screamed at him, 'What are you trying to do? Spy on me? Get out of here or I'll throw this water on you!' He said he was so surprised he couldn't move for a minute, and before he knew it, Miss Sasagawara just up and threw that water at him, pail and all. Oh, he said he got out of that place fast, but fast. Madwoman, he called her."

But Elsie had already met Miss Sasagawara, too, over at the apartment of the Murakamis, where Miss Sasagawara was borrowing Mrs. Murakami's Singer, and had found her quite amiable. "She said she was thirty-nine years old—imagine, thirty-nine, she looks so young, more like twenty-five; but she said she wasn't sorry she never got married, because she's had her fun. She said she got to go all over the country a couple of times, dancing in the ballet."

And after we emerged from the latrine, Elsie and I, slapping mosquitoes in the warm, gathering dusk, sat on the stoop of her apartment and talked awhile, jealously of the scintillating life Miss Sasagawara had led until now and nostalgically of the few ballets we had seen in the world outside. (How faraway Los Angeles seemed!) But we ended up as we always did, agreeing that our mission in life, pushing twenty as we were, was first to finish college somewhere when and if the war ever ended and we were free again, and then to find good jobs and two nice, clean young men, preferably handsome, preferably rich, who would cherish us forever and a day.

My introduction, less spectacular, to the Rev. Sasagawara came later, as I noticed him, a slight and fragile-looking old man, in the Block mess hall (where I worked as a waitress, and Elsie, too) or in the laundry room or going to and from the latrine. Sometimes he would be farther out, perhaps going to the post office or canteen or to visit friends in another Block or on some business to the Administration buildings, but wherever he was headed, however doubtless his destination, he always seemed to be wandering lostly. This may have been because he walked so slowly, with such negligible steps, or because he wore perpetually an air of bemusement, never talking directly to a person, as though, being what he was, he could not stop for an instant his meditation on the higher life.

I noticed, too, that Miss Sasagawara never came to the mess hall herself. Her father ate at the tables reserved for the occupants, mostly elderly, of the end barracks known as the bachelors' dormitory. After each meal, he came up to the counter and carried away a plate of food, protected with one of the pinkish apple wrappers we waitresses made as wrinkleless as possible and put out for napkins, and a mug of tea or coffee. Sometimes Miss Sasagawara could be seen rinsing out her empties at the one double-tub in the laundry that was reserved for private dishwashing.

If any one in the Block or in the entire camp of 15,000 or so people had talked at any length with Miss Sasagawara (everyone happening to speak of her called her that, although her first name, Mari, was simple enough and rather pretty) after her first and only visit to use Mrs. Murakami's sewing machine, I never heard of it. Nor did she ever willingly use the shower room, just off the latrine, when anyone else was there. Once, when I was up past midnight writing letters and went for my shower, I came upon her under the full needling force of a steamy spray, but she turned her back to me and did not answer my surprised hello. I hoped my body would be as smooth and spare and well-turned when I was thirty-nine. Another time Elsie and I passed in front of the Sasagawara apartment, which was really only a cubicle because the once-empty barracks had soon been partitioned off into six units for families of two, and we saw her there on the wooden steps, sitting with her wide, wide skirt spread splendidly about her. She was intent on peeling a grapefruit, which her father had probably brought to her from the mess hall that morning, and Elsie called out, "Hello there!" Miss Sasagawara looked up and stared, without recognition. We were almost out of earshot when I heard her call, "Do I know you?" and I could have almost sworn that she sounded hopeful, if not downright wistful, but Elsie, already miffed at having expended friendliness so unprofitably, seemed not to have heard, and that was that.

Well, if Miss Sasagawara was not one to speak to, she was certainly one to speak of, and she came up quite often as topic for the endless conversations which helped along the monotonous days. My mother said she had met the late Mrs. Sasagawara once, many years before the war, and to hear her tell it, a sweeter, kindlier woman there never was. "I suppose," said my mother, "that I'll never meet anyone like her again; she was a lady in every sense of the word." Then she reminded me that I had seen the Rev. Sasagawara before. Didn't I remember him as one of the three bhikshus who had read the sutras at Grandfather's funeral?

I could not say that I did. I barely remembered Grandfather, my mother's father. The only thing that came back with clarity was my nausea at the wake and the funeral, the first and only ones I had ever had occassion to attend, because it had been reproduced several times since—each time, in fact, that I had crossed again the actual scent or suspicion of burning incense. Dimly I recalled the inside of the Buddhist temple in Los Angeles, an immense, murky auditorium whose high and huge platform had held, centered in the background, a great golden shrine touched with black and white. Below this platform, Grandfather, veiled by gauze, had slept in a long grey box which just fitted him. There had been flowers, oh, such flowers, everywhere. And right in front of Grandfather's box had been the incense stand, upon which squatted two small bowls, one with a cluster of straw-thin sticks sending up white tendrils of smoke, the other containing a heap of coarse, grey powder. Each mourner in turn had gone up to the stand, bowing once, his palms touching in prayer before he reached it; had bent in prayer over the stand; had taken then a pinch of incense from the bowl of crumbs and, bowing over it reverently, cast it into the other, the active-bowl; had bowed, the hands praying again; had retreated a few steps and bowed one last time, the hands still joined, before returning to his seat. (I knew the ceremony well from having been severely coached in it on the evening of the wake.) There had been tears and tears and here and there a sudden sob.

And all this while, three men in black robes had been on the platform, one standing in front of the shining altar, the others sitting on either side, and the entire trio incessantly chanting a strange, mellifluous language in unison. From time to time there had reverberated through the enormous room, above the sing-song, above the weeping, above the fragrance, the sharp, startling whang of the gong.

So, one of those men had been Miss Sasagawara's father. . . . This information brought him closer to me, and I listened with interest later when it was told that he kept here in his apartment a small shrine, much more intricately constructed than that kept by the usual Buddhist household, before which, at regular hours of the day, he offered incense and chanted, tinkling (in lieu of the gong) a small bell. What did Miss Sasagawara do at these prayer periods, I wondered; did she participate, did she let it go in one ear and out the other, or did she abruptly go out on the steps, perhaps to eat a grapefruit?

Elsie and I tired one day of working in the mess hall. And this desire for greener fields came almost together with the Administration annoucement that henceforth the wages of residents doing truly vital labor, such as in the hospital or on the garbage trucks that went from mess hall to mess hall, would be upped to nineteen dollars a month instead of the common sixteen.

"Oh, I've always wanted to be a nurse!" Elsie confided, as the Block manager sat down to his breakfast after reading out the day's bulletin in English and Japanese.

"What's stopped you?" I asked.

"Mom," Elsie said. "She thinks it's dirty work. And she's afraid I'll catch something. But I'll remind her of the extra three dollars."

"It's never appealed to me much, either," I confessed. "Why don't we go over to garbage? It's the same pay."

Elsie would not even consider it. "Very funny. Well, you don't have to be a nurse's aide, Kiku. The hospital's short all kinds of help. Dental assistants, reception-ists. . . . Let's go apply after we finish this here."

So, willy-nilly, while Elsie plunged gleefully into the pleasure of wearing a trim blue-and-white striped seersucker, into the duties of taking temperatures and carry-ing bedpans, and into the fringe of medical jargon (she spoke very casually now of catheters, enemas, primiparas, multiparas), I became a relief receptionist at the hospital's front desk, taking my hours as they were assigned. And it was on one of my midnight-to-morning shifts that I spoke to Miss Sasagawara for the first time.

The cooler in the corridor window was still whirring away (for that desert heat in summer had a way of lingering intact through the night to merge with the warmth of the morning sun), but she entered bundled in an extraordinarily long black coat, her face made petulant, not unprettily, by lines of pain.

"I think I've got appendicitis," she said breathlessly, without preliminary.

"May I have your name and address?" I asked, unscrewing my pen.

Annoyance seemed to outbalance agony for a moment, but she answered soon enough, in a cold rush, "Mari Sasagawara, Thirty-three-seven C."

It was necessary also to learn her symptoms, and I wrote down that she had chill and a dull aching at the back of her head, as well as these excruciating flashes in her lower right abdomen.

"I'll have to go wake up the doctor. Here's a blanket, why don't you lie down over there on the bench until he comes?" I suggested.

She did not answer, so I tossed the Army blanket on the bench, and when I returned from the doctors' dormitory, after having tapped and tapped on the door of young Dr. Moritomo, who was on night duty, she was still standing where I had left her, immobile and holding onto the wooden railing shielding the desk.

"Dr. Moritomo's coming right away," I said. "Why don't you sit down at least?" Miss Sasagawara said, "Yes," but did not move.

"Did you walk all the way?" I asked incredulously, for Block 33 was a good mile off, across the canal.

She nodded, as if that were not important, also as if to thank me kindly to mind my own business.

Dr. Moritomo (technically, the title was premature; evacuation had caught him with a few months to go on his degree), wearing a maroon bathrobe, shuffled in sleepily and asked her to come into the emergency room for an examination. A short while later, he guided her past my desk into the laboratory, saying he was going to take her blood count.

When they came out, she went over to the electric fountain for a drink of water, and Dr. Moritomo said reflectively, "Her count's all right. Not appendicitis. We should keep her for observation, but the general ward is pretty full, isn't it? Hm, well, I'll give her something to take. Will you tell one of the boys to take her home?"

This I did, but when I came back from arousing George, one of the ambulance boys, Miss Sasagawara was gone, and Dr. Moritomo was coming out of the laboratory where he had gone to push out the lights. "Here's George, but that girl must have walked home," I reported helplessly.

"She's in no condition to do that. George, better catch up with her and take her home," Dr. Moritomo ordered.

Shrugging, George strode down the hall; the doctor shuffled back to bed; and soon there was the shattering sound of one of the old Army ambulances backing out of the hospital drive.

George returned in no time at all to say that Miss Sasagawara had refused to get on the ambulance.

"She wouldn't even listen to me. She just kept walking and I drove alongside and told her it was Dr. Moritomo's orders, but she wouldn't even listen to me."

"She wouldn't?"

"I hope Doc didn't expect me to drag her into the ambulance."

"Oh, well," I said. "I guess she'll get home all right. She walked all the way up here."

"Cripes, what a dame!" George complained, shaking his head as he started back to the ambulance room. "I never heard of such a thing. She wouldn't even listen to me."

Miss Sasagawara came back to the hospital about a month later. Elsie was the one who rushed up to the desk where I was on day duty to whisper, "Miss Sasagawara just tried to escape from the hospital!"

"Escape? What do you mean, escape?" I said.

"Well, she came in last night, and they didn't know what was wrong with her, so they kept her for observation. And this morning, just now, she ran out of the ward in just a hospital nightgown and the orderlies chased after her and caught her and brought her back. Oh, she was just fighting them. But once they got her back to bed, she calmed down right away, and Miss Morris asked her what was the big idea, you know, and do you know what she said? She said she didn't want any more of those doctors pawing her. Pawing her, imagine!"

After an instant's struggle with self-mockery, my curiosity led me down the entrance corridor after Elsie into the longer, wider corridor admitting to the general ward. The whole hospital staff appeared to have gathered in the room to get a look at Miss Sasagawara, and the other patients, or those of them that could, were sitting up attentively in their high, white, and narrow beds. Miss Sasagawara had the corner bed to the left as we entered and, covered only by a brief hospital apron, she was sitting on the edge with her legs dangling over the side. With her head slightly bent, she was staring at a certain place on the floor, and I knew she must be aware of that concentrated gaze, of trembling old Dr. Kawarnoto (he had retired several years before the war, but he had been drafted here), of Miss Morris, the head nurse, of Miss Bowman, the nurse in charge of the general ward during the day, of the other patients, of the nurse's aides, of the orderlies, and of everyone else who tripped in and out abashedly on some pretext or other in order to pass by her bed. I knew this by her smile, for as she continued to look at that same piece of the floor, she continued, unexpectedly, to seem wryly amused with the entire proceedings. I peered at her wonderingly through the triangular peephole created by someone's hand on hip, while Dr. Kawamoto, Miss Morris, and Miss Bowman tried to persuade her to lie down and relax. She was as smilingly immune to tactful suggestions as she was to tactless gawking.

There was no future to watching such a war of nerves as this; and besides, I was supposed to be at the front desk, so I hurried back in time to greet a frantic young mother and father, the latter carrying their small son who had had a hemorrhage this morning after a tonsillectomy yesterday in the out-patient clinic.

A couple of weeks later on the late shift I found George, the ambulance driver, in high spirits. This time he had been the one selected to drive a patient to Phoenix, where special cases were occasionally sent under escort, and he was looking forward to the moment when, for a few hours, the escort would permit him to go shopping around the city and perhaps take in a new movie. He showed me the list of things his friends had asked him to bring back for them, and we laughed together over the request of one plumpish nurse's aide for the biggest, richest chocolate cake he could find.

"You ought to have seen Mabel's eyes while she was describing the kind of cake she wanted," he said. "Man, she looked like she was eating it already!"

Just then one of the other drivers, Bobo Kunitomi, came up and nudged George, and they withdrew a few steps from my desk.

"Oh, I ain't particularly interested in that," I heard George saying.

There was some murmuring from Bobo, of which I caught the words, "Well, hell, you might as well, just as long as you're getting to go out there."

George shrugged, then nodded, and Bobo came over to the desk and asked for pencil and paper. "This is a good place . . . " he said, handing George what he had written.

Was it my imagination, or did George emerge from his chat with Bobo a little ruddier than usual? "Well, I guess I better go get ready," he said, taking leave. "Oh, anything you want, Kiku? Just say the word."

"Thanks, not this time," I said. "Well, enjoy yourself."

"Don't worry," he said. "I will!"

He had started down the hall when I remembered to ask, "Who are you taking, anyway?"

George turned around. "Miss Sa-sa-ga-wa-ra," he said, accenting every syllable. "Remember that dame? The one who wouldn't let me take her home?"

"Yes," I said. "What's the matter with her?"

George, saying not a word, pointed at his head and made several circles in the air with his first finger.

"Really?" I asked.

Still mum, George nodded in emphasis and pity before he turned to go.

How long was she away? It must have been several months, and when, towards late autumn, she returned at last from the sanitarium in Phoenix, everyone in Block 33 was amazed at the change. She said hello and how are you as often and easily as the next person, although many of those she greeted were surprised and suspicious, remembering the earlier rebuffs. There were some who never did get used to Miss Sasagawara as a friendly being.

One evening when I was going toward the latrine for my shower, my youngest sister, ten-year-old Michi, almost collided with me and said excitedly, "You going for your shower now, Kiku?"

"You want to fight about it?" I said, making fists.

"Don't go now, don't go now! Miss Sasagawara's in there," she whispered wickedly.

"Well," I demanded. "What's wrong with that, honey?"

"She's scary. Us kids were in there and she came in and we finished, so we got out, and she said, 'Don't be afraid of me. I won't hurt you.' Gee, we weren't even afraid of her, but when she said that, gee!"

"Oh, go home and go to bed," I said.

Miss Sasagawara was indeed in the shower and she welcomed me with a smile. "Aren't you the girl who plays the violin?"

I giggled and explained. Elsie and I, after hearing Menuhin on the radio, had in a fit of madness sent to Sears and Roebuck for beginners' violins that cost five dollars each. We had received free instruction booklets, too, but unable to make heads or tails from them, we contented ourselves with occasionally taking the violins out of their paper bags and sawing every which way away.

Miss Sasagawara laughed aloud—a lovely sound. "Well, you're just about as good as I am. I sent for a Spanish guitar. I studied it about a year once, but that was so long ago I don't remember the first thing and I'm having to start all over again. We'd make a fine orchestra."

That was the only time we really exchanged words and some weeks later I understood she had organized a dancing class from among the younger girls in the Block. My sister Michi, becoming one of her pupils, got very attached to her and spoke of her frequently at home. So I knew that Miss Sasagawara and her father had decorated their apartment to look oh, so pretty, that Miss Sasagawara had a whole big suitcase full of dancing costumes, and that Miss Sasagawara had just lots and lots of books to read.

The fruits of Miss Sasagawara's patient labor were put on show at the Block Christmas party, the second such observance in camp. Again, it was a gay, if odd, celebration. The mess hall was hung with red and green crepe paper streamers and the greyish mistletoe that grew abundantly on the ancient mesquite surrounding the camp. There were even electric decorations on the token Christmas tree. The oldest occupant of the bachelors' dormitory gave a tremulous monologue in an exaggerated Hiroshima dialect; one of the young boys wore a bow-tie and whispered a popular song while the girls shrieked and pretended to be growing faint. My mother sang an old Japanese song; four of the girls wore similar blue dresses and harmonized on a sweet tune; a little girl in a grass skirt and superfluous brassiere did a hula; and the chief cook came out with an ample saucepan and, assisted by the waitresses, performed the familiar *dojo-sukui,* the comic dance about a man who is merely trying to scoop up a few loaches from an uncooperative lake. Then Miss Sasagawara shooed her eight little girls, including Michi, in front, and while they formed a stiff pattern and waited, self-conscious in the rustly crepe paper dresses they had made themselves, she set up a portable phonograph on the floor and vigorously turned the crank.

Something was past its prime, either the machine or the record or the needle, for what came out was a feeble rasp but distantly related to the Mozart minuet it was supposed to be. After a bit I recognized the melody; I had learned it as a child to the words,

> When dames wore hoops and powdered hair,
> And very strict was e-ti-quette,
> When men were brave and ladies fair,
> They danced the min-u-et. . . .

And the little girls, who might have curtsied and stepped gracefully about under Miss Sasagawara's eyes alone, were all elbows and knees as they felt the Block's one-hundred-fifty or more pairs of eyes on them. Although there was sustained applause after their number, what we were benevolently approving was the great effort, for the achievement had been undeniably small. Then Santa came with a pillow for a stomach, his hands each dragging a bulging burlap bag. Church people outside had kindly sent these gifts, Santa announced, and every recipient must write and thank the person whose name he would find on an enclosed slip. So saying, he called by name each Block child under twelve and ceremoniously presented each eleemosynary package, and a couple of the youngest children screamed in fright at this new experience of a red and white man with a booming voice.

At the last, Santa called, "Miss Mari Sasagawara!" and when she came forward in surprise, he explained to the gathering that she was being rewarded for her help with the Block's younger generation. Everyone clapped and Miss Sasagawara, smiling graciously, opened her package then and there. She held up her gift, a peach-colored bath towel, so that it could be fully seen, and everyone clapped again.

Suddenly I put this desert scene behind me. The notice I had long awaited, of permission to relocate to Philadelphia to attend college, finally came, and there was a prodigious amount of packing to do, leave papers to sign, and goodbyes to say. And once the wearying, sooty train trip was over, I found myself in an intoxicating new world of daily classes, afternoon teas, and evening concerts, from which I dutifully emerged now and then to answer the letters from home. When the beautiful semester was over, I returned to Arizona, to that glowing heat, to the camp, to the family; for although the war was still on, it had been decided to close down the camps, and I had been asked to go back and spread the good word about higher education among the young people who might be dispersed in this way.

Elsie was still working in the hospital, although she had applied for entrance into the cadet nurse corps and was expecting acceptance any day, and the long conversations we held were mostly about the good old days, the good old days when we had worked in the mess hall together, the good old days when we had worked in the hospital together.

"What ever became of Miss Sasagawara?" I asked one day, seeing the Rev. Sasagawara go abstractedly by. "Did she relocate somewhere?"

"I didn't write you about her, did I?" Elsie said meaningfully. "Yes, she's relocated all right. Haven't seen her around, have you?"

"Where did she go?

Elsie answered offhandedly. "California."

"California?" I exclaimed. "We can't go back to California. What's she doing in California?"

So Elsie told me: Miss Sasagawara had been sent back there to a state institution, oh, not so very long after I had left for school. She had begun slipping back into her aloof ways almost immediately after Christmas, giving up the dancing class and not speaking to people. Then Elsie had heard a couple of very strange, yes, very strange things about her. One thing had been told by young Mrs. Sasaki, that next-door neighbor of the Sasagawaras.

Mrs. Sasaki said she had once come upon Miss Sasagawara sitting, as was her habit, on the porch. Mrs. Sasaki had been shocked to the core to see that the face of this thirty-nine-year-old woman (or was she forty now?) wore a beatific expression as she watched the activity going on in the doorway of her neighbors across the way, the Yoshinagas. This activity had been the joking and loud laughter of Joe and Frank, the young Yoshinaga boys, and three or four of their friends. Mrs. Sasaki would have let the matter go, were it not for the fact that Miss Sasagawara was so absorbed a spectator of this horseplay that her head was bent to one side and she actually had one finger in her mouth as she gazed, in the manner of a shy child confronted with a marvel. "What's the matter with you, watching the boys like that?" Mrs. Sasaki had cried. "You're old enough to be their mother!" Startled, Miss Sasagawara had jumped up and dashed back into her apartment. And when

Mrs. Sasaki had gone into hers, adjoining the Sasagawaras', she had been terrified to hear Miss Sasagawara begin to bang on the wooden walls with something heavy like a hammer. The banging, which sounded as though Miss Sasagawara were using all her strength on each blow, had continued wildly for at least five minutes. Then all had been still.

The other thing had been told by Joe Yoshinaga who lived across the way from Miss Sasagawara. Joe and his brother slept on two Army cots pushed together on one side of the room, while their parents had a similar arrangement on the other side. Joe had standing by his bed an apple crate for a shelf, and he was in the habit of reading his sports and western magazines in bed and throwing them on top of the crate before he went to sleep. But one morning he had noticed his magazines all neatly stacked inside the crate, when he was sure he had carelessly thrown some on top the night before, as usual. This happened several times, and he finally asked his family whether one of them had been putting his magazines away after he fell asleep. They had said no and laughed, telling him he must be getting absent-minded. But the mystery had been solved late one night, when Joe gradually awoke in his cot with the feeling that he was being watched. Warily he had opened one eye slightly and had been thoroughly awakened and chilled in the bargain by what he saw. For what he saw was Miss Sasagawara sitting there on his apple crate, her long hair all undone and flowing about her. She was dressed in a white nightgown and her hands were clasped on her lap. And all she was doing was sitting there watching him, Joe Yoshinaga. He could not help it, he had sat up and screamed. His mother, a light sleeper, came running to see what had happened, just as Miss Sasagawara was running out the door, the door they had always left unlatched or even wide open in summer. In the morning Mrs. Yoshinaga had gone straight to the Rev. Sasagawara and asked him to do something about his daughter. The Rev. Sasagawara, sympathizing with her indignation in his benign but vague manner, had said he would have a talk with Mari.

And, concluded Elsie, Miss Sasagawara had gone away not long after. I was impressed, although Elsie's sources were not what I would ordinarily pay much attention to, Mrs. Sasaki, that plump and giggling young woman who always felt called upon to explain that she was childless by choice, and Joe Yoshinaga, who had a knack of blowing up, in his drawling voice, any incident in which he personally played even a small part (I could imagine the field day he had had with this one). Elsie puzzled aloud over the cause of Miss Sasagawara's derangement and I, who had so newly had some contact with the recorded explorations into the virgin territory of the human mind, sagely explained that Miss Sasagawara had no doubt looked upon Joe Yoshinaga as the image of either the lost lover or the lost son. But my words made me uneasy by their glibness, and I began to wonder seriously about Miss Sasagawara for the first time.

Then there was this last word from Miss Sasagawara herself, making her strange legend as complete as I, at any rate, would probably ever know it. This came some time after I had gone back to Philadelphia and the family had joined me there, when I was neck deep in research for my final paper. I happened one day to be looking through the last issue of a small poetry magazine that had suspended publication midway through the war. I felt a thrill of recognition at the name, Mari

Sasagawara, signed to a long poem, introduced as " . . . the first published poem of a Japanese-American woman who is, at present, an evacuee from the West Coast making her home in a War Relocation center in Arizona."

It was a *tour de force,* erratically brilliant and, through the first readings, tantalizingly obscure. It appeared to be about a man whose lifelong aim had been to achieve Nirvana, that saintly state of moral purity and universal wisdom. This man had in his way certain handicaps, all stemming from his having acquired, when young and unaware, a family for which he must provide. The day came at last, however, when his wife died and other circumstances made it unnecessary for him to earn a competitive living. These circumstances were considered by those about him as sheer imprisonment, but he had felt free for the first time in his long life. It became possible for him to extinguish within himself all unworthy desire and consequently all evil, to concentrate on that serene, eight-fold path of highest understanding, highest mindedness, highest speech, highest action, highest livelihood, highest recollectedness, highest endeavor, and highest meditation.

This man was certainly noble, the poet wrote, this man was beyond censure. The world was doubtless enriched by his presence. But say that someone else, someone sensitive, someone admiring, someone who had not achieved this sublime condition and who did not wish to, were somehow called to companion such a man. Was it not likely that the saint, blissfully bent on cleansing from his already radiant soul the last imperceptible blemishes (for, being perfect, would he not humbly suspect his own flawlessness?), would be deaf and blind to the human passions rising, subsiding, and again rising, perhaps in anguished silence, within the selfsame room? The poet could not speak for others, of course; she could only speak for herself. But she would describe this man's devotion as a sort of madness, the monstrous sort which, pure of itself, might possibly bring troublous, scented scenes to recur in the other's sleep.

SCENT OF APPLES

Bienvenido Santos

When I arrived in Kalamazoo it was October and the war was still on. Gold and silver stars hung on pennants above silent windows of white and brick-red cottages. In a backyard an old man burned leaves and twigs while a grey-haired woman sat on the porch, her red hands quiet on her lap, watching the smoke rising above the elms, both of them thinking of the same thought perhaps, about a tall, grinning boy with blue eyes and flying hair, who went out to war: where could he be now this month when leaves were turning into gold and the fragrance of gathered apples was in the wind?

It was a cold night when I left my room at the hotel for a usual speaking engagement. I walked but a little way. A heavy wind coming up from Lake Michigan was icy on the face. It felt like winter straying early in the northern woodlands. Under the lampposts the leaves shone like bronze. And they rolled on the pavements like the ghost feet of a thousand autumns long dead, long before the boys left for faraway lands without great icy winds and promise of winter early in the air, lands without apple trees, *the singing and the gold!*

It was the same night I met Celestino Fabia, "just a Filipino farmer" as he called himself, who had a farm about thirty miles east of Kalamazoo.

"You came all that way on a night like this just to hear me talk?" I asked.

"I've seen no Filipino for so many years now," he answered quickly. "So when I saw your name in the papers where it says you come from the Islands and that you're going to talk, I come right away."

Earlier that night I had addressed a college crowd, mostly women. It appeared that they wanted me to talk about my country; they wanted me to tell them things about it because my country had become a lost country. Everywhere in the land the enemy stalked. Over it a great silence hung; and their boys were there, unheard from, or they were on their way to some little known island on the Pacific, young boys all, hardly men, thinking of harvest moons and smell of forest fire.

It was not hard talking about our own people. I knew them well and I loved them. And they seemed so far away during those terrible years that I must have spoken of them with a little fervor, a little nostalgia.

In the open forum that followed, the audience wanted to know whether there was much difference between our women and the American women. I tried to answer the question as best as I could, saying, among other things, that I did not know much about American women, except that they looked friendly, but differences or similarities in inner qualities such as naturally belonged to the heart or to the mind, I could only speak about with vagueness.

While I was trying to explain away the fact that it was not easy to make comparisons, a man rose from the rear of the hall, wanting to say something. In the distance, he looked slight and old and very brown. Even before he spoke, I knew that he was, like me, a Filipino.

"I'm a Filipino," he began, loud and clear, in a voice that seemed used to wide open spaces, "I'm just a Filipino farmer out in the country." He waved his hand towards the door. "I left the Philippines more than twenty years ago and have never been back. Never will perhaps. I want to find out, sir, are our Filipino women the same like they were twenty years ago?"

As he sat down, the hall filled with voices, hushed and intrigued. I weighed my answer carefully. I did not want to tell a lie yet I did not want to say anything that would seem platitudinous, insincere. But more important than these considerations, it seemed to me that moment as I looked towards my countryman, I must give him an answer that would not make him so unhappy. Surely, all these years, he must have held on to certain ideals, certain beliefs, even illusions peculiar to the exile.

"First," I said as the voices gradually died down and every eye seemed upon me, "First, tell me what our women were like twenty years ago."

The man stood to answer. "Yes," he said, "you're too young. . . . Twenty years ago our women were nice, they were modest, they wore their hair long, they dressed proper and went for no monkey business. They were natural, they went to church regular, and they were faithful." He had spoken slowly, and now in what seemed like an afterthought, added, "It's the men who ain't."

Now I knew what I was going to say.

"Well," I began, "it will interest you to know that our women have changed—but definitely! The change, however, has been on the outside only. Inside, here," pointing to the heart, "they are the same as they were twenty years ago. God-fearing, faithful, modest, and *nice*."

The man was visibly moved. "I'm very happy, sir," he said, in the manner of one who, having stakes on the land, had found no cause to regret one's sentimental investment.

After this, everything that was said and done in that hall that night seemed like an anti-climax; and later, as we walked outside, he gave me his name and told me of his farm thirty miles east of the city.

We had stopped at the main entrance to the hotel lobby. We had not talked very much on the way. As a matter of fact, we were never alone. Kindly American friends talked to us, asked us questions, said goodnight. So now I asked him whether he cared to step into the lobby with me and talk.

"No, thank you," he said, "you are tired. And I don't want to stay out too late."

"Yes, you live very far."

"I got a car," he said, "besides . . . "

Now he smiled, he truly smiled. All night I had been watching his face and I wondered when he was going to smile.

"Will you do me a favor, please," he continued smiling almost sweetly. "I want you to have dinner with my family out in the country. I'd call for you tomorrow afternoon, then drive you back. Will that be all right?"

"Of course," I said. "I'd love to meet your family." I was leaving Kalamazoo for Muncie, Indiana, in two days. There was plenty of time.

"You will make my wife very happy," he said.

"You flatter me."

"Honest. She'll be very happy. Ruth is a country girl and hasn't met many Filipinos. I mean Filipinos younger than I, cleaner looking. We're just poor farmer folk, you know, and we don't get to town very often. Roger, that's my boy, he goes to school in town. A bus takes him early in the morning and he's back in the afternoon. He's nice boy."

"I bet he is," I agreed. "I've seen the children of some of the boys by their American wives and the boys are tall, taller than the father, and very good looking."

"Roger, he'd be tall. You'll like him."

Then he said goodbye and I waved to him as he disappeared in the darkness.

The next day he came, at about three in the afternoon. There was a mild, ineffectual sun shining; and it was not too cold. He was wearing an old brown tweed jacket and worsted trousers to match. His shoes were polished, and although the green of his tie seemed faded, a colored shirt hardly accentuated it. He looked younger than he appeared the night before now that he was clean shaven and seemed ready to go to a party. He was grinning as we met.

"Oh, Ruth can't believe it. She can't believe it," he kept repeating as he led me to his car—a nondescript thing in faded black that had known better days and many hands. "I says to her, I'm bringing you a first class Filipino, and she says, aw, go away, quit kidding, there's no such thing as first class Filipino. But Roger, that's my boy, he believed me immediately. What's he like, daddy, he asks. Oh, you will see, I says, he's first class. Like you daddy? No, no, I laugh at him, your daddy ain't first class. Aw, but you are, daddy, he says. So you can see what a nice boy he is, so innocent. Then Ruth starts griping about the house, but the house is a mess, she says. True it's a mess, it's always a mess, but you don't mind, do you? We're poor folks, you know."

The trip seemed interminable. We passed through narrow lanes and disappeared into thickets, and came out on barren land overgrown with weeds in places. All around were dead leaves and dry earth. In the distance were apple trees.

"Aren't those apple trees?" I asked wanting to be sure.

"Yes, those are apple trees," he replied. "Do you like apples? I got lots of 'em. I got an apple orchard, I'll show you."

All the beauty of the afternoon seemed in the distance, on the hills, in the dull soft sky.

"Those trees are beautiful on the hills," I said.

"Autumn's a lovely season. The trees are getting ready to die, and they show their colors, proud-like."

"No such thing in our own country," I said.

That remark seemed unkind, I realized later. It touched him off on a long deserted tangent, but ever there perhaps. How many times did the lonely mind take unpleasant detours away from the familiar winding lanes towards home for fear of this, the remembered hurt, the long lost youth, the grim shadows of the years; how many times indeed, only the exile knows.

It was a rugged road we were travelling and the car made so much noise that I could not hear everything he said, but I understood him. He was telling his story for the first time in many years. He was remembering his own youth. He was thinking of home. In these odd moments there seemed no cause for fear, no cause at all, no pain. That would come later. In the night perhaps. Or lonely on the farm under the apple trees.

In this old Visayan town, the streets are narrow and dirty and strewn with corral shells. You have been there? You could not have missed our house, it was the biggest in town, one of the oldest, ours was a big family. The house stood right on the edge of the street. A door opened heavily and you enter a dark hall leading to the stairs. There is the smell of chickens roosting on the low-topped walls, there is the familiar sound they make and you grope your way up a massive staircase, the bannisters smooth upon the trembling hand. Such nights, they are no better than the days, windows are closed against the sun; they close heavily.

Mother sits in her corner looking very white and sick. This was her world, her domain. In all these years I cannot remember the sound of her voice. Father was different. He moved about. He shouted. He ranted. He lived in the past and talked of honor as though it were the only thing.

I was born in that house. I grew up there into a pampered brat. I was mean. One day I broke their hearts. I saw mother cry wordlessly as father heaped his curses upon me and drove me out of the house, the gate closing heavily after me. And my brothers and sisters took up my father's hate for me and multiplied it numberless times in their own broken hearts. I was no good.

But sometimes, you know, I miss that house, the roosting chickens on the low-topped walls. I miss my brothers and sisters. Mother sitting in her chair, looking like a pale ghost in a corner of the room. I would remember the great live posts, massive tree trunks from the forests. Leafy plants grew on the sides, buds pointing downwards, wilted and died before they could become flowers. As they fell on the floor, father bent to pick them and throw them out into the corral streets. His hands were strong. I have kissed those hands . . . many times, many times.

Finally we rounded a deep curve and suddenly came upon a shanty, all but ready to crumble in a heap on the ground, its plastered walls were rotting away, the floor was hardly a foot from the ground. I thought of the cottages of the poor colored folk in the south, the hovels of the poor everywhere in the land. This one stood all by itself as though by common consent all the folk that used to live here had decided to stay away, despising it, ashamed of it. Even the lovely season could not color it with beauty.

A dog barked loudly as we approached. A fat blonde woman stood at the door with a little boy by her side. Roger seemed newly scrubbed. He hardly took his eyes off me. Ruth had a clean apron around her shapeless waist. Now as she shook my hands in sincere delight I noticed shamefacedly (that I should notice) how rough her hands, how coarse and red with labor, how ugly! She was no longer young and her smile was pathetic.

As we stepped inside and the door closed behind us, immediately I was aware of the familiar scent of apples. The room was bare except for a few ancient pieces of second-hand furniture. In the middle of the room stood a stove to keep the family warm in winter. The walls were bare. Over the dining table hung a lamp yet unlighted.

Ruth got busy with the drinks. She kept coming in and out of a rear room that must have been the kitchen and soon the table was heavy with food, fried chicken legs and rice, and green peas and corn on the ear. Even as we ate, Ruth kept standing, and going to the kitchen for more food. Roger ate like a little gentleman.

"Isn't he nice looking?" his father asked.

"You are a handsome boy, Roger," I said.

The boy smiled at me. "You look like Daddy," he said.

Afterwards I noticed an old picture leaning on the top of a dresser and stood to pick it up. It was yellow and soiled with many fingerings. The faded figure of a woman in Philippine dress could yet be distinguished although the face had become a blur.

"Your . . . " I began.

"I don't know who she is," Fabia hastened to say. "I picked that picture many years ago in a room on La Salle Street in Chicago. I have often wondered who she is."

"The face wasn't a blur in the beginning?"

"Oh, no. It was a young face and good."

Ruth came with a plate full of apples.

"Ah," I cried, picking out a ripe one, "I've been thinking where all the scent of apples came from. The room is full of it."

"I'll show you," said Fabia.

He showed me a backroom, not very big. It was half-full of apples.

"Every day," he explained, "I take some of them to town to sell to the groceries. Prices have been low. I've been losing on the trips."

"These apples will spoil," I said.

"We'll feed them to the pigs."

Then he showed me around the farm. It was twilight now and the apple trees stood bare against a glowing western sky. In apple blossom time it must be lovely here, I thought. But what about wintertime?

One day, according to Fabia, a few years ago, before Roger was born, he had an attack of acute appendicitis. It was deep winter. The snow lay heavy everywhere. Ruth was pregnant and none too well herself. At first she did not know what to do. She bundled him in warm clothing and put him on a cot near the stove. She shoveled the snow from their front door and practically carried the suffering man on her shoulders, dragging him through the newly made path towards the road where they waited for the U.S. Mail car to pass. Meanwhile snowflakes poured all over them and she kept rubbing the man's arms and legs as she herself nearly froze to death.

"Go back to the house, Ruth!" her husband cried, "you'll freeze to death."

But she clung to him wordlessly. Even as she massaged his arms and legs, her tears rolled down her cheeks. "I won't leave you, I won't leave you," she repeated.

Finally the U.S. Mail car arrived. The mailman, who knew them well, helped them board the car, and, without stopping on his usual route, took the sick man and his wife direct to the nearest hospital.

Ruth stayed in the hospital with Fabia. She slept in a corridor outside the patients' ward and in the day time helped in scrubbing the floor and washing the dishes and cleaning the men's things. They didn't have enough money and Ruth was willing to work like a slave.

"Ruth's a nice girl," said Fabia, "like our own Filipino women."

Before nightfall, he took me back to the hotel. Ruth and Roger stood at the door holding hands and smiling at me. From inside the room of the shanty, a low light flickered. I had a last glimpse of the apple trees in the orchard under the darkened sky as Fabia backed up the car. And soon we were on our way back to town. The dog had started barking. We could hear it for some time, until finally, we could not hear it anymore, and all was darkness around us, except where the head lamps revealed a stretch of road leading somewhere.

Fabia did not talk this time. I didn't seem to have anything to say myself. But when finally we came to the hotel and I got down, Fabia said, "Well, I guess I won't be seeing you again."

It was dimly lighted in front of the hotel and I could hardly see Fabia's face. Without getting off the car, he moved to where I had sat, and I saw him extend his hand. I gripped it.

"Tell Ruth and Roger," I said, "I love them."

He dropped my hand quickly. "They'll be waiting for me now," he said.

"Look," I said, not knowing why I said it, "one of these days, very soon, I hope, I'll be going home. I could go to your town."

"No," he said softly, sounding very much defeated but brave, "Thanks a lot. But, you see, nobody would remember me now."

Then he started the car, and as it moved away, he waved his hand.

"Goodbye," I said, waving back into the darkness. And suddenly the night was cold like winter straying early in these northern woodlands.

I hurried inside. There was a train the next morning that left for Muncie, Indiana, at a quarter after eight.

Watershed Years

12

CHANGING LIVES

WORLD WAR II AND THE POSTWAR YEARS

Yen Le Espiritu

World War II marked an important turning point in the history of Asians in the United States. During the war years, Japanese America was ripped apart as more than 100,000 persons of Japanese ancestry were relocated in concentration camps. The wartime internment devastated the lives of all internees but permanently eroded the Issei (first-generation) men's economic position and weakened their patriarchal authority over the family. The lives of Chinese, Koreans, Filipinos, and Asian Indians, in contrast, improved because their ancestral nations were allies of the United States. The wartime services of these men did a great deal to reduce white prejudice against Asians, earned many of them U.S. citizenship, and helped to rescind exclusion laws, thus renewing immigration from Asia. In particular, the War Brides Act of 1945, which allowed Asian wives and children of U.S. servicemen to enter as nonquota immigrants, brought large numbers of Asian immigrant women to the United States. Their arrival revitalized family life but also wreaked havoc in these male-dominated and resource-starved communities. The longtime bachelors were unable to meet the material needs of their newly (re)established families and were ill prepared for the day-to-day relationships with their wives. Finally, the wartime labor shortage and postwar economic prosperity generated unprecedented occupational opportunities not only for U.S.-born Asian men but also for many U.S.-born Asian women. These social and economic changes pushed more Asian Americans into contact with the larger U.S. society, accorded more economic independence to U.S.-born Asians, and fragmented Asian America more clearly than in the past along class lines. All these changes challenged the traditional patriarchal structure as many young men and women were freed for the first time from the confinement of the previously closed ethnic communities.

CHANGING POWER RELATIONS: THE WARTIME INTERNMENT OF JAPANESE AMERICANS

> Birds
> Living in a cage,
> The human spirit.
> Nikaido Gensui (1976: 116)

Immediately after the bombing of Pearl Harbor, the incarceration of Japanese Americans began. On the night of December 7, 1941, the Federal Bureau of Investigation (FBI) began taking into custody persons of Japanese ancestry who had connections to the Japanese government. Working on the principle of guilt by association, the security agencies simply rounded up most of the Issei leaders of the Japanese community. Initially, the federal government differentiated between alien and citizen Japanese Americans, but this distinction gradually disappeared. On February 19, 1942, President Franklin Delano Roosevelt signed Executive Order 9066, arbitrarily suspending civil rights of U.S. citizens by authorizing the "evacuation" of 120,000 persons of Japanese ancestry into concentration camps, of whom approximately 50 percent were women and 60 percent were U.S.-born citizens (Matsumoto 1989: 116). It was during this period that the Japanese American community discovered that the legal distinction between citizen and alien was not nearly so important as the distinction between white and yellow (Daniels 1988: chap. 6). Years later, in a speech in support of redress and reparations, Congressman Robert Matsui, who had been an infant in 1942, asked in anguish, "How could I as a 6-month-old child born in this country be declared by my own government to be an enemy alien?" (1987: 7584). Calling attention to the construction of Asian Americans as the "foreigner-within," Lisa Lowe has argued that Americans of Asian descent, even as citizens, remain the symbolic "alien"—metonym for Asia who by definition cannot share in the American nation.

The camp environment, with its lack of privacy, regimented routines, and new power hierarchy, inflicted serious and lasting wounds on Japanese American family life. In the crammed 20-by-25-foot "apartment" units, tensions were high as men, women, and children struggled to recreate family life under very trying conditions. The disappearance of the traditional family meal also increased the distance between parent and child. In the camps, the internees ate mass-prepared meals in large mess halls, and children often preferred to sit with their friends at separate tables from their parents (Kitagawa 1967: 84). A former Nisei (second-generation immigrant) internee recounted the havoc mess-hall living wreaked on her extended family:

> Before Manzanar,[1] mealtime had always been the center of our family scene. In camp, and afterward, I would often recall with deep yearning the old round wooden table in our dining room in Ocean Park . . . large enough to seat twelve or thirteen of us at once. . . . Now, in the mess halls, after a few weeks had passed, we stopped eating as a family. Mama tried to hold us together for a while, but it was hopeless. Granny was too feeble to walk across the block three times a day, especially during heavy weather, so May brought food to her in the barracks. My older brothers and sisters, meanwhile, began eating with their friends, or eating somewhere blocks away, in the hope of finding better food. (Houston and Houston 1973: 30–31)

The internment also transformed the balance of power in families: husbands lost some of their power over wives, as did parents over children. Until the internment, the Issei man had been the undisputed authority over his wife and children: he had been both the breadwinner and the decision maker for the entire family. Now "he had no rights, no home, no control over his own life" (Houston and Houston 1973: 62). Most important, the internment reversed the economic roles, and thus the status and authority, of family members. With their means of livelihood cut off indefinitely, Issei men lost their role as breadwinners. Despondent over the loss of almost everything they had worked so hard to acquire, many Issei men felt useless and frustrated, particularly as their wives and children became less dependent on them. Daisuke Kitagawa reported that in the Tule Lake relocation center, "The [Issei] men looked as if they had suddenly aged ten years. They lost the capacity to plan for their own futures, let alone those of their sons and daughters" (1967: 91).

Issei men responded to this emasculation in various ways. By the end of three years' internment, formerly enterprising, energetic Issei men had become immobilized with feelings of despair, hopelessness, and insecurity. Charles Kikuchi remembered his father, who "used to be a perfect terror and dictator," spending all day lying on his cot: "He probably realizes that he no longer controls the family group and rarely exerts himself so that there is little family conflict as far as he is concerned" (Modell 1973: 62). But others, like Jeanne Wakatsuki Houston's father, reasserted their patriarchal power by abusing their wives and children. Stripped of his roles as the protector and provider for his family, Houston's father "kept pursuing oblivion through drink, he kept abusing Mama, and there seemed to be no way out of it for anyone. You couldn't even run" (Houston and Houston 1973:

61). The experiences of the Issei men underscore the intersections of racism and sexism, showing how men of color live in a society that creates sex-based norms and expectations (e.g., man as breadwinner) that racism operates simultaneously to deny (Crenshaw 1989: 155).

Whereas camp life eroded the status and authority of the Issei men, it provided comparative benefit to Issei women. Ever since their arrival in the United States, most Issei women had endured lives of continuous drudgery: they had reared children, kept house, and toiled alongside their husbands in labor-intensive jobs. For these women, life in the camps was a "highly deserved holiday" (Kitagawa 1967: 89). The communally prepared meals and minimal living quarters (with no running water or cooking facilities) freed Issei wives from most domestic responsibilities and enabled them to attend to themselves (Kim 1990: 73–74). A good number of women filled their newfound spare time with adult classes, hobbies, religious meetings, cultural programs, and visits with friends—all activities previously prohibited because of their long workdays both inside and outside the home (Matsumoto 1989: 116–117). Daisuke Kitagawa recorded the changing lives of Issei women in the Tule Lake relocation center:

> For the first time in their lives, they had something akin to free time in a substantial amount, and in many different ways they blossomed out. Most of them took employment of some kind with the work corps . . . [but] the work was not too hard; moreover, they had the companionship of women from a similar situation and like background. Once the day's work was done, the rest of the time was completely at their disposal. . . . Issei women unwittingly became the happiest people in the relocation center. They even began to look younger. (1967: 89–90)

This is not to say that Issei women enjoyed their internment years, but only that their lives improved relative to those of the Issei men. Also, as much as Issei women relished their newfound independence, they also missed their position as "queen of the household." Deprived of their homes, the traditional site of the construction of their womanhood, some Issei women fought to regain their household authority. Charles Kikuchi recalled that his mother

> will do anything to retain her place in the family and won't be pushed aside. Even at meals she has her methods. Since she doesn't do the cooking, she attempts to maintain her position by carrying all the plates home and by dividing the desserts or watching our [younger siblings] unnecessarily. (Modell 1973: 140)

Camp life also widened the distance and deepened the conflict between the Issei and their U.S.-born children. At the root of these tensions were growing cultural rifts between the generations as well as a decline in the power and authority of the Issei fathers. The cultural rifts not only reflected a general process of acculturation but were accelerated by the degradation of everything Japanese and the simultaneous promotion of Americanization in the camps (Chan 1991: 128; see also Okihiro 1991: 229–232). The younger Nisei also spent much more time away from their parents' supervision. With no competition from white students, the

Nisei snatched the leadership positions in the schools: they became class presidents, yearbook editors, pom-pom girls, athletic heroes, and social "ins" (Kim 1982: 162–163; Kitano 1991a: 155). Enamored with their newfound social positions, the Nisei spent most of their "waking hours without either seeing or being seen by their parents" (Kitagawa 1967: 86). According to a former Nisei internee, "Once the weather warmed up, it was an out-of-doors life, where you only went 'home' at night, when you finally had to: 10,000 people on an endless promenade inside the square mile of barbed wire that was the wall around our city" (Houston and Houston 1973: 35). In such a setting, Issei parents lost their ability to discipline their children, whom they seldom saw during the day. Much to the chagrin of their conservative parents, young men and women began to spend more time with each other unchaperoned at sports events, dances, and other school functions. According to Charles Kikuchi, camp life broke down some of the parents' protectiveness toward their daughters: "Many of the parents who would never let their daughters go to dances before do not object so strenuously now" because they realized that their children could not "stay home night after night doing nothing without some sort of recreational release" (Modell 1973: 81–82). Freed from some of the parental constraints, the Nisei women socialized more with their peers and also expected to choose their own husbands and to marry for "love"—a departure from the old customs of arranged marriage (Matsumoto 1989: 117). Once this occurred, the prominent role fathers played in marriage arrangements—and by extension in their children's lives—declined (Okihiro 1991: 231).

Privileging U.S. citizenship and U.S. education, War Relocation Authority (WRA) policies regarding camp life further reversed the power hierarchy between the Japan-born Issei and their U.S.-born children. In the camps, only Nisei were eligible to vote and to hold office in the community council; Issei were excluded because of their alien status. Daisuke Kitagawa recorded the impact of this policy on parental authority: "In the eyes of young children, their parents were definitely inferior to their grown-up brothers and sisters, who as U.S. citizens could elect and be elected members of the Community Council. For all these reasons many youngsters lost confidence in, and respect for, their parents" (1967: 88). Similarly, the WRA salary scales were based on English-speaking ability and on citizenship status. As a result, the Nisei youths and young adults could earn relatively higher wages than their fathers. This shift in earning abilities eroded the economic basis for parental authority (Matsumoto 1989: 116). College-educated Nisei who had been trained as doctors, dentists, or teachers found work in their professions for the first time behind barbed wire. These Nisei professionals were at the top of the (albeit low) pay scale, earning $19 per month. Other workers were paid $16 for skilled work and $12 for unskilled or menial work (Kitagawa 1967: 80).

Though no mass evacuation of Japanese took place in Hawai'i,[2] the territory's martial law plans—applied to all of Hawai'i's residents but contrived specifically to contain the Japanese—also reversed the roles of parent and child. In a study of the anti-Japanese movement in Hawai'i, historian Gary Okihiro detailed this military-induced social inversion:

> The status of *issei* fell as the standing of *nisei* rose with the differential treatment given the generations by the military. *Issei* bore the stigma of enemy alien, *nisei* were tainted,

but nevertheless wooed and cajoled toward Anglo conformity. *Issei* spoke the language of the enemy; *nisei* translated government orders, radio and print news, and social cues, intonations, and sanctions for parents who did not know English well. *Issei* represented an obsolete mentality, an Old World flavor that had become distasteful. *Nisei* symbolized the future, a new direction and style, in full pursuit of the American dream. (1991: 231)

A young Nisei woman in Hawai'i praised this transition: "Like a symbol of medieval restraint, the kimono has been almost forsaken, and women have been freed of the stiff obi bindings and wrappings" (cited in Okihiro 1991: 231). Okihiro argued that this reversal of roles contributed to social disruption in the Japanese community, which was "a goal of the strategy for defense because it weakened the will and ability to resist" (1991: 229).

Women's work experiences also changed in complex ways during the internment years. In one of the many ironies the internment produced, Nisei women found more job opportunities in the relocation camps than they did on the outside. Organized as model cities, each camp offered a wide array of jobs for these young women, ranging from clerical work in the administration offices, medical care in the hospitals, and busing tables in the mess halls to serving as assistant teachers in the makeshift classrooms or as writers and artists for the camp newspapers. Although many Nisei women had worked before the war, the relative parity in wages in the camps altered family dynamics and accorded them relatively more status in the family (Matsumoto 1989: 116–117; Nakano 1990: 150–151).

The student relocation programs further removed Nisei men and women from the patriarchal constraints of their families. In 1942, concerned educators organized the nongovernmental National Japanese American Student Relocation Council (NJASRC) to enable Nisei college students to complete their education. NJASRC persuaded colleges and universities outside the restricted western defense zone to accept Nisei students, facilitated the admission of these students, and secured their leave clearances. In the years 1942 to 1946, NJASRC placed 4,084 Nisei students in colleges. Of the first 400 students to leave camps, a third were women. Matsumoto (1989) attributed the women's desire to relocate to the increasing sense of independence and self-confidence they developed in the camps. A Nisei woman recounted her determination to leave: "Mother and father do not want me to go out. However, I want to go so very much that sometimes I feel I'd go even if they disowned me. What shall I do? I realize the hard living conditions outside but I think I can take it" (quoted in Matsumoto 1989: 118). In yet another relaxation of patriarchal control, Issei parents, despite their initial reservations, gradually sanctioned their daughters' departures for education and employment in the Midwest and East. A postwar study of a group of 1,000 relocated students found that 40 percent were women. Many Nisei women gravitated to the field of nursing; by July 1944, there were more than 300 Nisei women in over 100 nursing programs in 24 states (Matsumoto 1989: 118–120).

At war's end in August 1945, Japanese Americans had lost much of the economic ground they had gained in more than a generation. The majority of Issei women and men no longer had their farms, businesses, and financial savings; those who still owned property found their homes dilapidated and vandalized and their personal belongings stolen or destroyed (Broom and Riemer 1949). The internment also ended Japanese Americans' concentration in agriculture and small businesses. In their absence, other groups had taken over these ethnic niches. This loss further eroded the economic basis of parental authority, because Issei men no longer had businesses to hand down to their Nisei sons (Broom and Riemer 1949: 31). Historian Roger Daniels declared that by the end of World War II, "the generational struggle was over: the day of the Issei had passed" (1988: 286). Issei men, now in their 60s, no longer had the vigor to start over from scratch. Forced to find employment quickly after the war, many Issei couples who had owned small businesses before the war returned to the forms of manual labor in which they had begun a generation ago. Most men found work as janitors, gardeners, kitchen helpers, and handymen; their wives toiled as domestic servants, garment workers, and cannery workers (Yanagisako 1987: 92). An Issei woman likened the effort to find the first job out of camp to "a race" (Glenn 1986: 79–83). As the Issei strove to eke out a living, their children struggled to join mainstream postwar United States-with varying degrees of success.

IMPROVED LIVES: CHINESE, KOREAN, FILIPINO, AND INDIAN AMERICANS

While the lives of Japanese Americans were being ripped apart, the lot of persons of Chinese, Korean, Filipino, and Asian Indian ancestry improved because their ancestral nations were allies of the United States. The start of World War II dramatically changed American public attitudes toward these groups, particularly toward Filipinos and Chinese (Feria 1946–1947; Chan 1991: 121). The military exploits of Filipino soldiers, both in the Philippines and in the United States, did a great deal to reduce white prejudice against Filipino Americans. When the United States declared war against Japan in December 1941, President Roosevelt incorporated the Philippine armed forces into the United States Armed Forces in the Far East (USAFFE). Fighting alongside American soldiers in defending Bataan and Corregidor during the spring of 1942, Filipino troops were widely praised in newsreels and newspaper headlines across the United States for their heroism and courage. Meanwhile, large numbers of Filipinos in the United States were inducted into the armed forces. Their status as U.S. nationals forgotten, many became citizens through mass naturalization ceremonies held before induction. A. B. Santos, a Filipino immigrant who came to the United States in the 1920s, recounted his experience with the draft and subsequent naturalization:

> When World War II came, I got drafted into the U.S. Army. They drafted me in 1943 even though I was a foreigner, a noncitizen. . . . On Saturday morning, I reported to Los Angeles. When I got there, they swore me in as a U.S. citizen. I did not even have to file an application. So that was how I became a U.S. citizen. (Espiritu 1995: 42)

Because most Filipinos were males of draft age, some 16,000 were called up under the first draft in 1942 (Espiritu 1995: 17).

Sizable numbers of Chinese also joined and served in the U.S. armed forces. According to a New York City survey, almost 40 percent of the Chinese population were drafted, the highest draft rate of any ethnic group. Historian Peter Kwong (1979) noted the historical origin of this high draft rate: "Because of the Exclusion Act, most Chinese had no dependents and according to the law were the first called" (pp. 114–115). Thomas Chinn estimated that between 15,000 and 20,000 Chinese men and women served in all branches of the U.S. military (1989: 147–150). Previously maligned as the "heathen Chinee," and "mice-eaters," the Chinese were characterized in a 1942 Gallup poll as "hardworking, honest, brave, religious, intelligent, and practical" (Chan 1991: 121). Harold Liu of New York's Chinatown expounded on the improved images of Chinese in the United States:

> In the 1940s for the first time Chinese were accepted by Americans as being friends because at that time, Chinese and Americans were fighting against the Japanese and the Germans and the Nazis. Therefore, all of a sudden, we became part of the American dream. . . . It was just a whole different era and in the community we began to feel very good about ourselves. . . . My own brother went into the service. We were so proud that they were in uniform. (cited in Takaki 1989: 373)

In late 1943, as a gesture of goodwill toward China and of U.S. commitment to democracy, Congress rescinded all Chinese exclusion laws, granted Chinese immigrants the right of naturalization, and provided for the admission of 105 Chinese each year. In 1946, the Luce-Celler bill conferred similar naturalization rights and an immigration quota of 100 to Asian Indians and Filipinos. In contrast, Japanese and Koreans did not receive these same rights until 1952 (Chan 1991: 122). As discussed below, these new rights renewed immigration from Asia and transformed forever the family and community life of Asians in the United States.

Eligibility for naturalization, coupled with President Roosevelt's 1941 Executive Order prohibiting racial discrimination in employment, also spearheaded the socio-economic advancement of the Asian American population. As citizens, qualified Asians were able to secure professional licenses and subsequently to participate in all those economic activities hitherto denied to them as "aliens ineligible for citizenship" (Wong 1980: 520). The right of naturalization also came at a fortuitous time—when defense industries were experiencing an extraordinary boom and were desperately short of human resources. The acute labor shortage; the confinement of the Japanese in relocation camps, creating a sudden vacuum; and the improvement in public images of (non-Japanese) Asians all created employment opportunities for Asians. As the country's industrial base expanded, many Filipino men found jobs in factories, trades, and wholesale and retail sales. Sociologist R. T. Feria (1946–1947) reported that in southern California, the shipyards of Wilmington and San Pedro and the plants of Lockheed, Douglas, and Vultee clamored for Filipino labor. Chinese Americans likewise entered the shipyards and aircraft factories as engineers, technicians, workers, and clerks. Finally able to break away from the Chinatown economy, thousands of laundrymen and waiters rushed to the higher-paying industrial jobs. In Los Angeles, some 300 Chinese laundry workers left their shops to work on the construction of the ship China Victory. In 1943, Chinese constituted approximately 15 percent of the shipyard labor force in the San Francisco Bay Area. They also seized the high-paying jobs in the defense industries at the Seattle-Tacoma Shipbuilding Corporation, the shipyards of Delaware and Mississippi, and the airplane factories on Long Island (Wong 1980: 511–512; Takaki 1989: 374).

Although there exist no detailed statistics on the wartime employment of Asian Americans, fluctuations between the 1940 and 1950 censuses provide a rough indication of changes in their occupational status. According to Ling-chi Wang's analysis of census data, in 1940 only about 1,000 Chinese held professional and technical jobs among 36,000 gainfully employed. Ten years later, some 3,500 held such jobs among 48,000 workers. The majority of these were Chinese male professionals who worked as engineers and technicians in war industries. The war also opened up employment opportunities for Chinese women: the number of women in the labor force increased from 2,800 in 1940 to 8,300 in 1950 (Chan 1991: 122).[3] The majority of these women worked as office clerks in defense industries; the number of Chinese female clerical workers increased from 750 in 1940 to 3,200 in 1950. But others also worked as mechanics and as professionals in private companies. In 1940, 200 Chinese women held professional or technical jobs; in 1950, more than 1,150 did (Yung 1986: 67; Chan 1991: 122).

In sum, World War II changed the economic fortunes of Asians in the United States by opening employment in labor-starved defense industries. This wartime employment opportunity helped many Asian men and women to break down race-based and gender-based occupational barriers and to launch new careers outside their ethnic communities not only during but also after the war (Yung 1986: 67; Chan 1991: 122).

ASIAN AMERICANS AND POSTWAR AMERICA: THE EMERGING MIDDLE CLASS

The fifteen years after World War II marked a period of largely positive change for Asian Americans. By the end of World War II, the U.S. economy had emerged as the preeminent urban industrial economy, generating numerous high-paying semiskilled jobs in the manufacturing sector. Other postwar conditions—the infrastructure development, the housing boom, the increasing U.S. military role around the world, and the expanding role of both the local and federal governments—likewise produced a wealth of high-wage jobs. As is usual during economic boom periods, race relations improved considerably during the postwar years. Legal restrictions based on race were removed due to the relatively affluent times and the growing civil rights movement. As a result of these changes in race relations and the strength of the U.S. economy, significant numbers of U.S.-born Asians—the children of the 1910s and 1920s—became increasingly middle class (Daniels 1988: chap. 7; Mar and Kian 1994: 19–20).

As detailed below, Japanese and Chinese Americans, particularly the women, benefited from the postwar expanding economic opportunities. Although the postwar period was marked by the increasing labor force participation of all U.S. women, Chinese and Japanese women entered the labor force in even greater numbers. By 1960, 47 percent of Japanese American women and 42 percent of Chinese American women were in the labor force, as compared with 34 percent of all U.S. women. In contrast, because few Filipina women immigrated prior to the war, there was not a significant number of American-born Filipino workers entering the postwar labor market. Although some immigrant Filipino workers left farm work as a result of the economic expansion, most remained in low-paying service or manufacturing jobs (Mar and Kim 1994: 23).

The postwar years marked a turning point for Japanese Americans in the labor force. The wartime destruction of their family businesses coupled with the postwar economic expansion moved Japanese Americans away from a community-based economy to one that depended on employment in the general economy (Mar and Kim 1994). As Japan became America's "junior partner" in containing Communism in eastern Asia, the U.S. public perception of Japanese Americans grew correspondingly more favorable. With the lessening of overt discrimination, more Nisei men and women were finally able to use their U.S. education to enter the mainstream labor market—in engineering, medical, sales, and clerical occupations—and to make steady and uninterrupted economic progress. As indicated above, the postwar years registered a sharp increase in the number of Japanese American women in the labor force. This increase reflects not only expanded job opportunities but also women's desire to help their families recover the internment losses, and the movement of Issei and Nisei women out of unpaid family labor (due in large part to the losses of family businesses) and into the general labor force. Whereas Nisei men still encountered discrimination in white-collar work, Nisei women workers were in high demand to fill clerical and civil service positions. Though some—primarily Issei women—still toiled as domestics and garment workers, the majority of second-generation women worked as typists, stenographers, and office clerks (Matsumoto 1989: 121–122; Nakano 1990: 189; Nishi 1995: 122). By 1970, well over half of all working Nisei women were in white-collar professional, managerial, sales, or clerical positions (Glenn 1986: 83–89).

Though the second-generation Chinese Americans also moved away from the traditional prewar occupations, they did so at a slower pace than the Japanese Americans. The greater survival of Chinese ethnic enterprises meant the continuation of employment in low-paying restaurant and garment work, particularly for the aging old-timers and the impoverished immigrants arriving in the 1950s (see below). At the same time, substantial numbers of American-born men and women landed professional and technical jobs, again concentrating in engineering and medical fields (Mar and Kim 1994: 23). Though their progress was temporarily halted during the "Cold War," when Communist China became the despised enemy, Chinese Americans managed to survive and steadily prospered (Chan 1991: 141–142).

In sum, compared to the pre-World War II period, the postwar years brought unprecedented economic and social progress for Asian American women and men. U.S.-born Asians, particularly Chinese and Japanese, were able for the first time to find employment in the growing professional and technical occupations. But we must not overemphasize the extent of this progress. The tide did turn; Asian Americans did benefit. On the other hand, many Asian Americans continued to be denied access to high-paying craft, manufacturing, and construction jobs (Mar and Kim 1994: 23). Another recurrent problem was discrimination in earnings. According to a 1965 report published by the California Trade Employment Practices Commission, for every $51 earned by a white male Californian, Japanese males earned $43 and Chinese males $38—even though Chinese and Japanese men did become slightly better educated than the white majority. No corresponding figures were reported for women (Daniels 1988: 315). Finally, well-qualified Japanese and Chinese Americans continued to be passed over for promotions to administrative and supervisory positions (Kitano and Daniels 1988: 47).

New Arrivals: The "Separated" Wives, War Brides, and Refugees

Unlike previous immigration flows, Asian immigration during the postwar period (1946–1965) was overwhelmingly female (Chan 1991: 140). The partial liberalization of immigration policies permitted many "split households" to be reunited and encouraged many single Asian men to rush "home" to find wives (Kitano 1991b: 199; Wong 1995: 65). Of great importance to the Asian American community—particularly to the Chinese American community—was the 1946 act permitting Asian spouses of U.S. citizens to skirt restrictive immigration quotas by entering as "nonquota immigrants" (Lee 1956: 14). Another important piece of immigration legislation was the War Brides Act of 1945. Amended in 1947 to include veterans of Asian ancestry, this act gave many Asian GIs a three-year window of opportunity to marry in Asia and to bring their brides back to the United States, where they started families. Together, these immigration policies brought an unprecedented number of Asian women—mostly "separated" wives and war brides—to the United States and in so doing changed forever the previously male-dominated bachelor societies (Lee 1956; Hsiao 1992: 153).

Between 1945 and 1953, more than 12,000 Chinese immigrants entered the United States, of whom 89 percent were women (Lee 1956: 15). This female dominance continued through the 1950s, when women constituted from 50 to 90 percent of the Chinese entries during particular years (Chan 1991: 140). Among this wave of immigrant women were older wives who had been separated from their Chinese American husbands for as many as fifteen years. The end of the war and changes in immigration policies finally allowed them to join their husbands in the United States (Lee 1956: 14). Despite their nonquota immigration status, these women, at the point of entry, were still harassed, detained, and threatened with deportation. In 1948, forty-one-year-old Wong Loy attempted to jump from the fourteenth floor of an immigration building when told that she would be deported. That same year, thirty-two-year-old Leong Bick Ha hanged herself from a shower pipe after having been detained for three months and performing poorly at her interrogation. In protest, 100 Chinese women detainees went on a hunger strike. Confronted with such adverse publicity as well as pressure from the American Civil Liberties Union and Chinese American organizations, the U.S. Immigration

Service finally agreed to stop detainment procedures and to settle an immigrant's right of entry at the point of departure instead of at the point of entry (Yung 1986: 81). Thousands of Chinese women were also admitted under the War Brides Act. In fact, Chinese women were the main group admitted under this act (Chan 1991: 140). Facing a 3-to-1 male-female ratio in the Chinese community, some 6,000 Chinese American soldiers married women in China and brought them back to the United States before the act expired on December 30, 1949. "Since the War Brides Act," testified Lim P. Lee before a Congressional committee hearing in 1947, "every ship arriving from Hong Kong or Canton carried about 200 to 250 war brides and their dependents" (quoted in Takaki 1989: 417). As a result of this massive influx of immigrants, the Chinese population in the United States rose substantially from 77,000 to 117,000 during the 1940s, a jump of just over 50 percent (Daniels 1988: 191). The women's arrival also balanced the sex ratio: it became 1.3 to 1 by 1960, a substantial drop from the 2.8 to 1 in 1940 (Wong 1980: 520–521; Daniels 1988: 191; Chan 1991: 140).

Whereas Chinese war brides married mainly coethnics, Japanese, Korean, and Filipino wives of GIs more often than not married non-Asian men. Most of these women entered not under the War Brides Act but as nonquota immigrants (i.e., as spouses of U.S. citizens). During the 1950s, 80 percent of the more than 45,000 Japanese immigrants were women, almost all of them wives of U.S. servicemen whom they had met during the postwar U.S. occupation of Japan (Nishi 1995: 100). These women scattered all over the United States, leading isolated lives in the hometowns of their husbands (Strauss 1954; Schriepp and Yui 1955). U.S. military presence in Korea likewise produced an influx of Korean immigrants. Between the years 1950 and 1964, more than 15,000 Koreans were admitted to the United States, almost 40 percent of whom came as G.I. wives (Min 1995: 202). The postwar years also brought a large number of Filipino immigrants. The arrival of 16,000 women—almost all wives of U.S. servicemen (including a sizable number of Filipino Americans serving in the U.S. Navy)—revitalized the Filipino American community and reduced the ratio of Filipino men to women to 3.5 to 1 (Agbayani-Siewert and Revilla 1995). Many scholars have documented the cultural and marital adjustment of Asian military wives of non-Asian men (Strauss 1954; Schnepp and Yui 1955; Kim 1972, 1977).

The male-dominant communities of Asian America were ill prepared in many ways for the influx of immigrants. Though the arrival of women and children transformed Asian America into more gender-balanced, family-oriented communities, it also exacerbated growing problems of substandard housing, underemployment, poor health conditions, and inadequate social services. Arriving in the late 1940s and early 1950s, Asian women discovered that it was well-nigh impossible—due to their limited means and race-based discrimination—to find housing outside the ethnic ghettos. Thus, for a time, many of the newly formed or reconstituted families were packed into barely furnished one-or two-room apartments, many of which had up to then housed mainly single men (Yung 1986; Chan 1991: 141). Rose Hum Lee (1956: 16) reported that in the San Francisco-Oakland area, many Chinese families were forced to live in one hotel room or hastily converted bachelors' quarters with limited kitchen and bath facilities.

With their meager incomes, Asian men also had a difficult time providing for their new families. To supplement their husbands' wages, many newly arrived women worked in Chinatown restaurants and sweatshops, where they labored long hours for less than minimum wage, received no overtime or health and vacation benefits, and toiled under dangerous and unsanitary conditions. The life of Dong Zem Ping, as documented in *Sewing Woman,* a film by Arthur Dong (1982), exemplifies the hardships experienced by many Chinatown seamstresses in the post-World War II era. Married off at age thirteen to a Gold Mountain man, Dong had no contact with her husband during the Sino-Japanese War and was able to join him in the United States after the war only by posing as a war bride. With limited English language and job skills, Dong could find work only as a seamstress. For the rest of her working life in the United States, she was bound to her sewing machine:

> I can still recall the times when I had one foot on the pedal and another one on an improvised rocker, rocking one son to sleep while the other was tied to my back. Many times I would accidentally sew my finger instead of the fabric because one child screamed or because I was falling asleep on the job. (quoted in Yung 1986: 81)

Confronted with language barriers, cultural differences, limited economic opportunities, and the sheer pressure of daily survival, many post-World War II wives were disillusioned and disappointed with their new lives—and by extension, with their husbands. The "separated wives"—those older women who had lived apart from their husbands for many years—had the most difficult time. Though they had been married for years, these women had seen their husbands only briefly during the husbands' periodic visits; and many had not seen their husbands for eighteen to twenty-five years. As long as the husbands provided economically for the family and the wives reared the children, the prolonged separation did not seem to threaten this "split-household" arrangement. Once reunited, however, spouses complained of incompatibility, conflicting goals and values, and "unreasonable" sexual demands. Money was a source of constant friction. Many wives were deeply disappointed in their husbands' menial jobs or the type of business they operated. They could not accept the minimal earnings, the long workdays, and the physical labor their husbands invested in these modest enterprises. "I was so . . . shocked by our home," declared Lee Wai Lan, who reunited with her husband and four children in 1946, "a filthy house with a small hole between two bricks for a toilet. I wanted to die." Determined to make it in the United States, Lee found a job washing dishes and peeling vegetables in a Chinese restaurant, rented a small house for her family, and later saved and borrowed enough money to start her own restaurant (Yung 1986: 81). Other disillusioned wives returned to China. One wife flatly declared that she had a return plane ticket and would leave alone if her husband did not sell his business at once and reestablish himself in China (Lee 1956: 23).

In these reconstituted families, husbands and wives had to renegotiate their roles and institute a new gender division of labor. In some instances, a more egalitarian division of labor emerged. For example, the domestic skills men had been forced to learn in their wives' absence—cooking, ironing, grocery shopping—

were still put to use (see Hondagneu-Sotelo 1994: 113). On the other hand, the habits some migrant husbands acquired during the separation—the drinking and gambling—stressed the family's budget and caused considerable friction between the spouses (Nakano 1990: 38). The reconstituted family also threatened the authority of these "separated" wives. During the prolonged absence of their husbands, these women had assumed total family governance and spent as they deemed best the periodic but large remittances from their husbands. In the United States, these women resented having to share or relinquish their authority to their husbands, especially in the matter of household finances (Yung 1986).

Given the brief courtship period, the war brides, like the "separated" wives, were not well acquainted with their husbands. However, younger than the latter by at least ten years, these wives had an easier time adapting to life in the United States. In a study of war wives, Rose Hum Lee reported that the more "modern" wives wore Western-style clothes, styled their hair, adopted American names, and walked arm in arm or holding hands with their husbands in public. In these families, wives relied on husbands' "superior" knowledge of American culture and accepted the latter's choice and taste in home furnishings, clothing, and personal accessories. Following the patterns of the older immigrant men, some of the younger husbands assumed more domestic responsibilities, such as buying groceries and performing household chores. In fact, many husbands taught wives how to cook—a skill they had learned as bachelors and as restaurant cooks or kitchen helpers (Lee 1956: 20). However, in the marriages that failed to thrive, the husband, with his greater social, economic, and sexual freedom, could escape through alcoholism, gambling, extramarital relations, or prolonged absence. In contrast, as women, and as newly arrived immigrants who possessed limited English-language and job skills, their wives had fewer forms of escapism available to them and often had to confine their frustrations, anxieties, and hostilities within the family (Lee 1956: 21).

The influx of women immigrants in the late 1940s produced a Chinese American baby boom. Like the second-generation Asian Americans of the 1930s and 1940s, many young Chinese American women growing up in the 1950s experienced race-based and culture-based gender discrimination. In many Chinese families, sons continued to receive preferential treatment over daughters. "When we were growing up," complained Bettie Luke Kan of Seattle of the double standards in her family,

> Marge and I had to work part-time, applying for scholarships, and pay our own way. But with Robert [brother], it was like, "Do you need more money?" It was just constant. He could go to the movies, play with friends, go downtown, and have spending money. Marge and I—in those growing up years when we had the grocery store—we were allowed one movie a year on New Year's Day; that was it. (cited in Yung 1986: 88)

These young women also had to combat sexist stereotypes of Asian American women in the media, particularly the image of the sexy, submissive prostitute popularized by Nancy Kwan in the 1960 film *The World of Suzie Wong*. Besieged by mass media images that constructed and reinforced U.S. standards of beauty as "blond, blue eyed, and big breasted," young Chinese American women of the

1950s received a message of inferiority from the larger society as strong as that which they received at home (Yung 1986: 88).

Political refugees composed the final group of Asians who came in under special legislation during the post-World War II period. After the Communist victory in China in 1949, some 23,000 highly educated and well-trained Chinese men and women were granted political asylum in the United States under the 1948 Displaced Persons Act and the 1953 Refugee Relief Act. Primarily Mandarin speakers from central and northern China, these refugees were some of China's brightest intellectuals, most of whom were from well-to-do families (Chan 1991: 141). Their educational background, ability to speak English, and previous exposure to Western ideas eased their integration into U.S. society. Due to the high demand for their scientific and technical skills, these men and women found work in academic and professional fields. Because of dialect and class differences, this new group bought homes in the suburbs away from the impoverished Chinatowns and seldom associated with the old-time Chinese immigrants (Yung 1986: 82). Their presence augmented the Chinese American middle class and further bifurcated the Chinese American community along class lines.

CONCLUSION

World War II and the postwar years brought significant changes to the lives of Asians in the United States, all of which led to shifts in the roles of men and women. The wartime internment, for example, resulted in the subversion of male dominance over women and parental authority over children in the Japanese American communities. The internment years stripped Issei men of their role as the family breadwinner and transferred some of the power and status to their U.S.-born children. The camp experience also decreased male dominance over women, as older Issei women gained more leisure time and younger Nisei women found unprecedented job opportunities in the camp enterprises and service divisions. After the war, these role changes persisted as Issei men faced limited job opportunities while their college-educated children moved into predominantly white-collar, managerial, and professional occupations. In other Asian American communities, particularly the Chinese American community, the influx of women and the subsequent (re)establishment of conjugal families "created havoc, throwing the male dominant community out of kilter" (Hsiao 1992: 152). As the Chinatown community changed from a community of aging bachelors to a community of young families, husbands and wives had to renegotiate their gender roles—a process that led at times to a more egalitarian division of labor. Although the postwar immigrants brought new vitality into Asian American communities, family separation was to remain common until the immigration reform of 1965.

NOTES

1. Manzanar Camp, located in Owens, California, was the first of the permanent concentration camps to open; it began operation in 1942.

2. In Hawai'i, just over 1,400, or less than 1 percent, of the territory's Japanese were interned (Okihiro 1991).
3. Xiaojian Zhao (in press) has estimated that by 1943, about 5,000 Chinese Americans were working (or had worked) for defense-related industries in the San Francisco Bay Area and that between 500 and 600 of them were women. Most of these working women were second-generation daughters of immigrant women.

REFERENCES

Agbayani-Siewert, P., and L. Revilla (1995). Filipino Americans. In P. G. Min, ed., *Asian Americans: Contemporary Trends and Issues,* 134–168. Thousand Oaks, Calif.: Sage.

Broom, L., and R. Riemer (1949). *Removal and Return: The Socio-economic Effects of the War on Japanese Americans.* Berkeley: University of California Press.

Chan, S. (1991). *Asian Americans: An Interpretive History.* Boston: Twayne.

Chinn, T. (1989). *Bridging the Pacific: San Francisco Chinatown and Its People.* San Francisco: Chinese Historical Society of America.

Crenshaw, K. (1989). Demarginalizing the intersection of race and sex: A black feminist critique of antidiscrimination doctrine, feminist theory and antiracist politics. In *University of Chicago Legal Forum: Feminism in the Law: Theory, Practice, and Criticism,* 139–167. Chicago: University of Chicago Press.

Daniels, R. (1988). *Asian America: Chinese and Japanese in the United States since 1850.* Seattle: University of Washington Press.

Espíritu, Y. L. (1992). *Asian American Panethnicity: Bridging Institutions and Identities.* Philadelphia: Temple University Press.

Feria, R. T. (1946–1947). War and the status of Filipino immigrants. *Sociology and Social Research* 31: 48–53.

Gensui, N. (1976). Footprints: Poetry of the American relocation camp experience. Translated by Constance Hayashi and Keiho Yamanaka. *Amerasia Journal* 3: 115–117.

Glenn, E. N. (1986). *Issei, Nisei, War Bride: Three Generations of Japanese American Women at Domestic Service.* Philadelphia: Temple University Press.

Hondagneu-Sotelo, P. (1994). *Gendered Transition: Mexican Experiences in Immigration.* Berkeley: University of California Press.

Houston, J. W., and J. D. Houston (1973). *Farewell to Manzanar.* San Francisco: Houghton Mifflin.

Hsiao, R. Y. (1992). Facing the incurable: Patriarchy in *Eat a Bowl of Tea.* In S. G. Lim and A. Ling, eds., *Reading the Literatures of Asian America,* 151–162. Philadelphia: Temple University Press.

Kim, E. (1982). *Asian American Literature: An Introduction to the Writings and Their Social Context.* Philadelphia: Temple University Press.

Kitagawa, D. (1967). *Issei and Nisei: The Internment Years.* New York: Seabury.

Kitano, H.H.L. (1991a). The effects of the evacuation on the Japanese Americans. In R. Daniels, S. C. Taylor, and H.H.L. Kitano, eds., *Japanese Americans: From Relocation to Redress,* 151–162. Seattle: University of Washington Press.

———— (1991b). *Race Relations.* Englewood Cliffs, N.J.: Prentice Hall.

Kitano, H.H.L., and R. Daniels (1988). *Asian Americans: Emerging Minorities.* Englewood Cliffs, N.J.: Prentice Hall.

Kwong, P. (1979). *Chinatown, N.Y.: Labor and Politics, 1930–1950.* New York: Monthly Review.

Lee, R. H. (1956). The recent immigrant Chinese families of the San Francisco-Oakland area. *Marriage and Family Living* 18: 14–24.

Lowe, L. (1996). *Immigrant Acts: On Asian American Cultural Politics.* Durham, N.C.: Duke University Press.

Mar, D., and M. Kim (1994). Historical trends. In P. Ong, ed., *The State of Asian Pacific America: Economic Diversity, Issues, and Policies,* 13–30. Los Angeles: LEAP Asian Pacific

American Public Policy Institute and University of California at Los Angeles, Asian American Studies Center.

Matsui, R. (1987). Speech in the House of Representatives on the 442 Bill for redress and reparations, September 17. *Cong. Rec. 7584.* Washington, D.C.: Government Printing Office.

Matsumoto, V. (1989). Nisei women and resettlement during World War II. In Asian Women United of California, ed., *Making Waves: An Anthology of Writing By and About Asian American Women,* 115–126. Boston: Beacon.

Min, P. G. (1995). Korean Americans. In P. G. Min, ed., *Asian Americans: Contemporary Trends and Issues,* 199–231. Thousand Oaks, Calif.: Sage.

Modell, J., ed. (1973). *The Kikuchi Diary: Chronicle from an American Concentration Camp.* Urbana: University of Illinois Press.

Nakano, M. T. (1990). *Japanese American Women: Three Generations, 1890–1990.* Berkeley, Calif.: Mina.

Nishi, S. M. (1995). Japanese Americans. In P. G. Min, ed., *Asian Americans: Contemporary Trends and Issues,* 95–133. Thousand Oaks, Calif.: Sage.

Okihiro, G. Y. (1994). *Margins and Mainstreams: Asians in American History and Culture.* Seattle: University of Washington Press.

Schnepp, G., and A. M. Yui (1955). Cultural and marital adjustment of Japanese war brides. *American Journal of Sociology* 61: 48–50.

Strauss, A. (1954). Strain and harmony in American-Japanese war bride marriages. *Journal of Marriage and Family Living* 16: 99–106.

Takaki, R. (1989). *Strangers from a Different Shore: A History of Asian Americans.* Boston: Little, Brown.

Wong, M. (1980). Changes in socioeconomic status of the Chinese male population in the United States from 1960 to 1970. *International Migration Review* 14: 511–524.

Yung, J. (1986). *Chinese Women in America: A Pictorial Essay.* Seattle: University of Washington Press.

——— (1990). *Unbinding the Feet, Unbinding Their Lives: Social Change for Chinese Women in San Francisco, 1902–1945.* Ph.D. dissertation, University of California, Berkeley.

Zhao, X. (in press). Chinese American women defense workers in World War II. *California History.*

SUCCESS STORY OF ONE MINORITY GROUP IN U.S.*

U.S. News and World Report, 1966

At a time when Americans are awash in worry over the plight of racial minorities—one such minority, the nation's 300,000 Chinese-Americans, is winning wealth and respect by dint of its own hard work. In any Chinatown from San Francisco to New York, you discover youngsters at grips with their studies. Crime and delinquency are found to be further minor in scope. Still being taught in Chinatown is the old idea that people should depend on their own efforts—not a welfare check—in order to reach America's "promised land."

Reported from SAN FRANCISCO, LOS ANGELES and NEW YORK. Visit Chinatown U.S.A. and you find an important racial minority pulling itself up from hardship and discrimination to become a model of self-respect and achievement in today's America. At a time when it is being proposed that hundreds of billions be spent to uplift Negroes and other minorities, the nation's 300,000 Chinese-Americans are getting ahead on their own, with no help from anyone else.

LOW RATE OF CRIME

In crime-ridden cities, Chinese districts turn up as islands of peace and stability. Of 4.7 million arrests reported to the Federal Bureau of Investigation in 1965,

*We include this piece as a historical document to pinpoint when the currently widespread concept of Asian Americans as the model minority was conceived. We strongly disagree with the contents of the article, since it was based on inaccurate data and analyses of Asian American communities across the nation, and thus presents an extremely distorted picture of Asian American realities. The article was published in 1966, when the civil rights movement was calling attention nationwide to the second-class citizenship of racial minorities in American society. Today, many historians and social scientists agree that the message in the piece—namely, that the Asian American case demonstrates that a racial minority can "make it" in America with hard work and sacrifice—was designed to scold other disenfranchised racial minorities, especially vocal African Americans, by stating: if Asians can achieve so much with so little in this society, other racial minorities could succeed if they tried harder; if they fail, the fault lies in their lack of initiative and not in the deep structural inequalities based on race.

only 1,293 involved persons of Chinese ancestry. A Protestant pastor in New York City's Chinatown said: "This is the safest place in the city." Few Chinese-Americans are getting welfare handouts—or even want them. Within a tight network of family and loyalties, relatives continue to help each other. Mrs. Jean Ma, publisher of a Chinese-language newspaper in Los Angeles, explained: "We're a big family. If someone has trouble, usually it can be solved within the family. There is no need to bother anyone else. And nobody will respect any member of the family who does not work and who just plays around."

Today, Chinese-American parents are worrying somewhat about their young people. Yet, in every city, delinquency in Chinatown is minor compared with what goes on around it.

STRICT DISCIPLINE

Even in the age of television and fast automobiles, Chinese-American children are expected to attend school faithfully, work hard at their studies—and stay out of trouble. Spanking is seldom used, but supervision and verbal discipline are strict.

A study of San Francisco's Chinatown noted that "if school performance is poor and the parents are told, there is an immediate improvement." And, in New York City, schoolteachers reportedly are competing for posts in schools with large numbers of Chinese-American children.

Recently Dr. Richard T. Sollenberger, professor of psychology at Mount Holyoke College, made a study of New York City's Chinatown and concluded: "There's a strong incentive for young people to behave." As one informant said, "When you walk around the streets of Chinatown, you have a hundred cousins watching you."

What you find, behind this remarkable group of Americans, is a story of adversity and prejudice that would shock those now complaining about the hardships endured by today's Negroes. It was during California's gold rush that large numbers of Chinese began coming to America. On the developing frontier, they worked in mines, on railroads and in other hard labor. Moving into cities, where the best occupations were closed to them, large numbers became laundrymen and cooks because of the shortage of women in the West.

PAST HANDICAPS

High value was placed on Chinese willingness to work long hours for low pay. Yet Congress, in 1882, passed an Exclusion Act denying naturalization to Chinese immigrants and forbidding further influx of laborers. A similar act in 1924, aimed primarily at the Japanese, prohibited laborers from bringing in wives.

In California, the first legislature slapped foreign miners with a tax aimed at getting Chinese out of the gold-mining business. That state's highest court ruled Chinese could not testify against whites in court. Chinese-Americans could not own land in California, and no corporation or public agency could employ them. These curbs, in general, applied also to Japanese-Americans, another Oriental minority that has survived discrimination to win a solid place in the nation.

The curbs, themselves, have been discarded in the last quarter century. And, in recent years, immigration quotas have been enlarged with 8,800 Chinese allowed to enter the country this year. As a result, the number of persons of Chinese ancestry living in the United States is believed to have almost doubled since 1950. Today, as in the past, most Chinese are to be found in Hawai'i, California and New York. Because of ancient emphasis on family and village, most of those on the U.S. mainland trace their ancestry to communities southwest of Canton.

HOW CHINESE GET AHEAD

Not all Chinese-Americans are rich. Many, especially recent arrivals from Hong Kong, are poor and cannot speak English. But the large majority are moving ahead by applying the traditional virtues of hard work, thrift and morality.

Success stories have been recorded in business, science, architecture, politics and other professions. Dr. Sollenberger said of New York's Chinatown: "The Chinese people here will work at anything. I know of some who were scholars in China and are now working as waiters in restaurants. That's a stopgap for them, of course, but the point is that they're willing to do something, they don't sit around moaning."

The biggest and most publicized of all Chinatowns is in San Francisco. Since 1960, the inflow of immigrants has raised the Chinese share of San Francisco's population from 4.9 percent to 5.7 percent. Altogether 42,600 residents of Chinese ancestry were reported in San Francisco last year.

SHIFT TO SUBURBS

As Chinese-Americans gain in affluence, many move to the suburbs. But about 30,000 persons live in the 25 blocks of San Francisco's Chinatown. Sixty-three percent of these are foreign-born, including many who are being indoctrinated by relatives in the American way of life.

Irvin Lum, an official of the San Francisco Federal Savings and Loan Community House, said: "We follow the custom of being good to our relatives. There is not a very serious problem with our immigrants. We're a people of ability, adaptable and easy to satisfy in material wants. I know of a man coming here from China who was looked after by his sister's family, worked in Chinatown for two years, then opened a small restaurant of his own." Problems among newcomers stir worries, however. A minister said: "Many are in debt when they arrive. They have a language problem. They are used to a rural culture, and they have a false kind of expectation."

A youth gang of foreign-born Chinese, known as "the Bugs" or "Tong San Tsai," clashes occasionally with a gang of Chinese-American youngsters. And one group of Chinese-American teenagers was broken up after stealing as much as $5,800 a week in burglaries this year.

Yet San Francisco has seen no revival of the "tong wars" or opium dens that led to the organizing of a "Chinese squad" of policemen in 1875. The last trouble between Chinese clans or "tongs" was before World War II. The special squad was abolished in 1956.

Streets are Safer

A University of California team making a three-year study of Chinatown in San Francisco reported its impression "that Chinatown streets are safer than most other parts of the city," despite the fact that it is one of the most densely populated neighborhoods in the United States. In 1965, not one San Francisco Chinese, young or old, was charged with murder, manslaughter, rape or an offense against wife or children. Chinese accounted for only two adult cases out of twenty-five of assault with a deadly weapon. Only one of San Francisco's Chinese youths, who comprise 17 percent of the city's high-school enrollment, was among 118 juveniles arrested last year for assault with a deadly weapon. Meantime, 25 percent of the city's semifinalists in the California state scholarship competition were Chinese.

Most Chinese-Americans continue to send their youngsters to Chinese schools for one or two hours a day so they can learn Chinese history, culture and, in some cases, language. A businessman said: "I feel my kids are Americans, which is a tremendous asset. But they're also Chinese, which is another great asset. I want them to have and keep the best of both cultures."

Much of the same picture is found in mainland America's other big Chinatowns, Los Angeles and New York.

Riots of 1871

Los Angeles has a memory of riots in 1871 when white mobs raged through the Chinese section. Twenty-three Chinese were hanged, beaten, shot, or stabbed to death.

Today, 25,000 persons of Chinese ancestry live in Los Angeles County, 20,000 in the city itself. About 5,000 alien Chinese from Hong Kong and Formosa are believed to be in southern California.

In Los Angeles, as elsewhere, Chinese-Americans are worrying about their children. Superior Judge Delbert E. Wong said: "Traditionally, the family patriarch ruled the household, and the other members of the family obeyed and followed without questioning his authority. As the Chinese become more Westernized, women leave the home to work and the younger generation finds greater mobility in seeking employment, we see greater problems within the family unit, and a corresponding increase in crime and divorce."

A Chinese-American clergyman complained that "the second- and third-generation Chinese feel more at home with Caucasians. They don't know how to act around the older Chinese any more because they don't understand them."

The Family Unit

On the other hand Victor Wong, president of the Chinese Consolidated Benevolent Association in Los Angeles, said: "Basically, the Chinese are good citizens. The parents always watch out for the children, train them, send them to school and make them stay home after school to study. When they go visiting it is as a family group. A young Chinese doesn't have much chance to go out on his own and get into trouble."

A high-ranking police official in Los Angeles found little evidence of growing trouble among Chinese. He reported: "Our problems with the Chinese are at a minimum. This probably is due to strict parental supervision. There is still a tradition of respect for parents."

New York City, in 1960, had a population of 32,831 persons of Chinese ancestry. Estimates today run considerably higher, with immigrants coming in at the rate of 200 or 300 a month.

Many Chinese have moved to various parts of the city and to the suburbs. But newcomers tend to settle in Chinatown and families of eight and ten have been found living in two-room apartments. "The housing shortage here is worse than in Harlem," one Chinese-American said. Altogether, about 20,000 persons are believed living in the eight-block area of New York's Chinatown at present. The head of the Chinatown Planning Council said recently that, while most Chinese are still reluctant to accept public welfare, somewhat more are applying for it than in the past. "We are trying to let Chinese know that accepting public welfare is not necessarily the worst thing in the world," he said.

However, a Chinese-American banker in New York took this view: "There are at least sixty associations whose main purpose is to help our own people. We believe welfare should be used only as a last resort." A sizable number of Chinese-Americans who could move out if they wanted to are staying in New York's Chinatown, not because of fears of discrimination on the outside, but because they prefer their own people and culture. And Chinatown, despite its proximity to the Bowery, remains a haven of law and order. Dr. Sollenberger said: "If I had a daughter, I'd rather her live in Chinatown than any place else in New York City." A police lieutenant said: "You don't find any Chinese locked up for robbery, rape or vagrancy."

There has been some rise in Chinese-American delinquency in recent years. In part, this is attributed to the fact that the ratio of children in Chinatown's total population is going up as more women arrive and more families are started.

Even so, the proportion of Chinese-American youngsters getting into difficulty remains low. School buildings used by large numbers of Chinese are described as the cleanest in New York. Public recreational facilities amount to only one small park, but few complaints are heard.

Efforts at Progress

Over all, what observers are finding in America's Chinatowns are a thrifty, law-abiding and industrious people, ambitious to make progress on their own. In Los Angeles, a social worker said:

> If you had several hundred thousand Chinese-Americans subjected to the same economic and social pressures that confront Negroes in major cities, you would

have a good deal of unrest among them. At the same time, it must be recognized that the Chinese and other Orientals in California were faced with even more prejudice than faces the Negro today. We haven't stuck Negroes in concentration camps, for instance, as we did the Japanese in World War II. The Orientals came back, and today they have established themselves as strong contributors to the health of the whole community.

The "Four Prisons" and the Movements of Liberation

Asian American Activism from the 1960s to the 1990s

Glenn Omatsu

According to Ali Shariati, an Iranian philosopher, each of us exists within four prisons.[1] First is the prison imposed on us by history and geography; from this confinement, we can escape only by gaining a knowledge of science and technology. Second is the prison of history; our freedom comes when we understand how historical forces operate. The third prison is our society's social and class structure; from this prison, only a revolutionary ideology can provide the way to liberation. The final prison is the self. Each of us is composed of good and evil elements, and we must each choose between them.

The analysis of our four prisons provides a way of understanding the movements that swept across America in the 1960s and molded the consciousness of one generation of Asian Americans. The movements were struggles for liberation from many prisons. They were struggles that confronted the historical forces of racism, poverty, war, and exploitation. They were struggles that generated new ideologies, based mainly on the teachings and actions of Third World leaders. And they were struggles that redefined human values—the values that shape how people live their daily lives and interact with each other. Above all, they were struggles that transformed the lives of "ordinary" people as they confronted the prisons around them.

For Asian Americans, these struggles profoundly changed our communities. They spawned numerous grassroots organizations. They created an extensive network of student organizations and Asian American Studies classes. They recovered buried cultural traditions and produced a new generation of writers, poets, and artists. But most importantly, the struggles deeply affected Asian American consciousness. They redefined racial and ethnic identity, promoted new ways of thinking about communities, and challenged prevailing notions of power and authority.

Yet, in the two decades that have followed, scholars have reinterpreted the movements in narrower ways. I learned about this reinterpretation when I attended a class recently in Asian American Studies at UCLA. The professor described the period from the late 1950s to the early 1970s as a single epoch involving the persistent efforts of racial minorities and their white supporters to secure civil rights. Young Asian Americans, the professor stated, were swept into this campaign and by later anti-war protests to assert their own racial identity. The most important influence on Asian Americans during this period was Dr. Martin Luther King Jr., who inspired them to demand access to policy makers and initiate advocacy programs for their own communities. Meanwhile, students and professors fought to legitimize Asian American Studies in college curricula and for representation of Asians in American society. The lecture was cogent, tightly organized, and well received by the audience of students—many of them new immigrants or the children of new immigrants. There was only one problem: the reinterpretation was wrong on every aspect.

Those who took part in the mass struggles of the 1960s and early 1970s will know that the birth of the Asian American movement coincided not with the initial campaign for civil rights but with the later demand for black liberation; that the leading influence was not Martin Luther King Jr., but Malcolm X; that the focus of a generation of Asian American activists was not on asserting racial pride but on reclaiming a tradition of militant struggle by earlier generations; that the movement was not centered on the aura of racial identity but embraced fundamental questions of oppression and power; that the movement consisted of not only college students but large numbers of community forces, including the elderly, workers, and high school youth; and that the main thrust was not one of seeking legitimacy and representation within American society but the larger goal of liberation.

It may be difficult for a new generation—raised on the Asian American code words of the 1980s stressing "advocacy," "access," "legitimacy," "empowerment," and "assertiveness"—to understand the urgency of Malcolm X's demand for freedom "by any means necessary," Mao's challenge to "serve the people," the slogans of "power to the people" and "self-determination," the principles of "mass line" organizing and "united front" work, or the conviction that people—not elites—make history. But these ideas galvanized thousands of Asian Americans and reshaped our communities. And it is these concepts that we must grasp to understand the scope and intensity of our movement and what it created.

But are these concepts relevant to Asian Americans today? In our community—where new immigrants and refugees constitute the majority of Asian Americans—can we find a legacy from the struggles of two decades ago? Are the ideas of the movement alive today, or have they atrophied into relics—the curiosities of a bygone era of youthful and excessive idealism?

By asking these questions, we, as Asian Americans, participate in a larger national debate: the reevaluation of the impact of the 1960s on American society today. This debate is occurring all around us: in sharp exchanges over "family values" and the status of women and gays in American society; in clashes in schools over curricular reform and multiculturalism; in differences among policy makers over the urban crisis and approaches to rebuilding Los Angeles and other inner cities after the 1992 uprisings; and continuing reexaminations of U.S. involvement in Indochina more than two decades ago and the relevance of that war to U.S. military intervention in Iraq, Somalia, and Bosnia.

What happened in the 1960s that made such an impact on America? Why do discussions about that decade provoke so much emotion today? And do the movements of the 1960s serve as the same controversial reference point for Asian Americans?

THE UNITED STATES DURING THE 1960S

In recent years, the movements of the 1960s have come under intense attack. One national bestseller, Allan Bloom's *Closing of the American Mind,* criticizes the movements for undermining the bedrock of Western thought.[2] According to Bloom, nothing positive resulted from the mass upheavals of the 1960s. He singles out black studies and affirmative action programs and calls for eliminating them from universities.

Activists who have continued political work provide contrasting assessments. Their books include Todd Gitlin's *The Sixties: Years of Hope, Days of Rage;* James Miller's *"Democracy Is in the Streets": From Port Huron to the Siege of Chicago;* Ronald Fraser's *1968: A Student Generation in Revolt;* Tom Hayden's *Reunion: A Memoir;* Tariq Ali's *Street Fighting Years;* George Katsiaficas's *The Imagination of the New Left: A Global Analysis of 1968;* and special issues of various journals, including *Witness, Socialist Review,* and *Radical America.*

However, as Winifred Breines states in an interesting review essay titled "Whose New Left?" most of the retrospectives have been written by white male activists from elite backgrounds, and reproduce their relationship to these movements.[3] Their accounts tend to divide the period into two phases: the "good" phase of the early 1960s, characterized by participatory democracy; followed by the post-1968 phase, when movement politics "degenerated" into violence and sectarianism.

"Almost all books about the New Left note a turning point or an ending in 1968 when the leadership of the movement turned toward militancy and violence and SDS [Students for a Democratic Society] as an organization was collapsing," Breines observes. The retrospectives commonly identify the key weaknesses of the movements as the absence of effective organization, the lack of discipline, and utopian thinking. Breines disagrees with these interpretations:

> The movement was not simply unruly and undisciplined; it was experimenting with antihierarchical organizational forms. . . . There were many centers of action in the movement, many actions, many interpretations, many visions, many experiences. There was no [organizational] unity because each group, region, campus, commune, collective, and demonstration developed differently, but all shared in a spontaneous opposition to racism and inequality, the war in Vietnam, and the repressiveness of American social norms and culture, including centralization and hierarchy.[4]

Breines believes that the most important contributions of activists were their moral urgency, their emphasis on direct action, their focus on community building, and their commitment to mass democracy.

Similarly, Sheila Collins in *The Rainbow Challenge,* a book focusing on the Jesse Jackson presidential campaign of 1984 and the formation of the National Rainbow Coalition, assesses the movements of the sixties very positively.[5] She contends that the Jackson campaign was built on the grassroots organizing experience of activists who emerged from the struggles for civil rights, women's liberation, peace and social justice, and community building during the sixties. Moreover, activists' participation in these movements shaped their vision of America, which, in turn, became the basis for the platform of the Rainbow Coalition twenty years later.

According to Collins, the movements that occurred in the United States in the sixties were also part of a worldwide trend, a trend Latin American theologians call the era of the "eruption of the poor" into history. In America, the revolt of the "politically submerged" and "economically marginalized" posed a major ideological challenge to ruling elites:

> The civil rights and black power movement exploded several dominant assumptions about the nature of American society, thus challenging the cultural hegemony of the white ruling elite and causing everyone else in the society to redefine their relationship to centers of power, creating a groundswell of support for radical democratic participation in every aspect of institutional life.[6]

Collins contends that the mass movements created a "crisis of legitimation" for ruling circles. This crisis, she believes, was "far more serious than most historians— even those of the left—have credited it with being."

Ronald Fraser also emphasizes the ideological challenge raised by the movements due to their mass, democratic character and their "disrespect for arbitrary and exploitative authority." In *1968: A Student Generation in Revolt,* Fraser explains how these concepts influenced one generation of activists:

> [T]he anti-authoritarianism challenged almost every shibboleth of Western society. Parliamentary democracy, the authority of presidents . . . and [the policies of] governments to further racism, conduct imperialist wars or oppress sectors of the population at home, the rule of capital and the fiats of factory bosses, the dictates of university administrators, the sacredness of the family, sexuality, bourgeois culture—nothing was in principle sacrosanct. . . . Overall . . . [there was] a lack of deference towards institutions and values that demean[ed] people and a concomitant awareness of peoples' rights.[7]

THE SAN FRANCISCO STATE STRIKE'S LEGACY

The retrospectives about the sixties produced so far have ignored Asian Americans. Yet, the books cited above—plus the review essay by Winifred Breines—provide us with some interesting points to compare and contrast. For example, 1968 represented a turning point for Asian Americans and other sectors of American society.

But while white male leaders saw the year as marking the decline of the movement, 1968 for Asian Americans was a year of birth. It marked the beginning of the San Francisco State strike and all that followed.

The strike, the longest student strike in U.S. history, was the first campus uprising involving Asian Americans as a collective force.[8] Under the Third World Liberation Front—a coalition of African American, Latino, American Indian, and Asian American campus groups—students "seized the time" to demand ethnic studies, open admissions, and a redefinition of the education system. Although their five-month strike was brutally repressed and resulted in only partial victories, students won the nation's first School of Ethnic Studies.

Yet, we cannot measure the legacy of the strike for Asian Americans only in the tangible items it achieved, such as new classes and new faculty; the strike also critically transformed the consciousness of its participants, who in turn profoundly altered their communities' political landscape. Through their participation, a generation of Asian American student activists reclaimed a heritage of struggle—linking their lives to the tradition of militancy of earlier generations of Pilipino farm workers, Chinese immigrant garment and restaurant workers, and Japanese American concentration camp resisters. Moreover, these Asian American students—and their community supporters—liberated themselves from the prisons surrounding their lives and forged a new vision for their communities, creating numerous grassroots projects and empowering previously ignored and disenfranchised sectors of society. The statement of goals and principles of one campus organization, Philippine-American Collegiate Endeavor (PACE), during the strike captures this new vision:

> We seek . . . simply to function as human beings, to control our own lives. Initially, following the myth of the American Dream, we worked to attend predominantly white colleges, but we have learned through direct analysis that it is impossible for our people, so-called minorities, to function as human beings, in a racist society in which white always comes first. . . . So we have decided to fuse ourselves with the masses of Third World people, which are the majority of the world's peoples, to create, through struggle, a new humanity, a new humanism, a New World Consciousness, and within that context collectively control our own destinies.[9]

The San Francisco State strike is important not only as a beginning point for the Asian American movement, but also because it crystallizes several themes that would characterize Asian American struggles in the next decade. First, the strike occurred at a working-class campus and involved a coalition of Third World students linked to their communities. Second, students rooted their strike in the tradition of resistance by past generations of minority peoples in America. Third, strike leaders drew inspiration—as well as new ideology—from international Third World leaders and revolutions occurring in Asia, Africa, Latin America, and the Middle East. Fourth, in its demands for open admissions, community control of education, ethnic studies, and self-determination, the strike confronted basic questions of power and oppression in America. Finally, strike participants raised their demands through a strategy of mass mobilizations and militant, direct action.

In the decade following the strike, several themes would reverberate in the struggles in Asian American communities across the nation. These included housing and anti-eviction campaigns, efforts to defend education rights, union organizing drives, campaigns for jobs and social services, and demands for democratic rights, equality, and justice. Mo Nishida, an organizer in Los Angeles, recalls the broad scope of movement activities in his city:

> Our movement flowered. At one time, we had active student organizations on every campus around Los Angeles, fought for ethnic studies, equal opportunity programs, high potential programs at UCLA, and for students doing community work in "Serve the People" programs. In the community, we had, besides [Asian American] Hard Core, four area youth-oriented groups working against drugs (on the Westside, Eastside, Gardena, and the Virgil district). There were also parents' groups, which worked with parents of the youth and more.[10]

In Asian American communities in Los Angeles, San Francisco, Sacramento, Stockton, San Jose, Seattle, New York, and Honolulu, activists created "serve the people" organizations—mass networks built on the principles of "mass line" organizing. Youth initiated many of these organizations—some from college campuses and others from high schools and the streets—but other members of the community, including small-business people, workers, senior citizens, and new immigrants, soon joined.

The *mass* character of community struggles is the least appreciated aspect of our movement today. It is commonly believed that the movement involved only college students. In fact, a range of people, including high-school youth, tenants, small-business people, former prison inmates, former addicts, the elderly, and workers embraced the struggles. But exactly who were these people, and what did their participation mean to the movement?

Historian George Lipsitz has studied similar, largely "anonymous" participants in civil rights campaigns in African American communities. He describes one such man, Ivory Perry of St. Louis:

> Ivory Perry led no important organizations, delivered no important speeches, and received no significant recognition or reward for his social activism. But for more than 30 years, he had passed out leaflets, carried the picket signs, and planned the flamboyant confrontations that made the civil rights movements effective in St. Louis and across the nation. His continuous commitment at the local level had goaded others into action, kept alive hopes of eventual victory in the face of short-term defeats, and provided a relatively powerless community with an effective lever for social change. The anonymity of his activism suggests layers of social protest activity missing from most scholarly accounts, while the persistence of his involvement undermines prevailing academic judgments about mass protests as outbursts of immediate anger and spasmodic manifestations of hysteria.[11]

Those active in Asian American communities during the late 1960s and early 1970s know there were many Ivory Perrys. They were the people who demonstrated at eviction sites, packed City Hall hearing rooms, volunteered to staff health fairs, and helped with day-to-day operations of the first community drop-in centers, legal defense offices, and senior citizen projects. They were the women and men who took the concept of "serve the people" and turned it into a material force, transforming the political face of our communities.

THE "CULTURAL REVOLUTION" IN ASIAN AMERICAN COMMUNITIES

But we would be wrong to describe this transformation of our communities as solely "political"—at least as our society narrowly defines the term today. The transformation also involved a cultural vitality that opened new ways of viewing the world. Unlike today—where Asian American communities categorize "culture" and "politics" into different spheres of professional activity—in the late 1960s they did not divide them so rigidly or hierarchically. Writers, artists, and musicians were "cultural workers," usually closely associated with communities, and saw their work as "serving the people." Like other community activists, cultural workers defined the period as a "decisive moment" for Asian Americans—a time for reclaiming the past and changing the future.

The "decisive moment" was also a time for questioning and transforming moral values. Through their political and cultural work, activists challenged systems of rank and privilege, structures of hierarchy and bureaucracy, forms of exploitation and inequality, and notions of selfishness and individualism. Through their activism in mass organizations, they promoted a new moral vision centered on democratic participation, cooperative work styles, and collective decision making. Pioneer poet Russell C. Leong describes the affinity between this new generation of cultural workers and their communities, focusing on the work of the Asian American Writers Workshop, located in the basement of the International Hotel in San Francisco Chinatown/Manilatown:

> We were a post-World War II generation mostly in our twenties and thirties; in or out of local schools and colleges. . . . [We] gravitated toward cities—San Francisco, Los Angeles, New York—where movements for ethnic studies and inner city blocks of Asian communities coincided. . . . We read as we wrote—not in isolation—but in the company of our neighbors in Manilatown pool halls, barrio parks, Chinatown basements. . . . Above all, we poets were a tribe of storytellers. . . . Storytellers live in communities where they write for family and friends. The relationship between the teller and listener is neighborly, because the teller of stories must also listen.[12]

But as storytellers, cultural workers did more than simply describe events around them. By witnessing and participating in the movement, they helped to shape community consciousness. San Francisco poet Al Robles focuses on this process of vision making:

> While living and working in our little, tiny communities, in the midst of towering highrises, we fought the oppressor, the landlord, the developer, the banks, City Hall.

But most of all, we celebrated through our culture; music, dance, song and poetry—not only the best we knew but the best we had. The poets were and always have been an integral part of the community. It was through poetry—through a poetical vision to live out the ritual in dignity as human beings.[13]

The transformation of poets, writers, and artists into cultural workers and vision makers reflected larger changes occurring in every sector of the Asian American community. In education, teachers and students redefined the learning process, discovering new ways of sharing knowledge different from traditional, authoritarian, top-down approaches. In the social-service sector, social workers and other professionals became "community workers," and under the slogan "serve the people" redefined the traditional counselor/client relationship by stressing interaction, dialogue, and community building. Within community organizations, members experimented with new organizational structures and collective leadership styles, discarding hierarchical and bureaucratic forms where a handful of commanders made all the decisions. Everywhere, activists and ordinary people grappled with change.

Overall, this "cultural revolution" in the Asian American community echoes themes we have encountered earlier: Third World consciousness, participatory democracy, community building, historical rooting, liberation, and transformation. Why were these concepts so important to a generation of activists? What did they mean? And do they still have relevance for Asian American communities today?

Political analyst Raymond Williams and historian Warren Susman have suggested the use of "keywords" to study historical periods, especially times of great social change.[14] Keywords are terms, concepts, and ideas that emerge as themes of a period, reflecting vital concerns and changing values. For Asian Americans in the 1980s and 1990s, the keywords are "advocacy," "access," "legitimacy," "empowerment," and "assertiveness." These keywords tell us much about the shape of our community today, especially the growing role of young professionals and their aspirations in U.S. society. In contrast, the keywords of the late 1960s and early 1970s—"consciousness," "theory," "ideology," "participatory democracy," "community," and "liberation"—point to different concerns and values.

The keywords of two decades ago point to an approach to political work that activists widely shared, especially those working in grassroots struggles in Asian American neighborhoods, such as the Chinatowns, Little Tokyos, Manilatowns, and International Districts around the nation. This political approach focused on the relationship between political consciousness and social change, and can be best summarized in a popular slogan of the period: "Theory becomes a material force when it is grasped by the masses." Asian American activists believed that they could promote political change through direct action and mass education that raised political consciousness in the community, especially among the unorganized—low-income workers, tenants, small-business people, high-school youth, and so on. Thus, activists saw political consciousness as rising not from study groups, but from involving people in the process of social change—through their confronting the institutions of power around them and creating new visions of community life based on these struggles.

Generally, academics studying the movements of the 1960s—including academics in Asian American Studies—have dismissed the political theory of that time as murky and eclectic, characterized by ultra-leftism, shallow class analysis, and simplistic notions of Marxism and capitalism.[15] To a large extent, the thinking was eclectic; Asian American activists drew from Marx, Lenin, Stalin, and Mao—and also from Frantz Fanon, Malcolm X, Che Guevara, Kim Il-sung, and Amilcar Cabral, as well as Korean revolutionary Kim San, W.E.B. Du Bois, Frederick Douglass, Paulo Freire, the Black Panther Party, the Young Lords, the women's liberation movement, and many other resistance struggles. But in their obsessive search for theoretical clarity and consistency, these academics miss the bigger picture. What is significant is not the *content* of ideas activists adopted, but what activists *did* with the ideas. What Asian American activists *did* was use the ideas drawn from many different movements to redefine the Asian American experience.

Central to this redefinition was a slogan that appeared at nearly every Asian American rally during that period: "The people, and the people alone, are the motive force in the making of world history." Asian American activists adapted the slogan, which originated in the Chinese revolution, to the tasks of community building, historical rooting, and creating new values. Thus, the slogan came to capture six new ways of thinking about Asian Americans:

- Asian Americans became active participants in the making of history, reversing standard accounts that had treated Asian Americans as marginal objects.
- Activists saw history as created by large numbers of people acting together, not by elites.
- This view of history provided a new way of looking at our communities. Activists believed that ordinary people could make their own history by learning how historical forces operated and by transforming this knowledge into a material force to change their lives.
- This realization defined a political strategy: political power came from grassroots organizing, from the bottom up.
- This strategy required activists to develop a broad analysis of the Asian American condition-to uncover the interconnections in seemingly separate events, such as the war in Indochina, corporate redevelopment of Asian American communities, and the exploitation of Asian immigrants in garment shops. In their political analyses, activists linked the day-to-day struggles of Asian Americans to larger events and issues. The anti-eviction campaign of tenants in Chinatown and the International District against powerful corporations became one with the resistance movements of peasants in Vietnam, the Philippines, and Latin America—or, as summarized in a popular slogan of the period, there was "one struggle, [but] many fronts."
- This new understanding challenged activists to build mass, democratic organizations, especially within unorganized sectors of the community. Through these new organizations, Asian Americans expanded democracy for all sectors of the community and gained the power to participate in the broader movement for political change taking place throughout the world.

The redefinition of the Asian American experience stands as the most important legacy from this period. As described above, this legacy represents far more than an ethnic awakening. The redefinition began with an analysis of power and domination in American society. It provided a way of understanding the historical forces surrounding us. And most importantly, it presented a strategy and challenge for changing our future. This challenge, I believe, still confronts us today.

The Late 1970s: Reversing Direction

As we continue to delve into the vitality of the movements of the 1960s, one question becomes more and more persistent: Why did these movements, possessing so much vigor and urgency, seem to disintegrate in the late 1970s and early 1980s? Why did a society in motion toward progressive change seem suddenly to reverse direction?

As in the larger Left movement, Asian American activists heatedly debate this question.[16] Some mention the strategy of repression—including assassinations—U.S. ruling circles launched in response to the mass rebellions. Others cite the accompanying programs of cooptation that elites designed to channel mass discontent into traditional political arenas. Some focus on the New Right's rise, culminating in the Reagan presidency. Still others emphasize the sectarianism among political forces within the movement, or target the inability of the movement as a whole to base itself more broadly within communities.

Each of these analyses provides a partial answer. But missing in most analyses by Asian American activists is the most critical factor: the devastating corporate offensive of the mid-1970s. We will remember the 1970s as a time of economic crisis and staggering inflation. Eventually, historians may more accurately describe it as the years of "one-sided class war." Transnational corporations based in the United States launched a broad attack on the American people, especially African American communities. Several books provide an excellent analysis of the corporate offensive. One of the best, most accessible accounts is *What's Wrong with the U.S. Economy?*, written in 1982 by the Institute for Labor Education and Research.[17] My analysis draws from that source.

Corporate executives based their offensive on two conclusions: first, the economic crisis in the early 1970s—marked by declining corporate profits—occurred because American working people were earning too much; and second, the mass struggles of the previous decades had created "too much democracy" in America. The Trilateral Commission—headed by David Rockefeller and composed of corporate executives and politicians from the United States, Europe, and Japan—posed the problem starkly: either people would have to accept less, or corporations would have to accept less. An article in *Business Week* identified the solution: "Some people will obviously have to do with less. . . . Yet it will be a hard pill for many Americans to swallow—the idea of doing with less so that big business can have more."

But in order for corporations to "have more," U.S. ruling circles had to deal with the widespread discontent that had erupted throughout America. We sometimes forget today that in the mid-1970s a large number of Americans had grown cynical about U.S. business and political leaders. People routinely called politicians—including President Nixon and Vice President Agnew—crooks, liars, and criminals. Increasingly, they began to blame the largest corporations for their economic problems. One poll showed that half the population believed that "big business is the source of most of what's wrong in this country today." A series of Harris polls found that those expressing "a great deal of confidence" in the heads of corporations had fallen from 55 percent in 1966 to only 15 percent in 1975. By the fall of 1975, public opinion analysts testifying before a congressional committee reported, according to the *New York Times,* "that public confidence in the government and in the country's economic future is probably lower than it has ever been since they began to measure such things scientifically." These developments stunned many corporate leaders. "How did we let the educational system fail the free-enterprise system?" one executive asked.

U.S. ruling elites realized that restoring faith in free enterprise could only be achieved through an intensive ideological assault on those challenging the system. The ideological campaign was combined with a political offensive, aimed at the broad gains in democratic rights that Americans, especially African Americans, had achieved through the mass struggles of previous decades. According to corporate leaders, there was "too much democracy" in America, which meant too little "governability." In a 1975 Trilateral Commission report, Harvard political scientist Samuel Huntington analyzed the problem caused by "previously passive or unorganized groups in the population [which were] now engaged in concerted efforts to establish their claims to opportunities, positions, rewards, and privileges which they had not considered themselves entitled to before." According to Huntington, this upsurge in "democratic fervor" coincided with "markedly higher levels of self-consciousness on the part of blacks, Indians, Chicanos, white ethnic groups, students and women, all of whom became mobilized and organized in new ways." Huntington saw these developments as creating a crisis for those in power:

> The essence of the democratic surge of the 1960s was a general challenge to existing systems of authority, public and private. In one form or another, the challenge manifested itself in the family, the university, business, public and private associations, politics, the government bureaucracy, and the military service. People no longer felt the same obligation to obey those whom they had previously considered superior to themselves in age, rank, status, expertise, character, or talents.[18]

The mass pressures, Huntington contended, had "produced problems for the governability of democracy in the 1970s." The government, he concluded, must find a way to exercise more control. And that meant curtailing the rights of "major economic groups."

The ensuing corporate campaign was a "one-sided class war": plant closures in U.S. industries and transfer of production overseas, massive layoffs in remaining industries, shifts of capital investment from one region of the country to other regions and to other parts of the globe, and demands by corporations for concessions in wages and benefits from workers in nearly every sector of the economy.

The Reagan presidency culminated and institutionalized this offensive. The

Reagan platform called for restoring "traditional" American values, especially faith in the system of free enterprise. Reaganomics promoted economic recovery by getting government "off the backs" of business people, reducing taxation of the rich, and cutting social programs for the poor. Meanwhile, racism and exploitation became respectable under the new mantle of patriotism and economic recovery.

The Winter of Civil Rights

The corporate assault ravaged many American neighborhoods, but African American communities absorbed its harshest impact. A study by the Center on Budget and Policy Priorities measures the national impact:

- Between 1970 and 1980, the number of poor African Americans rose by 24 percent from 1.4 million to 1.8 million.
- In the 1980s, the overall African American median income was 57 percent that of whites, a decline of nearly four percentage points from the early 1970s.
- In 1986, females headed 42 percent of all African American families, the majority of which lived below the poverty line.
- In 1978, 8.4 percent of African American families had incomes under $5,000 a year. By 1987, that figure had grown to 13.5 percent. In that year, a third of all African Americans were poor.[19]
- By 1990, nearly half of all African American children grew up in poverty.[20]

Manning Marable provides a stark assessment of this devastation in *How Capitalism Underdeveloped Black America:*

What is qualitatively *new* about the current period is that the racist/capitalist state under Reagan has proceeded down a public policy road which could inevitably involve the complete obliteration of the entire Black reserve army of labor and sections of the Black working class. The decision to save capitalism at all costs, to provide adequate capital for restructuring of the private sector, fundamentally conflicts with the survival of millions of people who are now permanently outside the workplace. Reaganomics must, if it intends to succeed, place the onerous burden of unemployment on the shoulders of the poor (Blacks, Latinos and even whites) so securely that middle to upper income Americans will not protest in the vicious suppression of this stratum.[21]

The corporate offensive, combined with widespread government repression, brutally destroyed grassroots groups in the African American community. This war against the poor ripped apart the social fabric of neighborhoods across America, leaving them vulnerable to drugs and gang violence. The inner cities became the home of the "underclass" and a new politics of inner-directed violence and despair.

Historian Vincent Harding, in *The Other American Revolution,* summarizes the 1970s as the "winter" of civil rights, a period in which there was "a dangerous loss of hope among black people, hope in ourselves, hope in the possibility of any real change, hope in any moral, creative force beyond the flatness of our lives."[22]

In summary, the corporate offensive—especially its devastation of the African American community—provides the necessary backdrop for understanding why the mass movements of the 1960s seemed to disintegrate. Liberation movements, especially in the African American community, did not disappear, but a major focus of their activity shifted to issues of day-to-day survival.

THE 1980S: AN AMBIGUOUS PERIOD FOR ASIAN AMERICAN EMPOWERMENT

For African Americans and many other people of color, the period from the mid-1970s through the Reagan and Bush presidencies became a winter of civil rights, a time of corporate assault on their livelihoods and an erosion of hard-won rights. But for Asian Americans, the meaning of this period is much more ambiguous. On the one hand, great suffering marked the period: growing poverty for increasing numbers of Asian Americans, especially refugees from Southeast Asia; a rising trend of racist hate crimes directed toward Asian Americans of all ethnicities and income levels; and sharpening class polarization within our communities—with a widening gap between the very rich and the very poor. But advances also characterized the period. With the reform of U.S. immigration laws in 1965, the Asian American population grew dramatically, creating new enclaves—including suburban settlements-and revitalizing more established communities, such as Chinatowns, around the nation. Some recent immigrant business people, with small capital holdings, found economic opportunities in inner city neighborhoods. Meanwhile, Asian American youth enrolled in record numbers in colleges and universities across the United States. Asian American families moved into suburbs, crashing previously lily-white neighborhoods. And a small but significant group of Asian American politicians, such as Mike Woo and Warren Furutani, scored important electoral victories in the mainstream political arena, taking the concept of political empowerment to a new level of achievement.

During the winter of civil rights, Asian American activists also launched several impressive political campaigns at the grassroots level. Japanese Americans joined together to win redress and reparations. Pilipino Americans rallied in solidarity with the "People's Power" movement in the Philippines to topple the powerful Marcos dictatorship. Chinese Americans created new political alignments and mobilized community support for the pro-democracy struggle in China. Korean Americans responded to the massacre of civilians by the South Korean dictatorship in Kwangju with massive demonstrations and relief efforts, and established an important network of organizations in America, including Young Koreans United. Samoan Americans rose up against police abuse in Los Angeles; Pacific Islanders demanded removal of nuclear weapons and wastes from their homelands; and Hawai'ians fought for the right of self-determination and recovery of their lands. And large numbers of Asian Americans and Pacific Islanders worked actively in the 1984 and 1988 presidential campaigns of Jesse Jackson, helping to build the Rainbow Coalition.

Significantly, these accomplishments occurred in the midst of the Reagan presidency and U.S. politics' turn to the right. How did certain sectors of the Asian

American community achieve these gains in the midst of this burgeoning conservatism?

There is no simple answer. Mainstream analysts and some Asian Americans have stressed the "model minority" concept. According to this analysis, Asian Americans—in contrast to other people of color in America—have survived adversity and advanced because of their emphasis on education and family values, their community cohesion, and other aspects of their cultural heritage. Other scholars have severely criticized this viewpoint, stressing instead structural changes in the global economy and shifts in U.S. government policy since the 1960s. According to their analysis, the reform of U.S. immigration laws and sweeping economic changes in advanced capitalist nations, such as deindustrialization and the development of new technologies, brought an influx of highly educated new Asian immigrants to America. The characteristics of these new immigrants stand in sharp contrast to those of past generations, and provide a broader social and economic base for developing our communities. Still other political thinkers have emphasized the key role played by political expatriates—both right-wing and left-wing—in various communities, but most especially in the Vietnamese, Pilipino, and Korean communities. These expatriates brought political resources from their homelands—e.g., political networks, organizing experience, and, in a few cases, access to large amounts of funds—and have used these resources to change the political landscape of ethnic enclaves. Still other analysts have examined the growing economic and political power of nations of the Asian Pacific and its impact on Asians in America. According to these analysts, we can link the advances of Asian Americans during this period to the rising influence of their former homelands and the dawning of what some call "the Pacific Century." Finally, some academics have focused on the significance of small-business activities of new Asian immigrants, arguing that this sector is most responsible for the changing status of Asian Americans in the 1980s. According to their analysis, Asian immigrant entrepreneurs secured an economic niche in inner city neighborhoods because they had access to start-up capital (through rotating credit associations or from family members) and they filled a vacuum created when white businesses fled.[23]

Thus, we have multiple interpretations for why some sectors of the Asian American community advanced economically and politically during the winter of civil rights. But two critical factors missing from the analyses can help us better understand the peculiar shape of our community in the 1980s and its ambiguous character when compared to other communities of color. First is the legacy of grassroots organizing from the Asian American movement, and second is the dramatic rise of young professionals as a significant force in the community.

A stereotype about the movements of the 1960s is that they produced nothing enduring—they flared brightly for an instant and then quickly died. However, evidence from the Asian American movement contradicts this commonly held belief. Through meticulous organizing campaigns, Asian American activists created an extensive network of grassroots formations. Unlike similar groups in African American communities—which government repression targeted and brutally destroyed—a significant number of Asian American groups survived the 1980s. Thus far, no researcher has analyzed the impact of the corporate offensive and government repression on grassroots organizations in different communities of color during the late 1970s. When this research is done, I think it will show that U.S. ruling elites viewed the movement in the African American community as a major threat due to its power and influence over other communities. In contrast, the movement in the Asian American community received much less attention due to its much smaller size and influence. As a result, Asian American grassroots formations during the 1970s escaped decimation and gained the time and space to survive, grow, and adapt to changing politics.

The survival of grassroots organizations is significant because it helped to cushion the impact of the war against the poor in Asian American communities. More important, the grassroots formations provided the foundation for many of the successful empowerment campaigns occurring in the 1980s. For example, Japanese Americans built their national effort to win reparations for their internment during World War II on the experiences of grassroots neighborhood organizations' housing and anti-eviction struggles of the early 1970s. Movement activists learned from their confrontations with systems of power and applied these lessons to the more difficult political fights of the 1980s. Thus, a direct link exists between the mass struggles of activists in the late 1960s and the "empowerment" approach of Asian Americans in the 1980s and 1990s.

But while similarities exist in political organizing of the late 1960s and the 1980s, there is one crucial difference: who is being empowered? In the late 1960s and 1970s, activists focused on bringing "power to the people"—the most disenfranchised of the community, such as low-income workers, youth, former prisoners and addicts, senior citizens, tenants, and small-business people. In contrast, the "empowerment" of young professionals in Asian American communities marks the decade of the 1980s. The professionals—children of the civil rights struggles of the 1950s and 1960s—directly benefited from the campaigns for desegregation, especially in the suburbs; the removal of quotas in colleges and professional schools; and the expansion of job opportunities for middle-class people of color in fields such as law, medicine, and education.

During the 1980s, young professionals altered the political terrain in our communities.[24] They created countless new groups in nearly every profession: law, medicine, social work, psychology, education, journalism, business, and arts and culture. They initiated new political advocacy groups, leadership training projects, and various national coalitions and consortiums. They organized political caucuses in the Democratic and Republican parties. And they joined the governing boards of many community agencies. Thus, young professionals—through their sheer numbers, their penchant for self-organization, and their high level of activity—defined the Asian American community of the 1980s, shaping it in ways very different from other communities of color.

The emergence of young professionals as community leaders also aided mass political mobilizations. By combining with grassroots forces from the Asian American movement, young professionals advanced struggles against racism and discrimination. In fact, many of the successful Asian American battles of the past decade resulted from this strategic alignment.

The growing power of young professionals has also brought a diversification of political viewpoints to our communities. While many professionals embrace concerns originally raised by movement activists, a surprisingly large number have moved toward neoconservatism. The emergence of neoconservatism in our community is a fascinating phenomenon, one we should analyze and appreciate. Perhaps more than any other phenomenon, it helps to explain the political ambiguity of Asian American empowerment in the 1980s.

STRANGE AND NEW POLITICAL ANIMALS: ASIAN AMERICAN NEO-CONSERVATIVES

Item: At many universities in recent years, some of the harshest opponents of affirmative action have been Chinese Americans and Korean Americans who define themselves as political conservatives. This, in and of itself, is not new or significant. We have always had Asian American conservatives who have spoken out against affirmative action. But what is new is their affiliation. Many participate actively in Asian American student organizations traditionally associated with campus activism.

Item: In the San Francisco newspaper *Asian Week*, one of the most interesting columnists is Arthur Hu, who writes about anti-Asian quotas in universities, political empowerment, and other issues relating to our communities. He also regularly chastises those he terms "liberals, progressives, Marxists, and activists." In a recent column, he wrote: "The left today has the nerve to blame AIDS, drugs, the dissolution of the family, welfare dependency, gang violence, and educational failure on Ronald Reagan's conservatism." Hu, in turn, criticizes the Left for "tearing down religion, family, structure, and authority; promoting drugs, promiscuity, and abdication of personal responsibility."[25]

Item: During the militant, three-year campaign to win tenure for UCLA Professor Don Nakanishi, one of the key student leaders was a Japanese American Republican, Matthew J. Endo. Aside from joining the campus-community steering committee, he also mobilized support from fraternities, something that progressive activists could not do. Matt prides himself on being a Republican and a life member of the National Rifle Association. He aspires to become a CEO in a corporation but worries about the upsurge in racism against Asian Pacific peoples and the failure of both Republicans and Democrats to address this issue.

The Asian American neoconservatives are a new and interesting political phenomenon. They are new because they are creatures born from the Reagan-Bush era of supply-side economics, class and racial polarization, and the emphasis on elitism and individual advancement. And they are interesting because they also represent a legacy from the civil rights struggles, especially the Asian American movement. The neoconservatives embody these seemingly contradictory origins.

- They are proud to be Asian American. But they denounce the Asian American movement of the late 1960s and early 1970s as destructive.
- They speak out against racism against Asian Americans. But they believe that only by ending affirmative action programs and breaking with prevailing civil rights thinking of the past four decades can we end racism.

- They express concern for Asian American community issues. But they contend that the agenda set by the "liberal Asian American establishment" ignores community needs.
- They vehemently oppose quotas blocking admissions of Asian Americans at colleges and universities. But they link anti-Asian quotas to affirmative action programs for "less qualified" African Americans, Latinos, and American Indians.
- They acknowledge the continuing discrimination against African Americans, Latinos, and American Indians in U.S. society. But they believe that the main barrier blocking advancement for other people of color is "cultural"—that unlike Asians, these groups supposedly come from cultures that do not sufficiently emphasize education, family cohesion, and traditional values.

Where did these neoconservatives come from? What do they represent? And why is it important for progressive people to understand their presence?

Progressives cannot dismiss Asian American neoconservatives as simple-minded Republicans. Although they hold views similar at times to Patrick Buchanan and William Buckley, they are not clones of white conservatives. Nor are they racists, fellow travelers of the Ku Klux Klan, or ideologues attached to Reagan and Bush. Perhaps the group they most resemble are the African American neoconservatives: the Shelby Steeles, Clarence Thomases, and Tony Browns of this period. Like these men, they are professionals and feel little kinship for people of lower classes. Like these men, they oppose prevailing civil rights thinking, emphasizing reliance on government intervention and social programs. And like these men, they have gained from affirmative action, but they now believe that America has somehow become a society where other people of color can advance through their own "qualifications."

Neoconservative people of color have embraced thinkers such as the late Martin Luther King Jr., but have appropriated his message to fit their own ideology. In his speeches and writings, King dreamed of the day when racism would be eliminated—when African Americans would be recognized in U.S. society for the "content of our character, not the color of our skin." He called upon all in America to wage militant struggle to achieve this dream. Today, neoconservatives have subverted his message. They believe that racism in U.S. society has declined in significance, and that people of color can now abandon mass militancy and advance individually by cultivating the content of their character through self-help programs and educational attainment, and retrieving traditional family values. They criticize prevailing "civil rights thinking" as overemphasizing the barriers of racism and relying on "external forces" (i.e., government intervention through social programs) to address the problem.

Asian American neoconservatives closely resemble their African American counterparts in their criticism of government "entitlement" programs and their defense of traditional culture and family values. But Asian American neoconservatives are not exactly the same as their African American counterparts. The growth of neoconservative thinking among Asian Americans during the past 25 years reflects the peculiar conditions in our community, notably the emerging power of young professionals. Thus, to truly understand Asian American neoconservatives, we need to look at their evolution through the prism of Asian American politics from the late 1960s to the early 1990s.

Twenty-five years ago, Asian American neoconservatives did not exist. Our community then had only traditional conservatives—those who opposed ethnic studies, the antiwar movement, and other militant grassroots struggles. The traditional conservatives denounced Asian American concerns as "special interest politics" and labeled the assertion of Asian American ethnic identity as "separatist" thinking. For the traditional conservative, a basic contradiction existed in identifying oneself as Asian American and conservative.

Ironically, the liberation struggles of the 1960s—and the accompanying Asian American movement—spawned a new conservative thinker. The movement partially transformed the educational curriculum through ethnic studies, enabling all Asian Americans to assert pride in their ethnic heritage. The movement accelerated the desegregation of suburbs, enabling middle-class Asian Americans to move into all-white neighborhoods. Today, the neoconservatives are mostly young, middle-class professionals who grew up in white suburbs apart from the poor and people of color. As students, they attended the elite universities. Their only experience with racism is name-calling or "glass ceilings" blocking personal career advancement—and not poverty and violence.

It is due to their professional status and their roots in the Asian American movement that the neoconservatives exist in uneasy alliance with traditional conservatives in our community. Neoconservatives are appalled by the violence and rabid anticommunism of reactionary sectors of the Vietnamese community, Chinese from Taiwan tied to the oppressive ruling Kuomintang party, and Korean expatriates attached to the Korean Central Intelligence Agency. They are also uncomfortable with older conservatives, those coming from small-business backgrounds who eye the neoconservatives warily, considering them political opportunists.

Neoconservatives differ from traditional conservatives not only because of their youth and their professional status but most important of all, their political coming of age in the Reagan era. Like their African American counterparts, they are children of the corporate offensive against workers, the massive transfer of resources from the poor to the rich, and the rebirth of so-called "traditional values."

It is their schooling in Reaganomics and their willingness to defend the current structure of power and privilege in America that gives neoconservative people of color value in today's political landscape. Thus, Manning Marable describes the key role played by African American neoconservatives:

> The singular service that [they] . . . provide is a new and more accurate understanding of what exactly constitutes conservatism within the Black experience. . . . Black conservatives are traditionally hostile to Black participation in trade unions, and urge a close cooperation with white business leaders. Hostile to the welfare state, they call for increased "self-help" programs run by Blacks at local and community levels. Conservatives often accept the institutionalized forms of patriarchy, acknowledging a secondary

role for Black women within economics, political life and intellectual work. They usually have a pronounced bias towards organizational authoritarianism and theoretical rigidity.[26]

Marable's analysis points to the basic contradiction for African American neoconservatives. They are unable to address fundamental problems facing their community: racist violence, grinding poverty, and the unwillingness of corporate and government policymakers to deal with these issues.

Asian American neoconservatives face similar difficulties when confronted by the stark realities of the post-Reagan period:

- The neoconservatives acknowledge continuing discrimination in U.S. society but deny the existence of institutional racism and structural inequality. For them, racism lies in the realm of attitudes and "culture" and not institutions of power. Thus, they emphasize individual advancement as the way to overcome racism. They believe that people of color can rise through merit, which they contend can be measured objectively through tests, grades, and educational attainment.

- The neoconservatives ignore questions of wealth and privilege in American society. In their obsession with "merit," "qualifications," and "objective" criteria, they lose sight of power and oppression in America. Their focus is on dismantling affirmative action programs and "government entitlements" from the civil rights era. But poverty and racism existed long before the civil rights movement. They are embedded in the system of inequality that has long characterized U.S. society.

- The neoconservatives are essentially elitists who fear expansion of democracy at the grassroots level. They speak a language of individual advancement, not mass empowerment. They propose a strategy of alignment with existing centers of power and not the creation of new power bases among the disenfranchised sectors of society. Their message is directed to professionals, much like themselves. They have nothing to offer to immigrant workers in sweatshops, the homeless, Cambodian youth in street gangs, or community college youth.

- As relative newcomers to Asian American issues, the neoconservatives lack understanding of history, especially how concerns in the community have developed over time. Although they aggressively speak out about issues, they lack experience in organizing around these issues. The neoconservatives function best in the realm of ideas; they have difficulty dealing with concrete situations.

However, by stimulating discussion of how Asian Americans define community problems, the neoconservatives bring a vibrancy to community issues by contributing a different viewpoint. Thus, the debate between Asian American neoconservatives and progressives is positive because it clarifies issues and enables both groups to reach constituencies that each could not otherwise reach.

Unfortunately, this debate is also occurring in a larger and more dangerous context: the campaign by mainstream conservatives to redefine civil rights in America. As part of their strategy, conservatives in the national political arena have targeted our communities. There are high stakes here, and conservatives regard the Asian American neoconservatives as small players to be sacrificed.

The high stakes are evident in an article by William McGurn entitled "The Silent Minority" appearing in the conservative digest *National Review*.[27] In his essay, he urges Republicans to actively recruit and incorporate Asian Americans into party activities. According to McGurn, a basic affinity exists between Republican values and Asian American values: many Asian immigrants own small businesses; they oppose communism; they are fiercely pro-defense; they boast strong families; they value freedom; and in their approach to civil rights, they stress opportunities not government "set-asides." McGurn then chastises fellow Republicans for their "crushing indifference" to Asian American issues. He laments how Republicans have lost opportunities by not speaking out on key issues such as the conflict between Korean immigrant merchants and African Americans, the controversy over anti-Asian quotas in universities, and the upsurge in anti-Asian violence.

McGurn sees Republican intervention on these issues strategically—as a way of redefining the race question in American society and shifting the debate on civil rights away from reliance on "an increasingly narrow band of black and liberal interest groups." According to McGurn:

> Precisely because Asian Americans are making it in their adoptive land, they hold the potential not only to add to Republican rolls but to define a bona-fide American language of civil rights. Today we have only one language of civil rights, and it is inextricably linked to government intervention, from racial quotas to set-aside government contracts. It is also an exclusively black-establishment language, where America's myriad other minorities are relegated to second-class citizenship.[28]

McGurn's article presages a period of intense and unprecedented conservative interest in Asian American issues. We can expect conservative commentaries to intensify black-Asian conflicts in inner cities, the controversy over affirmative action, and the internal community debate over designating Asian Americans as a "model minority."

Thus, in the coming period, Asian American communities are likely to become crowded places. Unlike the late 1960s, issues affecting our communities will no longer be the domain of progressive forces only. Increasingly, we will hear viewpoints from Asian American neoconservatives as well as mainstream conservatives. How well will activists meet this new challenge?

GRASSROOTS ORGANIZING IN THE 1990s: THE CHALLENGE OF EXPANDING DEMOCRACY

Time would pass, old empires would fall and new ones take their place, the relations of countries and the relations of classes had to change, before I discovered that it is not quality of goods and utility which matter, but movement; not where you are or what you have, but where you have come from, where you are going and the rate at which you are getting there.[29]

—C.L.R. James

On the eve of the twenty-first century, the Asian American community is vastly different from that of the late 1960s. The community has grown dramatically. In 1970, there were only 1.5 million Asian Americans, almost entirely concentrated in Hawai'i and California. By 1980, there were 3.7 million, and in 1990, 7.9 million—with major Asian communities in New York, Minnesota, Pennsylvania, and Texas. According to census projections, the Asian American population should exceed 10 million by the year 2000, and will reach 20 million by the year 2020.[30]

Moreover, in contrast to the late 1960s—when Chinese and Japanese Americans made up the majority of Asian Americans, today's community is ethnically diverse—consisting of nearly thirty major ethnic groups, each with a distinct culture. Today's community is also economically different from the 1960s. Compared to other sectors of the U.S. population, there are higher proportions of Asian Americans who are very rich and very poor. This gap between wealth and poverty has created a sharp class polarization in our community, a phenomenon yet to be studied.

But the changes for Asian Americans during the past twenty-five years have not been simply demographic. The political landscape has also changed due to new immigrants and refugees, the polarization between rich and poor, and the emergence of young professionals as a vital new force. Following the approach of C.L.R. James, we have traced the origins of these changes. We now need to analyze where these changes will take us in the decade ahead.

Ideologically and politically, activists confront a new and interesting paradox in the Asian American community of the 1990s. On the one hand, there is a great upsurge of interest in the community and all things Asian American. Almost daily, we hear about new groups forming across the country. In contrast to twenty-five years ago, when interest in the community was minimal and when only progressive activists joined Asian American organizations, we now find a situation where many different groups—including conservatives and neoconservatives, bankers and business executives, and young professionals in all fields—have taken up the banner of Asian American identity.

On the other hand, we have not seen a corresponding growth in consciousness—of what it means to be Asian American as we approach the twenty-first century. Unlike African Americans, most Asian Americans today have yet to articulate the "particularities" of issues affecting our community, whether these be the debate over affirmative action, the controversy regarding multiculturalism, or the very definition of empowerment. We have an ideological vacuum, and activists will compete with neoconservatives, mainstream conservatives, and others to fill it.

We have a political vacuum as well. In recent years, growing numbers of Asian Americans have become involved in community issues. But almost all have come from middle-class and professional backgrounds. Meanwhile, vast segments of our community are not coming forward. In fact, during the past decade the fundamental weakness for activists has been the lack of grassroots organizing among the disenfranchised sectors of our community: youth outside of colleges and universities, the poor, and new immigrant workers. Twenty-five years ago, the greatest strength of the Asian American movement was the ability of activists to organize the unorganized and to bring new political players into community politics. Activists targeted high school youth, tenants, small-business people, former prison inmates, gang members, the elderly, and workers. Activists helped them build new grassroots organizations, expanding power and democracy in our communities. Can a new generation of activists do the same?

To respond to this challenge, activists will need both a political strategy and a new ideological vision. Politically, activists must find ways to expand democracy by creating new grassroots formations, activating new political players, and building new coalitions. Ideologically, activists must forge a new moral vision, reclaiming the militancy and moral urgency of past generations and reaffirming the commitment to participatory democracy, community building, and collective styles of leadership.

Where will this political strategy and new consciousness come from? More than fifty years ago, revolutionary leader Mao Zedong asked a similar question:

> Where do correct ideas come from? Do they drop from the skies? No. Are they innate in the mind? No. They come from social practice, and from it alone. . . . In their social practice, people engage in various kinds of struggle and gain rich experience, both from their successes and their failures.[31]

In the current "social practice" of Asian American activists across the nation, several grassroots organizing projects can serve as the basis for a political strategy and new moral vision for the 1990s. I will focus on three projects that are concentrating on the growing numbers of poor and working poor in our community. Through their grassroots efforts, these three groups are demonstrating how collective power can expand democracy, and how, in the process, activists can forge a new moral vision.

The three groups—the Chinese Progressive Association (CPA) Workers Center in Boston, Asian Immigrant Women Advocates (AIWA) in Oakland, and Korean Immigrant Worker Advocates (KIWA) in Los Angeles—address local needs. Although each organization works with different ethnic groups, their history of organizing has remarkable similarities. Each organization is composed of low-income immigrant workers. Each has taken up more than "labor" issues. And each group has fashioned very effective "united front" campaigns involving other sectors of the community. Thus, although each project is relatively small, collectively their accomplishments illustrate the power of grassroots organizing, the creativity and talents of "ordinary" people in taking up difficult issues, and the ability of grassroots forces to alter the political landscape of their community. Significantly, the focus of each group is working people in the Asian American community—a sector that is numerically large and growing larger. However, despite their numbers, workers in the Asian American community during the past decade have become voiceless and silent. Today, in discussions about community issues, no one places garment workers, nurses' aides, waiters, and secretaries at the forefront of the debate to define priorities. And no one thinks about the working class as the cutting edge of the Asian American experience. Yet, if we begin to list the basic questions now confronting Asian Americans—racism and sexism, economic justice and human rights, coalition building, and community empowerment—we would find that it is the working class, of all sectors in our community, that is making the most interesting breakthroughs on these questions. They are doing this through groups such as KIWA, AIWA, and the CPA Workers Center. Why, then, are the voices of workers submerged in our community? Why has the working class become silent?

Three trends have pushed labor issues in our community into the background during the past two decades: the rising power of young professionals in our community; the influx of new immigrants and refugees, and the fascination of social scientists and policy institutes with the phenomenon of immigrant entrepreneurship; and the lack of grassroots organizing by activists among new immigrant workers.

Thus, although the majority of Asian Americans work for a living, we have relatively little understanding about the central place of work in the lives of Asian Americans, especially in low-income industries such as garment work, restaurant work, clerical and office work, and other service occupations. Moreover, we are ignorant about the role labor struggles have played in shaping our history.[32] This labor history is part of the legacy that activists must reclaim.

In contrast to the lack of knowledge about Asian American workers, we have a much greater understanding about the role of young professionals, students, and, most of all, small-business people. In fact, immigrant entrepreneurs, especially Korean immigrants, are perhaps the most studied people of our community. However, as sociologist Edna Bonacich notes, the profile of most Asian immigrant entrepreneurs closely resembles that of workers, due to their low earning power, their long work hours, and their lack of job-related benefits. Thus, Bonacich suggests that while the world outlook of Asian immigrant entrepreneurs may be petit bourgeoisie, their life conditions are those of the working class and might better be studied as a "labor" question. Asian immigrant small businesses, she contends, play the role of "cheap labor in American capitalism."[33]

Other researchers have only begun to investigate the extent of poverty among Asian Americans and the meaning of poverty for our community. In California, the rate of poverty for Asian Americans rose from about 10 percent in 1980 to 18 percent in 1990. But more important, researchers found that there are higher numbers of "working poor" (as opposed to "jobless poor") in the Asian American community than for other ethnic groups. Thus, in contrast to other Americans, Asian Americans are poor not because they lack jobs but because the jobs they have pay very low wages. According to researchers Dean Toji and James Johnson Jr., "Perhaps contrary to common belief, about half of the poor work—including about a quarter of poor adults who work full-time and year-round. Poverty, then, is a labor question."[34]

Activists in groups such as KIWA, AIWA, and the CPA Workers Center are strategically focusing on the "working poor" in the Asian American community. KIWA—which was founded in 1992—is working with low-income Korean immigrants in Los Angeles Koreatown, including garment workers and employees in small businesses. AIWA—founded in 1983—organizes Chinese garment workers,

Vietnamese garment and electronics workers, and Korean hotel maids and electronics assemblers. And the CPA Workers Center—which traces its roots to the landmark struggle of Chinese garment workers in Boston in 1985—is composed primarily of Chinese immigrant women. Although their main focus is on workers, each group has also mobilized students and social service providers to support their campaigns. Through these alliances, each group has carried out successful community organizing strategies.

The focus of the three groups on community-based organizing distinguishes them from traditional unions. Miriam Ching Louie of AIWA explains this distinction:

> AIWA's base is simultaneously worker, female, Asian, and immigrant, and the organization has developed by blending together several different organizing techniques. As compared to the traditional union organizing strategy, AIWA's approach focuses on the needs of its constituency. *Popular literacy / conscientization / transformation* [based on the teachings of Paulo Freire] is a learning and teaching method which taps into people's life experiences as part of a broader reality, source of knowledge, and guide to action. *Community-based organizing* takes a holistic view of racial/ethnic people and organizes for social change, not only so that the people can win immediate improvements in their lives, but so that they can also develop their own power in the course of waging the fight.[35]

AIWA's focus on grassroots organizing is illustrated by its "Garment Workers' Justice Campaign," launched in late 1992 to assist Chinese immigrant women who were denied pay by a garment contractor. AIWA organizers shaped the campaign to respond to the peculiar features of the garment industry. The industry in the San Francisco Bay Area is the nation's third largest—behind New York and Los Angeles—and employs some 20,000 seamstresses, 85 percent of them Asian immigrant women. The structure of the industry is a pyramid with retailers and manufacturers at the top, contractors in the middle, and immigrant women working at the bottom. Manufacturers make the main share of profits in the industry; they set the price for contractors. Meanwhile, immigrant women work under sweatshop conditions.

In their campaign, AIWA and the workers initially confronted the contractor for the workers' back pay. When they discovered that the contractor owed a number of creditors, they took the unusual step of holding the garment manufacturer, Jessica McClintock, accountable for the unpaid wages. McClintock operates ten boutiques and sells dresses through department stores. The dresses—which garment workers are paid $5 to make—retail in stores for $175. AIWA and the workers conducted their campaign through a series of high-profile demonstrations at McClintock boutiques, including picket lines and rallies in ten cities by supporters. AIWA designed these demonstrations not only to put pressure on McClintock and educate others in the community about inequities in the structure of the garment industry, but also to serve as vehicles for empowerment for the immigrant women participating in the campaign. Through this campaign, the women workers learned how to confront institutional power, how to forge alliances with other groups in the community, and how to carry out effective tactics based on their collective power.[36]

Thus, through its activities promoting immigrant women's rights, AIWA is expanding democracy in the community. It is bringing labor issues to the forefront of community discussions. It is creating new grassroots caucuses among previously unorganized sectors of the community, and forming new political alignments with supporters, such as students, young professionals, labor unions, and social service providers. Finally, AIWA is developing a cadre of politically sophisticated immigrant women and promoting a new leadership style based on popular literacy, community building, and collective power.

Similarly, in Boston, the CPA Workers Center is expanding democracy through its grassroots efforts around worker rights. The Center emerged out of the Chinese immigrant women's campaign to deal with the closing of a large garment factory in Boston in 1985.[37] The shutdown displaced 350 workers and had a severe impact on the local Chinese community due to the community's high concentration of jobs in the garment industry. However, with the assistance of the Chinese Progressive Alliance, the workers formed a labor-community-student coalition and waged an 18–month campaign to win job retraining and job replacement. Lydia Lowe, director of the CPA Workers Center, describes how the victory of Chinese immigrant women led to creation of the Workers Center, which, in turn, has helped other workplace campaigns in the Chinese community:

> This core of women activated through the campaign joined with community supporters from the CPA to found a community-based workers' mutual aid and resource center, based at CPA. . . . Through the Workers Center, immigrant workers share their experience, collectively sum up lessons learned, find out about their rights, and develop mutual support and organizing strategies. Today, the Workers Center involves immigrant workers from each of its successive organizing efforts, and is a unique place in the community where ordinary workers can walk in and participate as activists and decision-makers.[38]

Moreover, forming the Workers Center reshaped politics in the local Chinese community, turning garment workers and other immigrant laborers into active political players. "Previously the silent majority, immigrant workers are gaining increasing respect as a force to be reckoned with in the local Chinese community," states Lowe.

In Los Angeles, the formation of KIWA in March 1992—only a month before the uprisings—has had a similar impact. Through its programs, KIWA is bringing labor issues to the forefront of the Asian American community, educating labor unions about the needs of Asian American workers, and forming coalitions with other grassroots forces in the city to deal with interethnic tensions. KIWA is uniquely positioned to take up these tasks. Out of the multitude of Asian American organizations in Los Angeles, KIWA distinguishes itself as the only organization governed by a board of directors of mainly workers.

KIWA's key role in the labor movement and community politics is evident in the recent controversy involving the Koreana Wilshire Hotel.[39] The controversy began in late 1991 when Koreana Hotel Co. Ltd., a South Korean corporation, bought the Wilshire Hyatt in Los Angeles. The change in ownership meant that 175 unionized members, predominantly Latino immigrants, were out of jobs. Meanwhile, the new hotel management hired a new work force, paying them an average of $1.50 per hour less than the former unionized work force. The former workers, represented by Hotel Employees and Restaurant Employees (HERE) Local 11, called upon labor unions and groups from the Asian American, African American, and Latino communities to protest Koreana's union-busting efforts. Local 11 defined the dispute as not only a labor issue, but a civil rights issue. With the help of groups such as KIWA and the Asian Pacific American Labor Alliance, Local 11 initiated a letter-writing campaign against Koreana, began a community boycott of the hotel, and organized militant actions outside the hotel, including rallies, marches, and a picket line, as well as civil disobedience at the nearby Korean consulate. In each of these actions, Local 11 worked closely with KIWA and members of the Asian American community. Due to the mass pressure, in late 1992 the Koreana management agreed to negotiate with Local 11 to end the controversy and rehire the union members.

Throughout the campaign, KIWA played a pivotal role by helping Local 11 build alliances with the Asian American community. In addition, KIWA members promoted labor consciousness in the Korean community by urging the community to boycott the hotel. KIWA members also spoke at Local 11 rallies, mobilized for picket lines, and worked with the union in its efforts to put pressure on the South Korean government. By taking these steps, KIWA prevented the controversy from pitting the Korean community against Latinos and further inflaming interethnic tensions in Los Angeles.

Also, through campaigns such as this one, KIWA is educating Asian immigrants about unions; training workers around the tasks of political leadership; and creating new centers of power in the community by combining the resources of workers, young professionals, and social service providers.

Thus, through grassroots organizing, KIWA—like AIWA and the CPA Workers Center—is expanding democracy in the Asian American community. Moreover, the three groups collectively are reshaping community consciousness. They are sharpening debate and dialogue around issues and redefining such important concepts as empowerment. What is their vision of empowerment, and how does it differ from prevailing definitions?

THE TWENTY-FIRST CENTURY: BUILDING AN ASIAN AMERICAN MOVEMENT

[A] movement is an idea, a philosophy. . . . Leadership, I feel, is only incidental to the movement. The movement should be the most important thing. The movement must go beyond its leaders. It must be something that is continuous, with goals and ideas that the leadership can then build on.[40]

—PHILIP VERA CRUZ

In the late 1960s, Asian American activists sought to forge a new approach to leadership that would not replicate traditional Eurocentric models—i.e., rigid hierarchies with a single executive at the top, invariably a white male, who commanded an endless chain of assistants. In their search for alternatives, activists experimented with various ideas borrowed from other movements, but most of all, activists benefited from the advice and guidance of "elders" within the Asian American community—women and men with years of grassroots organizing experience in the community, the workplace, and the progressive political movement. One such "elder" was Pilipino immigrant labor leader Philip Vera Cruz, then in his sixties. Vera Cruz represented the *manong* generation—the first wave of Pilipinos who came to the United States in the early twentieth century and worked in agricultural fields, canneries, hotels, and restaurants.

Now eighty-eight years old, Vera Cruz continues to educate a new generation of activists. His lifetime of experience in grassroots organizing embodies the historic themes of Asian American activism: devotion to the rights of working people, commitment to democracy and liberation, steadfast solidarity with all who face oppression throughout the world, and the courage to challenge existing institutions of power and to create new institutions as the need arises. These themes have defined his life and shaped his approach to the question of empowerment—an approach that is different from standard definitions in our community today.

Vera Cruz is best known for his role in building the United Farm Workers (UFW), a culmination of his many years of organizing in agricultural fields. In 1965, he was working with the Agricultural Workers Organizing Committee, AFL–CIO, when Pilipino farmworkers sat down in the Coachella vineyards of central California. This sit-down launched the famous grape strike and boycott, eventually leading to the formation of the UFW. Many books and articles have told the story of the UFW and its leader, Cesar Chavez. But until recently, no one has focused on the historic role of Pilipinos in building this movement. Craig Scharlin and Lilia Villanueva have filled that vacuum with their new publication about Vera Cruz's life.

Following the successful grape boycott, Vera Cruz became a UFW vice president and remained with the union until 1977, when he left due to political differences with the leadership. He was critical of the lack of rank-and-file democracy in the union, and of the leadership's embrace of the Marcos dictatorship in the Philippines. Since 1979, Vera Cruz has lived in Bakersfield, California, and has continued to devote his life to unionism and social justice, and to the education of a new generation of Asian American youth.

Vera Cruz's life experiences have shaped a broad view of empowerment. For Vera Cruz, empowerment is grassroots power: the expansion of democracy for the many. Becoming empowered means gaining the capacity to advocate not only for one's own concerns but for the liberation of all oppressed peoples. Becoming empowered means being able to change fundamentally the relationship of power and oppression in society. Thus, Vera Cruz's vision is very different from that of today's young professionals. For them, empowerment is leadership development for an elite. Becoming empowered means gaining the skills to advocate for the community by gaining access to decision makers. Thus, for young professionals, the key leadership quality to develop is assertiveness. Through assertiveness, leaders gain access to policy makers as well as the power to mobilize their followers. In contrast, Vera Cruz stresses the leadership trait of humility. For him, leaders are "only incidental to the movement"—the movement is "the most important thing." For Vera Cruz, empowerment is a process where people join to develop goals and ideas to create a larger movement—a movement "that the leadership can then build on."

Vera Cruz's understanding of empowerment has evolved from his own social practice. Through his experiences in the UFW and the AFL–CIO, Vera Cruz learned about the empty democracy of bureaucratic unions and the limitations of the charismatic leadership style of Cesar Chavez. Through his years of toil as a farmworker, he recognized the importance of worker solidarity and militancy and the capacity of common people to create alternative institutions of grassroots power. Through his work with Pilipino and Mexican immigrants, he saw the necessity of coalition-building and worker unity that crossed ethnic and racial boundaries. He has shared these lessons with several generations of Asian American activists.

But aside from sharing a concept of empowerment, Vera Cruz has also promoted a larger moral vision, placing his lifetime of political struggle in the framework of the movement for liberation. Three keywords distinguish his moral vision: "compassion," "solidarity," and "commitment." Vera Cruz's lifetime of action represents compassion for all victims of oppression, solidarity with all fighting for liberation, and commitment to the ideals of democracy and social justice.

Activists today need to learn from Vera Cruz's compassion, solidarity, commitment, and humility to create a new moral vision for our community. In our grassroots organizing, we need a vision that can redefine empowerment—that can bring questions of power, domination, and liberation to the forefront of our work. We need a vision that can help us respond to the challenge of conservatives and neoconservatives, and sharpen dialogue with young professionals. We need a new moral vision that can help fill the ideological vacuum in today's community.

Nowhere is this ideological challenge greater than in the current debate over the model minority stereotype. This stereotype has become the dominant image of Asian Americans for mainstream society, and has generated intense debate among all sectors of our community. This debate provides an opportunity for activists to expand political awareness and, in the process, redefine the Asian American experience for the 1990s.

In the current controversy, however, activists criticize the model minority stereotype politically but not ideologically. Activists correctly target how the concept fails to deal with Asian American realities: the growing population of poor and working poor, the large numbers of youth who are not excelling in school, and the hardships and family problems of small-business people who are not "making it" in U.S. society. Activists also correctly point out the political ramifications of the model minority stereotype: the pitting of minority groups against each other, and growing interethnic tensions in U.S. society. In contrast, conservative and neoconservative proponents of the model minority concept argue from the standpoint of both political realities and a larger moral vision. They highlight Asian American accomplishments: "whiz kids" in elementary schools; growing numbers of Asian Americans in business, politics, and the professions; and the record enrollment of youth in colleges and universities. Conservatives and neoconservatives attribute these accomplishments to Asian culture and tradition, respect for authority, family cohesion, sacrifice and toil, rugged individualism, and self-reliance—moral values they root in conservative thinking. Conservatives and neoconservatives recognize that "facts" gain power from attachment to ideologies. As a result, they appropriate Asian culture and values to promote their arguments.

But is Asian culture inherently conservative—or does it also have a tradition of militancy and liberation? Do sacrifice, toil, and family values fit with a conservative moral vision only—or do these qualities also constitute the core of radical and revolutionary thinking? By asking these questions, activists can push the debate over the model minority concept to a new, ideological level. Moreover, by focusing on ideology, activists can delve into the stereotype's deeper meaning. They can help others understand the stereotype's origins and why it has become the dominant image for Asian Americans today.

Historically, the model minority stereotype first arose in the late 1950s—the creation of sociologists attempting to explain low levels of juvenile delinquency among Chinese and Japanese Americans.[41] The stereotype remained a social-science construct until the 1960s when a few conservative political commentators began to use it to contrast Asian Americans' "respect for law and order" with African Americans' involvement in civil rights marches, rallies, and sit-ins. By the late 1970s, the stereotype moved into the political mainstream, coinciding with the influx of new Asian immigrants into all parts of the United States. But the widespread acceptance of the stereotype was not simply due to the increase in the Asian American population or the new attention focused on our community from mainstream institutions. More importantly, it coincided with the rise of the New Right and the corporate offensive against the poor. As discussed earlier, this offensive economically devastated poor communities and stripped away hard-won political gains. It also included an ideological campaign designed to restore trust in capitalism and values associated with free enterprise. Meanwhile, conservatives and neoconservatives fought to redefine the language of civil rights by attacking federal government "entitlement" programs while criticizing the African American "liberal establishment."

In this political climate, the model minority stereotype flourished. It symbolized the moral vision of capitalism in the 1980s: a celebration of traditional values, an emphasis on hard work and self-reliance, a respect for authority, and an attack on prevailing civil rights thinking associated with the African American community. Thus, the stereotype took on an ideological importance above and beyond the Asian American community. The hard-working immigrant merchant and the refugee student winning the local spelling bee have become the symbols for the resurrection of capitalist values in the last part of the twentieth century.

Yet, we know a gap exists between symbol and reality. Today, capitalism in America is not about small-business activities; it is about powerful transnational corporations and their intricate links to nation-states and the world capitalist system. Capitalist values no longer revolve around hard work and self-reliance; they deal with wealth and assets, and the capacity of the rich to invest, speculate, and obtain government contracts. And the fruits of capitalism in the last part of the twentieth century are not immigrant entrepreneurship and the revival of urban areas; they are more likely to be low-paying jobs, unemployment, bankruptcies, and homelessness.

However, as corporations, banks, and other institutions abandon the inner city, the immigrant merchant—especially the Korean small-business person—emerges as the main symbol of capitalism in these neighborhoods. For inner city residents, the Asian immigrant becomes the target for their wrath against corporate devastation of their neighborhoods. Moreover, as this symbol merges with other historical stereotypes of Asians, the result is highly charged imagery, which perhaps underlies the ferocity of anti-Asian violence in this period, such as the destruction of Korean small businesses during the Los Angeles uprisings. The Asian immigrant becomes a symbol of wealth—and also greed; a symbol of hard work—and also materialism; a symbol of intelligence—and also arrogance; a symbol of self-reliance—and also selfishness and lack of community concern. Thus, today the model minority stereotype has become a complex symbol through the confluence of many images imposed on us by social scientists, the New Right, and the urban policies of corporate and political elites.

Pioneer Korean immigrant journalist K. W. Lee—another of our Asian American "elders"—worries about how the melding of symbols, images, and stereotypes is shaping the perception of our community, especially among other people of color. "We are not seen as a compassionate people," states Lee. "Others see us as smart, hard-working, and good at making money—but not as sharing with others. We are not seen as a people who march at the forefront of the struggle for civil rights or the campaign to end poverty."[42] Like Philip Vera Cruz, Lee believes that Asian Americans must retrieve a heritage of compassion and solidarity from our past and use these values to construct a new moral vision for our future. Asian Americans must cast off the images imposed on us by others.

Thus, as we approach the end of the twentieth century, activists are confronted with a task similar to that confronting activists in the late 1960s: the need to redefine the Asian American experience. And as an earlier generation discovered, redefining means more than ethnic awakening. It means confronting the fundamental questions of power and domination in U.S. society. It means expanding democracy and community consciousness. It means liberating ourselves from the prisons still surrounding our lives.

In our efforts to redefine the Asian American experience, activists will have the guidance and help of elders like K. W. Lee and Philip Vera Cruz. And we can also draw from the rich legacy of struggle of other liberation movements.

In closing this chapter, I want to quote from two great teachers from the 1960s: Malcolm X and Martin Luther King Jr. Their words and actions galvanized the consciousness of one generation of youth, and their message of compassion continues to speak to a new generation in the 1990s.

Since their assassinations in the mid-1960s, however, mainstream commentators have stereotyped the two men and often pitted one against the other. They portray Malcolm X as the angry black separatist who advocated violence and hatred against white people. Meanwhile, they make Martin Luther King Jr. the messenger of love and nonviolence. In the minds of most Americans, both men—in the words of historian Manning Marable—are "frozen in time."[43]

But as Marable and other African American historians note, both King and Malcolm evolved, and became very different men in the years before their assassinations. Both men came to see the African American struggle in the United States in a worldwide context, as part of the revolutionary stirrings and mass uprisings happening across the globe. Both men became internationalists, strongly condemning U.S. exploitation of Third World nations and urging solidarity among all oppressed peoples. Finally, both men called for a redefinition of human values; they believed that people in the United States, especially, needed to move away from materialism and embrace a more compassionate worldview.

If we, too, as Asian Americans, are to evolve in our political and ideological understanding, we need to learn from the wisdom of both men. As we work for our own empowerment, we must ask ourselves a series of questions. Will we fight only for ourselves, or will we embrace the concerns of all oppressed peoples? Will we overcome our own oppression and help to create a new society, or will we become a new exploiter group in the present American hierarchy of inequality? Will we define our goal of empowerment solely in terms of individual advancement for a few, or as the collective liberation for all peoples?

> These are revolutionary times. All over the globe men are revolting against old systems of exploitation and oppression, and out of the wombs of a frail world, new systems of justice and equality are being born. The shirtless and barefoot people of the land are rising up as never before. "The people who sat in the darkness have seen a great light." We in the West must support these revolutions. It is a sad fact that, because of comfort, complacency, a morbid fear of communism, and our proneness to adjust to injustice, the Western nations that initiated so much of the revolutionary spirit of the modern world have now become the arch anti-revolutionaries. . . . Our only hope today lies in our ability to recapture the revolutionary spirit and go out into a sometimes hostile world declaring eternal hostility to poverty, racism, and militarism. —Martin Luther King Jr.[44]

> I believe that there will ultimately be a clash between the oppressed and those who do the oppressing. I believe that there will be a clash between those who want freedom, justice and equality for everyone and those who want to continue the system of exploitation. I believe that there will be that kind of clash, but I don't think it will be based on the color of the skin. —Malcolm X[45]

NOTES

1. Iranian philosopher Ali Shariati's four prisons analysis was shared with me by a member of the Iranian Students Union, Confederation of Iranian Students, San Francisco, 1977.

2. Allan Bloom, *The Closing of the American Mind* (New York: Simon & Schuster, 1987).

3. Winifred Breines, "Whose New Left?" *Journal of American History* 75, no. 2 (September 1988).

4. Ibid., 543.

5. Sheila D. Collins, *The Rainbow Challenge: The Jackson Campaign and the Future of U.S. Politics* (New York: Monthly Review Press, 1986).

6. Ibid., 16.

7. Ronald Fraser, *1968: A Student Generation in Revolt* (New York: Pantheon Books, 1988), 354–355.

8. Karen Umemoto, " 'On Strike!' San Francisco State College Strike, 1968–69: The Role of Asian American Students," *Amerasia Journal* 15, no. 1 (1989).

9. "Statement of the Philippine-American Collegiate Endeavor (PACE) Philosophy and Goals," mimeograph; quoted in Umemoto, " 'On Strike!' " 15.

10. Mo Nishida, "A Revolutionary Nationalist Perspective of the San Francisco State Strike," *Amerasia Journal* 15, no. 1 (1989): 75.

11. George Lipsitz, "Grassroots Activists and Social Change: The Story of Ivory Perry," *CAAS Newsletter,* UCLA Center for Afro-American Studies, 1986. See also George Lipsitz, *A Life in the Struggle. Ivory Perry and the Culture of Opposition* (Philadelphia: Temple University Press, 1988).

12. Russell C. Leong, "Poetry Within Earshot: Notes of an Asian American Generation, 1968–1978," *Amerasia Journal* 15, no. 1 (1989): 166–167.

13. Al Robles, "Hanging On to the Carabao's Tail," *Amerasia Journal* 15, no. 1 (1989): 205.

14. Warren J. Susman, *Culture as History: The Transformation of American Society in the Twentieth Century* (New York: Pantheon Books, 1973); and Raymond Williams, *Keywords: A Vocabulary of Culture and Society,* revised edition (New York: Oxford University Press, 1976).

15. John M. Liu and Lucie Cheng, "A Dialogue on Race and Class: Asian American Studies and Marxism," in *The Left Academy,* vol. 3, ed. Bertell Ollman and Edward Vernoff (Westport, Conn.: Praeger, 1986).

16. See Mary Kao, compiler, "Public Record, 1989: What Have We Learned from the 60s and 70s?" *Amerasia Journal* 15, no. 1 (1989): 95–158.

17. Institute for Labor Education and Research, *What's Wrong with the U.S. Economy? A Popular Guide for the Rest of Us* (Boston: South End Press, 1982). See especially chapters 1 and 19.

18. Samuel Huntington, "The United States," in *The Crisis of Democracy: Report on the Governability of Democracies to the Trilateral Commission,* ed. Michel Crozier (New York: New York University Press, 1975).

19. Center on Budget and Policy Priorities, *Still Far from the Dream: Recent Developments in Black Income, Employment and Poverty* (Washington, D.C., 1988).

20. Center for the Study of Social Policy, *Kids Count: State Profiles of Child Well-Being* (Washington, D.C., 1992).

21. Manning Marable, *How Capitalism Underdeveloped Black America* (Boston: South End Press, 1983), 252–253.

22. Vincent Harding, *The Other American Revolution* (Los Angeles: UCLA Center for Afro-American Studies, and Atlanta: Institute of the Black World, 1980), 224.

23. For analyses of the changing status of Asian Americans, see Lucie Cheng and Edna Bonacich, eds., *Labor Immigration Under Capitalism: Asian Workers in the United States Before World War II* (Berkeley: University of California Press, 1984); Paul Ong, Edna Bonacich, and Lucie Cheng, eds., *Struggles for a Place: The New Asian Immigrants in the Restructuring Political Economy* (Philadelphia: Temple University Press, 1993); and Sucheng Chan, *Asian Americans: An Interpretive History* (Boston: Twayne Publishers, 1991).

24. For an analysis of the growing power of Asian American young professionals, see Yen Espiritu and Paul Ong, "Class Constraints on Racial Solidarity among Asian Americans," in *Struggles for a Place* (Philadelphia: Temple University Press, 1993).

25. Arthur Hu, "AIDS and Race," *Asian Week,* 13 December 1991.

26. Marable, *How Capitalism Underdeveloped Black America,* 182.

27. William McGurn, "The Silent Minority," *National Review,* 24 June 1991.

28. Ibid., 19.

29. C.L.R. James, *Beyond a Boundary* (New York: Pantheon Books, 1983), 116–117.

30. LEAP Asian Pacific American Public Policy Institute and UCLA Asian American Studies Center, *The State of Asian Pacific America: Policy Issues to the Year 2020* (Los Angeles: LEAP and UCLA Asian American Studies Center, 1993).

31. Mao Zedong, "Where Do Correct Ideas Come From?" in *Four Essays on Philosophy* (Beijing: Foreign Languages Press, 1966), 134.

32. See "Asian Pacific American Workers: Contemporary Issues in the Labor Movement," ed. Glenn Omatsu and Edna Bonacich, *Amerasia Journal* 18, no. 1 (1992).

33. Edna Bonacich, "The Social Costs of Immigrant Entrepreneurship," *Amerasia Journal* 14, no. 1 (1988).

34. Dean S. Toji and James H. Johnson Jr., "Asian and Pacific Islander American Poverty: The Working Poor and the Jobless Poor," *Amerasia Journal* 18, no. 1 (1992): 85.

35. Miriam Ching Louie, "Immigrant Asian Women in Bay Area Garment Sweatshops: 'After Sewing, Laundry, Cleaning and Cooking, I Have No Breath Left to Sing,'" *Amerasia Journal* 18, no. 1 (1992): 12.

36. Miriam Ching Louie, "Asian and Latina Women Take On the Garment Giants," *Cross-Roads,* March 1993.

37. Peter N. Kiang and Man Chak Ng, "Through Strength and Struggle: Boston's Asian American Student/Community/Labor Solidarity," *Amerasia Journal* 15, no. 1 (1989).

38. Lydia Lowe, "Paving the Way: Chinese Immigrant Workers and Community-based Labor Organizing in Boston," *Amerasia Journal* 18, no. 1 (1992): 41.

39. Namju Cho, "Check Out, Not In: Koreana Wilshire/Hyatt Take-over and the Los Angeles Korean Community," *Amerasia Journal,* 18, no. 1 (1992).

40. Craig Scharlin and Lilia V. Villanueva, *Philip Vera Cruz: A Personal History of Filipino Immigrants and the Farmworkers Movement* (Los Angeles: UCLA Labor Center and UCLA Asian American Studies Center, 1992), 104.

41. For an overview of the evolution of the "model minority" stereotype in the social sciences, see Shirley Hune, *Pacific Migration to the United States: Trends and Themes in Historical and Sociological Literature* (New York: Research Institute on Immigration and Ethnic Studies of the Smithsonian Institution, 1977), reprinted in *Asian American Studies: An Annotated Bibliography and Research Guide,* ed. Hyung-chan Kim (Westport, Conn.: Greenwood Press, 1989). For comparisons of the "model minority" stereotype in two different decades, see "Success Story of One Minority Group in U.S.," *U.S. News and World Report,* 26 December 1966, reprinted in *Roots: An Asian American Reader,* ed. Amy Tachiki et al. (Los Angeles: UCLA Asian American Studies Center, 1971) and in the present volume, chapter 13; and the essay by William McGurn, "The Silent Minority," *National Review,* 24 June 1991.

42. Author's interview with K. W. Lee, Los Angeles, California, October 1991.

43. Manning Marable, "On Malcolm X: His Message & Meaning" (Westfield, N.J.: Open Magazine Pamphlet Series, 1992).

44. Martin Luther King Jr., "Beyond Vietnam," speech delivered at Riverside Church, New York, April 1967.

45. Malcolm X, interview on Pierre Breton Show, 19 January 1965, in *Malcolm X Speaks,* ed. George Breitman (New York: Grove Press, 1966), 216.

wo:
Social
Issues
and Literatures

Racial Formations and the Question of Class

ON THE THEORETICAL STATUS OF THE CONCEPT OF RACE

Michael Omi and Howard Winant

INTRODUCTION

Race used to be a relatively unproblematic concept; only recently have we seriously challenged its theoretical coherence. Today there are deep questions about what we actually mean by the term "race." But before (roughly) World War II, before the rise of Nazism, before the end of the great European empires and before the decolonization of Africa, before the urbanization of the U.S. black population and the rise of the modern civil rights movement, race was still largely seen in Europe and North America (and elsewhere as well) as an essence, a natural phenomenon, whose meaning was fixed—constant as a southern star.

In the earlier years of this century only a handful of pioneers, people like W.E.B. Du Bois and Franz Boas, conceived of race in a more social and historical way.

Other doubters included avant-garde racial theorists emerging from the intellectual ferment of the Harlem Renaissance; black nationalists and pan-Africanists who sought to apply the rhetoric of national self-determination expressed at Versailles to the mother continent, and who returned from the battlefields of France to the wave of antiblack race riots that swept the country in 1919; a few Marxists (whose perspectives had their own limitations); and to some extent the Chicago school of sociology led by Robert Ezra Park. But even these intellectuals and activists made incomplete breaks with essentialist notions of race, whether biological or otherwise deterministic.

That was then; this is now. Today the theory of race has been utterly transformed. The socially constructed status of the concept of race, which we have labeled the *racial formation* process, is widely recognized (Omi and Winant 1986), so much so that it is now often *conservatives* who argue that race is an illusion. The main task facing racial theory today, in fact, is no longer to problematize a seemingly "natural" or "common-sense" concept of race—although that effort has not been entirely completed by any means. Rather, our central work is to focus attention on the *continuing significance and changing meaning of race.* It is to argue against the recent discovery of the illusory nature of race; against the supposed contemporary transcendence of race; against the widely reported death of the concept of race; and against the replacement of the category of race by other, supposedly more objective categories like ethnicity, nationality, or class. All these initiatives are mistaken at best, and intellectually dishonest at worst.

In order to substantiate these assertions, we must first ask, what is race? Is it merely an illusion, an ideological construct utilized to manipulate, divide, and deceive? This position has been taken by a number of theorists, and activists as well, including many who have heroically served the cause of racial and social justice in the United States. Or is race something real, material, objective? This view too has its adherents, including both racial reactionaries and racial radicals. From our perspective both these approaches miss the boat. The concept of race is not an ideological construct, nor does it reflect an objective condition. In this essay we first reflect critically on these two opposed viewpoints on the contemporary theory of race. Then we offer an alternative perspective based on the approach of racial formation.

RACE AS AN IDEOLOGICAL CONSTRUCT

The assertion that race is an ideological construct—understood in the sense of a "false consciousness" that explains other "material" relationships in distorted fashion—seems to us highly problematic. This is the position taken by the prominent historian Barbara Fields in a well-known article, "Slavery, Race and Ideology in the United States of America" (1990). Although Fields inveighs against various uses of the concept of race, she directs her critical barbs most forcefully against historians who "invoke race as a historical explanation" (1990: 101).

According to Fields, the concept of race arose to meet an ideological need: its original effectiveness lay in its ability to reconcile freedom and slavery. The idea of race provided "the means of explaining slavery to people whose terrain was a

republic founded on radical doctrines of liberty and natural rights" (1990: 114).
But, Fields says, to argue that race—once framed as a category in thought, an
ideological explanation for certain distinct types of social inequality—"takes on a
life of its own" in social relationships is to transform (or "reify") an illusion into
a reality. Such a position could be sustained "only if race is defined as innate and
natural prejudice of color."

> Since race is not genetically programmed, racial prejudice cannot be genetically pro-
> grammed either, but must arise historically. . . . The preferred solution is to suppose
> that, having arisen historically, race then ceases to be a historical phenomenon and
> becomes instead an external motor of history; according to the fatuous but widely
> repeated formula, it "takes on a life of its own." In other words, once historically
> acquired, race becomes hereditary. The shopworn metaphor thus offers camouflage
> for a latter-day version of Lamarckism. (1990: 101)

Thus race is either an illusion that does ideological work, or an objective biological
fact. Since it is certainly not the latter, it must be the former. No intermediate
possibility—for instance, the Durkheimian notion of a "social fact"—is considered.

Some of this account—for example, the extended discussion of the origins of
North American race-thinking—can be accepted without major objection.[1] Furthermore, Fields effectively demonstrates the absurdity of many commonly held ideas
about race. But her position is so extreme that at best it can only account for the
origins of race-thinking, and then only in one social context. To examine how race-
thinking evolved from these origins, how it responded to changing sociocultural
circumstances, is ruled out. Why and how did race-thinking survive after emancipation? Fields cannot answer, because her theoretical approach rules out the very
perpetuation of the concept of race. As a relatively orthodox Marxist, Fields could
argue that changing "material conditions" continued to give rise to changes in
racial "ideology," except that even the limited autonomy this would attach to the
concept of race would exceed her standards. Race cannot take on "a life of its
own"; it is a pure ideology, an illusion.

Fields simply skips from emancipation to the present, where she disparages
opponents of "racism" for unwittingly perpetuating it. In denunciatory terms she
concludes by arguing for the concept's abolition:

> Nothing handed down from the past could keep race alive if we did not constantly
> reinvent and re-ritualize it to fit our own terrain. If race lives on today, it can do so
> only because we continue to create and re-create it in our social life, continue to verify
> it and thus continue to need a social vocabulary that will allow us to make sense, not
> of what our ancestors did then, but of what we choose to do now. (1990: 118)

Fields is unclear about how "we" should jettison the ideological construct of
race, and one can well understand why. By her own logic, racial ideologies cannot
be abolished by acts of will. One can only marvel at the ease with which she
distinguishes the bad old slavery days of the past from the present, when we
anachronistically cling, as if for no reason, to the illusion that race retains any

meaning. We foolishly "throw up our hands" and acquiesce in race-thinking, rather than . . . doing what? Denying the racially demarcated divisions in society? Training ourselves to be "color-blind"?[2]

We venture to say that only a historian (however eminent) could have written such an article. Because at the least a sociologist would know W. I. Thomas's famous dictum that if people "define situations as real, they are real in their consequences" (Thomas and Thomas 1928: 572). Nor is Fields alone in claiming that racial ideology persists because people insist on thinking racially. Her position is espoused by many, on both the left and the right of racial debates.[3]

In any case the view that race is a kind of false consciousness is not held only by intellectuals, based on both well-intentioned and ulterior motivations; it also has a common-sense character. One hears in casual discussion, or in introductory social science classes, variations on the following statement: "I don't care if a person is black, white, or purple, I treat them exactly the same; a person's just a person to me." Furthermore, some of the integrationist aspirations of racial minority movements, especially the civil rights movement, invoke this sort of idea. Consider the famous phrases from the "I Have a Dream" speech, the line that made Shelby Steele's career: "that someday my four little children will be judged, not by the color of their skin, but by the content of their character."

The core criticisms of this "race as ideology" approach, in our view, are two. First, it fails to recognize that the salience of a social construct can develop over half a millennium or more of diffusion, or should we say enforcement, as a fundamental principle of social organization and identity formation. The longevity of the race concept, and the enormous number of effects race-thinking (and race-acting) have produced, guarantee that race will remain a feature of social reality across the globe, and *a fortiori* in our own country, despite its lack of intrinsic or scientific merit (in the biological sense).

Our second, and related, criticism of this approach is that it fails to recognize that at the level of experience, of everyday life, race is an almost indissoluble part of our identities. Our society is so thoroughly racialized that to be without racial identity is to be in danger of having no identity. To be raceless is akin to being genderless. Indeed, when one cannot identify another's race, a microsociological "crisis of interpretation" results, something perhaps best interpreted in ethnomethodological or perhaps Goffmanian terms. To complain about such a situation may be understandable, but it does not advance understanding.

RACE AS AN OBJECTIVE CONDITION

On the other side of the coin, it is clearly problematic to assign objectivity to the race concept. Such theoretical practice puts us in quite heterogeneous, and sometimes unsavory, company. Of course the biologistic racial theories of the past do this: here we are thinking of the prototypes of fascism such as Gobineau and Chamberlain (see Mosse 1978), of the eugenicists such as Lothrop Stoddard and Madison Grant, and of the "founding fathers" of scientific racism such as Agassiz, Broca, Terman, and Yerkes (see Kevles 1985; Chase 1977). Indeed, up to our own time we can find an extensive legacy of this sort of thinking. Stephen Jay Gould makes devastating critiques of such views (1981).

But much liberal and even radical social science, though firmly committed to a social, as opposed to biological, interpretation of race, nevertheless also slips into a kind of objectivism about racial identity and racial meaning. This is because race is all too frequently treated as an *independent variable*. Thus, to select only prominent examples, Daniel Moynihan, William Julius Wilson, Milton Gordon, and many other mainstream thinkers theorize race in terms that downplay its variability and historically contingent character. Even these major thinkers, who explicitly reject biologistic forms of racial theory, fall prey to a kind of creeping objectivism of race. For in their analyses a modal explanatory approach emerges: as sociopolitical circumstances change over historical time, racially defined groups adapt or fail to adapt to these changes, achieving mobility or remaining mired in poverty, and so on. In this logic there is no problematization of group identities, of the constantly shifting parameters through which race is understood, group interests are assigned, statuses are ascribed, agency is attained, and roles are performed.

Contemporary racial theory, then, is often "objectivistic" about its fundamental category. Although abstractly acknowledged to be a sociohistorical construct, race in practice is often treated as an objective fact: one simply *is* one's race; in the contemporary United States, if we discard euphemisms, we have five color-based racial categories: black, white, brown, yellow, and red.

This is problematic, indeed ridiculous, in numerous ways. Nobody really belongs in these boxes; they are patently absurd reductions of human variation. But even accepting the nebulous "rules" of racial classification—such as "hypodescent" (see Harris 1964; Davis 1991)—many people don't fit anywhere. Into what categories should we place Arab Americans, for example? Brazilians? South Asians? Such a list could be extended almost indefinitely. Objectivist treatments, lacking a critique of the *constructed* character of racial meanings, also clash with experiential dimensions of the issue. If one doesn't act black, white, or whatever, that's just deviance from the norm. There is in these approaches an insufficient appreciation of the *performative* aspect of race, as postmodernists might call it.[4]

To summarize, then, the critique of this race-as-objective-condition approach fails on three counts. First, it cannot grasp the process-oriented and relational character of racial identity and racial meaning. Second, it denies the historicity and social comprehensiveness of the race concept. And third, it cannot account for the way actors, both individual and collective, have to manage incoherent and conflictual racial meanings and identities in everyday life. It has no concept, in short, of what we have labeled racial formation.

Toward a Critical Theory of the Concept of Race

The foregoing clearly sets forth the agenda any adequate theorization of the race concept must fulfill. Such an approach must be constructed so as to steer between the Scylla of "race as illusionary" and the Charybdis of "racial objectivism." Such a critical theory can be consistently developed, we suggest, drawing upon the racial formation approach. Such a theoretical formulation, too, must be explicitly historicist. It must recognize the importance of historical context and contingency in the framing of racial categories and the social construction of racially defined experiences.

What would be the minimum conditions for the development of such a critical, process-oriented theory of race? We suggest that it must meet three requirements:

- It must apply to contemporary political relationships.
- It must apply in an increasingly global context.
- It must apply across historical time.

Let us address each of these points briefly.

Contemporary Political Relationships

The meaning and salience of race are forever being reconstituted in the present. Today such new relationships emerge chiefly at the point where some counterhegemonic or postcolonial power is attained. At that point the meanings and the political articulations of race proliferate.

A central example is the appearance of competing racial projects, by which we mean efforts to institutionalize racial meanings and identities in particular social structures, notably those of individual, family, community, and state (see Winant 1990, 1991). As egalitarian movements contend with racial "backlash" over sustained periods of time, as binary logics of racial antagonism (white/black, ladino/indio, settler/native, etc.) become more complex and decentered, political deployments of the concept of race come to signal qualitatively new types of political domination, as well as new types of opposition.

Consider the case of the United States. It is now possible to perpetuate racial domination without making any explicit reference to race at all. Subtextual or "coded" racial signifiers, or the mere denial of the continuing significance of race, may suffice. Similarly, in terms of opposition, it is now possible to resist racial domination in entirely new ways, particularly by limiting the reach and penetration of the political system into everyday life, by generating new identities, new collectivities, new (imagined) communities that are relatively less permeable to the hegemonic system.[5] Much of the rationale for Islamic currents among blacks in the United States, for the upsurge in black anti-Semitism, and to some extent for the phenomenon of Afrocentrism, can be found here. Thus the old choices, integration vs. separatism and assimilation vs. nationalism, are no longer the only options.

In the "underdeveloped" world, proliferation of so-called postcolonial phenomena also has significant racial dimensions, as the entire Fanonian tradition (merely to select one important theoretical current) makes clear. Crucial debates have now been occurring for a decade or more on issues such as postcolonial subjectivity and identity, the insufficiency of the simple dualism of "Europe and its others," and the subversive and parodic dimensions of political culture at and beyond the edges of the old imperial boundaries.[6]

The Global Context of Race

The geography of race is becoming more complex. Once more easily seen in terms of imperial reach, in terms of colonization, conquest, and migration, racial space is becoming *globalized* and thus accessible to a new kind of comparative analysis. This only becomes possible now, at a historical moment when the distinction "developed/underdeveloped" has been definitively overcome. Obviously by this we don't mean that now there are no disparities between North and South or rich and poor. We mean that the movement of capital and labor has internationalized all nations, all regions. Today we have reached the point where "the empire strikes back" (see Centre for Contemporary Cultural Studies 1982), as former (neo)colonial subjects, now redefined as "immigrants," challenge the majoritarian status of the formerly metropolitan group (the whites, the Europeans, the "Americans" or "French," etc.). Meanwhile such phenomena as the rise of "diasporic" models of blackness, the creation of "pan-ethnic" communities of Latinos and Asians (in such countries as the United Kingdom or the United States), and the breakdown of borders in both Europe and North America all seem to be internationalizing and racializing previously national polities, cultures, and identities. To take just one example, popular culture now internationalizes racial awareness almost instantaneously, as reggae, rap, samba, and various African pop styles leap from continent to continent.[7]

Because of these transformations it becomes possible to make a global comparison of hegemonic social/political orders based on race. We think that in a highly specified form, i.e., not as mere reactions to or simple negations of "Western" cultural/theoretical dominance, such notions as diasporic consciousness or racially informed standpoint epistemologies deserve more serious attention as efforts to express the contemporary globalization of racial space (see Mudimbe 1988; Rabinow 1986; Harding 1986). Indeed, recent developments such as the construction of new racial identities or the phenomenon of pan-ethnicity simply cannot be understood without recognizing that the territorial reach of racial hegemony is now global.

The dissolution of the transparent racial identity of the formerly dominant group—that is to say, the increasing racialization of whites in Europe and the United States—must also be recognized as proceeding from the increasingly globalized dimensions of race. As previous assumptions erode, white identity loses its transparency and the easy elision with "racelessness" that accompanies racial domination. "Whiteness" becomes a matter of anxiety and concern.

The Emergence of Racial Time

Some final notes are in order in respect to the problem of the epochal nature of racial time. Classical social theory had an enlightenment-based view of time, a perspective that understood the emergence of modernity in terms of the rise of capitalism and the bourgeoisie. This view was by no means limited to Marxism. Weberian disenchantment and the rise of the Durkheimian division of labor also partake of this temporal substrate. Only rarely does the racial dimension of historical temporality appear in this body of thought, as for example in Marx's excoriation of the brutalities of "primitive accumulation":

The discovery of gold and silver in America, the extirpation, enslavement, and entomb-
ment in mines of the aboriginal population, the beginning of the conquest and looting
of the East Indies, the turning of Africa into a warren for the commercial hunting of
blackskins, signalized the rosy dawn of the era of capitalist production. These idyllic
proceedings are the chief momenta of primitive accumulation. On their heels treads
the commercial war of the European nations with the globe for a theater. It begins
with the revolt of the Netherlands from Spain, assumes giant dimensions in England's
AntiJacobin War, and is still going on in the opium wars with China, etc. (Marx 1967:
751)

Yet even Marx frequently legitimated such processes as the inevitable and ultimately
beneficial birth-pangs of classlessness—enacted by the ceaselessly revolutionary
bourgeoisie.

Today such teleological accounts seem hopelessly outmoded. Historical time
could well be interpreted in terms of something like a racial *longue dureé*. For has
there not been an immense historical rupture represented by the rise of Europe,
the onset of African enslavement, the *conquista,* and the subjugation of much of
Asia? We take the point of much poststructural scholarship on these matters to
be quite precisely an effort to explain "Western" or colonial time as a huge project
demarcating human "difference," or more globally, as Todorov for example would
argue, of framing partial collective identities in terms of externalized "others"
(Todorov 1985). Just as, for example, the writers of the *Annales* school sought to
locate the deep logic of historical time in the means by which material life was
produced—diet, shoes, and so forth (Braudel 1981)—so we might usefully think of
a racial *longue dureé* in which the slow inscription of phenotypical signification took
place upon the human body, in and through conquest and enslavement to be sure,
but also as an enormous act of expression, of narration.

In short, just as the noise of the "big bang" still resonates through the universe,
so the overdetermined construction of world "civilization" as a product of the rise
of Europe and the subjugation of the rest of us still defines the race concept. Such
speculative notes, to be sure, can be no more than provocations. Nor can we
conclude this effort to reframe the agenda of racial theory with a neat summation.
There was a long period—centuries—in which race was seen as a natural condition,
an essence. This was only recently succeeded, although not entirely superseded,
by a way of thinking about race as subordinate to more supposedly concrete,
"material" relationships; thus we have become used to thinking about race as an
illusion, an excrescence. Perhaps now we are approaching the end of this racial
epoch too.

We may, to our dismay, have to give up our familiar way of thinking about race
once more. If so, there may also be some occasion for delight. For it may be
possible to glimpse yet another view of race, in which the concept operates neither
as a signifier of comprehensive identity, nor as one of fundamental difference,
both of which are patently absurd, but rather as a marker of the infinity of variations
we humans hold as a common heritage and hope for the future.

Notes

1. Minor objections would have to do with Fields's functionalist view of ideology, and her claim that the race concept only "came into existence" when needed by whites in North American colonies beginning in the late seventeenth century. The concept of race, of course, has a longer history than that (Fields 1990: 101).
2. Fields's admirer David Roediger also criticizes her on this point. "At times she nicely balances the ideological creation of racial attitudes with their manifest and ongoing importance and their (albeit ideological) reality. . . . But elsewhere, race disappears into the 'reality' of class" (see Roediger 1991: 7–8).
3. Another important thinker who has at least flirted with the idea of race as illusion is Kwame Anthony Appiah. See "The Uncompleted Argument: DuBois and the Illusion of Race" (in Gates, ed., 1985); idem, "Racisms" (in Goldberg, ed., 1990).
4. "The question of identification is never the affirmation of a pregiven identity, never a self-fulfilling prophecy—it is always the production of an image of identity and the transformation of the subject in assuming that image" (Bhabha 1990b: 188).
5. The work of Paul Gilroy, which focuses on the British racial situation, is particularly revealing in regard to these matters. Gilroy's analysis of the significance of popular music in the African diaspora is indispensable (see Gilroy 1991).
6. There is a vast literature by now on these matters, whose founding statement is undoubtedly Edward Said's *Orientalism* (1978); also useful is Bhabha, ed., 1990a.
7. David Lopez and Yen Espiritu define pan-ethnicity as "the development of bridging organizations and solidarities among subgroups of ethnic collectivities that are often seen as homogeneous by outsiders." Such a development, they claim, is a crucial feature of ethnic change—"supplanting both assimilation and ethnic particularism as the direction of change for racial/ethnic minorities." While pan-ethnic formation is facilitated by an ensemble of cultural factors (e.g., common language and religion) and structural factors (e.g., class, generation, and geographical concentration), Lopez and Espiritu conclude that a specific concept of race is fundamental to the construction of pan-ethnicity (Lopez and Espiritu 1990: 198).

References

Appiah, K. A. (1985). "The uncompleted argument: DuBois and the illusion of race." In H. L. Gates, ed., *"Race," Writing, and Difference*. Chicago: University of Chicago Press.
———. (1990). "Racisms." In D. T. Goldberg ed., *Anatomy of Racism*. Minneapolis: University of Minnesota Press.
Bhabha, H. K. ,ed. (1990a). *Nation and Narration*. New York: Routledge.
———. (1990b). "Interrogating identity: The postcolonial prerogative." In D. T. Goldberg, ed., *Anatomy of Racism*. Minneapolis: University of Minnesota Press.
Braudel, E. (1981). *The Structures of Everyday Life: The Limits of the Possible*. Vol. 1 of *Civilization and Capitalism, 15th–18th Century*, trans. S. Reynolds. New York: Harper.
Centre for Contemporary Cultural Studies. (1982). *The Empire Strikes Back: Race and Racism in 70s Britain*. London: Hutchinson.
Chase, A. (1977). *The Legacy of Malthus: The Social Costs of the New Scientific Racism*. New York: Knopf.
Davis, F. J. (1991). *Who Is Black? One Nation's Definition*. University Park: Pennsylvania State University Press.
Fields, B. (1990). "Slavery, race, and ideology in the United States of America." *New Left Review* 181: 95–118.
Gilroy, P. (1991). *"There Ain't No Black in the Union Jack": The Cultural Politics of Race and Nation*. Chicago: University of Chicago Press.
Harding, S. (1986). *The Science Question in Feminism*. Ithaca, N.Y.: Cornell University Press.
Harris, Wilson. (1964). *Patterns of Race in the Americas*. New York: Norton.

Kevles, D. J. (1985). *In the Name of Eugenics: Genetics and the Uses of Human Heredity.* New York: Knopf.

Lopez, D., and Y. Espiritu (1990). "Pan-ethnicity in the United States: A theoretical framework." *Ethnic and Racial Studies* 13: 198–224.

Marx, K. (1967). *Capital,* vol. 1. New York: International Publishers.

Mosse, G. L. (1978). *Toward the Final Solution: A History of European Racism.* New York: Fertig.

Mudimbe, V. Y. (1988). *The Invention of Africa: Gnosis, Philosophy, and the Order of Knowledge.* Bloomington: Indiana University Press.

Omi, M., and H. Winant (1986). *Racial Formation in the United States: From the 1960s to the 1980s.* New York: Routledge.

Rabinow, P. (1986). "Representations are social facts: Modernity and post-modernity in anthropology." In J. Clifford and G. E. Marcus, eds., *Writing Culture: The Poetics and Politics of Anthropology.* Berkeley: University of California Press.

Roedinger, D. (1991). *The Wages of Whiteness: Race and the Making of the American Working Class.* London: Verso.

Said, E. (1978). *Orientalism.* New York: Pantheon.

Thomas, W. I., and D. S. Thomas (1928). *The Child in America: Behavior Problems and Programs.* New York: Knopf.

Todorov, T. (1985). *The Conquest of America: The Question of the Other,* trans. R. Howard. New York: Harper.

Winant, H. (1990). "Postmodern racial politics in the United States: Difference and inequality." *Socialist Review* 90, no.1: 121–147.

_____. (1991). Rethinking race in Brazil. *Journal of Latin American Studies* 24, no. 1: 173–192.

A Borderless World?

From Colonialism to Transnationalism

And the Decline of the Nation-State

Masao Miyoshi

Discourse and practice are interdependent. Practice follows discourse, while discourse is generated by practice. As for the discourse on colonialism, there is a long lineage of engagements with the history of colonialism. One recalls papers by practitioners such as John Locke, Edmund Burke, James Mill, and Thomas Macaulay early on, and critiques of the practice by Hobson, Lenin, Luxemburg, and Schumpeter among many others since the height of imperialism. Numerous metropolitan fiction writers are obsessed by the presence of remote colonies, from Melville and Flaubert to Conrad and Gide. Actually, hardly any Western writer from Jane Austen to Thomas Mann, from Balzac to D. H. Lawrence could manage to escape from the spell of modern expansionism. The modern West depends on its colonies for self-definition, as Edward Said's newest book, *Culture and Imperialism,* argues.[1]

In the area of literary theory and criticism, however, the discourse on colonialism has a surprisingly brief history. One needs to remember that writers of the Negritude Movement and other Third World writers such as Aimé Césaire, C.L.R. James, Frantz Fanon, and George Lamming[2] began to voice their views from the oppositionist perspective soon after the end of World War II.[3] And yet it was only fifteen years ago—well after the disappearance of administrative colonization from most regions of the world—that the discourse on colonialism entered the mainstream of Western theory and criticism.[4] Examining history from the perspective of personal commitment to resistance, Said's *Orientalism* in 1978 dramatically heightened the consciousness of power and culture relations, vitally affecting segments of disciplines in the humanities.[5] In other words, it was not until years after the end of formal colonialism between 1945 and 1970 that theory was enabled to negotiate issues of colonialism as an admissible factor in criticism. The time gap of a good many decades in literary history here is interesting enough if only because it demonstrates the discipline's habitual unease and disinclination in recent times to engage with extratextual matters, especially those concerning the imminent transfer of powers and resources. The history of decolonization and the memory of administrative and occupational colonialism, dangerously verging on nostalgia at times, form the base on which colonial and minority discourses have been built in recent years.[6]

The circumstances surrounding this process of liberation and independence, however, have no widely accepted narrative as yet. Does colonialism only survive today in a few places such as Israel, South Africa, Macao, Ireland, and Hong Kong? Does the rest of the world enjoy the freedom of postcolonialism? The problem we face now is how to understand today's global configuration of power and culture that is both similar and different vis-à-vis the historical metropolitan-colonial paradigm. This chapter is concerned with such transformation and persistence in the neocolonial practice of displacement and ascendancy, and with its specular engagements in discourse. The current academic preoccupation with "postcoloniality" and multiculturalism looks suspiciously like another alibi to conceal the actuality of global politics. This chapter argues that colonialism is even more active now in the form of transnational corporatism.

We might begin with the beginning of the decolonization process.[7] The end of the cold war in 1989 has enabled us to look back at the history of the past half-century—or even longer—from a perspective informed by truly radical change. We are, for instance, once again reassessing the end of World War II, which fundamentally altered the world system. The destruction of German and Japanese aggressions did not result in the full resuscitation of the hegemony of the European industrial states. The Western European nations, especially Britain and France, were too profoundly injured to be able simultaneously to rebuild their domestic industrial bases and to sustain their military forces to dominate their colonies. In retrospect, we see that the Soviet Union kept up the front of a military superpower while disastrously wrecking its production and distributive systems. The avowed war objective of Germany and Japan—liberation and decolonization through a new world order (*die neue Ordnung* and *sekai Shin chitsujo* in Axis slogans)—was a total sham; the colonized of the world that had sided with their master states in World War II seized the day and would not settle for less than independence and autonomy. Liberation was demanded and allowed to take place over several subsequent decades, albeit under varying circumstances.

After World War II, independence appeared to have ended the humiliating and exploitive colonial domination that had lasted anywhere from decades to centuries in countries covering at least 85 percent of the earth's land surface. And yet freedom and self-rule—for which the colonized had bitterly struggled, often at the cost of immense sacrifice—were unexpectedly elusive. Decolonization neither effected emancipation and equality nor provided new wealth or peace. Instead, suffering and misery continued nearly everywhere in an altered form, at the hands of different agencies. Old compradors took over, and it was far from rare that they went on to protect their old masters' interest in exchange for compensation. Thus the welfare of the general population saw little improvement; in fact, in recent years it has worsened in many old colonies with the possible exceptions of the East Asian Newly Industrialized Economies (NIEs) and the Association of Southeast Asian

Nations (ASEAN).[8] The "postcolonial" deterioration Basil Davidson called "the black man's burden" was a result of double processes of colonization and decolonization, which were inextricably intermeshed.[9] We are all familiar with the earlier stage. As the colonizers drew borders at will, inscribing their appropriation on a map, tribes were joined or fragmented. Those who were encircled by a more or less arbitrary cartographic form were inducted into servitude on behalf of the distant and unseen metropolis. Western culture was to be the normative civilization, and the indigenous cultures were banished as premodern and marginal. And although subaltern resistance proved far more resilient than anticipated, and colonial programs were never really fulfilled anywhere, the victor's presence was powerful enough in most places to maintain a semblance of control and order despite unceasing resistance and opposition.

With the removal of formal colonialism after World War II, the cartographic unit that constituted a colony was now perceived by both the departing colonizers and the newly freed to be a historically autonomous territory, that is to say, a modern nation-state, with a national history, national language, national culture, national coherence, and finally a state apparatus of its own as symbolized by a national anthem, flag, museum, and map. In many places, however, the entity was no more than a counterfeit reproduction of, and by, its former Conqueror, having neither a discrete history nor logic that would convince the newly independent citizens of its legitimacy or authenticity. Earlier, while struggling against the oppressors, self-definition was not difficult to obtain: opposition articulated their identity. Once the Europeans were gone, however, the residents of a colonial territory were thrown back on their old disrupted site, which had in the precolonial days operated on a logic and history altogether different. The liberated citizens of a colony now had to renegotiate the conditions of a nation-state in which they were to reside thereafter. Retroversion to nativism might have been an option, but the Third World was fraught with inequalities and contradictions among various religions, tribes, regions, classes, genders, and ethnicities that had been thrown together in any given colonial territory. And production and distribution were often horrendously inefficient. The golden age of a nation-state's memory proved to be neither pure nor just, nor even available, but a utopian dream often turned into a bloody nightmare. The hatred of the oppressors was enough to mobilize toward liberation, but was inadequate for the management of an independent state. As Fanon had predicted early in the game, attempts at nativism indeed ended in disastrous corruption and self-destruction, and they are still ongoing events in many parts of the world. Once absorbed into the "chronopolitics" of the secular West, colonized space cannot reclaim autonomy and seclusion; once dragged out of their precolonial state, the indigenes of peripheries have to deal with the knowledge of the outside world, irrespective of their own wishes and inclinations. And yet the conditions of the modern nation-state are available to most former colonies.[10]

One recalls that Western industrialized nations had the luxury of several centuries—however bloody—to resolve civil strifes, religious wars, and rural/urban or agricultural/industrial contradictions. Former colonies had far less time to work them out, and they had been under the domination of alien powers. Thus most former colonies have yet to agree on the logic and objective of a geographic and demographic unit. The will to fragmentation battles with the will to totalization.

One cannot forget that there were countless cases of overt and covert interventions by the United States and other colonial powers through economic, political, and military means. Peaceful progress has been structurally denied to them. Alliances among Third World states against First World domination such as the Bandung Conference (1955), the Organization of Petroleum Exporting Countries (OIXEC, 1960), UN Conference on Trade and Development (UNCTAD, 1964), and the New International Economic Order (NIEO, 1974) have all performed poorly, ultimately surrendering to the Bretton Woods system, which the victorious West established in 1944 for the postwar management of the ruined world with the World Bank, International Monetary Fund (IMF), and General Agreement on Tariffs and Trade (GATT) as the three central economic instruments.

It is widely agreed that the nation-state is a modern Western construction. It can be further argued that the gradual ascendancy of the nation-state around 1800 in the West was a function of colonialism. Earlier, at the beginning of the modern period, the European monarchs sponsored adventurist projects, which were further propelled thereafter by the bourgeoisie's greater need for markets and resources to form a policy of colonial expansion. About the same time, as the industrial revolution increased production efficiency, urban areas received a large influx of agricultural laborers, creating a pool of surplus population.[11] These potentially rebellious unemployed and displaced workers needed to be depressurized in the marginal areas of the labor market. Toward that end, the organizers of colonialism had to persuade their recruits and foot soldiers of the profitability as well as the nobility of their mission. Voyaging into distant and savage regions of the world was frightening enough, and the prospects of sharing the loot were far from assured. Above all, bourgeois leaders had to conceal their class interests, which sharply conflicted with the interests of the populace at large. They needed crusaders and supporters who trusted their good faith, believed in the morality of their mission, and hoped for the eventual wealth promised them. Thus they made the myth of the nation-state (that is, the belief in the shared community ruled by a representative government) and the myth of *mission civilisatrice* (that is, the voyagers' racial superiority over the heathen barbarians) seem complementary and indispensable. In such an "imagined [or manufactured] community," the citizens were bound by kinship and communality; they were in it together.[12] In the very idea of the nation-state, the colonialists found a politicoeconomical as well as moral-mythical foundation on which to build their policy and apology.

Thus the development of Western colonialism from the sixteenth to the mid-twentieth century coincides with the rise and fall of the nation-state. The fate of the nation-state in recent years, however, is not synonymous with the "rise and fall of the great powers," as Paul Kennedy argues.[13] The bourgeois capitals in the industrialized world are now as powerful, or even far more powerful, than before. But the logic they employ, the clients they serve, the tools available to them, the sites they occupy—in short, their very identities—have all changed. They no longer wholly depend on the nation-state of their origin for protection and facilitation. They still make use of the nation-state structure, of course, but their power and energy reside in a different locus, as I will argue below.

Even before 1945, Winston Churchill sensed that Britain had to yield its imperial scepter to the United States. If not at the Yalta Conference, by the time he was voted out of 10 Downing Street, he knew the management of the world was now in the hands of the United States. He was, of course, right. Colonial history since 1945 converges with U.S. history. At the end of World War II, the United States' economy was finally free from all scars of the Depression. In peacetime, however, prospects were far from rosy. To downscale wartime economy would mean a drastic rise in unemployment (a miniscule 1.2 percent in 1942) as well as an absolute plunge in production and consumption, resurrecting the nightmare of 1930. There were a series of labor strikes (steel, coal, rail, and port) in 1946; President Truman's veto of the Taft-Hartley Labor Act, which sought to curb strikes, was overturned by the Congress in 1947. It was under such circumstances of economic tension and unease that the president decided to contain "Communist terrorism" in Greece and Turkey in 1947, and the Marshall Plan was inaugurated to aid European reconstruction. The GNP had sunk ominously by 19 percent in 1946 but only by 2.8 percent in 1947; and if it remained at a stagnant 0.02 percent in 1949, the Korean War (whose origins are not as yet unambiguous)[14] saved the day: the GNP rose by 8.5 percent in 1950 and 10.3 percent in 1951.[15] Similarly, just about the time the peace treaty with North Korea was signed in 1953 (resulting in a minor recession), the United States began to aid the French government in its anti-insurgency war in Southeast Asia, shouldering 75 percent of the cost; and the training of South Vietnamese troops commenced in 1955 after the catastrophic defeat of the French army at Dien Bien Phu in 1954. When President Eisenhower warned Americans against "the potential for the disastrous rise of misplaced power" in the hands of the "military-industrial complex" and the "scientific-technological elite," the security state system had already been firmly—perhaps irretrievably—established in the United States.[16] (One notes that this was the decade in which the universities expanded to absorb the returned GIs, lowering the female-male college attendance ratio well below the level in the 1920s.[17] And in literary theory and practice, conservative ideology and formalist aestheticism of course dominated.)

The cold war, regularly reinforced by hot "anti-Communist" skirmishes, then, was a dependable instrument for the U.S. economy to organize its revenues and expenditures and to maintain a certain level of production and distribution. One notes in this connection that "in every year from 1951 to 1990, the Defense Department budget has exceeded the combined net profits of all American corporations." The U.S. Constitution does not accord the president the top economic power; nevertheless, he has acquired that capacity from his role as chief executive of the military economy's management. Subordinate to the President/C.E.O. are the managers of 35,000 prime contracting firms and about 100,000 subcontractors. The Pentagon uses 500,000 people in its own Central Administrative Office acquisition network."[18] The Pentagon, in short, is the U.S. equivalent of Japan's Ministry of International Trade and Industry (MITI); it plans and executes a centrally organized economic policy. Thus it is more accurate to say that national security questions were essentially economic in nature. The U.S. economy, rather than merely reacting to uncontrollable foreign threats, actually guided world relations.

Soon after the recession in 1957 and 1958, the Kennedy administration sought to expand international trade by lowering the European Community tariffs through the GATT Kennedy Round. The so-called liberalization of trade in the early 1960s restored the integrated world market and encouraged direct foreign investment. The result was a marked rise in European investment by American enterprises. This expansion in international trade led to the rapid development of "multinational enterprises" and "transnational corporations," that is, giant companies that not only import and export raw and manufactured goods but also transfer capital, factories, and sales outlets across national borders, as will be explained more fully later on. And this history of economic organizations needs to be recalled here in the context of global decolonization.

The fracture of the British empire was accelerating throughout the 1960s with the loss of innumerable colonies one after another—from Cyprus, Nigeria, and Kenya to Jamaica, Malaysia, and Singapore.[19] Having lost Indochina and other colonies in the 1950s, France finally yielded Algeria in 1962. At the same time, the U.S. GNP increased at a brisk pace—7 to 9 percent, with fairly low inflation and unemployment rates. Economically and militarily invincible, the United States was ready to protect capitalist interests everywhere, but especially in Vietnam. If President Johnson was trying to win support for his Great Society programs and the war on poverty by offering a Southeast Asian expedition to the conservative positions, his gamble was calamitous. As no one can easily forget, protests raged across the country, splitting the nation into doves and hawks, Clintons and Gores. On the antiwar demonstrators' enemy list, the names of defense-related corporations were conspicuous: General Motors, General Electric, DuPont, and Dow Chemical, to name a few. And it was many of these corporations that began during the 1960s to set the pattern of systematic transfer of capital and factories overseas. There were other factors, too; technological innovations in automation, synthetic chemistry, and electronic engineering produced an enormous accumulation of capital and a remarkable improvement in communication and transportation as well. The U.S. policy of liberal trade was both a response to and an instigation of such a development.

In the late 1960s, the global domination of U.S. multinational corporations was unchangeable. Mainly centered in the Western hemisphere, less in Africa and Asia, U.S. foreign direct investment (FDI) amounted to one half of all the cross-border investments worldwide, far surpassing the British FDI that stood at 20 percent and the French FDI at less 10 percent.[20] Transnational corporations meant U.S. transnationals, then, and this pattern remained unchanged until the mid-1970s. The concentration of U.S. investments in Western Europe can be explained by four factors: high interest rates in Europe; the emergence of the European Economic Community (EEC); the U.S. tax laws favorable to overseas profits; and comparatively low costs of skilled labor in Europe. The serious task of controlling the world order for the West was still assigned to the U.S. government with its military and political programs of aid and intervention.[21]

Around 1970, European and Japanese transnational corporations (TNCs) emerged rapidly to compete with their U.S. counterparts, and their main target was none other than the advanced manufacturing industries in the United States itself. This bold move is explainable by several economic developments. First, the U.S. dollar was devalued after the Nixon administration froze wages and prices and suspended conversion of dollars into gold in 1971, making the U.S. attractive for foreign investment. Second, the U.S. market also became attractive again after the political instability and unpredictability in the rest of the world as a result of the fourth Middle East war of 1973 and its consequent oil embargo. Third, the European and Japanese industrial recovery was strong enough to wage a vigorous investment campaign in the United States. Finally, trade friction intensified in time, and European and Japanese manufacturers saw an advantage in building plants inside the U.S. market. The U.S. share of TNCs was still overwhelming, but in the 1980s it fell to 33 percent as against Britain at 18 percent, West Germany at 10 percent, and Japan at 8 percent.

In 1985 the United States negotiated a depreciation of the dollar at the G5 (or Group of 5) meeting in New York. The Plaza Agreement forced the dollar down by one half against the yen, raising Japan's currency value by 100 percent. Though aimed at an increase of U.S. export to Japan and a decrease of Japan's export to the United States, the measure was not really effective. Before long, moreover, Japanese TNCs realized the power of the strengthened yen, with which they proceeded to stage an aggressive campaign of investment, while cutting prices as much as they could to maintain their market share. What characterizes this stage of multinational development is, in addition to continued investment in the United States, a general concentration on four regional targets: tax havens (for example, Curaçao in the Dutch Caribbean); OPEC nations; Asian NIEs (South Korea, Taiwan, Hong Kong, and Singapore); and ASEAN countries (Thailand, Malaysia, Indonesia, the Philippines, Singapore, and Brunei). Many of these nations were ruled by authoritarian governments that banned labor unions and opposition parties, thus achieving political "stability"—a minimal requirement for a large-scale TNC commitment. There has also been a gradual development of TNCs among OPEC, NIEs, Mexico, and India, investing in each other as well as in the United States. Also, smaller corporations (that is, those with capital outlays of between 100 and 500 million dollars) in both industrialized and less industrialized nations were active in transnationalizing their operations. And this coexistence of TNCs of various origins (including joint ventures) is what makes the analysis of economic hegemony so complicated and difficult.

What emerges from this is an increasingly tightly woven network of multinational investments among EC, North American, and East Asian countries, gradually transforming the multinational corporations into transnational corporations. The distinction between the two corporate categories is certainly problematic: the terms are frequently used interchangeably. If there are differences, they are more or less in the degree of alienation from the countries of origin. The range of international trading might be explained developmentally as follows. First, domestic companies simply undertake export/import activities, linking up with local dealers. Then the companies take over overseas distribution and carry out their manufacturing, marketing, and sales overseas. Finally, the transnational corporations denationalize their operations by moving the old business system, including capital, personnel, and research and development. This final stage is reached when a corporation promotes loyalty to itself among shareholders, employees, and clients rather than to its country of origin or host countries. Thus, a multinational corporation (MNC) is one that is headquartered in a nation, operating in a number of countries. Its high-echelon personnel largely consist of the nationals of the country of origin, and the corporate loyalty is, though increasingly autonomous, finally tied to the home nation. A truly transnational corporation, on the other hand, might no longer be tied to its nation of origin but is adrift and mobile, ready to settle anywhere and exploit any state including its own, as long as the affiliation serves its own interest.[22]

Let me repeat here that a sharp distinction between a TNC and a MNC is impossible because the precise extent of the denationalization of a corporation is not readily determinable. There is, for instance, no systematic study of the TNC tax obligations as against their MNC counterparts, or of their comparative patterns of foreign direct investment. MNCs are as self-regarding as TNCs; however, a recent tendency toward lesser national identification and greater corporate self-interest is discernible. In other words, despite the ongoing dependence on the state apparatus (for example, the military), multinational corporations are in the process of denationalization and transnationalization.

There are still relatively few corporations that completely fit the TNC specification, but there are examples such as Asea Brown Bovari (ABB) among large-scale companies and Yaohan among smaller ones. Started in Sweden, ABB, with annual revenues of more than $25 billion, has no geographic center.[23] Yaohan began as a Japanese grocery store chain, severed its Japanese ties, and moved first to Brazil and then to Hong Kong, where it is located at least for now. It should be noted here that the corporate tax in Japan was 49.9 percent, whereas in Hong Kong it stood at 16.5 percent in 1989.[24] Yaohan's chairman declares that his real target in the twenty-first century is the one billion Chinese.[25] Many MNCs on the other hand are alertly comparing opportunities in their home countries and host countries as they map out their strategies for maximizing profits

TNCs of this type became more visible in the 1980s, although the loss of national sovereignty to the multinational companies had been discussed since the 1960s, and even earlier.[26] That this development should take place in the 1980s was no accident. After President Carter's stagflation in the late 1970s, President Reagan had a clearly defined program to promote private interests, supposedly with the conviction that strong private sectors would necessarily benefit the populace as a whole (but, in all likelihood, by simply following the cue cards handed over by the corporate designers of the policy). During this decade the transfer of wealth from the poor to the rich was carried out with remarkable efficiency. Corporate taxes were cut. Public services such as education, welfare, and medicine were reduced in the name of efficiency, resulting in a marked reliance on private enterprises such as Federal Express and private security services instead of "inefficient" public institutions such as the U.S. Postal Service or municipal police departments. There has even been talk of privatizing penal systems and public universities.[27] The 1980s also witnessed the reduction of the income tax rates for the higher brackets. The top tax on wages in 1945 was 94 percent, and in the 1950s though the 1970s it was in the 87 to 70 percent range; with the advent of President Reagan's administration the top tax on wages fell to 50 percent, and in 1991 under Bush it stood at 28 percent.[28] Thus the top one percent of Americans received 60 percent of the after-tax income gains between 1977 and 1989, while the bottom 40 percent of families had actual declines in income. According to the May 6, 1991 issue of *Business Week,* the typical CEO's pay was more than eighty-five times that of a typical manufacturing worker's pay in the United States, while the comparable ratio in Japan was only seventeen times.[29] Kevin Phillips reports, however, that "the pay of top corporate executives . . . soared to 130 to 140 times that of average workers, even while real or inflation-adjusted wages continued their 1980's decline."[30] Examples of illicit and semi-illicit business practices are too many to be enumerated here—from dubious mergers and appropriations and junk-bond scams to the savings and loan industry scandal. The number of poor people in 1991 increased to 35.7 million, that is, 14.2 percent of the total population, which is the highest figure since 1964.[31] In such an atmosphere of intensified self-regard and self-interest, corporate managers took it for granted that their business was to maximize profits with almost total disregard for consequences. They would go wherever there were lower taxes and greater profits.

It should be emphasized here that this move toward transnationalization was not just American but global. Leslie Sklair, in one of the most comprehensive studies to date of TNCs (from a Gramscian and feminist perspective), points out that "while there is no convincing evidence that the TNCs can bring salvation to the Third World, in many poor countries the TNCs are seen as responsible for the only bright spots in the economy and society. . . . [TNCs] are very widely sought after and they carry high prestige."[32] As mentioned earlier, not only industrialized nations but NIEs and other economies also produce corporations that maximize profits by freely crossing national borders. However one may view the TNC practice, TNCs are not beholden to any nation-states but seek their own interests and profits globally. They represent neither their home countries nor their host nations but simply their own corporate selves.

There are of course many other contributing factors. TNCs are immensely powerful. Sklair points out that "in 1986, according to the World Bank, 64 out of 120 countries had a GDP (gross domestic product) of less than $10 billion. United Nations data for 1985–86 show that 68 TNCs in mining and manufacturing had annual sales in excess of ten billion dollars, while all the top 50 banks, the top 20 securities firms, and all but one of the top 30 insurance companies had net assets in excess of ten billion" (pp. 48–49). That is, of the largest one hundred economic units in the world, more than fifty are TNCs.[33] Because of the rapid development in sophisticated computer technology—often justifiably called the third industrial revolution—in communication, transportation, and manufacturing, the transfer of capital, products, facilities, and personnel has been unprecedentedly efficient. Private funds—to the amount of billions of dollars at one transaction—flow from one industrial center to another, totalling every business day nearly 1 trillion dollars at the Clearing House Inter-bank Payment System (CHIPS) in New York City alone.[34] It goes without saying that this development weakens the interventionary power of central national banks, such as the Bundes Bank of Germany, Nihon Ginko of Japan, and the Federal Reserve of the United States.

Post-Fordist production methods enable TNCs to move their factories to any site that can offer trained and trainable cheap labor forces as long as there are tax inducements, political stability, adequate infrastructure, and relaxed environmental protection rules. Low civil rights consciousness, too, including underdeveloped unionism and feminism, is crucial; although female labor is abused everywhere, the wage difference between the sexes is still greater in the Third World—the target area for TNCs.[35] Global transportation is so efficient that the division of labor across national borders is now a given. Parts are produced in many places to be assembled—depending on particular tariffs, labor conditions, and other factors—at a locale strategically close to the targeted market.[36] There are innumerable joint ventures, such as GM and Toyota, or GE, RCA, and Thomson SA. Banks and other financial institutions also move across borders with fewer and fewer impediments.

In this MNC/TNC operation, at any rate, manufactured products are advertised and distributed globally, being identified only by brand name, not country of origin. In fact, the country of origin is itself becoming more and more meaningless. The "Buy American" drive is increasingly a hollow battle plan: the Honda Accord is manufactured in Ohio from 75 percent U.S.-made parts, while the Dodge Stealth is made in Japan by Mitsubishi.[37] "In the new Boeing 777 program, the Boeing Company is manufacturing only the wings, nose structure and engine nacelles. The rest of the wide-body airplane will come from hundreds of subcontractors in North America, Japan and Europe."[38] Almost no TV sets are wholly domestic products. It was announced in 1992 that "Zenith Electronics Corp., the last U.S.-owned television company, is moving final assembly of all of its large-screen sets to Mexico."[39] A TNC selects the place of operation, in short, solely by a fine calculus of costs and profits, involving the entire process of research, development, production, distribution, advertising, marketing, financing, and tax obligations.

TNCs are faced with the task of recruiting workers thoroughly familiar with local rules and customs as well as the specific corporate policies for worldwide operation. For that purpose, their work force usually comprises various nationalities and ethnicities. This aspect is significant in several ways. First, TNCs will increasingly require from all workers loyalty to the corporate identity rather than to their own national identities. Second, employees of various nationalities and ethnicities must be able to communicate with each other. In that sense, TNCs are at least officially and superficially trained to be color-blind and multicultural.[40] Despite the persistent recurrence of violent racist events in the United States, its immigration regulations were radically changed in 1965 to reject the ethnically defined quota system set out by the 1952 McCarran-Walter Act. In the revised Immigration Reform and Control Act of 1986 and the November 1990 reform bill, priorities are given to skills rather than ethnicities. TNCs, especially, are allowed to claim a quota from the category of 40,000 aliens with special abilities in addition to the general category of skilled experts and professionals.[41] Third, the need for a huge pool of such skilled workers creates a transnational class of professionals who can live and travel globally, while freely conversing with their colleagues in English, the lingua franca of the TNC era. The formation of the transnational class, or what Robert Reich in his *Work of Nations* calls "symbolic analysts," is itself a development that calls for further study, especially as this exclusive and privileged class relates—or does not relate—to those kept outside: the unemployed, the underemployed, the displaced, and the homeless.[42] The third industrial revolution, very much like the first two, creates an immense semiskilled and unskilled surplus labor, causing a huge demographic movement across the world and feeding into the mass underclass in every industrialized region.

Reich has little to say about the fate that awaits those who won't be able to move up to the class of privilege. The question remains, then, as to how the new elite managers compare to the professional class of modern industrial society and how they relate to those left marginalized and abandoned in the TNC structure.

Earlier, as traditional society transformed itself into bourgeois capitalist society in the West, intellectuals and professionals who served in the planning and execution of the capitalist agenda were led to think of themselves as free and conscientious critics and interpreters. In the age of TNCs, they are even more shielded and mediated by the complexity and sophistication of the situation itself because transnational corporatism is by definition unprovincial and global, that is, supposedly free from insular and idiosyncratic constrictions. If clear of national and ethnic blinders, the TNC class is not free of a new version of "ideologyless" ideology that is bent on the efficient management of global production and consumption, hence of world culture itself. Are the intellectuals of the world willing to participate in transnational corporatism and be its apologists? How to situate oneself in this neo-Daniel Bell configuration of transnational power and culture without being trapped by a dead-end nativism seems to be the most important question that faces every critic and theorist the world over at this moment, a question to which I will return later.

The decline of the nation-state has been accelerated by the end of the cold war. War activates nationalism and patriotism inasmuch as hostility deepens the chasm that cuts "them" off from "us." The binary alignment that was present in all foreign relations during the cold war was abruptly removed in 1989. With the demise of authoritarian socialist states, bourgeois capitalism looked to have triumphed over all rivals. Whether such a reading is right or wrong, the disappearance of "the other side," together with the end of administrative colonialism, has placed the nation-state in a vacant space that is ideologically uncontested and militarily constabularized. The choreographed display of high-tech destruction by the United States during the Gulf War could not conceal the lack of objective and meaning in that astounding military exercise. The Gulf War was the war of ultimate snobbery, all style, demonstrating power for the sake of power in a world after the cold war. The war expressed the contempt of the rich for the poor, just as military and political force were being replaced in importance by economic and industrial power. The single superpower, the United States, executed the war, of course, but as the "sharing" of the military expenses among the "allied nations" demonstrates, the war was fought on behalf of the dominant corporate structure rather than the United States, which served after all as no more than a mercenary. Does this mean that from now on the armed forces of the United States are in the service of a corporate alliance with little regard for its own people's interests? Is the state apparatus being even more sharply cut off than before from the welfare of the people? Wealth that generates right and might seems to have overwhelmed power that creates wealth.[43]

Against the effective operation of TNCs, the nation-states more and more look undefined and inoperable. Although the end of the cold war also loosened the ties that bound nation-states such as the Soviet Union and Yugoslavia while encouraging separatist movements in Scotland, Spain, India, Canada, and many other places, these are expressions of ethnicism, not nationalism.[44] To quote from *The New International Economy*, these independence movements are "a kind of mirrored reflection of the decline of the viability of nationalism as a politically unifying force, a decline occasioned moreover, by the economic and political internationalization."[45]

Admittedly, it is more customary nowadays to regard as "nationalistic" the "ethnic cleansing" by the Serbs, the Muslim and Hindu antagonism in India, or Islamic fundamentalism, but it seems at least as sensible to think of such neorevivalism, neoracism, and neoethnicism in conjunction with the decline of the nation-state. The fragmenting and fragmented units in these embattled areas in the world are newly wakened agents not for the construction of autonomous nations but for the abandonment of the expectations and responsibilities of the politico-economic national projects. Ethnicity and raciality are being brandished as the refuge from the predicaments of an integrated political and economic body. As globalization intensifies, neoethnicism is appealing because of its brute simplicity and reductionism in this rapidly altering and bewilderingly complex age. But over all the separatist aspirations—from Czechoslovakia, Yugoslavia, India, and Myanmar—hover the dark shadows of economic anxieties that none of these "nationalist" units have sufficiently recognized as they rush toward independence and purification. It seems almost that the inadequacy of the nation-state is now fully realized, and the provincial strongmen are all trying to grab a piece of real estate for keeps before all is incorporated and appropriated by transnational corporations.

Those who have thought of the nation-state as a historical bourgeois invention for the sake of protecting a national economy from the threats of free democracy might hail transnationalism's negative effect on the nation-state. To the extent that war was an unavoidable product of national economy, as argued by Marx in his 1848 *Communist Manifesto*, there is something exhilarating about the demise of the nation-state. At the same time, the state did, and still does, perform certain functions, for which there is as of now no substitute agency. It defines citizenship, controls currency, imposes law, protects public health, provides general education, maintains security, and, more importantly, guides the national economy (though little acknowledged in the United States, as I pointed out earlier), all with revenues raised through taxation. As we enumerate these functions, however, it becomes indisputably clear that the list is not one of achievements but of failures. In all these items, the state as a political authority seems biased and compromised. It is not the nation as an integrated whole but certain classes, the privileged in it, that receive a major portion of benefits from the state performing these tasks. The state fails to satisfy most of its sectors and leaves most of its citizenry resentful. Thus, there is a palpable aversion to taxation among all segments of the population, rich or poor, although everyone knows that tax is the glue that keeps the nation-state coherent. The nation-state, in this sense, no longer works; it is thoroughly appropriated by transnational corporations. Thus for some it is a sheer annoyance, but for a vast majority it serves as a nostalgic and sentimental myth that offers an illusion of a classless organic community of which everyone is an equal member. Such an illusion of national community stubbornly persists.

Let me give one more example of the use of the concept of nation-states. The formation of a highly complex web across national borders of industrial production and distribution—in a word, transnationalization—largely invalidates disputes over surpluses and deficits in trade. Reich rightly argues that wealth is accumulated at the site where managers and technicians carry out research and development, not where the corporations or manufactured goods originate.[46] As I mentioned above, the identification of the countries of origin of manufactured goods is becoming increasingly impossible, and parts of a product come from all over. The "local content" regulations are nearly impossible to enforce. The United States, for instance, imports as much as 30 percent from U.S. transplants that have been established overseas over the last several decades.[47] Further, MNCs and TNCs are indifferent as they create regions of poverty in the middle of their own countries of origin such as the United States and Britain. It is quite possible to argue that the trade protectionists, such as the so-called revisionists in the United States-Japan trade discourse, are conscious or unconscious participants in a patriotic scam to conceal the class interests involved in the bilateral trade friction. Protectionism benefits certain sectors of industry and hurts others, just as free trade does. In other words, protectionism and free trade grant favors to different portions of industry in the short run, although protectionism invariably hurts consumers. Only when the coherence of a total nation-state is unswervingly desired and maintained can the practice of protectionism persuade the population at large. In the present world, however, there is no example of such unquestioned national coherence—not even the notorious Japan, Inc. The "revisionists" merely stir the residual patriotic sentiment so that they can keep the illusion of national unity a while longer.[48]

TNCs are obviously not agents of progress for humanity. First, since the raison d'etre of TNCs is maximum profits, the welfare of the people they leave behind, or even the people in the area where they operate, is of little or no concern to them. The host governments that are eager to invite TNCs cannot be expected to be particular about the workers' employment conditions or the general citizens' public welfare. The framework of the nation-state is deteriorating also in the host nations, which are often controlled by dictators and oligarchs. All TNCs are finally in alliance, though competitive in several basic aspects.[49] The transnational class is self-concerned, though aggressively extroverted in cross-border movement. Labor unions, on the other hand, which might be expected to offer assistance to workers, still operate within the framework of a national economy. It is at present simply unthinkable that transnational labor unions will take joint actions across national borders, equalizing their wages and working conditions with their cross-border brothers and sisters. Imagine UAW officials meeting with Mexican union representatives to negotiate together a contract with the GM management in a *maquila* plant.[50] TNCs might raise GNP or even per capita income, but such a raise does not guarantee a better living for all citizens. So who finally protects the workers inside the United States or elsewhere? The TNCs are far more transnational than the labor unions, generating the unemployed and underemployed everywhere, from Detroit to Manila, from Taipei to San Diego. There is little to be expected as of now from the residual nation-state or its alternatives in the way of protecting these people. What we have heard so far in relation to the North America Free Trade Agreement from the Bush administration, the Clinton administration, or U.S. university experts promises very little indeed.[51] As Sklair summarizes, "The choice is more likely to be between more or less efficient foreign exploitative transnational corporations and highly protected and perhaps corrupt local, state, parastatal or private firms" (p. 117).

Second, the rapid formation of the transnational class is likely to develop a certain homogeneity among its members. Even without the formation of TNCs, the world has been turning toward all-powerful consumerism in which brand names command recognition and attraction. Everywhere commodities are invented, transported, promoted, daydreamed over, sold, purchased, consumed, and discarded. And they are the cultural products of the transnational class. The members of such a class are the leaders, the role models, of the 1990s and beyond; their one gift is, needs to be, an ability to converse and communicate with each other. Cultural eccentricities are to be avoided, if not banned altogether. National history and culture are not to intrude or to be asserted oppositionally or even dialectically. They are merely variants of one "universal"—as in a giant theme park or shopping mall. Culture will be kept to museums, and the museums, exhibitions, and theatrical performances will be swiftly appropriated by tourism and other forms of commercialism. No matter how subversive at the beginning, variants will be appropriated aggressively by branches of consumerism, such as entertainment and tourism, as were rap music, graffiti art, or even classical music and high arts. Cable TV and MTV dominate the world absolutely. Entertainment and tourism are huge transnational industries by themselves. The return to "authenticity," as mentioned earlier, is a closed route. There is nothing of the sort extant any longer in much of the world. How then to balance the transnationalization of economy and politics with the survival of local culture and history—without mummifying them with tourism and in museums—is the crucial question, for which, however, no answer has yet been found.[52]

Third, workers in search of jobs all over the world are changing global demography in this third industrial revolution. They come, legally or illegally, from everywhere to every industrial center in either industrialized or developing nations. TNCs are in need of them, though they are unwilling to provide them with adequate pay or care. Cut off from their homes, migrant workers disappear into huge urban slums without the protection of a traditional rural mutual dependence system. The struggle for survival does not allow any leisure in which to enjoy their pastoral memory. For those exploited alien workers in inner cities, consumerism alone seems to offer solace, if they are fortunate enough to have money for paltry pleasures. In Mexico City or Seoul, in Berlin or Chicago, migrants mix and compromise alongside other aliens from other regions. Neither nativism nor pluralism are in their thoughts, only survival. "Multiculturalism" is a luxury largely irrelevant to those who live under the most wretched conditions. It is merely an "import strategy" of the TNC managers, as Mike Davis calls it.[53] In fact, it may very well turn out to be the other side of the coin of neoethnicism and neoracism.

Fourth, environmental destruction is a major consequence of the development of TNCs. Because TNCs often move across borders to escape from stringent environmental regulations, the host government is not likely to enforce the pollution control rules. The effects of the damage caused in industrialized areas as well as NIEs and Third World regions, however, is not confined to these specific localities. The proposal made by Lawrence Summers of Harvard and the World Bank to shift polluting industries from developed countries to the "'underpolluted'" Third World is as foolish as it is invidious.[54] The effects of environmental violence inescapably visit everyone, everywhere. Air pollution, ozone layer depletion, acid rain, the greenhouse effect, ocean contamination, and a disrupted ecosystem are finally unavoidable no matter where the damage originates. The TNCs might escape from the regulators, but we are all—without exception—victims. Who is there to control the environmental performance of TNCs globally? Are we to rely on the good sense of corporate planners to fight off catastrophe? Can we trust the fugitives from law to protect the law?[55]

Finally, academia, the institution that might play the principal role in investigating transnational corporatism and its implications for humanity, seems all too ready to cooperate rather than deliberate. The technical complexity of the TNC mechanism requires academic expertise in sophisticated research, explanation, and management of immense quantities of data. Those in economics, political science, sociology, and anthropology, as well as business administration and international relations, are not expected to be harsh critics of the TNC practice, being compliant enough to be its explicators and apologists. Critics and theorists in the humanities, too, are not immune to the attraction of global exchange, as I will argue once more before I close.

TNCs continue colonialism. Like pre-1945 colonialism, they operate over distance. While they homogenize regions, they remain aliens and outsiders in each place, faithful only to the exclusive clubs of which they are members. True, old colonialism operated in the name of nations, ethnicities, and races, and transnational corporatism tends toward nationlessness. But as I have already mentioned, even the historical nation-state was actually an enabling institution for international enterprises. British colonialism made possible the East India Company, just as the U.S. government made possible the dominance of the United Fruit Company in Central America. Colonialism never benefited the whole population of an adventurist nation. As J. A. Hobson argued nearly a century ago and scholars since have confirmed, colonialism enriched the rich and powerful of the home country and the *compradors* at the expense of the populace at large.[56] The trickle-down theory of the 1980s was, as always, a wishful fantasy or, more likely, an unadulterated con game. It is indeed sobering to remember that the war in Vietnam was conducted at a huge cost to the United States as a whole, which of course gained nothing from the old exhausted Southeast Asian colony of France. And yet there were a good number of stockholders, executives, entrepreneurs, and employees of the U.S. defense industry who amassed fortunes over the millions of dead and wounded bodies and impoverished souls, both Vietnamese and American. Japanese industrial recovery, too, owes a great deal to the Korean and Vietnam wars.

TNCs are unencumbered by nationalist baggage. Their profit motives are unconcealed. They travel, communicate, and transfer people and plants, information and technology, money and resources globally. TNCs rationalize and execute the objectives of colonialism with greater efficiency and rationalism. And unlike imperial invaders, they are welcomed by the leaders of developing nations. In order to exploit the different economic and political conditions among the current nation-states, they ignore the borders to their own advantage. When the need arises, however, they can still ask for the aid of the armed forces of their home or host states. And in the process patriotic rhetoric can be resurrected to conceal the true state of affairs, as the Gulf War clearly demonstrated. The military, in the meantime, is increasingly assuming the form of a TNC itself, being nearly nation-free. TNC employees, too, are satisfied with their locally higher wages. And yet there is no evidence that the whole population of a host country enjoys an improvement in welfare: let me repeat, a higher GNP or per capita income does not mean an equally enjoyed increase in wealth. As the host government represses labor organization and urban industrial centers generate surplus labor, wages can be lowered and inequality can intensify at least temporarily.[57] Authoritarianism is unlikely to diminish. Oppression and exploitation continue. Ours, I submit, is an age not of postcolonialism but of intensified colonialism, though under an unfamiliar guise.[58]

I am raising these issues as a participant in the discourse on colonialism. I have myself participated in a number of workshops and conferences on the subject. It is curious, however, how quickly "colonial" discourse has been replaced by "postcolonial" discourse. There was a conference in Berkeley called "After 'Orientalism'" in the spring of 1992. Soon thereafter, there was another at Santa Cruz, this time entitled "Beyond Orientalism." During the subsequent fall, there were at least two more: one at Scripps College, called "Writing the Postcolonial," and another, though slightly different in orientation, at Santa Barbara, entitled "Translating Cultures: The Future of Multiculturalism?" And above all there is a three-year project on minority discourse at the Humanities Research Institute, at University of California, Irvine. These are all recent California events, but there are many meetings and conferences on the subject everywhere, converting academics—us—into frequent fliers and globetrotters. And there is, of course, an outpouring of articles in scholarly publications.[59]

Such activities are presumably politically engaged intellectual exercises. But if practice follows discourse, discourse must follow practice. Very much like studies in New Historicism, these are efforts once again to distance political actuality from direct examination. Once again, we are sanitizing our academic discourse on the ongoing political conditions—this time around TNCs and their eager host governments. We might even be masking a secret nostalgia as we devote our scholarly attention to "postcoloniality," a condition in history that is safely distant and inert, instead of seeking alternatives in this age after the supposed end of history. Similarly, multiculturalism looks suspiciously like a disguise of transnational corporatism that causes, of necessity, havoc with a huge mass of displaced workers helplessly seeking jobs and sustenance. Los Angeles and New York, Tokyo and Hong Kong, Berlin and London are all teeming with "strange-looking" people. And U.S. academics quite properly study them as a plurality of presences. But before we look distantly at them and give them over to their specialists, we need to know why they are where they are. What are the forces driving them? How do they relate to our everyday life? Who is behind all this drifting? The plurality of cultures is a given of human life: "our own tradition" is a fabrication, as it has always been, everywhere. It is impossible not to study cultures of others; the American curricula must include "alien" histories. But that is merely a beginning. In the recent rise in cultural studies and multiculturalism among cultural traders and academic administrators, inquiry stops as soon as it begins. What we need is a rigorous political and economic scrutiny rather than a gesture of pedagogic expediency. We should not be satisfied with recognizing the different subject-positions from different regions and diverse backgrounds. We need to find reasons for such differences—at least in the political and economic aspects—and to propose ways to erase such "differences," by which I mean political and economic inequalities. To the extent that cultural studies and multiculturalism provide students and scholars with an alibi for their complicity in the TNC version of neocolonialism, they are serving, once again, merely as one more device to conceal liberal self-deception. By allowing ourselves to be absorbed into the discourse on "postcoloniality" or even post-Marxism, we are fully collaborating with the hegemonic ideology, which looks, as usual, as if it were no ideology at all.

NOTES

Many of my friends have read this paper in various stages. I am thankful to the following for detailed and insightful comments and suggestions; any remaining errors and misinterpretations are, of course, entirely my own: Martha L. Archibald, Carlos Blanco-Aguinaga, Paul Bové, Noam Chomsky, Arif Dirlik, Joseba Cabilondo, H.D. Harootunian, Takeo Hoshi, Stephanie McCurry, and Anders Stephanson.

1. See Edward W. Said, *Culture and Imperialism* (New York: Knopf, 1993).
2. Some examples are Aimé Césaire, *Discours sur le colonialisme* (Paris: Presence africaine, 1989); C.L.R. James, *The Black Jacobins: Tousaint Louverture and the San Domingo Revolution* (New York: Dial Press, 1938), *A History of Negro Revolt* (London: Fact, Ltd., 1938), *Beyond a Boundary* (London: Hutchinson, 1963), and many others; Frantz Fanon, *The Wretched of the Earth*, trans. Constance Farrington (New York: Grove Press, 1961), and *Studies in a Dying Colonialism*, trans. Haakon Chevalier (New York: Monthly Review Press, 1965); and George Lamming, *In the Castle of My Skin* (New York: McGraw-Hill, 1953), and *The Pleasures of Exile* (London: Allison and Busby, 1984).
3. During the 1960s, black writers began to express to the white audience their anticolonialist views as activists were promoting civil rights. Politically acceptable to many liberal academics, they were at the same time dismissed by "respectable" critics and scholars in academic disciplines.
4. Perhaps this is more conspicuously an Anglo-American phenomenon. In South America, for instance, the discourse on colonialism started everywhere—from Mexico to Argentina—much earlier, at the latest in the 1960s.
5. See Edward Said, *Orientalism* (New York: Pantheon, 1978). Of course, there had been numerous studies in history and political science in relation to imperialism, racism, slavery, colonies, and so on, and the political activism of the 1960s and 1970s had also made contributions to the change in the political consciousness of Western intellectuals. But before the appearance of Said's book, no text had made a serious inroad into the mainline Anglo-American disciplines of the humanities.
6. The state of colonialization is obviously much harder to define than this abbreviated argument might suggest. Any example—say, of Palestine or Hong Kong—will at once

display the particular complexities of individual circumstances. It does seem undeniable, however, that while oppression and suffering continue unabated, the administrative and occupational mode of colonialism is irreversibly being replaced by an economic version—especially after the end of the cold war. To complicate the situation further, the status of the aborigines settlement societies such as Australia, Taiwan, the United States, Canada, and the Pacific islands, to take random examples, is far from clarified. Serious legal disputes are distinct possibilities in the near future in some of these areas, for example, in Hawai'i and Australia.

7. There are six interrelated developments in post-World War II history, none of which should or could be considered in isolation. It is indeed possible to argue that any one of these developments needs to be studied in close conjunction *with every other.* They are: (1) the cold war (and its end); (2) decolonization; (3) transnational corporatism; (4) high-tech revolution; (5) feminism; (6) the environmental crisis. There are adjacent cultural coordinates such as postmodernism, popularization of culture, cultural studies, de-disciplinization, ethnicism, economic regionalism (tripolarism), and so on. The relationship between the two groups is neither homologic nor causal, but its exact nature requires further examination in a different context.

8. In many regions of the world, there were some improvements in general welfare. As to starvation, for instance, the ratio of the chronically undernourished to the total population in the Middle East, South America, and Asia has been reduced by nearly one-half between 1970 and 1990. In Africa, however, there is hardly any change in the same period. See *Sekai o yomu kii waado* (Tokyo, 1992), 82–83.

9. See Basil Davidson, *The Black Man's Burden: Africa and the Curse of the Nation-State* (New York: Times Books, 1992). An Africanist journalist, Davidson may be overly influenced by his observations of Africa when he writes about the rest of the world. He is, for instance, much too pessimistic—and Orientalist!—as he predicts that aside from Japan no Third World nation will become industrialized.

10. This narrative of colonization/decolonization is obviously oversimplified and, worse, totalized. Again, the case of South America, for instance, is an exception in many important aspects. However, for an inclusive discussion of the decolonization/recolonization process, one would have to consult an entirely different essay with a different focus and emphasis.

11. A typically preindustrial society has about 80 percent of its population engaged in agriculture. A fully industrialized society has a very small agricultural worker population of about 5 percent. This transformation from agriculture to manufacturing and other industries has taken most industrialized nations around 200 years. Japan went through the process in less than a century, while the East Asian NIEs are changing at the speed of less than a generation. The high cost paid for such a social change is to be expected. Industrialization and colonization converge in this development. And thus all industrialized nations are former colonizers. There is a later development of this process in industrialized societies now. As manufacturing technology improves productivity, manufacturing jobs are rapidly disappearing everywhere, and they are being replaced by service jobs. The manufacturing worker surplus urgently needs to find outlets that are nowhere visibly available. There is not even an equivalent of old colonies for these surplus workers. See Sylvia Nasar, "Clinton Job Plan in Manufacturing Meets Skepticism," *New York Times,* 27 December 1992, A1. See also Motoyama Yoshihiko, *Minami to kita* (Tokyo, 1991), 223–225.

12. See Benedict Anderson, *Imagined Communities: Reflections on the Origin and Spread of Nationalism,* 2d ed. (London: Verso, 1991). The book does not explain who imagined the community, however.

13. See Paul Kennedy, *Rise and Fall of the Great Powers: Economic Change and Military Conflict from 1500 to 2000* (New York: Random House, 1987).

14. See Bruce Cumings, *The Origins of the Korean War,* 2 vols. (Princeton, N.J. : Princeton University Press, 1981, 1990).

15. The figures are based on Table B-2—Gross National Product in 1982 Dollars 1929–87, *The Annual Report of the Council of Economic Advisers,* in Economic Report of the President (Washington, D.C., 1988), 251.

16. Dwight D. Eisenhower, "Liberty Is at Stake" (1961), in *Super-State: Readings in the Military-Industrial Complex,* ed. Herbert I. Schiller and Joseph D. Phillips (Urbana: University of Illinois Press, 1970), 32

17. U.S. Office of Education, "Institutions of Higher Education—Degrees Conferred, by Sex, 1870–1970," *Biennial Survey of Education in the United States.*

18. Seymour Melman, "Military State Capitalism," *The Nation,* 20 May 1991, 666, 667. Melman's *The Demilitarized Society: Disarmament and Conversion* (Nottingham: Spokesman, 1988), *Profits without Production* (New York: Knopf, 1983), and *The Permanent War Economy: American Capitalism in Decline* (New York: Simon and Schuster, 1974) are important studies on the subject.

19. Others include Tanzania (1964), Zanzibar (1963), Somaliland (1960), Aden (1967), Kuwait (1961), Malta (1964), Borneo (1963), and Trinidad and Tobago (1962).

20. See Okumura Shigeji, "Takokuseki kigyo to hatten tojo koku," in *Takokuseki kigyo to hatten tojo koku* (Tokyo, 1977), 11–12.

21. The history of U.S. interventions since the Vietnam War is long and wide-ranging. To pick only the most conspicuous (overt) operations: the Dominican Republic, Lebanon, Grenada, Panama, and the Persian Gulf. In addition, there were of course numerous covert operations in Iran, Nicaragua, El Salvador, and other places.

22. These terms are used differently depending on the region and the times. In South Africa, for instance, the term "multinational" was not used in the 1960s and 1970s because it was felt that those giant corporations were all U.S.-based and not multinational. The term "transnational," on the other hand, was felt to be more accurate because it suggested the *transgressiveness* of these U.S. corporate managements. Now that there are Mexico-originated "multinational" giant corporations (such as Televisa, the biggest TV network in the world outside the United States), the term is becoming more commonly accepted. See John Sinclair, "Televisa: Mexico's Multinational," *Centro: Puerto Rican Studies Bulletin* 2, no. 8 (n.d.): n.p.

    There are numerous publications treating the development of transnational corporatism. For instance, see Peter E Drucker, *The New Realities: In Government and Politics, in Economies and Business, in Sociology and World View* (New York: Harper and Row, 1989); and Kenichi Ohmae, *The Borderless World: Power and Strategy in the Interlinked Economy* (New York: Harper Business, 1990), 91–99. Perhaps the most important source of information, though little known, is the United Nations Center on Transnational Corporations, which publishes the biannual CTC Reporter as well as numerous specific reports on transnational corporate activities. The center published the Bibliography on Transnational Corporations in 1979.

23. Percy Barnevik, CEO of ABB, concluded a recent interview by remarking, "Are we above governments? No. We answer to governments. We obey the laws in every country in which we operate, and we don't make the laws. However, we do change relations between countries. We function as a lubricant for worldwide economic integration. . . . We don't create the process, but we push it. We make visible the invisible hand of global competition" (William Taylor, "The Logic of Global Business: An Interview with ABB's Percy Barnevik," *Harvard Business Review* 69 [March-April 1991]: 105).

24. See Terajima Jitsuro, *Chikyugi o te ni kangaeru Amerika: 21 seiki Nishi-Bei kanki e no koso* (Tokyo, 1991), 78–79.

25. There are several books on this supposedly family-owned but un-Japanese enterprise, all by admiring—and commissioned?—Japanese authors. See, for instance, Itagaki Hidenori, *Yaohan: Nihon dasshutsu o hakaru tairiku-gata shoho no hasso* (Tokyo, 1990); and Tsuchiya Takanori, *Yaohan Wada Kazuo: Inoru keikei to hito zakuri* (Tokyo, 1991). Reflecting the owner's faith, Yaohan is aggressive in evangelizing the doctrine of the Seicho-no-ie Temple among its local employees. Despite predictable conflicts with employees of

other religions (for example, Muslims in Singapore), Yaohan insists that the doctrine is the key to its success.

26. For specific comments on this aspect of TNCs, see, for instance, Raymond Vernon, *Sovereignty at Bay: The Multinational Spread of U.S. Enterprises* (New York: Basic Books, 1971); and Stephen Hymer, *The International Operations of National Firms: A Study of Direct Foreign Investment* (Cambridge, Mass.: The MIT Press, 1976). In this connection J. A. Hobson's foresight in his *Imperialism* (London: Allen and Unwin, Ltd., 1902), especially in part 1, "The Economics of Imperialism," cannot be forgotten.

27. Amidst the fiscal crisis in the State of California, there have been rumors that the University of California, Berkeley, and UCLA are being considered for privatization. Though there has been no confirmation of the rumor, there has been no official denial either.

28. See Tom Petruno, "A Return to Rational Rates," *Los Angeles Times,* 29 January 1992, D1.

29. See "Are CEOs Paid Too Much?" *Business Week,* 6 May 1991. The Japanese are very proud of this "democratic" distribution of wealth. Though it is to a large extent true and suitable, wealth equity is not quite so real. For one thing, there is a huge sum being spent every year on executive perks such as free housing, free chauffeured car, free parking (no admittance in space-scarce Japan), plus the notorious entertainment expenses annually estimated, by one study, at $35.5 billion. See Robert Neff and Joyce Barnathan, "How Much Japanese CEOs Really Make," *Business Week,* 27 January 1992, 31. The manifestation of wealth, power, and privilege obviously takes different forms from society to society.

30. Kevin Phillips, "Down and Out," *New York Times Magazine,* 10 January 1993, 20.

31. See Robert Pear, "Ranks of U.S. Poor Reach 35.7 Million, the Most Since '64," *New York Times,* 4 September 1992, Al, A14. After President Bush's visit to Japan in late 1993, the comparative figures of the rich and the poor in the United States attracted a good deal of media attention. See also Nasar, "The 1980s: A Very Cood Time for the Very Rich," *New York Times,* 5 March 1992, A1, A22; Petruno, "Investors Seeking Voice on Execs' Pay May Get It," *Los Angeles Times,* 7 February 1992, D1, D3; Linda Grant, "Corporations Search for Answers on Executive Pay," *Los Angeles Times,* 23 February 1992, Dl, D9; James E. Ellis, "Layoffs on the Line, Bonuses in the Executive Suite," *Business Week,* 21 October 1991, 34; Anne B. Fisher, "The New Debate over the Very Rich," *Fortune,* 29 June 1992, 42–55; and Louis S. Richman, "The Truth about the Rich and the Poor," *Fortune,* 21 September 1992, 134–146; Lee Smith, "Are You Better Off?" *Fortune,* 24 February 1992, 38–48; Geoffrey Colvin, "How to Pay the CEO Right," 6 April 1992, 60–69. See also the feature on executive pay in *Business Week,* 30 March 1992, 52–58.

32. Leslie Sklair, *Sociology of the Global System* (Baltimore: Johns Hopkins University Press, 1995), 101–102. Among numerous books on the subject Sklair's is singular for a sociopolitical vision that informs its economic analysis.

33. Also, it was said in 1973 that "of the 100 largest economic units in the world, only half are nation-states, the others multinational companies of various sorts" (Harry M. Makler, Alberto Martinelli, and Neil J. Smelser, "Introduction," in *The New International Economy,* ed. Makler, Martinelli, and Smelser [Beverly Hills, Calif.: Sage Publications, 1982], 25).

34. See June Kinoshita, "Mapping the Mind," *New York Times Magazine,* 18 October 1992, 43–47, 50, 52, 54.

35. Female labor is cheaper than male labor everywhere, especially in the Third World. Thus the sexual division of labor is attracting some attention among economists. An extremely important topic, it urgently requires further study. See Sklair, *Sociology of the Global System* 96–101, 108–109, 233–235. See also Maria Mies, *Patriarchy and Accumulation on a World Scale: Women in the International Division of Labour* (London: Atlantic Highlands, 1986), esp. chaps. 3 and 4.

36. There is a good deal of literature available on this subject. See, for instance, Folker

Frobel, Jurgen Heinrichs, and Otto Kreye, *The New International Division of Labour: Structural Unemployment in Industrialized Countries and Industrialization in Developing Countries*, trans. Pete Burgess (Cambridge: Cambridge University Press, 1980); and Michael I. Piore and Charles E. Sabel, *The Second Industrial Divide: Possibilities for Prosperity* (New York: Basic Books, 1984).

37. Lee Iacocca, the former Chrysler chairman, said little about the Nagoya Mitsubishi factory when he accompanied President Bush to Japan in 1991 to complain about the Japanese automobile imports. The Stealth is made entirely in Japan except for the word "Dodge" etched in the front bumper. See David E. Sanger, "Detroit Leaning on Japan, in Both Senses," *New York Times*, 27 February 1992, A1.

38. John Holusha, "International Flights, Indeed," *New York Times*, 1 january 1992, 49.

39. "'Made in America' Gets Tougher to Determine," *San Diego Union-Tribune*, 2 February 1992, A33.

40. This does not mean that TNCs are all capable of rationally and skillfully dealing with complex race issues in all regions. The Japanese MNC/TNC managers in the United States, for instance, have had many serious difficulties in understanding the racial and ethnic problems, often provoking their employees of both majority and minority ethnicities to take legal action against them. The problem as I see it, however, arises not from their informed policies but from their inexperience and ignorance in execution. The corporate managers are becoming alert enough to what is expected and demanded of them for the maintenance of their operation in alien lands.

41. See Kuwahara Yasuo, *Kokkyo o koeru rodosha* (Tokyo, 1991), 127–143. The movements of both skilled and unskilled labor in the European community, too, offers an economic integration model par excellence.

42. See Robert B. Reich, *The Work of Nations: Preparing Ourselves for Twenty-First-Century Capitalism* (New York: Knopf, 1991). In his contribution to *The New International Economy*, Voker Bornschier concludes, "we know that personal income distribution is more unequal if the level of [multinational corporation] penetration is high. No empirical evidence is reported that MNCs reduce inequality in less-developed countries in the course of their operation, whereas there are several hypotheses with preliminary empirical support for the contrary" (Volker Bornschier, "World Economic Integration and Policy Responses: Some Developmental Impacts," in *The New International Economy*, 68–69).

43. The first large-scale war after the end of the cold war, the war in the Persian Gulf, requires further analysis. First World intellectuals hardly protested, although the U.S. Congress was nearly evenly divided about the land force invasion of Iraq before the actual event. Among several collections of essays about the war in the gulf see *The Gulf War Reader: History, Documents, Opinions*, ed. Micah L. Sifry and Christopher Cerf (New York: Times Books, 1991). See also Christopher Norris, *Uncritical Theory: Postmodernism, Intellectuals, and the Gulf War* (London: Lawrence and Wishart, 1992).

44. David Binder and Barbara Crossette count forty-eight ethnic wars in the world in their "As Ethnic Wars Multiply, U.S. Strives for a Policy," *New York Times*, 7 February 1993, A1, A12.

45. Makler, Martinelli, and Smelser, "Introduction," in *The New International Economy*, 26–27.

46. See Reich, *The Work of Nations*, esp. chap. 12.

47. The ratio of the overseas production totals of TNCs to the TNC sales totals is 79 percent for Switzerland, 48 percent for Britain, 33 percent for the United States, and 12 percent for Japan. And among the top three countries, the overseas production totals were greater than the export totals. The 1981 U.S. export totals were $233.6 billion, while the overseas production totals were more than twice as much, $482.9 billion. The Japanese export totals were $152 billion, while its overseas production totals were merely $30 billion (Motoyama Yoshihiko, *Minami to Kita: Kuzureyuku daisan sekai* [Tokyo, 1991], 196–197; my trans. See also Jitsuro, *Chikyugi o te ni kangaeru Amerika*, 68, 69, 160–162).

48. Reich's comments occasioned by the publication of Crichton's *Rising Sun* are eloquent on this. "The purpose of having a Japanese challenge is to give us a reason to join

together. That is, we seem to need Japan as we once needed the Soviet Union—as a means of defining ourselves, our interests, our obligations to one another. We should not be surprised that this wave of Japan-as-enemy books coincides exactly with the easing of cold-war tensions" (Reich, "Is Japan Really out to Get Us?" *New York Times Book Review*, 9 February 1992). To quote from Sklair, protectionism "acts as a bargaining counter for the rich, and a bluff for the poor, and mainly comes to life in its use as a rhetorical device to satisfy domestic constituencies. For example, desperate politicians tend to fall back on it to appease working class voters in the United States and the United Kingdom" (*Sociology of the Global System*, 71). Among the "revisionists" are Clyde V. Prestowitz Jr., James Fallows, Karel van Wolferen, and Chalmers Johnson.

49. Chiu Yen Liang, "The Moral Politics of Industrial Conflict in Multinational Corporations Located in Hong Kong: An Anthropological Case Study," 2 vols. (Ph.D. diss., University of Chicago, 1991) discusses a strike at a Japanese TNC in Hong Kong. Although overly detailed in description and confusing in analysis, this work offers many interesting observations of the TNC practice.

50. "In some, though not all, export oriented zones (EOZs) the right of workers to organize is curtailed, either formally or in practice, and . . . trade unions are either suppressed or manipulated through government-TNC collaboration" (*Sociology of the Global System*, 95).

51. Some labor unions and some Democrats, including Bill Clinton, support NAFTA with reservations concerning worker retraining and enforcement of adequate environmental regulations in Mexico. But the specifics are not available. As to the overall gains and losses, obviously some industrial sectors will gain while others will lose. The questions are who will gain how much, who will lose how much, and when will the disparity be balanced out? As to the prospects of worker displacement, a group of researchers at the University of Michigan predicted that "as few as 15,000 to 75,000 American workers— out of a work force of 120 million—could lose their jobs over 10 years as a result of the pact" (Nasar, "Job Loss in Pact Is Called Small," *New York Times*, 17 August 1992, D3). The details are not offered, but the prediction as reported is totally unconvincing. Nearly all in the management side agree that NAFTA will benefit everyone in the long run. No one spells out, however, how long that means. It remains to be proven that NAFTA will not be a disaster to the U.S. workers for a foreseeable future. See also Bob Davis, "Fighting 'Nafta': Free-Trade Pact Spurs a Diverse Coalition of Grass-Roots Foes," *Wall Street Journal*, 23 December 1992, 1.

52. There are numerous works by the members of the Frankfurt School on this, especially Adorno and Benjamin. Also, see Sklair, *Sociology of the Global System*, 42; and Dean MacCannell, *Empty Meeting Grounds: The Tourist Papers* (London: Routledge, 1992). Arif Dirlik in his forthcoming essay, "Post-Socialism/Flexible Production: Marxism in Contemporary Radicalism," advocates a neo-Marxist localism to deal with this problem.

53. Mike Davis, *City of Quartz: Excavating the Future in Los Angeles* (London: Verso, 1990), 80–81. See also Edward W. Soja, *Postmodern Geographies: The Reassertion of Space in Critical Social Theory* (London: Verso, 1989).

54. James Risen, "Economists Watch in Quiet Fury," *Los Angeles Times*, 8 January 1993, A20.

55. See, for example, United Nations Centre on Transnational Corporations, *Environmental Aspects of the Activities of Transnational Corporations: A Survey* (New York: United Nations, 1985).

56. For recent studies, see, for instance, Lance E. Davis and Robert A. Huttenback, *Mammon and the Pursuit of Empire: The Economics of British Imperialism* (Cambridge: Cambridge University Press, 1986). They argue that the elite members of British society gained economically and the middle-class British taxpayers lost during the nation's imperial expansion.

57. See Kuwahara, *Kokkyo o koeru rodosha*.

58. See Noam Chomsky, *Year 501: The Conquest Continues* (Boston: South End Press, 1993), esp. chapters 3 and 4.

59. To name a few, Kawame Anthony Appiah, "Is the Post- in Postmodernism the Post- in Post-Colonialism?" *Critical Inquiry* 17 (winter 1991): 336–357; Homi Babha, "Of Mimicry and Man: The Ambivalence of Colonial Discourse," *October* 28 (spring 1984): 125–133; Sara Suleri, "Women Skin Deep: Feminism and the Postcoloniality of the Artifice of History: Who Speaks for 'Indian' Pasts?" *Representations* 37 (winter 1992): 1–26; and, most important, issue no. 31–32 of *Social Text,* which addresses the question of postcolonialism and the Third World. None of the articles, however, directly discusses the development of the TNC.

The Chinese and
the American Labor Unions

Peter Kwong

Since the mid-1970s, classes in Chinatown have polarized, and exploitation of workers has increased. So far, social-service agencies have not helped workers deal with workplace problems. Union organizing, it would seem, is the logical alternative.

Although working people constitute the overwhelming majority of the population, they are poorly organized and politically weak. There are dozens of merchants' associations of all types, but not a single traditional organization has formed around workers. In fact, the very idea that workers should organize into unions that cut across clan, village, and trade lines is an alien concept. At the same time, American labor unions, partly because of their racial attitudes, are unwilling to break into Chinatown to help develop a workers' movement. Thus, by 1987 less than 2 percent of Chinatown restaurants were unionized. And while most of the garment workers are members of the International Ladies Garment Workers Union, management is still able to get away with sweatshop conditions.

Unions in Chinatown

Chinatown before the 1960s was not fertile ground for labor organizing. Most Chinese worked in small service-oriented laundry and restaurant trades, and were either self-employed or partners in proprietorships invariably formed by people originally from the same clan or village in China. When workers were needed, they gave preference to fellow clansmen. Furthermore, the skill required in these trades was so minimal that there was no division between masters and apprentices. This gave these establishments a cooperative character: while normal capitalistic development creates a definite distinction between owners and workers, Chinese firms did not usually differentiate between employer and employees.

Small businessmen realized that survival depended on successful competition with larger, modernized, white-owned firms. For instance, white-owned laundries during the 1930s made major breakthroughs by introducing washing machines and large automatic steam presses, often operated by low-paid black or immigrant female labor. Chinese laundrymen attracted customers by providing extra services, such as free mending, free pickup and delivery, and low prices. As a result, there was constant friction between the modernized laundries and the small Chinese hand laundries, always with racial overtones. Further, the Chinese laborers developed little affinity for other American workers, and viewed unions as a threat, since the survival of Chinese firms depended on keeping costs down and wages as low as possible.

In the 1930s, at the height of the American industrial labor movement, some Chinese were exposed to American radical movements and labor attempted to organize unions in Chinatown. Except for attracting some members into the welfare-relief-oriented Chinese Unemployed Council during the Great Depression, they made few inroads. In 1935 a Chinese leftist organization, the Chinese Anti-Imperialist Alliance, recruited twenty restaurant workers into the Restaurant and Food Production Union, a branch of the International Labor Union, but these individuals worked neither in Chinatown nor in Chinese restaurants.[1] However, at that time, the New China Restaurant, which was located outside Chinatown, near City Hall, was the only Chinese restaurant organized by an American union, the Cafeteria Employees.

LABOR AND THE CHINATOWN ESTABLISHMENT

Today, the composition of the Chinatown work force has changed. With the expanded economy and the development of manufacturing industries, there is a large working class and serious division between labor and capital. Yet Chinese workers are still not part of the larger American labor force, because they work in an underground economy with its own informal political structure. This structure has historically been dominated by property owners and merchants; in recent years it has been able to incorporate manufacturers. Thus, on the owners' side, there is a powerful structure through which to exert control. The workers have no such counterforce.

To deter workers from organizing or being too active, owners have an effective weapon—the blacklist. Troublemakers are fired and are unable to find another job in Chinatown. Blacklisting is effective because there is no possibility of appeal, either to the traditional associations, to the CCBA, or to the media.

The Chinatown media are locked into this system. Reporters are enjoined from reporting anything that might stir up community conflicts. For example, in the summer of 1984, waiters picketed against the owners of the Hong Kong Restaurant on Pell Street, whom they accused of union busting. An editorial in the Chinese-language *Pei-Mei Daily* commented:

> If only both sides could sit down and negotiate in good faith, and if each side would make some compromises, this situation could be resolved without resorting to American courts. After all, we are all the offspring of our ancient emperor Wang-te, we have the same skin color, we speak the same language, we have sprung from the same roots; why should we be so impatient with each other? In the face of racial

discrimination, which we all suffer, and relentless competition from American businesses, it is wrong to fight among us brothers.[2]

Workers in the Chinese community have no effective organization to represent
them, nor a leader to champion their interests. Even federal and state authorities
are not troubled by widespread violations of minimum-wage laws in Chinatown.
The Department of Labor won't take any action unless the Chinese complain, and
the workers cannot complain for fear of retaliation.

Under these circumstances, the only way for Chinese workers to improve their
lot is through organizing. Yet the American unions have not responded. Typical
is the attitude of the AFL/CIO Hotel and Restaurant Employees and Bartenders
Union, which has frustrated the activism of Chinese workers.

THE RESTAURANT WORKERS UNION MOVEMENT

There are 450 restaurants in Chinatown and another thousand or so Chinese-
owned restaurants elsewhere in the New York metropolitan area. Before 1978 very
few Chinese restaurants were organized. The AFL/CIO Hotel and Restaurant
Employees and Bartenders Union, Local 69, tended to focus its energy on expensive
restaurants and hotel, hospital, and company dining rooms; because they have a
large number of workers concentrated in one place, they are relatively easy to
organize. The union claims that Chinese restaurants are too scattered and too
costly to organize. Thus, the initiative for unionization of Chinese restaurants in
New York City had to develop from the workers themselves.

In the late 1970s, there were (and still are, of course) a number of expensive
and well-known Chinese restaurants on the Upper East Side of Manhattan. The
owners of these very profitable establishments, who had never worried about
unions, treated their workers badly. Waiters, for instance, were paid low wages
and worked long hours; they had neither job security nor benefits. It was common
for management to order them to do chores that they were not hired to do, such
as dumping garbage, mopping floors, cleaning bathrooms, or running errands for
the owners.[3] Some establishments provided only leftover or inferior food for the
workers and charged them for it. Most of the employees were non-Cantonese
immigrants who spoke English and had been in this country for a number of years;
many were over forty years old. The few who were more politically active, frustrated
by their working conditions, eventually asked the Hotel and Restaurant Employees
and Bartenders Union, Local 69, for help. The union had no plans to organize
the Chinese, but agreed to help as long as the workers themselves assumed the
responsibility. In May 1978, Uncle Tai's, a fancy Upper East Side establishment
serving Szechuan food, became the first Chinese restaurant in the city in almost
forty years to become organized.

Others soon followed. By 1979 workers in at least four other non-Chinatown
Chinese restaurants had joined Local 69. They were organized with overwhelming
support, because the workers, having accumulated grievances over a long period,
had finally found a vehicle for dealing with their problems. Even so, the process
of organizing was not easy, because the owners resisted fiercely. Although Local

69 had not hired professional union organizers, many Chinese waiters were so excited by the prospect of unionization that they volunteered to help.

However, the waiters who joined the union were soon dissatisfied. Local 69 regularly refused to enforce contracts and allowed management to get away with violations of labor codes. At several restaurants workers contended that Local 69 had settled for inadequate medical benefits. Members at one restaurant accused the representative from their local of sitting by while they were replaced by nonunion workers.[4]

Local 69 was a typical "business union," more interested in collecting dues than in representing its members. Once a restaurant was organized, the union rarely enforced contracts aggressively, because any dispute with management would require costly litigation. Further, this type of union prefers to organize from the top down: to reach an agreement with management permitting unionization, the union promises lenient contract enforcement. Complaints by the workers had little effect. After all, the union had never been keen on organizing the Chinese in the first place.

In response to these complaints, union activists formed the Chinese Staff and Workers Association. While it claimed to be a social club, its main objective was to promote unionization in the Chinese community. Thus, the association worked to develop a strong voice responsive to the needs of its Chinese members. Some even hoped that eventually the union would establish a Chinese section in Local 69.

The response of Local 69 was not encouraging. The case of Peng's Restaurant shows the union bureaucracy at its worst. In 1978, organizers from Local 69 approached the workers about joining the union. Since the majority were reluctant, the unionization effort failed; in addition, two union supporters were fired. In 1980 the union went back again. This time, despite warnings of dismissal and threats by the owner, the workers voted 14 to 2 to join the union. So the owner closed the restaurant and reopened it three months later under a new name. The "new" owner allowed the workers to be organized by Local 69 but refused to rehire those who had voted for the union under the "old" management. The union went along with this arrangement. The old workers had to sue the new management for unfair labor practice. They won in the end—after five long years of court proceedings—but during the trial the union testified for the management.

In 1979, a whole year after the first wave of Chinese restaurants had been organized, Local 69 reluctantly agreed to hire a part-time Chinese organizer. In short order, the organizer persuaded workers in five uptown restaurants to sign up. However, the union business agents were incompetent and passive; in subsequent efforts to negotiate contracts, all the organizing efforts were fruitless. It seemed that the union did not really care. The workers suspected that some officials had been paid off by management. The defeat was bitter and cost many workers their jobs. By then, almost all the Chinese union activists realized that working with Local 69 would turn Chinese workers against unions altogether and end the growing movement.

In February 1980 a dispute broke out at the largest Chinatown restaurant, the Silver Palace. The dispute was triggered when management asked the waiters to kick in additional shares of their tips for the busboys, the business managers, and the maître d'. Customarily, a waiter's tip was divided into thirty shares, two of which went into the pool. In the Silver Palace case, management argued that since business was so good and tips plentiful, waiters should contribute two additional shares. The waiters, who were paid less than $150 a month and counted on tips for a large part of their income, protested. Management fired fifteen of them. The waiters asked for their jobs back, but management refused and hired new workers to take their place.[5]

The waiters then approached the Staff and Workers Association for advice. After discussion, they decided to picket to force management to negotiate. The Staff and Workers Association quickly mobilized other waiters from uptown unionized restaurants along with its membership and contacts in Chinatown. Mass meetings were organized and a support committee was formed. The association headquarters on East Broadway became the command center. Fired waiters took turns on the picket line. The support committee called in union activists from around the city, so that during business hours there were forty to fifty individuals circling the front door of the restaurant. On weekends, when the restaurant was busiest, there were almost one hundred pickets. Other volunteers, including community activists, young lawyers and other professionals, wrote bilingual leaflets and issued news stories to the media. At the same time, waiters visited workers in other restaurants to explain the issues and ask for pledges of support. In almost every instance, workers from these restaurants contributed money for the strikers and their families.

Such open defiance in Chinatown was a shock to the community. Previously, union drives had taken place outside Chinatown. Many believed that organizing within the community was not possible because restaurant owners had rigid control of the immigrant work force. It was even more surprising that the workers had dared to take on the management of the Silver Palace, since it was the most respectable restaurant in the community, specializing in elaborate, large dinner parties and formal banquets. It could accommodate one thousand guests at one sitting; it was booked months in advance for important association celebrations and political fundraising dinners, suggesting that management had powerful connections. In fact, one of the restaurant's partners was the president of the Chinatown Restaurants Association, and several others were well-known leaders of a prominent tong. In one respect, though, it was logical that the Silver Palace should be the first Chinatown restaurant to have a labor/management dispute: it employed more than one hundred workers, making it a likely place for union consciousness to develop.

The picketing severely reduced business at the Silver Palace. The community honored the picket line, because countless residents either were working, or had worked, or had close family members working in restaurants. Even some owners of other restaurants believed that the Silver Palace management was arrogant and had pushed the workers too far. The pro-worker sentiment in the community alarmed the owners. Many people pressured the Silver Palace to settle quickly, and finally management agreed to rehire the strikers and to withdraw its demand for an additional share of the tips. The owners' capitulation represented an overwhelming victory for the waiters.

When the workers realized that they had won, they understood that simply getting their jobs back would not ensure job security. They needed to form a union to protect their gains and to improve working conditions. Should they join Local 69? Several heated debates were held at the association headquarters, those in favor of joining Local 69 arguing that without the backing of a large union workers would have neither the organizational nor the financial strength to protect themselves. On the other hand, uptown workers who had had dealings with Local 69 spoke against affiliation, and the experience of the Silver Palace waiters with the local had been instructive. At the beginning of the strike, workers had approached union officials for support in their attempts to win back their jobs, but the officials refused to help unless the waiters joined their union. This only deepened the Chinese suspicion of the purely business nature of Local 69. Finally, and perhaps not surprisingly, the Silver Palace workers voted overwhelmingly (27 to 7) in favor of forming an independent union not affiliated with Local 69.

Once rehired, the waiters negotiated with management for formal recognition of their union. Although these negotiations went on for months, it was clear that management was in no position to block the union. Thus, the Silver Palace became the first restaurant in Chinatown to be organized, and its workers the first to set up an independent union.[6]

The union contract included all the basic terms and benefits guaranteed outside Chinatown: a forty-hour work week, overtime pay, a minimum wage, health benefits, paid holidays, collective bargaining, and job security. The terms of the contract were revolutionary as far as the Chinese community was concerned. No other Chinatown workers enjoyed anything comparable. Most of the larger restaurants in Chinatown quietly improved conditions in order to avoid unionization. Within two years, workers at three other restaurants organized independent unions.

However, after these early successes, the momentum of the independent union movement slackened. Workers had shown militancy, but in order to maintain their gains, they needed organizational strength. Since workers in each restaurant formed an independent union, the organizational base was weak. There was a loose alliance of independent unions through the Chinese Staff and Workers Association. Dues were collected to provide funds for health insurance, pensions, and strikes. However, each union had very limited resources. In cases involving expensive legal battles or drawn-out strikes, the independent unions had to turn to the Staff and Workers Association for support. The association, a voluntary membership organization, was not even able to hire full-time organizers, and without organizers, the independent union movement could not grow, further contributing to its weakness.

Restaurants have become shrewder in dealing with unions; they sabotage organizing efforts by resorting to legal maneuvers. Stanley Mark, an attorney for the Asian American Legal Defense and Education Fund, which represents Chinese workers, observed: "We have had four cases in one year alone where owners closed the restaurants after the workers voted for unions. These places reopened months later, with new names and reshuffled corporate ownership. Usually we are able to win court cases against them, but only after long months of deliberation. By then the workers had found work elsewhere." Mark also suggested that with the Reagan Administration's antilabor policies and the recent Supreme Court decision allowing weakened businesses to file for bankruptcy under Chapter 11, businesses can legally evade union contracts. The job security of the workers and the power of their unions in the restaurant industry have been jeopardized.

Moreover, in Chinatown management remains strong because of its institutional and ideological hold over the community. In order to counter that power, union members must go beyond the workplace; they need to join with other Chinatown residents to form a new base of power from which to address a variety of issues.

This is a difficult task, requiring time and resources. Nevertheless the restaurant workers have dramatically changed the political landscape of Chinatown. Widespread restaurant unionization is accepted as certain. The owners' argument that unions would kill their business has been shown to be invalid: the Silver Palace since unionization is still the most popular restaurant, with prices no higher than other establishments'. Moreover, under the union contract, service has improved and the tension between management and workers has lessened. In the meantime, the Chinese Staff and Workers Association has developed into a solid, mass-based organization which restaurant workers in Chinatown can claim as their own. They come to it whenever they face problems and need advice.

The success of independent unions has pressured Local 69 (recently renamed Local 100) to improve its work in the community. The local finally hired several Chinese organizers and unionized a number of Chinese restaurants (mostly uptown). Local 100 officials have also developed a mutually supportive relationship with the Staff and Workers Association and the Chinese independent unions. On occasion, the two groups join each other's picket lines.

However, the problems between community activists and Local 100 continue. The Chinese Progressive Association (CPA) argued during the formation of independent unions that activists should continue to work within American unions, even if they were corrupt, in order to reform them from within. Subsequently, several CPA members were hired as organizers for Local 100. However, almost all eventually quit because of the impossible situation in the union. One CPA member and organizer became so outraged that he joined a workers' picket line in front of a unionized Chinatown restaurant in defiance of the union, which had branded the picket line an illegal wildcat strike.

In the final analysis, Chinatown restaurant workers want the advantages of a large American union. However, the unions have not shown sensitivity to the needs of immigrants in ethnic communities, and until they do, the Chinese will not join. Chinatown garment workers, on the other hand, do have a large union behind them.

The ILGWU and Chinatown Sweatshops

The International Ladies Garment Workers Union started to organize the Chinese as early as 1957. By 1974 all Chinatown garment workers had joined Local 23–25 of the union. Unlike the Hotel and Restaurant Employees and Bartenders Union, the ILGWU wanted the Chinese. Since the early 1970s Chinatown has been New York's leading center for the production of women's apparel, the city's most important manufacturing industry. While the ILGWU's general membership had declined drastically, membership in Chinatown had increased dramatically. Local 213–25, whose membership is 85 percent Chinese, has become the most important ILGWU local. In fact, the last manager-secretary of Local 23–25, Jay Mazur, who presided over its rapid expansion, has moved up to become president of the ILGWU.

The Chinese belonging to the ILGWU presumably have all the advantages that the restaurant workers in independent unions do not. The ILGWU is a national union, with a membership of over 200,000, staff and business agents in the thousands, and a large budget that enables it to organize and recruit new members and to withstand long strikes. Historically, the union has also played an influential role in the Democratic Party. In addition to its powerful political allies, it has lobbyists in Washington to support legislation beneficial to its members.

But despite all its power, the ILGWU has not yet brought full union benefits to its Chinese members. The union negotiates a new contract with Chinese management every three years, but working conditions are still well below minimum union standards. The complex piece-rate system is not enforceable, because the employers always concoct their own formula to underpay the workers. Working conditions are hazardous to safety and health. On the average, Chinese garment workers are on the job ten to twelve hours a day, six days a week, and make only about $9,000 a year. These are nineteenth-century sweatshop conditions. The only protection the union members truly enjoy are the health and pension benefits, although the union has even cut back on them, because of the decline in contributions from the contractors and manufacturers.

Most Chinese contractors have small business operations in comparison to the large union, yet they do what they want on the shop floors. Union officials have never been willing to organize an active rank and file in order to defend the workers' interests. This reluctance is rooted in the union's peculiar strategy of organizing.

UNION STRATEGY IN CHINATOWN

In the early 1970s, when manufacturers recognized the productive environment of Chinatown, they willingly signed an agreement with the ILGWU to stabilize the labor situation. Once the manufacturers took the initiative, all the other arrangements followed. The union got the most out of it, since it was able to sign up all the workers in Chinatown factories. Because of the unstable nature of the garment industry, the ILGWU prefers to organize workers from the top down. At present, the garment industry is divided into four sectors: manufacturers, contractors, the union, and the workers. The manufacturers don't manufacture anything; they provide design specifications, determine production volume, and secure the necessary capital. The contractors get orders from the manufacturers and hire women to do the work. And the union represents the workers in the contractors' factories. However, the ILGWU does not aggressively confront the contractors because, after all, they operate marginal businesses. Further, negotiations usually begin with the manufacturers, who provide the money which affects the wage scale. The union appeals to the manufacturers' desire for stable production conditions by having them award jobs only to contractors who hire union workers. So the ILGWU normally beings its organizing efforts with the manufacturers. Once the union comes to terms with the large manufacturers, it then goes to the contractors. The contractors usually accept the union's terms, because the union has commitments for work supplied by manufacturers. Finally, the union, with the approval of the contractors, organizes the workers. This organizing method may not require serious shop struggle at all. The critical point is to convince the contractors that it is in their self-interest to agree to recognize the union.

Under these circumstances, the union has divided loyalties. It represents the workers, but it also must be sensitive to the problems of the manufacturers and contractors, in order to hold the whole package together. If the manufacturers and contractors were to move their operations elsewhere, there would be few jobs and fewer union members. As a result, the union moderates its demands to make sure they stay in business. In carrying out this constructive role, the union is not singlemindedly representing the workers. For this reason, it is sensitive to any movement among the rank and file that might lessen its ability to carry on its delicate negotiations. The union is centralized and does not appreciate activism from its members.

U NION L OCAL 2 3 – 2 5

The garment factories in Chinatown were unionized by organizing the contractors. It was the easiest, quickest, and cheapest way for the union to succeed. So women became members of the union without the experience of struggle. Once they joined, the ILGWU made little effort to establish its presence on the factory floor. In many factories shop representatives, whose job it is to take up workers' complaints with the bosses, were, in fact, chosen by the owners. In some cases the ILGWU business agents, who represent the union in overseeing individual shops, get along better with the owners than with their own members. This is not surprising, since the success of the union clearly depends more on cooperation with the contractors than with the rank and file.

Most women who work in the industry are recent immigrants with no previous union experience. Furthermore, the union local consists almost entirely of Chinese. The women are not exposed to other American workers; nor are they familiar with working conditions in other American industries. The power of management is dominant. The contractors do what they like, violating contracts at will and blacklisting those who dare to speak out. When dissident workers are fired, the union is not able to get their jobs back because the business agents regularly side with management. There have also been innumerable charges of officials taking bribes.

Formal contracts are in effect, but violations are pervasive and the union acts as though nothing is wrong. When asked why there are so many clear violations in Chinatown factories, officials reply that the union always prosecutes these cases vigorously *if* the workers file formal complaints. Few Chinese ever do, because it is a complex and treacherous process, inviting possible retaliation from the contractors and betrayal by union officials.

The union claims that the Chinese cooperate with management by knowingly working off the books, not reporting management's cheating on piece rates, secretly working on jobs from nonunionized manufacturers, and even taking work home. On the other hand, the union has made no effort to educate its members: it prefers to emphasize the services it provides the workers. To many Chinese, the union is nothing more than a health-insurance company.

MILITANT CHINESE WOMEN

The ILGWU seems to consider Chinese women difficult to organize, because they are thought to be passive and tied to Chinatown's political and social structure. But in the summer of 1982, during the negotiation of a new contract, this stereotype still shared by so many was shattered. The negotiation involved renewal of a three-year contract and called for standard wage increases. The manufacturers signed the agreement; the union and the negotiating unit for the contractors (the Greater Blouse, Skirts, and Undergarment Association, translated as the "Foreigners Garment Merchants Association") also agreed to its terms. In fact, this same contract had already been signed to cover 120,000 non-Chinese garment workers on the East Coast. Unexpectedly, all the Chinese contractors balked, claiming that the negotiating unit did not represent them, since they had not been consulted during the negotiations. They were angry because even though 85 percent of the firms affected by the contract were Chinese-owned, there were no Chinese on the negotiating team. Furthermore, Chinatown's shops were the only ones in the industry that were doing well. As the backbone of New York's garment industry, and the most vital segment of Chinatown's economy, the contractors expected the community to rally behind them, particularly in this clear instance of racial discrimination. The contractors said to the workers, "We are all Chinese and should be able to settle this in our own house; there is no need to go to the white man's union." And knowing that the Chinese women were particularly concerned about health benefits, the contractors promised to provide the same benefits if they got out of the union.

The union had not expected this roadblock; it decided to head off the challenge by a show of force. It called for demonstrations in Columbus Park, on the edge of Chinatown, to defend the contract. According to some accounts, the union leaders had no idea how the Chinese women would react to the decision, since its staff was not close to the membership. Some doubted that the Chinese women would turn out to confront their own establishment in Chinatown.

But the reaction was overwhelming. Hundreds of women volunteered help: some operated phone banks to contact individual members, others wrote bilingual leaflets, banners, and propaganda material. Shops were mobilized by militant leaders who emerged from the rank and file. On the day of the first demonstration, 20,000 workers turned out. This was a historic event. Never before had so many Chinese, much less Chinese women, turned out over a labor issue. One of the leaders, Alice Tse, a new immigrant, spoke during the rally: "We cannot accept any treatment that is inferior. Chinese workers are people, too! We should receive equal treatment. . . . This is the true eternal spirit of being Chinese! If we cooperate and stand together behind our union, we will win! Let's celebrate our coming victory! Let's celebrate our historical show of unity demonstrated today."[7]

After two demonstrations, the Chinese contractors backed off and the workers won a new contract. The militancy of the Chinese women had been the key to victory. They had not been able to act on factory floors, because they were isolated and silenced by the community's conservative establishment, which represents owners; but the ILGWU's call for mass mobilization unleashed their militancy. The critical point was that the union had shown its support for the workers, who then realized that they did not have to be passive and cooperate with management: in fact, they repudiated those who did.

For many garment workers, the events of 1982 were their first real experience with collective protest. Afterwards they began to see new possibilities for improving conditions in their shops. If they maintained their solidarity, they could stop owners from violating labor codes. And if the power of the rank and file was consolidated, the union could pose a serious challenge to the community's traditional political order. Workers would then no longer fear intimidation and blacklisting.

However, the ILGWU as an institution has never been comfortable with a militant and active rank and file;[8] militant workers threaten the maneuverability of the union leadership in negotiations and the delicate balance of the industry. Many union officials have turned into career bureaucrats, concerned primarily with maintaining their jobs. Over the years, leadership has remained in the hands of white males, particularly those of Jewish origin,[9] even though the membership has been overwhelmingly female. The ILGWU's ethnic composition has changed from Jewish to Italian, to black, to Puerto Rican; today, it is mainly Chinese and Hispanic. Although at present 85 percent of Local 23–25 members are Chinese, only in the past few years has the union opened staff jobs to Chinese; none, however, is in a decision-making position.

During the serious, closed-door negotiations in the 1985 contract talks, all the representatives of the manufacturers and contractors were male; on the union side also, there were only males. Women, who are in fact the foundation of the whole industry, had no chance to voice their concerns—their interests are still being represented by male officials who are not even aware of their own chauvinism.

After the events of 1982, the union did not use the opportunity to strengthen the rank-and-file structure at the shop level. It did not improve the training of shop representatives, it did not replace the passive business agents, nor did it institute labor-education programs for its membership. It did, however, recruit the most militant workers to join its staff; there they could no longer organize fellow workers, but had to channel their energies in "acceptable" directions. They were assigned to so many high-profile projects that members began to see them as clever public-relations ploys. For example, some of the union's staff were shown in Chinese papers demonstrating against apartheid at the South African consulate. It was a worthy cause, except that most union members at the time were more upset about cutbacks in health benefits. No wonder a critic observed that the ILGWU has a complete "foreign policy" but no position on its own members.

A UNION IN CRISIS

Today, the American garment industry is in crisis. In the last twenty years clothing imports have jumped from 11 percent to a 54 percent share of the U.S. market.

Manufacturers, including those who originally signed contracts with the union, have switched their production to Third World countries and now import the finished products to the United States at much lower prices. Of the three hundred or so American manufacturers that used to provide jobs for Chinatown contractors, only about eighty are still doing so. The rest either moved their entire production abroad or contracted work out to nonunion shops. Chinese contractors complain that orders from unionized manufacturers keep only 40 percent of their work force busy. And since the union is no longer able to deliver enough work from the manufacturers, contractors are demanding concessions, most specifically permission to take on jobs from nonunion manufacturers. The union has refused to let Chinese contractors do so unless they contribute a high percentage of their income from those contracts to union membership funds. Violators are subject to fines.

But it is widely known that Chinese contractors, fearful of going out of business, have solicited jobs from nonunion manufacturers to keep their factories busy. They are doing this without telling the union. The response from the union when it learns of these violations has been mild. In November 1985, the Department of Labor indicted five men for conspiring to evade taxes by falsifying records. The accused were owners of the Leung Family Group garment factories. According to the charges, they were accepting work from noncontract manufacturers, and in order to cover up this violation they had the manufacturers pay them through a bank account opened under a fictitious name. Each check was to be in an amount less than $10,000, in order to evade scrutiny by banking authorities. In all, the Leung Family Group has allegedly avoided paying federal income tax and contributions for union health benefits on unreported income totaling $3 million.[10]

The Labor Department's action was the first major crackdown of its kind in the Chinese community. The immediate response was panic: every factory owner wondered who would be indicted next. Nobody denied such practices had been going on, but the main question was who had told the authorities. Who sold them out? Eventually the finger pointed to the ILGWU. The contention was that the union was upset because the violations cut into its income. After questioning, the president of Local 23–25 admitted that his office had provided records to the federal authorities. However, he said that the union would have never reported to the authorities had it not been subpoenaed by the government. It had to comply, lest it be found in contempt of court.[11] The answer was curious. Why should the union be defensive about reporting actions that violated its contract and thus hurt its members? Furthermore, if the union had records showing contractors' violations, why had it not exposed the matter earlier, rather than waiting for a federal summons?

In any event, the union's curious attitude has only emboldened contractors to ignore the contracts even more. Its attitude also discourages vigilant workers from reporting violations. Conditions in the shops have deteriorated further. The situation is so bad that more and more Chinese women have ventured uptown to work in non-Chinese-operated factories in the Seventh Avenue Garment District. Workers there belong to the same union, but to a different local, and Chinese workers have found conditions there much better than those in Chinatown. They no longer have to work from seven in the morning until seven at night, they get overtime pay, and piece rates are calculated correctly. Some women say they are much happier there, and swear never to work in Chinatown shops again. Local 23–25 is clearly not enforcing union contracts in the Chinatown shops.

However, the ILGWU still tries to shift the blame to imports. And since the union has no leverage over the manufacturers' investment decisions, its response has been to lobby in Congress for a rollback of imports to 25 percent of the U.S. market. In fact, the union has sponsored several citywide protests against imports. One can imagine how difficult it is for Chinese women to demonstrate against imports made by Chinese women in Hong Kong, Taiwan, and the People's Republic—where many have only recently come from. Lobbying Congress to pass import restrictions is an uphill battle. There is stiff opposition from many forces, including retailers who profit from markups of several hundred percent on imported items, and export industries—such as the aircraft and chemical industries—that fear import retaliation from other nations. In 1986 Congress passed a resolution to protect the domestic textile industry, a close ally of the garment industry, but President Reagan vetoed the bill, claiming that a trade war with other textile-exporting countries would harm the national interest.

Underlying the union's failure to enforce contracts is the belief that enforcement would put contractors out of business. But it is not clear whether the problem is real. While Chinese contractors complain about loss of business, every day there are dozens of want ads for seamstresses in the Chinese-language papers. The contractors' complaints may simply be a ploy to force the union to accept lower wages for the workers. Moreover, in recent years retailers have developed a strategy of encouraging fast-changing fashions. To keep up with rapidly changing styles, they need faster deliveries and greater production volume. This growing "spot market" has led to increases in jobs for Chinatown factories. While some individual shops may not be doing well, it is not necessarily true of the industry in Chinatown as a whole. Incompetent contractors who use obsolete production methods create their own problems; they would not survive in any event. Recently there has been a new development: two Hong Kong garment companies have set up factories in Chinatown. They evidently believe that, even with the higher wages, they will be able to make money in New York by employing modern production methods and locating nearer to the retail markets.[12]

Ultimately, whatever problems face the industry, the union is not expected to solve them. However, that is no excuse for the union to accept the contractors' view of the situation and not enforce contracts. If the industry is declining, does that justify the union's failure to enforce labor standards? Why should Chinese workers be the victims of this arrangement?

WOMEN'S RIGHTS

The blatant contradictions are hard to cover up. Since their mobilization in 1982, Chinese women have been stirred up and have shown more interest in union affairs. They now expect more from their union, and certainly they are more critical of its leadership. Some women realize that unless they mobilize, the union's commitment to them will remain limited. Thus, a group of activists gathered soon after the summer of 1982. At first they met as members of a Chinese choral group, to avoid union attention. After a few meetings one issue became paramount—the need for a children's daycare center. Among the 20,000 members of the local, there are mothers with an estimated 1,000 preschool children. Since the women work long hours and cannot leave their children at home, they bring them to work. But factory conditions are hardly suitable: several children were severely injured when they fell into elevator shafts. The women appealed to the union for help, but the president was outraged at the suggestion, declaring that child care was not its concern. Furthermore, he argued, if the union set up a daycare center for the Chinese, all other ethnic groups in the union would want one, too. And finally, he claimed the union had no money for such a project. Eventually, after much discussion, the union did raise enough funds and took credit for establishing a daycare center, presently accommodating seventy-five children. Its original reluctance is ironic, considering the ILGWU's proud tradition of practicing "social unionism." In the 1940s, the union built housing cooperatives for its members, set up a Workers' University, and was one of the first unions to establish welfare and retirement funds.[13]

As more rank-and-file Chinese women have become involved in the daycare issue, the union leadership has had to make some concessions, because of the important role its Chinese members play in the industry and because of their impact on the union. Since 1982 it understands the potentially militant nature of the rank and file. In recent years, the union has become more involved in Chinatown's community affairs, taking positions on housing, civil rights, immigration, and even public safety issues. However, these involvements, if continued, may push the union into community politics and ultimately shift the focus of its power from the union local to the community. This "decentralizing" development is not what the union leadership wants, and that's why at present none of its leaders is Chinese.

THE NEED TO BUILD COMMUNITY-BASED LABOR ORGANIZATIONS

The needs of today's Chinatown workers seem at odds with the nature of American unions. They need active unions that can protect them against exploitation, but militant unionism long ago declined in this country. Today the Chinese usually have flabby business unions, interested primarily in collecting dues and protecting the union bureaucracy, and not concerned with the complex problems facing workers in an ethnic community.

The Chinese need decentralized, community-oriented labor organizations to deal with their problems; this pattern is contrary to the model of American unions in the last fifty years, which stresses centralized, nationwide, big unions, able to confront big businesses.

But the labor movement may be forced to change in ways favorable to Chinese as well as other workers. The economy has undergone drastic transformations in the last decade: manufacturing industries are in decline; service industries and high-tech production are expanding. New production systems tend to require automation and decentralization, with fewer employees. There is, at the same time, a growing underground economy that requires immigrant labor and subcontracting systems. All these changes undermine the foundations of established American unions. If they are to survive, unions will have to make fundamental changes. One of the most important would be to organize labor effectively in ways and places that are ignored today, including industries employing minority and immigrant workers. As we have seen, the problems of Chinatown's workers are those that the ILGWU and the Hotel and Restaurant Employees and Bartenders Union will have to confront and solve in order to survive.

NOTES

1. Peter Kwong, *Chinatown, New York: Labor and Politics, 1930–1950* (New York: Monthly Review Press, 1979), 89.
2. *Pei-mei jih-pao* [*North American Daily News*, New York City], 31 March 1984, 8.
3. *Mei-chou jih-pao* [*Chinese Journal*, New York City], 14 June 1966, 7.
4. "Teamsters Plan an Organizing Drive in Chinatown," *The New York Times*, 13 May 1979, 36; and *Szù-chieh jih-pao* [*Singtao Daily News*, New York City], 13 May 1979, 2.
5. *Kung-jen Kuan-tién* [*Workers' Viewpoint*], 4 May 1980, 1.
6. *Hua-yü k'uài-pao* [*Sino Daily News*], 5 July 1980, 4.
7. Shiree Teng, "Women, Community and Equality," *East Wind* (spring/summer 1983): 20.
8. See discussion by Robert Laurentz, "Racial/Ethnic Conflict in the New York City Garment Industry, 1933–1980" (Ph.D. dissertation, SUNY Binghamton, 1980), 119.
9. See discussion by Herbert Hill of the similar kind of problems in the 1960s, "The ILGWU Today—The Decay of the Labor Union," *New Politics* (summer 1962): 3–14.
10. *Chung-pao* [*Central Daily News*, New York City], 29 November 1985, 20.
11. Ibid., 1 December 1985, 20.
12. Ibid., 21 June 1986, 20; 5 August 1986, 20; and Scott Davis, "From Rags to Real Estate," *The Christian Science Monitor*, 30 September 1986, 6.
13. Leon Stein, ed., *Out of the Sweatshops* (New York: Quadrangle, 1977), 244–272.

Panethnicity

18

NOT ASIAN, BLACK, OR WHITE?
REFLECTIONS ON SOUTH ASIAN
AMERICAN RACIAL IDENTITY

Nazli Kibria

Several friends have been urging me to watch *Late Night with David Letterman* to see the two Bangladeshi brothers who have become a semipermanent feature of the show. (I am of Bangladeshi origin.) On the occasion of July Fourth, Sirajul and Mujibur, operators of a small convenience store in New York, are shown holding American flags in front of the White House. In their familiar-sounding "accented" English, they respond in polite monosyllables ("yes," "no," "very nice") to Letterman's pesky questions as the audience screams with laughter, often for no apparent reason. I watch transfixed, feeling disturbed and perversely fascinated. Who are these men? Do they feel themselves to be the objects of ridicule or of affectionate

amusement? And how did the audience view and socially identify Sirajul and
Mujibur? As naive greenhorn immigrants? As clever entrepreneurs cashing in on
the American penchant for foreign oddities? As "Bangladeshis"? As "Indians"? As
"South Asians"? As "Asians"?

As South Asian Americans[1] become a more visible presence in the United States,
the need for a dialogue about questions of South Asian American identity has
become more pressing than ever. Here I would like to explore one aspect of South
Asian American identity—that of race. As a Bangladeshi immigrant, I am very aware
of the fact that as a signifier of identity, the term "South Asian" is itself highly
problematic, masking deeply salient divisions of nationality, culture, religion, and
language.[2] However, the issue of race calls for an analysis of South Asian rather
than Bangladeshi or Asian Indian identity because of the fact that in U.S. society,
persons of South Asian origin are not generally distinguished from one another
since they are judged to "look alike."

Although there are some signs of change, I believe that at present the racial
identity of South Asians in the United States is ambiguous in certain respects.
Among the consequences of this racial ambiguity is a sense of marginality for South
Asian Americans in a variety of social contexts, including that of the pan-Asian
movement.

SOUTH ASIAN AMERICANS AS "AMBIGUOUS NONWHITES"

I am teaching a small-sized undergraduate class on the sociology of race and ethnic
relations. The highly diverse group is unusually gregarious, frank, and talkative.
We are discussing the meaning of "race." At one point I casually ask, "Well, what
race do you think I am?" Stony silence. I fight back the urge to break the awkward
quietness. After what seems like several minutes, I am rewarded for my patience
with a barrage of comments:

"Aren't Indians[3] Caucasians? I remember reading somewhere that Indians from
India are from the same racial stock as Europeans. Their features are white; except
for their skin color they're basically white."

"But the skin color is what matters. Asian Indians have dark skin. No one in
America would ever look at Professor Kibria and say that she is white."

"The only thing I know about this is from watching *Mississippi Masala*. And from
that it seemed to me that Indians don't see themselves as black."

"As far as race, it's clear that you're not white or black or Asian. So what does
that leave us with? How do you feel about Latino?" (laughter)

"It's a ridiculous question. I don't see why we have to put these labels on people.
We don't have to accept the system."

In the United States, race is a commonsense aspect of reality, one that works as a
basic reference scheme by which to order and interpret social relations and encounters.[4] Race is, furthermore, viewed as "pure," and thus adequately defined by a

limited and discrete set of categories.[5] Those persons who lack a clear "race" because they are not easily placed into available racial categories (such as "Black," "White," or "Asian") are likely then to be a source of some unease to others, who wonder about the exact social identity of the person they have encountered. More important, perhaps, than the danger of causing social discomfort and awkwardness, such "raceless" persons run the risk of being ignored, of being invisible due to their inability to fit into established racial schemes. As Omi and Winant observe, "without a racial identity, one is in danger of having no identity."[6]

Studies of racial attitudes in the United States show that South Asians are clearly perceived to be racially distinct from the white population. There is, however, considerable confusion about the exact "race" of South Asians, who are categorized by the majority population inconsistently, as members of any of the major racial groupings in the United States.[7] So while it would be going too far to say that South Asian Americans have no "race," I believe that ambiguity is a prominent element of current South Asian racial identity in the United States. For lack of a more elegant term, South Asian Americans are ambiguous nonwhites.

A fundamental dynamic of the U.S. racial system is the division of people into a dichotomous scheme of white and nonwhite, based loosely on skin color.[8] South Asian Americans are clearly nonwhites within this scheme. Historically, for example, despite the fact that South Asians were "scientifically" classified to be "Caucasian," the U.S. courts judged them to be "nonwhite" in popular U.S. understanding and thus ineligible for the privileges of white status, such as the acquisition of citizenship, and, along with that, the right to own land.[9] The racial ambiguity of South Asians does not then stem from the question of whether they are white or nonwhite, but rather, from who exactly they are as nonwhites.

As I have mentioned, U.S. racial thinking is characterized by an understanding of race as "pure" and thus easily divided into a series of limited and mutually exclusive categories. These categories, while powerfully real in their consequences, are shifting and emergent in character. In the United States, the established racial categories that are popularly used, in everyday social encounters, to classify non-whites include Asian ("Oriental"), Black, American Indian, and Hispanic.[10] These categories are the outcome of complex historical processes in which both racial labeling and group self-definition have played a role.[11] Although South Asians do not fit well into any of these categories, they, like everyone else, encounter a social dynamic that insists on pigeonholing people into "a race." As a result, South Asian Americans are, in a certain sense, racially marginalized. This position of racial marginality is clearly not unique to South Asian Americans, but one that is shared by growing numbers of biracial and multiracial persons, as well as groups such as Arab Americans.

In some complex ways, South Asian Americans have themselves exacerbated the ambiguities of their racial identity. Like other minority groups in the United States, South Asian Americans view issues of identity in ways that are influenced by conceptions of race that are carried or transmitted from their countries of origin. Because the South Asian American communities tend to be transnational—maintaining active relations between multiple countries of origin and settlement—

the influence of these "native" conceptions of race may be particularly sharp for them. For South Asian Americans, these "native" conceptions of race may provide a means or frame of reference by which to resist dominant society racial thinking. But they also contribute to the group's racial ambiguity by allowing or facilitating South Asian American efforts to ignore or bypass the issue of South Asian racial status in the United States.[12]

Unfortunately, empirical research on how South Asian Americans understand their racial identity is currently limited. The studies we do have suggest that there is considerable resistance to both the categorical character and the skin color logic of U.S. racial thinking. For example, in her study of Asian Indians in New York City, Maxine Fisher describes the lack of consensus among Asian Indian immigrants about an appropriate racial designation for the group. Instead, the Asian Indians suggested a whole range of possible racial terms, including Aryan, Dravidian, Indo-Aryan, Indian, Oriental, Asian, and Mongol. Fisher further describes the consistent separation of race from skin color among Asian Indians, in contrast to U.S. racial thinking in which skin color is a major indicator of race. The Asian Indians she interviewed emphasized the diversity of skin color among Asian Indians, as well as the lack of relationship between skin color and race: "My uncle is very dark and my aunt is very fair. Their son is very fair and one daughter is very dark; one is in the middle. Their colors are different, but the race is the same."[13]

Such conceptions of race, which are so different from the principles of U.S. racial thinking, have helped South Asian Americans to remain ideologically disengaged from the U.S. racial order. In other words, confronted with the fact of their nonwhite ambiguity, South Asian Americans can turn to alternative conceptions of race to interpret their identity. Perhaps further reinforcing the tenacity of this response is the historical South Asian experience with white colonialism, which has fostered a powerful tradition of cultural resistance to colonial ways of thinking.

The changing composition of the South Asian American community is, however, making it increasingly difficult to maintain this position of ideological disengagement from the U.S. racial order. South Asian Americans are collectively experiencing a heightened sense of their nonwhiteness. Over the course of the past decade or so, South Asian Americans have moved from being a relatively invisible and benign presence to one that is increasingly visible as well as economically and culturally threatening to portions of U.S. society. Underlying this ongoing transformation are structural shifts within the South Asian American communities. On the one hand are the sheer numbers. The 1990 census, for example, showed the number of Asian Indians to have increased by 125.6 percent in the 1980s, from 387,223 to 815,447.[14] There is, furthermore, the growing socioeconomic diversity of the South Asian American communities. In the immediate aftermath of the 1965 Immigration Act, South Asian immigrants to the United States were largely professionals who were sheltered by the privileges of their class status from the most blatant forms of racism against nonwhites in the United States. Today, however, a growing number of South Asian Americans are to be found in labor-intensive and high-risk enterprises, such as the operation of convenience stores, gas stations, taxicabs and motels, in which they are highly vulnerable to racial hostility. Besides socioeconomic diversity, there is also the growing generational diversity of the South Asian American communities. "Native" conceptions of racial identity are likely to have far less meaning for second-generation South Asian Americans than for the immigrant generation. Particularly given their exposure and socialization into a post-civil rights political environment, one that has been characterized by a heightened consciousness of race, second-generation South Asian Americans may find it more necessary than their parents did to confront directly the dynamics of U.S. racial thinking. In short, for the South Asian American communities, a posture of distance from issues of race will become harder to maintain over time.

While the precise outcome of these developments is difficult to predict, it does seem likely that they will engender a more active dialogue among and between South Asians and other minority groups about South Asian American racial identity. Given the contested and shifting character of racial meaning in the United States, this dialogue has a potentially important role to play in the construction of South Asian American identity.

RACE, SOUTH ASIANS, AND (OTHER) ASIAN AMERICANS

I am at a fundraising reception for Asian American student scholarships where I am introduced to a bright young Korean American college student. We talk for awhile about the courses she is taking and her future career plans. Quite abruptly, she asks me if I consider myself "Asian." A little taken aback, but curious about her thinking on the issue, I replied that I did indeed consider myself Asian. But what had prompted the question?

"Quite frankly, you're the only Indian person here, so it got me thinking about the whole thing. I mean, there's a natural bond among most of the Asian groups because of the way we look, everyone sees us as Oriental. But that's not the case with Indians. The only bond with Indians is geographical—we're all from Asia. And maybe there are some cultural similarities with us, although I don't know because India's not really a Confucian-based society like a lot of the Asian ones. It's really very hard to figure out. I've wanted to ask someone about these things for awhile, but I'm usually too embarrassed."

The need for the South Asian American communities to enter into a dialogue about race with the larger Asian American community seems especially pressing. The ongoing immigration from Asia following the 1965 Immigration Act has increased the ethnic, generational, and class diversity of the Asian population in the United States. The new immigration has thus challenged the pan-Asian movement by enhancing potential sources of division and conflict. As exemplified by the experience of South Asians, one of the most important but least talked about of these axes of diversity is racial difference.

Within Asian American academic and political circles, South Asians tend to feel like outsiders, in ways that are somewhat similar to the experiences of Southeast Asians and Filipinos. This marginality reflects, in part, the more recent immigrant character of the South Asian American population and concurrently, its shorter history of involvement with the Asian American movement. But beyond all of this, there is the issue of perceived racial difference between South Asians and other Asian Americans. A rare public and explicit expression of this perceived racial difference occurred during the 1991 debate in San Francisco about whether or not South Asians should be included as Asians in the city's minority set-aside programs. In this now infamous incident, the effort to exclude South Asians (eventually overruled) was supported by a segment of the Chinese American business community, which felt "it would be wrong to mix two groups who were clearly different physically."[15]

More commonly, however, certainly in the academic circles with which I am most familiar, the issue of racial difference among Asian Americans is simply ignored. During a panel discussion on teaching at the 1994 Asian American Studies meetings in Ann Arbor, a South Asian American scholar raised the issue of South Asian marginality among Asian Americans. She cited her experience as a teaching assistant for an Asian American Studies course, in which students (largely Asian American) questioned the legitimacy of her position as a T.A. for the course because she was "not Asian." Who was she, as a South Asian, to tell them about "their history"? Further reinforcing her sense of being an outsider were the course materials, which purported to represent the Asian American experience, but with virtually no reference to South Asians. Her comments at the meeting were greeted with awkward silence, and soon the audience hurriedly moved on to discuss a far more comfortable issue—the thorny intricacies of interactions between white students and instructors teaching Asian American Studies courses and topics. Later, in private conversations, South Asians in attendance at the meeting talked of how the incident was symptomatic of the general tendency of the field of Asian American Studies to ignore South Asians.

On a variety of levels, the South Asian Americans I talked to at the conference expressed a powerful sense of marginality. As reflected in the inclusion of chapters on South Asians (or Asian Indians, to be more exact) in anthologies dealing with Asian Americans, there is growing recognition of the need to expand the subject matter of Asian American Studies beyond its traditional boundaries. However, South Asians remain largely at the margins rather than the center of scholarship and writing on Asian America. There is also the touchy issue of resources. Are South Asians being excluded from whatever resources are available within the field of Asian American Studies? An Asian Indian graduate student spoke of how the opening up of Asian American Studies to excluded groups such as South Asians had to go beyond token representation on organizational committees. What about, she angrily asked, the "real stuff"—the teaching and research positions, the fellowships, the publishing opportunities?

But for South Asian scholars and activists working on Asian American issues, perhaps the most personally painful expression of marginality occurs in the subtle signals of suspicion (e.g., offhand comments, distrustful gazes) that surround their very presence in Asian American forums. These suspicions are driven in part by questions regarding intent: what motivates the South Asians to join in the Asian American fray? Is it pure self-interest? At the heart of these questions about motivation and integrity is the issue of who is a real Asian American. South Asian claims to legitimate "Asian American-ness" are suspect because of perceived racial difference.

In *Asian American Panethnicity,* Yen Le Espiritu portrays panethnicity as a shifting phenomenon, one that emerges out of the complex interaction of structural circumstances and group efforts. The forces that foster panethnicity include "racial lumping" by the dominant society as well as structural incentives, or the development of situations in which the competitive advantages of banding together as a larger group are clear. Also critical to panethnic unity is the emergence of a panethnic consciousness, which "involves the creation of a common [Asian American] heritage out of diverse histories."[16]

What is the potential for the development of an Asian American consciousness that includes South Asians? For those who are interested in fostering such a common consciousness, one strategy might be to stress points of similar experience in the United States. In fact, United States history is replete with examples of the similar reception and treatment accorded immigrants from Asia. In 1910, for example, the San Francisco Japanese and Korean Exclusion League changed its name to the Asiatic Exclusion League so that it could also target Asian Indian immigrants. An inclusive panethnic Asian consciousness can be fostered not only by reference to the common aspects of the past, but also based on contemporary instances of successful and inclusive pan-Asian unity. Since the 1970s, South Asian Americans have been an important part of various pan-Asian political efforts, especially those in which the competitive advantage of unity and larger numbers has been clear. The demand for a revision of the 1980 census, for example, was one in which South Asians joined with other Asian groups. In recent years South Asian American college students have joined with other Asian students to protest unofficial quotas against the admission of Asian Americans to colleges and universities. In Detroit, Asian Indians were part of the Vincent Chin campaign, launched to protest the weak judicial response to hate crimes against Asian Americans.

These and other instances of successful solidarity are potentially important elements in the creation of a common heritage and thus consciousness among Asian Americans, one that includes South Asians. However, I remain pessimistic about the meaningful inclusion of South Asians in the pan-Asian fold as long as the issue of race is avoided by members of the pan-Asian movement. To the extent that the pan-Asian movement is self-defining, it may be possible to move beyond what Lisa Lowe describes as "the racist discourse that constructs Asians as a homogeneous group, that implies we are 'all alike' and conform to 'types.' "[17] But to move beyond the dominant racial discourse requires something that has been relatively absent: a frank and open discussion of the meaning of race, both within and between the South Asian and other Asian American communities.

NOTES

Thanks to Yen Le Espiritu, Madhulika Khandelwal, and Naheed Islam for their comments on earlier drafts.

1. "South Asia" includes Bangladesh, Bhutan, India, Pakistan, Maldives, Nepal, and Sri

Lanka. Most of the empirical studies I cite in this chapter are on the Indian population because of the absence of research on the other groups.

2. For further discussion of the problem of the "South Asian" category, see Naheed Islam, "In the Belly of the Multicultural Beast I Am Named South Asian," in *Our Feet Walk the Sky: Women of the South Asian Diaspora,* ed. Women of South Asian Descent Collective (San Francisco: Aunt Lute Books, 1993), 242–245.

3. Like other non-Indian South Asians, I am frequently referred to as "Indian." This reflects both the dominance of India in popular American understandings of the South Asian region and the dynamic of "lumping" into one group that all South Asians experience.

4. See Lucius Outlaw, "Toward a Critical Theory of 'Race,'" in *Anatomy of Racism,* ed. David T. Goldberg (Minneapolis: University of Minnesota Press, 1990), 58–82.

5. Sharon Lee, "Racial Classifications in the US Census: 1890–1990," *Ethnic and Racial Studies* 16, no. 1 (1993): 75–94.

6. Michael Omi and Howard Winant, *Racial Formation in the United States* (New York: Routledge, 1986), 62.

7. Maxine Fisher, *The Indians of New York City: A Study of Immigrants from India* (New Delhi: Heritage Publishers, 1980); and Rosaland Dworkin, "Differential Processes in Acculturation: The Case of Asiatic Indians in the United States," *Plural Societies* 11 (1980): 43–57.

8. See Sharon Lee and Maria Root, eds., "Within, Between, and Beyond Race," in *Racially Mixed People in America* (Newbury Park, Calif.: Sage Publications, 1992), 3–11.

9. Joan Jensen, *Passage from India* (New Haven, Conn.: Yale University Press, 1988).

10. These categories refer to contemporary commonsense understandings about racial divisions and not necessarily to official government racial classification schemes. Hispanics, for example, are not a racial category of the U.S. census, although the group is often seen as a "race" in the United States.

11. Stephen Cornell, "Land, Labour and Group Formation: Blacks and Indians in the United States," *Ethnic and Racial Studies* 13, no. 3 (1990): 368–388.

12. For an analysis of the South Asian unwillingness to come to terms with the U.S. racial order, see Sucheta Mazumdar, "Race and Racism: South Asians in the United States," in *Frontiers of Asian American Studies,* ed. Gail Nomura, Russell Endo, Stephen Sumida, and Russell Leon (Pullman: Washington State University Press, 1989), 25–39.

13. Fisher, *Indians of New York City,* 126.

14. Sucheta Mazumdar, "South Asians in the U.S. with a Focus on Asian Indians," in *The State of Asian Pacific Americans: A Public Policy Report* (Los Angeles: LEAP Asian Pacific American Public Policy Institute and UCLA Asian American Studies Center, 1993), 283–302.

15. Batuk Vora, "Indians Win Minority List Battle," *India West, 28* June 1991.

16. Yen Le Espíritu, *Asian American Panethnicity: Bridging Institutions and Identities* (Philadelphia: Temple University Press, 1992).

17. Lisa Lowe, "Heterogeneity, Hybridity, Multiplicity: Marking Asian American Differences," *Diaspora* 1, no. 1 (1991): 24–44.

WHAT MUST I BE?

ASIAN AMERICANS AND THE QUESTION

OF MULTIETHNIC IDENTITY

Paul R. Spickard

In 1968, Asian American Studies was born out of the Third World Strike at San Francisco State University; in 1995, Stanford announced it would finally join the rest of West Coast higher education by offering a major in Asian American Studies. Times and institutions change, as has the definition of what is an Asian American.

When I took the first Asian American Studies class at the University of Washington in 1970, "Asian American" meant primarily Japanese and Chinese Americans, with a few Filipinos allowed a place on the margin. Now "Asian American" includes Koreans, Vietnamese, Thais, Burmese, Laotians, Cambodians, Hmong, Asian Indians, and other Asians and Pacific Islanders. The multiplication of significant Asian and Pacific American populations, and their relative inclusion or lack of inclusion in the pan-Asian group, is the subject of another essay.[1] The topic here is more elusive and perhaps more subtle: the inclusion or lack of inclusion in Asian American Studies of people of multiple ancestries who are, as some would say, "part Asian."

THE IDENTITY QUESTION

Is it possible to have more than one ethnic identity? In *Hunger of Memory,* Richard Rodriguez asserts that members of ethnic minority groups must choose between private and public identities. By this he means that, in order to make satisfactory places for themselves in American society, minorities must either retain the ethnic culture of their youth, family, and community, or eschew their ethnicity and adopt the culture, values, and viewpoints of the dominant Anglo-American group. The ethnic, or "private," identity Rodriguez regards as inferior and limiting; the dominant group, or "public," identity he finds superior and liberating, even as he recounts the emotional costs of choosing to flee his own ethnicity.[2] According to Rodriguez and Pat Buchanan and Malcolm X, to name just three examples, a person can have only one ethnic identity, and cannot live in more than one community simultaneously. One cannot be black *and* white, Asian *and* American.[3]

W.E.B. Du Bois had a different view. He contended that every African American possessed and was possessed by a double consciousness, two identities in dialectical conversation. In an *Atlantic Monthly* essay, Du Bois wrote in 1897:

> [T]he Negro is a sort of seventh son, born with a veil, and gifted with second-sight in this American world,—a world which yields him no self-consciousness, but only lets him see himself through the revelation of the other world. It is a peculiar sensation, this double-consciousness, this sense of always looking at one's self through the eyes of others, of measuring one's soul by the tape of a world that looks on in amused contempt and pity. One ever feels his two-ness, an American, a Negro; two souls, two thoughts, two unreconciled strivings; two warring ideals in one dark body, whose dogged strength alone keeps it from being torn asunder.[4]

Such questions of double identity—of ethnicity and nationality—are issues for nearly all people of color in the United States. For no group of people is the dilemma of double identity more pointed than for people of multiple ancestry. They find themselves continually defined by people other than themselves. Regardless of how they construct their own identities, they always find themselves in dialogue with others who would define them from the outside.

Amerasian Santa Cruz poet Douglas Easterly rebels against being defined by whites, in this excerpt from "Guessing Game":

> Five seconds and they've gotta have you figured
> or it gnaws at them all night in a tiny
> part of their brain till they come up and ask you
> what *are* you?
> like you're from another planet
> *   *   *
> . . . Leaving you
> a footnote
> in race relation theory
> a symbol
> for the intersection of two worlds,
>   one foot in each of them
> so you can be dissected
> stuffed into labeled boxes—
> What *are* you?[5]

Cindy Cordes, a woman of Caucasian and Filipino ancestry raised in Hawai'i, puts it this way:

> I have a *hapa* [multiple-identity] mentality. I look white but I don't identify with white culture. I grew up with a Filipino mother in an Asian household. We ate Asian food,

had Filipino relationships, Filipino holidays, with Filipino values of family. In Hawai'i,
I always felt comfortable, so much of our culture is a conglomeration of cultures.

But then she went to Columbia University and found that other Asian Americans
"look at me as white." When she went to a meeting of an Asian American student
group, "They asked me, 'Why are you here?'"[6]

For multiracial Asians like Cordes and Easterly, one task is to defend themselves
against the *dominant discourse* imposed by white America, in order to establish
control of their own identity. But there is a second task that Cordes sees as equally
important: to defend herself against the *subdominant discourse* imposed by Asian
Americans. Throughout their history, Asian Americans have also defined people
of part-Asian descent,[7] without regard to their actual life situations or wishes. In
thus specifying identities for mixed people of Asian ancestry, some Asian Americans
have been as guilty of stereotyping and oppressing, of mythologizing and dominating, as have whites. Throughout their history, however, multiracial Asian Americans
have also chosen identities for themselves. They have created patterns of choosing
identities that are the portents for the future.

THE DOMINANT AND SUBDOMINANT DISCOURSES: PRE-1960S

For most of the history of mixing between Asians and non-Asians in the United
States, people of part-Asian ancestry have not had much choice about how to
identify themselves. Either the Asian minority or the white majority told them what
they must be.

Prior to the 1960s, most Asian American peoples were so opposed to intermarriage that they shunned not only the intermarried couples but also their mixed
children. That is in marked contrast to the situation for multiracial people of
African American descent, who found at least a grudging welcome among African
Americans, and who were in any case forced by white Americans to identify as
black. Chinese-Hawai'ians in the 1930s, by far the largest group of Amerasians in
that era, were far more readily accepted in the Hawai'ian community than in the
Chinese community.[8] In that same period, Japanese Americans thrust out of their
midst most mixed people. The Los Angeles Japanese community ordinarily took
care of any of its members who were in need. One result was that only 101 orphans
had to be taken care of by the Japanese American Children's Village in 1942. But
nineteen of them were people of mixed ancestry. That was far more than their
percentage in the Japanese American child population at large. Most of them,
probably, were children who had been abandoned and whom no Japanese family
would adopt.

White Americans also opposed intermarriage with Asians, and they were not
inclined to celebrate the presence in their midst of multiracial people of Asian
descent. But the number of Amerasians was so small that whites could ignore such
individuals and let them slide by on the margins of white society.

Strange and vicious ideas about multiracial people of Asian descent have
emerged historically from white racism. Those ideas are important because they
shaped people's life chances then and now. The fullest exploration of this topic is

in a recent essay by Cynthia Nakashima.[9] White ideas about mixed-race people proceeded from biological ideas propounded by pseudoscientific racists in the late nineteenth and early twentieth centuries.[10] Reasoning from the physical properties of plants and animals to the physical and moral qualities of human beings, pseudo-scientific racists put on the American intellectual agenda a set of assumptions about multiracial people that still plague mixed people today. Nakashima summarizes these ideas:

> [T]hat it is "unnatural" to "mix the races"; that multiracial people are physically, morally, and mentally weak; that multiracial people are tormented by their genetically divided selves; and that intermarriage "lowers" the biologically superior White race . . . that people of mixed race are socially and culturally marginal, doomed to a life of conflicting cultures and unfulfilled desire to be "one or the other," neither fitting in nor gaining acceptance in any group, thus leading lives of confused loneliness and despair.[11]

Most dominant discourse about Amerasians has been in terms of these myths of degeneracy, confusion, conflict, and despair. Edward Byron Reuter, the foremost academic authority on racial mixing in his day, had this to say in 1918:

> Physically the Eurasians are slight and weak. Their personal appearance is subject to the greatest variations. In skin color, for example, they are often darker even than the Asiatic parent. They are naturally indolent and will enter into no employment requiring exertion or labor. This lack of energy is correlated with an incapacity for organization. They will not assume burdensome responsibilities, but they make pass-able clerks where only routine labor is required.[12]

About the same time, a white California journalist wrote: "The offspring are neither Japanese nor American, but half-breed weaklings, who, doctors declare, have neither the intelligence nor healthfulness of either race, in conformity with the teaching of biology, that the mating of extreme types produces deficient off-spring."[13] Even whites who fancied themselves defenders of Asians found themselves debating in terms set by the pseudobiological argument. Sidney L. Gulick, who opposed Japanese exclusion, felt compelled to give evidence that (1) unlike mules, Amerasians were not sterile, and (2) far from being weak and imbecilic, they were stout and smart.[14]

Within popular culture, Amerasians are perceived as sexual enthusiasts. This is related to a mechanism of dominance that attributes lack of sexual control to dominated peoples—women especially—as a way to excuse white male abuses of women.[15] This dynamic, the "myth of the erotic exotic," is compounded for women of mixed race.[16] Speaking of Amerasians, Nakashima writes, "The mixed-race person is seen as the product of an immoral union between immoral people, and is thus expected to be immoral him- or herself. . . . [M]ultiracial females are especially likely targets for sexual objectification because of their real and perceived vulnerability as a group."[17]

During World War II, when Japanese Americans were placed in concentration camps on account of their ancestry, a small but significant number of mixed-race people—perhaps 700 Amerasians—also shared that experience. The army and the War Relocation Authority (WRA) ruled that all persons of full Japanese ancestry living on the West Coast had to be imprisoned. Some had non-Japanese spouses; the spouses could choose whether or not to go to the government's prison camps. Amerasians presented a special problem. Were they more Japanese, in which case they should be required to go to prison camp? or were they more American, in which case they might remain at liberty with their non-Japanese parent? First the government incarcerated all the multiracial people of Japanese ancestry, then they tried to figure out what to do with them.

The WRA eventually made a judgment about each Amerasian's prewar environment. This judgment was made on the basis of the gender of the non-Japanese parent. Amerasian children who had white fathers and Japanese mothers could leave the camps and return to their presumably "Caucasian" (the army's term) prewar homes. Amerasian children who had Japanese fathers and non-Japanese mothers were presumed to have been dominated by their fathers, so while they could leave the prison camp, they were not allowed to return to the West Coast until late in the war. Adult Amerasians could leave the camps, but only if they had "fifty per cent, or less, Japanese blood," and could demonstrate that their prewar environment had been "Caucasian."[18]

Whites were confused about Amerasians and uncertain exactly where to place them. They had a number of stereotypes about multiracial people (Amerasians especially) that were perverse and demeaning. Asians were less confused than whites: generally speaking, they did not want multiracial people of Asian ancestry, and they told them they could not be Asians.[19]

This made life problematic for many multiracial people of Asian descent. Take the case of Kathleen Tamagawa. Born at the turn of the century, she did not like being an Amerasian. She opened her autobiography with the words, "The trouble with me is my ancestry. I really should not have been born."[20] There follows a tale of tortured passage through her young life in America and Japan, undermined rather than supported by parents who had problems of their own. She was, by her own reckoning, a "citizen of nowhere," but by that she meant that she could find no place for herself in Japan. In time, in fact, she married a nondescript, middle-class white American and faded into white suburban life.

Peter, a Japanese-Mexican boy, had a tougher time of it in Los Angeles in the 1920s. His Mexican mother died when he was very young, and he never established ties to any Chicanos. His father remarried, this time to a Japanese woman who did not like Peter. She beat him, ridiculed him, refused to feed him, and finally threw him out of the house. School authorities found him running unsupervised in the streets at age seven. Peter's father told him that "he wished that I had never been born; and at times I have even wished that myself. I have often wished that I were an American and not a Japanese or Mexican." Juvenile court authorities found Peter "an outcast" from both Japanese and Chicano communities. They tried to find a foster home for Peter, but no one would take him because of his mixed ancestry. He finally was sent to the state reformatory.[21]

For every Kathleen or Peter who suffered for their mixed raciality, however, there were others much happier. Kiyoshi Karl Kawakami, a prominent writer and interpreter of Japan to America and of America to Japan, married Mildred Clark of Illinois and had two children, Clarke and Yuri. The younger Kawakamis spoke positively of their Eurasianness when interviewed in 1968. They grew up from the 1910s to the 1930s, mainly in the Midwest, well-educated and insulated from life's blows by their father's money and status. They had almost nothing to do with Japanese Americans except for their father, and in fact looked down on Nisei as people suffering from an "inferiority complex.[22] The common thread is that nearly all mixed-race people of Asian descent prior to the 1960s had to make their way outside of Asian American communities, for Asian communities would not have them.

This was true even for the great Asian American writer Sui Sin Far. Born Edith Maud Eaton in 1865, daughter of an English father and a Chinese mother, she was raised and lived her adult life in several parts of Canada and the United States. She chose to identify with Chinese people to the extent of choosing Chinese themes and a Chinese pseudonym, and she wrote prose sympathetic to the sufferings, fears, and hopes of Chinese North Americans. But she was nonetheless always more on the white side than the Chinese, in relation to where she lived and worked, who her friends were, and the point of view from which she wrote. In Sui Sin Far's writing, there were always people and Chinese. Partly it was because her literary aspirations demanded that her work be intelligible to a white audience, partly because Chinese people treated her as an outsider, albeit a friendly one. For example,

> Some little Chinese women whom I interview are very anxious to know whether I would marry a Chinaman. I do not answer No. They clap their hands delightedly, and assure me that the Chinese are much the finest and best of all men. They are, however, a little doubtful as to whether one could be persuaded to care for me, full-blooded Chinese people having a prejudice against the half-white.[23]

Like other part-Asians before the 1960s, Sui Sin Far spent her life racially on the white side.

WINDS OF CHANGE: POST-1960S

Substantial numbers of Asian Americans began to marry non-Asians in the 1960s. By the 1970s, the numbers of Chinese and Japanese who married outside their respective groups and then had children were so large that Asian American communities were forced to begin to come to terms with and accept the existence of mixed people. There were some limitations on this acceptance, however. Those involved in the Asian American movement of the 1960s and 1970s seldom had a place for people of multiple ancestry or their distinctive issues. Stephen Murphy-Shigematsu describes the dynamic:

> [I]t has been difficult to include biracial Asian Americans in Asian American communities.

The subject of biracial Asian Americans relates directly to interracial couples—an issue that is often seen as threatening to Asian American communities and individuals. There is a feeling that openly discussing this topic amounts to sanctioning interracial marriage and endorsing the death of Asian American ethnic groups.[24]

Today multiracial people of Asian descent take a number of paths to ethnic identity. Very few are inclined or able to identify solely with one part of their inheritance. Many adopt what Amy Iwasaki Mass calls "situational ethnicity." They feel mainly white or black or Latino (according to their mix) when among white or black or Latino relatives and friends, and act mainly Asian when among Asians.[25]

Joy Nakamura (a pseudonym) grew up in Brooklyn. She was in most respects a normal Jewish girl in a Jewish neighborhood, except that her father was Japanese. Her Nisei father seldom talked about his childhood in California, her Japanese American relatives were far away, and although she felt somehow connected to Japan, she never had an opportunity to explore the connection until she entered a large eastern university. "I met more Asians my first year [in college] than I had ever known. When one Japanese American called me on the phone to invite me to join a Japanese American discussion group, I was very excited. I went to the group meetings a few times, but my 'white-half' began to feel uncomfortable when the others began putting down whites," so she stopped going. She took classes on Japanese language and culture and enrolled in a seminar on Asian Americans. "I was desperately trying to find myself as an Asian-American woman, but I was not succeeding." She had clashes with her white boyfriend over racial issues, and she tried to ignore her Jewishness. Pressure from an African American activist friend helped Nakamura clarify her feelings. He said,

> "You must decide if you are yellow, or if you are white. Are you part of the Third World, or are you against it?" I laughed at his question. How could I possibly be one and not the other? I was born half-yellow and half-white. I could not be one and not the other anymore than I could cut myself in half and still exist as a human being.

At length she decided, "I do not feel guilty about not recognizing my Asianness. I have already done so. I have just readjusted my guilt feelings about ignoring my Jewish half. . . . My Jewishness is something that can be easily hidden. I do not want to hide that fact. I want to tell the world that I am a Jew and a Japanese American."[26]

When I told Joy Nakamura's story at a conference on Jewish history and identity, one member of the audience—a distinguished Jewish scholar—snorted loudly that Nakamura was obviously a sick person. On the contrary, she is healthy and whole. Her choice to embrace both halves of her identity in the mid-1970s is a point of self-understanding which increasing numbers of multiracial people have reached in the two decades since. There is no question that to embrace both (or all) parts of one's identity is a healthier situation than to cling to one and pretend that the other does not exist. The general thinking here is to overturn the idea of a tortured "half-breed," torn between two irreconcilable identities. One has, not a split consciousness, but an integrated identity fused from two—"I am a whole from two wholes," is the way one Japanese-Caucasian man put it.[27]

In recent years a number of organizations of multiracial Asian Americans have sprung up around the country—the Amerasian League in West Los Angeles is an outstanding example—where people can come to explore their multiraciality. There has also grown up a veritable cottage industry of scholarly studies by and about multiracial people of Asian descent.[28]

ASIAN AMERICAN RESPONSES

Many mainstream Asian American groups still do not know quite what to do with multiracial Asians. Until very recently, there has been no place for them in Asian American Studies curricula.[29]

Asian Americans have, until recently, merely adopted the biases and boundaries set by white America. In so doing, they internalize the oppression that circumscribes their lives and project that oppressive vision on Amerasians. The 1990–91 controversy over the Broadway version of the hit musical *Miss Saigon* illustrates this point. The play's lead character was a Eurasian pimp. The play's producer and director chose a white person for the role. Asian American actors and community activists protested bitterly, saying the role should go to an Asian. Lost in the shuffle was the fact that, if ethnicity were the casting criterion, the only appropriate actor would be neither a Caucasian nor an Asian, but a person of mixed ancestry.[30] Multiracial Asian Americans exist (and in large numbers), and no amount of ignoring them will cause them to go away.

Increasing numbers of Amerasians are inclined to regard themselves as a variety of Asian Americans, and increasingly they find that Asians of unmixed ancestry will accept them as fellow ethnics. Across the country, it is hard to find a Japanese American or Chinese American church that does not have interracial couples and biracial children; there are even a few biracial adults. Sometimes, as Nakamura complained, Asian groups will accept Amerasians only if they renounce their non-Asian background. But with increasing frequency Asian American institutions, from athletic leagues to community newspapers to social welfare organizations, seem inclined to admit Amerasians as something like full participants.

CREATING AMERASIAN CULTURE

In this new era, most Amerasians do not link up primarily with other Amerasians. But in some cultural respects they nonetheless constitute a distinct group. Those who grew up in Japan, for example, the children of American soldiers and Japanese women, have created a social world of their own, different from but not walled off from the Japanese or the Americans around them. They socialize more with each other than with non-Amerasians, and have begun to form a third culture that mixes the languages, values, and symbol systems of their two parental cultures.[31]

INTRA-ASIAN ETHNIC VARIATIONS

In all this, one must remember that there are large differences among multiracial Asians. No one has yet studied the meaning of multiethnicity for multiracial Asians of differing derivations.

A few observations can be made. The community acceptance level for Filipino Amerasians has long been much higher than for other groups. This is because the Filipino immigrant population was so heavily male that, until after World War II, almost any Filipino man who married had to find a non-Filipina mate. The majority of the American-born generation was multiracial.[32]

The situation for multiracial Japanese Americans differs from that of multiracial Chinese Americans, who are fewer in number. The difference has to do not only with the relatively greater numbers of Japanese Amerasians, but also with structural differences in the two communities. Japanese Americans are an almost entirely American-born ethnic group. The bulk of the adult population are members of the third or fourth generation. By contrast, more than half the current Chinese American population is made up of immigrants. The unmixed Japanese Americans are, as a group, much more assimilated to American society and culture at large, and somewhat more accepting of intermarriage and multiracial people.[33]

A third example of difference is between Korean and Vietnamese Amerasians, on the one hand, and Amerasians whose Asian ancestry is from the other countries mentioned above on the other. Most Amerasians are American-born and raised, the children of Asian Americans and other sorts of Americans. Nearly all Korean and Vietnamese Amerasians, however, were born in Asia, the children of American GIs and Asian women. Many of the Korean Amerasians were given up for adoption and came to the United States at a very young age. They were raised by people with names like Lund and Anderson in the Midwest. Their life trajectories and their identity issues are quite different from other sorts of Amerasians. These frequently revolve around how to connect with their Korean background when they grew up in rural Minnesota knowing only Swedish American culture. Most of the Vietnamese Amerasians, like the Koreans, were born in Asia. But the Vietnamese typically came to the United States only recently, in their teens and twenties. Generally speaking, the Korean and Vietnamese communities have been less eager to include Amerasians than have other Asian groups.[34]

GEOGRAPHICAL DIFFERENCES

If there are intra-Asian ethnic differences, there are also substantial differences depending on one's geographical location. Ethnic dynamics in Hawai'i, for example, are quite different from those on the mainland. For over a century, there has been a great deal of intermarriage in Hawai'i, and therefore a large number of Hapas, or people of mixed ancestry.

To some extent, in Hawai'i the mainland patterns of ethnic acceptance are inverted. Island Chinese these days seem more accepting of multiracial Asians than do island Japanese communities. The Chinese community in Hawai'i may once have shunned people of mixed parentage, but in the last several decades that community has learned to make room for part-Chinese. One finds people in Chinese churches with Chinese names who look Hawai'ian and went to the Kamehameha Schools, which are reserved for people of Hawai'ian ancestry. By comparison, island Japanese communities and institutions have less room for multiracial Japanese Americans. There is a substantial number of Japanese Amerasians in Hawai'i, but generally they are not tightly connected to Japanese community institutions. They find places in the social system, but usually in a wider, mixed sector that includes whites, various Asians, some Polynesians, and other mixed people. To be *Hapa* among Chinese in Hawai'i is more acceptable; to be *Hapa* among Japanese in Hawai'i is less acceptable. A Japanese-Caucasian woman recently reported from Hawai'i that a Japanese relative twirled the *Hapa* woman's red hair in her finger and snorted, "What part of you is Japanese—your big toe?"[35]

The reverse is true for most West Coast cities. There, intermarriage by Japanese Americans is more frequent than in Hawai'i, and mixed people are more likely to be included in Japanese American communities. By contrast, multiracial Chinese Americans in cities like San Francisco and Seattle are more likely to be treated with suspicion and are less likely to be included in Chinese community institutional life.[36]

Perhaps the biggest difference, however, is between the Pacific states, where there are large Asian communities, and most of the rest of the country, where Asians are more of a novelty. Those large communities keep down the rate of Asian outmarriage.[37] But they also encourage non-Asians to regard Asian Americans as ordinary parts of the social fabric. That acceptance of Asians extends to Amerasians: Amerasians (like unmixed Asians) are less likely to be harassed by whites in Monterey Park, California, than they are in Columbus, Birmingham, or Boston.[38]

PHYSICAL APPEARANCE

Another way the experiences of multiracial people of Asian descent vary has to do with their physical appearance. University of Washington professor Jim Morishima tells the story of Kimiko Johnson (a pseudonym), whom, on the basis of her last name and appearance, he took to be a Japanese American married to a Caucasian. When Morishima asked her about her husband, she replied cryptically that she was not married and had never been married, but would show him his mistake. Soon she reappeared with an African American youth whom she introduced as her brother. The brother spoke black English and identified himself as black. The two Johnsons had the same set of parents—an African American father and a Japanese American mother—yet they identified themselves differently, one as Japanese, one as black, because that is the way they looked, and therefore the way other people treated them.[39]

Physical appearance, however, does not completely determine one's identity. Christine Hall, Michael Thornton, and Teresa Williams, in studying children of Japanese-American intermarriages, all found some people whose features appeared to favor the Japanese side, but who nonetheless identified more strongly with their American heritage (white or black). Conversely, they found others who appeared physically more American, but who for reasons of their upbringing felt more attached to their Japanese identities. Williams found,

> darker-skinned Afroasians did not automatically relate to African Americans, nor did lighter-skinned Afroasians necessarily identify with their Japanese parentage. Eurasians who appeared more Caucasian did not always blend in naturally with Euro-Americans;

those who looked relatively more Asian did not always accept their Japanese background willingly and readily.[40]

Only in instances of conspicuous achievement are Asian communities willing to treat mixed people of African American parentage as insiders. This is related to what Cynthia Nakashima calls the "claim-us-if-we're-famous syndrome."[41] It is not likely that many San Francisco Japanese Americans thought of attorney Camille Hamilton as one of their own until she was named by *Ebony* magazine as one of "Fifty Black Leaders of the Future" in 1990. But then *Hokubei Mainichi* was quick to feature her accomplishments.[42]

IMPLICATIONS OF MULTIPLE IDENTITIES

An increasing number of people who are of mixed ancestry are choosing to embrace multiple identities. Psychological studies by Amy Iwasaki Mass, George Kitahara Kich, and others suggest that the choice of a biracial identity is, for most mixed people, a healthier one than being forced to make an artificial choice.[43] In helping individuals make their way to identity choices, family support is crucial. One must add here, however, that since the pull of the dominant Anglo-American culture is so strong in America, if a child is of mixed Asian and White descent, it is prudent to emphasize the Asian heritage.[44]

In addressing multiracial people of Asian descent, the task for the dominant group in America is to rearrange its understandings to accommodate the reality of biracial identity. Asian Americans must also rearrange their understandings. This means redefining in more inclusive terms what it means to be an Asian American. In the case of some Asian groups—certainly Japanese Americans, and probably Chinese, Koreans, and Filipinos before long—their very survival in an era of high intermarriage depends on coming to terms with and incorporating multiracial Asians.

Asian American Studies programs, to take just one example, ought to do more to include Amerasians. Stephen Murphy-Shigematsu states:

> When biracial people see their concerns expressed as legitimate within the context of Asian American issues, there is a greater opportunity for continued interest and involvement and less chance of alienation. When they are free to acknowledge their non-Asian heritage as an integral part of who they are as a people, without fear of rejection, then their ability to study and work among other Asian Americans will grow.[45]

The good news is that a growing number of Asian American Studies programs—and many other Asian institutions—are doing just that: changing to include the issues and persons of multiracial people of Asian descent.

NOTES

1. See Yen Le Espiritu, *Asian American Panethnicity* (Philadelphia: Temple University Press, 1992); William Wei, *The Asian American Movement* (Philadelphia: Temple University Press, 1993).

2. Richard Rodriguez, *Hunger of Memory: The Education of Richard Rodriguez* (New York: Godine, 1982).

3. Buchanan's sentiments on the necessity of obliteration of ethnic differences, and the need to put strict limits on non-northwest European immigrants because they are, in his view, harder to "assimilate," were much in the news during his 1992 run for the U.S. presidency, and they threaten to appear again. See, for example, DeWayne Wickham, "Buchanan Is Mounting a Racist Campaign," *Honolulu Star Bulletin,* 16 December 1991. Malcolm X called on African Americans, most of whom shared his mixed ancestry, to denounce their white background and embrace the black. In his autobiography he recounted how "I learned to hate every drop of that white rapist's blood that is in me." When he came to self-consciousness as a member of the Nation of Islam, he changed his name: "For me, my X replaced the white slave-master name of 'Little' which some blue-eyed devil named Little had imposed upon my paternal forebears." *The Autobiography of Malcolm X* (New York: Grove, 1965), 2:199.

4. W. E. Burghardt Du Bois, "Strivings of the Negro People," *Atlantic Monthly* 80 (August 1897): 194–195.

5. Douglas P. Easterly, "Guessing Game," in Asian/Pacific Islander Student Alliance, *Seaweed Soup,* vol. 2 (Santa Cruz, Calif.: University of California, Santa Cruz, Pickled Plum Press, 1990), 26–27.

6. Susan Yim, "Growing Up 'Hapa,'" *Honolulu Star-Bulletin and Advertiser,* 5 January 1992.

7. Terminology for mixed-descent people is problematic and cumbersome, and there is no standard. I use the term "Amerasian" most frequently here, as a label for people who have Asian ancestry on one side and American (white, black, Native American, etc.) on the other. "Eurasian" refers specifically to people whose non-Asian heritage is European. I also use a number of descriptions, such as "multiracial Asians," "mixed people of Asian ancestry," and "people of part-Asian ancestry," more or less interchangeably. I do not wish here to enter into a discussion of the difference or nondifference between "race" and "ethnicity" (see Paul R. Spickard, *Mixed Blood: Intermarriage and Ethnic Identity in Twentieth-Century America* [Madison: University of Wisconsin Press, 1989], 9–10, for that discussion). Here I use "multiethnic" and "multiracial" interchangeably. By describing a person as having "part-Asian ancestry" I specifically do *not* mean to imply that she is less than a fully integrated personality, nor that she is less than fully entitled to membership in an Asian American community. If in any of this I offend a reader, I can only apologize, plead that the offense is unintentional, and ask that the reader attend to the argument and evidence presented here rather than to taxonomy.

8. Doris M. Lorden, "The Chinese-Hawaiian Family," *American Journal of Sociology* 40 (1935): 453–463; Everett V. Stonequist, *The Marginal Man* (New York: Russell and Russell, 1965; orig. New York: Scribner's, 1937), 41.

9. Cynthia L. Nakashima, "An Invisible Monster: The Creation and Denial of Mixed-Race People in America," in Maria P. P. Root, ed., *Racially Mixed People in America* (Beverly Hills, Calif.: Sage, 1991), 162–178. Nakashima writes about the images of all sorts of mixed-race people, but her findings apply particularly well to the Amerasian case.

10. On American ideas about race, see Paul R. Spickard, "The Illogic of American Racial Categories," in Root, *Racially Mixed People,* 12–23; James C. King, *The Biology of Race* (Berkeley: University of California Press, 1981).

11. Nakashima, "Invisible Monster," 165.

12. Edward Byron Reuter, *The Mulatto in the United States* (New York: Negro Universities Press, 1969; orig. Ph.D. dissertation, University of Chicago, 1918), 29. See also E. B. Reuter, "The Personality of Mixed Bloods," in Reuter, *Race Mixture* (New York: Negro Universities Press, 1969; orig. New York: Whittlesey House, 1931), 205–216.

13. Quoted in Kiyoshi K. Kawakami, *Asia at the Door* (New York. Revell, 1914), 71.

14. Sidney L. Gulick, *The American Japanese Problem* (New York: Scribner's, 1914), 153–157.

15. For fuller treatment of this theme, see Spickard, *Mixed Blood,* 35–42, 252–259; Calvin

Hernton, *Sex and Racism* (New York: Grove, 1965); Winthrop D. Jordan, *White Over Black* (Chapel Hill: University of North Carolina Press, 1968), 154.

16. Elaine Louie speaks of Asian women in general, not specifically of Amerasians, in "The Myth of the Erotic Exotic," *Bridge* 2 (April 1973): 19–20.

17. Nakashima, "Invisible Monster," 168–169.

18. Paul R. Spickard, "Injustice Compounded: Amerasians and Non-Japanese Americans in World War II Concentration Camps," *Journal of American Ethnic History* 5, no. 2 (spring 1986): 5–22.

19. Rejection of multiracial people of Asian descent was common in China and Japan as well as among Chinese and Japanese Americans. Filipino communities were an exception to this rule of rejection (see below).

20. Kathleen Tamagawa Eldridge, *Holy Prayers in a Horse's Ear* (New York: Long and Smith, 1932), 1, 220.

21. William C. Smith, "Life History of Peter," Survey of Race Relations Papers, Hoover Institution Archives, Stanford University, Major Document 251–A; William C. Smith, "Adjutant M. Kobayashi on the Second Generation," Survey of Race Relations Papers, Major Document 236.

22. Clarke Kawakami and Yuri Morris, interviewed by Joe Grant Masaoka and Lillian Takeshita, 22 May 1968, Bancroft Library, Berkeley, Calif., Phonotape 1050B:10. Other elite Eurasian children inhabited similarly comfortable positions, aware of the Asian aspect to their identities—even trading on it in their careers—but essentially white in outlook and connections. See, for example, the autobiographical portions of Isamu Noguchi, *Isamu Noguchi: A Sculptor's World* (Tokyo: Thames and Hudson, 1967); *The Life and Times of Sadakichi Hartmann* (Riverside, Calif.: Rubidoux, 1970); and (also on Hartmann) Gene Fowler, *Minutes of the Last Meeting* (New York: Viking, 1954). Others in less comfortable circumstances had to struggle—psychically, interpersonally, and financially—to make places for themselves. See, for example, Sui Sin Far, "Leaves from the Mental Portfolio of an Eurasian," *The Independent* 66, no. 3136 (7 January 1909): 125–132.

23. Sui Sin Far, *Mrs. Spring Fragrance and Other Writings,* ed. Amy Ling and Annette White-Parks (Urbana: University of Illinois Press, 1995), 223. The essay is titled "Leaves from the Mental Portfolio of an Eurasian." See also Paul Spickard and Laurie Mengel, "Deconstructing Race: The Multi-ethnicity of Sui Sin Far," *Books and Culture,* November 1996.

24. Stephen Murphy-Shigematsu, "Addressing Issues of Biracial/Bicultural Asian Americans," in Gary Y. Okihiro et al., eds., *Reflections on Shattered Windows* (Pullman: Washington State University Press, 1988), 111.

25. Amy Iwasaki Mass, "Interracial Japanese Americans: The Best of Both Worlds or the End of the Japanese American Community?" in Root, *Racially Mixed People,* 265–279. See also Maria P. P. Root, "Resolving 'Other' Status: Identity Development of Biracial Individuals," in L. Brown and M.P.P. Root, eds., *Complexity and Diversity in Feminist Theory and Therapy* (New York: Haworth, 1990), 185–205.

26. Joy Nakamura (pseud.), letter to the author, 22 May 1974.

27. Jean Y. S. Wu, "Breaking Silence and Finding Voice: The Emergence of Meaning in Asian American Inner Dialogue and a Critique of Some Current Psychological Literature" (Ed.D. dissertation, Harvard University, 1984), 173–182.

28. See, for example, Nakashima, "Invisible Monster"; Cynthia Nakashima, "Research Notes on Nikkei Hapa Identity," in Okihiro, *Reflections on Shattered Windows,* 206–213; Barbara Posadas, "Mestiza Girlhood: Interracial Families in Chicago's Filipino American Community since 1925," in Asian Women United of California, eds., *Making Waves* (Boston: Beacon Press, 1989), 273–282; Murphy-Shigematsu, "Biracial/Bicultural Asian Americans"; Stephen Murphy-Shigematsu, "The Voices of Amerasians: Ethnicity, Identity, and Empowerment in Interracial Japanese Americans" (Ed.D. dissertation, Harvard University, 1986); Hall, "Please Choose One"; Christine C. I. Hall, "The Ethnic Identity of Racially Mixed People: A Study of Black-Japanese" (Ph.D. dissertation, UCLA, 1980);

Strong, "Japan's Konketsuji"; Teresa Kay Williams, "Prism Lives: Identity of Binational Amerasians," in Root, *Racially Mixed People*, 280–303; Mass, "Interracial Japanese Americans"; George Kitahara Kich, "The Developmental Process of Asserting a Biracial, Bicultural Identity," in Root, *Racially Mixed People*, 304–317; George Kitahara Kich, "Eurasians: Ethnic/Racial Identity Development of Biracial Japanese/White Adults" (Ph.D. dissertation, Wright Institute, 1982); Michael C. Thornton, "A Social History of a Multiethnic Identity: The Case of Black Japanese Americans" (Ph.D. dissertation, University of Michigan, 1983); Kieu-Linh Caroline Valverde and Chung Hoang Chuong, "From Dust to Gold: The Vietnamese Amerasian Experience," in Root, *Racially Mixed People*, 144–161; Ana Mari Cauce et al., "Between a Rock and a Hard Place: Social Adjustment of Biracial Youth," in Root, *Racially Mixed People*, 207–222; Ronald C. Johnson, "Offspring of Cross-Race and Cross-Ethnic Marriages in Hawaii," in Root, *Racially Mixed People*, 239–249; Cookie White Stephan and Walter G. Stephan, "After Intermarriage: Ethnic Identity among Mixed Heritage Japanese-Americans and Hispanics," *Journal of Marriage and the Family* 51 (1989): 507–519; Ronald C. Johnson and Craig T. Nagoshi, "The Adjustment of Offspring of Within-Group and Interracial/Intercultural Marriages: A Comparison of Personality Factor Scores," *Journal of Marriage and the Family* 48 (1986): 279–284; Lorraine K. Duffy, "The Interracial Individual: Self-Concept, Parental Interaction, and Ethnic Identity" (M.A. thesis, University of Hawai'i, 1978).

29. In just the past few years, Asian American studies programs at the University of California campuses at Berkeley and Santa Barbara have begun to teach about Amerasian issues.

30. It has been asserted by some that the part was originally written for an Asian pimp, and then transformed into a Eurasian so that a Caucasian could play the part. If that be true, then the situation is similar to the controversy over the *Kung Fu* television series of the early 1970s, where an originally Chinese leading character was rewritten as a Eurasian so that a white actor could play the part. If that is the situation here, then my analysis must be revised. However, to my knowledge this assertion has never been supported by any hard evidence.

31. Williams, "Prism Lives"; Strong, "Japan's Konketsuji."

32. Posadas, "Mestiza Girlhood."

33. Spickard, *Mixed Blood*, 61–70; Betty Lee Sung, *Chinese American Intermarriage* (New York: Center for Migration Studies, 1990), 74–86.

34. Kieu-Linh Caroline Valverde and Chung Hoang Chuong, "From Dust to Gold: The Vietnamese Amerasian Experience," in Root, *Racially Mixed People*, 144–161; Nancy Cooper, "'Go Back to Your Country': Amerasians Head for Their Fathers' Homeland," *Newsweek*, 18 March 1988, 34–35; K. W. Lee, "Korean War Legacy," *Boston Herald Advertiser*, 24 March 1974.

35. Private communication with the author.

36. A unique transition occurred for one group of Amerasians during the period 1930–1960. These were the children of mixed Chinese-Black families in the Delta region of Mississippi. During that period, according to sociologist James W. Loewen, Chinese gradually made a climb in status, from being segregated along with African Americans into the bottom layer of Mississippi life, to being granted a kind of acceptance at the lower margin of the white group. In the decades before that transition, quite a few Chinese immigrant men had married African American women. Those mixed couples and their offspring, according to Loewen, were left behind by the unmixed Chinese as they made their ascent. See Loewen, *The Mississippi Chinese: Between Black and White* (Cambridge, Mass.: Harvard University Press, 1971), 135–153.

37. Spickard, *Mixed Blood*, 73–84.

38. There is also, of course, the enormous difference between the ways multiracial Asians are perceived and treated in the United States and the ways they are treated in various Asian countries. See, for example, Strong, "Japan's Konketsuji"; Williams, "Prism Lives"; "Court Rejects Japan Nationality for Children of U.S. Fathers," *Japan Times Weekly*, 4 April 1981; Elizabeth Anne Hemphill, *The Least of These: Miki Sawada and Her Children*

(New York: Weatherhill, 1980); Valverde and Chuong, "From Dust to Gold." There is another difference in harassment that is very difficult to express clearly. Insofar as Asians or whites may be bothered by the presence of multiracial people of Asian descent, whites are more likely than Asians to be open about their opposition. Whites are more likely to use a racist epithet in public or to snub a person openly. Some of that may be because Asians are more likely to be indirect, even passive-aggressive in the ways they express disapproval. But also the characteristic—the Asianness of the Amerasian—that sets off a white bigot is perceived by the white to be a disempowering thing. The white person's sense of advantage over the Amerasian may encourage the white bigot to express openly her or his hostility. By contrast, the distinct characteristic—the American-ness of the Amerasian—that sets off the Asian bigot is perceived by the Asian to be an empowering thing. The Asian's sense of threat or disadvantage relative to the Amerasian may encourage the Asian bigot to keep quiet about her or his hostility.

39. James Morishima, "Interracial Issues among Asian Americans" (Panel discussion before the Association for Asian/Pacific American Studies, Seattle, 1 November 1980).

40. Christine Hall finds that whites and people of color emphasize different characteristics when they consider the physical aspects of racial identity: "It seems that Whites concentrate primarily on skin color, while people of color (who vary tremendously in skin color and ancestry) attend to other features, such as eyes, hair, nose, body build, and stature." Hall, "Please Choose One"; Williams, "Prism Lives"; Thornton, "Multiethnic Identity"; Mass, "Interracial Japanese Americans."

41. Nakashima, "Invisible Monster."

42. That a Japanese American community newspaper would claim a black Japanese American as one of their own was in itself a remarkable step forward; it could not have happened a decade earlier (*Hokubei Mainichi,* April 1990). Rex Walters, a Eurasian from San Jose, is also an object of the claim-us-if-we're-famous syndrome, on the basis of his basketball exploits for the University of Kansas and in the National Basketball Association. "Japanese American Athletes," *Hokubei Mainichi,* 1 January 1992.

43. Mass, "Interracial Japanese Americans"; Kich, "Eurasians"; Hall, "Ethnic Identity of Racially Mixed People."

44. Mass, "Interracial Japanese Americans."

45. Murphy-Shigematsu, "Biracial/Bicultural Asian Americans."

HOME IS WHERE THE *HAN* IS

A KOREAN AMERICAN PERSPECTIVE ON

THE LOS ANGELES UPHEAVALS

Elaine H. Kim

About half of the estimated $850 million in material losses incurred during the Los Angeles upheavals was sustained by a community no one seems to want to talk much about. Korean Americans in Los Angeles, suddenly at the front lines when violence came to the buffer zone they had been so precariously occupying, suffered profound damage to their means of livelihood.[1] But my concern here is the psychic damage which, unlike material damage, is impossible to quantify.

I want to explore the questions of whether or not recovery is possible for Korean Americans, and what will become of our attempts to "become American" without dying of *han*. *Han* is a Korean word that means, loosely translated, the sorrow and anger that grow from the accumulated experiences of oppression. Although the word is frequently and commonly used by Koreans, the condition it describes is taken quite seriously. When people die of *han*, it is called dying of *hwabyong*, a disease of frustration and rage following misfortune.

Situated as we are on the border between those who have and those who have not, between predominantly Anglo and mostly African American and Latino communities, from our current interstitial position in the American discourse of race, many Korean Americans have trouble calling what happened in Los Angeles an "uprising." At the same time, we cannot quite say it was a "riot." So some of us have taken to calling it *sa-i-ku*, April 29, after the manner of naming other events in Korean history—3.1 (*sam-il*) for March 1, 1919, when massive protests against Japanese colonial rule began in Korea; 6.25 (*yook-i-o*) for June 25, 1950, when the Korean War began; and 4.19 (*sa-il-ku*) for April 19, 1960, when the first student movement in the world to overthrow a government began in South Korea. The ironic similarity between 4.19 and 4.29 does not escape most Korean Americans.

Los Angeles Koreatown has been important to me, even though I visit only a dozen times a year. Before Koreatown sprang up during the last decade and a half,[2] I used to hang around the fringes of Chinatown, although I knew that this habit was pure pretense.[3] For me, knowing that Los Angeles Koreatown existed made a difference; one of my closest friends worked with the Black-Korean Alliance there,[4] and I liked to think of it as a kind of "home"—however idealized and hypostatized—for the soul, an anchor, a potential refuge, a place in America where I could belong without ever being asked, "Who are you and what are you doing here? Where did you come from and when are you going back?"

Many of us watched in horror the destruction of Koreatown and the systematic targeting of Korean shops in South Central Los Angeles after the Rodney King verdict. Seeing those buildings in flames and those anguished Korean faces, I had the terrible thought that there would be no belonging and that we were, just as I had always suspected, a people destined to carry our *han* around with us wherever we went in the world. The destiny (*p'aljja*) that had spelled centuries of extreme suffering from invasion, colonization, war, and national division had smuggled itself into the United States with our baggage.

AFRICAN AMERICAN AND KOREAN AMERICAN CONFLICT

As someone whose social consciousness was shaped by the African American-led civil rights movement of the 1960s, I felt that I was watching our collective dreams for a just society disintegrating, cast aside as naive and irrelevant in the bitter and embattled 1990s. It was the courageous African American women and men of the 1960s who had redefined the meaning of "American," who had first suggested that a person like me could reject the false choice between being treated as a perpetual foreigner in my own birthplace, on the one hand, and relinquishing my identity for someone else's ill-fitting and impossible Anglo-American one on the other. Thanks to them, I began to discern how institutional racism works and why Korea was never mentioned in my world history textbooks. I was able to see how others besides Koreans had been swept aside by the dominant culture. My American education offered nothing about Chicanos or Latinos, and most of what I was taught about African and Native Americans was distorted to justify their oppression and vindicate their oppressors.

I could hardly believe my ears when, during the weeks immediately following *sa-i-ku,* I heard African American community leaders suggesting that Korean American merchants were foreign intruders deliberately trying to stifle African American economic development, when I knew that they had bought those liquor stores at five times gross receipts from African American owners, who had previously bought them at two times gross receipts from Jewish owners after Watts.[5] I saw anti-Korean flyers that were being circulated by African American political candidates and read about South Central residents petitioning against the reestablishment of swap meets, groups of typically Korean immigrant-operated market stalls. I was disheartened with Latinos who related the pleasure they felt while looting Korean stores they believed "had it coming," and who claimed that it was because of racism that more Latinos were arrested during *sa-i-ku* than Asian Americans.[6] And I was filled with despair when I read about Chinese Americans wanting to dissociate themselves from us. According to one Chinese American reporter assigned to cover Asian American issues for a San Francisco daily, Chinese and Japanese American shop-keepers, unlike Koreans, always got along fine with African Americans in the past.[7] "Suddenly," admitted another Chinese American, "I am scared to be Asian. More specifically, I am afraid to be mistaken for Korean."[8] I was enraged when I overheard European Americans discussing the conflicts as if they were watching a dogfight or a boxing match. The situation reminded me of the Chinese film "Raise the Red Lantern," in which we never see the husband's face. We only hear his mellifluous voice as he benignly admonishes his four wives not to fight among themselves. He can afford to be kind and pleasant because the structure that pits his wives against each other is so firmly in place that he need never sully his hands or even raise his voice.

BATTLEGROUND LEGACY

Korean Americans are squeezed between black and white and also between U.S. and South Korean political agendas. Opportunistic American and South Korean presidential candidates toured the burnt ruins, posing for the television cameras but delivering nothing of substance to the victims. Like their U.S. counterparts, South Korean news media seized upon *sa-i-ku*, featuring sensational stories that depicted the problem as that of savage African Americans attacking innocent Koreans for no reason.[9] To give the appearance of authenticity, Seoul newspapers even published articles using the names of Korean Americans who did not in fact write them.[10]

Those of us who chafe at being asked whether we are Chinese or Japanese as if there were no other possibilities or who were angered when the news media sought Chinese and Japanese but not Korean American views during *sa-i-ku* are sensitive to an invisibility that seems particular to us. To many Americans, Korea is but the gateway to or the bridge between China and Japan, or a crossroads of major Asian conflicts.[11]

Although little known or cared about in the Western world, Korea has been a perennial battleground. Besides the Mongols and the Manchus, there were the *Y<o>jin* (Jurched), the *Koran* (Khitan), and the *Waegu* (Wäkö) invaders. In relatively recent years, there was the war between China and Japan that ended in 1895 and the war between Japan and Russia in 1905, both of which were fought on Korean soil and resulted in extreme suffering for the Korean people. Japan's thiryt-six years of brutal colonial rule ended with the United States and what was then the Soviet Union dividing the country in half at the 38th parallel. Thus, Korea was turned into a cold war territory that ultimately became a battleground for world superpowers during the conflict of 1950–53.

BECOMING AMERICAN

One of the consequences of war, colonization, national division, and superpower economic and cultural domination has been the migration of Koreans to places like Los Angeles, where they believed their human rights would be protected by law. After all, they had received U.S.-influenced political educations. They started learning English in the seventh grade. They all knew the story of the poor boy from Illinois who became president. They all learned that the U.S. Constitution and Bill of Rights protected the common people from violence and injustice. But they who grew up in Korea watching "Gunsmoke," "Night Rider," and "McGyver" dubbed in Korean were not prepared for the black, brown, red, and yellow America they encountered when they disembarked at the Los Angeles International Airport.[12] They hadn't heard that there is no equal justice in the United States. They had to learn about American racial hierarchies. They did not realize that, as immigrants of color, they would never attain political voice or visibility but would instead be used to uphold the inequality and the racial hierarchy they had no part in creating.

Most of the newcomers had underestimated the communication barriers they would face. Like the Turkish workers in Germany described in John Berger and Jean Mohr's *A Seventh Man,*[13] their toil amounted to only a pile of gestures and the English they tried to speak changed and turned against them as they spoke it. Working fourteen hours a day, six or seven days a week, they rarely came into sustained contact with English-speaking Americans and almost never had time to study English. Not feeling at ease with English, they did not engage in informal conversations easily with non-Koreans and were hated for being curt and rude. They did not attend churches or do business in banks or other enterprises where English was required. Typically, the immigrant, small-business owners utilized unpaid family labor instead of hiring people from local communities. Thanks to Eurocentric American cultural practices, they knew little or nothing good about African Americans or Latinos, who in turn and for similar reasons knew little or nothing good about them. At the same time, Korean shopowners in South Central and Koreatown were affluent compared with the impoverished residents, whom they often exploited as laborers or looked down upon as fools with an aversion to hard work.[14] Most Korean immigrants did not even know that they were among the many direct beneficiaries of the African American-led civil rights movement, which helped pave the way for the 1965 reforms that made their immigration possible.

Korean immigrant views, shaped as they were by U.S. cultural influences and official, anticommunist, South Korean education,[15] differed radically from those of many poor people in the communities Korean immigrants served: unaware of the shameful history of oppression of nonwhite immigrants and other people of color in the United States, they regarded themselves as having arrived in a meritocratic "land of opportunity" where a person's chances for success are limited only by individual lack of ability or diligence. Having left a homeland where they foresaw their talents and hard work going unrecognized and unrewarded, they were desperate to believe that the "American dream" of social and economic mobility through hard work was within their reach.

S A - I - K U

What they experienced on April 29 and 30 was a baptism into what it really means for a Korean to "become American" in the 1990s.[16] In South Korea, there is no

911, and no one really expects a fire engine or police car if there is trouble. Instead, people make arrangements with friends and family for emergencies. At the same time, guns are not part of Korean daily life. No civilian in South Korea can own a gun. Guns are the exclusive accoutrement of the military and police, who enforce order for those who rule the society. When the Korean Americans in South Central and Koreatown dialed 911, nothing happened. When their stores and homes were being looted and burned to the ground, they were left completely alone for three horrifying days. How betrayed they must have felt by what they had believed was a democratic system that protects its people from violence. Those who trusted the government to protect them lost everything; those who took up arms after waiting for help for two days were able to defend themselves. It was as simple as that. What they had to learn was that, as in South Korea, protection in the United States is by and large for the rich and powerful. If there were a choice between Westwood and Koreatown, it is clear that Koreatown would have to be sacrificed. The familiar concept of privilege for the rich and powerful would have been easy for the Korean immigrant to grasp if only those exhortations about democracy and equality had not obfuscated the picture. Perhaps they should have relied even more on whatever they brought with them from Korea instead of fretting over trying to understand what was going on around them here. That Koreatown became a battleground does seem like the further playing out of a tragic legacy that has followed them across oceans and continents. The difference is that this was a battle between the poor and disenfranchised and the invisible rich, who were being protected by a layer of clearly visible Korean American human shields in a battle on the buffer zone.

This difference is crucial. Perhaps the legacy is not one carried across oceans and continents but one assumed immediately upon arrival, not the curse of being Korean but the initiation into becoming American, which requires that Korean Americans take on this country's legacy of five centuries of racial violence and inequality, of divide and rule, of privilege for the rich and oppression of the poor. Within this legacy, they have been assigned a place on the front lines. Silenced by those who possess the power to characterize and represent, they are permitted to speak only to reiterate their acceptance of this role.

SILENCING THE KOREAN AMERICAN VOICE

Twelve years ago, in Kwangju, South Korea, hundreds of civilians demonstrating for constitutional reform and free elections were murdered by U.S.-supported and -equipped South Korean elite paratroopers. Because I recorded it and played it over and over again, searching for a sign or a clue, I remember clearly how what were to me heartrendingly tragic events were represented in the U.S. news media. For a few fleeting moments, images of unruly crowds of alien-looking Asians shouting unintelligible words and phrases and wearing white headbands inscribed with unintelligible characters flickered across the screen. The Koreans were made to seem like insane people from another planet. The voice in the background stated simply that there were massive demonstrations but did not explain what the protests were about. Nor was a single Korean ever given an opportunity to speak to the camera.

The next news story was about demonstrations for democracy in Poland. The camera settled on individuals' faces, which one by one filled the screen as each man or woman was asked to explain how he or she felt. Each Polish person's words were translated in a voiceover or subtitle. Solidarity leader Lech Walesa, who was allowed to speak often, was characterized as a heroic human being with whom all Americans could surely identify personally. Polish Americans from New York and Chicago to San Francisco, asked in man-on-the-street interviews about their reactions, described the canned hams and blankets they were sending to Warsaw.

This was for me a lesson in media representation, race, and power politics. It is a given that Americans are encouraged by our ideological apparatuses to side with our allies (here, the Polish resisters and the anticommunist South Korean government) against our enemies (here, the communist Soviet Union and protesters against the South Korean government). But visual-media racism helps craft and reinforce our identification with Europeans and whites while distancing us from fearsome and alien Asiatic hordes.

In March 1992, when two delegates from North Korea visited the Bay Area to participate in community-sponsored talks on Korean reunification, about 800 people from the Korean American community attended. The meeting was consummately newsworthy, since it was the first time in history that anyone from North Korea had ever been in California for more than twenty-four hours just passing through. The event was discussed for months in the Korean-language media—television, radio, and newspapers. Almost every Korean-speaking person in California knew about it. Although we sent press releases to all the commercial and public radio and television stations and to all the Bay Area newspapers, not a single mainstream media outfit covered the event. However, whenever there was an African American boycott of a Korean store or whenever conflict surfaced between Korean and African Americans, community leaders found a dozen microphones from all the main news media shoved into their faces, as if they were the president's press secretary making an official public pronouncement. Fascination with interethnic conflicts is rooted in the desire to excuse or minimize white racism by buttressing the mistaken notion that all human beings are "naturally" racist, and when Korean and African Americans allow themselves to be distracted by these interests, their attention is deflected from the social hierarchies that give racism its destructive power.

Without a doubt, the U.S. news media played a major role in exacerbating the damage and ill will toward Korean Americans, first by spotlighting tensions between African Americans and Koreans above all efforts to work together and as opposed to many other newsworthy events in these two communities, and second by exploiting racist stereotypes of Koreans as unfathomable aliens, this time wielding guns on rooftops and allegedly firing wildly into crowds.[17] In news programs and on talk shows, African and Korean American tensions were discussed by blacks and whites, who pointed to these tensions as the main cause of the uprising. I heard some European Americans railing against rude and exploitative Korean merchants for ruining peaceful race relations for everyone else. Thus, Korean Americans were used to deflect attention from the racism they inherited and the economic injustice and poverty that had been already well woven into the fabric of American life, as evidenced by a judicial system that could allow not only the Korean store owner who killed Latasha Harlins but also the white men who killed Vincent Chin and the white police who beat Rodney King to go free, while Leonard Peltier still languishes in prison.

As far as I know, neither the commercial nor the public news media has mentioned the many Korean and African American attempts to improve relations, such as joint church services, joint musical performances and poetry readings, Korean merchant donations to African American community and youth programs, African American volunteer teachers in classes for Korean immigrants studying for citizenship examinations, or Korean translations of African American history materials.

While Korean immigrants were preoccupied with the mantra of day-to-day survival, Korean Americans had no voice, no political presence whatsoever in American life. When they became the targets of violence in Los Angeles, their opinions and views were hardly solicited except as they could be used in the already constructed mainstream discourse on race relations, which is a sorry combination of blaming the African American and Latino victims for their poverty and scapegoating the Korean Americans as robotic aliens who have no "real" right to be here in the first place and therefore deserve whatever happens to them.

THE *NEWSWEEK* EXPERIENCE

In this situation, I felt compelled to respond when an editor from the "My Turn" section of *Newsweek* magazine asked for a 1,000–word personal essay.[18] Hesitant because I was given only a day and a half to write the piece, not enough time in light of the vastness of American ignorance about Koreans and Korean Americans, I decided to do it because I thought I could not be made into a sound bite or a quote contextualized for someone else's agenda.

I wrote an essay accusing the news media of using Korean Americans and tensions between African and Korean Americans to divert attention from the roots of racial violence in the United States. I asserted that these lie not in the Korean-immigrant-owned corner store situated in a community ravaged by poverty and police violence, but reach far back into the corridors of corporate and government offices in Los Angeles, Sacramento, and Washington, D.C. I suggested that Koreans and African Americans were kept ignorant about each other by educational and media institutions that erase or distort their experiences and perspectives. I tried to explain how racism had kept my parents from ever really becoming Americans, but that having been born here, I considered myself American and wanted to believe in the possibility of an American dream.

The editor of "My Turn" did everything he could to frame my words with his own viewpoint. He faxed his own introductory and concluding paragraphs that equated Korean merchants with cowboys in the Wild West and alluded to Korean/African American hatred. When I objected, he told me that my writing style was not crisp enough and that as an experienced journalist, he could help me out. My confidence wavered, but ultimately I rejected his editing. Then he accused me of being overly sensitive, confiding that I had no need to be defensive—because his wife was a Chinese American. Only after I had decided to withdraw the piece did he agree to accept it as I had written it.

Before I could finish congratulating myself on being able to resist silencing and the kind of decontextualization I was trying to describe in the piece, I started receiving hate mail. Some of it was addressed directly to me, since I had been identified as a University of California faculty member, but most of it arrived in bundles, forwarded by *Newsweek*. Hundreds of letters came from all over the country, from Florida to Washington state and from Massachusetts to Arizona. I was unprepared for the hostility expressed in most of the letters. Some people sent the article, torn from the magazine and covered with angry, red-inked obscenities scratched across my picture. "You should see a good doctor," wrote someone from Southern California, "you have severe problems in thinking, reasoning, and adjusting to your environment."

A significant proportion of the writers, especially those who identified themselves as descendants of immigrants from Eastern Europe, wrote *Newsweek* that they were outraged, sickened, disgusted, appalled, annoyed, and angry at the magazine for providing an arena for the paranoid, absurd, hypocritical, racist, and childish views of a spoiled, ungrateful, whining, bitching, un-American bogus faculty member who should be fired or die when the next California earthquake dumps all of the "so-called people of color" into the Pacific Ocean.

I was shocked by the profound ignorance of many writers' assumptions about the experiences and perspectives of American people of color in general and Korean and other Asian Americans in particular. Even though my essay revealed that I was born in the United States and that my parents had lived in the United States for more than six decades, I was viewed as a foreigner without the right to say anything except words of gratitude and praise about America. The letters also provided some evidence of the dilemma Korean Americans are placed in by those who assume that we are aliens who should "go back" and at the same time berate us for not rejecting "Korean-American identity" for "American identity."

How many Americans migrate to Korea? If you are so disenchanted, Korea is still there. Why did you ever leave it? Sayonara.

Ms. Kim appears to have a personal axe to grind with this country that has given her so much freedom and opportunity. . . . I should suggest that she move to Korea, where her children will learn all they ever wanted about that country's history.

[Her] whining about the supposedly racist U.S. society is just a mask for her own acute inferiority complex. If she is so dissatisfied with the United States why doesn't she vote with her feet and leave? She can get the hell out and return to her beloved Korea—her tribal afinity [*sic*] where her true loyalty and consciousness lies [*sic*].

You refer to yourself as a Korean American and yet you have lived all your life in the United States . . . you write about racism in this country and yet you are the biggest racist by your own written words. If you cannot accept the fact that you are an American, maybe you should be living your life in Korea.

My stepfather and cousin risked their lives in the country where your father is buried to ensure the ideals of our country would remain. So don't expect to find a sympathetic ear for your pathetic whining.

Many of the letter writers assumed that my family had been the "scum" of Asia and that I was a college teacher only because of American justice and largesse. They were furious that I did not express gratitude for being saved from starvation in Asia and given the opportunity to flourish, no doubt beyond my wildest dreams, in America.

Where would she be if her parents had not migrated to the United States? For a professor at Berkeley University [sic] to say the American dream is only an empty promise is ludicrous. Shame, shame, shame on Elaine!

[Her father and his family] made enough money in the USA to ship his corpse home to Korea for burial. Ms. Kim herself no doubt has a guaranteed life income as a professor paid by California taxpayers. Wouldn't you think that she might say kind things about the USA instead of whining about racism?

At the same time some letters blamed me for expecting freedom and opportunity: "It is wondrous that folks such as you find truth in your paranoia. No one ever promised anything to you or your parents."

Besides providing indications of how Korean Americans are regarded, the letters revealed a great deal about how American identity is thought of. One California woman explained that although her grandparents were Irish immigrants, she was not an Irish American, because "if you are not with us, you are against us." A Missouri woman did not seem to realize that she was conflating race and nationality and confusing "nonethnic" and "nonracial," by which she seems to have meant "white," with "American." And, although she insists that it is impossible to be both "black" and "American," she identifies herself at the outset as a "white American."

I am a white American. I am proud to be an American. You cannot be black, white, Korean, Chinese, Mexican, German, French, or English or any other and still be an American. Of course the culture taught in schools is strictly American. That's where we are and if you choose to learn another [culture] you have the freedom to settle there. You cannot be a Korean American which assumes you are not ready to be an AMERICAN. Do you get my gist?

The suggestion that more should be taught in U.S. schools about America's many immigrant groups and people of color prompted many letters in defense of Western civilization against non-Western barbarism:

You are dissatisfied with current school curricula that exclude Korea. Could it possibly be because Korea and Asia for that matter has [sic] not had . . . a noticeable impact on the shaping of Western culture, and Korea has had unfortunately little culture of its own?

Who cares about Korea, Ms. Kim? . . . And what enduring contributions has the Black culture, both here in the US and on the continent contributed to the world, and mankind? I'm from a culture, Ms. Kim, who put a man on the moon 23 years ago, who established medical schools to train doctors to perform open heart surgery, and . . . who created a language of music so that musicians, from Beethoven to the Beatles, could easily touch the world with their brilliance forever and ever and ever. Perhaps the dominant culture, whites obviously, "swept aside Chicanos . . . Latinos . . . African-Americans . . . Koreans," because they haven't contributed anything that made—be mindful of the cliche—a world of difference?

Koreans' favorite means of execution is decapitation. . . . Ms. Kim, and others like her, came here to escape such injustice. Then they whine at riots to which they have contributed by their own fanning of flames of discontent. . . . Yes! Let us all study more about Oriental culture! Let us put matters into proper perspective.

Fanatical multiculturalists like you expect a country whose dominant culture has been formed and influenced by Europe . . . nearly 80% of her population consisting of persons whose ancestry is European, to include the history of every ethnic group who has ever lived here. I truly feel sorry for you. You and your bunch need to realize that white Americans are not racists. . . . We would love to get along, but not at the expense of our own culture and heritage.

Kim's axe-to-grind confirms the utter futility of race-relations—the races were never meant to live together. We don't get along and never will. . . . Whats [*sic*] needed is to divide the United States up along racial lines so that life here can finally become livable.

What seemed to anger some people the most was their idea that, although they worked hard, people of color were seeking handouts and privileges because of their race, and the thought of an ungrateful Asian American siding with African Americans, presumably against whites, was infuriating. How dare I "bite the hand that feeds" me by siding with the champion "whiners who cry 'racism'" because to do so is the last refuge of the "terminally incompetent"?

The racial health in this country won't improve until minorities stop erecting "me first" barriers and strive to be Americans, not African-Americans or Asian-Americans expecting privileges.

Ms. Kim wants preferential treatment that immigrants from Greece-to-Sweden have not enjoyed. . . . Even the Chinese . . . have not created any special problems for themselves or other Americans. Soon those folk are going to express their own resentments to the insatiable demands of the Blacks and other colored peoples, including the wetbacks from Mexico who sneak into this country then pilfer it for all they can.

The Afroderived citizens of Los Angeles and the Asiatic derivatives were not suffering a common imposition. . . . The Asiatics are trying to build their success. The Africans are sucking at the teats of entitlement.

As is usual with racists, most of the writers of these hate letters saw only themselves in their notions about Korea, America, Korean Americans, African Americans. They felt that their own sense of American identity was being threatened and that they were being blamed as individuals for U.S. racism. One man, adept at manipulating various fonts on his word processor, imposed his preconceptions on my words:

> Let me read between the lines of your little hate message:
> . . . "The roots . . . stretch far back into the corridors of corporate and government offices in Los Angeles, Sacramento, and Washington, D.C."
> **All white America and all American institutions are to blame for racism.**
> . . . "I still want to believe the promise is real."
> **I have the savvy to know that the American ideals of freedom and justice are a joke but if you want to give me what I want I'm willing to make concessions.**
> Ms. Kim . . . if you want to embody the ignorant, the insecure, and the emotionally immature, that's your right! just stop preaching hate and please, please, quit whining.
> Sincerely, A proud White-American
> teaching my children not to be prejudicial

Especially since my essay had been subdued and intensely personal, I had not anticipated the fury it would provoke. I never thought that readers would write over my words with their own. The very fact that I used words, and English words at that, particularly incensed some: one letter writer complained about my use of words and phrases like "manifestation" and "zero-sum game," and "suzerain relationship," which is the only way to describe Korea's relationship with China during the T'ang Dynasty. "Not more than ten people in the USA know what [these words] mean," he wrote. "You are on an ego trip." I wondered if it made him particularly angry that an Asian American had used those English words, or if he would make such a comment to George Will or Jane Bryant Quinn.

Clearly I had encountered part of America's legacy, the legacy that insists on silencing certain voices and erasing certain presences, even if it means deportation, internment, and outright murder. I should not have been surprised by what happened in Koreatown or by the ignorance and hatred expressed in the letters to *Newsweek*, any more than African Americans should have been surprised by the Rodney King verdict. Perhaps the news media, which constituted *sa-i-ku* as news, as an extraordinary event in no way continuous with our everyday lives, made us forget for a moment that as people of color many of us simultaneously inhabit two Americas: the America of our dreams and the America of our experience.

Who among us does not cling stubbornly to the America of our dreams, the promise of a multicultural democracy where our cultures and our differences might be affirmed instead of distorted in an effort to destroy us?

After *sa-i-ku*, I was able to catch glimpses of this America of my dreams because

I received other letters that expressed another American legacy. Some people identified themselves as Norwegian or Irish Americans interested in combating racism. Significantly, while most of the angry mail had been sent not to me but to *Newsweek*, almost all of the sympathetic mail, particularly the letters from African Americans, came directly to me. Many came from Korean Americans who were glad that one of their number had found a vehicle for self-expression. Others were from Chinese and Japanese Americans who wrote that they had had similar experiences and feelings. Several were written in shaky longhand by women fervently wishing for peace and understanding among people of all races. A Native American from Nashville wrote a long description of cases of racism against African, Asian, and Native Americans in the U.S. criminal justice system. A large number of letters came from African Americans, all of them supportive and sympathetic—from judges and professors who wanted better understanding between Africans and Koreans to poets and laborers who scribbled their notes in pencil while on breaks at work. One man identified himself as a Los Angeles African American whose uncle had married a Korean woman. He stated that as a black man in America, he knew what other people feel when they face injustice. He ended his letter apologizing for his spelling and grammar mistakes and asking for materials to read on Asian Americans. The most touching letter I received was written by a prison inmate who had served twelve years of a thirty-five-to-seventy-year sentence for armed robbery during which no physical injuries occurred. He wrote:

> I've been locked in these prisons going on 12 years now . . . and since being here I have studied fully the struggles of not just blacks, but all people of color. I am a true believer of helping "your" people "first," but also the helping of all people no matter where there at or the color of there skin. But I must be truthful, my struggle and assistance is truly on the side of people of color like ourselves. But just a few years ago I didn't think like this.
>
> I thought that if you wasn't black, then you was the enemy, but . . . many years of this prison madness and much study and research changed all of this. . . . [I]t's not with each other, blacks against Koreans or Koreans against blacks. No, this is not what it's about. Our struggle(s) are truly one in the same. What happened in L.A. during the riot really hurt me, because it was no way that blacks was suppose to do the things to your people, my people (Koreans) that they did. You're my sister, our people are my people. Even though our culture may be somewhat different, and even though we may worship our God(s) different . . . white-Amerikkka [doesn't] separate us. They look at us all the same. Either you're white, or you're wrong. . . . I'm just writing you to let you know that, you're my sister, your people's struggle are my people's struggle.

This is the ground I need to claim now for Korean American resistance and recovery, so that we can become American without dying of *han*.

Although the sentiments expressed in these letters seemed to break down roughly along racial lines—that is, all writers who were identifiably people of color wrote in support—and one might become alarmed at the depth of the divisions they imply, I like to think that I have experienced the desire of many Americans, especially Americans of color, to do as Rodney King pleaded on the second day of *sa-i-ku*: "We're all stuck here for awhile. . . . Let's try to work it out."

In my view, it's important for us to think about *all* of what Rodney King said and not just the words "we all can get along," which have been depoliticized and transformed into a Disneyesque catchphrase for Pat Boone songs and roadside billboards in Los Angeles. It seems to me the emphasis is on the being "stuck here for awhile" together as we await "our day in court."[19]

Like the African American man who wrote from prison, the African American man who had been brutally beaten by white police might have felt the desire to "love everybody," but he had to amend—or rectify—that wish. He had to speak last about loving "people of color." The impulse to "love everybody" was there, but the conditions were not right. For now, the most practical and progressive agenda may be people of color trying to "work it out."

FINDING COMMUNITY THROUGH NATIONAL CONSCIOUSNESS

The place where Korean and American legacies converge for Korean Americans is the exhortation to "go home to where you belong."

One of the letters I received was from a Korean American living in Chicago. He had read a translation of my essay in a Korean-language newspaper. "Although you were born in the U.S.A.," he wrote, noticing what none of the white men who ordered me to go back to "my" country had, "your ethnical background and your complexion belong to Korea. It is time to give up your U.S. citizenship and go to Korea."

Some ruined merchants are claiming that they will pull up stakes and return to Korea, but I know that this is not possible for most of them. Even if their stores had not been destroyed, even if they were able to sell their businesses and take the proceeds to Korea, most of them would not have enough to buy a home or business there, since both require total cash up front. Neither would they be able to find work in the society they left behind because it is plagued by recession, repression, and fierce economic competition.

Going back to Korea. The dream of going back to Korea fed the spirit of my father, who came to Chicago in 1926 and lived in the United States for sixty-three years, during which time he never became a U.S. citizen, at first because the law did not allow it and later because he did not want to. He kept himself going by believing that he would return to Korea in triumph one day. Instead, he died in Oakland at eighty-eight. Only his remains returned to Korea, where we buried him in accordance with his wishes.

Hasn't the dream of going back home to where you belong sustained most of America's unwanted at one time or another, giving meaning to lives of toil and making it possible to endure other people's hatred and rejection? Isn't the attempt to find community through national consciousness natural for people refused an American identity because racism does not give them that choice?

Korean national consciousness, the resolve to resist and fight back when threatened with extermination, was all that could be called upon when the Korean Americans in Los Angeles found themselves abandoned. They joined together to guard each other's means of livelihood with guns, relying on Korean-language radio and newspapers to communicate with and help each other. On the third day after the outbreak of violence, more than 30,000 Korean Americans gathered for a peace march in downtown L.A. in what was perhaps the largest and most quickly organized mass mobilization in Asian American history. Musicians in white, the color of mourning, beat traditional Korean drums in sorrow, anger, and celebration of community, a call to arms like a collective heartbeat.[20] I believe that the mother of Edward Song Lee, the Los Angeles-born college student mistaken for a looter and shot to death in the streets, has been able to persevere in great part because of the massive outpouring of sympathy expressed by the Korean-American community that shared and understood her *han*.

I have been critical lately of cultural nationalism as detrimental to Korean Americans, especially Korean American women, because it operates on exclusions and fosters intolerance and uniformity of thought while stifling self-criticism and encouraging sacrifice, even to the point of suicide. But *sa-i-ku* makes me think again: what remains for those who are left to stand alone? If Korean Americans refuse to be victims or political pawns in the United States while rejecting the exhortation that we go back to Korea where we belong, what will be our weapons of choice?

In the darkest days of Japanese colonial rule, even after being stripped of land and of all economic means of survival, Koreans were threatened with total erasure when the colonizers rewrote Korean history, outlawed the Korean language, forced the subjugated people to worship the Japanese emperor, and demanded that they adopt Japanese names. One of the results of these cultural-annihilation policies was the fierce insistence on the sanctity of Korean national identity that persists among Koreans to this day. In this context, it is not difficult to understand why nationalism has been the main refuge of Koreans and Korean Americans.

While recognizing the potential dangers of nationalism as a weapon, I for one am not ready to respond to the antiessentialists' call to relinquish my Korean American identity. It is easy enough for the French and Germans to call for a common European identity and an end to nationalisms, but what of the peoples suppressed and submerged while France and Germany exercised their national prerogatives? I am mindful of the argument that the resurgence of nationalism in Europe is rooted in historical and contemporary political and economic inequality among the nations of Europe. Likewise, I have noticed that many white Americans do not like to think of themselves as belonging to a race, even while thinking of people of color almost exclusively in terms of race. In the same way, many men think of themselves as "human beings" and of women as the ones having a gender. Thus crime, small businesses, and all Korean-African American interactions are seen and interpreted through the lens of race in the same dominant culture that angrily rejects the use of the racial lens for viewing yellow/white or black/white interactions and insists suddenly that we are all "American" whenever we attempt to assert our identity as people of color. It is far easier for Anglo-Americans to call for an end to cultural nationalisms than for Korean Americans to give up the national consciousness that makes it possible for us to survive the vicious racism that would deny our existence as either Korean Americans or Americans.

Is there anything of use to us in Korean nationalism? During one thousand years of Chinese suzerainty, the Korean ruling elite developed a philosophy called *sadaejui,* or reliance of the weak on the strong. In direct opposition to this way of thought is what is called *jaju* or *juche sasang,* or self-determination.[21] Both *sadaejui* and *juche sasang* are ways of dealing with unequal power relationships and resisting the transformation of one's homeland into a battlefield for others, but *sadaejui* has never worked any better for Koreans than it has for any minority group in America. *Juche sasang,* on the other hand, has the kind of oppositional potential needed in the struggle against silence and invisibility. From Korean national consciousness, we can recover this fierce refusal to accept subjugation, which is the first step in the effort to build community, so that we can work with others to challenge the forces that would have us annihilate each other instead of our mutual oppression.

What is clear is that we cannot "become American" without dying of *han* unless we think about community in new ways. Self-determination does not mean living alone. At least for now, that may mean mining the rich and haunted lode of Korean national consciousness while we struggle to understand how our fate is entwined with the fate of others lying prostrate before the triumphal procession of the winners of History.[22] During the past fifteen years or so, many young Korean nationalists have been studying the legacies of colonialism and imperialism that they share with peoples in many Asian, African, and Latin American nations. At the same time that we take note of this work, we can also try to understand how nationalism and feminism can be worked together to demystify the limitations and reductiveness of each as a weapon of empowerment. If Korean national consciousness is ever to be such a weapon for us, we must use it to create a new kind of nationalism-in-internationalism to help us call forth a culture of survival and recovery, so that our *han* might be released and we might be freed to dream fiercely of different possibilities.

NOTES

1. According to a September 1992 Dun and Bradstreet survey of 560 business owners in Koreatown in South Central Los Angeles, an estimated 40 percent of the businesses damaged during *sa-i-ku* have closed their doors permanently. Moreover, almost 40 percent had no insurance or were insured for 50 percent or less of their total losses ("L.A. Riot Took Heavy Toll on Businesses," *San Francisco Chronicle,* 12 September 1992).

2. Following quota changes in U.S. immigration laws in 1965, the Korean population in America increased more than eightfold to almost one million. Between 1970 and 1990, Los Angeles Koreatown grew from a few blocks of stores and businesses into a community base for all sorts of economic and cultural activities.

3. Pretense, of course, because I was only passing for Chinese. The temporary comfort I experienced would come to an end whenever it was discovered that I could speak no Chinese and that I had no organic links to Chinese Americans, who frequently underscored both our commonalities and our differences by telling me that everything Ko-

rean—even *kimchi,* that quintessentially Korean vegetable eaten at every Korean meal—was originally Chinese.

4. The Black-Korean Alliance (BKA) was formed, with the assistance of the Los Angeles County Human Relations Commission, to improve relations between the Korean and African American communities after four Korean merchants were killed in robberies during April 1986. The BKA sponsored activities and events, such as joint church services, education forums, joint cultural events, and seminars on crime prevention and community economic development. The BKA never received political or financial support from the public or private sectors. The organization had neither its own meeting place nor a telephone. Grassroots participation was not extensive, and despite the good intentions of the individuals involved, the BKA was unable to prevent the killing of a dozen more Korean merchants in southern California between 1990 and *sa-i-ku,* or to stop the escalation of tensions between the two communities after the shooting of fifteen-year-old Latasha Harlins by Korean merchant Soon Ja Du in March 1991. By June of that year, after police declared the killing of an African American man by a Korean liquor store owner "justifiable homicide," African American groups began boycotting the store, and the BKA failed to convince African American boycotters and Korean merchants to meet together to negotiate an end to the conflict. Nor were the members of the BKA successful in obtaining the help of members of the Los Angeles City Council or the California State Legislature, who might have been instrumental in preventing the destructive violence of *sa-i-ku* if they had had the integrity and farsightedness to address the intensifying hostilities before it was too late. After *sa-i-ku,* the BKA was in disarray, and as of this writing, its members are planning to dissolve the group.

5. According to John Murray, founder of the southern California chapter of Cal-Pac, the black beverage and grocers' association, African American liquor store owners "sold stores they had bought in the mid-1960s for two times monthly gross sales—roughly $80,000 at the time, depending on the store—for five times monthly gross, or about $300,000" After the Jews fled in the wake of the Watts riots, African Americans were enabled by civil rights legislative mandates to obtain for the first time credit from government-backed banks to start a number of small businesses. But operating liquor stores, although profitable, was grueling, dangerous, and not something fathers wanted their sons to do, according to interviews with African American owners and former owners of liquor stores in African American communities. Former liquor merchant Ed Piert exclaimed: "Seven days a week, 20 hours a day, no vacations, people stealing. That's slave labor. I wouldn't buy another liquor store." When liquor prices were deregulated in 1978 and profit margins shrank in the face of competition from volume buyers, many African American owners sold out to Korean immigrants carrying cash collected in rotating credit clubs called *kye* (Susan Moffat, "Shopkeepers Fight Back: Blacks join with Koreans in a Battle to Rebuild Their Liquor Stores," *Los Angeles Times,* 15 May 1992).

6. In a newspaper interview, Alberto Machon, an eighteen-year-old junior at Washington Preparatory High School who had moved to South Central Los Angeles with his family from El Salvador ten years ago, said that he was laughing as he watched every Korean store looted or burned down because "I felt that they deserved it for the way they was treatin' people . . . the money that we are giving to the stores they're taking it to their community, Koreatown." Thirty-two-year-old Arnulfo Nunez Barrajas served four days in the Los Angeles County jail for curfew violation. He was arrested while going from Santa Ana to Los Angeles to see his aunt, whose son had been killed during the upheavals. According to Nunez, "[T]he ones they've caught are only from the black race and the Latin race. I haven't seen any Koreans or Chinese. Why not them? Or white? Why only the black race and the Latinos? Well, it's racism" (*Los Angeles Times,* 13 May 1992).

7. L. A. Chung, "Tensions Divide Blacks, Asians," *San Francisco Chronicle,* 4 May 1992.

8. *Los Angeles Times,* 5 May 1992.

9. They were also given to gloating over the inability of American authorities to maintain social order as well as the South Korean government can. In an interview, a South Korean diplomat in Los Angeles remarked to me that he was astonished at how ill-prepared the Los Angeles police and the National Guard were for "mass disturbances." They did not react quickly enough, they were very inefficient, they had no emergency plan, and even their communications network broke down, he observed. He could not imagine "riots" getting out of control in South Korea, which was ruled by the military from 1961 to 1987; there, he commented, "the police are very effective. They work closely with the military."

10. For example, a story about the "black riots" in the 6 May 1992 *Central Daily News* in Seoul listed the writer as Korean-American sociologist Edward T'ae-han Chang, who was astonished when he saw it because he hadn't written it (personal communication).

11. In 1913, a group of Korean-American laborers was run out of Hemet Valley, California by a mob of anti-Japanese whites. The Koreans responded by insisting that they were Korean, not Japanese. What might seem a ludicrous response to racist expulsion has to be viewed in light of the fact that the United States sanctioned Japan's 1909 annexation of Korea, closing all Korean delegations and placing Korean immigrants under the authority of Japanese consulates. Since they were classified as Japanese, Korean Americans were subject to the Alien Land Acts that, in California and nine other states, targeted Japanese by denying them the right afforded all others regardless of race, nativity, or citizenship: the right to own land. Also, foreign-born Koreans were able to become naturalized U.S. citizens only after the McCarran-Walter Act of 1952 permitted naturalization of Japanese. I have heard some Asian Americans equate the Chinese and Japanese American use of signs and buttons reading "I Am Not Korean" during *sa-i-ku* with the Korean American (and, not coincidentally, Chinese American) practice of wearing buttons saying "I Am Not Japanese" during World War II. But, in light of the specificities of Korean and Korean American history, this cannot be a one-to-one comparison.

12. In a 23 July 1992 interview, a fifty-year-old Korean immigrant woman whose South Central Los Angeles corner grocery store had been completely destroyed during *sa-i-ku* told me, "The America I imagined [before I arrived here] was like what I saw in the movies—clean, wide streets, flowers everywhere. I imagined Americans would be all big, tall . . . with white faces and blond hair. . . . But the America here is not like that. When I got up to walk around the neighborhood the morning after we arrived in Los Angeles from Korea, it was as if we had come to Mexico."

13. John Berger and Jean Mohr, *A Seventh Man: A Book of Images and Words about the Experiences of Migrant Workers in Europe* (New York: Penguin Books, 1975). I want to thank Barry Maxwell for bringing this work to my attention.

14. I am not grappling directly with social class issues here because, although I am cognizant of their crucial importance, I am simply not qualified to address them at the present time. The exploited "guest workers" in Europe described by Berger and Mohr, unlike the Korean immigrants to the United States, brought with them their laboring bodies but not capital to start small businesses. Because they are merchants, the class interests of Korean American shopowners in Los Angeles differ clearly from the interests of poor African American and Latino customers. But working with simple dyads is impossible, since Korean American shopowners are also of color and mostly immigrants from a country colonized by the United States. At the same time, it seems to me that class factors have been more important than race factors in shaping Korean-American immigrants' attitudes toward African American and Latino populations. Perhaps because of the devastation caused by Japanese colonization and the Korean War, many Koreans exhibit intensely negative attitudes toward the poor and indeed desperately fear being associated with them. I have often marveled at the importance placed on conspicuous consumer items, especially clothing, in South Korean society, where a shabbily dressed

person can expect only shabby treatment. In the 1960s, a middle-class American could make a social statement against materialistic values by dressing in tattered clothing without being mistaken for a homeless person. Now that this is no longer true, it seems to me that middle-class Americans exhibit some of the fears and aversions I witnessed in South Korea. Ironically, in the society where blackness and brownness have historically been almost tantamount to a condemnation to poverty, prejudice against the poor brought from Korea is combined with homegrown U.S. racism, and the results have been explosive.

At the same time, I have also noticed among Korean merchants profound empathy with the poor, whose situation many older immigrants know from firsthand past experiences. I personally witnessed many encounters between Korean merchants who lost their stores and African American neighbors in South Central during July 1992, when I accompanied the merchants as they visited their burned-out sites. None of the encounters were hostile. On the contrary, most of the African American neighbors embraced the Korean shopowners and expressed concern for them, while the merchants in turn asked warmly after the welfare of their neighbors' children. Although Korean-African American interaction has been racialized in the dominant culture, the quality of these relationships, like the quality of all human relationships, proved far more individual than racial schematizing allows for.

15. Every South Korean middle school, high school, and college student is required to take a course in "National Ethics," formerly called "Anticommunism." This course, which loosely resembles a civics class on Western civilization, government, constitutionalism, and political ideology, emphasizes the superiority of capitalism over communism and the importance of the national identity and the modern capitalist state. From the early 1960s through the 1970s, when most of the Los Angeles Korean immigrant merchants studied "Anticommunism" or "National Ethics," they were taught that "capitalism" and "democracy" are the same, and that both are antithetical to "communism" or "socialism." According to this logic, criticisms of the United States, a "democracy," are tantamount to praise of "communism." Such a view left little room for acknowledgment of racism and other social problems in American society. Indeed, the South Korean National Security Law formerly prosecuted and jailed writers who depicted Americans negatively and filmmakers who portrayed North Koreans as good-looking or capable of falling in love. Today, however, the interpretation of what constitutes antistate activity is far narrower, and although the South Korean government maintains that "pro-North Korea" activities are against the law, anti-U.S. sentiments have been common in South Korea since the mid-1980s.

16. I cannot help thinking that these violent baptisms are an Asian American legacy of sorts, for in some sense it was the internment that forced the Japanese Americans to "become American" half a century ago.

17. Many Korean Americans have criticized the *Los Angeles Times* and local television news, and the ABC network in particular, for repeatedly running stories about Soon Ja Du shooting Latasha Harlins (the tape was the second-most-played video during the week of the riots, according to the media-watch section of *A Magazine: An Asian American Quarterly* 1, no. 3 [1991]: 4). They complained that the Los Angeles ABC affiliate aired the store videotape in tandem with the King footage. ABC even inserted the Du-Harlins tape segment into its reportage of the height of the *sa-i-ku* upheavals. Korean Americans have also protested the media focus on armed Korean American merchants. In particular, they objected to the repeated use of the image of a Korean merchant pointing a gun at an unseen, off-camera target. They knew that he was being shot at and that he was firing only at the ground, but they felt that the image was used to depict Korean immigrants as violent and lawless. They argued that by blocking out the context, the news media harmed Korean Americans, about whom little positive was known by the American public. Tong S. Suhr wrote in a Korean American newspaper:

> The Harlins killing is a tragic but isolated case. . . . This is not to condone the
> Harlins killing; nor is it to justify the death by countering with how many merchants
> in turn have been killed. Our complaint is directed to the constant refrain of "the
> Korean-born grocer killing a black teen-ager," which couldn't help but sow the
> seeds of racial hatred . . . [and make me wonder]: Was there any conspiracy among
> the . . . white-dominated media to pit one ethnic group against another and sit
> back and watch them destroy one another? . . . Why were the Korean American
> merchants portrayed as gun-toting vigilantes shooting indiscriminately when they
> decided to protect their lives and businesses by arming themselves because no
> police protection was available? Why wasn't there any mention of the fact that they
> were fired upon first? Why such biased reporting? ("Time for Soul Searching by
> Media," *Korea Times,* 29 June 1992)

I would challenge representatives of the news media who argue that visual images of
beatings and shootings, especially when they are racialized or sexualized, are "exciting"
and "interesting," even when they are aired hundreds or thousands of times, when
compared with "boring" images of the everyday. Three months after *sa-i-ku,* I visited a
videotape brokerage company in search of generic footage that could be used in a
documentary about the Korean immigrant experience of losing their means of livelihood. Almost every inch of the stringers' footage contained images of police cars, fire
engines, and uniformed men heroically wiping their brows as they courageously prepared to meet the challenges before them. Since there were neither police nor firemen
anywhere in sight in South Central or Koreatown during the first three days of *sa-i-ku,*
none of this footage was of use to me. No doubt the men who shot these scenes chose
what seemed to them the most "interesting" and "exciting" images. But if I, a woman
and a Korean American, had had a camera in my hands, I would have chosen quite
different ones.

18. *Newsweek,* 18 May 1992.
19. The text of King's statement was printed in the *Los Angeles Times* (2 May 1992) as follows:

> People I just want to say . . . can we all get along? Can we get along? Can we stop
> making it horrible for the older people and the kids? . . . We've got enough smog
> here in Los Angeles, let alone to deal with the setting of those fires and things.
> It's just not right. It's not right, and it's not going to change anything.
>
> We'll get our justice. They've won the battle but they haven't won the war. We
> will have our day in court and that's all we want. . . . I'm neutral. I love everybody.
> I love people of color. . . . I'm not like they're . . . making me out to be.
>
> We've got to quit. We've got to quit. . . . I can understand the first upset in the
> first two hours after the verdict, but to go on, to keep going on like this, and to
> see a security guard shot on the ground, it's just not right. It's just not right because
> those people will never go home to their families again. And I mean, please, we
> can get along here. We all can get along. We've just got to, just got to. We're all
> stuck here for awhile. . . . Let's try to work it out. Let's try to work it out.

20. The news media that did cover this massive demonstration invariably focused on the
    Korean musicians because they looked and sounded alien and exotic. Ironically, most
    of them were young, American-born or at least American-educated Korean Americans
    who learned traditional music as a way to recover their cultural heritage. They perform
    at many events: I remember them in the demonstrations against the 1991 Gulf War.
21. *Juche sasang,* the concept of self-determination, was attractive to Koreans before the

division of the country after the defeat of Japan in World War II. However, since the term *juche* is central to the official political ideology in communist North Korea, the synonym *jaju* is used in South Korean officialdom.

22. I borrow this image from Walter Benjamin, "Theses on the Philosophy of History," in *Illuminations* (New York: Schocken Books, 1969), 256. I would like to thank Shelley Sunn Wong for helping me see its relevance to Korean Americans in the 1990s.

THE VIETNAMESE
AMERICAN EXPERIENCE

FROM DISPERSION TO THE DEVELOPMENT

OF POST-REFUGEE COMMUNITIES

Linda Trinh Võ

Old Saigon is no more, the Communists have seen to that. We wanted to created something here in America that will remind us of who we are. (Tony Lam, Westminster City Council member, first Vietnamese American elected to public office and one of the first to open a business in Little Saigon, Orange County, California. Quoted in Bert Eljera, "Big Plans for Little Saigon," AsianWeek, 17 May 1996)

Here, the smoke-filled coffee-houses, bakeries, boutiques and restaurants—all reminiscent of the fallen capital of the former South Vietnam—beckoned to the expatriates who, in their hearts, still yearned for the tastes and textures of their homeland. (Lily Dizon, "Little Saigon is Big in Hearts of Vietnamese," *Los Angeles Times*, 14 June 1994)

Before 1975, there were approximately fifteen thousand Vietnamese living in the United States and most were exchange students or wives of U.S. servicemen (Gordon 1987). The aftermath of the Communist takeover of South Vietnam led to a mass exodus of Vietnamese, many of whom came to the United States. By 1980 there were a quarter million Vietnamese in this country; by 1990, the number had increased to half a million; and by the late 1990s, it is estimated that this population numbers approximately one million (Bouvier and Agresta 1987; Lee 1998). It is predicted that by the turn of the century they will be one of the largest Asian groups, outnumbered only by Filipinos, Chinese, and Asian Indians. Unlike most immigrants, refugees do not leave their country voluntarily, but are compelled to leave by life-threatening circumstances or are forcibly expelled.[1] Their status as exiled political refugees affects their arrival in this country as well as their settlement and adaptation process. This chapter explores how the U.S. government's policy to resettle the refugees and make them financially self-sufficient by dispersing them across the country and isolating them from co-ethnics was later counteracted by the refugees' own efforts to build concentrated ethnic communities. The Federal Resettlement Program chose to separate these involuntary immigrants, while neglecting the importance of ethnic networks and ethnic communities that could have assisted the refugees in adapting to their host society. With the process of secondary migration and chain migration, these refugees, through a process of self-selected segregation, gravitated toward certain urban areas and developed distinct ethnic Vietnamese communities—using them as a vital form of mutual support.

REFUGEE WAVES

Since 1975, the political turmoil and economic instability in Vietnam forced many Vietnamese to flee and seek refuge in other countries, with more than half a million arriving in the United States during this exodus.[2] They came in two major refugee flows: the 1975 evacuees and the "boat people," many of whom are ethnic Chinese. The first wave of refugees, most often families, left as South Vietnam was being overtaken by Communist forces. These 1975 evacuees feared political reprisals because of their position of employment, their economic status, or their religious beliefs. Many worked for the American government or for the South Vietnamese military or government. These evacuees, most of whom were airlifted out during a U.S.-assisted evacuation, spent a short time in the processing camps temporarily set up at military bases in the United States before being relocated, and the majority were given three years' monetary assistance. By the end of 1975, more than 130,000 refugees were settled in the United States under the direction of the federal agencies and the voluntary agencies (VOLAGs), many of which were religious charities. These refugees were a select group primarily from middle-class and elite backgrounds; half of the heads of households had completed high school, and one fourth had been to college.[3] In addition, some had previous contact with Americans, half were Catholic, and almost two-thirds had some English fluency—all factors that eased their transition and distinguished them from later flows.

Many officials thought the 1975 refugees would be the only wave to arrive, but later turmoil in the area led to the arrival of more refugees, referred to as the boat people. This group lacked the resources of the earlier arrivals and encountered far different obstacles. In 1976–77, the U.S. attorney general, under the Indochinese Parole Program, authorized the admission of a limited number of refugees, but in 1978–80, a mass exodus of refugees fled their home country by boats, which they navigated through treacherous seas to neighboring countries. These refugees had lived under the communist regime for a number of years and some had been sent to be "reeducated" in the new economic zones in Vietnam. Their escape was more perilous, and some spent considerable time in the refugee camps of first asylum in Indonesia, Malaysia, the Philippines, Thailand, and Hong Kong. A large number of refugees were young males, partly because the conditions of escape precluded departure by the older generation, and to some extent by women and children. They endured the boredom of the camps, ill health, inadequate nutrition, and psychological traumas. Unlike the first wave, this group went directly from the processing centers abroad to the settlement areas in the United States, and some requested to be placed near kin already in this country. The United States accepted 44,500 Vietnamese refugees in 1979; 95,000 in 1980; 86,000 in 1981; 44,000 in 1982; and 20,000 each subsequent year until 1986 (Tollefson 1989: 10). These later flows were closely scrutinized, and those classified as "economic" refugees were denied entrance to the United States, which recognizes only "political" refugees—categories that can be quite arbitrary. Generally, this group of refugees was primarily from rural areas, less formally educated, and came with fewer marketable job skills in comparison to their 1975 counterparts, factors which made their resettlement more difficult. To add to their problems, in 1982 financial assistance from the government was cut from 36 months to 18 months, and there were fewer programs overall to facilitate refugee adjustment.

In the second wave, many of the refugees were ethnic Chinese, Vietnam's ethnic minority group, who began leaving Vietnam in 1978 when border hostilities between China and Vietnam flared up. With an estimated population of 2 million, they were a marginalized entrepreneurial class who made up a small percentage of the population but controlled most of the retail trade (Knoll 1982: 260; Desbarats 1986). Some ethnic Chinese identified themselves as Vietnamese and intermarried, but many retained their Chinese affiliation and maintained their separate communities in Vietnam. After 1975, the Communist regime, in the process of nationalizing the economy, targeted this group and increased the persecution of these ethnic minorities, directly encouraging them to leave. Estimated to account for 25 percent of the refugee population, the majority of ethnic Chinese escaped by boat and were placed in refugee camps under the same conditions as the second wave of refugees. Their socioeconomic background and their minority status differentiates them from other Vietnamese refugee groups as a whole, though in the resettlement process this distinction was often not recognized. The ethnic Chinese received some assistance from the Chinese American community, but for the most part they do not fit neatly in either the Chinese community or the Vietnamese community in the United States (Espiritu 1989).

THE RESETTLEMENT AND DISPERSION PROCESS

The resettlement programs coordinated by the government and the VOLAGs were created to disperse the refugees throughout the United States, hoping to facilitate their acceptance by American communities and also to expedite their assimilation (Yu and Liu 1986). This refugee group differs from other refugees who entered the United States in this century, such as the Jewish case, which has an established population and ethnic concentrations (Gold 1992). In the mid-1970s, there was no established Vietnamese population that could act as sponsors or provide a network of support to the newly arrived group. The Vietnamese in this country at the time, mainly students and women married to American husbands, could provide only limited assistance. Refugees entering under the Indochina Migration and Refugee Assistance Act of 1975 or under the Refugees Act of 1980 were provided with financial assistance in their resettlement process (Gordon 1987).[4] Yet their numbers were unprecedented, and there was no explicit guideline, so ad hoc policies were created in setting up the camps, facilitating health tests and matching sponsors. The refugees were provided with basic needs, such as housing, clothing, and job placement, with the assistance of government funds, but much of the direct settlement was handled by local charity organizations.[5] With the first and subsequent waves, federal funds went largely to occupational retraining, English language courses, and reimbursements to states for public assistance, all of which were significantly reduced in the early 1980s.

While there was a great sense of sympathy for the fleeing refugees, public sentiment was not in favor of admitting them to the United States. The Gallup Poll and the Harris Survey reported that more than half of the American public did not favor the resettlement of Vietnamese in the United States (Reimers 1985: 176). The fact that the Vietnam War was an unpopular war in this country undoubtedly contributed to the antipathy felt toward these refugees (Roberts 1988). The refugees were a reminder that America had suffered high casualties and had been defeated by those they considered to be "backward peasants." The U.S. government had intervened in a Vietnamese civil war and although there were political distinctions made between their pro-democracy south Vietnamese "allies" and their pro-Communist north Vietnamese "enemies," physically the two ideological factions were indistinguishable to the American public, who were wary of these "foreigners" now invading their shores. Hein (1993: ix) refers to the Vietnamese refugees as "allied aliens," since they are technically foreigners who became the responsibility of the interventionist state. Similar to the Cuban refugee crisis, American officials were compelled to accept their Vietnamese allies in conjunction with their policies to undermine the communist regimes and also because of obligations of moral responsibility. Nonetheless, the economic downturn with high unemployment and high inflation during the mid-1970s added to this anti-Vietnamese sentiment, as there was concern that these foreigners would take away jobs from Americans and burden the stagnating economy along with straining the welfare system (Liu, Lamanna, and Mirata 1979: 63–73). With these dilemmas in mind, the government, along with the nonprofit organizations, had two main objectives: to make the refugees economically self-sufficient and to assimilate them as quickly as possible into the mainstream, thereby reducing any negative impact they might have on American society (Mortland and Ledgerwood 1987).

For government officials, the most effective method to pacify all sides was through geographic distribution, by scattering families in different locales across the United States, with the intent of making the refugees less conspicuous and forcing them to assimilate. Every state received at least 100 refugees and within these states, the Vietnamese were dispersed into small groups through various cities and towns to maintain their low visibility (Gordon 1987). Two-thirds moved to zip code areas with fewer than 500 refugees and 8.5 percent settled in areas with more than 3,000 Vietnamese (Baker and North 1984). Those who came in the second wave were placed near first waves, but this was closely monitored to prevent overburdening areas. Even with these precautionary measures to avoid conflict, there were tensions between refugees and the surrounding white, African American, and Latino communities, particularly over socioeconomic concerns such as housing and jobs (Rutledge 1992).

Individuals or groups who suggested the refugees be allowed to form their own ethnic communities for mutual support were ignored by officials, who were more concerned with the financial and political aspects of resettlement than with the social or cultural components (Skinner and Hendricks 1979). Since the government's main concern was to match the evacuees with willing sponsors quickly, they neglected to consider how this could lead to the fragmentation of extended kinship ties and the atomization of natural social support networks. Yu and Liu (1986) are critical of the Select Commission on Immigration and Refugees, which only accounts for "neutral" factors in terms of economic self-sufficiency, such as job procurement, welfare usage, and employment training, to evaluate refugee adaptation levels, neglecting central issues such as cultural, social, and mental adjustment. Newcomers who were sent to small towns throughout the United States felt culturally and spatially isolated from other Vietnamese and even other Asians. They could not depend on the basic resources of these communities, such as Asian markets where they could purchase food items suited to their dietary habits or ethnic organizations to accommodate them with culturally and linguistically appropriate social services.

The prevailing theory of assimilation, that immigrants should forsake their own culture and adopt the dominant culture in order to succeed, was the underlying objective of these policies. After the settlement of the 1975 group, it was assumed that the refugees would remain at their settlement sites and there would be no new arrivals, both of which were unrealistic perceptions given the inadequacies of the dispersion plans and the continuing instability in Southeast Asia (Desbarats and Holland 1983).

SELF-SELECTED SEGREGATION: SECONDARY MIGRATION AND CHAIN MIGRATION

By dispersing the refugees across the nation, it was hoped they would blend into American society. Instead, a trend toward internal secondary migration and chain migration became apparent as the refugees reorganized themselves and established their own distinct ethnic communities through a process of self-selected segregation. The process of moving from the original place of settlement to a new community is referred to as secondary migration. Unlike earlier Asian immigrants, who were forcibly segregated into economic and residential sites known as Chinatowns and Japantowns, these contemporary Asians were volunteering to form insular communities. Although there were no legal rules prohibiting the mobility of refugees, the government was concerned they would abandon the support of their sponsors and would burden the public assistance services in the new areas of residency. Another component leading to the expansion of ethnic concentrations is the pattern of chain migration, which is based on primary social relationships among co-ethnics.[6] In this process of chain migration, Vietnamese settled at a particular site either directly sponsored relatives or assisted other co-ethnics, thereby encouraging them to migrate to the same location (Haines 1982).

Often neglected is that many refugees are second-time migrants, who chose or were forced to move when circumstances deemed it necessary, so internal migration is not a novel concept for them (Kelly 1986). About 900,000 migrated from North to South Vietnam in the 1950s when the country was divided in half after the Geneva agreement, with the communists dominating the North (Tollefson 1989: 24). Many of them were Catholics who would eventually leave Vietnam when the communists overtook the South as well. The Vietnamese of Chinese ancestry had been moving from China since the late 1800s to the northern part of Vietnam, and some of them migrated again to the southern region in the 1950s. Between 1965 and 1973, as the war spread in Vietnam, it is estimated that 10 million refugees flooded the urban areas of South Vietnam, primarily peasants who were displaced from their villages in the fighting zone (ibid.). Since exact statistics are not available, one can only speculate on how many refugees who entered the United States were twice or thrice migrants and whose families had been forced to migrate within Vietnam. This may help to understand how geographic mobility within the United States is not incongruent with their personal experiences or the experiences of the Vietnamese in general.

The reason the refugees migrated within the United States was that they felt minimal connection to the assigned place of settlement—they were not structurally integrated into these communities, either socially or economically. The U.S. government assumed that economic self-sufficiency was viable only if the Vietnamese were forced to assimilate into the American mainstream. Clearly, the refugees desired self-sufficiency, but they felt it could be accomplished in conjunction with ethnic retention and ethnic segregation. Forcibly scattering the refugees was an attempt to prevent a pattern of ethnic clustering; however, the Vietnamese counteracted federal policy by making a concerted effort to create ethnic pockets. Ironically, the refugees often moved to these areas because it provided them with more socioeconomic opportunities, which facilitated their adaptation process rather than inhibiting it. In order to understand the process of self-selected segregation, which is marked by secondary migration and chain migration, one must examine the reasons for leaving the place of settlement and the motivation for reuniting with co-ethnics as well as why particular sites where chosen for resettlement.

ECONOMIC REASONS FOR SECONDARY MIGRATION

The refugees were sent to places where there were limited job opportunities, so they were not economically integrated into the community. Many of the private American families and churches that sponsored the refugees could only provide minimal assistance, so the refugees relied on public assistance, which also could be received in other locations. Sometimes, abuses occurred when Americans came forward to sponsor refugees with the intention of using them as cheap laborers, taking advantage of their desperation. Even well-intentioned sponsors, such as the religious charity organizations that assisted the refugees, were often located in areas with limited economic opportunities, such as the Lutheran Immigration and Refugee Service based in the northern Midwest or the United Hebrew Immigration and Assistance Service in the urban northeast (Andrews and Stropp 1985). American families who sponsored the refugees could provide food, clothing, and shelter, but could not provide all the jobs or social links the refugees desired. Thus, there were few economic reasons for them to remain in these locations and greater incentive to migrate to locations with better socioeconomic opportunities.

Ethnic ties are salient factors for these refugees who arrived during a recessionary period in the United States, since job prospects were limited and even more so in isolated locations. In the massive distribution of refugees, economic background became insignificant, so little effort was made to match their skills to job opportunities. Therefore, many were employed in occupations that differed from their former jobs. As a result of cultural barriers, many refugees were consigned to unskilled employment where little formal education, English language skills, and experience were required. The trend for those in rural areas and smaller towns was to migrate to urban areas within their state or across the country where job opportunities were more abundant. They often heard about better job prospects through informal channels, such as family members, friends, and other associates. Interestingly enough, when many refugees' families became marginally self-supporting and no longer had to rely on their individual or organizational sponsors, they chose to relocate to more ideal locations. From this perspective, secondary migration and linking up with other Vietnamese for economic betterment can be regarded as a means of becoming integated into American society.

SOCIAL REASONS FOR SECONDARY MIGRATION

As a survival strategy, the Vietnamese chose to relocate in order to be reunited with families and friends who could assist them in tangible ways, such as finding employment and housing, but also in intangible ways, as sources of emotional and psychological support. The development of these communities is an indication of the importance of maintaining and strengthening ties with co-ethnics who have endured the traumas of escaping a war-torn country and who have contended with starting a new life. They can share with other co-ethnics their feelings of displacement, homesickness, depression, loss, or guilt for having survived the war or the escape from Vietnam, while others less fortunate were not able to do so. These displaced persons have experienced downward social mobility because their qualifications and occupational status were often not transferable. Yet living among compatriots allows them to regain some of their class status, since other co-ethnics may acknowledge and recognize previous distinctions and statuses (Skinner and Hendricks 1989). Furthermore, among compatriots they can share their feelings about racial discrimination and other hardships they encounter in this country.

The turmoil of the war, the perils of their exodus, and the dilemma of their resettlement have dramatically affected the meaning and boundaries of kinship networks for refugees (Hein 1993: 135). Kinship networks include immediate and extended family members and even distant relatives helping one another. While 3 percent of white families have relatives outside the nuclear family (children or spouse) living with them, 13 percent of Vietnamese households include distant relatives (Bureau of Census 1993a). Thus, the refugees tried to counter the breakup of extended family units by regrouping themselves. For many Vietnamese, social networks are also based on non-kin affiliates. Seven percent of Vietnamese households include non-relatives, in contrast to only 4 percent of white households (ibid.). This can include those who lived in the same village or perhaps those who met in the refugee camps but treat one another as family members. The 1990 census indicates that whites average 2.5 persons per household and Asians average 3.3 persons, while the Vietnamese average is 4 persons (Lee 1998). By living together, they can rely on "patchworking," in which kin and non-kin household members pool their financial and human resources for survival with individuals sharing income, public assistance payments, household chores, and child care responsibilities (Desbarats and Holland 1983; Kibria 1993).

EMERGENCE OF ETHNIC SITES

Prior to the mid-1970s, there were no discernible Vietnamese communities; however, by the late 1970s, the formation of such areas was quite noticeable with the appearance of Vietnamese ethnic clusters comprising residences, restaurants, retail shops, markets, professional businesses, places of entertainment, festivals, and community centers. In these sites, there exist multigenerational families and non-kin networks. For example, one can find grandparents, parents, children, aunts, uncles, cousins, friends from the old village, and other associates who form the foundation of an ethnic community. Unlike some other Asian ethnic enclaves that have become tourist attractions to the general public, most of these Vietnamese business communities cater primarily to co-ethnics. As they become part of the American landscape, these "Little Saigons," as they are often called, symbolize a sense of stability and permanence for the Vietnamese.

Six months after their original settlement many refugees began to move away from their sponsors to other locations (Kelly 1977: 200) and chose to congregate in certain areas, particularly in the South and West. By 1980, it was reported that 45 percent of the refugees had resettled in another state and that Vietnamese living in zip code areas with fewer than five hundred refugees dropped from about 60 percent to 40 percent, while Vietnamese residing in locations with more than three thousand co-ethnics increased from 8.5 percent to 20 percent (Rumbaut 1995). With the 1975 evacuees, the selection of sites and sponsors was more restricted, but later arrivals could ask to rejoin family members who had relocated.

The Vietnamese are primarily concentrated in the Western (54.3 percent) and Southern (27.4 percent) regions of the United States, but there are also concentrations in the Northeast (9.8 percent) and Midwest (8.5 percent) regions (Bureau of the Census 1993c: 353). In 1990, the top ten states of residence for the Vietnamese were California with 46 percent, Texas with 11 percent, and Virginia, Washington, Louisiana, Florida, Pennsylvania, New York, Massachusetts, and Illinois with three percent or less in each (Bureau of the Census 1993b, Population and Housing). Most refugees in California are clustered in five counties: Los Angeles, Orange, San Diego, San Francisco, and Santa Clara (Knoll 1982: 152). Additionally, the Vietnamese comprise the largest Asian subgroup in a number of states: Texas, Louisiana, Mississippi, Arkansas, Kansas, and Oklahoma.

Sites of segregation in particular states, counties, or cities are not arbitrary, but are dependent on various incentives. Peters (1987) found that after better climate, refugees cited rejoining relatives and friends, and then better jobs, as the main reasons for migration, which correlates with other findings. A viable explanation for some geographic concentrations was that they developed near the original receiving stations temporarily set up in Camp Pendleton, California; Fort Indiantown Gap, Pennsylvania; Fort Chaffee, Arkansas (near the Texas border); and Fort Elgin, Florida. Sponsors were found for these first-wave refugees within the vicinity, particularly California and Texas, and eventually the first-wavers were joined by secondary migrants through chain migration. Coming from a tropical climate, many Vietnamese disliked the cold temperatures in the states where they were assigned, preferring to live in the warmer climates of the Western and Southern states. However, weather fails to explain the expansion of Vietnamese concentrations in the Midwest and East Coast regions that face severe winters.

Some have stressed that states such as California have more "liberal" welfare policies that attract refugee populations, yet there are twenty-five other states with similar policies that do not have the same density of refugees. Additionally, this fails to explain why many have settled in Texas, which has not adopted these policies (Daniels 1991). Although it did not have high welfare benefits or a thriving economy, Versailles Garden in the New Orleans area attracted numerous Vietnamese and has experienced residential growth because of its proximity to fishing opportunities, a strong Catholic charity service and community, and a climate similar to Vietnam (Zhou and Bankston 1998).

Noticeable is a trend toward selecting metropolitan destinations. In some cases, ethnic businesses have attracted new settlers, while in other instances the reverse actually occurs—business owners establish their businesses in proximity to ethnic residences (Lou 1989). Desbarats and Holland (1983) found that in Orange County, which has the largest Vietnamese community with close to three hundred thousand, the clustering of ethnic businesses that provide necessary services correlates with the high concentration of refugees who moved to the vicinity. In cities such as Seattle, Oakland, Los Angeles, New York, and Chicago, the Vietnamese business community is within or adjacent to the more established Chinese business and residential community, likely a byproduct of the ethnic Chinese Vietnamese population. The Vietnamese also have revitalized certain areas, such as sections of the downtown San Jose area where they own a number of ethnic businesses (Lou 1989). The concentrations in San Diego, Oakland, San Francisco, Philadelphia, Minneapolis-St. Paul, and Boston are typical of Vietnamese settlements that are located in economically depressed areas, which are often in racially mixed neighborhoods marked by low rents for housing and business enterprises, but also by high crime. Modest yet noticeable Vietnamese business clusters can be found in cities across the country, such as Salt Lake City, Wichita, Arlington (Virginia), and Oklahoma City.

Economic opportunities attracted the Vietnamese to particular urban locations. There they found work as machine operators, assembly line laborers, electronics technicians, service sector employees, or in other unskilled or low-skilled jobs. In many of these manufacturing industries, Vietnamese with limited English skills can work side by side with co-ethnics and can be managed by a co-ethnic as well. The expanding high-tech Silicon Valley companies in Santa Clara County in northern California employ Vietnamese, particularly females, as low-level technicians or assemblers. Clearly, many medium and small businesses that catered to co-ethnics led to the largest economic development in Westminster, Santa Ana, and Garden Grove, located in Orange County in southern California. The fishing industry along the Texas Gulf coast originally attracted many Vietnamese, which in turn brought more Vietnamese to the state, especially to Houston and to a lesser extent Dallas, which has more affordable housing prices and greater availability of unskilled jobs. Although economic self-sufficiency has been achieved by some members in these urban niches, for others it is still an elusive goal.

The Vietnamese selected regional areas for their self-sustained clusterings, especially those that were amenable to their residential expansion and that created favorable economic conditions. Having both a strong local economy and an existing Asian population lessens the impact of concentrated refugees (Finnan and Cooperstein 1983; Gordon 1987). Despite this fact, conflicts do arise, especially since the Vietnamese are more conspicuous in concentrated numbers and have amassed more area as their communities expand. Racial and economic conflicts between Vietnamese and other groups, such as have occurred with Chicanos in Denver, with whites on the Texas Gulf Coast, and with blacks in New Orleans over housing and employment issues in the earlier settlement period, seem to have subsided (Skinner 1980; Starr 1981).

During an interview as part of a larger project on Asian Americans, an elderly Vietnamese community leader explained to me his experiences as a first-wave refugee. Born in North Vietnam, he fled with his Catholic parents to South Vietnam, where he was raised. He was employed as a high school science teacher and worked on educational projects with Americans in Vietnam. Fearing persecution for his contact with Americans, he escaped with his wife and three young children to the United States in 1975. After three months in Fort Chaffee, Arkansas, his family was sponsored by a Baptist deacon in a Tennessee town with a population of fifteen thousand. The fifteen Vietnamese in the town consisted of his family, his brother's family, and a friend's family. He worked as a janitor, a cook, and in an office supply store before returning to school and eventually finding work as an engineer. Although he was able to support his family and had purchased a modest house and car, he and his family felt isolated from other Vietnamese. Through regular phone conversations with friends in California, they heard about the mild winters, the educational opportunities, the numerous Asian markets, and the growing Vietnamese population, particularly Catholics. These contacts led to their decision to relocate to San Diego in 1977, against the wishes of their sponsors and other townsfolk in Tennessee. He continued his education to improve his job skills, yet he realized that his limited English skills would prevent him from gaining promotions in a mainstream firm, so he eventually opened up his own small electronics company that employed mainly co-ethnics. He also became a leader in the Vietnamese Catholic community and in the Vietnamese Federation, an umbrella organization that incorporates local Vietnamese political, educational, economic, social, and cultural associations. The sponsorship program was effective in assisting this family's economic transition; however, the program did not address their social and cultural isolation, so they chose to relocate to a site that could provide them with ethnic comforts.

In the 1980s and 1990s, much of the growth in these concentrated communities has been in the form of resettled refugees who attain citizenship and sponsor second-and third-wave compatriots, who then join them in their communities directly from the camps overseas. These newcomers do not enter under the refugee status, but are admitted as immigrants. In 1979, the United Nations High Commission for Refugees and the Socialist Republic of Vietnam created the Orderly Departure Program to permit Vietnamese to leave the country legally. As a receiving country, the United States allows these immigrants entrance under the family reunification plan, although many are still unable to get permission to leave Vietnam or are ineligible for admission to the United States. There are estimates that by 1983 about half of the Vietnamese entering were not assisted by an intermediary agency, but instead were sponsored by relatives.

Other categories for entrance include (1) former U.S. employees and South Vietnamese military personnel; and (2) Amerasians and their families. Through humanitarian efforts the employees and military personnel, many of whom became political prisoners in reeducation camps in the post-1975 period, were allowed special admission to the United States if they had family members willing to sponsor them (Chan 1991: 164). The U.S. Congress passed the 1987 Amerasian Homecoming Act, which allows the children of Vietnamese women and American servicemen who served in Vietnam, along with immediate family members, to resettle in the United States. They joined other Amerasians who had previously used the Orderly Departure Program to emigrate, and this racially mixed population has helped to enlarge and diversify the Vietnamese ethnic concentrations. The pattern of chain migration of these new arrivals from abroad, along with those who migrate internally, contributes to the growth of Vietnamese communities in the United States.

ETHNIC ENCLAVES OR ETHNIC COMMUNITIES

The formation and maintenance of these ethnic enclaves defies the assimilationist theories, which suggest that the longer the immigrants are here, the more Americanized they will become.[7] Some consider these communities as ethnic enclaves that will marginalize the ethnic groups and prevent full participation in American society; others see these ethnic clusters as a resource (Gold 1992). In the Vietnamese case, while ethnic ghettoization and co-ethnic exploitation may occur in these communities, geographic concentrations provide access to beneficial social networks and resources. Desbarats and Holland state, "For newcomers and secondary migrants alike, emotional and economic dependence on traditional kinship and ethnic networks makes the pull of established refugee enclaves difficult to resist" (1983). These spaces provide displaced populations with a site where they can feel socially, culturally, and linguistically comfortable. Thus, the Vietnamese choice of self-selected segregation was justified based on a need for economic and social survival.

Depending on size, these communities can be self-contained with their own internal power structure. Within these communities, refugees have formed their own local social, cultural, professional, political, and religious organizations for mutual support, some of which are a continuation of institutions in their homeland, others arising from their experiences in the United States (Gold 1992). One of the first formal organizations developed was the Indochinese Mutual Assistance Associations (IMAAs), supported by federal and private grants and also by refugee contributions, which allowed members of the community to assist in their own adaptation process. Vietnamese Catholic priests are reestablishing or creating Vietnamese parishes (Kelly 1977; Andrews and Stopp 1985), and Vietnamese Buddhist temples are often the center for community cultural affairs.

Although the Vietnamese in America have formed ethnic communities and organizations, it would be premature and inaccurate to say that they are a cohesive group. Upon their arrival, they were lumped together as "refugees," yet there are numerous differences, not noticeable to outsiders, that still separate and divide members internally. For the Vietnamese, demarcations still exist based on regional affiliation (northern, central, or southern part of Vietnam), peasant vs. urbanite, rich vs. poor, educated vs. uneducated, Christian vs. Buddhist, ethnic majority vs. minority, and so on. Even language differentiates them by region, since there are northern, central, and southern dialects. Most noticeable is the factionalism that stems from ideological differences, such as the difference of opinions on the current efforts by the United States to normalize relations with Vietnam. Also apparent is the generational split between the older generation of traditional leaders, who dominate community politics, and the younger generation who hold more progressive views but at this point lack political clout. The diversity of these communities also manifests itself in the fact that some Vietnamese Americans are gaining university credentials and are attaining middle-class status, while others are dropping out of high school, going on welfare, and dealing with mental health problems (Le 1993).

These differences make it difficult to form community organizations and select leaders who can adeptly address the needs of the community or articulate their concerns to outsiders. It is only recently that Vietnamese formally organized a nationally based umbrella organization that unites the numerous Vietnamese organizations. Thus, being Vietnamese is not a natural affinity or a primordial identity; rather, the refugees have had to reorganize themselves according to an external label that lumps them together upon their arrival to this country. The Vietnamese, irrespective of the ethnic Chinese Vietnamese, have been the majority in Vietnam, yet in the United States they are categorized as an ethnic minority, which requires adjusting to a new identity (Espiritu 1989). In this regard, hyphenated identities such as Vietnamese-Americans are labels imposed by outsiders for matters of convenience, rather than self-imposed identifiers (Skinner 1980). Moreover, these people have been lumped into the Indochinese or Southeast Asian categories with other refugees from Laos and Cambodia, which has forced them to form temporary alliances, mainly for social service resources. In addition, though included under the rubric of Asian Americans, it is questionable whether the Vietnamese have internalized this label, and furthermore, whether they consider their interests aligned with other Asian Americans. Issues that unite them with other Asians include anti-Asian hate crimes, problems with juvenile delinquency, and the lack of adequate social service programs (Võ 1995).

CONCLUSION

It has been more than twenty-five years since the initial arrival of Vietnamese refugees, yet it would be incorrect to conclude that they have assimilated into the American mainstream. Although the circumstances that prompted their massive emigration were unique, the Vietnamese, like immigrants and refugees who arrived on American shores before them, did not merely assimilate. Instead, they chose to retain their ethnicity and develop their ethnic communities as a strategy for economic and social survival. This is a lesson that should not be forgotten should the United States face another large influx of refugees in the future. The Vietnamese have been transformed by their adopted society; simultaneously, their ethnic communities have changed the face of this country. Many refugees who left during the aftermath of 1975 thought they would return within a short period of time, but this has not been the case. Whether defined as refugee, immigrant, or ethnic communities, Vietnamese American communities are a permanent entity and are growing spatially and demographically.

Although immigration has decreased, a relatively young population and accompanying high fertility rate suggest that the Vietnamese population in the United States will increase steadily. There are two factors to consider that can dramatically affect the formation and resilience of these ethnic communities: the American-born Vietnamese and the normalization of relations between the United States and Vietnam. In 1990, approximately 80 percent of the population was foreign-born (Bureau of the Census 1993d: 1), but there is a new generation of Vietnamese, born and raised in the United States. The 1990 census showed that 92 percent of the native-born Vietnamese are under age fifteen (Lee 1998). They will only hear about the refugee experience, and it is difficult to ascertain if this acculturated U.S.-born population will choose to maintain its connection to the ethnic communities. With ongoing migration to revitalize the population and thriving ethnic enclaves, cultural transmission is still strong. Furthermore, intramarriage or marrying co-ethnics is generally encouraged (Nguyen 1998); however, this does not mean that the new generation of Vietnamese Americans will reside in the ethnic neighborhoods and patronize ethnic businesses. Although the second-generation Vietnamese may be acculturated, they, like other Asians, still need to contend with their treatment as a racial minority in a country that does not accept them as bona fide Americans.

Secondly, with travel possible to Vietnam since the late 1980s, many individuals are visiting their former homeland, especially during the annual Tet (Lunar New Year) celebration, and have been reunited with relatives. Some have returned with the intention of seeking economic opportunities there. Others refuse to even visit their former homeland with the current Communist regime still in existence and are critical of the human rights violation and corruption, as well as skeptical about the economic reforms being proposed. It is unlikely that normalizing political and economic relations between Vietnam and the United States will drastically affect the ethnic communities in America. Even though some first-generation Vietnamese refugees or immigrants may want to return permanently, they find it difficult, since this means being separated from their American-born children and grandchildren, who have established roots in the United States. For some, their old lives cannot simply be reestablished upon their return to a Vietnam, which has changed in their absence. For others, their experiences in this country transformed them, and in some cases provided them with opportunities unattainable in Vietnam. In many ways, Americans of Vietnamese ancestry may visit their homeland, but there is no returning home.

NOTES

1. This is not to say that those in the immigrant category do not leave because of life-threatening circumstances; often it is a variety of factors which motivates their emigration.
2. As a result of the turmoil in Southeast Asia, refugees from Cambodia and Laos also arrived in the United States. Although their experiences are distinct, they shared experiences similar to the Vietnamese. For the purposes of this chapter, I intend to focus on the Vietnamese experience.
3. This is in contrast to the fact that 16 percent of the population in Vietnam attended secondary school and 1 percent attended college (see Kelly 1986).
4. The 1980 Act provided $405 million for resettlement; half of which was set aside to reimburse individual states for cash disbursements, medical care, and social services for the refugees.
5. Active VOLAGs include: the United States Catholic Conference, the Lutheran Immigration and Refugee Service, the International Rescue Committee, the United Hebrew Immigrant Aid Society, World Church Service, the Tolstoy Foundation, the American Fund for Czechoslovak Refugees, the American Council for Nationalities Service, and Travelers' Aid-International Social Services.
6. For further discussion on chain migration, see MacDonald and MacDonald (1964: 82–97).
7. For an example of the assimilationist model, see Montero (1979: 62). Using his Spontaneous International Migration Model, Montero predicted that Vietnamese ethnicity would quickly erode and ethnic enclaves would cease to exist.

REFERENCES

Andrews, Alice C., and G. Harry Stopp Jr. (1985). "The Indochinese." In *Ethnicity in Contemporary America: A Geographical Appraisal*, ed. Jess O. McKee, 217–239. Dubuque, Iowa: Kendall/Hunt Publishing.

Arnold, Fred, Urmil Minocha, and James T. Fawcett (1987). "The Changing Face of Asian Immigration to the United States." In *Pacific Bridges: The New Immigration from Asia and the Pacific Islands*, ed. James T. Fawcett and Benjamin V. Carino, 105–152. Staten Island, N.Y.: Center for Migration Studies.

Baker, Reginald P., and David S. North (1984). *The 1975 Refugees: Their First Five Years in America.* Washington, D.C.: New TransCentury Foundation.

Bouvier, Leon F., and Anthony J. Agresta (1987). "The Future Asian Population of the United States." In *Pacific Bridges: The New Immigration from Asia and the Pacific Islands,* ed. James T. Fawcett and Benjamin V. Carino, 285–301. Staten Island, N.Y.: Center for Migration Studies.

Chan, Sucheng (1991). *Asian Americans: An Interpretive History.* Boston: Twayne Publishers.

Daniels, Roger (1991). *Coming to America: A History of Immigration and Ethnicity in American Life.* New York: Harper Perennial.

Desbarats, Jacqueline (1986). "Ethnic Differences in Adaptation: Sino-Vietnamese Refugees in the United States." *International Migration Review* 20, no. 2: 405–427.

Desbarats, Jacqueline, and Linda Holland (1983). "Indochinese Settlement Patterns in Orange County." *Amerasia Journal* 10, no. 1 (spring/summer): 23–46.

Espiritu, Yen Le (1989). "Beyond the 'Boat People': Ethnicization of American Life." *Amerasia Journal* 15, no. 2: 49–67.

Finnan, Christine R., and Rhonda Cooperstein (1983). *Southeast Asian Refugee Resettlement at the Local Level: The Role of Ethnic Community and the Nature of Refugee Impact.* Menlo Park, Calif.: SRI International.

Gold, Steven J. (1992). *Refugee Communities: A Comparative Field Study.* Newbury Park, Calif.: Sage Publications.

Gordon, Linda (1987). "Southeast Asian Refugee Migration to the United States." In *Pacific Bridges: The New Immigration from Asia and the Pacific Islands,* ed. James T. Fawcett and Benjamin V. Carino, 153–173. Staten Island, N.Y.: Center for Migration Studies.

Haines, David W. (1982). "Southeast Asian Refugees in the United States: The Interaction of Kinship and Public Policy." *Anthropological Quarterly* 55, no. 3 (July): 170–181.

Hein, Jeremy (1993). *States and International Migrants: The Incorporation of Indochinese Refugees in the United States and France.* Boulder, Colo.: Westview Press.

Kelly, Gail (1977). *From Vietnam to America: A Chronicle of the Vietnamese Immigration to the United States.* Boulder, Colo.: Westview Press.

——— (1986). "Coping with America: Refugees from Vietnam, Cambodia, and Laos in the 1970s and 1980s." *Annals, AAPSS* 487 (September): 138–149.

Kibria, Nazli (1992). *Family Tightrope: The Changing Lives of Vietnamese Americans.* Princeton, N.J.: Princeton University Press.

Knoll, Tricia (1982). *Becoming Americans: Asian Sojourners, Immigrants, and Refugees in the Western United States.* Portland, Ore.: Coast to Coast Books.

Le, Ngoan (1993). "The Case of the Southeast Asian Refugees: Policy for a Community At-Risk." In *The State of Asian Pacific America, A Public Policy Report: Policy Issues to the Year 2000,* 167–188. Los Angeles: LEAP Asian Pacific American Public Policy Institute and UCLA Asian American Studies Center.

Lee, Sharon M. (1998). "Asian Americans: Diverse and Growing." *Populations Bulletin* 53, no. 2 (June).

Liu, William T., Maryanne Lamanna, and Alice Mirata (1979). *Transition to Nowhere: Vietnamese Refugees in America.* Nashville, Tenn.: Charter House.

Lou, Raymond (1989). "The Vietnamese Business Community of San Jose." In *Frontiers of Asian American Studies: Writing, Research, and Commentary,* ed. Gail M. Nomura, Russell Endo, Stephen H. Sumida, and Russell C. Leong, 98–112. Pullman: Washington State University Press.

MacDonald, John S., and Leatrice D. MacDonald (1964). "Chain Migration, Ethnic Neighborhood Formation and Social Networks." *Milbank Memorial Fund Quarterly* 42, no. 1.

Montero, Darrel (1979). *Vietnamese Americans: Patterns of Resettlement and Socioeconomic Adaptation in the United States.* Boulder, Colo.: Westview Press.

Mortland, Carol, and Judy Ledgerwood (1987). "Secondary Migration Among Southeast Asian Refugees in the United States." *Urban Anthropology* 16, nos. 3–4: 291–326.

Nguyen, Ly Thi (1998). "To Date or Not to Date a Vietnamese: Perceptions and Expectations of Vietnamese American College Students." *Amerasia Journal* 24, no. 1: 143–170.

Peters, Gary L. (1987). "Migration Decision-Making Among the Vietnamese in Southern California." *Sociology and Social Research* 71, no. 3 (April): 280–286.

Reimers, David M. (1985). *Still the Golden Door: The Third World Comes to America*. New York: Columbia University Press.

Roberts, Alden E. (1988). "Racism Sent and Received: Americans and Vietnamese View One Another." *Research in Race and Ethnic Relations* 5: 75–97.

Rumbaut, Ruben G. (1995). "Vietnamese, Laotian, and Cambodian Americans." In *Asian Americans: Contemporary Trends and Issues*, ed. Pyong Gap Min. Thousand Oaks, Calif.: Sage Publications.

Rutledge, Paul James (1992). *The Vietnamese Experience in America*. Bloomington: Indiana University Press.

Skinner, Kenneth A. (1980). "Vietnamese in America: Diversity in Adaptation." *California Sociologist* 3, no. 2 (summer): 103–124.

Skinner, Kenneth A., and Glenn L. Hendricks (1979). "The Shaping of Ethnic Self-Identity Among Indochinese Refugees." *The Journal of Ethnic Studies* 7, no. 3 (fall): 25–41.

Starr, Paul D. (1981). "Troubled Waters: Vietnamese Fisherfolk on America's Gulf Coast." *International Migration Review* 15, no. 1: 226–238.

Tollefson, James W. (1989). *Alien Winds: The Reeducation of America's Indochinese Refugees*. New York: Praeger.

U.S. Bureau of the Census (1993a). *1990 Census of Population, Social and Economic Characteristics, United States* CP-2–1 (November), Tables 41 and 105. Washington, D.C.: U.S. Government Printing Office.

———— (1993b). *U.S. Census of Population and Housing, 1980 and 1990*. Washington, D.C.: U.S. Government Printing Office.

———— (1993c). *1990 Census of Population, General Population Characteristics, The United States*, CP-1–1, Table 353. Washington, D.C.: U.S. Government Printing Office.

———— (1993d). *1990 Census of the Population, Asians and Pacific Islanders in the United States*, CP-3–5, Table 1. Washington, D.C.: U.S. Government Printing Office.

Võ, Linda Trinh (1995). "Paths to Empowerment: Panethnic Mobilization in San Diego's Asian American Community." Ph.D. dissertation, University of California, San Diego.

Yu, Elena S. H., and William T. Liu (1986). "Methodological Problems and Policy Implications in Vietnamese Refugee Research." *International Migration Review* 20, no. 2: 483–501.

Zaharlick, Amy, and Jean Brainard (1987). "Demographic Characteristics, Ethnicity and the Resettlement of Southeast Asian Refugees in the United States." *Urban Anthropology* 16, nos. 3–4: 327–373.

Zhou, Min, and Carl L. Bankston III (1998). *Growing Up American: How Vietnamese Children Adapt to Life in the United States*. New York: Russell Sage Foundation.

Gender

THE WOMAN WARRIOR VERSUS THE CHINAMAN PACIFIC

MUST A CHINESE AMERICAN CRITIC CHOOSE BETWEEN FEMINISM AND HEROISM?

King-Kok Cheung

The title of this anthology notwithstanding, I shall speak primarily not about topics that divide feminists but about conflicting politics of gender, as reflected in the literary arena, between Chinese American women and men.[1] There are several reasons for my choice. First, I share the frustrations of many women of color that while we wish to engage in a dialogue with "mainstream" scholars, most of our potential readers are still unfamiliar with the historical and cultural contexts of various ethnic "minorities." Furthermore, whenever I encounter words such as "conflicts," "common differences," or "divisive issues" in feminist studies, the authors more often than not are addressing the divergences either between French and Anglo-American theorists or, more recently, between white and nonwhite women. Both tendencies have the effect of re-centering white feminism. In some instances, women of color are invited to participate chiefly because they take issue with white feminists and not because what they have to say is of inherent interest to the audience. Finally, I believe that in order to understand conflicts among diverse groups of women, we must look at the relations between women and men, especially where the problems of race and gender are closely intertwined.

It is impossible, for example, to tackle the gender issues in the Chinese American cultural terrain without delving into the historically enforced "feminization" of Chinese American men, without confronting the dialectics of racial stereotypes and nationalist reactions or, above all, without wrestling with diehard notions of masculinity and femininity in both Asian and Western cultures. It is partly because these issues touch many sensitive nerves that the writings of Maxine Hong Kingston have generated such heated debate among Chinese American intellectuals. As a way into these intricate issues, I will structure my discussion around Kingston's work and the responses it has elicited from her Chinese American male critics, especially those who have themselves been influential in redefining both literary history and Asian American manhood.

Attempts at cultural reconstruction, whether in terms of "manhood" and "womanhood," or of "mainstream" versus "minority" heritage, are often inseparable from a wish for self-empowerment. Yet many writers and critics who have challenged the monolithic authority of white male literary historians remain in thrall to the norms and arguments of the dominant patriarchal culture, unwittingly upholding the criteria of those whom they assail. As a female immigrant of Cantonese descent, with the attendant sympathies and biases, I will survey and analyze what I construe to be the "feminist" and "heroic" impulses that have invigorated Chinese American literature but at the same time divided its authors and critics.

I

Sexual politics in Chinese America reflect complex cultural and historical legacies. The paramount importance of patrilineage in traditional Chinese culture predisposes many Chinese Americans of the older generations to favor male over female offspring (a preference even more overt than that which still underlies much of white America). At the same time Chinese American men, too, have been confronted with a history of inequality and of painful "emasculation." The fact that 90 percent of early Chinese immigrants were male, combined with antimiscegenation laws and laws prohibiting Chinese laborers' wives from entering the United States, forced these immigrants to congregate in the bachelor communities of various Chinatowns, unable to father a subsequent generation. While many built railroads, mined gold, and cultivated plantations, their strenuous activities and contributions in these areas were often overlooked by white historians. Chinamen were better known to the American public as restaurant cooks, laundry workers, and waiters, jobs traditionally considered "women's work."[2]

The same forms of social and economic oppression of Chinese American women and men, in conjunction with a long-standing Orientalist tradition that casts the Asian in the role of the silent and passive Other,[3] have in turn provided material for degrading sexual representations of the Chinese in American popular culture. Elaine H. Kim notes, for instance, that the stereotype of Asian women as submissive and dainty sex objects has given rise to an "enormous demand for X-rated films featuring Asian women and the emphasis on bondage in pornographic materials about Asian women," and that "the popular image of alluring and exotic 'dream girls of the mysterious East' has created a demand for 'Oriental' bath house workers in American cities as well as a booming business in mail order marriages."[4] No less insidious are the inscriptions of Chinese men in popular culture. Frank Chin, a well-known writer and one of the most outspoken revisionists of Asian American history, describes how the American silver screen casts doubts on Chinese American virility:

> The movies were teachers. In no uncertain terms they taught America that we were lovable for being a race of sissies . . . living to accommodate the whitemen. Unlike the white stereotype of the evil black stud, Indian rapist, Mexican macho, the evil of the evil Dr. Fu Manchu was not sexual, but homosexual. . . . Dr. Fu, a man wearing a long dress, batting his eyelashes, surrounded by muscular black servants in loin clothes, and with his bad habit of caressingly touching white men on the leg, wrist, and face with his long fingernails is not so much a threat as he is a frivolous offense to white manhood. [Charlie] Chan's gestures are the same, except that he doesn't touch, and instead of being graceful like Fu in flowing robes, he is awkward in a baggy suit and clumsy. His sexuality is the source of a joke running through all of the forty-seven Chan films. The large family of the bovine detective isn't the product of sex, but animal husbandry. . . . He *never gets into violent things.* [my emphasis][5]

According to Chin and Jeffery Paul Chan, also a writer, "Each racial stereotype comes in two models, the acceptable model and the unacceptable model. . . . The unacceptable model is unacceptable because he cannot be controlled by whites. The acceptable model is acceptable because he is tractable. There is racist hate and racist love."[6] Chin and Chan believe that while the "masculine" stereotypes of blacks, Indians, and Mexicans are generated by "racist hate," "racist love" has been lavished on Chinese Americans, targets of "effeminate" stereotypes:

> The Chinese, in the parlance of the Bible, were raw material for the "flock," pathological sheep for the shepherd. The adjectives applied to the Chinese ring with scriptural imagery. We are meek, timid, passive, docile, industrious. We have the patience of Job. We are humble. A race without sinful manhood, born to mortify our flesh. . . . The difference between [other minority groups] and the Chinese was that the Christians, taking Chinese hospitality for timidity and docility, weren't afraid of us as they were of other races. They loved us, protected us. Love conquered.[7]

If "racist love" denies "manhood" to Asian men, it endows Asian women with an excess of "womanhood." Elaine Kim argues that because "the characterization of Asian men is a reflection of a white male perspective that defines the white man's virility, it is possible for Asian men to be viewed as asexual and the Asian woman as only sexual, imbued with an innate understanding of how to please and serve." The putative gender difference among Asian Americans—exaggerated out of all proportion in the popular imagination—has, according to Kim, created "resentment and tensions" between the sexes within the ethnic community.[8]

Although both the Asian American and the feminist movements of the late sixties have attempted to counter extant stereotypes, the conflicts between Asian American men and women have been all the more pronounced in the wake of the two movements. In the last two decades many Chinese American men—especially such writers and editors as Chin and Chan—have begun to correct the distorted images of Asian males projected by the dominant culture. Astute, eloquent, and incisive as they are in debunking racist myths, they are often blind to the biases resulting from their own acceptance of the patriarchal construct of masculinity. In Chin's discussion of Fu Manchu and Charlie Chan and in the perceptive contrast he draws between the stock images of Asian men and those of other men of color, one can detect not only homophobia but perhaps also a sexist preference for stereotypes that imply predatory violence against women over "effeminate" ones. Granted that the position taken by Chin may be little more than a polemicist stance designed to combat white patronage, it is disturbing that he should lend credence to the conventional association of physical aggression with manly valor. The hold of patriarchal conventions becomes even more evident in the following passage:

> The white stereotype of the Asian is unique in that it is the only racial stereotype completely devoid of manhood. Our nobility is that of an efficient housewife. At our worst we are contemptible because we are womanly, effeminate, devoid of all the traditionally masculine qualities of originality, daring, physical courage, creativity. We're neither straight talkin' or straight shootin'. The mere fact that four of the five American-born Chinese-American writers are women reinforces this aspect of the stereotype.[9]

In taking whites to task for demeaning Asians, these writers seem nevertheless to be buttressing patriarchy by invoking gender stereotypes, by disparaging domestic efficiency as "feminine," and by slotting desirable traits such as originality, daring, physical courage, and creativity under the rubric of masculinity.[10]

The impetus to reassert manhood also underlies the ongoing attempt by Chin, Chan, Lawson Inada, and Shawn Wong to reconstruct Asian American literary history. In their groundbreaking work *Aiiieeeee! An Anthology of Asian-American Writers,* these writers and coeditors deplored "the lack of a recognized style of Asian-American manhood." In a forthcoming sequel entitled *The Big Aiiieeeee! An Anthology of Asian American Writers,* they attempt to revive an Asian heroic tradition, celebrating Chinese and Japanese classics such as *The Art of War, Water Margin, Romance of the Three Kingdoms, Journey to the West,* and *Chushingura,* and honoring the renowned heroes and outlaws featured therein.[11]

The editors seem to be working in an opposite direction from that of an increasing number of feminists. While these Asian American spokesmen are recuperating a heroic tradition of their own, many women writers and scholars, building on existentialist and modernist insights, are reassessing the entire Western code of heroism. While feminists question such traditional values as competitive individualism and martial valor, the editors seize on selected maxims, purportedly derived from Chinese epics and war manuals, such as "I am the law," "life is war," and "personal integrity and honor is the highest value," and affirm the "ethic of private revenge."[12]

The *Aiiieeeee!* editors and feminist critics also differ on the question of genre. According to Chin, the literary genre that is most antithetical to the heroic tradition is autobiography, which he categorically denounces as a form of Christian confession:

> The fighter writer uses literary forms as weapons of war, not the expression of ego alone, and does not [waste] time with dandyish expressions of feeling and psychological attitudinizing. . . . A Chinese Christian is like a Nazi Jew. Confession and autobiography celebrate the process of conversion from an object of contempt to an object of acceptance. You love the personal experience of it, the oozings of viscous putrescence and luminous radiant guilt. . . . It's the quality of submission, not assertion that counts, in the confession and the autobiography. The autobiography combines the thrills and guilt of masturbation and the porno movie.[13]

Feminist critics, many of whom are skeptical of either/or dichotomies (in this instance fighting vs. feeling) and impatient with normative definitions of genre (not that Chin's criteria are normative), believe that women have always appropriated autobiography as a vehicle for *asserting*, however tentatively, their subjectivity. Celeste Schenck writes:

> the poetics of women's autobiography issues from its concern with constituting a female subject—a precarious operation, which . . . requires working on two fronts at once, *both* occupying a kind of center, assuming a subjectivity long denied, *and* maintaining the vigilant, disruptive stance that speaking from the postmodern margin provides—the autobiographical genre may be paradigmatic of all women's writing.[14]

Given these divergent views, the stage is set for a confrontation between "heroism" and "feminism" in Chinese American letters.

I I

The advent of feminism, far from checking Asian American chauvinism, has in a sense fueled gender antagonism, at least in the literary realm. Nowhere is this antagonism reflected more clearly than in the controversy that has erupted over Maxine Hong Kingston's *The Woman Warrior*. Classified as autobiography, the work describes the protagonist's struggle for self-definition amid Cantonese sayings such as "Girls are maggots in the rice," "It is more profitable to raise geese than daughters," "Feeding girls is feeding cowbirds" (pp. 51, 54). While the book has received popular acclaim, especially among feminist critics, it has been censured by several Chinese American critics—mostly male but also some female—who tax Kingston for misrepresenting Chinese and Chinese American culture, and for passing fiction off as autobiography. Chin (whose revulsion for autobiography we already know) wrote a satirical parody of *The Woman Warrior*; he casts aspersions on its historical status and places Kingston in the same company as the authors of Fu Manchu and Charlie Chan for confirming "the white fantasy that everything sick and sickening about the white self-image is really Chinese."[15] Jeffery Paul Chan castigates Knopf for publishing the book as "biography rather than fiction (which it obviously is)" and insinuates that a white female reviewer praises the book indiscriminately because it expresses "female anger."[16] Benjamin Tong openly calls it a "fashionably feminist work written with white acceptance in mind."[17] As Sau-ling Wong points out, "According to Kingston's critics, the most pernicious of the stereotypes which might be supported by *The Woman Warrior* is that of Chinese American men as sexist," and yet some Chinese American women "think highly of *The Woman Warrior* because it confirms their personal experiences with sexism."[18] In sum, Kingston is accused of falsifying culture and of reinforcing stereotype in the name of feminism.

At first glance the claim that Kingston should not have taken the liberty to infuse autobiography with fiction may seem to be merely a generic, gender-neutral criticism, but as Susan Stanford Friedman has pointed out, genre is all too often gendered.[19] Feminist scholars of autobiography have suggested that women writers often shy away from "objective" autobiography and prefer to use the form to reflect a private world, a subjective vision, and the life of the imagination. *The Woman Warrior*, though it departs from most "public" self-representations by men, is quite in line with such an autobiographical tradition. Yet for a "minority" author to exercise such artistic freedom is perilous business because white critics and reviewers persist in seeing creative expressions by her as no more than cultural history.[20] Members of the ethnic community are in turn upset if they feel they have been "misrepresented" by one of their own. Thus where Kingston insists on shuttling between the world of facts and the world of fantasy, on giving multiple versions of "truth" as subjectively perceived, her Chinese American detractors demand generic purity and historical accuracy. Perhaps precisely because this author is female, writing amid discouraging realities, she can only forge a viable and expansive identity by refashioning patriarchal myths and invoking imaginative possibilities.[21] Kingston's autobiographical act, far from betokening submission, as Chin believes, turns the self into a "heroine" and is in a sense an act of "revenge" (a word represented in Chinese by two ideographs which Kingston loosely translates as "report a crime") against both the Chinese and the white cultures that undermine her self-esteem. Discrediting her for taking poetic license is reminiscent of those white reviewers who reduce works of art by ethnic authors to sociohistorical documentary.

The second charge concerning stereotype is more overtly gender-based. It is hardly coincidental that the most unrelenting critics (whose grievance is not only against Kingston but also against feminists in general) have also been the most ardent champions of Chinese American "manhood." Their response is understandable. Asian American men have suffered deeply from racial oppression. When Asian American women seek to expose antifemale prejudices in their own ethnic community, the men are likely to feel betrayed.[22] Yet it is also undeniable that sexism still lingers as part of the Asian legacy in Chinese America and that many American-born daughters still feel its sting. Chinese American women may be at once sympathetic and angry toward the men in their ethnic community: sensitive to the marginality of these men but resentful of their male privilege.

I I I

Kingston herself seems to be in the grips of these conflicting emotions. The opening legend of *China Men* captures through myth some of the baffling intersections of gender and ethnicity in Chinese America and reveals the author's own double allegiance. The legend is borrowed and adapted from an eighteenth-century Chinese novel entitled *Flowers in the Mirror,* itself a fascinating work and probably one of the first "feminist" novels written by a man.[23] The male protagonist of this novel is Tang Ao, who in Kingston's version is captured in the Land of Women, where he is forced to have his feet bound, his ears pierced, his facial hair plucked, his cheeks and lips painted red—in short, to be transformed into an Oriental courtesan.

Since Kingston explicitly points out at the end of her legend that the Land of Women was in North America, critics familiar with Chinese American history will readily see that the ignominy suffered by Tang Ao in a foreign land symbolizes the emasculation of Chinamen by the dominant culture. Men of Chinese descent have encountered racial violence in the United States, both in the past and recently.[24] Kingston's myth is indeed intimating that the physical torment in their peculiar case is often tied to an affront to their manhood.

But in making women the captors of Tang Ao and in deliberately reversing masculine and feminine roles, Kingston also foregrounds constructions of gender. I cannot but see this legend as double-edged, pointing not only to the mortification of Chinese men in the New World but also to the subjugation of women both in old China and in America. Although the tortures suffered by Tang Ao seem palpably cruel, many Chinese women had for centuries been obliged to undergo similar mutilation. By having a man go through these ordeals instead, Kingston, following the author of *Flowers in the Mirror,* disrupts the familiar and commonplace acceptance of Chinese women as sexual objects. Her myth deplores on the one hand the racist debasement of Chinese American men, and on the other the sexist objectification of Chinese women. Although *China Men* mostly commemorates the founding fathers of Chinese America, this companion volume to *The Woman Warrior* is also suffused with "feminist anger." The opening myth suggests that the author objects as strenuously to the patriarchal practices of her ancestral culture as to the racist treatment of her forefathers in their adopted country.

Kingston reveals not only the similarities between Chinamen's and Chinese women's suffering but also the correlation between these men's umbrage at racism and their misogynist behavior. In one episode, the narrator's immigrant father, a laundryman who seldom opens his mouth except to utter obscenities about women, is cheated by a gypsy and harassed by a white policeman:

> When the gypsy baggage and the police pig left, we were careful not to be bad or noisy so that you [father] would not turn on us. We knew that it was to feed us you had to endure demons and physical labor. You screamed wordless male screams that jolted the house upright. . . . Worse than the swearing and the nightly screams were your silences when you punished us by not talking. You rendered us invisible, gone. (p. 8)

Even as the daughter deplores the father's "male screams" and brooding silences, she attributes his bad temper to his sense of frustration and emasculation in a white society. As in the analogous situations of Cholly Breedlove in Toni Morrison's *The Bluest Eye* and Grange Copeland in Alice Walker's *The Third Life of Grange Copeland,* what seems to be male tyranny must be viewed within the context of racial inequality. Men of color who have been abused in a white society are likely to attempt to restore their sense of masculinity by venting their anger at those who are even more powerless—the women and children in their families.

Kingston's attempt to write about the opposite sex in *China Men* is perhaps a tacit call for mutual empathy between Chinese American men and women. In an interview, the author likens herself to Tang Ao: just as Tang Ao enters the Land of Women and is made to feel what it means to be of the other gender, so Kingston, in writing *China Men,* enters the realm of men and, in her own words, becomes "the kind of woman who loves men and who can tell their stories." Perhaps, to extend the analogy further, she is trying to prompt her male readers to participate in and empathize with the experiences of women.[25] Where Tang Ao is made to feel what his female contemporaries felt, Chinese American men are urged to see parallels between their plight and that of Chinese American women. If Asian men have been emasculated in America, as the aforementioned male critics have themselves argued, they can best attest to the oppression of women who have long been denied male privilege.

I V

An ongoing effort to revamp Chinese American literary history will surely be more compelling if it is informed by mutual empathy between men and women. To return to an earlier point, I am of two minds about the ambitious attempt of the *Aiiieeeee!* editors to restore and espouse an Asian American heroic tradition. Born and raised in Hong Kong, I grew up reading many of the Chinese heroic epics—along with works of less heroic modes—and can appreciate the rigorous effort of the editors to introduce them to Asian American and non-Asian readers alike.[26] But the literary values they assign to the heroic canon also function as ideology. Having spoken out against the emasculation of Asian Americans in their introduction to *Aiiieeeee!,* they seem determined to show further that Chinese and Japanese Americans have a heroic—which is to say militant—heritage. Their propagation of the epic tradition appears inseparable from their earlier attempt to eradicate effeminate stereotypes and to emblazon Asian American manhood.[27] In this light, the special appeal held by the war heroes for the editors becomes rather obvious. Take, for example, Kwan Kung, in *Romance of the Three Kingdoms*: loud, passionate, and vengeful, this "heroic embodiment of martial self-sufficiency" is antithetical in every way to the image of the quiet, passive, and subservient Oriental houseboy. Perhaps the editors hope that the icon of this imposing Chinese hero will dispel myths about Chinese American tractability.

While acquaintance with some of the Chinese folk heroes may induce the American public to acknowledge that Chinese culture too has its Robin Hood and John Wayne, I remain uneasy about the masculinist orientation of the heroic tradition, especially as expounded by the editors who see loyalty, revenge, and individual honor as the overriding ethos that should be inculcated in (if not already absorbed by) Chinese Americans. If white media have chosen to highlight and applaud the submissive and nonthreatening characteristics of Asians, the Asian American editors are equally tendentious in underscoring the militant strain of their Asian literary heritage.[28] The refutation of effeminate stereotypes through the glorification of machismo merely perpetuates patriarchal terms and assumptions.

Is it not possible for Chinese American men to recover a cultural space without denigrating or erasing "the feminine"? Chin contends that "use of the heroic tradition in Chinese literature as the source of Chinese American moral, ethical and esthetic universals is not literary rhetoric and smartass cute tricks, not wishful thinking, not theory, not demagoguery and prescription, but simple history."[29] However, even history, which is also a form of social construct, is not exempt from critical scrutiny. The Asian heroic tradition, like its Western counterpart, must be reevaluated so that both its strengths and its limitations can surface. The intellectual excitement and the emotional appeal of the tradition is indisputable: the strategic brilliance of characters such as Chou Yu and Chuko Liang in *Romance of the Three Kingdoms* rivals that of Odysseus, and the fraternal bond between the three sworn brothers—Liu Pei, Chang Fei, and Kuan Yu (Kwan Kung)—is no less moving than that between Achilles and Patrocles. But just as I no longer believe that Homer speaks for humanity (or even all mankind), I hesitate to subscribe wholeheartedly to the *Aiiieeeee!* editors' claim that the Asian heroic canon (composed entirely of work written by men, though it contains a handful of heroines) encompasses "Asian universals."

Nor do I concur with the editors that a truculent mentality pervades the Chinese heroic tradition, which generally places a higher premium on benevolence than on force and stresses the primacy of kinship and friendship over personal power. By way of illustration I will turn to the prototype for Kingston's "woman warrior"—Fa Mu Lan (also known as Hua Mulan and Fa Muk Lan). According to the original "Ballad of Mulan" (which most Chinese children, including myself, had to learn by heart), the heroine in joining the army is prompted neither by revenge nor by personal honor but by filial piety. She enlists under male disguise to take the place of her aged father. Instead of celebrating the glory of war, the poem describes the bleakness of the battlefield and the loneliness of the daughter (who sorely misses her parents). The use of understatement in such lines as "the general was killed after hundreds of combats" and "the warriors returned in ten years" (my translation) connotes the cost and duration of battles. The "Ballad of Mulan," though it commits the filial and courageous daughter to public memory, also contains a pacifist subtext—much in the way that the *Iliad* conceals an antiwar message beneath its martial trappings. A reexamination of the Asian heroic tradition may actually reveal that it is richer and more sophisticated than the *Aiiieeeee!* editors, bent on finding belligerent models, would allow.[30]

Kingston's adaptation of the legend in *The Woman Warrior* is equally multivalent. Fa Mu Lan as recreated in the protagonist's fantasy does excel in martial arts, but her power is derived as much from the words carved on her back as from her military skills. And the transformed heroine still proves problematic as a model since she can only exercise her power when in male armor. As I have argued elsewhere, her military distinction, insofar as it valorizes the ability to be ruthless and violent—"to fight like a man"—affirms rather than subverts patriarchal mores.[31] In fact, Kingston discloses in an interview that the publisher is the one who entitled the book "The Woman Warrior"; she herself (who is a pacifist) resists complete identification with the war heroine:

> I don't really like warriors. I wish I had not had a metaphor of a warrior, a person who uses weapons and goes to war. I guess I always have in my style a doubt about wars as a way of solving things.[32]

Aside from the fantasy connected with Fa Mu Lan, the book has little to do with actual fighting. The real battle that runs through the work is one against silence and invisibility. Forbidden by her mother to tell a secret, unable to read aloud in English while first attending American school, and later fired for protesting against racism, the protagonist eventually speaks with a vengeance through writing—through a heroic act of self-expression. At the end of the book her tutelary genius has changed from Fa Mu Lan to Ts'ai Yen—from warrior to poet.

Kingston's commitment to pacifism—through re-visioning and recontextualizing ancient "heroic" material—is even more evident in her most recent book, *Tripmaster Monkey*. As though anticipating the editors of *The Big Aiiieeeee!*, the author alludes frequently to the Chinese heroic tradition, but always with a feminist twist. The protagonist of this novel, Wittman Ah Sing, is a playwright who loves *Romance of the Three Kingdoms* (one of the aforementioned epics espoused by Chin). Kingston's novel culminates with Wittman directing a marathon show he has written based on the *Romance*. At the end of the show he has a rather surprising illumination:

> He had made up his mind: he will not go to Viet Nam or to any war. He had staged the War of the Three Kingdoms as heroically as he could, which made him start to understand: The three brothers and Cho Cho were masters of the war; they had worked out strategies and justifications for war so brilliantly that their policies and their tactics are used today, even by governments with nuclear-powered weapons. And they lost. The clanging and banging fooled us, but now we know—they lost. Studying the mightiest war epic of all time, Wittman changed—beeen!—into a pacifist. Dear American monkey, don't be afraid. Here, let us tweak your ear, and kiss your other ear.[33]

The seemingly easy transformation of Wittman—who is curiously evocative of Chin in speech and manner—is achieved through the pacifist author's sleight of hand. Nevertheless, the novel does show that it is possible to celebrate the ingenious strategies of the ancient warriors without embracing, wholesale, the heroic code that motivates their behavior, and without endorsing violence as a positive expression of masculinity.[34]

Unfortunately, the ability to perform violent acts implied in the concepts of warrior and epic hero is still all too often mistaken for manly courage; and men who have been historically subjugated are all the more tempted to adopt a militant stance to manifest their masculinity. In the notorious Moynihan report on the black family, "military service for Negroes" was recommended as a means to potency:

> Given the strains of the disorganized and matrifocal family life in which so many Negro youth come of age, the Armed Forces are a dramatic and desperately needed change: a world away from women, a world run by strong men of unquestioned authority.[35]

Moynihan believed that placing black men in an "utterly masculine world" would strengthen them. The black men in the sixties who worshipped figures that exploited and brutalized women likewise conflated might and masculinity. Toni Cade, who cautions against "equating black liberation with black men gaining access to male privilege," offers an alternative to patriarchal prescriptions for manhood:

> Perhaps we need to let go of all notions of manhood and femininity and concentrate on Blackhood. . . . It perhaps takes less heart to pick up the gun than to face the task of creating a new identity, a self, perhaps an androgynous self.[36]

If Chinese American men use the Asian heroic dispensation to promote male aggression, they may risk remaking themselves in the image of their oppressors—albeit under the guise of Asian panoply. Precisely because the racist treatment of Asians has taken the peculiar form of sexism—insofar as the indignities suffered by men of Chinese descent are analogous to those traditionally suffered by women—we must refrain from seeking antifeminist solutions to racism. To do otherwise reinforces not only patriarchy but also white supremacy.

Well worth heeding is Althusser's caveat that when a dominant ideology is integrated as common sense into the consciousness of the dominated, the dominant class will continue to prevail.[37] Instead of tailoring ourselves to white ideals, Asian Americans may insist on alternative habits and ways of seeing. Instead of drumming up support for Asian American "manhood," we may consider demystifying popular stereotypes while reappropriating what Stanford Lyman calls the "kernels of truth" in them that are indeed part of our ethnic heritage. For instance, we need not accept the Western association of Asian self-restraint with passivity and femininity. I, for one, believe that the respectful demeanor of many an Asian and Asian American indicates, among other things, a willingness to listen to others and to resolve conflict rationally or tactfully.[38] Such a collaborative disposition—be it Asian or non-Asian, feminine or masculine—is surely no less valid and viable than one that is vociferous and confrontational.

V

Although I have thus far concentrated on the gender issues in the Chinese American cultural domain, they do have provocative implications for feminist theory and criticism. As Elizabeth Spelman points out, "It is not easy to think about gender, race, and class in ways that don't obscure or underplay their effects on one another."[39] Still, the task is to develop paradigms that can admit these crosscurrents and that can reach out to women of color and perhaps also to men.

Women who value familial and ethnic solidarity may find it especially difficult to rally to the feminist cause without feeling divided or without being accused of betrayal, especially when the men in their ethnic groups also face social iniquities. Kingston, for instance, has tried throughout her work to mediate between affirming her ethnic heritage and undermining patriarchy. But she feels that identification with Asian men at times inhibits an equally strong feminist impulse. Such split loyalties apparently prompted her to publish *The Woman Warrior* and *China Men* separately, though they were conceived and written together as an "interlocking story." Lest the men's stories "undercut the feminist viewpoint," she separated the female and the male stories into two books. She says, "I care about men . . . as much as I care about women. . . . Given the present state of affairs, perhaps men's and women's experiences have to be dealt with separately for now, until more auspicious times are with us."[40]

Yet such separation has its dangers, particularly if it means that men and women will continue to work in opposing directions, as reflected in the divergences between the proponents of the Asian heroic tradition and Asian American feminists. Feminist ideas have made little inroad in the writing of the *Aiiieeeee!* editors, who continue to operate within patriarchal grids. White feminists, on the other hand, are often oblivious to the fact that there are other groups besides women who have been "feminized" and seem puzzled when women of color do not readily rally to their camp.

The recent shift from feminist studies to gender studies suggests that the time has come to look at women and men together. I hope the shift will also entice both men and women to do the looking and, by so doing, strengthen the alliance between gender studies and ethnic studies. Lest feminist criticism remain in the wilderness, white scholars must reckon with race and class as integral experiences for both men and women, and acknowledge that not only female voices but the voices of many men of color have been historically silenced or dismissed. Expanding the feminist frame of reference will allow certain existing theories to be interrogated or reformulated.[41] Asian American men need to be wary of certain pitfalls in using what Foucault calls "reverse discourse," in demanding legitimacy "in the same vocabulary, using the same categories by which [they were] disqualified."[42] The ones who can be recruited into the field of gender studies may someday see feminists as allies rather than adversaries, and proceed to dismantle not just white but also male supremacy. Women of color should not have to undergo a self-division resulting from having to choose between female and ethnic identities. Chinese American women writers may find a way to negotiate the tangle of sexual and racial politics in all its intricacies, not just out of a desire for "revenge" but also out of a sense of "loyalty." If we ask them to write with a vigilant eye against possible misappropriation by white readers or against possible offense to "Asian American manhood," however, we will end up implicitly sustaining racial and sexual hierarchies. All of us need to be conscious of our "complicity with the gender ideologies" of patriarchy, whatever its origins, and to work toward notions of gender and ethnicity that are nonhierarchical, nonbinary, and nonprescriptive; that can embrace tensions rather than perpetuate divisions.[43] To reclaim cultural traditions without getting bogged down in the mire of traditional constraints, to attack stereotypes without falling prey to their binary opposites, to chart new topographies for manliness and womanliness, will surely demand genuine heroism.

NOTES

1. Research for this essay is funded in part by an Academic Senate grant and a grant from the Institute of American Cultures and the Asian American Studies Center, UCLA. I wish to thank the many whose help, criticism, and encouragement have sustained me through the mentally embattled period of writing this essay: Kim Crenshaw, Donald Goellnicht, Marianne Hirsch, Evelyn Fox Keller, Elaine Kim, Elizabeth Kim, Ken Lincoln, Gerard Mard, Rosalind Melis, Jeff Spielberg, Sau-ling Wong, Richard Yarborough, and Stan Yogi. A version of this chapter was delivered at the 1989 MLA Convention in Washington, D.C. My title alludes not only to Maxine Hong Kingston's *The Woman Warrior* and *China Men* but also Frank Chin's *The Chickencoop Chinaman* and *The Chinaman Pacific & Frisco R. R. Co.* The term "Chinamen" has acquired divers connotations through time: "In the early days of Chinese American history, men called themselves 'Chinamen' just as other newcomers called themselves 'Englishmen' or 'Frenchmen': the term distinguished them from the 'Chinese' who remained citizens of China, and also showed that they were not recognized as Americans. Later, of course, it became an insult. Young Chinese Americans today are reclaiming the word because of its political and historical precision, and are demanding that it be said with dignity and not for name-calling" (Kingston, "San Francisco's Chinatown: A View from the Other Side of Arnold Genthe's Camera," *American Heritage,* December 1978, 37). In my article the term refers exclusively to men.
2. The devaluation of daughters is a theme explored in *The Woman Warrior* (1976; New York: Vintage, 1977); as this book suggests, this aspect of patriarchy is upheld no less by women than by men. The "emasculation" of Chinese American men is addressed in *China Men* (1980; New York: Ballantine, 1981), in which Kingston attempts to reclaim the founders of Chinese America. Subsequent page references to these two books will appear in the text. Detailed accounts of early Chinese immigrant history can be found in Victor G. Nee and Brett De Bary Nee, *Longtime Californ': A Documentary Study of an American Chinatown* (1973; New York: Pantheon, 1981); and Ronald Takaki, *Strangers from a Different Shore: A History of Asian Americans* (Boston: Little, Brown, 1989), 79–131.
3. See Edward Said, *Orientalism* (New York: Vintage, 1979). Although Said focuses on French and British representations of the Middle East, many of his insights also apply to American perceptions of the Far East.
4. "Asian American Writers: A Bibliographical Review," *American Studies International* 22, no. 2 (October 1984): 64.
5. "Confessions of the Chinatown Cowboy," *Bulletin of Concerned Asian Scholars* 4, no. 3 (1972): 66.

6. "Racist Love," in *Seeing through Shuck,* ed. Richard Kostelanetz (New York: Ballantine, 1972), 65, 79. Although the cinematic image of Bruce Lee as a Kung-fu master might have somewhat countered the feminine representations of Chinese American men, his role in the only Hollywood film in which he appeared before he died was, in Elaine Kim's words, "less a human being than a fighting machine" ("Asian Americans and American popular Culture," in *Dictionary of Asian American History,* ed. Hyung-Chan Kim [New York: Greenwood Press, 1986], 107).

7. "Racist Love," 69.

8. "Asian American Writers: A Bibliographical Review," 64.

9. "Racist Love," 68. The five writers under discussion are Pardee Lowe, Jade Snow Wong, Virginia Lee, Betty Lee Sung, and Diana Chang.

10. Similar objections to the passage have been raised by Merle Woo in "Letter to Ma," in *This Bridge Called My Back: Writings by Radical Women of Color,* ed. Cherríe Moraga and Gloria Anzaldúa (1981; New York: Kitchen Table, 1983), 145; and Elaine Kim in *Asian American Literature: An Introduction to the Writings and Their Social Context* (Philadelphia: Temple University Press, 1982), 189. Richard Yarborough delineates a somewhat parallel conundrum about manhood faced by African American writers in the nineteenth century and which, I believe, persists to some extent to this day; see "Race, Violence, and Manhood: The Masculine Ideal in Frederick Douglass's 'Heroic Slave,'" in *Frederick Douglass: New Literary and Historical Essays,* ed. Eric J. Sundquist (Cambridge: Cambridge University Press, 1990). There is, however, an important difference between the dilemma faced by the African American men and that faced by Asian American men. While writers such as William Wells Brown and Frederick Douglass tried to reconcile the white inscription of the militant and sensual Negro and the white ideal of heroic manhood, several Chinese American male writers are tying to disprove the white stereotype of the passive and effeminate Asian by invoking its binary opposite.

11. *Aiiieeeee! An Anthology of Asian-American Writers* (1974; Washington, D.C.: Howard University Press, 1983), xxxviii; *The Big Aiiieeeee! An Anthology of Chinese American and Japanese American Literature,* ed. Jeffrey Chan et al. (New York: Meridian, 1991). All the Asian classics cited are available in English translations: Sun Tzu, *The Art of War,* trans. Samuel B. Griffith (London: Oxford University Press, 1963); Shi Nai'an and Luo Guanzhong, *Outlaws of the Marsh* [*The Water Margin*], trans. Sidney Shapiro (Beijing: Foreign Language Press, and Bloomington: Indiana University Press, 1981); Luo Guan-Zhong, *Romance of the Three Kingdoms,* trans. C. H. Brewitt-Taylor (Singapore: Graham Brash, 1986), 2 vols.; Wu Ch'eng-en, *Journey to the West,* trans. Anthony Yu (Chicago: University of Chicago Press, 1980), 4 vols.; Takeda Izumo, Miyoshi Shoraku, and Namiki Senryu, *Chushingura (The Treasury of Loyal Retainers),* trans. Donald Keene (New York: Columbia University Press, 1971). I would like to thank Frank Chin for allowing me to see an early draft of *The Big Aiiieeeee!.* For a foretaste of his exposition of the Chinese heroic tradition, see "This Is Not an Autobiography," *Genre* 18 (1985): 109–130.

12. The feminist works that come to mind include Paula Gunn Allen, *The Sacred Hoop: Recovering the Feminine in American Indian Traditions* (Boston: Beacon, 1986); Nina Auerbach, *Communities of Women: An Idea in Fiction* (Cambridge: Harvard University Press, 1978); Zillah R. Eisenstein, *The Radical Future of Liberal Feminism* (New York: Longman, 1981); Carol Gilligan, *In a Different Voice: Psychological Theory and Women's Development* (Cambridge: Harvard University Press, 1982); Christa Wolf, *Cassandra: A Novel and Four Essays,* trans. Jan van Heurck (New York: Farrar, 1984). The Chinese maxims appear in the introduction to *The Big Aiiieeeee! An Anthology of Chinese American and Japanese American Literature,* ed. Jeffrey Chan, et al. (New York: Meridian 1991) and are quoted with the editors' permission. The same maxims are cited in Frank Chin, "This Is Not an Autobiography."

13. Chin, "This Is Not An Autobiography," 112, 122, 130.

14. "All of a Piece: Women's Poetry and Autobiography," in *Life/Lines: Theorizing Women's Autobiography,* ed. Bella Brodzki and Celeste Schenck (Ithaca, N.Y.: Cornell University

Press, 1988), 286. See also Estelle Jelinek, ed., *Women's Autobiography: Essays in Criticism* (Bloomington: Indiana University Press, 1980); Donna Stanton, *The Female Autograph* (New York: New York Literary Forum, 1984); Sidonie Smith, *Poetics of Women's Autobiography: Marginality and the Fictions of Self-Representation* (Bloomington: Indiana University Press, 1987).

15. "The Most Popular Book in China," in *Quilt 4,* ed. Ishmael Reed and Al Young (Berkeley, Calif.: Quilt, 1984), 12. The essay is republished as the "Afterword" in *The Chinaman Pacific & Frisco R. R. Co.* The literary duel between Chin, a self-styled "Chinatown Cowboy," and Kingston, an undisguised feminist, closely parallels the paper war between Ishmael Reed and Alice Walker.

16. "The Mysterious West," *New York Review of Books,* 28 April 1977, 41.

17. "Critic of Admirer Sees Dumb Racist," *San Francisco Journal,* 11 May 1977, 20.

18. "Autobiography as Guided Chinatown Tour?" in *Multicultural Autobiography: American Lives,* ed. James Robert Payne (Knoxville: University of Tennessee Press, 1992). See also Deborah Woo, "The Ethnic Writer and the Burden of 'Dual Authenticity': The Dilemma of Maxine Hong Kingston," forthcoming in *Amerasia Journal.* Reviews by Chinese American women who identify strongly with Kingston's protagonist include Nellie Wong, "The Woman Warrior," *Bridge* (Winter 1978): 46–48; and Suzi Wong, review of *The Woman Warrior, Amerasia Journal* 4, no. 1 (1977): 165–167.

19. "Gender and Genre Anxiety: Elizabeth Barrett Browning and H. D. as Epic Poets," *Tulsa Studies in Women's Literature* 5, no. 2 (fall 1986): 203–228.

20. Furthermore, a work highlighting sexism within an ethnic community is generally more palatable to the reading public than a work that condemns racism. *The Woman Warrior* addresses both forms of oppression, but critics have focused almost exclusively on its feminist themes.

21. Susanne Juhasz argues that because women have traditionally lived a "kind of private life, that of the imagination, which has special significance due to the outright conflict between societal possibility and imaginative possibility, [Kingston] makes autobiography from fiction, from fantasy, from forms that have conventionally belonged to the novel" ("Towards a Theory of Form in Feminist Autobiography," *International Journal of Women's Studies* 2, no. 1 [1979]: 62).

22. Cf. similar critical responses in the African American community provoked by Alice Walker's *The Color Purple* and Toni Morrison's *Beloved.* Although I limit my discussion to sexual politics in Chinese America, Asian American women are just as vulnerable to white sexism, as the denigrating stereotypes discussed earlier by Kim suggest.

23. Li Ju-Chen, *Flowers in the Mirror,* trans. and ed. Lin Tai-Yi (London: Peter Owen, 1965).

24. A recent case has been made into a powerful public television documentary: "Who Killed Vincent Chin?" (directed by Renee Tajima and Christine Choy, 1989). Chin, who punched a white auto worker in Detroit in response to his racial slurs, was subsequently battered to death with a baseball bat by the worker and his stepson.

25. The interview was conducted by Kay Bonetti for the American Audio Prose Library (Columbia, Mo., 1986). Jonathan Culler has discussed the various implications, for both sexes, of "Reading as a Woman" (*On Deconstruction: Theory and Criticism after Structuralism* [Ithaca, N.Y.: Cornell University Press, 1982], 43–64); see also *Men in Feminism,* ed. Alice Jardine and Paul Smith (New York: Methuen, 1987).

26. The other modes are found in works as diverse as T'ao Ch'ien's poems (pastoral), Ch'u Yuan's *Li sao* (elegiac), selected writings by Lao Tzu and Chuang Tzu (metaphysical), and P'u Sung-ling's *Liao-Chai Chih I* (Gothic). (My thanks to Shu-mei Shih and Adam Schorr for helping me with part of the romanization.) One must bear in mind, however, that Asian and Western generic terms often fail to correspond. For example, what the *Aiiieeeee!* editors call "epics" are loosely classified as "novels" in Chinese literature.

27. Epic heroes, according to C. M. Bowra, are "the champions of man's ambitions" seeking to "win as far as possible a self-sufficient manhood" (*Heroic Poetry* [London: Macmillan, 1952], 14). Their Chinese counterparts are no exception.

28. Benjamin R. Tong argues that the uneducated Cantonese peasants who made up the majority of early Chinese immigrants were not docile but venturesome and rebellious, that putative Chinese traits such as meekness and obedience to authority were in fact "reactivated" in America in response to white racism ("The Ghetto of the Mind," *Amerasia Journal* 1, no. 3 [1971]: 1–31). Chin, who basically agrees with Tong, also attributes the submissive and "unheroic" traits of Chinese Americans to Christianity ("This Is Not an Autobiography"). While Tong and Chin are right in distinguishing the Cantonese folk culture of the early immigrants from the classical tradition of the literati, they underestimate the extent to which mainstream Chinese thought infiltrated Cantonese folk imagination, wherein the heroic ethos coexists with Buddhist beliefs and Confucian teachings (which do counsel self-restraint and obedience to parental and state authority). To attribute the "submissive" traits of Chinese Americans entirely to white racism or to Christianity is to discount the complexity and the rich contradictions of the Cantonese culture and the resourceful flexibility and adaptability of the early immigrants.

29. "This Is Not an Autobiography," 127.

30. Conflicting attitudes toward Homeric war heroes are discussed in Katherine Callen King, *Achilles: Paradigms of the War Hero from Homer to the Middle Ages* (Berkeley: University of California Press, 1987). Pacifist or at least antikilling sentiments can be found in the very works deemed "heroic" by Chin and the editors. *Romance of the Three Kingdoms* not only dramatizes the senseless deaths and the ravages of war but also betrays a wishful longing for peace and unity, impossible under the division of "three kingdoms." Even *The Art of War* sets benevolence above violence and discourages actual fighting and killing: "To subdue the enemy without fighting is the acme of skill" (77).

31. "'Don't Tell': Imposed Silences in *The Color Purple* and *The Woman Warrior*," *PMLA* (March 1988): 166. I must add, however, that paradoxes about manhood inform Chinese as well as American cultures. The "contradictions inherent in the bourgeois male ideal" are pointed out by Yarborough: "the use of physical force is, at some levels, antithetical to the middle-class privileging of self-restraint and reason: yet an important component of conventional concepts of male courage is the willingness to use force" ("Race, Violence, and Manhood "). Similarly, two opposing ideals of manhood coexist in Chinese culture, that of a civil scholar who would never stoop to violence and that of a fearless warrior who would not brook insult or injustice. Popular Cantonese maxims such as "a superior *man* would only move his mouth but not his hands" (i.e., would never resort to physical combat) and "he who does not take revenge is not a superior man" exemplify the contradictions.

32. Interview conducted by Kay Bonetti.

33. *Tripmaster Monkey: His Fake Book* (New York: Knopf, 1989), 348.

34. I am aware that a forceful response to oppression is sometimes necessary, that it is much easier for those who have never encountered physical blows and gunshots to maintain faith in nonviolent resistance. My own faith was somewhat shaken while watching the tragedy of Tiananmen on television; on the other hand, the image of the lone Chinese man standing in front of army tanks reinforced my belief that there is another form of heroism that far excels brute force.

35. Lee Rainwater and William L. Yancey, *The Moynihan Report and the Politics of Controversy* (Cambridge: The M.I.T. Press, 1967), 88 (p. 42 in the original report by Daniel Patrick Moynihan).

36. "On the Issue of Roles," in *The Black Woman: An Anthology,* ed. Toni Cade (York, Ont.: Mentor-NAL, 1970), 103; see also bell hooks, *Ain't I a Woman: Black Women and Feminism* (Boston: South End Press, 1981), 87–117.

37. *Lenin and Philosophy and Other Essays* (New York: Monthly Review Press, 1971), 174–183.

38. Of course, Asians are not all alike, and most generalizations are ultimately misleading. Elaine Kim pointed out to me that "It's popularly thought that Japanese strive for peaceful resolution of conflict and achievement of consensus while Koreans—for material as much as metaphysical reasons—seem at times to encourage combativeness in one

another" (personal correspondence, quoted with permission). Differences within each national group are no less pronounced.

39. *Inessential Woman: Problems of Exclusion in Feminist Thought* (Boston: Beacon, 1988), 115. I omitted class from my discussion only because it is not at the center of the literary debate.

40. Elaine Kim, *Asian American Literature: An Introduction to the Writings and Their Social Context* (Philadelphia: Temple University Press, 1982), 209.

41. Donald Goellnicht, for instance, has argued that a girl from a racial minority "experiences not a single, but a double subject split; first, when she becomes aware of the gendered position constructed for her by the symbolic language of patriarchy; and second, when she recognizes that discursively and socially constructed positions of racial difference also obtain . . . [that] the 'fathers' of her racial and cultural group are silenced and degraded by the Laws of the Ruling Fathers" ("Father Land and/or Mother Tongue: The Divided Female Subject in *The Woman Warrior* and *Obasan*," paper delivered at the MLA Convention, 1988).

42. *The History of Sexuality,* vol. 1, trans. Robert Hurley (New York: Vintage, 1980), 101.

43. Teresa de Lauretis, *Technologies of Gender: Essays on Theory, Film, and Fiction* (Bloomington: Indiana University Press, 1987), 11.

WOMEN IN EXILE

GENDER RELATIONS IN THE ASIAN INDIAN

COMMUNITY IN THE UNITED STATES

Sayantani DasGupta and Shamita Das Dasgupta

CHARTING THE CHASM

"It would be much easier if you were a lesbian," my friend Sanjay[1] recently suggested in response to my queries about available Indian men. "There are so many wonderful Indian women, political and progressive, who would fit you perfectly," he added. "Can't think of one man though!" I sighed. Being heterosexual, I thought, was clearly not all it was cracked up to be.

Despite my raising her with strong feminist values, and trying to inculcate in her the importance of women's self-sufficiency, it became apparent early on that my daughter intended to eventually marry a man and have children. I suppose my own example, as a wife, mother, and feminist activist, was a stronger motivator than all my warnings. However, as my daughter grew older, it became clear that finding a partner would not be very easy. Her pride in and identification with her Indian heritage inclined her toward choosing a compatriot, yet there were invisible obstacles that seemed to thwart this sympathy at its roots. Often, to my judicious inquiries about why she would not go out with Indian men, she exasperatedly replied, "You don't seem to understand, Indian men don't like women like me."

I recently saw the movie Waiting to Exhale, *adapted from Terry Macmillan's novel, in which four African American women mourn the lack of "good" (read: educated, sensitive, kind, honest, loving, truthful, steadfast) African American men. Despite being awed by both Angela Basset's superb acting and phenomenal biceps, I hated the film. Having been brought up on strong feminist ethics, I have no patience for the idea that women, in this case, strong, intelligent, beautiful women, are somehow unfulfilled without men. I also have minimal tolerance for conversations that begin with the query, "Where are all the good (insert the relevant ethnic group) men out there?" Yet, as an Indian American woman in my mid-*

twenties, I find myself holding my breath, waiting to find a "good" (read: all that Macmillan's characters were searching for, plus politically progressive/socially conscious) Indian American man. And many of my fellow heterosexual Indian American activist women friends are doing the same. Yet, what's going on is more than a mere manhunt. There is an interesting dynamic at work among heterosexual Indian American men and women, and only by analyzing and defining the parameters of this dynamic can we fully exhale.

More and more young women of Indian descent complain that they are unable to find a partner within the community who is supportive and encouraging of their independence, assertiveness, activism, and ambition. Although statistics are not yet available, there seems to be a greater number of South Asian women marrying outside the community than their male counterparts. An immigrant mother once remarked ruefully about this phenomenon, "All the accomplished young women in our community seem to be leaving the fold by marriage!"

Indeed, the phenomenon of female exogamy in the Indian American community appears to be predominantly among outgoing, outspoken, and often activist young women. While many highly achieving second-generation women are becoming exogamous, many more of their male counterparts are voluntarily returning to their parents' natal land to find brides. There is obviously a mutual vote of no confidence being cast between the genders in the second generation of heterosexual Indian Americans. The question is, why?

As two members of the Indian American community, an immigrant mother and a U.S.-born daughter, we have witnessed this gender interplay with both personal and professional interest. While it clearly affects our own lives, the phenomenon of female exogamy also illuminates pivotal community issues such as gender role recreation, consolidation of male power, heterosexual relational models, and finally, community integrity. Our different perspectives and life experiences have allowed us, as collaborators, to view these issues from varied vantage points. Thus, we have jointly written this essay examining heterosexual relations and gender roles within the Indian American community, while maintaining our different voices through changes in the typeface. We are, however, only two unique voices: a mother and a daughter, a psychology professor and a medical student, a community activist and a writer. We do not presume to dictate any answers, rather, we aim to introduce questions and ultimately, to open a dialogue through which we can recognize the phenomena at work around us, and strive to define them rather than allow them to define us.

RECREATING GENDER ROLES

The Indian American community as we know it today comprises primarily those immigrants who came to this country after the relaxation of immigration laws in 1965. There is no doubt that these immigrants have found economic and professional success quickly in this country.[2] As a result, Indians, like other Asian immigrant communities, have been labeled as the "model minority," an idea created in the 1970s when journalists publicized the high educational levels and median incomes, as well as low crime rates, among Asian Americans. At the time, this brand of "model minority" was an argument against social welfare programs;

however, it has ultimately created political schisms between Asian Americans and other minority communities. Indeed, it is the "model minority" myth that is responsible for propagating the notion that Indians are free from social problems such as unemployment, poverty, racism, and delinquency. Popularization of the myth has not only colored the political and social attitudes of the mainstream, but has also been deeply internalized by Indians themselves. Consequently, Indian immigrants have become preoccupied with living up to, as well as participating in, the creation of the image of a perfect group.

On a recent trip to Nashville, where I had been invited to facilitate a series of gender workshops at an Indian American "Youth" Conference, I came face to face with a breakdown of the "model minority" stereotype. As a daughter of immigrants who came to the United States in the late 1960s for graduate studies, the Indian community I know is basically made up of "first-wave" immigrants: white-collar and professional workers. Having been raised in primarily white professional towns, the overt racism I faced during my life was confined almost entirely to the schoolyard. As soon as I grew older, the prejudice I faced based on culture or skin color was definitely insidious. "I don't even think of you as a minority," white Americans would say to me. "I mean, Asians are just like us." During my recent trip to Nashville, however, I was shocked to hear my workshop participants describe stereotypes pertaining to themselves. "Americans think we're all motel and 7–11 owners," commented the men. "They think we're cheap." The women added, "American men think Indian women are ditzy and stupid, that we're only good for having babies and cleaning the house." As a daughter of the first-wave immigrants, I had been protected from these stereotypes. Indeed, I had always struggled against the idea that Indian Americans were nothing but upwardly mobile, asexual, nerdy doctor/engineer/computer programmer types. Never did it occur to me that Indian American women of different communities were being labeled as "ditzy" or "stupid." I was deeply startled as the "model minority" myth crumbled before my eyes.

When the post-1965 immigrants moved to America, they left behind a familiar world of relatives and friends along with cultural institutions and information. Settling down in the United States required not only finding economic stability, but reinventing immigrant identities in the new context. Without any established standards and reference points, everything had to be renegotiated, and Indian American immigrants proceeded to rebuild the "familiar essentials" in their new home.[3]

The Indian American community's reconstruction of itself has been based primarily upon a reinvention of what it means to be a "good Indian." Faced with the external threats of racism, assimilation, and cultural dissolution, as well as the internal pressures of maintaining a "good face" consistent with the model minority image, the Indian American communities of the United States have closed ranks. Their redefinition of self involves an extremely rigid notion of "Indian-ness" that homogenizes diversity, rejects variety, and silences dissent.

Construction of this exemplary public face has been dominated by the wealthy and powerful Indian male bourgeoisie, which controls the community's religious, political, informational, and cultural institutions. This bourgeoisie created certain representations to embody the integrity of its idealized community. Primary among these icons is that of the Indian woman as chaste, modest, nurturing, obedient, and loyal. According to Anannya Bhattacharjee, "[T]he woman becomes a metaphor for the purity, the chastity, and the sanctity of the Ancient Spirit that is India."[4] Through this creation of an unblemished Asian Indian public face, the immigrant patriarchy has rested the validity of the entire community upon the submissiveness of the community's women. Thus, the "proper" behavior of both first-and second-generation Indian women in America has become a litmus test of community solidarity. In turn, women deviating from this idea of traditional Indian womanhood are considered traitors to the community. There is, thus, a general denial of feminist activism and women's strength as a part of Indian traditions.

As I became active in feminist groups and domestic violence work in my new home, many of the men I knew became alarmed that their wives were acquainted with me. Many declared jokingly (!) that they did not want their wives to be corrupted by me. Some even renamed our South Asian woman's group, Manavi[5] (which means primordial woman), changing it to "danavi," demoness. A few more sympathetic souls tried to unearth the reasons for my untoward preoccupations. "What happened to you to make you this way? Were you abused as a child or something?" The subtext was loud and clear that such activities are engaged in only by women who have somehow been warped. I became a thorn in the community's side.

Feminists and other activists are systematically marginalized from the Indian American hegemonic construction of "community," exemplified by incidents such as the 1995 barring of all women's groups, gay/lesbian groups, and other "political" organizations from the India Day Parade in New York City organized by the FIA (Federation of Indians in America). While it is well protected from all hints of diversity or dissent, the reinvented identity of the Indian American hegemony is also being kept intact through its inculcation in the community's sons and daughters. Indeed, although community festivals initially served immigrants' own nostalgia, they have become vehicles for cultural training of the "second generation." Since Indian American youth often have no real connection to the subcontinent beyond their immigrant parents, their cultural teachings are not only anachronistic, dating back to the India of the 1960s and 1970s known by the immigrant parents, but also heavily entrenched in the idealized, reinvented "familiar essentials" of the hegemony.

"The central task of any youth conference," reads a 1992 opinion letter in *India Abroad,* "is to inculcate in the young our values, traditions and heritage . . . (however) due to the failings of their parents and due to their own nonchalance, (Indian American youth) fail to appreciate the richness of their ancient heritage and its timeless values. At the same time, like adolescents everywhere, they succumb to imbibing the undesirable elements in American society."[6] The "undesirable elements" referred to here undoubtedly are what Nita Shah calls "the American culture of drugs, promiscuity, and rebelliousness."[7] However, there is a gender discrepancy in the community's response to such threats. Indeed, since it is the icon of the perfect Indian woman that upholds community integrity, so too are the daughters of the community disproportionately burdened with the preservation of culture in the form of religion, language, dress, food, and child-rearing.

Throughout my life, I have been involved in Indian community dances, poetry recitals, musical festivals, and pujas. While I and countless other little Indian girls were sari-swathed, paper-flower-garlanded, primped, and prodded for most of our youth, our male counterparts got off, for the most part, scot-free. The young women I met at a recent Indian

American "Youth" Conference perhaps said it best. "We girls are expected to deck out in Indian clothes at every bhangra," they complained, "But the guys can just wear their baggy jeans and backwards baseball caps. They dress like homeboys and no one says anything."

Of central importance in the cultural schooling of community "youth" is the careful preservation of gender roles. To this end, the "chastity" and "purity" of community daughters is much prized, evidenced by unequal parental restrictions on the autonomous dating behavior of daughters, and the increased vigilance against exogamy of girls.[8] As second-generation women are expected to be "chaste" and "pure," so too are they expected to be "docile" and "obedient." Indeed, most "second-generation" community members are taught to believe that Indian culture and political activism do not go together. Young women are raised to believe feminism—and ultimately, perhaps, women's strength—is anti-Indian.

Heroines and Strong Women

In a community whose integrity is based upon the iconography of women's passivity, history must be rewritten. Indeed, in order to maintain its flawless community façade, the Indian American hegemony has ignored the rich history of Indian women's contributions to various social change movements. Yet, as Indian women, we carry a long history of activism and social awareness, both within and outside the subcontinent.[9]

My father, who had participated in the Indian nationalist movement, filled my childhood with stories of the revolution. In most of these anecdotes, women were integral. In many, they were heroines. I myself would later observe women in the thick of various other political movements, such as the Naxalite movement of the late 1960s. My own lifelong and active involvement in fighting for women's rights, therefore, was never a surprise, nor an anomaly. Both my family in India and I considered it to be a natural progression of my thinking and beliefs.

From politics to the environment, from indigenous people's rights to health issues, from displacement of families to workers' rights, Indian women have always played an active role in social movements. Interestingly, most such activist women did not embrace either activism or family in their lives, but combined their multiple roles successfully. By choosing the path of activism, women did not forego the happiness of having a family.

My role models emerged from mythology and real life: goddesses, queens, freedom fighters, participants in social and political movements—women who were at the center, rather than the margins of society. My upbringing, although quite traditional in many ways, never convinced me that being a wife and mother and a social change agent were oppositional to each other. Although my parents had arranged my marriage when I was sixteen, they had not emphasized only the traditional "good wife" role to me. I was raised on Mahatma Gandhi's proclamation, "A woman who does not raise her voice against social injustices is committing injustice herself." Thus, when my daughter was growing up in the United States, my goal was to raise a socially conscious and active person, someone with a sense of justice and integrity.

One of my earliest memories is of a "Take Back the Night" march. I must have been five or six. I remember holding my mother's hand as we marched among throngs of other women, holding candles and raising their voices to illuminate the darkness. Later, frustrated with the racism inherent in the mainstream American women's movement, my mother would found the first South Asian women's organization in the United States, Manavi. I was fifteen, and by that age, extremely familiar with and comfortable within women's organizations. I was brought up marching. Yet, activism was not something "American" to me, nor was it something unique to my mother. I had grown up seeing a strong tradition of women's strength in India: from the mythical ferocity of the warrior goddess Durga to the very formidable presence of the women in my family. While I grew up hearing stories about my great-aunts, who fought and died in the Indian Independence Movement, I was able to meet in person my grandmother's friends: elderly white-sari-clad ladies who turned out to be Black Belts in Judo, double Ph.D.s and international language experts. I had no doubt that I came from a heritage of insuperable women.

A long tradition of women's strength has most strategically been lost in the process of immigration and self re-creation. For many Indian American women raised in the West, being "Indian" and being "feminist" are antithetical concepts.

More than once, young women have come up to me after one of my talks on college campuses and remarked, "But, you look just like my mother!" The declaration is not about my age, but a comment on the apparent incompatibility of my appearance and work. How could I, a married, middle-aged mother carrying the symbols of sari and bindi, be an activist? These symbols marked me as a traditional woman, and therefore as complacent and compliant.

The common assumption among Americans is that only "Westernization" leads women to be involved in politics, social change movements, or any kind of social activism. We Indian American women are seen as essentially passive, subservient, conservative, dependent, slavish, oppressed, and tradition-bound (read: backward). It is only by coming to the West and internalizing its culture that we can be free and emancipated. This characterization of Indian women is unambiguously articulated in Bharati Mukherjee's novel, *Jasmine*.[10] Mukherjee's heroine undergoes transformation from Indian/Eastern to American/Western and thereby is delivered from the tyranny of patriarchal oppression.[11] Thus, when Asian Indian women do become active forces, Westernization is given credit for it. Too many academics and lay people alike believe that immigration is responsible for Indian American women's liberation, that acculturation to Western culture has made Indian American women "progressive."

"What do you consider yourself?" I was asked by a "progressive" white American woman, "an Indian or a feminist?" It is this mainstream notion, that progressive politics and Asian heritage are somehow irreconcilable, that has maintained the silence around Asian women's activism. For the Indian American community, this attitude is not only an external one, but an internal one as well. Feminists in the community risk being considered "un-Indian" community betrayers. My mother, a long-time activist in the Indian American community, has managed to confuse community nay-sayers by maintaining a happy thirty-year marriage and stable position in the mainstream Indian American community while continuing her work with issues of domestic violence. Half the time, neither mainstream Americans nor mainstream Indian Americans realize exactly how subversive a person she is, since they are somehow lulled into security by her "proper" Indian appearance, attire, and almost ever-

present bindi. I am lucky in having her example. I know that while my feminism arises from a long tradition of Indian women's strength, my very Indian-ness is dependent upon my being a feminist. Yet, with my short hair, Western education, clothes and accent, my activism risks being attributed to my Westernization, a betrayal of my heritage.

While I was teaching a course on Third World women, a young Indian woman student stayed back after one class. The class discussions that day had been bleak, elaborating the various injustices women face on a day-to-day basis. When the other students had left, this young woman came up to me and said dejectedly, "I am so upset! We are doomed unless we learn from the West." She is not the only person who has expressed these sentiments. Another young woman student asked me once whether my daughter was politically active. On hearing my affirmation, she proudly declared, "My family is very traditional. I live within my heritage. I would never do something like that."

Those with this ahistorical perspective and understanding of Indian women have dismissed our work and labeled activists as traitors to the community. Consequently, many young men of the community dispute the femininity as well as the "Indian-ness" of activist women.

"Indian men hate us," my friend Preeti, a fellow outspoken Indian American woman and frequent Indian "Youth" Conference speaker, told me recently. "They just don't like the package." She added, "You may confuse them at first. You look all demure and sweet from the outside, but then you open your big mouth and the illusion crumbles. The fact is, most Indian American men just can't deal with a strong Indian woman." I've had this discussion with many other Indian women and my experiences confirm these sentiments. At a recent conference, I met an interesting, smart, funny and warm Indian American man–a fellow writer. However, our day-long chummy camaraderie turned around 180 degrees as soon as this young man attended my workshop and heard me speak. Since he seemed a fairly liberal person, I don't think it was my politics that offended him. Rather, I believe I somehow intimidated him. While there are politically progressive, even feminist, Indian American men, it seems that many of our heterosexual male counterparts have more stringent and usually more unrealistic expectations for us than for non-Indian women. As my friend Preeti says, "It's okay for their American girlfriends to be whatever they are. But as soon as an Indian guy dates an Indian woman, she's no good unless she can cook "daal" just like his Ma."

Rather than encouraging and accommodating women's activism, postcolonial conceptualizations deny variability in women's roles. In the West, there are basically two dichotomous models of women: the goddess and the whore. In fact, the ubiquity of these images has washed the existence of any other models from our minds. Similar to the image of the Western goddess, South Asian Hindu cultures have Devi, the chaste and benevolent ideal woman who supports and upholds the patriarchal order. There is also the "whore"-like fallen woman. However, between these two extremes is another powerful model available in the Asian Indian schema: Shakti. In real life, this image has been translated into the Virangana, the brave warrior woman. Viranganas are the numerous women leaders, from the Rani of Jhansi to Indira Gandhi, who throughout history have led battles against the enemy and struggles against injustice. Although the gentle Devi is the one all parents hope their daughters will emulate, the virangana is not marginalized in South Asia. She is very much respected and worshiped. Furthermore, she is not just a Hindu image. Within Islamic culture also, there are many women leaders we can claim as our models, including Khadija and Ayesha from the time of the prophet; Noorjehan, Jahanara, and many others from the Mughal times; Rokeya Sakhawat Hossain, Halima Khatun, Badrunnessa Begum, and numerous other freedom fighters from the nationalist movement. This tradition of viranganas and activist foremothers creates a space within subcontinental cultures for women's strength.

My grandmother, while a fairly traditional woman, has never pressured me to be domestic or docile. Indeed, because I have always been academically successful, she seems to consider me outside of the traditional womanly expectations. "You will be a great doctor," she tells me, "and heal the poor. You don't have time to worry about a household. That will be taken care of by others." Clearly, there is a traditional Indian space for me, as a successful woman, that is beyond the expectations of womanly normalcy.

In their transmigration to the United States, Indian immigrants failed to bring over these traditional spaces for Indian women's strength. Indeed, the role of the virangana, while alive and well in subcontinental cultures, has been wiped out in Indian American communities in favor of the more constricting "goddess"/"whore" or "good Indian girl"/"bad Indian girl" dichotomy. Not only traditional spaces, but Indian women's chronicles of activism in this country are also being denied. Early immigrant women who came here in the 1800s carved out a space for themselves amidst virulent social and legal racism. However, the post-1965 immigrants have rendered invisible the work of these early activists in their struggle to redefine themselves with an unblemished and monolithic public face.

MASCULINITY UNDER FIRE

Racism is not gender-neutral, but strikes at the essential "masculinity" and "femininity" of minority peoples. This fact is recognized in the African American community, where the phenomenon of black men's "emasculation" by mainstream America is a galvanizing point for many male activists. Indeed, the recent "Million Man March" on Washington, D.C. was partially an attempt to redefine African American masculinity and reclaim it from the jaws of racist parameters. In the Indian American community, racism also plays out in gendered terms. Indeed, for Indian American women's groups, the linking of minority "otherness" to our femininity is a well-recognized phenomenon.

When I was a teenager, if a car full of white men hooted at me, I was convinced they were making fun of me–ridiculing me as ugly, brown and undesirable. If a car full of nonwhite men were to do the same, I would recognize it as sexual harassment without convoluting the incident with my own sexual insecurities. Growing up as the only little brown-skinned girl on the block in the heart of the U.S. midwest, I was too often told my brown skin was "ugly". The combined effect of this rejection and an omnipresent Farrah Fawcett/Cheryl Ladd/Barbie white beauty standard convinced me that I, with my dark skin, black hair, and "foreign" ways, would never be beautiful. As a college student on a liberal New England campus, my brown skin went from "ugly" to "exotic." It was difficult not to enjoy the "exoticization" and "spiritualization" of my sexual self after the ego bruises of childhood.

While the effect of racism upon Indian American women's sexual self-concepts has been explored by our community,[12] the role racism plays in the development of Indian American masculine self-concepts is perhaps left unexplored. The list of stereotypes given to Indian men, and for that matter all Asian American men, include: nerdy, weak, unassertive, sneaky, smelly, sexist, and short. In contrast, the characteristics that form a cluster around Western masculinity are related to instrumentality and aggression. Western macho men are independent, strong, large, go-getters, and fighters. Despite the "sensitive male" movement of the '60s and '70s, the image of Western man as aggressive, powerful, and omnipotent has remained largely unchanged over the years. Since this masculine model is based upon the Western male, Indian and Asian men can hardly hope to measure up to it. In all areas of popular ideals of masculinity such as physique, sexuality, aggression, and athletics, the Asian Indian man falls short of the standards in no uncertain terms.

Thus, Indian men are perhaps "emasculated" through their very status as a "model minority." While African American men are marginalized and rendered impotent through their association with criminality, joblessness, and the drug culture, and Latino men are disempowered through their association with laziness, stupidity, and slothfulness, both groups of minority men are still considered "masculine," if not hypersexual and animalistic. On the other hand, the stereotypes afforded Asian American men are more in accordance with a sexist notion of "femininity." Asian American men are weak, delicate, precise, fragile, and ultimately, quellable.

> [The stereotype is] . . . of black and Latino men being sexually hungry, ravenous beasts (white men are scared of them); and of Asian men as being nerdy, asexual and gay (white men patronizing them). . . . Asian men have 1000 per cent more pressure to "prove" their heterosexuality. . . . Asian men are seen as not being capable of having power in general (because they are not seen as having sexual power), and black and Latino men are seen as not being able to handle power in general.[13]

David Henry Hwang's play *M. Butterfly* explores this emasculation of the Asian man through imperialism and machismo. "The West thinks of itself as masculine," says the character Song, an Asian man who for years fools his French lover into thinking he is a woman. "[B]ig guns, big industry, big money—so the East is feminine—weak, delicate, poor . . . but good at art, and full of inscrutable wisdom—the feminine mystique."[14] To explain why it was so easy to fool his French lover, Song adds, "(Because) . . . I am an Oriental. And being an Oriental, I could never be completely a man."[15]

Although both Asian Indian men and women are victims of negative stereotypes in the United States, the fundamental gender identity of only Indian men is brought into question. Although Indian women's gender identity is a target for racist assault, they are rarely considered unfeminine. Indeed, through images of exoticism and Eastern mystique, Indian American women are often labeled as hyperfeminine. Conversely, due to the impossibility of reaching Western masculine ideals, the gender typing of Asian Indian men becomes suspect. As "Oriental" men, Indian Americans can perhaps never be considered "fully male."

In contrast to this deprecation of the outside world, most Indian American men are treated at home with special privileges. There they can do little wrong and are allowed concessions in line with traditional patriarchal advantages and the strong subcontinental tradition of son-privilege. In the immigrant community, however, there is a contradiction between this internal reality and the external forces of U.S. racism. Even though he is brought up as the "raja" of his home and believes that such treatment is due him, the racism and neglect of the external world do not allow the Indian American young man to feel privileged. Thus, cultural identification is a double-edged sword: to be an Indian American in the mainstream community means being feminized. Thus, only through their Indian identity can young men find power in being a community "raja."

Many of the young Indian American men I grew up with initially rejected their heritage. Indeed, since community girls were unequally burdened with upholding cultural continuity, young men were able to reject "Indian-ness" in dress, food, and language. Many young men I knew tried to be "ultra-American" by lifting weights, participating in sports, joining mainstream fraternities, guzzling beers, and even through dating only non-Indian women. However, I've been noticing a change among the men slightly younger than I am. Perhaps because the men my age were unable to compete successfully with American standards of masculinity, younger men seem to be finding their sense of manhood through cultural identification. "We come from a strong heritage, a good heritage," a young man recently proclaimed at an Indian American "youth" conference. "Do we really want to be like these Americans, sleeping around, dressing like women, having no morals at all?" As he became more and more agitated, he punched his arms in the air "bhangra"-style, shouting, "Jai Hind!"

This contradiction of an external racist emasculation and an internal "raja" syndrome leaves only one area where the Indian American male can assert his masculinity: his relationship with community women. Indeed, while discussing the hostility that women's organizations face in the United States, one of India's foremost journalists, Madhu Kishwar, remarked that she was flabbergasted by immigrant men's negative reactions. She claimed that Indian men had shown her and her women's magazine, *Manushi,* much more support than we could ever imagine here. This discrepancy between subcontinental and immigrant Indian men's reactions to women's strength can perhaps be traced to the pressures upon Indian masculinity in the New World.

Indeed, this threat to their masculinity from the mainstream community has prompted Indian men to impose strict limits on their sisters' behavior. It is only by defining their counterparts as passive, docile homebodies that Asian Indian men can ascertain their masculinity. Thus, in order to both secure a homogenous community face and ensure masculine privilege, they exile from the community women who do not fit the above characterization. Such women become branded as unfit to be wives. They are castrating females.

A few years back, my daughter and I were featured on the cover of a feminist magazine as a mother-daughter activist team. My proud husband took the issue to work for a round of "show and tell." One of his close Indian immigrant friends gently advised him that if not for his wife, for his daughter this was risky conduct. "She has to find a husband, you know," he observed. "It is going to be hard to find someone if she gets involved with such things. In our community, very few families want "smart" girls."

STRAYING FROM THE FOLD

Exogamy is not a new phenomenon in Asian American communities. Indeed, according to Tinker (1973) and Kikumura and Kitano (1973), approximately half the marriages in which one person was Japanese American did not involve a Japanese American partner.[16] However, these patterns may have changed with time. A. Magazine cites that "in 1980, 75 percent of different-nationality marriages among Asian Americans were to whites, 20 percent to other Asians and 5 percent to other minorities. Ten years later, 55 percent of the marriages were to other Asians, 40 percent to whites, and 5 percent to other minorities."[17] There are further gender discrepancies in Asian American outmarriage. For instance, Kitano and Yeung's 1979 research on Chinese American outmarriages in Los Angeles County suggested that the outmarriage rate was 44 percent for Chinese American males and 56 percent for Chinese American females.[18] The rationale for such gender disparity suggested by Kikumura and Kitano (1973) is that "Asian American females seem to acculturate faster than their male counterparts" primarily because "in a racist society, ethnic minority males may be viewed as more of a threat than females."[19] Acculturation, here, is directly linked to outmarriage. The "war bride" phenomenon, when U.S. servicemen increasingly began to bring their wartime Asian brides home, may also contribute to mainstream acceptance of Asian female/white male marriages. Other arguments are that Asian American women have more incentive to outmarry, since many are dissatisfied with traditional Asian female gender roles, while Asian American men may be inhibited from doing the same by "family pressures, the necessity to carry on the family name, 'saving face,' and physical height."[20] Finally, research on Asian American outmarriage suggests that sex differences in exogamy rates may be a function of stereotypes that label Asian American males as "quiet, shy, passive, and socially inept," while Asian American females are given more "positive" stereotypes such as being "exotic, sexy, compliant, agreeable, and domestic."[21]

In many ways, this research on Asian American exogamy cannot be used to analyze the Asian Indian immigrant communities. First and foremost, many of these previous studies ignored the huge subpopulation of South Asians when discussing Asian Americans. Findings on Asian Americans are further rendered inapplicable to South Asians due to our different immigration histories and patterns of community re-creation. For instance, Morishima (1980) speculates that the Japanese American community's history of evacuation and detainment led some Japanese Americans to encourage their children to marry Caucasians with the hopes that succeeding generations could become more and more "American" (the assumption being that internment occurred as a result of not being "American" enough). In stark contrast, the bulk of the Indian American community is made up of post-1965 immigrants who, in many ways, consider themselves "migrant workers" unwilling to give up ties to their motherland, including, most importantly, ties of marriage. Another vital factor differentiating the experiences of Indian Americans from other Asians is that of color. Indeed, while Asian outmarriage may be affected by the fact that "many Asian American groups are light-skinned, which may make them less different from Caucasian Americans,"[22] the skin color of Asian Indians, on the whole, does not resemble that of white Americans.

Although much of these previous findings may be inapplicable to Indian Americans, the idea that higher rates of Asian American female exogamy can be attributed to gendered stereotyping does ring true. Indeed, previous analyses of Indian American women's exogamy have focused solely upon the white American "exoticization" of the Asian woman, the idea being that the hyperfeminine South Asian woman is a fetish-like token for sexual appetites of the white American man. Although Indian American women are clearly exoticized in the mainstream perception, there are also internal community forces determining their exogamy. Indeed, perhaps it is the marginalization and rejection of successful, outspoken, and high-achieving women from the Indian American community fold that necessitates their seeking partners elsewhere. And, perhaps, the masculine role confusion of Indian American men is what makes them intolerant of strong Indian American women. Conversely, mainstream American men, whose masculine self-concepts are generally relatively intact and under no racist challenge, are perhaps more open to and supportive of their Indian American female partners' strength.

"I was attracted to you because you were so outspoken and strong," my non-Indian boyfriend tells me. "I love the fact that you can argue anyone into the ground." This is a sentiment I have heard from non-Indian American men. "You're going to be famous," he adds, "and I'll be able to brag about you." Whether or not I achieve any type of fame in my life, his support gives me tremendous encouragement. It is true, it would be much easier if he were Indian, but I'd rather have a supportive partner than one who is constantly made insecure by my strength.

COMPLEMENTARITY, NOT COMPETITION

This antagonism emerging between the genders may be a function of the differences in gender role conceptions in India and America. In India, gender roles are visualized as complementary. Despite many other problems, the flexibility inherent in this perception allows the genders to reverse roles at appropriate times. Thus, to the dynamic and militant Kali, there is the supportive and patient Siva. Although their female partners are powerful, neither Siva nor the spouses of viranganas are considered emasculated in the subcontinental context.

My commitment and association in women's rights work gradually converted my husband. For a number of years now, he has been an active member of Manavi. At many Indian parties I have heard his voice explaining the latest feminist doctrine or praxis regarding violence against women to a roomful of unresponsive men. His involvement with Manavi has at times drawn snide asides from many of our Indian male friends. Yet my husband has been my strongest supporter and comrade. However, I can hardly claim total responsibility for his understanding of women's activism. His mother was a motivated participant in the revolutionary wing of the nationalist movement.

In contrast to this idea of complementarity, gender roles in the West are considered dichotomous and oppositional. Thus, there is no room for women to be dynamic without the men being passive, for women to be aggressive without the men losing their machismo. Internalization of Western gender standards by the Asian Indian immigrants thereby necessitates marginalization of activist and feminist women.

Due to both the heterogeneity intrinsic to South Asian culture and the long tradition of viranganas in Indian society, there has always been space for autonomous and strong women. However, due to the homogeneity of Indian American society, artificially shaped by the immigration laws, a "model minority" myth, and the strict standards of community leaders, this recognition of women's power and energy is being effectively denied within our communities.

The intention of this essay is not to blame Indian men for all social ills, nor to tar them as ultimately oppressive. However, we believe it is important to recognize the intergender discord that is brewing in our community and begin a conversation aimed at an amelioration of the situation. It is our contention that the dichotomous conceptualization of gender roles allows little room for the existence of both strong women and men. It is only by accepting role complementarity or androgyny[23] as gender ideals that we can prevent the actual and psychological exclusion of activist and competent women from our ranks.

NOTES

1. All names have been changed to protect the privacy of the individuals.
2. A. W. Helweg and U M. Helweg 1990; P. Agarwal 1991.
3. A. Bharracharjee 1992.
4. Ibid., 30.
5. Manavi is the pioneering organization in the United States that focuses on violence against South Asian women. It was established in 1985.
6. *India Abroad,* 5 June 1992, 3.
7. N. Shah 1993.
8. L. Mani 1992; S. D. Dasgupta in press; S. D. Dasgupta and S. DasGupta 1996.
9. R. Kumar 1993.
10. B. Mukherjee 1989.
11. In *Jasmine,* Bharati Mukherjee's heroine transforms herself from Jyoti to Jasmine to Jane as she moves from Hasnapur to Iowa in search of liberation. In fact, Mukherjee characterizes "Jyoti" as already a "Jane" at birth, as she is a "fighter and adapter." Obviously, Mukherjee believes that only a "Jane" could be a "fighter and adapter," as opposed to Jyoti, who is doomed to be the opposite.
12. S. DasGupta 1993.
13. The 1995 National Asian American Sex Survey, *A. Magazine,* August/September 1995, 27.
14. D. H. Hwang 1986: 83.
15. Ibid.
16. S. Sue and J. K. Morishima 1982: 108.
17. T. Hong 1995: 21.
18. As cited in S. Sue and J. K. Morishima 1982: 109.

19. Ibid., 113.
20. Ibid., 114.
21. Ibid., 115.
22. Ibid., 112.
23. Androgyny as the third gender identity was elaborated by American psychologist Sandra Bern in 1974. According to Bern, androgynous individuals measure high on both "feminine" and "masculine" personality traits. The concept of androgyny has been noted in Hindu mythology as the "ardhanarishwar."

Bibliography

Agarwal, R. (1991). *Passage from India: Post 1965 Indian Immigrants and Their Children: Conflicts, Concerns, & Solutions*. Palos Verdes, Calif.: Yuvati Publications.

Bem, S. (1974). "The Measurement of Psychological Androgyny." *Journal of Consulting and Clinical Psychology* 42: 155–162.

Bhattacharjee, A. (1992). "The Habit of Ex-nomination: Nation, Women, and the Indian Immigrant Bourgeoisie." *Public Culture* 5: 19–44.

Dasgupta, S. D. (forthcoming). "The Gift of Utter Daring: Cultural Continuity in Asian Indian Communities." In *Women, Communities, and Cultures: South Asians in America*, ed. S. Mazumdar and J. Vaid. Unpublished manuscript.

Dasgupta, S. D. ed. 1998. *A Patchwork Shawl: Chronicles of South Asian Women in America*. New Brunswick, N.J.: Rutgers University Press.

Dasgupta, S. D., and DasGupta, S. (1996). "Public Face, Private Space: Asian Indian Women and Sexuality." In N. B. Maglin & D. Perry (Eds.), *"Bad Girls"/"Good Girls": Women, Sex & Power in the Nineties*, ed. N. B. Maglin and D. Perry. New Brunswick, N.J.: Rutgers University Press.

DasGupta, S. (1993). "Glass Shawls and Long Hair: A South Asian Woman Talks Sexual Politics." *Ms.* 111 (March/April): 76–77.

Hong, T. (1995). "Tying the Knot." *A Magazine* 16–21 (August/September): 38.

Hwang, D. H. (1986). *M. Butterfly*. New York: New American Library.

India Abroad (1992). "Letters to the Editor," 5 June, 3.

Kikumura, A., and Kitano, H.H.L. (1973). "Interracial Marriage: A Picture of the Japanese Americans." *Journal of Social Issues* 29: 67–81.

Kumar, R. (1993). *The History of Doing: An Illustrated Account of Movements for Women's Rights and Feminism in India, 1800–1990*. New York: Verso.

Morishima, J. K. (1980). "Asian American Racial Mixes: Attitudes, Self-Concept, and Academic Performance." Paper presented at Western Psychological Association convention, Honolulu, April.

Mukherjee, B. (1989). *Jasmine*. New York: Grove Weidenfeld.

Shah, N. (1993). *The Ethnic Strife: A Study of Asian Indian Women in the United States*. New York: Pinkerton and Thomas Publications.

Sue, S., and J. K. Morishima (1982). *The Mental Health of Asian Americans*. San Francisco: Jossey-Bass, Inc.

Tinker, J. N. (1973). "Intermarriage and Ethnic Boundaries: The Japanese American Case." *Journal of Social Issues* 29: 49–66.

Yang, J. (1995). "The 1995 National Asian American Sex Survey." *A. Magazine* 22–1 (August/September): 47.

LOOKING FOR MY PENIS

THE EROTICIZED ASIAN IN GAY VIDEO PORN

Richard Fung

Several scientists have begun to examine the relation between personality and human reproductive behavior from a gene-based evolutionary perspective. . . . In this vein we reported a study of racial difference in sexual restraint such that Orientals > whites > blacks. Restraint was indexed in numerous ways, having in common a lowered allocation of bodily energy to sexual functioning. We found the same racial pattern occurred on gamete production (dizygotic birthing frequency per 100: Mongoloids, 4; Caucasoids, 8; Negroids, 16), intercourse frequencies (premarital, marital, extramarital), developmental precocity (age at first intercourse, age at first pregnancy, number of pregnancies), primary sexual characteristics (size of penis, vagina, testis, ovaries), secondary sexual characteristics (salient voice, muscularity, buttocks, breasts), and biologic control of behavior (periodicity of sexual response predictability of life history from onset of puberty), as well as in androgen levels and sexual attitudes.[1]

This passage from the *Journal of Research in Personality* was written by University of Western Ontario psychologist Philippe Rushton, who enjoys considerable controversy in Canadian academic circles and in the popular media. His thesis, articulated throughout his work, appropriates biological studies of the continuum of reproductive strategies of oysters through chimpanzees and posits that degree of "sexuality"—interpreted as penis and vagina size, frequency of intercourse, buttock and lip size—correlates positively with criminality and sociopathic behavior and inversely with intelligence, health, and longevity. Rushton sees race as the determining factor and places East Asians (Rushton uses the word "Orientals") on one end of the spectrum and blacks on the other. Since whites fall squarely in the middle, the position of perfect balance, there is no need for analysis, and they remain free of scrutiny.

Notwithstanding its profound scientific shortcomings, Rushton's work serves as an excellent articulation of a dominant discourse on race and sexuality in Western society—a system of ideas and reciprocal practices that originated in Europe simultaneously with (some argue as a conscious justification for[2]) colonial expansion and slavery. In the nineteenth century these ideas took on a scientific gloss with social Darwinism and eugenics. Now they reappear, somewhat altered, in psychology journals from the likes of Rushton. It is important to add that these ideas have also permeated the global popular consciousness. Anyone who has been exposed to Western television or advertising images, which is much of the world, will have absorbed this particular constellation of stereotyping and racial hierarchy. In Trinidad in the 1960s, on the outer reaches of the empire, everyone in my schoolyard was thoroughly versed in these "truths" about the races.

Historically, most organizing against racism has concentrated on fighting discrimination that stems from the intelligence-social behavior variable assumed by Rushton's scale. Discrimination based on perceived intellectual ability does, after all, have direct ramifications for education and employment, and therefore for survival. Until recently, issues of gender and sexuality remained a low priority for those who claimed to speak for the communities.[3] But antiracist strategies that fail to subvert the race-gender status quo are of seriously limited value. Racism cannot be narrowly defined in terms of race hatred. Race is a factor in even our most intimate relationships.

The contemporary construction of race and sex as exemplified by Rushton has endowed black people, both men and women, with a threatening hypersexuality. Asians, on the other hand, are collectively seen as undersexed.[4] But here I want to make some crucial distinctions. First, in North America, stereotyping has focused almost exclusively on what recent colonial language designates as "Orientals"—that is, East and southeast Asian peoples—as opposed to the "Orientalism" discussed by Edward Said, which concerns the Middle East. This current, popular usage is based more on a perception of similar physical features—black hair, "slanted" eyes, high cheekbones, and so on—than through a reference to common cultural traits. South Asians, people whose backgrounds are in the Indian subcontinent and Sri Lanka, hardly figure at all in North American popular representations, and those few images are ostensibly devoid of sexual connotation.[5]

Second, within the totalizing stereotype of the "Oriental," there are competing and sometimes contradictory sexual associations based on nationality. So, for example, a person could be seen as Japanese and somewhat kinky, or Filipino and "available." The very same person could also be seen as "Oriental" and therefore sexless. In addition, the racial hierarchy revamped by Rushton is itself in tension with an earlier and only partially eclipsed depiction of all Asians as having an undisciplined and dangerous libido. I am referring to the writings of the early European explorers and missionaries, but also to antimiscegenation laws and such specific legislation as the 1912 Saskatchewan law that barred white women from employment in Chinese-owned business.

Finally, East Asian women figure differently from men both in reality and in representation. In "Lotus Blossoms Don't Bleed," Renee Tajima points out that in Hollywood films,

There are two basic types: the Lotus Blossom Baby (a.k.a. China Doll, Geisha Girl, shy Polynesian beauty, et al.) and the Dragon Lady (Fu Manchu's various female relations, prostitutes, devious madames). . . . Asian women in film are, for the most part, passive figures who exist to serve men—as love interests for white men (re: Lotus Blossoms) or as partners in crime for men of their own kind (re: Dragon Ladies).[6]

Further:

Dutiful creatures that they are, Asian women are often assigned the task of expendability in a situation of illicit love. . . . Noticeably lacking is the portrayal of love relationships between Asian women and Asian men, particularly as lead characters.[7]

Because of their supposed passivity and sexual compliance, Asian women have been fetishized in dominant representation, and there is a large and growing body of literature by Asian women on the oppressiveness of these images. Asian men, however—at least since Sessue Hayakawa, who made a Hollywood career in the 1920s of representing the Asian man as sexual threat[8]—have been consigned to one of two categories: the egghead/wimp, or—in what may be analogous to the lotus blossom-dragon lady dichotomy—the kung fu master/ninja/samurai. He is sometimes dangerous, sometimes friendly, but almost always characterized by a desexualized Zen asceticism. So whereas, as Fanon tells us, "the Negro is eclipsed. He is turned into a penis. He *is* a penis,"[9] the Asian man is defined by a striking absence down there. And if Asian men have no sexuality, how can we have homosexuality?

Even as recently as the early 1980s, I remember having to prove my queer credentials before being admitted with other Asian men into a Toronto gay club. I do not believe it was a question of a color barrier. Rather, my friends and I felt that the doorman was genuinely unsure about our sexual orientation. We also felt that had we been white and dressed similarly, our entrance would have been automatic.[10]

Although a motto for the lesbian and gay movements has been "we are everywhere," Asians are largely absent from the images produced by both the political and the commercial sectors of the mainstream gay and lesbian communities. From the earliest articulation of the Asian gay and lesbian movements, a principal concern has therefore been visibility. In political organizing, the demand for a voice, or rather the demand to be heard, has largely been responded to by the problematic practice of "minority" representation on panels and boards.[11] But since racism is a question of power and not of numbers, this strategy has often led to a dead-end tokenistic integration, failing to address the real imbalances.

Creating a space for Asian gay and lesbian representation has meant, among other things, deepening an understanding of what is at stake for Asians in coming out publicly.[12] As is the case for many other people of color and especially immigrants, our families and our ethnic communities are a rare source of affirmation in a racist society. In coming out, we risk (or feel that we risk) losing this support, though the ever-growing organizations of lesbian and gay Asians have worked against this process of cultural exile. In my own experience, the existence of a gay

Asian community broke down the cultural schizophrenia in which I related on the one hand to a heterosexual family that affirmed my ethnic culture, and on the other to a gay community that was predominantly white. Knowing that there was support also helped me come out to my family and further bridge the gap.

If we look at commercial gay sexual representation, it appears that the antiracist movements have had little impact: the images of men and male beauty are still of *white* men and *white* male beauty. These are the standards against which we compare both ourselves and often our brothers—Asian, black, native, and Latino.[13] Although other people's rejection (or fetishization) of us according to the established racial hierarchies may be experienced as oppressive, we are not necessarily moved to scrutinize our own desire and its relationship to the hegemonic image of the white man.[14]

In my lifelong vocation of looking for my penis, trying to fill in the visual void, I have come across only a handful of primary and secondary references to Asian male sexuality in North American representation. Even in my own video work, the stress has been on deconstructing sexual representation and only marginally on creating erotica. So I was very excited at the discovery of a Vietnamese American working in gay porn.

Having acted in six videotapes, Sum Yung Mahn is perhaps the only Asian to qualify as a gay porn "star." Variously known as Brad Troung or Sam or Sum Yung Mahn, he has worked for a number of different production studios. All of the tapes in which he appears are distributed through International Wavelength, a San Francisco-based mail order company whose catalog entries feature Asians in American, Thai, and Japanese productions. According to the owner of International Wavelength, about 90 percent of the Asian tapes are bought by white men, and the remaining 10 percent are purchased by Asians. But the number of Asian buyers is growing.

In examining Sum Yung Mahn's work, it is important to recognize the different strategies used for fitting an Asian actor into the traditionally white world of gay porn and how the terms of entry are determined by the perceived demands of an intended audience. Three tapes, each geared toward a specific erotic interest, illustrate these strategies.

Below the Belt (1985, directed by Philip St. John, California Dream Machine Productions), like most porn tapes, has an episodic structure. All the sequences involve the students and *sense* of an all-male karate *dojo*. The authenticity of the setting is proclaimed with the opening shots of a gym full of *gi*-clad, serious-faced young men going through their weapons exercises. Each of the main actors is introduced in turn; with the exception of the teacher, who has dark hair, all fit into the current porn conventions of Aryan, blond, shaved, good looks.[15] Moreover, since Sum Yung Mahn is not even listed in the opening credits, we can surmise that this tape is not targeted to an audience with any particular erotic interest in Asian men. Most gay video porn uses white actors exclusively; those tapes having the least bit of racial integration are pitched to the specialty market throughout outlets such as International Wavelengths.[16] This visual apartheid stems, I assume, from an erroneous perception that the sexual appetites of gay men are exclusive and unchangeable.

A karate *dojo* offers a rich opportunity to introduce Asian actors. One might image it as the gay Orientalist's dream project. But given the intended audience for this video, the erotic appeal of the *dojo*, except for the costumes and a few misplaced props (Taiwanese and Korean flags for a Japanese art form?) are completely appropriated into a white world.

The tape's action occurs in a gym, in the students' apartments, and in a garden. The one scene with Sum Yung Mahn is a dream sequence. Two students, Robbie and Stevie, are sitting in a locker room. Robbie confesses that he has been having strange dreams about Greg, their teacher. Cut to the dream sequence, which is coded by clouds of green smoke. Robbie is wearing a red headband with black markings suggesting script (if indeed they belong to an Asian language, they are not the Japanese or Chinese characters one would expect). He is trapped in an elaborate snare. Enter a character in a black ninja mask, wielding a *nanchaku*. Robbie narrates: "I knew this evil samurai would kill me." The masked figure is menacingly running the *nanchaku* chain under Robbie's genitals when Greg, the teacher, appears and disposes of him. Robbie explains to Stevie in the locker room: "I knew that I owed him my life, and I knew I had to please him [long pause] in any way that he wanted." During that pause we cut back to the dream. Amid more puffs of smoke, Greg, carrying a man in his arms, approaches a low platform. Although Greg's back is toward the camera, we can see that the man is wearing the red headband that identifies him as Robbie. As Greg lays him down, we see that Robbie has "turned Japanese"! It's Sum Yung Mahn.

Greg fucks Sum Yung Mahn, who is always face down. The scene constructs anal intercourse for the Asian Robbie as an act of submission, not of pleasure: unlike other scenes of anal intercourse in the tape, for example, there is no dubbed dialogue on the order of "Oh yeah . . . fuck me harder!" but merely ambiguous groans. Without coming, Greg leaves. A group of (white) men wearing Japanese outfits encircle the platform, and Asian Robbie, or "the Oriental boy," as he is listed in the final credits, turns to lie on his back. He sucks a cock, licks someone's balls. The other men come all over his body; he comes. The final shot of the sequence zooms in to a close-up of Sum Yung Mahn's headband, which dissolves to a similar close-up of Robbie wearing the same headband, emphasizing that the two actors represent one character.

We now cut back to the locker room. Robbie's story has made Stevie horny. He reaches into Robbie's pants, pulls out his penis, and sex follows. In his Asian manifestation, Robbie is fucked and sucks others off (Greek passive/French active/bottom). His passivity is pronounced, and he is never shown other than prone. As a white man, his role is completely reversed: he is at first sucked off by Stevie, and then he fucks him (Greek active/French passive/top). Neither of Robbie's manifestations veers from his prescribed role.

To a greater extent than most other gay porn tapes, *Below the Belt* is directly about power. The hierarchical *dojo* setting is mild for its evocation of dominance and submission. With the exception of one very romantic sequence midway through the tape, most of the actors stick to their defined roles of top or bottom. Sex, especially anal sex, as punishment is a recurrent image. In this genre of gay pornography, the role-playing in the dream sequence is perfectly apt. What is significant, however, is how race figures into the equation. In a tape that appropriates emblems of Asian power (karate), the only place for a real Asian actor is as a caricature of passivity. Sum Yung Mahn does not portray an Asian, but rather the liberalization of a metaphor, so that by being passive, Robbie actually becomes "Oriental." At a more practical level, the device of the dream also allows the producers to introduce an element of the mysterious, the exotic, without disrupting the racial status quo of the rest of the tape. Even in the dream sequence, Sum Yung Mahn is at the center of the frame as spectacle, having minimal physical involvement with the men around him. Although the sequence ends with his climax, he exists for the pleasure of others.

Richard Dyer, writing about gay porn, states:

> although the pleasure of anal sex (that is, of being anally fucked) is represented, the narrative is never organized around the desire to be fucked, but around the desire to ejaculate (whether or not following from anal intercourse). Thus, although at a level of public representation gay men may be thought of as deviant and disruptive of masculine norms because we assert the pleasure of being fucked and the eroticism of the anus, in our pornography this takes a back seat.[17]

Although Tom Waugh's amendment to this argument—that anal pleasure is represented in individual sequences[18]—also holds true for *Below the Belt*, as a whole the power of the penis and the pleasure of ejaculation are clearly the narrative's organizing principles. As with the vast majority of North American tapes featuring Asians, the problem is not the representation of anal pleasure per se, but rather that the narratives privilege the penis while always assigning the Asian the role of bottom; Asian and anus are conflated. In the case of Sum Yung Mahn, being fucked may well be his personal sexual preference. But the fact remains that there are very few occasions in North American video porn in which an Asian fucks a white man, so few, in fact, that International Wavelength promotes the tape *Studio X* (1986) with the blurb "Sum Yung Mahn makes history as the first Asian who fucks a non-Asian."[19]

Although I agree with Waugh that in gay as opposed to straight porn "the spectator's positions in relation to the representations are open and in flux,"[20] this observation applies only when all the participants are white. Race introduces another dimension that may serve to close down some of this mobility. This is not to suggest that the experience of gay men of color with this kind of sexual representation is the same as that of heterosexual women with regard to the gendered gaze of straight porn. For one thing, Asian gay men are men. We can therefore physically experience the pleasures depicted on the screen, since we too have erections and ejaculations and can experience anal penetration. A shifting identification may occur despite the racially defined roles, and most gay Asian men in North America are used to obtaining pleasure from all-white pornography. This, of course, goes hand in hand with many problems of self-image and sexual identity. Still, I have been struck by the unanimity with which gay Asian men I have met, from all over this continent as well as from Asia, immediately identify and resist these representations. Whenever I mention the topic of Asian actors in American porn, the first question I am asked is whether the Asian is simply shown getting fucked.

Asian Knights (1985, directed by Ed Sung, William Richhe Productions), the second tape I want to consider, has an Asian producer-director and a predominantly Asian cast. In its first scenario, two Asian men, Brad and Rick, are seeing a white psychiatrist because they are unable to have sex with each other:

> Rick: We never have sex with other Asians. We usually have sex with Caucasian guys.
> Counselor: Have you had the opportunity to have sex together?
> Rick: Yes, a coupla times, but we never get going.

Homophobia, like other forms of oppression, is seldom dealt with in gay video porn. With the exception of safe sex tapes that attempt a rare blend of the pedagogical with the pornographic, social or political issues are not generally associated with the erotic. It is therefore unusual to see one of the favored discussion topics for gay Asian consciousness-raising groups employed as a sex fantasy in *Asian Knights*. The desexualized image of Asian men I have described has seriously affected our relationships with one another, and often gay Asian men find it difficult to see each other beyond the terms of platonic friendship or competition, to consider other Asian men as lovers.

True to the conventions of porn, minimal counseling from the psychiatrist convinces Rick and Brad to shed their clothes. Immediately sprouting erections, they proceed to have sex. But what appears to be an assertion of gay Asian desire is quickly derailed. As Brad and Rick make love on the couch, the camera cross-cuts to the psychiatrist looking on from an armchair. The rhetoric of the editing suggests that we are observing the two Asian men from his point of view. Soon the white man takes off his clothes and joins in. He immediately takes up a position at the center of the action—and at the center of the frame. What appeared to be a "conversion fantasy" for gay Asian desire was merely a ruse. Brad and Rick's temporary mutual absorption really occurs to establish the superior sexual draw of the white psychiatrist, a stand-in for the white male viewer, who is the real sexual subject of the tape. And the question of Asian-Asian desire, though presented as the main narrative force of the sequence, is deflected, or rather reframed from a white perspective.

Sex between the two Asian men in this sequence can be related somewhat to heterosexual sex in some gay porn films, such as those produced by the Gage brothers. In *Heatstroke* (1982), for example, sex with a woman is used to establish the authenticity of the straight man who is about to be seduced into gay sex. It dramatizes the significance of the conversion from the sanctioned object of desire, underscoring the power of the gay man to incite desire in his socially defined superior. It is also tied up with the fantasies of (female) virginity and conquest in Judeo-Christian and other patriarchal societies. The therapy session sequence of *Asian Knights* also suggests parallels to representations of lesbians in straight porn, representations that are not meant to eroticize women loving women, but rather to titillate and empower the sexual ego of the heterosexual male viewer.

Asian Knights is organized to sell representations of Asians to white men. Unlike Sum Yung Mahn in *Below the Belt*, the actors are therefore more expressive and sexually assertive, as often the seducers as the seduced. But though the roles shift during the predominantly oral sex, the Asians remain passive in anal intercourse, except that they are now shown to want it! How much this assertion of agency represents a step forward remains a question.

Even in the one sequence of *Asian Knights* in which the Asian actor fucks the white man, the scenario privileges the pleasure of the white man over that of the Asian. The sequence begins with the Asian reading a magazine. When the white man (played by porn star Eric Stryker) returns home from a hard day at the office, the waiting Asian asks how his day went, undresses him (even taking off his socks), and proceeds to massage his back.[21] The Asian man acts the role of the mythologized geisha or "the good wife" as fantasized in the mail order bride business. And, in fact, the "house boy" is one of the most persistent white fantasies about Asian men. The fantasy is also a reality in many Asian countries where economic imperialism gives foreigners, whatever their race, the pick of handsome men in financial need. The accompanying cultural imperialism grants status to those Asians with white lovers. White men who for various reasons, especially age, are deemed unattractive in their own countries, suddenly find themselves elevated and desired.

From the opening shot of painted lotus blossoms on a screen to the shot of a Japanese garden that separates the episodes, from the Chinese pop music to the chinoiserie in the apartment, there is a conscious attempt in *Asian Knights* to evoke a particular atmosphere.[22] Self-conscious "Oriental" signifiers are part and parcel of a colonial fantasy—and reality—that empowers one kind of gay man over another. Though I have known Asian men in dependent relations with older, wealthier white men, as an erotic fantasy the house boy scenario tends to work one way. I know of no scenarios of Asian men and white house boys. It is not the representation of the fantasy that offends, or even the fantasy itself, but the uniformity with which these narratives reappear and the uncomfortable relationship they have to real social conditions.

International Skin (1985, directed by William Richhe, N'wayvo Richhe Productions), as its name suggests, features a Latino, a black man, Sum Yung Mahn, and a number of white actors. Unlike the other tapes I have discussed, there are no "Oriental" devices. And although Sum Yung Mahn and all the men of color are inevitably fucked (without reciprocating), there is mutual sexual engagement between the white and nonwhite characters.

In this tape Sum Yung Mahn is Brad, a film student making a movie for his class. Brad is the narrator, and the film begins with a self-reflexive "head and shoulders" shot of Sum Yung Mahn explaining the scenario. The film we are watching supposedly represents Brad's point of view. But here again the tape is not targeted to black, Asian, or Latino men; though Brad introduces all of these men as his friends, no two men of color ever meet on screen. Men of color are not invited to participate in the internationalism that is being sold, except through identification with white characters. This tape illustrates how an agenda of integration becomes problematic if it frames the issue solely in terms of black-white, Asian-white mixing: it perpetuates a system of white-centeredness.

The gay Asian viewer is not constructed as sexual subject in any of this work—not on the screen, not as a viewer. I may find Sum Yung Mahn attractive, I may desire his body, but I am always aware that he is not meant for me. I may lust after Eric Stryker and imagine myself as the Asian who is having sex with him, but the role the Asian plays in the scene with him is demeaning. It is not that there is anything wrong with the image of servitude per se, but rather that it is one of the few fantasy scenarios in which we figure, and we are always in the role of servant.

Are there, then, no pleasures for an Asian viewer? The answer to this question is extremely complex. There is first of all no essential Asian viewer. The race of the person viewing says nothing about how race figures in his or her own desires. Uniracial white representations in porn may not in themselves present a problem in addressing many gay Asian men's desires. But the issue is not simply that porn may deny pleasures to some gay Asian men. We also need to examine what role the pleasure of porn plays in securing a consensus about race and desirability that ultimately works to our disadvantage.

Though the sequences I have focused on in the preceding examples are those in which the discourses about Asian sexuality are most clearly articulated, they do not define the totality of depiction in these tapes. Much of the time the actors merely reproduce or attempt to reproduce the conventions of pornography. The fact that, with the exception of Sum Yung Mahn, they rarely succeed—because of their body type, because Midwestern-cowboy-porn dialect with Vietnamese intonation is just a bit incongruous, because they groan or gyrate just a bit too much—more than anything brings home the relative rigidity of the genre's codes. There is little seamlessness here. There are times, however, when the actors appear neither as simulated whites nor as symbolic others. There are several moments in *International Skin,* for example, in which the focus shifts from the genitals to hands caressing a body; these moments feel to me more "genuine." I do not mean this in the sense of an essential Asian sexuality; rather, a moment is captured in which the actor stops pretending. He does not stop acting, but he stops pretending to be a white porn star. I find myself focusing on moments like these, in which the racist ideology of the text seems to be temporarily suspended or rather eclipsed by the erotic power of the moment.

In "Pornography and the Doubleness of Sex for Women," Joanna Russ writes:

> Sex is ecstatic, autonomous and lovely for women. Sex is violent, dangerous and unpleasant for women. I don't mean a dichotomy (i.e., two kinds of women or even two kinds of sex) but rather a continuum in which no one's experience is wholly positive or negative.[23]

Gay Asian men are men and therefore not normally victims of the rape, incest, or other sexual harassment to which Russ is referring. However, there is a kind of doubleness, of ambivalence, in the way Asian men experience contemporary North American gay communities. The "ghetto," the mainstream gay movement, can be a place of freedom and sexual identity. But it is also a site of racial, cultural, *and* sexual alienation sometimes more pronounced than that in straight society. For me sex is a source of pleasure, but also a site of humiliation and pain. Released from the social constraints against expressing overt racism in public, the intimacy of sex can provide my (non-Asian) partner an opening for letting me know my place—sometimes literally, as when after we come, he turns over and asks where I come from.[24] Most gay Asian men I know have similar experiences.

This is just one reality that differentiates the experiences and therefore the political priorities of gay Asians and, I think, other gay men of color from those of white men. For one thing we cannot afford to take a libertarian approach. Porn can be an active agent in representing *and* reproducing a sex-race status quo. We cannot attain a healthy alliance without coming to terms with these differences.

The barriers that impede pornography from providing representations of Asian men that are erotic and politically palatable (as opposed to correct) are similar to those that inhibit the Asian documentary, the Asian feature, the Asian experimental film and videotape. We are seen as too peripheral, not commercially visible—not the general audience. *Looking for Langston* (1988),[25] which is the first film I have seen that affirms rather than appropriates the sexuality of black gay men, was produced under exceptional economic circumstances that freed it from the constraints of the marketplace.[26] Should we call for an independent gay Asian pornography? Perhaps I am, in a utopian sort of way, though I feel that the problems in North America's porn conventions are manifold and go beyond the question of race. There is such a limited vision of what constitutes the erotic.

In Canada, the major debate about race and representation has shifted from an emphasis on the image to a discussion of appropriation and control of production and distribution—who gets to produce the work. But as we have seen in the case of *Asian Knights,* the race of the producer is no automatic guarantee of "consciousness" about these issues or of a different product. Much depends on who is constructed as the audience for the work. In any case, it is not surprising that under capitalism, finding my penis may ultimately be a matter of dollars and cents.

DISCUSSION

Audience Member: You made a comment about perceived distinctions between Chinese and Japanese sexuality. I have no idea what you mean.

Richard Fung: In the West, there are specific sexual ambiences associated with the different Asian nationalities, sometimes based on cultural artifacts, sometimes on mere conjecture. These discourses exist simultaneously, even though in conflict with, totalizing notions of "Oriental" sexuality. Japanese male sexuality has come to be identified with strength, virility, perhaps a certain kinkiness, as signified for example by the clothing and gestures in *Below the Belt.* Japanese sexuality is seen as more "potent" than Chinese sexuality, which is generally represented as more passive and languorous. At the same time, there is the cliché that "all Orientals look alike." So in this paradox of the invisibility of difference lies the fascination. If he can ascertain where I'm from, he feels that he knows what he can expect from me. In response to this query about "ethnic origins," a friend of mine answers, "Where would you like me to be from?" I like this response because it gently confronts the question while maintaining the erotic possibilities of the moment.

Simon Watney: I wanted to point out that the first film you showed, *Below the Belt,* presents us with a classic anxiety dream image. In it there is someone whose identity is that of a top man, but that identity is established in relation to a competing identity that allows him to enjoy sexual passivity, which is represented as a racial identity. It's as if he were in racial drag. I thought this film was extraordinary. Under what other conditions are Caucasian men invited to fantasize ourselves as racially other? And it seems to me that the only condition that would allow the visibility of that fantasy to be acted out in this way is the prior anxiety about a desired role, about top and bottom positions. This film is incredibly transparent and unconscious about how it construes or confuses sexual role-playing in relation to race. And the thrust of it all seems to be the construction of the Asian body as a kind of conciliatory pseudoheterosexuality for the white "top," who has anus envy, as it were.

Fung: I completely agree. The film says too much for its own good by making this racist agenda so clear.

Ray Navarro: I think your presentation was really important, and it parallels research I'm doing with regard to the image of Latino men in gay male porn. I wondered if you might comment a bit more, however, about the class relations you find within this kind of work. For example, I've found a consistent theme running throughout gay white male porn of Latino men represented as either campesino or criminal. That is, it focuses less on body type—masculine, slight, or whatever— than on signifiers of class. It appears to be a class fantasy collapsed with a race fantasy, and in a way it parallels the actual power relations between the Latino stars and the producers and distributors, most of whom are white.

Fung: There are ways in which your comments can also apply to Asians. Unlike whites and blacks, most Asians featured in gay erotica are younger men. Since youth generally implies less economic power, class-race hierarchies appear in most of the work. In the tapes I've been looking at, the occupations of the white actors are usually specified, while those of the Asians are not. The white actors are assigned fantasy appeal based on profession, whereas for the Asians, the sexual cachet of race is deemed sufficient. In *Asian Knights* there are also sequences in which the characters' lack of "work" carries connotations of the housewife or, more particularly, the house boy.

But there is at least one other way to look at this discrepancy. The lack of a specified occupation may be taken to suggest that the Asian actor is the subject of the fantasy, a surrogate or the Asian viewer, and therefore does not need to be coded with specific attributes.

Tom Waugh: I think your comparison of the way the Asian male body is used in gay white porn to the way lesbianism is employed in heterosexual pornography is very interesting. You also suggested that racial markers in gay porn tend to close down its potential for openness and flux in identifications. Do you think we can take it further and say that racial markers in gay porn replicate, or function, in the same way as gender markers do in heterosexual pornography?

Fung: What, in fact, I intended to say with my comparison of the use of lesbians in heterosexual porn and that of Asian male bodies in white gay male porn was that they're similar but also very different. I think that certain comparisons of gender with race are appropriate, but there are also profound differences. The fact that Asian gay men are *men* means that, as viewers, our responses to this work are grounded in our gender and the way gender functions in this society. Lesbians are *women,* with all that that entails. I suspect that although most Asian gay men experience ambivalence with white gay porn, the issues for women in relation to heterosexual pornography are more fundamental.

Waugh: The same rigidity of roles seems to be present in most situations.

Fung: Yes, that's true. If you notice the way the Asian body is spoken of in Rushton's work, the terms he uses are otherwise used when speaking of women. But it is too easy to discredit these arguments. I have tried instead to show how Rushton's conclusions are commensurate with the assumptions everywhere present in education and popular thought.

Audience Member: I'm going to play devil's advocate. Don't you think gay Asian men who are interested in watching gay porn involving Asian actors will get ahold of the racially unmarked porn that is produced in Thailand or Japan? And if your answer is yes, then why should a white producer of gay porn go to the trouble of making tapes that cater to a relatively small gay Asian market? This is about dollars and cents. It seems obvious that the industry will cater to the white man's fantasy.

Fung: On the last point I partially agree. That's why I'm calling for an independent porn in which the gay Asian man is producer, actor, and intended viewer. I say this somewhat halfheartedly, because personally I am not very interested in producing porn, though I do want to continue working with sexually explicit material. But I also feel that one cannot assume, as the porn industry apparently does, that the desires of even white men are so fixed and exclusive.

Regarding the first part of your question, however, I must insist that Asian Americans and Asian Canadians are Americans and Canadians. I myself an a fourth-generation Trinidadian and have only a tenuous link with Chinese culture and aesthetics, except for what I have consciously searched after and learned. I purposely chose not to talk about Japanese or Thai productions because they come from cultural contexts about which I am incapable of commenting. In addition, the fact that porn from those countries is sometimes unmarked racially does not mean that it speaks to my experience or desires, my own culture of sexuality.

Isaac Julien: With regard to race representation or racial signifiers in the context of porn, your presentation elaborated a problem that came up in some of the safe sex tapes that were shown earlier. In them one could see a kind of trope that traces a circular pattern—a repetition that leads a black or Asian spectator to a specific realm of fantasy.

I wonder if you could talk a bit more about the role of fantasy, or the fantasy one sees in porn tapes produced predominantly by white producers. I see a fixing of different black subjects in recognizable stereotypes rather than a more dialectical representation of black identities, where a number of options or fantasy positions would be made available.

Fung: Your last film, *Looking for Langston,* is one of the few films I know of that has placed the sexuality of the black gay subject at its center. As I said earlier, my own work, especially *Chinese Characters* (1986), is more concerned with pulling apart the tropes you refer to than in constructing an alternative erotics. At the same time I feel that this latter task is imperative, and I hope that it is taken up more. It is in this context that I think the current attack on the National Endowment for the Arts and arts funding in the United States supports the racial status quo. If it succeeds, it effectively squelches the possibility of articulating counter-hegemonic views of sexuality.

Just before I left Toronto, I attended an event called "Cum Talk," organized by two people from Gay Asians Toronto and from Khush, the group for South Asian lesbians and gay men. We looked at porn and talked about the images people had of us, the role of "bottom" that we are constantly cast in. Then we spoke of what actually happened when we had sex with white men. What became clear was that we don't play out that role and are very rarely asked to. So there is a discrepancy between the ideology of sexuality and its practice, between sexual representation and sexual reality.

Gregg Bordowitz: When Jean Carlomusto and I began working on the porn project at Gay Men's Health Crisis, we had big ideas of challenging many of the roles and positionings involved in the dominant industry. But as I've worked more with porn, I find that it's really not an efficient arena in which to make such challenges. There is some room to question assumptions, but there are not many ways to challenge the codes of porn, except to question the conditions of production, which was an important point raised at the end of your talk. It seems to me that the only real way to picture more possibilities is, again, to create self-determining groups, make resources available for people of color and lesbians and other groups so that they can produce porn for themselves.

Fung: I only partly agree with you, because I think, so far as is possible, we have to take responsibility for the kinds of images we create, or recreate. *Asian Knights* had a Chinese producer, after all. But, yes, of course, the crucial thing is to activate more voices, which would establish the conditions for something else to happen. The liberal response to racism is that we need to integrate everyone—people should all become coffee-colored, or everyone should have sex with everyone else. But such an agenda doesn't often account for the specificity of desires. I have seen very little porn produced from such an integrationist mentality that actually affirms my desire. It's so easy to find my fantasies appropriated for the pleasures of a white viewer. In that sense, porn is most useful for revealing relationships of power.

José Arroyo: You've been talking critically about a certain kind of colonial imagery. Isaac's film *Looking for Langston* contains not only a deconstruction of this imagery in its critique of the Mapplethorpe photographs, but also a new construction of black desire. What kind of strategies do you see for a similar reconstructing of erotic Asian imagery?

Fung: One of the first thing that needs to be done is to construct Asians as viewing subjects. My first videotape, *Orientations* (1984), had that as a primary goal. I thought of Asians as sexual subjects, but also as viewing subjects to whom the work should be geared. Many of us, whether we're watching news or pornography or looking at advertising, see that the image or message is not really being directed at us. For example, the sexism and heterosexism of a disk jockey's attitudes become obvious when he or she says, "When you and your girlfriend go out tonight. . . . " Even though that's meant to address a general audience, it's clear that this audience is presumed not to have any women (not to mention lesbians) in it. The general audience, as I analyze him, is white, male, heterosexual, middle-class, and center-right politically. So we have to understand this presumption first, to see that only very specific people are being addressed.

When I make my videotapes, I know that I am addressing Asians. That means that I can take certain things for granted and introduce other things in a completely different context. But there are still other questions of audience. When we make outreach films directed at the straight community—the "general public"—in an effort to make lesbian and gay issues visible, we often sacrifice many of the themes that are important to how we express our sexualities: drag, issues of promiscuity, and so on. But when I made a tape for a gay audience, I talked about those same issues very differently. For one thing, I *talked* about those issues. And I tried to imagine them in ways that were very different from the way the dominant media image them. In *Orientations* I had one guy talk about park and washroom sex—about being a slut, basically—in a park at midday with front lighting. He talked very straightforwardly about it, which is only to say that there are many possibilities for doing this.

I think, however, that to talk about gay Asian desire is very difficult, because we need to swim through so much muck to get to it. It is very difficult (if even desirable) to do in purely positive terms, and I think it's necessary to do a lot of deconstruction along the way. I have no ready-made strategies; I feel it's a hit-and-miss sort of project.

Lei Chou: I want to bring back the issue of class. One of the gay Asian stereotypes that you mentioned was the Asian house boy. The reality is that many of these people are immigrants: English is a second language for them, and they are thus economically disenfranchised by being socially and culturally displaced. So when you talk about finding the Asian penis in pornography, how will this project work for such people? Since pornography is basically white and middle-class, what kind of tool is it? Who really is your target audience?

Fung: If I understand your question correctly, you are asking about the prognosis for new and different representations within commercial porn. And I don't think the prognosis is very good: changes will probably happen very slowly. At the same time, I think that pornography is an especially important site of struggle precisely for those Asians who are, as you say, economically and socially at a disadvantage, or those who are most isolated, whether in families or rural areas; print pornography is often the first introduction to gay sexuality—before, for example, the gay and lesbian press or gay Asian support groups. But this porn provides mixed messages: it affirms gay identity articulated almost exclusively as white. Whether we like it or not, mainstream gay porn is more available to most gay Asian men than any independent work you or I might produce. That is why pornography is a subject of such concern for me.

NOTES

I would like to thank Tim McCaskell and Helen Lee for their ongoing criticism and comments, as well as Jeff Nunokawa and Douglas Crimp for their invaluable suggestions in converting the original spoken presentation into a written text. Finally, I would like to extend my gratitude to Bad Object-Choices for inviting me to participate in "How Do I Look?"

1. Phillipe Rushton and Anthony Bogaert, "Race versus Social Class Difference in Sexual Behavior: A Follow-up Test of the r/K Dimension," *Journal of Research in Personality* 22 (1988): 259.
2. See Eric Williams, *Capitalism and Slavery* (New York: Capricorn, 1966).
3. Feminists of color have long pointed out that racism is phrased differently for men and women. Nevertheless, since it is usually heterosexual (and often middle-class) males whose voices are validated by the power structure, it is their interests that are taken up as "representing" the communities. See Barbara Smith, "Toward a Black Feminist Criticism," in *All the Women Are White, All the Blacks Are Men, But Some of Us Are Brave: Black Women's Studies* (Old Westbury, N.Y.: The Feminist Press, 1982), 182.
4. The mainstream "leadership" within Asian communities often colludes with the myth of the model minority and the reassuring desexualization of Asian people.
5. In Britain, however, more race-sex stereotypes of South Asians exist. Led by artists such as Pratibha Parmar, Sunil Gupta, and Hanif Kureishi, there is also a growing and already significant body of work by South Asians themselves, which takes up questions of sexuality.
6. Renee Tajima, "Lotus Blossoms Don't Bleed: Images of Asian Women," in *Anthologies of Asian American Film and Video* (New York: A distribution project of Third World Newsreel, 1984), 28.
7. Ibid., 29.
8. See Stephen Gong, "Zen Warrior of the Celluloid (Silent) Years: The Art of Sessue Hayakawa," *Bridge* 8, no. 2 (winter 1982–83): 37–41.
9. Frantz Fanon, *Black Skin, White Masks* (London: Paladin, 1970), 120. For a reconsideration of this statement in the light of contemporary black gay issues, see Kobena Mercer, "Imaging the Black Man's Sex," in *Photography / Politics: Two*, ed. Pat Holland, Jo Spence, and Simon Watney (London: Comedia/Methuen, 1987); reprinted in *Male Order: Unwrapping Masculinity*, ed. Rowena Chapman and Jonathan Rutherford (London: Lawrence and Wishart, 1988), 141.
10. I do not think this could happen in today's Toronto, which now has the second largest Chinese community on the continent. Perhaps it would not have happened in San Francisco. But I still believe that there is an onus on gay Asians and other gay people of color to prove our homosexuality.
11. The term "minority" is misleading. Racism is not a matter of numbers but of power. This is especially clear in situations where people of color constitute actual majorities, as in most former European colonies. At the same time, I feel that none of the current terms are really satisfactory and that too much time spent on the politics of "naming" can in the end be diversionary.
12. To organize effectively with lesbian and gay Asians, we must reject self-righteous condemnation of "closetedness" and see coming out more as a process or a goal, rather than as a prerequisite for participation in the movement.
13. Racism is available to be used by anyone. The conclusion that—because racism = power + prejudice—only white people can be racist is Eurocentric and simply wrong. Individuals have varying degrees and different sources of power, depending on the given moment in a shifting context. This does not contradict the fact that, in contemporary North American society, racism is generally organized around white supremacy.
14. From simple observation, I feel safe in saying that most gay Asian men in North America hold white men as their idealized sexual partners. However, I am not trying to construct an argument for determinism, and there are a number of outstanding problems that are not easily answered by current analyses of power. What of the experience of Asians who are attracted to men of color, including other Asians? What about white men who prefer Asians sexually? How and to what extent is desire articulated in terms of race as opposed to body type or other attributes? To what extent is sexual attraction exclusive

and/or changeable, and can it be consciously programmed? These questions are all politically loaded, as they parallel and impact the debates between essentialists and social constructionists on the nature of homosexuality itself. They are also emotionally charged, in that sexual choice involving race has been a basis for moral judgment.

15. See Richard Dyer, *Heavenly Bodies: Film Stars and Society* (New York: St. Martin's Press, 1986). In his chapter on Marilyn Monroe, Dyer writes extensively on the relationship between blondness, whiteness, and desirability.

16. Print porn is somewhat more racially integrated, as are the new safe sex tapes—by the Gay Men's Health Crisis, for example—produced in a political and pedagogical rather than a commercial context.

17. Richard Dyer, "Coming to Terms," *Jump Cut* 30 (March 1985): 28.

18. Tom Waugh, "Men's Pornography, Gay vs. Straight," *Jump Cut* 30 (March 1985): 31.

19. *International Wavelength News* 2, no. 1 (January 1991).

20. Tom Waugh, "Men's Pornography, Gay vs. Straight," 33.

21. It seems to me that the undressing here is organized around the pleasure of the white man in being served. This is in contrast to the undressing scenes, in, say, James Bond films, in which the narrative is organized around undressing as an act of revealing the woman's body, an indicator of sexual conquest.

22. Interestingly, the gay video porn from Japan and Thailand that I have seen has none of this Oriental coding. Asianness is not taken up as a sign but is taken for granted as a setting for the narrative.

23. Joanna Russ, "Pornography and the Doubleness of Sex for Women," *Jump Cut* 32 (April 1986): 39.

24. Though this is a common enough question in our postcolonial, urban environments, when asked of Asians it often reveals two agendas: first, the assumption that all Asians are newly arrived immigrants, and second, a fascination with difference and sameness. Although we (Asians) all supposedly look alike, there are specific characteristics and stereotypes associated with each particular ethnic group. The inability to tell us apart underlies the inscrutability attributed to Asians. This "inscrutability" took on sadly ridiculous proportions when during World War II the Chinese were issued badges so that white Canadians could distinguish them from "the enemy."

25. Isaac Julien (director), *Looking for Langston* (United Kingdom: Sankofa Film and Video, 1988).

26. For more on the origins of the black film and video workshops in Britain, see Jim Pines, "The Cultural Context of Black British Cinema," in *Blackframes: Critical Perspectives on Black Independent Cinema,* ed. Mybe B. Chain and Clair Andrade-Watkins (Cambridge, Mass.: MIT Press, 1988), 26.

MAIDEN VOYAGE

EXCURSION INTO SEXUALITY AND

IDENTITY POLITICS IN ASIAN AMERICA

Dana Y. Takagi

The topic of sexualities—in particular, lesbian, gay, and bisexual identities—is an important and timely issue in that place we imagine as Asian America. There are at least two compelling reasons to think about sexuality and Asian American history.

First, while there has been a good deal of talk about the "diversity" of Asian American communities, we are relatively uninformed about Asian American subcultures organized specifically around sexuality. There are Asian American gay and lesbian social organizations, gay bars that are known for Asian clientele, and conferences that have focused on Asian American lesbian and gay experiences. But gay Asian organizations are not likely to view themselves as a gay subculture within Asian America any more than they are likely to think of themselves as an Asian American subculture within gay America. If anything, I expect that many of us view ourselves as on the margins of both communities. That state of marginalization in both communities is what prompts this essay and makes the issues raised in it all the more urgent for all of us—gay, straight, somewhere-in-between. For, as Haraway has suggested, the view is often clearest from the margins where "The split and contradictory self is the one who can interrogate positionings and be accountable, the one who can construct and join rational conversations and fantastic imaginings that change history."[1]

To be honest, the very act of including lesbian and gay experiences in Asian American history, which seems important in a symbolic sense, produces in me a moment of hesitation. Not because I do not think that lesbian and gay sexualities are deserving of a place in Asian American history, but rather, because the inscription of nonstraight sexualities in Asian American history immediately casts theoretical doubt about how to do it. But the recognition of different sexual practices and identities that also claim the label *Asian American* presents a useful opportunity for rethinking and reevaluating notions of identity that have been used, for the most part, unproblematically and uncritically in Asian American Studies.

The second reason, then, that we ought to be thinking about gay and lesbian sexuality and Asian America is the theoretical trouble we encounter in our attempts to situate and think about sexual identity *and* racial identity. Just at the moment we attempt to rectify our ignorance by adding, say, the lesbian to Asian American history, we arrive at a stumbling block, an ignorance of how to add her. Surely the quickest and simplest way to add her is to think of lesbianism as a minority within a minority. But efforts to think of sexuality in the same terms that we think of race, yet simultaneously different from race in certain ways, and therefore to invite the inevitable "revelation" that gays/lesbians/bisexuals are like minorities but also different too, is often inconclusive, frequently ending in "counting" practice. While many minority women speak of "triple jeopardy" oppression—as if class, race, and gender could be disentangled into discrete additive parts—some Asian American lesbians could rightfully claim quadruple jeopardy oppression—class, race, gender, and sexuality. Enough counting. Marginalization is not as much about the *quantities* of experiences as it is about *qualities* of experience. And as many writers, most notably feminists, have argued, identities, whether drawn from sexual desire, racial origins, languages of gender, or class roots, are simply not additive.[2]

NOT COUNTING

Writing, speaking, acting queer. Against a backdrop of lotus leaves, sliding *shoji* panels, and the mountains of Guilin. Amid the bustling enclaves of Little Saigon, Koreatown, Chinatown, and Little Tokyo. Sexual identity, like racial identity, is one of many types of recognized "difference." If marginalization is a qualitative state of being and not simply a quantitative one, then what is it about being "gay" that is different from "Asian American"?

The terms "lesbian" and "gay," like "Third World," "woman," and "Asian American," are political categories that serve as rallying calls and personal affirmations. In claiming these identities we create and locate ourselves in phrases that seem a familiar fit: black gay man, Third World woman, working-class Chicana lesbian, Asian American bisexual, and so on. But is it possible to write these identities—like Asian American gay—without writing oneself into the corners that are either gay and only gay, or Asian American and only Asian American? Or, as Trinh T. Minh-ha put it, "How do you inscribe difference without bursting into a series of euphoric narcissistic accounts of yourself and your own kind?"[3]

It is in vogue these days to celebrate difference. But underlying much contemporary talk about difference is the assumption that differences are comparable things. For example, many new social activists, including those in the gay and lesbian movement, think of themselves as patterned on the "ethnic model."[4] And for many ethnic minorities, the belief that "gays are oppressed, too" is a reminder of a sameness, a common political project in moving margin to center, that unites race-based movements with gays, feminists, and Greens. The notion that our differences are "separate but equal" can be used to call attention to the specificity of experiences or to rally the troops under a collective banner. But in the heat of local political struggles and coalition building, it turns out that not all differences are created equal.

There are numerous ways that being "gay" is not like being "Asian." Two broad distinctions are worth noting. First is the relative invisibility of sexual identity compared with racial identity. While both can be said to be socially constructed, the former are performed, acted out, and produced, often in individual routines, whereas the latter tends to be more obviously "written" on the body and negotiated by political groups.[5] Put another way, there is a quality of voluntarism in being gay/lesbian that is usually not possible as an Asian American. One has the option to present onself as "gay" or "lesbian," or alternatively, to attempt to "pass," or to stay in "the closet," that is, to hide one's sexual preference.[6] However, these same options are not available to most racial minorities in face-to-face interactions with others. Put another way, homosexuality is more clearly seen as *constructed* than is racial identity.[7] As Asian Americans, we do not think in advance about whether or not to present ourselves as "Asian American"; rather, that is an identification that is worn by us, whether we like it or not, and which is easily read off of us by others.

A second major reason the category "gay" cannot be comparable to the category "Asian American" is the very different histories of each group. Studying the politics of being "gay" entails, on the one hand, an analysis of discursive fields, ideologies, and rhetoric about sexual identity, and, on the other hand, knowledge of the history of gays/lesbians as subordinated minorities relative to heterosexuals.... Similarly, studying "Asian America" requires analysis of semantic and rhetorical discourse in its variegated forms, racist, apologist, and paternalist, and requires in addition an understanding of the specific histories of the peoples who recognize themselves as Asian or Asian American. But the specific discourses and histories in each case are quite different. Even though we make the same intellectual moves to approach each form of identity, that is, a two-tracked study of ideology on the one hand, and history on the other, the particular ideologies and histories of each are very different.[8]

In other words, many of us experience the worlds of Asian America and gay America as separate places—emotionally, physically, intellectually. We sustain the separation of these worlds with our folk knowledge about the family-centeredness and suprahomophobic beliefs of ethnic communities. And we frequently take great care to keep those worlds distant from each other. What could be more different than the scene at gay bars like "The End Up" in San Francisco or "Faces" in Hollywood, and, on the other hand, the annual Buddhist church bazaars in the Japanese American community or Filipino revivalist meetings?[9] These disparate worlds occasionally collide through individuals who manage to move, for the most part stealthily, between these spaces. But it is the act of deliberately bringing these worlds closer together that seems unthinkable. Imagining your parents, clutching bento box lunches, thrust into the smoky haze of a South of Market leather bar in San Francisco is no less strange a vision than the idea of Lowie taking Ishi, the last of his tribe, for a cruise on Lucas's *Star Wars* Tour at Disneyland. "Cultural strain," the anthropologists would say. Or, as Wynn Young, laughing at the prospect of mixing his family with his boyfriend, said, "Somehow I just can't picture his conversation at the dinner table, over my mother's homemade barbecued pork:

'Hey, Ma, I'm sleeping with a sixty-year-old white guy who's got three kids, and would you please pass the soy sauce?"[10]

That the topic of *homo*-sexuality in Asian American studies is often treated in whispers, if mentioned at all, should be some indication of trouble. It is noteworthy, I think, that in the last major anthology on Asian American women, *Making Waves,* the author of the essay on Asian American lesbians was the only contributor who did not wish her last name to be published.[11] Of course, as we all know, a chorus of sympathetic bystanders is chanting about homophobia, saying, "She was worried about her job, her family, her community. . . . " Therefore, perhaps a good starting point for considering lesbian and gay identities in Asian American Studies is to problematize the silences surrounding homosexuality in Asian America. While it may seem politically efficacious to toss the lesbian onto the diversity pile, adding one more form of subordination to the heap of inequalities, such a strategy glosses over the particular or distinctive ways sexuality is troped in Asian America. One way homosexuality may be seen as a vehicle for theorizing identity in Asian America is through the missteps, questions, and silences that are often clearest in collisions at the margins (identities as opposed to people). In the following discussion, I describe two such confrontations—the coming out of a white student in an Asian American Studies class and the problem of authenticity in gay/lesbian Asian American writing. Each tells in its own way the awkward limits of ethnic-based models of identity.

THE COMING-OUT INCIDENT

Once, when I was a teaching assistant during the early 1980s, a lesbian, one of only two white students in my section, decided to come out during the first section meeting. I had asked each student to explain their interest, personal and intellectual, in Asian American Studies. Many students mentioned wanting to know "more about their heritage" and "knowing the past in order to understand the present." The lesbian was nearly last to speak. After explaining that she wanted to understand the heritage of a friend who was Asian American, she said, "And, I guess I also want you all to know that I am a lesbian." In the silence that followed I quickly surveyed the room. A dozen or so Asian American students whom I had forced into a semicircular seating arrangement stared glumly at their shoes. The two white students, both of whom were lesbians, glanced expectantly around the circle, and then they, too, looked at the ground. I felt as though my own world had split apart, and the two pieces were in front of me, drifting, surrounding, and at that moment, both silent.

I knew both parts well. On the one side, I imagined that the Asian American students in the class recoiled in private horror at the lesbian, not so much because she was a lesbian or white, but because she insisted on publicly baring her soul in front of them. I empathized with the Asian American students because they reminded me of myself as an undergraduate. While my fellow white students chatted effortlessly in section about readings or lectures, I was almost always mute. I marveled at the ease with which questions, thoughts, answers, and even half-baked ideas rolled off their tongues and floated discussion. For them, it all seemed so easy. As for me, I struggled with the act of talking in class. Occasionally, I managed to add a question to the discussion, but more often I found that by the time I had silently practiced my entry into a fast-moving exchange, the discussion had moved on. In my silence, I chastised myself for moving too slowly, for hesitating where others did not, and alternately, chastised the other students for their bulldozing, loose lips. I valorized and resented the verbal abilities of my fellow classmates. And I imagined how, like me, the Asian American students who sat in my class the day the lesbian decided to come out identified the ability to bare one's soul through words as "white." On the other side, I empathized as well with the lesbian. I identified with what I imagined as her compelling need to claim her identity, to be like the others in the class, indeed to be an "other" at all in a class where a majority of the students were in search of their "roots." I figured that being a lesbian, while not quite like being Asian American, must have seemed to the intrepid student as close to the ethnic model as she could get. Finally, I thought she represented a side of me that always wanted, but never could quite manage, to drop the coming-out bomb in groups that did not expect it. Part of the pleasure in being an "outsider" can be in the affirmation of the identity abhorred by "insiders." I imagined that she and her friend had signed up for my section because they *knew* I too was a lesbian, and I worried that they assumed that I might be able to protect them from the silence of the closet.

In the silence that followed the act of coming out, and, indeed, in the ten weeks of class in which no one spoke of it again, I felt an awkwardness settle over our discussions in section. I was never sure exactly how the Asian American students perceived the lesbian—as a wannabe "minority," as a comrade in marginality, as any white Other; or perhaps they did not think of it at all. Nor did I ever know if the lesbian found what she was looking for, a better understanding of the Asian American experience, in the silence that greeted her coming out.

More important, the coming-out incident suggests that marginalization is no guarantee for dialogue. If there is to be an interconnectedness between different vantage points, we will need to establish an art of political conversation that allows for affirmation of difference without choking secularization. The construction of such a politics is based implicitly on our vision of what ought to happen when difference meets itself—queer meets Asian, black meets Korean, feminist meets Green, and so on, at times all in one person.[12] What exactly must we know about these other identities in order to engage in dialogue?

THE QUESTION OF AUTHENTICITY

What we do know about Asian American gays and lesbians must be gleaned from personal narratives, literature, poetry, short stories, and essays. But first, what falls under the mantle *Asian American gay and lesbian* writings? Clearly, lesbians and gays whose writings are self-conscious reflections on Asian American identity and sexual identity ought to be categorized as Asian American gay/lesbian writers. For example, Kitty Tsui, Barbara Noda, Alice Hom, and Merle Woo are lesbians who write about themselves as lesbians, which grants them authorial voice *as lesbians*. But they also identify as *Asian American* and are concerned with the ways in which these different sources of community—lesbian and Asian American—function in their everyday lives.

But what then about those who do not write explicitly or self-consciously about their sexuality or racial identity? For example, an essay on AIDS and mourning by Jeff Nunokawa, while written by a Japanese American English professor, does not focus on issues of racial and sexual *identity,* and as such is neither self-consciously gay nor Asian American.[13] What are we to make of such work? On the one hand, we might wish to categorize the author as a gay Asian American writer, whether he wishes to take this sign or not—presuming, of course, that he is gay, since his essay appears in an anthology subtitled "gay theories," and in addition presuming that he is Asian American, or at least identifies as such given his last name. On the other hand, we might argue that it is the author's work, his subject matter, and not the status of the author, that marks the work as gay, Asian American, or both. . . . In this case, we might infer that since the topic of the essay is AIDS and men, the work is best categorized as "gay," but not Asian American.

The university is filled with those of us who, while we live under signs like gay, Asian, feminist, ecologist, middle-class, and so on, do not make such signs the central subject of our research. And what about those individuals who write about gays/lesbians, but who identify themselves as heterosexual? In the same way that colonizers write about the colonized, and more recently, the colonized write back, blacks write about whites and vice versa, "we" write about "them" and so on.

Not only is marginalization no guarantee for dialogue; the state of being marginalized itself may not be capturable as a fixed, coherent, and holistic identity. Our attempts to define categories like "Asian American" or "gay" are necessarily incomplete.

A politics of identity and whatever kind of politics ensues from that project—multiculturalism, feminism, and gay movements—is first of all a politics about identity. That is, about the lack of a holistic and "coherent narrative" derived from race, class, gender, and sexuality. . . . Because no sooner do we define, for example, "Japanese American" as a person of Japanese ancestry than we are forced back to the drawing board by the biracial child of a Japanese American and African American who thinks of herself as "black" or "feminist."

RETHINKING IDENTITY POLITICS

The gist of this essay has been to insist that our valuation of heterogeneity not be ad hoc and that we seize the opportunity to recognize non-ethnic-based differences—like homosexuality—as an occasion to critique the tendency toward essentialist currents in ethnic-based narratives and disciplines. In short, the practice of including gayness in Asian America rebounds into a reconsideration of the theoretical status of the concept of "Asian American" identity. The interior of the category "Asian American" ought not be viewed as a hierarchy of identities led by ethnic-based narratives, but rather, the complicated interplay and collision of different identities.

At the heart of my insistence on a qualitative, not quantitative, view of difference is a particular notion of subjectivity. That notion of the subject as nonunitary—that is, the notion that each of us has multiple identities—stands in sharp contrast to the holistic and coherent identities that find expression in much contemporary talk and writing about Asian Americans. At times, our need to "reclaim history" has been bluntly translated into a possessiveness about *the* Asian American experience (politics, history, literature) or perspective as if such experiences or perspectives were not diffuse, shifting, and often contradictory. Feminists and gay writers offer an alternative: to "theorize" the subject rather than assume its truth or, worse yet, assign to it a truth.

To theorize the subject means to uncover in magnificent detail the "situated-ness"[14] of perspectives or identities. The politics that result will be marked by moments of frustration and tension, because the participants will be pulling and pushing one another with statements such as "I am like you" and "I am not like you." But the reward for an identity politics that is not primarily ethnic-based, or essentialist along some other axis, will be that conversations like the one that never took place in my Asian American Studies section many years ago will finally begin.

NOTES

My special thanks to Russell Leong for his encouragement and commentary on this essay.

1. See Donna Haraway, "Situated Knowledges: The Science Question in Feminism and the Privilege of Partial Perspective," *Feminist Studies* 14, no. 3 (1988): 575–599.
2. See Teresa de Lauretis, "Feminist Studies/Critical Studies: Issues, Terms, and Contexts," in *Feminist Studies/Critical Studies,* ed. Teresa de Lauretis (Bloomington: Indiana University Press, 1986), 1–19; bell hooks, *Yearning: Race, Gender and Cultural Politics* (Boston: South End Press, 1990); Trinh T. Minh-ha, *Woman, Native, Other* (Bloomington: Indiana University Press, 1989); Chandra Talpade Mohanty, "Under Western Eyes: Feminist and Colonialist Discourses," in *Third World Women and the Politics of Feminism,* ed. Chandra Talpade Mohanty, Ann Russo, and Lourdes Torres (Bloomington: Indiana University Press, 1991), 52–80; Linda Alcoff, "Cultural Feminism versus Post-Structuralism: The Identity Crisis in Feminist Theory," *Signs* 13, no. 3 (1988): 405–437.
3. Trinh T. Minh-ha, *Woman, Native, Other,* 28.
4. Steven Epstein, "Gay Politics and Ethnic Identity: The Limits of Social Constructionism," *Socialist Review* 17, nos. 3/4 (May/August 1987): 9–54. Jeffrey Escoffier, editor of *Outlook* magazine, made this point in a speech at the American Educational Research Association meeting in San Francisco, April 24, 1992.
5. Of course there are exceptions—for example, blacks that "pass." Perhaps this is where homosexuality and racial identity come closest to one another, amongst those minorities who "pass" and gays who can also "pass."
6. I do not mean to suggest that there is only one presentation of self as lesbian. For example, one development is the evolution of "lipstick lesbians." The fashion issue has also been discussed in gay/lesbian publications.
7. See Judith Butler, *Gender Trouble* (New York: Routledge, 1990); Michel Foucault, *The History of Sexuality, Volume 1: An Introduction,* trans. Robert Hurley (New York: Vintage, 1980); Monique Wittig, *The Straight Mind and Other Essays* (Boston: Beacon Press, 1992); David Greenberg, *The Construction of Homosexuality* (Chicago: University of Chicago Press, 1988).
8. Compare for example the histories—Ronald Takaki's *Strangers from a Different Shore,* Sucheng Chan's *Asian Americans,* and Roger Daniels's *Chinese and Japanese in America—* with Jonathan Katz's *Gay American History,* Jeffrey Week's *The History of Sexuality,* Michel Foucault's *History of Sexuality,* and David Greenberg's *The Construction of Homosexuality.*
9. See Steffi San Buenaventura, "The Master and the Federation: A Filipino American

Social Movement in California and Hawaii," *Social Process in Hawaii* 33 (1991): 169–193.

10. Wynn Young, "Poor Butterfly," *Amerasia Journal* 17, no. 2 (1991): 118.

11. See Asian Women United, *Making Waves* (Boston: Beacon Press, 1989).

12. All too often we conceptualize different identities as separate, discrete, and given (as opposed to continually constructed and shifting). For an example of how "identity" might be conceptualized as contradictory and shifting moments rather than discrete and warring "homes" see Minnie Bruce Pratt, "Identity: Skin Blood Heart," in *Yours in Struggle: Three Feminist Perspectives on Anti-Semitism and Anti-Racism,* ed. Elly Bulkin, Minnie Bruce Pratt, and Barbara Smith (Ithaca, N.Y.: Firebrand Books, 1984), 11–63, and commentary by Biddy Martin and Chandra Talpade Mohanty, "Feminist Politics: What's Home Got to Do with It?" in *Feminist Studies, Clinical Studies,* ed. Teresa de Lauretis (Bloomington: Indiana University Press, 1986), 191–212.

13. See Jeff Nunokawa, "All the Sad Young Men: AIDS and the Work of Mourning," in *inside/out,* ed. Diana Fuss (New York: Routledge, 1991), 311–323.

14. Haraway, "Situated Knowledges: The Science Question in Feminism and the Privilege of Partial Perspective," in *Simians, Cyborgs, and Women* (New York: Routledge, 1991), 188.

Critical Race Theory

WHY WE NEED A CRITICAL ASIAN AMERICAN LEGAL STUDIES

Robert Chang

Asian Americans suffer from discrimination. Much of this discrimination is quantitatively and qualitatively different from that suffered by other disempowered groups. The qualitative difference, in that Asian Americans suffer as Asian Americans and not just generically as persons of color, has certain implications for the study of Asian Americans and the law. I realize that this may raise the (obligatory) essentialist question. I do not make the claim that there is a unitary, essential Asian American experience. Such a claim would be foolhardy given the diversity encompassed in the category "Asian American" and in its intersection with gender, class, sexual orientation, and disability. However, acknowledging the limitations behind the category "Asian American" does not render the term meaningless. One may still talk about "Asian Americans" despite the heterogeneity, hybridity, and multiplicity contained within the term and the bodies that constitute it and that it constitutes.[1] Further, "Asian American" can be used as a "strategic identity."[2] Even though the category "Asian American" can (and perhaps should) be subverted, one can, as has been argued in the context of gay and lesbian rights, still "tak[e] advantage of a civil rights heritage that is grounded on identity politics," despite the "desire to deconstruct the imprisoning category itself."[3]

However, care must be taken when engaging in traditional civil rights work, which has a tendency to emphasize color-blindness and to deny substantial difference. To deny difference may erase Asian American identities and may be inadequate to address fully the needs of Asian Americans. Instead of traditional civil rights work, we might turn to critical race theory, a legal movement that began in the late 1980s as a racial intervention in critical legal studies and as a leftist intervention in liberal race discourse.[4] Richard Delgado describes critical race scholarship as having the following themes:

> (1) an insistence on "naming our own reality"; (2) the belief that knowledge and ideas are powerful; (3) a readiness to question basic premises of moderate/incremental civil rights law; (4) the borrowing of insights from social science on race and racism; (5) critical examination of the myths and stories powerful groups use to justify racial subordination; (6) a more contextualized treatment of doctrine; (7) criticism of liberal legalisms; and (8) an interest in structural determinism—the ways in which legal tools and thought-structures can impede law reform.[5]

John Calmore describes critical race theory in the following manner:

> [C]ritical race theory can be identified as such not because a random sample of people of color are voicing a position, but rather because certain people of color have deliberately chosen race-conscious orientations and objectives to resolve conflicts of interpretation in acting on the commitment to social justice and antisubordination.[6]

One problem, though, with critical race theory is that while it has made the powerful claim that race matters, it has yet to show how different races matter differently. Part two of this chapter is an attempt to correct this by developing a critical legal studies focused on Asian Americans.

In making this distinction between traditional civil rights work, which seeks to minimize differences, and a critical Asian American legal studies with its (partial) claim of distinctiveness, it might seem that I am setting up what Anthony Appiah calls "the classic dialectic of reaction to prejudice":

> The thesis in this dialectic . . . is the denial of difference. Du Bois' antithesis is the acceptance of difference, along with a claim that each group has its part to play; that the white race and its racial Other are related not as superior to inferior but as complementaries; that the Negro message is, with the white one, part of the message of humankind. I call this pattern the classic dialectic for a simple reason: we find it in feminism also—on the one hand, a simple claim to equality, a denial of substantial difference; on the other, a claim to a special message, revaluing the feminine Other not as the helpmate of sexism, but as the New Woman.[7]

However, a critical Asian American legal studies, in making its claim of distinctiveness, is not simply the antithesis of Asian American civil rights work. It is not a matter of either sameness or difference, but rather, both/and.

This critical Asian American legal studies will provide a framework that will encompass and mediate between the notions of liberalism underlying civil rights work and the critical perspectives contained within critical race theory. I have several goals in mind:

- A critical Asian American legal studies will recognize that Asian Americans are differently situated historically with respect to other disempowered groups. A study of race relations in the United States cannot focus solely on the relationship between the dominant white majority and each subordinate minority group. It must also focus on interethnic and interracial relations. This expansion of the study of "Majority-Minority Relations" to include "Minority-Minority Relations" represents a necessary shift in the current paradigm of racial dynamics in the United States.[8]
- Despite the historical differences in the treatment of different minority groups, the commonality found in shared oppression can bring different disempowered groups together to participate in each others' struggles.
- The exclusion of Asian Americans from the political and legal processes has led to an impoverished notion of politics and law that furthers the oppression of Asian Americans. A critical Asian American legal studies will offer the inclusion of Asian American voices in the form of narrative, personal and otherwise, in the practice of legal scholarship as a powerful method to combat the effects of exclusion.[9]
- Finally, by including narratives in law review articles, briefs, and law teaching, this legal scholarship will more effectively persuade decision makers, practitioners, law professors, and students.

Present-day attitudes often demonstrate a lack of understanding about the history and current status of Asian Americans. For example, during the spring of 1991, a national poll conducted by the *Wall Street Journal* and NBC News "revealed that the majority of American voters believe that Asian Americans are not discriminated against in the United States" and that "[s]ome even believe that Asian Americans receive 'too many special advantages.'"[10] In 1992 the United States Commission on Civil Rights called this a misconception and compiled evidence confirming that Asian Americans face widespread prejudice, discrimination, and barriers to equal opportunity. A first step then is to counter the misperception that Asian Americans occupy a privileged position in U.S. society. Because a comprehensive overview of Asian American history is beyond the scope of this book, I will discuss two major issues here: nativistic violence and discrimination against Asian Americans, and the "model minority" myth.[11]

While all disempowered groups have suffered from exclusion and marginalization, Asian Americans have been subjected to unique forms of these problems. Traditional civil rights advocates and critical race scholars have failed to account sufficiently for these differences. A critical Asian American legal studies is needed to change the current racial paradigm, which is inadequate to support a more complete discourse on race and the law.

THAT WAS THEN, THIS IS NOW: VARIATIONS ON A THEME

Part of the problem is that many people remain unaware of the violence and discrimination that have plagued Asian Americans since their arrival in this country. Much of this ignorance can be attributed to school textbooks that fail to include Asian Americans in the history of this nation.[12] Moreover, those who know the history often fail to make the connection between this history and the ongoing problems that continue to affect Asian Americans today. I attribute this lack of awareness in part to history textbooks that "routinely omit the word 'because.' . . . Students must guess whether facts strung together are causally related. Texts present a 'crabgrass' or 'natural disaster' theory of history; problems unaccountably grow until they become serious, at which time they keep on going until they stop."[13] If things are going to improve, we should remember what the philosopher George Santayana said: "Progress, far from consisting in change, depends on retentiveness."[14] When I look at certain recent events, such as the rise in the incidence of hate crimes directed toward Asian Americans, or the rhetoric of the official English movement and of politicians such as Patrick Buchanan, or even the uproar caused by the sale of the Rockefeller Center and the Seattle Mariners to Japanese investors, I question how much progress we have made. When I look at those events, I see that we have not retained in our cultural memory the history of discrimination against Asian Americans, and we are left to replay variations on the tired theme of anti-Asian violence.

VIOLENCE AGAINST ASIAN AMERICANS

Anti-Asian sentiment has historically expressed itself in violent attacks against Asian Americans. The 1982 killing of Vincent Chin in Detroit by two white auto workers is one variation on this theme. Vincent Chin, a Chinese American, was punished by the two white men for being of Asian ancestry and for paying attention to a white woman. People like him were displacing "real" Americans like them from their jobs; people like him were displacing "real" Americans like them from their rightful place with their women. This threat to their white masculinity and to their sense of economic and sexual entitlement pushed them to hunt Vincent for twenty to thirty minutes, to sneak up on him and grab him, and to beat him to death with a baseball bat. The physical violence was then compounded by the light sentences—a fine of $3,780, probation for three years, and no jail time—given to the two attackers, who, according to the judge, had simply been administering a punishment that got out of hand.[15]

I relate this story not to point out a miscarriage of justice (and I know that our judicial system is not perfect). Instead, I tell the story to begin developing the thesis that the killing of Vincent Chin is not an isolated episode. Violence stems from, and is causally related to, anti-Asian feelings that arise during times of economic hardship and the resurgence of nativism, the "intense opposition to an internal minority on the grounds of its foreign (i.e., 'un-American') connections."[16]

Another variation on the theme of anti-Asian sentiment is the killing of Navroze Mody. Mody was an Asian Indian who was beaten to death in 1987 in Jersey City by a gang of eleven youths who did not harm Mody's white friend. No murder or bias charges were brought; instead, three of the assailants were convicted of assault while one was convicted of aggravated assault. This attack took place in the context of other racially motivated hostilities directed against Asian Indians, who were the fastest-growing immigrant group in New Jersey. Earlier in the month that Navroze Mody was killed, a Jersey City gang called the Dotbusters (named after the bindi, the dot that Indian women often wear as a sign of marital fidelity) had published a letter in the *Jersey Journal* saying that they "would 'go to any extreme' to drive Indians from Jersey City."[17] Violence against Asian Indians began the next day, with an attack on an Asian Indian in his home after his name had been picked out of a phone book by the assailants. One community leader said that "the violence worked. . . . People moved out, and others thinking of moving here from the city moved elsewhere."[18]

These recent events read in some ways like a page from the book of history. They resemble other racially motivated incidents of the past. In the late 1800s, a white supremacist organization known as the Order of Caucasians was active throughout California. They blamed the Chinese for the economic woes suffered by all workers. Their tactics included threatening letters sent to people who employed Chinese laborers:

> Dear Sir: You are respectfully requested without further warning to discharge the Chinamen in your employ, and give your work to whites instead, whom you well know are suffering from the effects of all those heathens in our midst. Think well of the country of your adoption, and try to assist the poor white man in making an honest living. Take heed lest the course you are now pursuing shall fall upon your own head with tenfold vengeance. [Signed]— Native Americans.[19]

Even though many members of the Order of Caucasians were in fact immigrants from Europe, their white skins were sufficient to grant them functional membership as "native" Americans.

One example of their work took place in 1877 in Chico, California. While attemping to burn down all of Chico's Chinatown, members of a labor union associated with the Order of Caucasians murdered four Chinese workers by tying them up, dousing them with kerosene, and setting them on fire. The attackers were convicted but were released long before the end of their sentences.

The Chinese Massacre of 1885 also took place in the context of a struggling economy and a growing nativist movement. In Rock Springs, Wyoming, a mob of white miners, angered by the Chinese miners' refusal to join their strike, killed twenty-eight Chinese laborers, wounded fifteen, and chased several hundred out of town. It should be remembered that the Chinese miners were not permitted to join the white miners' union. In this incident, as in many others, a grand jury failed to indict a single person.[20]

My informal count, based on a very limited survey of the literature, came up with more than three hundred Chinese killed in racially motivated assaults in the West between 1860 and 1887.[21] I hesitate to provide even this number because much of the violence was not documented and we will never know the actual extent of violence directed against Chinese workers. Part of the problem lies in the failure of school textbooks and historians to acknowledge the extent of this violence. For example, in a recent work entitled "Historiography of Violence in the American West," Richard Brown limits his discussion of anti-Chinese violence to two paragraphs.[22] This lack of coverage is odd because even though the Western frontier was a violent place, no group, except for American Indians, encountered as much violence as did the Chinese.[23]

I could go on, but my point is not merely to describe. I seek to link the present with the past. In linking these late-nineteenth-century events with present events, I may seem to be drawing improper associations by taking things out of context. In fact, I am doing the reverse. I am placing present events into context to show that today's rising incidence of hate crimes against Asian Americans, like the violence of the past, is fostered by a climate of anti-Asian sentiment spurred by economic troubles and nativism. As Stanley Fish stated in a different context, "I am arguing for a match at every level, from the smallest detail to the deepest assumptions. It is not simply that the books written today bear some similarities to the books that warned earlier generations of the ethnic menace: they are the same books."[24] Fish was discussing books, but there is, of course, a sometimes unfortunate link between words and deeds.

NATIVISTIC RACISM

The words accompanying the violent deeds of the present also grow out of the resurgence of nativism. This resurgence is apparent in some of the arguments marshaled against multiculturalism. Stanley Fish presents a cogent summary of one of the leading critics of multiculturalism, Arthur M. Schlesinger Jr.:

> [Schlesinger] finds the threat in what he calls the "ethnic upsurge," an "unprecedented . . . protest against the Anglocentric culture" that "today threatens to become a counter-revolution against the original theory of America as . . . a common culture, a single nation." Schlesinger deplores the rejection of what he calls "the old American ideal of assimilation"—the ideal that asks immigrants and minorities to "shed their ethnicity" in favor of the Western Anglo-Saxon tradition. . . . "White guilt," he declares, "can be pushed too far," and he predicts that the multiculturalist ethnic upsurge will be defeated by the fact that "the American synthesis has an inevitable Anglo-Saxon coloration."[25]

As Fish correctly surmises, "It is clear from these quotations that for Schlesinger the danger of multiculturalism is not confined to the classroom, but extends to the very fabric of our society."[26] Some politicians have used the rhetoric of nativism to great effect, gaining support among segments of the population. An obvious example is Patrick Buchanan, who said, "Who speaks for the Euro-Americans who founded the United States? . . . Is it not time to take America back?"[27]

Nativism, with its message of America first, has a certain allure. Indeed, to reject its message seems unpatriotic. However, present-day nativism is grounded in racism, and should be termed nativistic racism, which differs from the traditional paradigm of racism by including the element of "foreign."[28] Nativistic racism lurks behind the specter of "the Japanese 'taking over,'" which appeared when Mitsubishi Corporation bought a 51 percent share of the Rockefeller Center and when Nintendo purchased "a piece of America's national pastime," the Seattle Mariners, an American League baseball team. These sentiments were not just the views of those on the fringe. When the sale of the Mariners baseball team was being contemplated, surveys revealed that a majority of Americans "disapproved of Japanese ownership in the national pastime."[29] The first problem with the notion of "the Japanese taking over" is that "Japan" did not buy Rockefeller Center; nor did "Japan" buy a piece of America's national pastime. In both instances, private corporations made the investments. The second problem is the different treatment of Japanese investors as compared to those from other Western nations. Why is there an outcry when Japanese investors buy institutions such as the Rockefeller Center or Columbia Pictures, but not when other Westerners buy similar institutions? Moreover, the notion of the Japanese "taking over" is factually unsupported. As of January 1992, in the midst of the clamor about the Japanese buying out America, Japanese investors owned less than 2 percent of United States commercial property. We might compare this with the level of British investments, which far exceeds that of Japanese investors in the United States.[30]

Similarly, in 1910, three years before California passed its first Alien Land Law—which targeted aliens ineligible for citizenship and prevented them from owning real property—Japanese Americans controlled just 2.1 percent of California's farms.[31] Nevertheless, Japanese Americans were perceived to be a threat of such magnitude that a law was passed "to discourage further immigration of Japanese aliens to California and to call to the attention of Congress and the rest of the country the desire of California that the 'Japanese menace' be crushed."[32] Through lobbying efforts by various chambers of commerce, boards of trade, merchants associations, and foreign oil and copper syndicates, the law was designed to be of limited applicability instead of one affecting all aliens. It did so by targeting Asian immigrants, particularly the Japanese, as aliens ineligible for citizenship. The naturalization statute in effect in 1913 restricted naturalization to free white persons and persons of African nativity or descent. Although the United States Supreme Court had yet to decide the issue of naturalization for Asian immigrants, these immigrants were apparently excluded from naturalization, as many lower courts held. By limiting the application of the Alien Land Law to aliens ineligible for citizenship, European interests were protected.[33]

These examples show that little has changed over the past hundred years in the way persons of Asian ancestry are seen as perpetual foreigners whose racialized bodies constitute a threat to the American way of life. It is this sense of "foreignness" that distinguishes the particular type of racism directed at Asian Americans. Understanding the way nativistic racism operates is one of the insights offered by a critical legal studies centered on Asian Americans. Bringing this to light is important because nativistic racism must first be represented and named before it can be combated.

THE MODEL MINORITY MYTH

One barrier to bringing nativistic racism to light is that the history of discrimination and violence and the contemporary problems of Asian Americans are obscured by the portrayal of Asian Americans as a "model minority." Asian Americans are portrayed as "hardworking, intelligent, and successful."[34] This description represents a sharp break from past stereotypes of Asians as "sneaky, obsequious, or inscrutable."[35] But the dominant culture's belief in the "model minority" allows it to justify ignoring the unique discrimination faced by Asian Americans. The portrayal of Asian Americans as successful permits the general public, government officials, and the judiciary to ignore or marginalize the contemporary needs of Asian Americans.

The phrase "model minority" was coined by William Petersen, a demographer-sociologist at the University of California, Berkeley. In a *New York Times Magazine* article in early 1966, Petersen used

> the term "model" in two senses: first, as a way of praising the superior performance of Japanese Americans; and second, as a way of suggesting that other ethnic groups should *emulate* the Japanese American example. The unstated major premise of Petersen's argument was that Horatio-Alger-bootstrap-raising was needed for success by such "non-achieving" minorities as blacks and Chicanos, rather than the social programs of Lyndon Johnson's "Great Society."[36]

Later that year, an article in *U.S. News & World Report* followed up on the same theme, focusing this time on Chinese Americans:

> At a time when Americans are awash in worry over the plight of racial minorities—
>
> One such minority, the nation's 300,000 Chinese-Americans, is winning wealth and respect by dint of its own hard work.
>
> In any Chinatown from San Francisco to New York, you discover youngsters at grips with their studies. . . .
>
> Still being taught in Chinatown is the old idea that people should depend on their own efforts—not a welfare check—in order to reach America's "promised land."
>
> Visit "Chinatown U.S.A." and you find an important racial minority pulling itself up from hardship and discrimination to become a model of self-respect and achievement in today's America.[37]

Again, the lesson is that there is something to be learned from the self-reliance of Chinese Americans who work hard instead of relying on welfare. This "model minority" theme has become a largely unquestioned assumption about current social reality. The early articulations have been reinforced by a spate of media stories in the mid-1980s:

In 1986, NBC Nightly News and the McNeil/Lehrer Report aired special news segments on Asian Americans and their success, and a year later, CBS's "60 Minutes" presented a glowing report on their stunning achievements in the academy. "Why are Asian Americans doing so exceptionally well in school?" Mike Wallace asked, and quickly added, "They must be doing something right. Let's bottle it." Meanwhile, *U.S. News & World Report* featured Asian-American advances in a cover story, and *Time* devoted an entire section on this meteoric minority in its special immigrants issue, "The Changing Face of America." Not to be outdone by its competitors, *Newsweek* titled the cover story of its college-campus magazine "Asian-Americans: The Drive to Excel" and a lead article of its weekly edition "Asian Americans: A 'Model Minority.'" *Fortune* went even further, applauding them as "America's Super Minority," and the *New Republic* extolled "The Triumph of Asian Americans" as "America's greatest success story."[38]

At its surface, the label "model minority" seems like a compliment. However, once one moves beyond this complimentary façade, one can see the label for what it is—a tool of oppression that works a dual harm by (1) denying the existence of present-day discrimination against Asian Americans and the present-day effects of past discrimination, and (2) legitimizing the oppression of other racial minorities and poor whites.

The notion that Asian Americans are a "model minority" is a myth. But the myth has gained a substantial following, both inside and outside Asian American communities. The successful inculcation of the model minority myth has created an audience unsympathetic to the problems of Asian Americans. Thus, when we try to make our problems known, our complaints of discrimination or calls for remedial action are seen as unwarranted and inappropriate and may spark resentment. For example, Mitsuye Yamada tells a story about the angry reactions of her Ethnic American Literature class to an anthology compiled by some outspoken Asian American writers. Her students were not offended by the militancy expressed by Black American, Chicano, or Native American writings because

> they "understood" the anger expressed by the Blacks and Chicanos and they "empathized" with the frustrations and sorrow expressed by the Native American. But the Asian Americans?? [*sic*]
>
> Then finally, one student said it for all of them: "It made me angry. *Their* anger made *me* angry, because I didn't even know the Asian Americans felt oppressed. I didn't expect their anger."[39]

This story illustrates the danger of the model minority myth, which renders the oppression of Asian Americans invisible. This invisibility has harmful consequences, especially when those in positions of power cannot see. Programs designed to help Asian Americans learn English and to find jobs have been denied funding by policy makers and government officials who believed that Asian Americans had succeeded and needed no aid. College administrators, believing the same, have sometimes excluded poor Asian American students from Educational Opportunity Programs even though eligibility for those programs is to include all students from low-income families.[40]

In this way, the model minority myth diverts much-needed attention from the problems of many segments of the Asian American community, particularly the Laotians, Hmong, Cambodians, and Vietnamese who have poverty rates of 34.7 percent, 63.6 percent, 42.6 percent, and 25.7 percent, respectively. These poverty rates compare with a national poverty rate of 13 percent.[41]

This distorted view of the current status of Asian Americans has infected not only government officials but at least one very influential member of the judiciary and legal academy. In a recent speech, Judge Richard Posner posed two questions: "Are Asians an oppressed group in the United States today? Are they worse off for lacking sizable representation on the faculties of American law schools?"[42] His questions were rhetorical because he already had answers, with figures to back them up: "In 1980, Japanese-Americans had incomes more than 32 percent above the national average income, and Chinese-Americans had incomes more than 12 percent above the national average; Anglo-Saxons and Irish exceeded the average by 5 percent and 2 percent, respectively."[43] He also pointed out that "in 1980, 17.8 percent of the white population aged 25 and over had completed four or more years of college, compared to 32.9 percent of the Asian-American population."[44] Unspoken but assumed in Posner's comments is the meritocratic thesis: "that, when compared to Whites, there are equal payoffs for qualified and educated racial minorities; education and other social factors, but not race, determine earnings."[45] If Posner is right, Asian Americans should make as much as their white counterparts, taking into account "education and other social factors, but not race." Yet when we look more carefully at the numbers, we find at least three anomalies that disprove the meritocratic thesis.

First, Posner's reliance on median family income as evidence for lack of discriminatory effects in employment is misleading. It does not take into account the fact that Asian American families have more workers per household than do white families. For example, in California, which has one of the highest concentrations of Asian Americans, in 1980 white familes had 1.6 workers per family, whereas Japanese families had 2.1 workers, immigrant Chinese families had 2.0, immigrant Filipino families had 2.2, and immigrant Korean familes had 1.8—although this last figure is artificially low because it does not reflect the fact that many Korean women are unpaid family workers.[46] One reason for the higher number of workers in Asian American families is that more Asian American women work because of the low wages earned by male family members.[47]

Second, the use of national income averages is misleading because most Asian Americans live in geographical locations that have both higher incomes and higher costs of living. In 1980, 59 percent of all Asian Americans lived in three states, California, Hawai'i, and New York, each of which have higher median incomes and higher costs of living than the national averages. This can be compared to 19 percent of the general population residing in those three states.[48] Further, many Asian Americans are concentrated in high-income and high-cost-of-living metropolitan areas such as Honolulu, San Francisco, Los Angeles, Chicago, and New York.[49] When geographic location is considered, wage disparities become apparent.

Third, the fact that Asian Americans have a higher percentage of college gradu-ates does not mean that they have economic opportunities commensurate to their level of education. Returns on education rather than educational level provide a better indicator of the existence of discrimination. Many Asian Americans have discovered that they, like other racial minorities, do not get the same return for their educational investment as do their white counterparts.[50]

Posner's meritocratic thesis is refuted when these factors are taken into consider-ation. Japanese Americans present the strongest case for Posner because of their high household income and high educational attainment. However, a closer look that takes into account individual income, geographic location, educational attain-ment, and hours worked reveals the flaws in his analysis. I use 1980 figures as Posner did, and I control for geography by considering California statistics. In 1980, Japanese American men in California earned incomes comparable to those of white men, but "they did so only by acquiring more education (17.7 years compared to 16.8 years for white men twenty-five to forty-four years old) and by working more hours (2,160 hours compared to 2,120 hours for white men in the same age category)."[51] The income disparities for men from other Asian American groups are more glaring. In California, Korean men earned only $19,200, or 82 percent of the income of white men, Chinese men only $15,900 or 68 percent, and Filipino men only $14,500 or 62 percent.[52] I use figures for men because calculations are more complex when both race and gender are considered. Com-plexity is, of course, not a good reason for avoiding this important issue, but I will defer the discussion to another time because the complexity is buttressed by contradictory comparisons of women's income based on race.[53]

The answer, then, to Posner's question, whether Asian Americans are an op-pressed group in America, is a resounding "Yes." Some Asian American groups are better off than other racial minorities, but to hold their "successes" up to deny the existence of ongoing racism and to hold them up as the poster child for the American Dream's equality of opportunity is offensive. To accept the myth of the model minority is to participate in the oppression of Asian Americans. In addition to hurting Asian Americans, this myth works a dual harm by hurting other racial minorities and poor whites who are blamed for not being successful like Asian Americans. This blame is justified by the meritocratic thesis supposedly proven by the example of Asian Americans; it is then used to campaign against government social services for these "undeserving" minorities and poor whites and against affirmative action. To the extent that Asian Americans accept the model minority myth, we are complicit in the oppression of other racial minorities and poor whites.

This blame and its consequences create resentment against Asian Americans among African Americans, Latinos, and poor whites. This resentment, fueled by poor economic conditions, can flare into anger and violence. Asian Americans, the "model minority," serve as convenient scapegoats, as Korean Americans in Los Angeles discovered during the 1992 civil disturbance where almost half of the looting and violence was directed at Korean American businesses.[54] According to Los Angeles attorney Angela Oh, many Korean Americans "now view themselves as 'human shields' in a complicated racial hierarchy," caught between "the racism of the white majority and the anger of the black minority."[55] The model minority myth plays a key role in establishing a racial hierarchy that denies the oppression of Asian Americans while simultaneously legitimizing the oppression of other racial minorities and poor whites.

THE INADEQUACY OF THE CURRENT RACIAL PARADIGM

Most discussions of race and the law focus on African Americans to the exclusion of non-African American racial minorities. To limit the discussion in this way is a mistake. Analogies may be drawn between the discrimination experienced by different disempowered groups, but care must be taken to avoid confusing one form of discrimination with another.[56] The dominant group has used various methods of discrimination, legal and extralegal, against different disempowered groups. The differences between these groups must be considered in a discourse on race and the law if we are to use law as a means to help end racial oppression. Both traditional civil rights work and critical race theory have failed to account sufficiently for these differences.

Traditional Civil Rights Work

Traditional civil rights work presents two problems for Asian Americans. The first is a matter of coverage; the second, a matter of theory. By coverage, I mean that civil rights advocates sometimes forget to consider Asian Americans when they are battling discrimination. For example, when civil rights advocates have sued to correct underrepresentation of minorities on police forces, Asian Americans have often not been included in the lawsuits. The United States Commission on Civil Rights in 1992 reported that representation of Asian Americans was not included in a court order that required the Los Angeles Police Department to increase its representation of women, African Americans, and Hispanics.[57] Asian Americans are afraid, though, to sue to be included in the existing consent decree because they fear that the entire decree, which benefits other minorities and women, could be jeopardized based on a 1989 United States Supreme Court decision.[58] Because Asian Americans were not considered when the hiring practices of many municipalities were being challenged, and because of the problems inherent in suing later to be included, Asian Americans have rarely been included in corrective measures following lawsuits.

Coverage, although problematic, is not fatal. It can be corrected if civil rights advocates consider the needs of Asian Americans. The theoretical difficulties may present a greater problem. First, traditional civil rights work, with its foundation in liberal political philosophy, is based upon conceptions of individual rights.[59] These rights are premised on the notion of an individuated autonomous self.[60] However, this individuated autonomous self may not reflect the reality of all Asian Americans and the cultures from which they come. Many Asian philosophies and cultures have at their center the concept of no-self.[61] And at least one Asian language does not have a word for "I" that corresponds to "I" in English.[62] Thus, for some Asian Americans, traditional civil rights work may be at odds with their self-conception and worldview.

Furthermore, traditional civil rights work has often resulted in court opinions advocating color-blind constitutionalism, which provides only incremental improvement while legitimizing white racial domination.[63] This form of color-blind constitutionalism does not allow for adequate consideration of difference. Thus, traditional civil rights work, while providing some important benefits, will ultimately be unable to meet the needs of Asian Americans because of its coverage and theoretical problems.

Critical Race Scholarship

Critical race scholarship presents only a problem of coverage for Asian Americans. Critical race scholars understand that differences between racial minorities are important.[64] However, these differences have yet to be fully developed. As a result, critical race scholarship tends to focus on the black-white racial paradigm, excluding Asian Americans and other racial minorities. For example, in a recent Colloquy entitled "Racism in the Wake of the Los Angeles Riots," the Korean American-African American conflict was not addressed, with the exception of two footnotes in one article and a discussion in another article of the actions taken by the Korean government to try to protect Korean citizens and immigrants.[65] Nor were the perspectives of Korean Americans represented in any of the articles. While the individual authors are not to be blamed for these omissions, the Colloquy, taken as a whole, has serious gaps. The result is that the Colloquy, and more generally, the discourse on race and the law, is not as rich or complete as it might or should be. These omissions foreclosed the possibility of reaching a greater understanding of why the racial tensions exist, how they have been fostered by legal decisions, and what might be done to bridge the differences.

To focus on the black-white racial paradigm is to misunderstand the complicated racial situation in the United States. It ignores such things as nativistic racism. It ignores the complexity of a racial hierarchy that has more than just a top and a bottom.

Asian Americans have a vested interest in helping to flesh out the racial paradigm. A critical Asian American legal studies is needed to address the coverage problem both in traditional civil rights work and in critical race scholarship. Perceptions fostered by the model minority myth contribute to the lack of coverage. An important tool to address these problems of coverage is the use of narrative. Narrative will allow us to speak our oppression into existence, for it must first be represented before it can be erased.[66] We need a critical Asian American legal studies to break the silence that surrounds our oppression.

NOTES

1. Lisa Lowe, *Immigrant Acts: On Asian American Cultural Politics* (1996).
2. See Angela P. Harris, "Race and Essentialism in Feminist Legal Theory," 42 *Stan. L. Rev.* 581, 610–12 (1990).
3. D. Hunter, "Life After Hardwick," 27 *Harv. C.R.-C.L.L. Rev.* 531, 546–47 (1992).
4. Kimberle Crenshaw, Remarks at Opening Plenary, Conference on Critical Race Theory, Yale Law School, 14 November 1997. See also "Introduction," in *Critical Race Theory: The Key Writings that Formed the Movement,* ed. Kimberle Crenshaw et al., 1995.
5. Richard Delgado, "When a Story Is Just a Story: Does Voice Really Matter?" 76 *Va. L. Rev.* 95, 95 n.1 (1990).

6. John O. Calmore, "Critical Race Theory, Archie Shepp, and Fire Music: Securing an Authentic Intellectual Life in a Multicultural World," 65 *S. Cal. L. Rev.* 2129, 2163 (1992).

7. Anthony Appiah, "The Uncompleted Argument: Du Bois and the Illusion of Race," in *"Race," Writing, and Difference,* ed. Henry L. Gates Jr., 21, 25 (1986).

8. See Shirley Hune, "An Overview of Asian Pacific American Futures: Shifting Paradigms," in *The State of Asian Pacific America[,] A Public Policy Report: Policy Issues to the Year 2020,* at 1, 5–6 (LEAP Asian Pac.Am.Pub. Policy Inst. and UCLA Asian Am. Studies Ctr. eds., 1993).

9. Narrative would include not just the personal narrative of the author, but also actual and fictional narratives of others told by the author. See, e.g., Derrick Bell, *And We Are Not Saved: The Elusive Quest for Racial Justice* (1987); Mari J. Matsuda, "Public Response to Racist Speech: Considering the Victim's Story," 87 *Mich. L. Rev.* 2320 (1989).

10. U.S. Commission on Civil Rights, Civil Rights Issues Facing Asian Americans in the 1990s [hereinafter Civil Rights Report], at 1 (1992) (quoting Michel McQueen, "Voters' Responses to Poll Disclose Huge Chasm Between Social Attitudes of Blacks and Whites," *Wall St. J.,* 17 May 1991, at A 16) (footnote omitted).

11. For general works discussing Asian American history, see Sucheng Chan, *Asian Americans: An Interpretive History* (1991); Roger Daniels, *Asian America: Chinese and Japanese in the United States Since 1850* (1988); Ronald Takaki, *Strangers from a Different Shore: A History of Asian Americans* (1989).

12. See Racism and Sexism Resource Ctr. for Educators, Council on Interracial Books for Children, *Stereotypes, Distortions and Omissions in U.S. History Textbooks* 33–54 (1977).

13. Stephen E. Gottlieb, "In the Name of Patriotism: The Constitutionality of 'Bending' History in Public Secondary Schools," 62 *N.Y.U. L. Rev.* 497, 510–11 (1987).

14. George Santayana, *The Life of Reason* 284 (2d ed. 1922).

15. Paula C. Johnson, "The Social Construction of Identity in Criminal Cases: Cinema Verité and the Pedagogy of Vincent Chin," 1 *Mich. J. Race & L.* 347, 401 (1996).

16. John Higham, *Strangers in the Land: Patterns of American Nativism, 1860–1925,* at 4 (2d ed. 1988).

17. Al Kamen, "When Hostility Follows Immigration: Racial Violence Sows Fear in New Jersey's Indian Community," *Washington Post,* 16 November 1992, at A1, A6.

18. Id.; see also Civil Rights Report, *supra* note 1, at 28–29.

19. Sucheng Chan, *This Bittersweet Soil: The Chinese in California Agriculture, 1860–1910,* at 370 (1986); Chan, *supra* note 2, at 49.

20. Paul Crane and Alfred Larson, "The Chinese Massacre," 12 *Annals of Wyoming* 47, 47–49 (1940).

21. See *Anti-Chinese Violence in North America,* ed. Roger Daniels (1978); Chan, *supra* note 2, at 48–51; Daniels, *supra* note 2, at 58–64 (1988).

22. See Richard M. Brown, "Historiography of Violence in the American West," in *Historians and the American West,* ed. Michael P. Malone, 234, 250–51 (1983).

23. Daniels, *supra* note 2, at 59 n.66.

24. Stanley Fish, "Bad Company," 56 *Transition* 60, 63 (1992).

25. Id. at 60–61 (quoting Arthur Schlesinger Jr., *The Disuniting of America: Reflections on a Multicultural Society* [1992], some alteration in original).

26. Id. at 61.

27. E. J. Dionne Jr., "Buchanan's Political Street Fight: Challenger's Conservatism Rooted in Catholic Upbringing," *Washington Post,* 15 February 1992, at A1, A20 (quoting a June 1990 article by Buchanan).

28. See Neil Gotanda, "'Other Non-Whites' in American Legal History," 85 *Colum. L. Rev.* 1186, 1188 (1985) (reviewing Peter Irons, *Justice at War* [1983]).

29. Mark Potts, "Japanese Cleared for Seattle Baseball Deal," *Washington Post,* 10 June 1992, at A1, A18.

30. See "Don't Reject Japanese Pitch," *USA Today,* 29 January 1992, at 10A; Mike Meyers,

"Enduring U.S.-Japanese Rivalry Has Roots That Precede World War II," *Star Tribune*, 8 December 1991, at 1A.

31. Edwin E. Ferguson, "The California Alien Land Law and the Fourteenth Amendment," 35 *Cal. L. Rev.* 61, 77 (1947). I refer to both Japanese-born aliens and their American-born offspring as Japanese Americans. I do not differentiate because the naturalization statutes prevented Japanese-born aliens from becoming United States citizens.

32. Id. at 62.

33. Id. at 66–67.

34. Civil Rights Report, *supra* note 1, at 19.

35. Id.

36. See Daniels, *supra* note 2, at 317–18 (citing William Petersen, "Success Story, Japanese American Style," *New York Times Magazine*, 6 January 1966, at 20).

37. "Success Story of One Minority Group in U.S.," *U.S. News & World Report*, 26 December 1966, at 73, 73, reprinted in *Roots: An Asian American Reader*, ed. Amy Tachiki et al., 6 (1971).

38. Takaki, *supra* note 2, at 474 (citations omitted).

39. Mitsuye Yamada, "Invisibility Is an Unnatural Disaster: Reflections of an Asian American Woman," in *This Bridge Called My Back: Writings By Radical Women of Color*, ed. Cherrie Moraga and Gloria Anzaldua, 35, 35 (1981).

40. Takaki, *supra* note 2, at 478; see also Civil Rights Report, *supra* note 1, at 20 (quoting U.S. Commission on Civil Rights, "Success of Asian Americans: Fact or Fiction?" 24 [1980]).

41. U.S. Dept. of Commerce, "We the Americans . . . Asians" 7 (1993) (based on 1990 census).

42. Richard A. Posner, "Duncan Kennedy on Affirmative Action," 1990 *Duke L. J.* 1157, 1157 (revised text of speech delivered on 4 January 1991, at Association of American Law Schools convention).

43. Id. at 1157 n.2.

44. Id.

45. Henry Der, "Asian Pacific Islanders and the 'Glass Ceiling'—New Era of Civil Rights Activism?: Affirmative Action Policy," in *The State of Asian Pacific America[,] A Public Policy Report: Policy Issues to the Year 2020*, at 215, 219 (LEAP Asian Pac. Am. Pub. Policy Inst. and UCLA Asian Am. Studies Ctr., 1993).

46. Takaki, *supra* note 2, at 475; see also Civil Rights Report, *supra* note 1, at 18.

47. Chan, *supra* note 2, at 169.

48. Takaki, *supra* note 2, at 475.

49. Chan, *supra* note 2, at 168.

50. One study reported that "for each additional year of education, whites earned $522 more, compared to $438 for Japanese, $320 for Chinese, $340 for Mexican Americans, and $284 for blacks." Id. at 168 (citing Robert M. Jiobu's 1976 study of American-born men in California).

51. Takaki, *supra* note 2, at 475.

52. Id. In New York the mean personal income for white men was $21,600, compared to only $18,900 or 88 percent for Korean men, $16,500 or 76 percent for Filipino men, and only $11,200 or 52 percent for Chinese men.

53. Compare Der, *supra* note 36, at 220: "[C]ontrolling for educational and occupational status when compared to white women, Asian Pacific Islander women do as well if not slightly better, in terms of earned median income." with Chan, *supra* note 2, at 169: "But despite their high educational level, [Asian American women] receive lower returns to their education than do white women." and Deborah Woo, "The Gap Between Striving and Achieving: The Case of Asian American Women," in *Making Waves: An Anthology of Writings By and About Asian American Women*, ed. Asian Women United of California, 185, 192 (1989): "While education enhances earnings capability, the return on education for Asian American women is not as great as that for other women."

Professors Chan and Woo note two factors that Henry Der may not have considered: that Asian American women live in localities with higher wages, and that a larger percentage of Asian American women work full-time than do their white counterparts. Chan, *supra* note 2, at 169; Woo, *supra* at 187–88. Also, the higher median income does not take into account the unpaid labor of many Asian American women in small, family-owned businesses, many of which operate with very low gross earnings. See Chan, *supra* note 2, at 169–70.

54. See Seth Mydans, "Giving Voice to the Hurt and Betrayal of Korean-Americans," *New York Times*, 2 May 1993, §, at 9.

55. Id.

56. See, e.g., Trina Grillo and Stephanie M. Wildman, "Obscuring the Importance of Race: The Implication of Making Comparisons Between Racism and Sexism (or Other -Isms)," 1991 *Duke L. J.* 397, 401–10.

57. See Civil Rights Report, *supra* note 1, at 59.

58. Id. at 59 n.53; *Martin v. Wilks*, 490 U.S. 755 (1989), recognizing a right to challenge as discriminatory a consent decree that orders an employer to hire minorities.

59. See, e.g., Ronald Dworkin, *Law's Empire* 381–87 (1986), discussing three forms of constitutional rights against discrimination.

60. See Robin West, "Jurisprudence and Gender," 55 *U. Chi. L. Rev.* 1, 5 (1988), discussing the autonomous individual celebrated by liberal legalism.

61. See, e.g., Walpola S. Rahula, *What the Buddha Taught* 51–66 (rev. ed. 1974), describing the doctrine of Anatta, which maintains that the notion of "self" is false and that all evil in the world can be traced to the idea of self. There is a large body of literature, much of it from critical legal scholars, that criticizes liberalism's celebration of individualism. See, e.g., Roberto M. Unger, *Knowledge and Politics* 277–78 (1975).

62. "In the Vietnamese language, the word 'I' (toi) . . . means 'your servant'; there is no 'I' as such. When you talk to someone, you establish a relationship." Patricia Williams, "Spirit-Murdering the Messenger: The Discourse of Fingerpointing as the Law's Response to Racism," 42 *U. Miami L. Rev.* 127, 140 (1987) (quoting Daniel Berrigan and Thich Nhat Hanh, *The Raft is Not the Shore* 38 [1975]).

63. See Neil Gotanda, "A Critique of 'Our Constitution is Color-Blind,'" 44 *Stan. L. Rev.* 1 (1991); see also Alan D. Freeman, "Legitimizing Racial Discrimination Through Antidiscrimination Law: A Critical Review of Supreme Court Doctrine," 62 *Minn. L. Rev.* 1049 (1978), tracing the Court's post-Brown approach to discrimination and maintaining that a focus on rights often legitimizes oppression. Many minority scholars have criticized critical legal studies scholars, such as Freeman, for their insensitivity to minorities' reliance on rights. See, e.g., Richard Delgado, "The Ethereal Scholar: Does Critical Legal Studies Have What Minorities Want?" 22 *Harv. C.R.-C.L. L. Rev.* 301, 305 (1987), criticizing CLS attacks on rights and noting that CLS fails to offer substitute protection.

64. See John Calmore, "Critical Race Theory, Archie Shepp, and Fire Music: Securing an Authentic Intellectual Life in a Multicultural World," 65 *S. Cal. L. Rev.* 2129, 2171–72 (1992).

65. Colloquy, "Racism in the Wake of the Los Angeles Riots," 70 *Denv. U. L. Rev.* 187 (1993), including contributions by The Honorable A. Leon Higginbotham Jr., The Honorable Nathaniel R. Jones, Jerome Culp, Henry Richardson, Deborah Post, Lynn Curtis, Kimberle Crenshaw, Gary Peller, and Anthony Cook; Jerome M. Culp Jr., "Notes from California: Rodney King and the Race Question," 70 *Denv. U. L. Rev.* 199, 202 nn.8–9 (1993); Henry J. Richardson III, "The International Implications of the Los Angeles Riots," 70 *Denv. U. L. Rev.* 213, 225–26 (1993).

66. I borrow this phrase from Barbara Johnson, who said, "Difference . . . must be represented in order to be erased." Barbara Johnson, "Thresholds of Difference: Structures of Address in Zora Neale Hurston," in *"Race," Writing, and Difference,* ed. Henry L. Gates Jr., 317, 323 (1986).

MULTICULTURALISM AND

RACIAL STRATIFICATION

Neil Gotanda

Overlooked by much of the national media in its coverage of the 1992 Los Angeles civil disturbances was the case of *People v Soon Ja Du.*[1] The trial of Du Soon Ja[2] for the grocery-store shooting of fifteen-year-old Latasha Harlins has helped to define subsequent relations between Asian Americans and African Americans.

Crucial to understanding the role of the courts in this incident is the judge's statement that accompanied her pronouncement of sentence. Instead of their stated goal of reducing tensions, I will argue that the judge's culturally coded comments show how institutions like the judicial system may manage "minority-minority" conflict.

Du Soon Ja, a fifty-one-year-old Korean immigrant mother and store owner, shot and killed a fifteen-year-old African American girl in a dispute and fight over a bottle of orange juice. Coming after a national series of incidents involving Korean grocers in African American neighborhoods, the case was followed closely in the press.

After a tense jury trial marked by demonstrations and courtroom outbursts, Du was convicted of voluntary manslaughter. Attention then focused on the sentence of newly appointed Los Angeles Superior Court Judge Joyce A. Karlin. Karlin was widely expected to sentence Du to prison time, with most speculation centering on the length of the sentence. However, instead of a prison sentence, Karlin sentenced Du to probation with prison time suspended, a small fine, and a requirement of community service.[3] Judge Karlin immediately became a center of controversy because the sentence was regarded as far too lenient. Many critics accused her of being at best insensitive, and at worst racist.[4] The Los Angeles County district attorney appealed the sentence, but the California Court of Appeal affirmed the decision.[5]

The statement explaining a sentence is referred to as a sentencing colloquy. I will use Karlin's short sentencing colloquy (reproduced at the end of this essay) as a text—interpreting her language to illustrate the hidden assumptions and implications in her statement and sentence.

Recognition and use of the idea of culture are sometimes offered as a positive alternative to the reenshrinement of racial subordination that comes with the repetition of traditional racial usages. The colloquy reveals how multicultural techniques can function to maintain the centerpiece of the old racial order—white privilege. As the racial, ethnic, and cultural complexities of Los Angeles continue to develop, this case illuminates some of the ongoing rearrangements of race, culture, subordination, and power.

KARLIN'S MULTICULTURALISM

Karlin makes extensive use of particular culturally specific characterizations. The defendant Du is portrayed as a good mother and wife, as a hardworking shopkeeper, as an innocent victim of circumstance acting in self-defense. The real victim, Latasha Harlins, is presented as a criminal shoplifter, as aggressive and violent, as associated with gangs. These portrayals are woven together from fact and speculation and extend existing racial stereotypes.

Judge Karlin structures the sentencing colloquy in a way that illustrates her adherence to the color-blind technique. Karlin specifically recognizes the African American and Korean communities in the opening and closing paragraphs of the colloquy (¶ 1–2, 41).[6] In her actual sentencing comments, however, Karlin makes no explicit reference to Koreans or African Americans.

Thus, the judge does not make specific reference to black, African American, Korean, or Asian in the main body of the colloquy. Instead, it is the use of the cultural characteristics themselves that emphasizes and circumscribes the contrasting groups—Korean and African American. Links to Koreans and African Americans are made in prefatory and concluding comments. The crucial racial connections lie in the background understanding that these individuals are representatives of communities in conflict.

The use of cultural markers and the avoidance of the Korean and African American labels are of particular importance in the legal context. Avoidance of racial or ethnic labels is supportive of the doctrine of constitutional color-blindness. Under that ideology, any consideration of race in governmental decision making is either questionable or unconstitutional.[7]

Karlin's use of multicultural markers goes beyond the traditional legal prescription for color-blindness. Instead of a judicial fiat that race shall not be taken into consideration in her deliberations, Karlin uses the various cultural attributes and stereotypes as a multicultural alternative to race. Her implicit adoption of these cultural markers as a substitute for race validates the significance of the cultural stereotypes she employs.

The specific content of these stereotypes and cultural attributes is also of significance. Within the boundaries of the cultural markers that substitute for race and ethnicity, Karlin utilizes attributes that differ from traditional black-white racial subordination. Instead of a model that emphasizes the subordinate position of *all* racial and ethnic minorities, Karlin creates a tiered, hierarchical structure *between* minorities. The cultural attributes of defendant Du are favorable, and portray a sympathetic, Korean "model minority." Placed in opposition is the more familiar cruel stereotype of African American as criminal and gang member.

The difference in this context is that the African American minority is not judged against the majority society. Rather, the African American minority is measured against and therefore "monitored" by the Korean minority. The Korean "model minority" is thus the measure of the African American "monitored minority."

Implicit also is the idea that "monitored" and "model" racial minorities are subordinate to an "invisible majority." That invisible majority is, I believe, the white majority and its position of white racial privilege.

JUDGE KARLIN'S SENTENCING COLLOQUY

In this section, my examination of the text of Judge Karlin's colloquy shows how Karlin sympathizes with Du and presents the victim Latasha Harlins in a harsh and unfavorable light. These contrasting portrayals are presented by associating Du and Harlins with various culturally based racial stereotypes.

The individualized racial characterizations of Du coincide with and reproduce the image and structure of Koreans and Asian Americans as a "model minority." Karlin emphasizes Du's "model minority" status by portraying her as an "innocent shopkeeper." Karlin does not articulate, but understands, and expects others to understand, that Du is a Korean shopkeeper. Du Soon Ja is a representative successful shopkeeper and, by implication, the Korean community is a successful "model minority."

Latasha Harlins is portrayed as a criminal and associated with gangs and gang violence. Judge Karlin emphasizes the "monitored minority" aspect of Harlins by improperly balancing Du against Harlins. In the traditional approach to sentencing, valuation of the "worth" of the victim is only one among many considerations. Judge Karlin, however, makes constant comparisons between the two throughout the colloquy. This use of Du as the "model" against which the victim Harlins is measured emphasizes the monitoring dimension to Karlin's social hierarchy.

Karlin describes Du as a fifty-one-year-old woman who is a victim of circumstances (¶ 29), including gang terror (¶ 29, 33), and a gun altered by unknown thieves (¶ 29). Further, Du was present on the day of the killing only because of her maternal loyalty to her son (¶ 33–34), to shield her son from the repeated robberies (¶ 33) and "to save him one day of fear" (¶ 34). And Karlin is generally sympathetic to the hardships faced by innocent shopkeepers who are under frequent attack (¶ 24–36).

Judge Karlin portrays defendant Du as an innocent victim. In the colloquy, Du is a hard worker and has no criminal record (¶ 19). Gangs terrorize Du's family while they operate the store (¶ 29–33). The actual killing was the result of the assault by Harlins upon Du (¶ 38) and the modification of the revolver by unknown thieves who had rendered the revolver "defective" (¶ 29, 32).[8]

Harlins is described as having likely committed a criminal assault upon Du (¶ 26–29) after an act of shoplifting (¶ 25). Harlins is an example of shoplifters who attack shopkeepers after being caught in the act (¶ 24–26). Further, Karlin associates Harlins with gang theft and terror (¶ 33); Harlins is the person who caused Du to commit a criminal act when Du had previously led a crime-free life (¶ 38).

Judge Karlin also stereotypes Harlins through continued references to gangs and gang terror. These references to gangs are not an allegation that Harlins was herself a gang member. Judge Karlin connects "gangness" with African Americans, ignoring the widespread presence of gangs made up largely of Asians. Karlin emphasizes her appreciation of "gangness" by using the word "terror" three times in her colloquy: "victimized and terrorized by gang members" (¶ 29); "the very real terror experienced by the Du family" (¶ 33); "repeated robberies and terrorism in the same store" (¶ 33).

Judge Karlin's omission of any humanizing information about Harlins works to demonize her. Karlin might have done well to note a number of facts related by the court of appeal about Latasha Harlins:

> The probation report also reveals that Latasha had suffered many painful experiences during her life, including the violent death of her mother. Latasha lived with her extended family (her grandmother, younger brother and sister, aunt, uncle and niece) in what the probation officer described as "a clean, attractively furnished three-bedroom apartment" in South Central Los Angeles. Latasha had been an honor student at Bret Harte Junior High School, from which she had graduated the previous spring. Although she was making only average grades in high school, she had promised that she would bring her grades up to her former standard. Latasha was involved in activities at a youth center as an assistant cheerleader, member of the drill team and a summer junior camp counselor. She was a good athlete and an active church member.[9]

Another significant dimension of Karlin's "humanizing" of Du and "demonizing" of Harlins occurs in the question of *punishment.* Karlin omits any direct consideration of punishment. Instead, she *balances* Harlins against Du, African American against Asian American.[10]

First, Karlin balances Du against Harlins by noting that in determining whether probation is appropriate, she must determine "the *vulnerability of the victim*" (¶ 23). Although the issue of vulnerability is in theory applicable only to the *victim,* Karlin proceeds to apply it to both Harlins *and* Du. Because Harlins "used her fists as weapons" Karlin declares that she was not vulnerable. Karlin does not mention the fact that Du shot Harlins in the *back* of the head, which demonstrates that Harlins was "vulnerable" to an attack by Du. Karlin follows this with a *non sequitur* implying that Harlins was not vulnerable because she was an accused shoplifter and therefore had not been justified in her assault upon Du (¶ 24–25). In contrast, Karlin describes Du's situation sympathetically: shopkeepers like Du seem unable even to accuse customers of shoplifting without fear of being assaulted.

Second, Karlin states that under the statute she is to consider "criminal sophistication" in deciding the propriety of probation. Although the consideration is meant to apply to the criminal sophistication of the *defendant,* Karlin ultimately balances Du's criminal sophistication against the victim's alleged criminality (¶ 27). Karlin describes Du as lacking "any degree of criminal sophistication in her offense," as a woman "who would not be here today" but for "unusual circumstances" (¶ 28–29). Judge Karlin believes that Harlins, on the other hand, would have had charges filed against her had she "not been shot" and had the "incident which preceded the shooting been reported" (¶ 26).

Karlin further reinforces her social hierarchy through the use of gendered images of Du and Harlins. Du is portrayed as a good wife—loyally working in the family store. She is even more dramatically portrayed as a good mother—volunteering to work in the store to protect her son. Karlin also focuses attention on Du Soon Ja's status as spouse and wife by never directly mentioning Du's husband. There are references to Du's family and her son, but her husband is omitted. The context for these images is the traditional stereotype of the family as a strength of Asian cultures.

By contrast, any of the available positive gendered images of Harlins as dutiful daughter, church member, and student are ignored and she is portrayed as a criminal. This contrast between Du and Harlins reinforces the social hierarchy through the greater social distance from Judge Karlin—a female lawgiver.

THE MODEL MINORITY

In this section, I argue that Karlin's racial characterizations of Du and Harlins are more than a byproduct of her personal sympathy or antipathy toward the two individuals. Karlin's racial stereotypes involve a racial map that includes more than just Du and Harlins as representative of Asian American and African American. By differentially distancing herself from Du and Harlins, she is producing a three-tier racial hierarchy that reinforces an existing set of stereotyped images.

The change from older stereotypes to the "model minority" can be illustrated by describing some of the older images that evolved in the early twentieth century and that have been only partly superseded today. At least one author has speculated on the connection of Edward Said's development of the complex construction of Oriental "otherness" to Europe and the West.[11] John Kuo Wei Tchen argues that British authors Sax Rohmer, creator of Fu Manchu in 1911, and Thomas Burke, author of "Limehouse Nights," set in the opium dens and shabby corners of London's small Chinese quarter, were themselves Orientalists, engaged in constructing racialized images of Chinese that would define American and British identity.[12]

As examples of demeaning stereotypes, Tchen points to Rohmer's Fu Manchu as embodying "evil incarnate," to caricatures of Chinese laundrymen who appeared as comic relief in early films, and to Sessue Hayakawa as an enslaving Japanese antique dealer in Cecil B. DeMille's 1915 film *The Cheat.* The images are not, however, uniform in their attitudes. Tchen examines D. W. Griffith's 1919 film *Broken Blossoms* and finds that Griffith "eschews the standard stereotype of the 'heathen Chinee' already well established in the previous century, and adapts the alternative image of the hardworking, good-for-the-West 'John Chinaman'."[13]

A much more unrelentingly harsh set of images is seen in John Dower's *War without Mercy,* an examination of the mutually hostile propaganda campaigns of

Japan and the United States throughout World War II. During the war, "yellow hordes" of Japanese were portrayed as apes, monkeys, and insects.

These images constituted the collective set of stereotypes and constructed identities of Asian Americans, accumulated over a century of Asian immigration to the United States. The transformation of the Asian American from the "heathen Chinee" and the "yellow horde" into a "model minority" has been dramatic and rapid.

The sharp change began in the mid-1960s with the appearance of several articles in major national news media commenting favorably on the success of the Asian Americans, at that time mostly second-and third-generation Japanese and Chinese Americans.[14] Especially noteworthy was a 1966 *New York Times Magazine* article entitled "Success Story: Japanese Style."[15] Those early articles, however, emphasized overcoming adversity, rather than focusing on Asians' economic success.

In the past decade the stereotype has shifted to emphasize economic success based on an extremely aggressive work ethic and strong family cohesion. Lisa Lowe has described the model-minority myth as including the image of Asians as "aggressively driven overachievers" who "assimilate well."[16] This version of the "model minority" places Asian Americans in reasonably well-to-do class position vis-à-vis other minorities, especially African Americans.

In the modern context, the image of the Korean grocery store owner has become the dominant media image of an Asian American.[17] Sales transactions between Korean grocers and African American patrons are now exemplary of all social interaction between Asians and African Americans, and the actions of Korean grocers are exemplary of all Asian American cultures.

The racial stratification provided by the "model minority" thus provides Judge Karlin with an ideological framework both to distance herself from Latasha Harlins individually and to absolve non-blacks generally, especially those in the highest tier of the three-tiered system of the "model minority," of any social responsibility for the effects of racial subordination on African Americans.

CONCLUSION

In conclusion, I offer some questions and suggestions for further exploration. One group of questions concerns the use of cultural forms to create ideological constructions like the "model minority." Another surrounds the difficulty of a racial analysis of Asian Americans and the troubling implications for political coalition.

Karlin's colloquy both reflects the myth of the "model minority" and advances it by providing greater specificity. Karlin ascribes to a Korean grocer a certain class privilege (shopkeeper status), higher social status (strong family), and high moral worth (law-abiding). These are balanced against the demonized Latasha Harlins, who lacks them. The result is that Korean Americans—and, by implication, Asian Americans—are defined by this short list and the resulting narrow stereotype. Omitted is any sense of personal or social history, community or real family life, religion or spirituality, all of which would be part of any historically textured description of Asian Americans.

This entire effort took place in the midst of a now familiar media circus, with full broadcast and print-media coverage. Karlin's efforts were therefore not limited to the courtroom or even to traditional legal texts, but became part of our everyday popular cultural discourse.

Work on the slippery terrain of popular culture and mass media is always difficult. Hampering efforts has been the near total absence of academic and popular studies of the representation of Asian Americans.[18] Presenting the varied and broad range of experiences encompassed by persons of Asian ancestry in America while combating both model-minority and yellow-peril stereotyping will require a depth of understanding and analysis that is only now emerging.

Perhaps even more difficult is the question of the depth of reality behind the "model minority." If one accepts that there really is a privileging of Asian Americans and that the "model minority" is not simply a fabricated illusion, then an examination of the racial status of Asian Americans in a multiracial model becomes intensely complex.

If one takes the position that "Asians have problems, just like African Americans," then one is implicitly using an analytical framework that says the racial status of Asian Americans is identical to that of African Americans—both are subordinated by whites. This two-category (white/non-white) framework suggests that the only "real" differences between Asian Americans and African Americans are minor variations in culture and economic achievement.

If, however, Asian Americans are coming to occupy a class position between whites and African Americans, then a different analysis is needed. A further exploration of Asian American as an intermediate racial category would examine whether or not social and economic privileges attach to those persons classified as Asian American. For example, in economic relations, research could determine whether real property values declined when an Asian American integrated a formerly all-white neighborhood. One could compare whether the decline in values, and any associated racial "tipping," was more severe for African Americans than for Asian Americans. An analysis of social attitudes might also reveal a differential between African Americans and Asian Americans around such issues as crime and morality. Similar studies could be carried out in other areas such as income, job discrimination, and portrayals in popular culture.

Recognizing that there is some truth in the "myth of the model minority" seems to me a better starting point for examining whether there is an emerging Asian American racial category. The difficulty comes in attempting to situate this racial category without succumbing to the "model minority" stereotype. On the one hand, if a real class privilege is emerging for Asian Americans, then long-term political coalitions cannot turn on simple calls for recognizing a common history of racial oppression by a white majority. Instead, one must explore more carefully the deeply intertwined issues of class and group privilege to explore where one can find both short- and long-term common interests.

What should not be forgotten amidst these complexities, however, is that interracial and interethnic conflict cannot be divorced from the broader American historical context of racial subordination. One of the historical axes of social subordination in America has been white privileging over African Americans. Even as the possibilities of racial stratification and the embedded ideological constructions of Orientalism are examined, awareness of the continuation of that basic axis of power and privilege must continue.

Sentencing Colloquy

[*Los Angeles Daily Journal,* 22 November 1991, 7: a transcript of remarks by Los Angeles Superior Court Judge Joyce A. Karlin in the sentencing of Soon Ja Du.]

[¶ 1] One thing I think both sides will agree on is that nothing I can do, nothing the judicial system can do, nothing will lessen the loss suffered by Latasha Harlins' family and friends. But the parties involved in this case and anyone truly interested in what caused this case can make sure that something positive comes out of this tragedy by having Latasha Harlins' death mark a beginning rather than an end—a beginning of a greater understanding and acceptance between two groups, some of whose members have until now demonstrated intolerance and bigotry toward one another.

[¶ 2] Latasha's death should be a catalyst to force members of the African American and Korean communities to confront an intolerable situation by creating constructive solutions. Through that process, a greater understanding and acceptance will hopefully result so that similar tragedies will not be repeated.

[¶ 3] Statements by the district attorney, (which) suggest that imposing less than the maximum sentence will send a message that a black child's life is not worthy of protection, (are) dangerous rhetoric, which serves no purpose other than to pour gasoline on a fire.

[¶ 4] This is not a time for revenge, and my job is not to exact revenge for those who demand it.

[¶ 5] There are those in this community who have publicly demanded in the name of justice that the maximum sentence be imposed in this case.

[¶ 6] But it is my opinion that justice is never served when public opinion, prejudice, revenge or unwarranted sympathy are considered by a sentencing court in resolving a case.

[¶ 7] In imposing sentence I must first consider the objectives of sentencing a defendant:

1) To protect society.
2) To punish the defendant for committing a crime.
3) To encourage the defendant to lead a law-abiding life.
4) To deter others.
5) To isolate the defendant so she can't commit other crimes.
6) To secure restitution for the victim.
7) To seek uniformity in sentencing.

[¶ 8] The question becomes, are any of these sentencing objectives achieved by Mrs. Du being remanded to state prison?

[¶ 9] Let us start with the last objective first: uniformity in sentencing. According to statistics gathered for the Superior Courts of California, sentences imposed on defendants convicted of voluntary manslaughter last year ranged from probation with no jail time to incarceration in state prison for several years.

[¶ 10] Because of the unique nature of each crime of voluntary manslaughter, and by that I mean the uniquely different factual situations resulting in that crime, uniformity in sentencing is virtually impossible to achieve.

[¶ 11] Which, then, of the other sentencing objectives lead to the conclusion that state prison is warranted?

[¶ 12] Does society need Mrs. Du to be incarcerated in order to be protected? I think not.

[¶ 13] Is state prison needed in order to encourage the defendant to lead a law-abiding life or isolate her so she cannot commit other crimes? I think not.

[¶ 14] Is state prison needed to punish Mrs. Du? Perhaps.

[¶ 15] There is, in this case, a presumption against probation because a firearm was used.

[¶ 16] In order to overcome that presumption, the court must find this to be an unusual case, as that term is defined by law.

[¶17] There are three reasons that I find this is an unusual case:

[¶ 18] First, the basis for the presumption against probation is technically present. But it doesn't really apply. The statute is aimed at criminals who arm themselves when they go out and commit other crimes. It is not aimed at shopkeepers who lawfully possess firearms for their own protection.

[¶ 19] Second, the defendant has no recent record, in fact, no record at any time of committing similar crimes or crimes of violence.

[¶ 20] Third, the defendant participated in the crime under circumstances of great provocation, coercion and duress. Therefore, this is, in my opinion, an unusual case that overcomes the statutory presumption against probation.

[¶ 21] Should the defendant be placed on probation?

[¶ 22] One of the questions a sentencing court is required to ask in answering that question is "whether the crime was committed because of unusual circumstances, such as great provocation." I find that it was.

[¶ 23] I must also determine the vulnerability of the victim in deciding whether probation is appropriate. Although Latasha Harlins was not armed with a weapon at the time of her death, she had used her fists as weapons just seconds before she was shot.

[¶ 24] The district attorney argues that Latasha was justified in her assault on Mrs. Du. Our courts are filled with cases which suggest otherwise.

[¶ 25] Our courts are filled with defendants who are charged with assault resulting in great bodily injury as a result of attacks on shopkeepers, including shopkeepers who have accused them of shoplifting.

[¶ 26] Had Latasha Harlins not been shot and had the incident which preceded the shooting been reported, it is my opinion that the district attorney would have relied on the videotape and Mrs. Du's testimony to make a determination whether to file charges against Latasha.

[¶ 27] Other questions I am required to address in determining whether probation is appropriate are "whether the carrying out of the crime suggested criminal sophistication and whether the defendant will be a danger to others if she is not imprisoned."

[¶ 28] Having observed Mrs. Du on videotape at the time the crime was committed and having observed Mrs. Du during this trial, I cannot conclude that there was any degree of criminal sophistication in her offense. Nor can I conclude that she is a danger to others if she is not incarcerated.

[¶ 29] Mrs. Du is a (51)-year-old woman with no criminal history and no history of violence. But for the unusual circumstances in this case, including the Du family's history of being victimized and terrorized by gang members, Mrs. Du would not be here today. Nor do I believe Mrs. Du would be here today if the gun she grabbed for protection had not been altered. This was a gun that had been stolen from the Du family and returned to them shortly before the shooting.

[¶ 30] The court has been presented with no evidence, and I have no reason to believe that Mrs. Du knew that the gun had been altered in such a way as to—in effect—make it an automatic weapon with a hairpin trigger.

[¶ 31] Ordinarily a .38 revolver is one of the safest guns in the world. It cannot go off accidentally. And a woman Mrs. Du's size would have to decide consciously to pull the trigger and to exert considerable strength to do so.

[¶ 32] But that was not true of the gun used to shoot Latasha Harlins. I have serious questions in my mind whether this crime would have been committed at all but for a defective gun.

[¶ 33] The district attorney would have this court ignore the very real terror experienced by the Du family before the shooting, and the fear Mrs. Du experienced as she worked by herself the day of the shooting. But there are things I cannot ignore. And I cannot ignore the reason Mrs. Du was working at the store that day. She went to work that Saturday to save her son from having to work. Mrs. Du's son had begged his parents to close the store. He was afraid because he had been the victim of repeated robberies and terrorism in that same store.

[¶ 34] On the day of the shooting Mrs. Du volunteered to cover for her son to save him one day of fear.

[¶ 35] Did Mrs. Du react inappropriately to Latasha? Absolutely.

[¶ 36] Was Mrs. Du's over-reaction understandable? I think so.

[¶ 37] If probation is not appropriate, and state prison time is warranted, then a short prison term would be an injustice. If Mrs. Du should be sent to prison because she is a danger to others or is likely to re-offend, then I could not justify imposing a short prison term.

[¶ 38] But it is my opinion that Mrs. Du is not a danger to the community and it is my opinion that she will not re-offend. She led a crime free life until Latasha Harlins walked into her store and there is no reason to believe that this is the beginning of a life of crime for Mrs. Du. But if I am wrong, Mrs. Du will face severe consequences.

[¶ 39] For all of these reasons it is hereby adjudged that: on her conviction for voluntary manslaughter, Mrs. Du is sentenced to the midterm of 6 years in state prison. On the personal use of a firearm enhancement, the defendant is sentenced to the midterm of 4 years, to run consecutive to the 6 years for a total of 10 years. Execution of this sentence is suspended.

[¶ 40] Mrs. Du is placed on formal probation for five years on the following terms and conditions:

[¶ 41] Mrs. Du is to perform 400 hours of community service. I strongly recommend that for the maximum impact on Mrs. Du and for the community, this service should be in connection with efforts to various groups to unite the Korean and African American communities.

[¶ 42] Mrs. Du is to pay $500 to the restitution fine [*sic*] and pay full restitution to the victim's immediate family for all out of court expenses for Latasha Harlins' funeral and any medical expenses related to Latasha Harlins' death.

[¶ 43] Mrs. Du is to obey all laws and orders of the probation department and the court.

[¶ 44] If I am wrong about Mrs. Du and she re-offends, then she will go to state prison for 10 years.

NOTES

1. Superior Court of Los Angeles County, no. BA037738; *People v Superior Court (Du)*, 5 Cal. App. 4th 822 (1992).
2. The titles of the superior court case and the reported opinion use "Soon Ja Du" and place Du's surname last. In referring to defendant Du in this article, I will follow standard Korean usage in my placement of the family surname.
3. Appeal, p. 829.
4. See, for example, "Blacks Voice Outrage over Sentence in Girl's Death; Reaction: Some Fear that Fragile Truce between Korean Merchants and African Americans Could Be in Danger," *Los Angeles Times*, 17 November 1991, 1; "Blacks Seek to Channel Anger over Sentence," *Los Angeles Times*, 17 November 1991, 1.
5. Largely fueled by sentiment against her sentence in *People v Soon Ja Du*, three challengers opposed Karlin in her confirmation election. A majority of voters, however, reelected her to a full judicial term. She is not currently assigned to try cases in the criminal division of the Los Angeles Superior Court.
6. References to the sentencing colloquy are by paragraph and are not footnoted.
7. See generally, my discussion in "A Critique of 'Our Constitution Is Colorblind,'" *Stanford Law Review* 44 (1991): 1.
8. Judge Karlin does not mention the choice by Du and her family to operate a store in a racially particularized neighborhood. The appeals court noted that the Du family sold one business and chose to purchase this business in a "bad neighborhood" (Appeal, p. 828). Had she recognized a "consenting shopkeeper" instead of an "innocent shop-keeper," Karlin could then have allowed an inference that Du understood some of the dangers of operating a small business in a poor neighborhood. Du's use of the revolver would take on a more calculated character. Instead of Du as the innocent victim of a "defective" revolver, her use of the revolver was part of the difficult and sometimes harsh environment in which the Du family had chosen to work. I am not suggesting that self-defense, including armed self-defense, is inappropriate. At issue here is Judge Karlin's understanding of the context for the use of firearms and how Karlin has characterized Du Soon Ja's use of the weapon as completely without fault.
9. Appeal, 829 n. 7.
10. This "measurement" of Du is an aspect of a judge's traditional sentencing function.
11. Edward W, Said, *Orientalism* (New York: Random House, 1978).
12. John Kuo Wei Tchen, "Modernizing White Patriarchy: Re-Viewing D. W. Griffith's *Broken Blossoms*," in *Moving the Image: Independent Asian Pacific American Media Arts*, ed. Russell Leong (Los Angeles: UCLA Asian American Studies Center and Visual Communications, 1991), 133. See also John W. Dower, *War without Mercy: Race and Power in the Pacific War* (New York: Pantheon, 1986), 147–180; Dennis M. Ogawa, *From Japs to Japanese: An Evolution of Japanese-American Stereotypes* (Berkeley, Calif.: McCutchan Publishing, 1971). More traditional treatments are found in Stuart Creighton Miller,

The Unwelcome Immigrant: The American Image of the Chinese, 1785–1882 (Berkeley: University of California Press, 1969); and Stuart Creighton Miller, *"Benevolent Assimilation": The American Conquest of the Philippines, 1899–1903* (New Haven, Conn.: Yale University Press, 1982).

13. Tchen, "Modernizing White Patriarchy," 136–137.

14. Bob Suzuki, "Education and the Socialization of Asian Americans: A Revisionist Analysis of the 'Model Minority' Thesis," *Amerasia Journal* 23 (1977): 4.

15. William Petersen, "Success Story: Japanese American Style," *New York Times Magazine,* 9 January 1966: vi–20. Similar articles included Julian Makaroff, "America's Other Racial Minority: Japanese Americans," *Contemporary Review* 210 (1967): 310–314; Barbara Varon, "The Japanese Americans: Comparative Occupational Status, 1960 and 1950–," *Demography* 4 (1967): 809–819. A recent article that discussed the model minority is Don T. Nakanishi, "Surviving Democracy's 'Mistake': Japanese Americans and the Enduring Legacy of Executive Order 9066," *Amerasia Journal* 19 (1993): 7–35.

16. Lisa Lowe, "Heterogeneity, Hybridity, Multiplicity: Marking Asian American Differences," *Diaspora* 1, no. 1 (spring 1991): 24–44.

17. More recently, the *Los Angeles Times* presented a photo essay with accompanying text about Korean grocers and African American patrons: photographs by Chang W. Lee, article by John W. Lee, "Counter Culture: In Los Angeles, Korean-American Stores Are Sometimes the Flash Point of Racial Animosity—But They Are Also the Proving Ground for Tolerance," *Los Angeles Times Magazine,* 17 October 1993, 20–21.

18. I am aware of only two book-length treatments of Asians in popular culture: James S. Moy, *Marginal Sights: Staging the Chinese in America* (Iowa City: University of Iowa Press, 1993); and Darrell Y. Hamamoto, *Monitored Peril: Asian Americans and the Politics of TV Representation* (Minneapolis: University of Minnesota Press, 1994).

(Mis)Identifying Culture

Asian Women and the "Cultural Defense"

Leti Volpp

Introduction

The "cultural defense"[1] is a legal strategy defendants use in attempts to excuse criminal behavior or to mitigate culpability based on a lack of requisite *mens rea*.[2] Defendants may also use "cultural defenses" to present evidence relating to state of mind when arguing self-defense or mistake of fact. The theory underlying the defense is that the defendant, usually a recent immigrant to the United States, acted according to the dictates of his or her "culture," and therefore deserves leniency.[3] There is, however, no formal "cultural defense"; individual defense attorneys and judges use their discretion to present or consider cultural factors affecting the mental state or culpability of a defendant.[4] In my discussion of this strategy, I focus on the significance of its use for Asian women. When examining the "cultural defense" and its effect on Asian women, I write from the subject position of an Asian American woman.[5] I also write with the benefit of the collective insight of Asian American women working with the Asian Women's Shelter in San Francisco, who created the "Cultural Defense" Study Group.[6] The Study Group arose from concern about the use of the "cultural defense" and from the pressing need for Asian American women to articulate a position on its use.

The "cultural defense" presents several complex problems inherent in essentializing a culture and its effect on a particular person's behavior. I analyze the use of the defense in two cases in order to illustrate problems with the defense and situations in which allowing cultural information into the courtroom might be appropriate. I argue that any testimony about a defendant's cultural background must embody an accurate and personal portrayal of cultural factors used to explain an individual's state of mind and should not be used to fit an individual's behavior into perceptions about group behavior.

Presentation of cultural factors must also be informed by a recognition of the multiple, intersectional layers of group-based oppression that may be relevant to understanding any particular case. The concept of intersectionality, which in this context refers to the interplay of racism and sexism in the experiences of women of color, provides a useful analytical tool.[7] Because of our identity as both women and persons of color within discourses shaped to respond to one categorization or the other, women of color exist at the margins of both discourses.[8] Because intersectionality is a methodology that disrupts the categorization of race and gender as exclusive or separable, I argue that an intersectional analysis is essential to an understanding of the relationship of the "cultural defense" to Asian women.[9]

I also explore why the choice of whether or not to support the use of the "cultural defense" is difficult and suggest a strategy for making this choice. I ultimately argue that the value of antisubordination should be used to mediate between a position that totally rejects the defense and a position that embraces a formalized "cultural defense" from the perspective of cultural relativism. I conclude that the formalization of a "cultural defense" should not be promoted, and that a commitment to ending all forms of subordination should inform the decision of whether or not to support the informal use of cultural information on behalf of a defendant in a given case.

I discuss in detail two cases, *People v Dong Lu Chen*[10] and *People v Helen Wu,*[11] because they are representative of the two kinds of cases in which "cultural defenses" involving Asian women have most often been attempted.[12] The first type of case, exemplified in *Chen,* involves an Asian man seeking a "cultural defense" for his violence toward an Asian woman.[13] The second factual pattern, seen in *Wu,* features an Asian woman seeking to admit cultural factors to explain her mental state when she attempted to commit parent-child suicide.[14]

Both of the cases involve Chinese Americans. I hesitate to focus on these cases because Chinese Americans are frequently used synecdochically to represent all Asian Americans, and I repeat that process here by describing my project as one about "Asian women."[15] Yet, paradoxically, because of the homogeneity into which the dominant community crushes the vast diversity of Asian America,[16] the legal system's treatment of two cases affecting Chinese Americans does reflect popular and legal conceptions of other Asian American communities.[17]

I use the terms "Asian" and "Asian American" at different points throughout this piece in order to emphasize how communities are identified in different contexts. The concept of a "cultural defense" rests on the idea of a community not fully "integrated" into the United States and assists "Asians in America," or "immigrants," as opposed to "Asian Americans." Asian Americans are those whom American society generally assumes to have assimilated into "American culture"[18] to the extent that we do not require a special defense.[19]

Drawing this distinction relies on the problematic positioning of recent immigrants from Asia as "not American." Reserving the term "American" for those who seem fully assimilated erases two important and related factors. The first is the fluid and shifting nature of American identity. The second is the fact that both immigrant and Asian experiences are integral and formative components of American identity. This failure to acknowledge its multiplicity leaves American identity, and specifically the identity of United States law, a neutral and unquestioned backdrop.[20]

One is left with an image of a spoonful of cultural diversity from immigrants ladled onto a flat, neutral base. Creating a "cultural defense" for immigrants in the United States thus rests on the implication that U.S. law is without a culture.[21] The flawed conception, inherent in a "cultural defense," that recent immigrants have a "culture" while U.S. law does not, promotes an anthropological relationship between the court and the immigrant defendant. The court, through testimony of "experts," conducts an examination of communities not considered to "fit" within the borders of U.S. law. This anthropological relationship is characterized by "expert" presentations of Asian culture that depict Asian communities as static, monolithic, and misogynist. This dynamic distances the subject of study by creating an unrecognizable "other" and allows the dominant anthropologist "expert" to subordinate members of the foreign culture through descriptive control.

This chapter begins by examining the use of the "cultural defense" in a case that clearly demonstrates its potential to render Asian women invisible by ignoring factors of subordination within their own communities. In the next section, I narrate the case of *People v Dong Lu Chen*.[22] In that case, an Asian woman, Jian Wan Chen, was murdered by her husband. Dong Lu Chen, the defendant, successfully used a "cultural defense" that presented essentialized notions of "Chinese culture" to excuse his actions. By analyzing the expert testimony and decision of the trial judge, I show how the "cultural defense" in that case used a description of "culture" that obliterated any notion of gender oppression.

I then analyze the response to the Chen case among white feminist organizations and Asian American community organizations, which paradigmatically illustrates the tensions that exist between these groups regarding the use of the "cultural defense." I survey reactions to the "cultural defense" both within these communities and within legal literature. I conclude that a new approach to the "defense" is necessary, both to guide appropriate presentations of cultural information within the courtroom and to inform the choice of whether and when to support admission of a defendant's cultural background.

Next I consider the case of *People v Helen Wu*,[23] in which the state of California convicted an Asian woman of killing her son. This case illustrates that, despite the problematic positioning of "immigrant," "culture," and "America" inherent in the "cultural defense," many cases will present compelling fact patterns that encourage admission of cultural evidence into the courtroom to explain the defendant's actions as shaped by her particular experiences. But *People v Helen Wu* also exemplifies the problem of cultural determinism inherent in the use of a "cultural defense": the defense rests on the notion that one's behavior is determined by one's identity. Because what defendants frequently present as "culture" in "cultural defenses" is static and particular, if a defendant's behavior does not sufficiently match what experts describe as "traditional" cultural behavior, she may lose the opportunity to offer testimony as to her cultural background.

In the next section I explain why a formal "cultural defense" would be problematic and why allowing informal testimony is preferable. As an instructive parallel that argues against the creation of a formalized "cultural defense," I describe difficulties engendered by a formalized battered women's syndrome. I explain the importance of an intersectional analysis to understanding how "cultural defenses" impact Asian women, and discuss the utility of "strategic essentialism" in determining when to allow "cultural" evidence.

I conclude by describing an approach to the "cultural defense" that supports what may appear to be the contradictory interests of Jian Wan Chen, "victim," and Helen Wu, "defendant." I argue that the value of antisubordination should be factored into the decision of whether or not to support use of the defense and that a commitment to antisubordination must entail a simultaneous recognition of material and descriptive oppression based on factors such as race, gender, immigrant status, and national origin.[24]

INVISIBLE WOMAN: *THE PEOPLE V DONG LU CHEN*[25]

In 1989, Brooklyn Supreme Court Justice Edward Pincus sentenced Chinese immigrant Dong Lu Chen to five years probation for using a claw hammer to smash the skull of his wife, Jian Wan Chen.[26] The defense sought to demonstrate that the requisite state of mind was lacking by introducing evidence about Chen's cultural background. After listening to a white anthropologist "expert," Burton Pasternak, provide a "cultural defense" for Dong Lu Chen, Pincus concluded that traditional Chinese values about adultery and loss of manhood drove Chen to kill his wife.

The defense introduced most of the information about Dong Lu Chen's cultural background through Pasternak's expert testimony. Defense Attorney Stewart Orden presented Pasternak with a lengthy hypothetical designed to evoke a response about the "difference" between how an "American" and a "Mainland Chinese individual"[27] might respond to a particular set of events. This hypothetical was in fact a history of Dong Lu Chen and provided the defense's explanation for why he killed Jian Wan Chen.[28] As Orden set forth in this "hypothetical," Dong Lu Chen was fifty-four years old at the time of trial. Since 1968 Dong Lu Chen had believed he was hearing voices around him; doctors told him there was something wrong with his mind.[29]

In September 1986, the Chen family immigrated to the United States. While Dong Lu Chen worked as a dishwasher in Maryland, Jian Wan Chen and their three children stayed in New York.[30] During a visit when Jian Wan Chen refused to have sex with him and "became abusive," Dong Lu Chen became suspicious she was having an affair. He returned to Maryland, burdened with the stress of his wife's assumed infidelity.[31]

In June 1987, Dong Lu Chen moved to New York.[32] On August 24 he rushed into his wife's bedroom and grabbed her breasts and vaginal area. They felt more developed to him and he took that as a sign she was having affairs.[33] When he confronted her the next day, she said she was seeing another man.[34] On September 7, when he again confronted her and said he wanted to have sex, "she said I won't let you hold me because I have other guys who will do this."[35] His head felt dizzy, and he "pressed her down and asked her for how long had this been going on. She responded, for three months."[36] Confused and dizzy, he picked something up and hit her a couple of times on the head. He passed out.[37]

After presenting the above "facts" as part of his hypothetical, Orden asked

Pasternak if this history was consistent with reactions "under normal conditions for people from Mainland China."[38] Pasternak responded:

> Yes. Well, of course, I can't comment on the mental state of this particular person. I am not a psychiatrist. I don't know this particular person. But the events that you have described, the reactions that you have described would not be unusual at all for Chinese in that situation, for a normal Chinese in that situation. Whether this person is normal or not I have no idea. . . . If it was a normal person, it's not the United States, they would react very violently. They might very well have confusion. It would be very likely to be a chaotic situation. I've witnessed such situations myself.[39]

Orden also asked Pasternak to verify that a "normal Chinese person from Mainland China" would react in a more extreme and much quicker way than an "American" to the history as given in the hypothetical.[40] Pasternak answered: "In general terms, I think that one could expect a Chinese to react in a much more volatile, violent way to those circumstances than someone from our own society. I think there's no doubt about it."[41]

This initial testimony highlights some important issues. First, the distinction Orden and Pasternak draw between "American," "someone from our own society," and "Chinese" implies that "Chinese" and "American" are two utterly distinct categories: "American" does not encompass immigrant Chinese.[42] This dichotomy rests on the lingering perception of Asians in America as somehow "foreign," as existing in "America" while not being "American."[43] Importantly, the perspective that Chinese living in the United States are not "American" is the very basis for the assertion of the "cultural defense," on the grounds that someone from a distinctly "non-American" culture should not be judged by "American" standards.

Perceiving Chinese living in the United States as American, as part of our *polis*, significantly affects our responses to Dong Lu Chen. Referring to Dong Lu Chen's identity as a hyphenated identity—Asian American—recognizes the specific histories of people of color in the United States while emphasizing the existence of a community of other Asian Americans that is best situated to evaluate and judge his actions. For reasons discussed further below, members of Asian American communities, particularly community organizations aware of internal power dynamics, should determine the use and content of the "cultural defense."[44]

After dichotomizing "American" and "Chinese," Orden and Pasternak's second step in creating a "cultural defense" was to assert that a man considered "normal" in the category "Chinese" would react very differently from someone in the category "American" to the belief that his wife was having an affair.[45] Their third step collapsed the history of a particular person with specific mental problems into the category "normal person from Mainland China."[46] Finally, Orden's and Pasternak's description of Dong Lu Chen's reaction was predicated on the "stress theory" of violence: abuse happened because the batterer experienced stress. This is a theory much criticized by battered women's advocates, who note that batterers choose to abuse power over their victims and that violence is not an automatic stress-induced response beyond batterers' control.[47] As the prosecuting attorney pointed out,

Chen waited from August 25, when he was allegedly informed by his wife that she was having an affair, until September 7 to confront his wife violently.[48]

To bolster Pasternak's assertions about Dong Lu Chen's behavior, Orden asked him to testify about the particularities of family life in China. Pasternak spoke of the "extraordinary" difference between "our own" ability and the ability of "the Chinese" to control the community through social sanctions.[49] He added to the "voices" that Dong Lu Chen heard in his head, earlier presented as a sign of mental difficulties, another set of "voices" controlling Chen.[50] Pasternak testified that his "Chinese friends" often said "there is no wall that the wind cannot penetrate," meaning that the voices of social control "will be heard everywhere."[51] Orden and Pasternak repeated these "voices of the community" throughout the trial to signify that in a tradition-bound society like Mainland China, social control is more strict and unchanging than in the West, and that a "Chinese individual" carries these "voices" of social control wherever he goes.

Continuing his description of Chinese family life and values, Pasternak asserted that "casual sex, adultery, which is an even more extreme violation, and divorce" are perceived as deviations from these social mores.[52] "In the Chinese context," adultery by a woman was considered a kind of "stain" upon the man, indicating that he had lost "the most minimal standard of control" over her.[53] Pasternak contrasted the condemnation of adultery in China with the United States, "where we take this thing normally in the course of an event."[54] He claimed that the Chinese woman was likely to be "thrown out" and that both parties would have difficulty remarrying.[55]

Pasternak proceeded to delineate the ramifications of a woman's adultery for the Chinese man and Chinese woman in the context of the United States.[56] Pasternak relied on his perception of the prevalence of "yellow fever" among white males and the desexualization of Asian men in America to assert that a Chinese "adulteress" would have no problem establishing a relationship with a white man, while the Chinese male cuckold would have no chance of finding a white woman. The Chinese male would be considered a "pariah" among Chinese women because he would be viewed as having been unable to "maintain the most minimal standard of control" within his family.[57]

Pasternak's bizarre portrayal of divorce and adultery in China in fact had little basis in reality.[58] When Assistant District Attorney Arthur Rigby pressed him for his sources during cross-examination, Pasternak mentioned fieldwork he did between the 1960s and 1988 (he could not remember the title of his own article), incidents he saw, such as a man chasing a woman with a cleaver, and stories he heard.[59] He admitted he could not recall having witnessed or indeed ever heard of a single instance in which a man in China killed his wife, yet he suggested that this was accepted in China.[60] Pasternak's description of "Chinese society" thus was neither substantiated by fact nor supported by his own testimony. The description was in fact his own American fantasy.

During his cross-examination of Pasternak, Rigby attempted to undermine Chen's "cultural defense" by deconstructing Pasternak's identification of "American," his description of Chinese as insulated from Western influence, and his depiction of Chinese Americans as completely non-assimilated. Rigby began his questioning by asking, "What would you consider your average American?" Pasternak responded, "I think you are looking at your average American."[61]

With this statement Pasternak situated his own subjective position as the definition of the "average American." In other words, Pasternak defined the "average American" to be a white, professional male. By situating himself as the "average American," Pasternak exposed his subjective identification as the "average American" against whom the "foreigner," Dong Lu Chen, was to be compared. He also demonstrated his identification with masculinity. He thereby abandoned any pretensions to "objectivity" he might have claimed as an anthropologist and revealed his personal investment in his identity as dominant anthropologist[62] and white male, vis-à-vis the subordinated Chinese male and female objects of study.

When Rigby pressed Pasternak about whether he meant "Anglo Saxon male" by "average American," Pasternak responded by positioning "us"/"American" and "them"/"Chinese" as "two extremes."[63] When asked to identify what he meant by "American," he replied by describing American as not "Chinese."[64] With this explanation, Pasternak followed a tradition, identified as "Orientalism," of dichotimizing the human continuum into "we" and "they" and essentializing the resultant "other."[65] When a dominant group essentializes a subordinated group by focusing on selected traits to describe the group as a whole, the dominant group defines its own characteristics in contrast to the subordinated group.[66] This fetishization of "difference" enabled Pasternak's creation of a "cultural defense" for Dong Lu Chen by depicting gender relations in China as vastly different from gender relations in the United States. The resulting image erased the prevalence of gendered violence in the United States and distanced the United States-based spectator from both Dong Lu Chen and Jian Wan Chen in a way that rendered them unrecognizable and inhuman.

After challenging Pasternak's definition of "average American," Rigby attacked his depiction of Chinese culture as insular and impermeable by outside influence. Rigby asked whether in the last ten years, since Nixon had opened relations with China, China had "embraced Western culture" and if this had a "liberalizing" or "awakening" effect. "No," said Pasternak.[67] This question demonstrated that Rigby as well as Pasternak accepted a construction of China as a "closed" or "conservative" nation slumbering away, as compared to the "advanced" West. Rigby's method of attack thus depended in part on the same stereotypes he was attempting to undermine.

Trying another approach, Rigby then asked: "Now in a situation where someone from China comes to the United States, let's say, for instance, comes to New York City, how quickly do they assimilate, if at all, the American culture?" Pasternak answered, "Very slowly, if ever. . . . Of all the Asians who come to this country, from my experience . . . the people who have the hardest time adjusting to this society are Chinese. The Japanese do a lot better."[68]

Pasternak's statement obviously served his construction of Dong Lu Chen as unassimilable alien. His response failed to problematize the concept of assimilation, and its complete lack of historical or contextual specification unmasked ludicrous generalizations. Which "Chinese" was Pasternak referring to? Which "Asians?"[69]

Although Orden attempted to point out some of the flaws inherent in Pasternak's characterizations of Chinese culture and its relationship to Jian Wan Chen's death, Justice Pincus was swayed by the "persuasiveness" of Pasternak's testimony about the "cultural" roots of Dong Lu Chen's actions. He held:

> Were this crime committed by the defendant as someone who was born and raised in America, or born elsewhere but primarily raised in America, even in the Chinese American community, the Court [*sic*] would have been constrained to find the defendant guilty of manslaughter in the first degree. But, this Court [*sic*] cannot ignore . . . the very cogent forceful testimony of Doctor Pasternak, who is, perhaps, the greatest expert in America on China and interfamilial relationships.[70]

Pincus specifically found significant Pasternak's testimony that Chen lacked a Chinese community to act as a "safety valve" to keep him from killing his wife.[71] Yet the alleged motivation for Chen's actions was his "shame" and humiliation before this very same community. The inconsistency in this reasoning is self-evident.[72]

Pincus attempted to incorporate his newly acquired, inaccurate and essentialized understanding of Chinese culture into his sentencing decisions. At the probation hearing Pincus tried to integrate these lessons about the "Chinese" and how a "Chinese" is motivated by "honor" and "face": "And I must have a promise from the defendant on his honor and his honor of his family he will abide by all of the rules and conditions that I impose. . . . And if he does not obey and he violates any of these conditions, not only does he face jail, but this will be a total loss of face."[73]

In his decision to grant probation rather than impose a jail sentence, Pincus also took other unrelated "cultural" considerations into account. Pincus believed that the possible effect of Chen's incarceration on his daughters' marriage prospects should be a factor in determining Chen's sentence. Pincus told a reporter, "Now there's a stigma of shame on the whole family. They have young, unmarried daughters. To make them marriageable prospects, they must make sure he succeeds so they succeed."[74] In the sentencing colloquy Pincus indicated that he also learned that Dong Lu Chen was a "victim":

> Based on the cultural background of this individual he has also succeeded in partially destroying his family and his family's reputation. . . . There are victims in this case: The deceased is a victim, her suffering is over. The defendant is a victim, a victim that fell through the cracks because society didn't know where or how to respond in time.[75]

Thus Pincus was able to justify his probationary sentencing: Dong Lu Chen did not serve time for killing his wife because in balancing this action and the surrounding circumstances he was just as much a "victim" as she was.[76]

But where was Jian Wan Chen in this story? The defense strategy rendered her invisible. She was most notably present in the testimony as a dead body[77] and as a reputed "adulteress," bringing a "stain" upon her husband.[78] Jian Wan Chen did not exist as a multifaceted person but was instead flattened into the description "adulteress." Any discussion of her at trial was premised upon her characterization as a woman who provoked her husband into jealousy. How should this flattening be interpreted? This invisibility and erasure of the woman, Jian Wan Chen?

Jian Wan Chen's invisibility involved more than the disappearance of a victim in a trial focused on the guilt or innocence of a defendant. The defense presented a narrative that relied on her invisibility as an Asian woman for its logical coherence. This invisibility was manifest through the absence of Jian Wan Chen as a subject, a void that was filled only by stereotypes of the sexual relationships of "Chinese women" and an image of her silent physicality. She appeared as an object whose silence devalued her humanity to the extent that the taking of her life did not merit a prison sentence.

Jian Wan Chen's invisibility is a legacy of an intersection of race and gender that erases the existence of women of color from the popular consciousness.[79] Because white male citizens personify what is considered "normal" in the United States, a status as "other" that is more than one deviation away from the "norm" rarely exists in popular consciousness.[80] The exclusion of Jian Wan Chen exemplifies the difficulty women of color have when attempting to express themselves as holistic subjects, as Asian women whose identity lies at the intersection of multiple forms of subordination.[81]

Applying an intersectional analysis, it is clear that what Pasternak presented as "Chinese culture" privileged race over any consideration of gender oppression. Pasternak's perspective was "male," obviating the possibility that a woman, and specifically a Chinese immigrant woman, might describe divorce, adultery, and male violence within "Chinese culture" very differently. The perspective, was, of course, also "white." The "whiteness" of Pasternak's perspective allowed him to situate Dong Lu Chen in a category labelled "Chinese" diametrically opposite to Pasternak's own "average," white, male citizen position. Yet this placement ignored that Jian Wan Chen was, in fact, the person categorically opposite to Pasternak: she was Chinese, immigrant, and female. Thus, the "cultural defense" served in this case to legitimize male violence against women by glossing over the gendered aspects of Pasternak's testimony about "culture."

The Chen trial suffered from a complete absence of any female perspective: Dong Lu Chen, Pasternak, Orden, Rigby, and Pincus were all male. Jian Wan Chen was dead, symbolizing how ideologies that subordinate groups of people literally transpire over the body of an "other." Thus, Jian Wan Chen's invisibility is not only the product of the racist notion that "Asian life is cheap,"[82] but also a remnant of the indifference with which many in the United States treat the epidemic of violence against women.[83] Furthermore, the complete disregard for her life also reflected the way racism and sexism intersect to render insignificant violence against women of color, and here specifically, Asian immigrant women.

The impact of the trial and probationary sentencing resonated beyond the courtroom, sending a message to the wider community. Jian Wan Chen's life was not valued; her life was worth less than other lives; her murderer did not deserve punishment in jail. Other Chinese immigrant women living with abuse at the hand of their partners and husbands identified with Jian Wan Chen and clearly understood that violence against them by their partners and husbands had the implicit approval of the state.[84]

The Chen decision sent a message to battered immigrant Asian women that they had no recourse against domestic violence. One battered Chinese woman told a worker at the New York Asian Women's Center, "Even thinking about that case makes me afraid. My husband told me: 'If this is the kind of sentence you get for killing your wife, I could do anything to you. I have the money for a good attorney.'"[85] In other words, her husband could afford to hire someone to testify as an expert to bolster a "cultural defense" that legitimized his violence.[86] The codirector of the New York Asian Women's Center reported that battered women who had previously threatened their husbands with legal sanctions also lost this threat as a means to stop the abuse: "For some women this has worked, but no more. They tell me their husbands don't buy it anymore because of this court decision."[87]

RESPONSE TO THE CASE: LIMITED POSITIONS

After Pincus's decision in the Chen case, a coalition of Asian American community activists and white feminists protested and planned to file a complaint against Pincus with the state Commission on Judicial Conduct.[88] The coalition, however, rapidly fragmented. White feminists like Elizabeth Holtzman[89] and the National Organization for Women wanted to completely ban any consideration of culture from the courtroom, while Asian American activists from the Organization of Asian Women, the Asian American Legal Defense and Education Fund, and the Committee Against Anti-Asian Violence were unable to agree with that position.[90] Asian American groups wanted to be able to retain the possibility of using the "cultural defense" in other contexts. Françoise Jacobsohn, president of the New York City chapter of the National Organization for Women, said she understood the concerns of the Asian American organizations but felt frustrated: "They were afraid that we were going to go around with a battering ram and destroy the whole concept of a cultural defense. But the judge needed to know that we did not find his statements acceptable."[91]

The philosophical division that fragmented this coalition is symptomatic of the split that exists between white feminists and feminists of color. White feminists saw the case as indicating that a defendant's cultural background should never be taken into account in deciding a sentence: according to Holtzman, we should have only "one standard of justice."[92] Holtzman's position is one of a number of different responses legal scholars have offered regarding the "cultural defense." As yet, none have effectively navigated between the extremes of condemning the defense in all cases and promoting the defense in the interest of cultural pluralism. Neither of the extremes is satisfying because they both fail to acknowledge that the multiple subordinations existing within immigrant communities are relevant to the choice of whether to support the use of the "cultural defense" in any one case.

The position that a defendant's cultural background should never be taken into account not only denies that our legal system already has a culture, but also rests on other troubling assumptions. Julia Sams's article is probably the most egregious example of law review literature that espouses this "no culture in the courtroom" position, and an examination of her article unmasks the xenophobia and positivism that can lurk underneath this stance.[93] Sams writes: "The response of United States courts to this [novel] theory is significant because it stems from an increasingly urgent problem in the United States—the collision of foreign cultures with the United States legal system."[94] She states in a footnote: "This conflict has been aggravated by the rising population of immigrants and refugees, most of whom are Asian."[95] In other words, Asian immigrants—whom she labels "foreign newcomers"—are responsible for the urgent problem of collision of their "foreign" cultures with the U.S. legal system.

Sams bases her dislike of a formalized "cultural defense" on the theory that "[l]ack of cultural conformity and ignorance of the United States law by such people pose serious threats to the court systems and communities in which they settle."[96] She expresses the concern that allowing a "cultural defense" will strip the criminal law of its deterrent function: "If [foreign newcomers'] incentive to learn about the judicial system is diminished, their communities will likely continue to fluctuate between following the newcomers' alien customs and those of their newly adopted American ways."[97] Allowing those immigrants to follow their "alien" ways through granting them a "cultural defense" is also unfair, says Sams, to the majority of Americans, who cannot use it.

Sams ultimately touts assimilation as the key to success.[98] She suggests that rejecting the "cultural defense" is a means to encourage and accelerate the assimilation process: "By rejecting the 'cultural defense' and therefore not excusing the immigrants' ignorance, the courts will encourage them to adapt more quickly to the legal system of their new homeland. This hastened assimilation by the newcomers to unfamiliar laws may aid their assimilation into other aspects of life in the United States."[99]

Finally, Sams makes the positivist argument that upholding the principle of legality is reason enough to disavow any "cultural defense." This is because "the necessary elements of a legal order are that rules of law with 'objective meanings' are declared by 'competent officials' and only those meanings of the rules are the law."[100] The legal regime "'opposes objectivity to subjectivity, judicial process to individual opinion, [and] official to lay opinion."[101]

Patricia Williams discusses this reliance on "objectivity," "judicial process," and "official opinion" in her description of the characterizations of Anglo-American jurisprudence.[102] Claims by subordinated groups are frequently met by assertions like Sams's of a competing claim of the need for social order, or for legal order in the form of hegemonic authority to control an unruly populace.[103] This claim for social order fails to recognize the inherent subjectivity of legal standards and masks the oppressive force of the law against subordinated communities.

Other scholars have taken a more sophisticated position than Sams by criticizing the "cultural defense" as justifying violence against women.[104] Generally, articles in this vein only examine "cultural defense" cases such as the Chen case that can be condemned easily within a Western feminist framework.[105] Melissa Spatz calls for human rights law as the universal standard to judge cases in which cultural contexts legally sanction the killing of wives.[106] This analysis does not address more thorny issues involving the use of culture in the courtroom, for example, in contexts that do not fit so neatly within a feminist framework. One such difficult case is the Wu case, which involved a mother who killed her son.[107]

White feminists' failure to broach the complex issues raised by cases that do not easily fit within the feminist framework exemplifies their difficulty in recognizing that women of color also belong to communities of color and that they are not "just women." Women of color must continually navigate and choose where and when to articulate allegiances that are often presented as antithetical. Many white feminists repeatedly fail to recognize this multiple subordination, and continue to deny that subordination along lines other than gender gravely impacts women of color.[108] Analyzing what underlies the notion of a "cultureless" courtroom demonstrates the trouble facing feminists who want to disavow any considerations of "culture" in favor of "American" law or "international human rights."[109]

To say that there should be no "culture" in the courtroom is to claim that non-immigrant Americans have no "culture." It is impossible to hold on to this dichotomy without falling into the paradigm of the "West" as somehow "neutral" and "standard." Embracing the diversity and plurality of the United States necessitates a decentering of this "neutral" standard as the "norm." A feminist position that equates "West" with "feminist" is also predicated upon the popular misconception that feminism only flourishes in the West.[110] This view relies on what Laura Nader describes as a "grid of positional superiority,"[111] whereby white feminists in the West tend to ignore the subordination of women in the West or of white women, exaggerate the subordination of women in non-Western countries or in communities of color, and deny the existence of feminist movements in non-Western countries or among women of color.[112] This sense of "positional superiority" also denies the devastation Western colonialism has wrought on women's status in the "Third World" and in communities of color in the United States.[113]

A different version of "feminist imperialism" does not privilege the status of women in the "West" or of white women as non- or less-oppressed, but rather posits all women as predominantly linked across history and culture by the force of sexual domination. This view, characterized for example by some of the work of Mary Daly[114] and Catharine MacKinnon,[115] is problematic in its tendency to essentialize women and to deny the importance of forces of subordination not based on gender. An exclusively gender-based perspective conceptualizes "culture" either as acting only as a source of subordination, or alternatively as not having a specific influence on women's experiences.

Yet a position on the "cultural defense" that has no gender content is also problematic for women. A 1986 Harvard Note[116] analyzes the "cultural defense" from a position of cultural relativism, an anthropological perspective that withholds any condemnation of "cultural practices" of communities not one's own.[117] The Note argues for recognition of a formal "cultural defense" in the interests of individualized justice,[118] cultural pluralism,[119] and social order.[120] I discuss below why a formalized "cultural defense" is problematic and should not be promoted. Although the Note author recognizes the prevalence of racism in the judicial system and is concerned that the values of immigrants be respected, the author does not problematize what constitutes "culture." The Note author is thus willing to accept executing an adulterous wife as a foreign cultural "value." The author explains:

> Immolating one's own children for the sake of honor, executing an adulterous wife, and lashing out at someone in order to break a voodoo speak may seem very bizarre—indeed barbaric and disturbing—to the majority. But this is no reason to attempt immediately to quash the values of foreign cultures. American society has thrived on tolerance, curiosity towards the unknown, and experimentation with new ideas.[121]

The Note suggests limiting the scope of the "cultural defense" on the basis of the likelihood of recurrence and the severity of the crime. Since the author asserts that the only way to differentiate cases is based on the severity of the crime, patterns of subordination within immigrant communities lie unexamined. The author fails to interrogate what "culture" really means, or to identify who labels what as "culture." The author does not recognize that differently situated people within a community experience "culture" differently, or that Asian women might not find violence against them a good basis for "tolerance" and "experimentation with new ideas." Thus, the author falls into the trap of advocating a position that could justify Pasternak's "defense."

The Note and Sams's article thus illustrate two extreme positions with regard to the defense: a formalized "cultural defense" or no consideration of "culture" at all. In response to the Chen case, organizations like the Asian American Legal Defense and Education Fund and the Committee Against Anti-Asian Violence attempted to navigate a middle ground between white feminist positions calling for "no culture," and the position of cultural relativism underlying Pasternak's "cultural defense" and the Harvard Note. Similarly, in this chapter I strive to mediate a new position in the chasm between an adoption of the "cultural defense" premised on cultural relativism, and a rejection of the defense based on xenophobia or the inability to understand that Asian women may benefit from some consideration of "culture." The next part, in which I describe the case of Helen Wu, demonstrates why community-based organizations may want to retain the opportunity to admit cultural information into criminal trials in contexts very different from the Dong Lu Chen case.

NOT A GOOD MOTHER: *THE PEOPLE V HELEN WU*[122]

After strangling her son, Sidney Wu, with the cord from a window blind, Helen Wu was convicted of second degree murder and was sentenced to a term of fifteen years to life by a California Superior Court.[123] She appealed, claiming in part that the trial court committed reversible error by refusing to give a jury instruction about the effect her cultural background might have had on her state of mind when she killed her son.[124]

Compared to Dong Lu Chen's case, Helen Wu's case presents a more compelling reason to admit cultural information and a more accurate and individualized portrayal of cultural factors influencing the defendant's behavior. The case, however, also highlights a second tier of problems inherent in the use of the "cultural defense"—the limitations posed by linking behavior to identity.

Helen Wu was born in 1943 in Saigon, China.[125] In 1963 she met Gary Wu, who emigrated to the United States that same year and married another woman. In 1978 or 1979 Gary Wu contacted Helen and said that he heard she had been married, was divorced, and had a daughter.[126] He told her that his marriage was unsatisfactory because his wife was infertile and that he planned to divorce her. They discussed the possibility of Helen emigrating to the United States and bearing a child for him. Helen, who was in love with him, believed that Gary would marry her after he divorced his wife.

Gary Wu sent Helen money so that she could apply for a visa, and in November 1979 she came to the United States. At his request, Helen brought most of the money he had sent her. Upon her arrival he told her his divorce proceedings would be completed soon and that he would marry her. Gary then obtained a divorce but did not tell Helen.[127]

Helen Wu conceived a child with Gary in early 1980. After Sidney was born, Gary still made no overtures regarding marriage. Helen was depressed, could not speak English, could not drive, and had no support system in the United States. She told Gary that she intended to return to Macau, thinking that he would persuade her to stay. After he failed to do so, she returned to Macau without Sidney because she did not wish people in Macau to know she had had a baby out of wedlock.[128]

For the next eight years Helen repeatedly asked Gary to bring Sidney to visit her in Macau. In 1987 he said that he needed money and agreed to bring Sidney in return. During his visit, Helen showed him a certificate of deposit for a million Hong Kong dollars, which belonged to a friend. He proposed marriage, but she declined, depressed because the proposal seemed to be for "her" money and because she did not know if he was still married. She was so distraught she tried to kill herself.[129]

Helen came to the United States again in 1989 and visited Gary's ill mother, who said that Helen should take Sidney when she died because Gary would not take good care of him. That September Gary and Helen were married in Las Vegas. On the drive back, she asked him if he married her for her money, and he responded that until she produced the money, she had no right to speak. Eight days later Helen saw Gary beat Sidney. Sidney then told her that the house they were staying in belonged to another woman, Rosemary, who was Gary's girlfriend. Sidney also told her that Gary called Helen "psychotic" and "very troublesome," and that Gary beat him.[130]

After hearing this, Helen began to experience heart palpitations and had trouble breathing. She told Sidney that she wanted to die and asked him if he would go too. He clung to her neck and cried. Helen cut the cord off a window blind and strangled her son. She stopped breathing, and when she started again, she was surprised how quickly he had died. Helen wrote Gary a note saying that he had bullied her too much and that "now this air is vented. I can die with no regret." After failing in an attempt to strangle herself, she then slashed her left wrist with a knife in the kitchen. Helen returned to the bedroom and lay down next to Sidney on the bed, after first placing a waste-paper basket under her wrist so the floor would not be dirtied with her blood. Gary returned several hours later to find Sidney dead and Helen in a decreased state of consciousness. She was taken to an emergency room and revived.[131]

Based on these facts and the evidence at trial, the appellate court reversed and remanded the case.[132] The court found that the trial judge should have instructed the jurors that they could choose to consider Helen Wu's cultural background in determining the presence or absence of the various mental states that were elements of murder.[133] The trial court had refused to give the instruction, commenting that it did not want to put the "stamp of approval on [defendant's] actions in the United States, which would have been acceptable in China."[134] The appellate court held that evidence of Helen's cultural background was relevant to the elements of premeditation and deliberation, and found that cultural information was also relevant to the issues of malice aforethought and the existence of heat of passion because it could potentially reduce an intentional killing to voluntary manslaughter.[135]

At the initial trial, the prosecution and defense attempted to paint very divergent views of Helen Wu. They both focused on whether she had "motherly" feelings toward Sidney, and whether she was a "traditional Chinese woman." Initially, we note that the facts presented at trial, while not in conflict as to certain specific events, did vary considerably as to whether defendant had "motherly" feelings toward the victim, her son, whether she was a "traditional" Chinese woman, and, based on the above noted factors, whether the motive for his death was a desire for revenge against Sidney's father or guilt over having not taken good care of the child and fear that he would be ill-treated in the future.[136]

On appeal, the prosecution argued that the court did not give the instruction because the evidence that Helen Wu had the values and motives of a traditional Chinese mother was contradicted by other evidence, and because their expert noted that nothing in Chinese culture or religion encouraged filicide. The appellate court responded that a conflict in evidence did not mean the jury should not have been given an instruction.[137]

The appellate court held that there was ample evidence of both Helen Wu's cultural background and the impact her background might have had on her mental state. Unlike in the Chen case, the defense offered some of this information through experts on "transcultural psychology."[138] These experts testified that Helen Wu's emotional state was intertwined with and explained by her cultural background. They described Helen's actions in killing her son as stemming not from an evil motive, but from her love for Sidney, her feeling of failure as a mother and her desire to be with her son in another life. One expert, Dr. Chien, testified about the cultural context within which Helen acted:

> She thought the only way to find out a way out is to bring Sidney to go together so the mother and son can finally live together in the other heaven, other world if that cannot be done in this realistic earth. . . . [S]he was under the heat of passion when she realized that her son was unwanted son, uncared by Gary, passed around from one woman to the other woman, and now the grandmother is dying and she was planning to leave, "What will happen to Sidney?" And all this information came up

to her mind to stimulate all her guilt feeling which was probably more than ordinary guilt feeling that some depressive person would feel . . . [I]n my expertise as a transcultural psychiatr[ist] . . . with my familiarity with the Chinese culture . . . and from the information interview I obtain from Helen, she thought she was doing that out from the mother's love, mother's responsibility. . . . It's a mother's altruism. This may be very difficult for the Westerner to understand. . . . But in the Asian culture when the mother commits suicide and leaves the children alone, usually they'll be considered to be a totally irresponsible behavior, and the mother will usually worry what would happen if she died.[139]

In addition to Dr. Chien, the defense called another expert to explain the influence of Helen's cultural context on her behavior. Psychologist Terry Gock stated:

[S]he in many ways is a product of her past experiences, including her culture. . . . [I]n some sense the kind of alternatives that she . . . saw how to get out of that situation was quite culturally determined . . . perhaps in this country, even with a traditional woman may, may see other options. But in her culture, in her own mind, there are no other options but to, for her at that time, but to kill herself and take the son along with her so that they could sort of step over to the next world where she could devote herself, all of herself to the caring of the son, caring of Sidney. . . . Her purpose . . . in many ways . . . is a benevolent one.[140]

This presentation of cultural information avoided some of the pitfalls exemplified by Pasternak's "cultural defense" of Dong Lu Chen.[141] Here, the "experts" extensively interviewed the defendant, so that the focus of their testimony was on the individual and how her behavior fit into their conceptions of "culture," in contrast to Pasternak's focus on "the Chinese" and his attempt to fit Dong Lu Chen into that generalization. In addition, Helen Wu's "experts" based their theory on "transcultural psychology." Their analysis was based on the experience of people who migrate to the United States rather than in "culture" as observed in the country of origin. Finally, the "experts" were experts in the sense that they were immigrants to the United States themselves and were thus invested in representing the experience of immigrants from a subjective position. Their position stands in contrast to the white anthropologist Pasternak, whose subjectivity was based on an oppositional position to the "other," Dong Lu Chen, veiled behind a pretense of objectivity.

Although arguing that expert witnesses offer a subjective point of view flies in the face of traditional reliance on "objective" testimony, subjective cultural experts may present a fuller, more human analysis of the defendant. This is especially true because the "othering" that Pasternak practiced will not transpire. In other words, it may be more difficult to obscure the power relations within an immigrant community through a monolithic description of "culture" if the person doing the describing is from that community. This increased accuracy may result because the experts' description is more suspect as "less objective" and therefore more closely examined. More importantly, someone from an immigrant community may have more difficulty describing another member of that community in a way that completely denies her humanity.

In addition to providing a "subjective" perspective on Helen Wu, the experts testifying on her behalf also successfully collapsed the "difference" created between the culture-less "American" and the "cultural" Chinese.[142] By flattening this difference between the person accorded with a "cultural defense" and Americans with an "invisible culture," the jury could envision the defendant without the bizarre and dehumanizing distance that resulted from the Chen defense. Helen Wu was not protrayed as alien and other.[143]

For example, Juris C. Draguns, a clinical psychologist and expert in the area of cross-cultural psychology, testified at Helen Wu's trial about parent-child suicide by American mothers in 1920s Chicago. These mothers apparently did not yet regard their infant children as separate personalities with a right to live, but rather as part of themselves. Draguns found this tendency to interpret the interests and attitudes of another in terms of one's own interests neither abnormal nor unusual. In cases where the attitude led to parent-child suicides, the mother did not regard herself as doing anything criminal or even wrong. She was motivated by love, pity, and sympathy, and acted to remove someone from suffering that she had endured and that the other would, in time, also encounter.[144] Draguns's testimony about similar occurences of parent-child suicide in the United States thus helped to collapse cultural differences between "American" and "Chinese" culture.

Despite an improved presentation of "culture" in the Wu case, the use of a "cultural defense" still presents problems because of the ease with which culture may be reduced to stereotype and the likelihood that an inquiry into the defendant's "culture" becomes one into the defendant's identity within her "cultural" group. Because the defense explained Helen Wu's actions on the basis of cultural determinism—arguing, in other words, that she acted in a particular way because of who she was—the focus of the inquiry became who she was rather than what she did. If Helen Wu could not meet the threshold test of showing that she fit into the category "traditional Chinese woman," as translated by the trial court as a "good mother," then she would not receive the benefit of cultural information that might have helped explain her actions.

The particular threshold test the trial court applied to Wu relied on a stereotype of Asian women as the self-sacrificing woman/mother.[145] We can speculate that the trial court felt persuaded that Helen Wu should not benefit from such a defense because she gave birth to Sidney out of wedlock and was thus not a "traditional Chinese woman." Thus, women whose actions do not fit whatever cultural stereotype the court adopts will not be able to utilize a "cultural defense." Alternatively, women whose actions do fit stereotypes that a jury or judge finds distasteful will not be treated leniently in either case.[146]

Positing a relationship between identity and behavior that, rather than using culture to explain what an individual was thinking, tries to fit an individual into general group behavior risks reducing cultural information to stereotype. This reduction takes place through the creation of a group-based identity such as "the Chinese immigrant battered woman" and what her "typical" reactions are.[147] Such a shift in inquiry from a defendant's behavior to her identity is one reason a formalized "cultural defense" should not be advocated.

THE RISK OF A FORMALIZED DEFENSE

In this section I outline the risks of a formalized "cultural defense," using battered women's syndrome as an example. I also explore the dangers of describing an individual's behavior as "cultural," especially for Asian women. Despite these drawbacks, I still advocate the admission of cultural information for immigrant defendants in strategic contexts, in an effort to explain the state of mind of a defendant whose actions may stem from multiple oppressions.

An examination of how the battered women's syndrome defense operates in some jurisdictions to evaluate women by their characteristics and not by the reasonableness of their actions helps explain the risks of a formalized defense. Feminist legal theorists developed the idea of using expert testimony for battered women who kill their partners in self-defense "to educate the judge and jury about the common experiences of battered women, [and] to explain the context in which an individual battered woman acted, so as to lend credibility and provide a context to her explanation of her actions."[148] The great majority of experts who testify in cases involving battered women who act in self-defense rely upon a model of battered women's syndrome that evolved out of the work of the sociologist Lenore Walker.[149] Walker developed her model of domestic violence to explain why battered women stay in battering relationships; she describes a cycle theory of violence[150] and the theory of learned helplessness.[151] Battered women's syndrome looks for these two factors and post-traumatic stress disorder—all factors describing women as passive and helpless.[152]

Expert testimony on battered women's syndrome has been ruled admissible in the majority of courts that have addressed the issue.[153] Replacing existing criminal standards with a separate standard for battered women, however, has not guaranteed an outcome favorable to battered women's interests. Some courts have created an objective standard of the "reasonable battered woman who kills," which is difficult for many women to meet.[154] The creation of a generalized model of battered women invites courts to prevent fair trials of women who are not "model" battered women.[155] Furthermore, since battered women's syndrome exemplifies a stereotype of passive married middle-class white women, it may be especially difficult for battered women of color and gay men and lesbians to fit the model.[156]

Thus, the experience with battered women's syndrome shows that creating a formalized separate standard can lead to defendants either being refused access to expert testimony or being unable to benefit from that testimony because they do not adequately fit the characteristics of the defense. Similarly, a formalized "cultural defense" could be disastrous for Asian women, since the pertinent characteristics defendants would need to show to fit an "Asian woman" standard are likely to be based on reductive stereotypes, and the behavior or identity of many defendants would not fit the standard. Finally, making a link between identity and behavior entails particular risks for Asian American women since we live in communities where notions of "culture" often mask the interaction of multiple oppressions.[157]

Discourse about "race" or "culture" must not obliterate the intersectional oppressions of Asian women, who exist at a nexus of societal racism and sexism in multiple contexts. "Cultural defenses" that focus solely on "cultural difference" with no analysis of gender subordination serve to block out gender oppression and gender difference within Asian American communities. Thus, in the Chen case, the "cultural defense" masked the fact that Jian Wan Chen suffered subordination as a woman and as a victim of gendered violence. The deployment of the "cultural defense" where gender subordination is at issue requires that we examine not only the way "cultural practices" among Asian men and Asian women are an expression of particular power arrangements, but also the different means by which these practices are maintained and legitimated.[158]

For example, the fact that domestic violence in Asian communities is frequently explained by both Asians and non-Asians as caused or promoted by "Asian culture" is particularly troublesome.[159] This explanation was precisely the "cultural defense" given by Dong Lu Chen. Popular conception in the United States too often understands Asians to be governed by cultural dictates. This misconception is related to the association of "Asian" with "foreign" and "culture" with "other," and leads to dehumanizing descriptions of Asians.[160] I do not mean to deny that there is something we can call "culture" that may explain behavior. My concern is that domestic violence among Asian American communities is explained as "cultural," when a similar description is rarely given to domestic violence in the heterosexual white community. This masks the severity of violence against Asian women by describing it as a "practice" rather than as a political problem. Moreover, to explain behavior as "cultural" implies that it is insular to Asian communities and that the dominant society bears no relationship to that behavior.[161] This hides the fact that Asian women are also subject to oppression from forces outside of Asian communities.

While a formalized "cultural defense" is problematic because it will force defendants' actions to be defined through a group-based identity and so will reify cultural stereotypes, in some circumstances a defense that presents cultural background will be appropriate. In formulating a legal recourse to the predicament of a particular individual whose behavior was influenced by forces such as racism, sexism, and subordination in the form of violence, admission of cultural factors should not function as a reductive "explanation" of that individual's actions as fitting into group behavior or "culture." Rather, the choice to provide an individual defendant with cultural information should be made for the purpose of explaining that individual's state of mind, in much the same way that the criminal law allows other information about a defendant's life history to mitigate sentences or charges in a criminal trial. Even when we attempt to use cultural information to explain an individual's oppressions or her state of mind, we are forced to label and define—in other words, to essentialize—certain behaviors as "cultural." This can be done in the spirit of what might be called "strategic essentialism"[162]—consciously choosing to essentialize a particular community for the purpose of a specific political goal.[163] Ideally, strategic essentialism should be undertaken by the affected community, which is best situated to undertake the process of selecting the appropriate circumstances in which to offer cultural information.

The defendant's community may be an important resource to provide the court with a "subjective" perspective that serves to explain her actions in the context of their own norms. In *State v Chong Sun France*,[164] for example, a Korean woman who left her small children alone at night and returned to find one dead was sentenced to twenty years for second degree murder and felonious child abuse. The trial transcript demonstrates a hearing rife with gender, race, and cultural biases, as well as incredible communication difficulties between France and the court.[165] Throughout the hearing, the prosecution portrayed France as a bad mother—irresponsible and negligent—and as an opportunistic and promiscuous immigrant woman. The court found France guilty, adopting the prosecution's argument that she deliberately placed her son in the bureau drawer and shut him inside, crushing him.[166]

Chong Sun France would have benefitted from "cultural information" from her community. Expert testimony could have provided information to the judge and jury, interpreting her actions as those of a caring but poor Asian woman with few resources to adequately care for her children. France was released on parole on December 31, 1992, after a massive campaign organized by Korean women, who pointed out the lack of culturally specific information in her representation. The campaign's petition provides "cultural information" explaining France's actions from the perspective of other Korean immigrant women and offering information about child care in Korea.[167] While the community's presentation of cultural information runs the risk of essentializing Korean immigrant women in the eyes of the court and of popular culture, the risk can be justified in that it was the affected community of Korean immigrant women who made that strategic choice and also made the choice of what characteristics to present as "cultural information."

MOVING TOWARD HOME

The juxtaposition of the cases of Dong Lu Chen and Helen Wu flushes into view what may seem to be a number of contradictions. How can one argue that the "cultural defense" for Dong Lu Chen was inappropriate while approving the use of cultural information for women like Helen Wu? Both defendants were accused of killing someone over whom they had power. Both alleged feelings of great stress. Both pointed to cultural determinants as a reason for their actions. I reconcile my divergent positions on the two cases by proposing that the value of antisubordination must be a criterion in the decision as to when and how cultural factors should be presented as a defense.

Antisubordination is a value the legal system must factor in when deciding whether to present testimony as to a defendant's cultural background.[168] Valuing the principle of antisubordination is more than a game of hierarchical rankings of "who's most oppressed"; it means a serious commitment to evaluating and eradicating all forms of oppression.[169] In the cases of Helen Wu and Dong Lu Chen, it can involve making identity-based claims to knowledge about the appropriate political choices to make in balancing the risks of perpetuating stereotypes against fairness to the parties involved. As described above, this process can be called "strategic essentialism."

Antisubordination does not posit that those who suffer oppression lack agency due to their victimization and therefore are not responsible for their crimes. Rather, the agency of an Asian American woman, or of anyone who is the subject of multiple oppressions, exists within a complex arena of fractured structural forces and pressures. A fair presentation of her situation should evaluate her agency within this context. In cases like *Chen* and *Wu,* such an evaluation reveals these to be cases about Jian Wan Chen and Helen Wu, both subordinated on the basis of gender as well as influenced by dynamic forces from within and without their communities. The point of antisubordination is not to read every story as a "subordinated woman's story"; rather, it is that one must never explain or close off any story into being just one story.[170]

One step in an antisubordination analysis can be to examine whether the defendant acted with a consciousness of her position within the social structure of her community. Helen Wu resisted what she perceived as subordination out of a set of very narrowly defined choices; Dong Lu Chen acted to constrain his wife's choices further. Understanding someone's location as marginal is crucial to understanding her actions.[171] While I do not intend to justify Helen Wu's killing her son, an antisubordination analysis would consider her position in relation to her family and the narrow options she perceived to ameliorate her suffering.[172]

Antisubordination, as premised on the vastness of oppression along unidirectional lines, such as male oppression of women and xenophobic oppression of immigrants, must be the value on which we base our choices of whether to support the use of cultural factors in a defense and what information should be presented. Because the use of a "cultural defense" reflects the myriad problems of identity politics, including the perpetuation of stereotypical notions that can operate to exclude other people from benefitting from its use, this tactic will be difficult to follow. Using a goal of antisubordination, however, to evaluate the appropriateness of these factors both combats decision making premised on problematic descriptions of Asian women, and reflects a normative vision of what is valuable in our communities. Such a framework will also help dislodge the backdrop of "neutrality" as it exposes the relationship between the dominant and immigrant communities. The baseline from which the "uses and abuses" of "culture" are evaluated must be examined: we must question the unstated presuppositions about the American political and cultural character.

A coherent position on the presentation of "cultural information" that highlights its effect on Asian women thus requires an intersectional analysis, which implicates the use of antisubordination as a value to determine how the defense should be presented and when it should be used. Questions of identity and assimilation, of "strategic essentialism" and self-determination are important elements of the discussion. In making choices about the use of cultural testimony it is difficult to maneuver among complicated and sometimes contradictory strategic moves within a system that relies on its lack of flexibility as a means of deriving authority.

Creation of a formalized "cultural defense" will result in fossilizing culture as a reductive stereotype, and will lead to inquiries into whether a defendant's identity matches that stereotype well enough to merit expert testimony. Cultural information should be allowed only as an informal factor to be considered in deliberations, with the following caveats.

Clearly, an awareness that "culture" is something that affects everybody's actions is essential in consideration of a "cultural defense." There must be an acknowledgment of the fluid and interdynamic nature of cultures.[173] Information that explains the actions of a defendant should be articulated by community members who are sensitive to the dynamics of power and subordination within the community of the defendant. For example, in cases involving women who are abused, such as Jian Wan Chen or Helen Wu, input from organizations that work with battered Asian women is imperative, whether in the form of expert testimony or in amicus briefs. Information about the defendant's culture should never be reduced to stereotypes about a community, but rather should concretely address the individual defendant's location in her community, her location in the diaspora, and her history. The information should be provided so as to give insight into an individual's thoughts, and should not be used for purposes of explaining how an individual fits into stereotypes of group behavior.

Moreover, advocates should be wary lest the presentation of cultural factors do more harm to Asian women defendants than good, given the ease with which Asian behavior slips into stereotype. There may often be sufficient evidence to show that a defendant lacked the requisite mental state, without admitting special cultural testimony. In fact, a careful distinction must be made between assuming that cultural factors are relevant because Asians are governed by culture, and presenting an individual defendant with pertinent cultural background.

Highlighting the problematic aspects of "cultural defenses" should promote greater awareness of the complications connected to their use. It should also elucidate the difficult yet imperative nature of committing to a future that fights the subordination of Asian women, whether in forms material or descriptive.

NOTES

*I am very grateful to Alison Bernstein, Jodi Danis, Gina Dent, Mallika Dutt, Neil Gotanda, Inderpal Grewal, Deeana Jang, Hyun Kim, Jayne Lee, Jennifer Middleton, Paul Sonn, Ed Swanson, John Hayakawa Torok, Kendall Thomas, Sophie Volpp, and Patricia Williams for their comments and suggestions. Special thanks to Kimberle Crenshaw for getting me started and to Brent Edwards for keeping me going.

1. I put "cultural defense" in quotes since, as discussed throughout the chapter, the use of the term is politically problematic and is a misnomer, given the nonexistence of a singular, formalized defense.
2. In many cases the lack of requisite *mens rea* is argued on the basis of insufficient mental capacity. An impaired mental state defense is based on the idea that the accused is unable to appreciate the wrongfulness of her act or conform her conduct to the requirements of the law because of a mental disease or defect that she was suffering at the time the offense was committed. *Model Penal Code* § 4.01(1) (1962).
3. There have also been attempts to use "cultural defenses" for non-immigrant defendants of color. See, e.g., *People v Rhines,* 182 *Cal. Rptr.* 487 (Cal. Ct. App. 1982). For a critique of the "cultural defense" attempted in that case and of Orlando Patterson's "cultural defense" of Clarence Thomas's "down home style of courting," see Kimberle Crenshaw, "Whose Story Is It, Anyway? Feminist and Antiracist Appropriations of Anita Hill," in *Race-ing Justice, En-Gendering Power,* ed. Toni Morrison, 422 (1992).

The defense strategy in the murder trial of Native American Patrick Hooty Croy was referred to as a "cultural defense." See Denise Ferry, "Capitalizing on Race and Culture: The Croy Acquittal and Its Application to Future Minority Cases," 19 *CACJ/Forum* 48, 48 (1992); David Talbot, "The Ballad of Hooty Croy," *Los Angeles Times Magazine*, 24 June 1990, 16. See Ferry, *supra*, 50.

4. Cultural factors may be admitted as part of expert testimony at trial or as part of jury instructions. They may also be presented as mitigating factors during the sentencing phase and in the plea bargaining stage.

5. My perspective also derives from my experiences working with Shakti Women's Aid, a resource center and refuge for battered women of color in Edinburgh, Scotland; with the Asian Women's Shelter, which works with battered Asian women in the San Francisco Bay area; and with the New York Asian Women's Center, which works with battered Asian women in the New York City metropolitan area.

6. Jacqueline Agtuca, Inderpal Grewal, Deeana Jang, Mimi Kim, Debbie Lee, Jayne Lee, Lata Mani, Leni Marin, Beckie Masaki, and Alexandra Tantranon-Saur composed the Study Group.

7. I identify this chapter as part of a growing body of literature that uses the concept of intersectionality to address how women of color are situated in the law. For examples of other works that use the intersectionality framework, see generally Paulette Caldwell, "A Hair Piece: Perspectives on the Intersection of Race and Gender," 1991 *Duke L.J.* 365; Kimberle Crenshaw, "Demarginalizing the Intersection of Race and Sex: A Black Feminist Critique of Antidiscrimination Doctrine, Feminist Theory, and Antiracist Politics," 1989 *U. Chi. Legal F.* 139; Angela Harris, "Race and Essentialism in Feminist Legal Theory," 42 *Stan. L. Rev.* 581 (1990); Marlee Kline, "Race, Racism and Feminist Legal Theory," 12 *Harv. Women's L.J.* 115 (1989); Dorothy Roberts, "Punishing Drug Addicts Who Have Babies: Women of Color, Equality, and the Right of Privacy," 104 *Harv. L. Rev.* 1419 (1991); Celina Romany, "Ain't I a Feminist?" 4 *Yale J.L. & Feminism* 23 (1991). This chapter also uses approaches found in the literature of critical race theory. For examples of critical race theory, see generally Derrick Bell, *And We Are Not Saved* (1987) and *Faces at the Bottom of the Well* (1993); Mari J. Matsuda et al., *Words that Wound: Critical Race Theory, Assaultive Speech, and the First Amendment* (1993); Patricia J. Williams, *The Alchemy of Race and Rights* (1991); Robert Williams, *The American Indian in Western Legal Thought* (1990); Kimberle Crenshaw, "Race, Reform, and Retrenchment: Transformation and Legitimation in Antidiscrimination Law," 101 *Harv. L. Rev.* 1331 (1988); Neil Gotanda, "A Critique of 'Our Constitution is Color Blind,'" 44 *Stan. L. Rev.* 1 (1991); Maivan Clech Lam, "The Kuleana Case Revisited: The Survival of Traditional Hawaiian Commoner Rights in Land," 64 *Wash. L. Rev.* 233 (1989); Kendall Thomas, "Rouge et Noir Reread: A Popular Constitutional History of the Angelo Herndon Case," 65 *S. Cal. L. Rev.* 2599 (1989).

8. See generally Crenshaw, "Demarginalizing the Intersection of Race and Sex," *supra* note 7.

9. Kimberle Crenshaw, "Mapping the Margins: Intersectionality, Identity Politics, and Violence Against Women of Color," 43 *Stan. L. Rev.* 1241, 1244, 9 (1991).

10. No. 87–7774 (N.Y. Sup. Ct. Dec. 2, 1988).

11. 286 Cal. Rptr. 868 (Cal. Ct. App. 1991), rev'g No. ICR 12873 (Super. Ct. Riverside Co. 1990), review denied Jan. 23, 1992.

12. My discussion of these two cases involves a textual analysis of the relevant court opinions. I use this methodology rather than a doctrinal analysis of precedential cases for the following reasons. First, cases involving "cultural defenses" rarely appear at the appellate level. Second, a rhetorical analysis of the cases allows deconstruction of the problematic yet unquestioned ideas underlying uses of the "cultural defense." Because no law review article has yet addressed these ideas, the focus of my chapter is on raising these issues.

13. This fact pattern occurs quite frequently. See Myrna Oliver, "Immigrant Crimes; Cultural Defense—a Legal Tactic," *Los Angeles Times*, 15 July 1988, 1. For other examples

of Asian men seeking a "cultural defense" for violence toward an Asian woman, see *People v King Moua*, No. 315972 (Fresno Super. Ct. 1985); *People v Aphaylath*, 510 N.Y.S.2d 83 (N.Y. 1986); Mary Ann Galante, "Asian Refugee Who Shot Wife Receives 8½-Year Prison Term," *Nat'l L.J.*, 16 December 1985, 40; Oliver, *supra*, at 1.

14. See, e.g., Oliver, *supra* note 13; *People v Fumiko Kimura*, No. A-091133 (L.A. City Super. Ct. filed Apr. 24, 1985); Deborah Woo, "The People v. Fumiko Kimura: But Which People?" 17 *Int'l. J. Soc. L.* 403 (1989).

15. Which specific groups are used to represent the entire Asian American community depends on context. See Lisa Ikemoto, "Traces of the Master Narrative in the Story of African American/Korean American Conflict: How We Constructed 'Los Angeles,'" 66 *S. Cal. L. Rev.* 1581, 1592 (1993).

16. Compare Note, "Racial Violence Against Asian Americans," 106 *Harv. L. Rev.* 1926, 1932 (1993).

17. I am, of course, repeating this homogenization by using these two cases to talk about "Asian women." Whether to use the category "Asian" or "Asian American," instead of categories such as Cambodian, Korean, or Thai, is a political decision entailing both risks and advantages. See Lisa Lowe, "Heterogeneity, Hybridity, Multiplicity, Marking Asian American Differences," 1 *Diaspora* 24, 30 (1991); see also Yen Le Espiritu, *Asian American Panethnicity: Bridging Institutions and Identities* (1992).

18. When I use the terms "American" or "America," I intend an implicit critique of the ethnocentricity of these terms.

19. Of course, Asian Americans are, with enormous frequency, not recognized as "American." This positioning as foreign is something that Asian Americans, including fifth-generation Asian Americans in this country, constantly face. For the relation of this perception to anti-Asian violence, see Note, *supra* note 16, at 1938.

20. None of the law review articles dealing with the question of the "cultural defense" recognize the cultural particularity of American law, nor do they offer a sophisticated analysis of what is being presented as "culture" in cases involving the "cultural defense"—in fact, they frequently attempt no analysis at all. See, e.g., Carolyn Choi, "Application of a Cultural Defense in Criminal Proceedings," 8 *Pac. Basin L.J.* 80 (1990); Donna Kotake, "Survey: Women and California Law," 23 *Golden Gate L. Rev.* 1069 (1993); Julia P. Sams, "The Availability of the 'Cultural Defense' as an Excuse for Criminal Behavior," 16 *Ga. J. Int'l. & Comp. L.J.* 335 (1986); Malek-Mithra Sheybani, "Cultural Defense: One Person's Culture is Another's Crime," 9 *Loy. L.A. Int'l. & Comp. L.J.* 751 (1987); Note, "The Cultural Defense in the Criminal Law," 99 *Harv. L. Rev.* 1293 (1986). Ahn Lam does question racial and sexual bias in the use of the "cultural defense." See Anh Lam, "Culture as a Defense: Preventing Judicial Bias Against Asians and Pacific Islanders," 1 *Asian Am. Pac. Islands L.J.* 49, 62–63 (1993). Two law review articles criticize "cultural defense" cases as validating violence against Asian women but do not address many of the problems identified in this chapter. See Nilda Rimonte, "A Question of Culture: Cultural Approval of Violence Against Women in the Pacific-Asian Community and the Cultural Defense," 43 *Stan. L. Rev.* 1311 (1991); Melissa Spatz, "A 'Lesser' Crime: A Comparative Study of Legal Defenses for Men Who Kill Their Wives," 24 *Colum. J.L. & Soc. Probs.*. 597 (1991).

21. Descriptions of societies that have "culture" and societies in which culture is invisible, e.g., for white America, coincide with the relative powerlessness and power of the societies. Thus, assimilation or social mobility in the United States is supposed to coincide with a stripping away of culture. See Renato Rosaldo, *Culture & Truth: The Remaking of Social Analysis* 209–12 (1989).

22. No. 87-7774 (N.Y. Sup. Ct. Dec. 2, 1988).

23. 286 Cal Rpt. 868 (Cal. Ct. App. 1991), rev'g No. ICR 12873 (Super. Ct. Riverside Co. 1990), review denied Jan. 23, 1992 (unpublished opinion).

24. While not a focus here, factors I also consider fundamental include class and sexuality.

25. No. 87-7774 (N.Y. Sup. Ct. Dec. 2, 1988).

26. After hearing the evidence during the course of the trial, Pincus convicted Chen of second degree manslaughter, which carried a maximum prison term of five to fifteen years. Record at 309–310, Chen (No. 87–7774).
27. Record at 58.
28. The reader should be mindful that this is what Dong Lu Chen's defense attorney presented as an explanation of what "happened." By placing Dong Lu Chen's version here, before the reader learns more about Jian Wan Chen, I reenact her erasure in the narrative of the trial. I do this to show the reader how an easy acceptance of Chen's "cultural" explanation is only made possible by Jian Wan Chen's absence from the narrative as a living, breathing person.
29. Chen was born in Toisan, China. After he left school he worked as a farmer. He married Jian Wan Chen in 1963 in an arranged marriage. They had three children, the oldest twenty-one at the time of the trial, the youngest fifteen. See Record at 58–61.
30. Record at 64. During the first eight months of separation he returned to New York three times. On the first visit Dong Lu Chen and Jian Wan Chen had sexual intercourse. The second visit she refused. On the third, she again refused and "became abusive towards him, including beating him" (Record at 64). Their children said that they never saw their mother beat their father. See Record at 183–184, 213, 217, 219.
31. Record at 64–65. He had difficulty sleeping and palpitations, and began to hear the voice of his wife's lover planning to hurt him. See Record at 65.
32. Record at 65. Jian Wan Chen "became increasingly more brutal . . . she was hitting him, telling him to drop dead and . . . she would not permit him to touch her." Record at 66. Dong Lu Chen noted that Jian Wan Chen, working as a seamstress, changed her site of work and assumed that this was to facilitate her rendezvous with other men. She took all her clothing from their apartment; he thought it was so she could wear the clothes for her lover (Record at 66).
33. Id. at 66.
34. Id. at 66–67.
35. Id. at 67.
36. Id.
37. Id.
38. Id. at 68.
39. Id. at 68–69.
40. Id. at 74.
41. Id.
42. Pasternak's assumption that "American" does not encompass immigrant Chinese ignores the fact that we do not live in hermetically sealed cultures that travel with us from cradle to grave. We are not completely unaffected by other communities and do not live in cultural compartments separating "natives" from "anthropologists" or "immigrants" from "Americans." See Rosaldo, *supra* note 21, at 44–45.
43. On the original and lingering perception of Asian Americans as "foreign," see Neil Gotanda, "Asian American Rights and the 'Miss Saigon Syndrome,'" in *Asian Americans and the Supreme Court*, ed. Hyung-chan Kim, 1087, 1095 (1992); Neil Gotanda, "'Other Non-Whites' in American Legal History: A Review of Justice at War," 85 *Colum. L. Rev.* 1186, 1188 (1985); Elaine Kim, "Asian Americans and American Popular Culture," in *Dictionary of Asian American History*, ed. Hyung-chan Kim, 99 (1986); John H. Torok, "Towards a Liberatory Approach to Asian American Legal History" (June 1993) (unpublished manuscript on file with the *Harvard Women's Law Journal*). For historical illustrations of judicial perceptions of Asian Americans as "foreign," see *Plessy v John H. Ferguson,* 163 U.S. 537, 561 (1896) (Harlan, J., dissenting); also, see *Fong Yue Ting v U.S.,* 149 U.S. 698 (1893).
44. For an example of the important role the defendant's community may play, see the discussion of *State v Chong Sun France,* infra notes 164–168 and accompanying text.
45. Pasternak's claim that "American" men would react less violently than "Chinese" men

to the belief that their wives were having affairs is belied by the very encoding of the manslaughter/provocation doctrine in American law, which is explicitly premised upon a violent reaction to this knowledge. The voluntary manslaughter law of most jurisdictions recognizes the sight of a wife's adultery as a motivation to kill. In fact, adultery is the paradigmatic example of provocation sufficient to mitigate a charge of murder to a voluntary manslaughter conviction. See Donna K. Coker, "Heat of Passion and Wife Killing: Men Who Batter/Men Who Kill," 2 S. *Cal. Rev. L. & Women's Stud.* 71, 72 (1992).

46. Dong Lu Chen did not plead an insanity defense. One can conclude that neither his attorney nor the judge found his actions to be insane, given the "cultural" context.

47. For example, batterers are careful to abuse women when no one else is around to witness the abuse. See *Domestic Violence in Immigrant and Refugee Communities: Asserting the Rights of Battered Women,* ed. D. Jang et al. (1991).

48. See Record at 293. This information should have substantially undermined any manslaughter defense based on provocation.

49. Id. at 53–54.

50. Compare Pasternak, Id.

51. Id. at 78. By continually returning to this "wall and wind" motif and throwing in picturesque details such as gossip during laundry washing by canals, Pasternak fetishized "difference" as a way to anchor the "foreignness" of the "Chinese," and structured his "Chinese friends" as native informants. For a critique of anthropology and the difficulty facing the anthropological subject who wishes to escape the role of native informant see Robert Ji-Song Ku, "Can the Native Informant Write? The Ethnographic Gaze and Asian American Literature," unpublished manuscript presented at the Association for Asian American Studies Conference, Cornell University, June 3, 1993, on file with the *Harvard Women's Law Journal.*

52. Record at 54. See Pasternak, Id.

53. Id. at 55.

54. Id. at 54.

55. See Pasternak, Id. at 55.

56. See Pasternak stated, Id. at 55–56.

57. Id. at 55.

58. The number of divorces has risen steadily since 1980, following the Cultural Revolution and the 1981 marriage law reform allowing for "no fault" divorce; the historical peak of divorces was in 1953 when marriage laws introduced by the Communist government enabled women to escape feudal marriages. Teresa Poole, "China Divorce is Too Close For Comfort," *Independent,* 13 April 1993, 8. See also "Survey Shows Divorce Rising Among Chinese," Chicago Tribune, 11 October 1992, 5; "Divorce Loses Stigma with 10% Annual Rise," BBC Summary of World Broadcasts, 8 October 1992.

59. Record at 105–108.

60. Id. at 106–107. Pasternak gratuitously remarked: "It also happens, by the way, that the men are beaten. It isn't only the women. Sometimes, it's the men. In Inner Mongolia, a man drowned himself because his wife was beating him this summer." Id. at 85.

61. Id. at 76.

62. By "dominant anthropologist" I refer to the power inherent in the relationship between anthropologist and subject of study, which is exercised through the anthropologist's dissemination of descriptive "knowledge."

63. Record at 76.

64. Id. Pasternak explicitly included white Anglo-Saxons, Jews, blacks, Puerto Ricans, and Roman Catholics in his notion of "Americans," and contrasted them all with "Chinese."

65. See Edward Said, *Orientalism* (1978). For a critique of white feminist essentialization of women of color see Caldwell, Harris, and Kline, *supra* note 7.

66. The "West" characterizes the "other" as unchanging and homogenous in order to measure Western "progress" as well as to justify Western imperialism. Describing

societies as "classically traditional" and governed by a set of fixed rules, as Pasternak did, masks power relations within those societies—for instance, Chinese men over Chinese women—and justifies the subjugation of those societies by the "West." Western anthropologists who subjugate in their descriptive function, missionaries who need to save the heathen, or colonists and imperialists who conquer in the name of bringing enlightenment and civilization are examples of subjugating forces. See Rosaldo, *supra* note 21, at 41–42. This fetishization of "difference" has historically enabled global conquest and imperialism; see Elaine Kim, *supra* note 43, at 111.

67. Record at 81.

68. Id. at 102.

69. On redirect, Orden asked Pasternak to state whether seeing Dong Lu Chen bow when he entered the courtroom could lead him to conclude that Chen had not assimilated himself as an American. Pasternak responded that "Chinese do it when they feel enormous respect and the Japanese do it, of course." Id. at 118–119. The "Chinese" Pasternak attempted to define were a monolithic construction of his fantasy, a group consisting exclusively of bowing "Orientals."

70. Id. at 301–302. After hearing the evidence and expert testimony during the course of the bench trial, Pincus considered counts of second degree murder, first degree manslaughter, and second degree manslaughter. See id. at 301.

71. Id. at 302.

72. Monona Yin of the Committee Against Anti-Asian Violence pointed out this inconsistency at a forum on the Chen case. Linda Anthony, "Women Discuss Protection for the Battered Following Controversial 'Cultural Defence' Verdict," *Korea Times,* 14 July 1989.

73. Record at 311.

74. Shaun Asseal, "Judge Defends Sentencing Wife-Killer to Probation," *Manhattan Law.,* 4–10 April 1989, 4. Asseal also noted that Brooklyn prosecutors had considered Pincus a very tough sentencer. Id.

75. Record at 355. See Patricia Hurtado, "Killer's Sentence Defended: 'He's Not a Loose Cannon,'" *Newsday,* 4 April 1989, 17.

76. In leniently treating a man who killed a woman, and in seeing male batterers as "victims," Justice Pincus was not unique. The Pace University Battered Women's Justice Center reports that sentences battered women receive for killing their abusive partners far exceed those for abusive men who kill their partners. The average sentence for a woman who kills her partner is fifteen to twenty years; for a man, two to six. Nancy Gibbs, "'Til Death Do Us Part': When a Woman Kills an Abusive Partner, Is It an Act of Revenge or of Self Defense?" *Time,* 18 January 1993, 38.

77. The forensic pathologist reported that Jian Wan Chen was five foot three and weighed 99 pounds. Her body was found with numerous carved lacerations on both sides of her head. She had contusions on both left and right forearms, a contusion on her right wrist, an abrasion at the back of her left hand, and a bruise on her left thumb. The marks on her head were consistent with having been hit by a hammer. There were depressed skull fractures under her lacerations, indicating that a great amount of force was applied to a small surface area. The injuries on her arms, wrist, and hand were consistent with someone holding her or with her warding off a blow from a hammer. They were also consistent with an individual holding her down and striking her in the face with a hammer. See Record at 132–143.

78. Two of their children testified that they had heard their parents arguing, their father accusing their mother of having another man, and their mother saying "So what, it is so," which could substantiate Dong Lu Chen's allegations that she was having an affair. Both children, however, stated that they had never seen their mother hit their father, as Dong Lu Chen contended. See Record at 183–184, 213, 217, 219.

79. See *supra* note 7. By focusing here on race and gender, I do not intend to assert that only race and gender are critical to the experiences of women of color. Factors such

as class, sexual orientation, language, and immigration status are often as critical. For an analysis using postcolonial discourse to examine the intersection of language, gender, race, class, and national origin in the lives of Latinas, see Celina Romany, "Sculpting Identities: Carving a Niche for Latinas in Feminist Legal Theory" (unpublished manuscript on file with the *Harvard Women's Law Journal*).

80. Many of the experiences women of color face are not subsumed within the traditional boundaries of race and gender, nor of race and gender discrimination. See, e.g., Crenshaw, "Demarginalizing the Intersection of Race and Sex," *supra* note 7.

81. The needs of women of color are not fully met by structures or political movements designed to address either race or gender. See, e.g., Margaretta Wan Ling Lin & Cheng Imm Tan, "Holding Up More than Half the Heavens: Domestic Violence in Our Communities, A Call for Justice," in *The State of Asian America: Activism and Resistance in the 1990s*, ed. Karin Aguilar-San Juan, 321 (1994); "Document to Share with the Anti-Asian Violence Movement" (unpublished manuscript on file with the *Harvard Women's Law Journal*).

82. During the Vietnam War, many in the United States propagated the idea that Asians did not place the same value on life as those in the "West." See Richard Reeves, "Guns and Foreigners in America," Sacramento Bee, 7 June 1993, B12.

83. A 1992 United States Surgeon General's report attributed the leading cause of death among women to domestic violence. "United States, Look at the Violence Against Women, Democrats Told," *IPS*, 14 July 1992.

84. See Alexis Jetter, "Fear is Legacy of Wife Killing in Chinatown, Battered Asians Shocked By Husband's Probation," *Newsday*, 26 November 1989, 4.

85. Id.

86. The importance of economic class in access to and experience in the legal system is often overlooked and cannot be underestimated. See Gerald Lopez, *Rebellious Lawyering: One Chicano's Vision of Progressive Law Practice* (1992); Lucie E. White, "Subordination, Rhetorical Survival Skills, and Sunday Shoes: Notes on the Hearing of Mrs. G.," 38 *Buff. L. Rev.* 1 (1990).

87. Jetter, *supra* note 84.

88. Hurtado, *supra* note 75. City University of New York Assistant Law Professor Sharon Hom charged: "This kind of thinking reinforces patriarchal and racial stereotypes— which don't even exist in China today. This is like saying, 'My goodness, Americans lynch blacks, let's let them do it,' just because lynchings have happened in the past." Id.

89. Elizabeth Holtzman was the district attorney for Kings County when the Chen case was heard.

90. See Jetter, *supra* note 84.

91. Id.

92. See Anthony, *supra* note 72.

93. See Sams, *supra* note 20.

94. Id. at 335–336.

95. Id. at 336 n.6.

96. Id. at 345.

97. Id. at 348.

98. Id.

99. Id. at 348–349. Also see Id. at 349 (citing Thompson, "The Cultural Defense," 14 *Student Law.* 25, 27 [1985]).

100. Id. at 351, quoting J. Hall, *General Principles of Criminal Law,* 2d ed. (1960).

101. Id. at 352, quoting Hall, *supra* note 100, at 383.

102. See Patricia J. Williams, *The Alchemy of Race and Rights,* 8–9 (1991).

103. See, e.g., *Korematsu v United States,* 323 U.S. 214 (1944); *Dred Scott v John Sandford,* 60 U.S. (19 How.) 393 (1857); *Fong Yue Ting v U.S.,* 149 U.S. 698, 717 (1893).

104. See, e.g., Rimonte, *supra* note 20; Spatz, *supra* note 20.

105. Rimonte's article focuses solely on the "cultural defense" in cases involving violence against women. She asserts that the "cultural defense" validates "Pacific-Asian patriar-

chal values" that promote or facilitate crimes against women. Her solution is to apply United States laws that proscribe violence uniformly. See Rimonte, *supra* note 20, at 1326. For a critique of using Asian culture to explain violence in the Asian community, see *infra* notes 159–161 and accompanying text.

106. See Spatz, *supra* note 20. This is a strategic move that characterizes the "women's rights as human rights" movement. For an explanation of this movement see Charlotte Bunch, "Women's Rights as Human Rights: Toward a Re-Vision of Human Rights," 12 *Hum. Rts. Q.* 486 (1990).

107. See *infra*, "Not a Good Mother.".

108. For an example of an interchange raising some of these issues, see Catharine A. MacKinnon, "From Practice to Theory, or What is a White Woman Anyway?" 4 *Yale J.L. & Feminism* 13 (1991) and the subsequent response from members of the Yale Collective on Women of Color and the Law, "Students, Open Letters to Catharine MacKinnon," 4 *Yale J.L. & Feminism* 177 (1991).

109. Turning to international human rights law seems somewhat less problematic because there is greater consciousness among feminists that the international instruments created through the "women's rights as human rights" movement are designed to be applied to women in highly diverse communities across the world. Thus, the legal instruments used will be contested by different groups. Fitting one feminist standard to different contexts is a challenging process, requiring recognition of how structures of power construct gender differences. See Celina Romany, "Women as Aliens: A Feminist Critique of the Public/Private Distinction in International Human Rights Law," 6 *Harv. Hum. Rts. J.* 87, 121.

110. The existence of a formation that can be called "West" relies on the same technique that Pasternak used to distinguish "American" and "Chinese." In other words, a "West" requires that there be an "East," or, as formerly named, "the Orient." While it is no longer in vogue for some to refer to the "Orient" (harkening to the "primitive" and "Oriental"), references to "Western," usually implying sophistication, advancement, and enlightenment, remain uninterrogated; we still refer to the "West" while only silently acknowledging that this paradigm relies upon an "East."

111. Laura Nader, Professor of Anthropology, University of California at Berkeley, Speech at Harvard University (1988). Nader points to the equal pay for equal work women get in many Islamic countries, unlike in the United States, and to the comparative percentages of women on the faculty in 1980 at U.C. Berkeley (approximately 10 percent) and at Rabat, Mohammed V University in Morocco (38 percent) as examples that should disrupt the "positional superiority" with which many American feminists look at Islamic countries. See Tanya Schevitz Wills, *San Francisco Examiner,* 11 October 1993, A8.

112. For example, Cathy Young, Heritage Foundation lecturer, contends that the use of "cultural defense" in the courtroom promotes sexism; she premises this argument upon her belief that non-Western cultures are more sexist than "American" culture, and thereby queries why one would want to recognize non-Western culture within American legal standards. Cathy Young, "Equal Cultures or Equality for Women? Why Feminism and Multiculturalism Don't Mix," *The Heritage Lectures* No. 387, 1992. For a more subtle version of this position, see Lori Heise, "Crimes of Gender," *World-Watch* (March-April 1989).

113. See generally Gita Sen and Caren Grown, *Development, Crises, and Alternative Visions* (1987).

114. See generally Mary Daly, *Gyn/Ecology* (1978); and Audre Lorde, "An Open Letter to Mary Daly," in *Sister Outsider* (1984).

115. See generally Catharine A. MacKinnon, *Feminism Unmodified* (1987). For a critique of feminist essentialism in this text, see Paulette Caldwell et al., *supra* note 7.

116. Note, *supra* note 20.

117. Cultural relativism is harmful because, in "a world of radical inequality, relativist resignation reinforces the status quo." Mary Hawkesworth, "Knowers, Knowing,

Known: Feminist Theory and Claims of Truth," 14 *Signs* 533, 557 (1989). Pasternak's testimony in the Chen case was premised upon a perspective of cultural relativism. See *supra* notes 38–69 and accompanying text.

118. This term refers to justice for the immigrant who does not yet know American law or who is compelled to commit "a criminal act solely because the values of her native culture compelled her to do so." Note, *supra* note 20, at 1300.

119. The author asserts that: a "cultural defense" would recognize cultural pluralism, which will maintain the "vigor" of the United States; would reflect American principles of equality for all; and would value the American commitment to liberty. See id. at 1300–1301.

120. According to the author, use of a "cultural defense" would not inhibit the social order or deterrent function of the law. In fact, recognizing other communities' cultural values is a way of ensuring that groups do not become alienated and subsequently hostile, disrupting social order. Thus, "[r]ecognition of a cultural defense is one way of preserving a nucleus of values that, although leading to undesirable behavior in some contexts, encourages law-abiding conduct in many others." Id. at 1305.

121. Id. at 1311.

122. *People v Helen Wu*, 286 *Cal. Rptr.* 868 (1991), rev'g No. ICR 12873 (Super. Ct. Riverside Co. 1990), rev. denied Jan. 23, 1992 (unpublished opinion). While the Reporter of Decisions was directed not to publish this opinion, it is still valuable for the fact pattern it presents and instructive as to problems inherent in the use of the "cultural defense."

123. Id. at 869.

124. She also contended that the court committed reversible error by refusing to instruct the jury on the defense of unconsciousness. Id. at 870.

125. The following presentation of facts is what the appellate court described as "the evidence . . . upon which defendant's requested instructions were predicated." Id. at 870. In other words, this is Helen Wu's version of the facts.

126. Her daughter was twenty-five at the time of trial. Id.

127. Id. at 870–871.

128. See id. at 871.

129. See id.

130. Id. at 871–72.

131. Id. at 872.

132. Id. at 887.

133. Id. at 882–883. A tailored jury instruction may not have been necessary, since jury instructions in California allow a great deal of leeway. In addition, the recommendation by the appellate court that "cultural difference" be a jury instruction was presumably the reason the case was unpublished, since there was no basis for the appellate court's recommendation in California law. Telephone interview with Jayne Lee, Spaeth Fellow, Stanford University (16 January 1994). The appellate court also held that the trial court committed reversible error by refusing to instruct the jury on the defense that she was unconscious when she strangled Sidney. Wu, 286 *Cal. Rptr.* at 873.

134. See id. at 880.

135. Id. at 883.

136. Id. at 870. Also see the court of appeals comments, Id.

137. Id. at 880.

138. Transcultural psychology involves "culturally sensitive" evaluations and treatment that recognize variations in mental illnesses among ethnic groups. Community Profile: Dr. Francis Lu, *AsianWeek*, 27 August 1993, 4.

139. Wu, 286 *Cal. Rptr.* at 885.

140. Id. at 886.

141. Differences in the expert testimony in the two cases may also reflect differences in litigants' choice of strategy for presenting expert testimony before a judge as opposed to a jury, or the different legal standards in California (where diminished capacity is not recognized) and New York.

142. On bridging the distance between "us" and the "other," see Isabelle Gunning, "Arrogant Perception, World-Travelling and Multicultural Feminism: The Case of Female Genital Surgeries," 23 *Colum. Hum. Rts. L. Rev.* 189 (1991–92).

143. As discussed *supra* note 45, Chen's actions could have been compared to the American provocation doctrine. Such a comparison would have demonstrated that what is often referred to as a sign of the barbarity and misogyny of Asia—that "Asian men kill their wives for looking at other men"—is in fact encoded into our common law as justifiable. The function of this omission is to deny the reality of our judicial system's sanction of oppression against women while exaggerating "difference."

144. See Wu, 286 *Cal. Rptr.* at 886–87.

145. For a critique of the stereotype of the self-sacrificing Asian woman/mother, see Yoko Yoshikawa, "The Heat is On Miss Saigon Coalition: Organizing Across Race and Sexuality," in *The State of Asian America, supra* note 81.

146. As an example, imagine a woman who is described at trial as having emigrated to the United States through marriage: this can be conceptualized as a "green card marriage," evoking the image of a deceitful, conniving, scheming Asian woman trying to take advantage of the United States.

147. Expert witness Terry Gock's expert testimony for Helen Wu fell into this trap to some extent.

148. Elizabeth Schneider, "Describing and Changing: Women's Self-Defense Work and the Problem of Expert Testimony on Battering," 9 *Women's Rts. L. Rep.* 195, 201 (1986).

149. Lenore F. Walker, *The Battered Woman Syndrome* (1984).

150. Walker describes the cycle of violence as consisting of three phases: (1) tension building; (2) acute battering; and (3) loving contrition. The cycle theory, however, does not appear to characterize many women's situations accurately. See id. at 97. Many domestic violence advocates thus prefer to describe domestic violence as characterized by abuses of power and control. See, e.g., *Domestic Violence in Immigrant and Refugee Communities, supra* note 47.

151. Learned helplessness is a term from social learning theory that Walker applied to explain "why women stay." See generally Martin E. Seligman, *Helplessness: On Depression, Development, and Death* (1982). Many domestic violence advocates find the concept of learned helplessness inaccurate. See, e.g., Julie Blackman, "Potential Uses for Expert Testimony: Ideas Toward the Representation of Battered Women Who Kill," 9 *Women's Rts. L. Rep.* 227, 230 (1986). The appropriate inquiry may be "why do men batter?" rather than "why women stay." Battered women are often active and resourceful in their efforts to avoid violence to themselves and their children within the context of the relationship. See Julie Blackman, *Intimate Violence: A Study of Injustice*, 48–52, 133–152 (1989). Some advocates thus prefer to view battered women as engaged in covert resistance. See, e.g., Hyun Sook Kim, "Theorizing Marginality: Violence Against Korean Women," Address before the Asian American Studies Conference, Cornell University, 4 June 1993 (unpublished manuscript, on file with the *Harvard Women's Law Journal*).

152. Battered women's syndrome, thus, while attempting to explain why women act, is problematically premised on a theory describing women as passive.

153. Denise Bricker, Note, "Fatal Defense: An Analysis of Battered Woman's Syndrome Expert Testimony for Gay Men and Lesbians Who Kill Abusive Partners," 58 *Brook. L. Rev.* 1379, 1420–1421 (1993). Even when admitted, however, the content and scope of expert testimony permitted by courts varies among states. For example, some states have limited expert testimony to a general description of battered women's syndrome without reference to the specific defendant. Others have permitted experts to offer an opinion on the ultimate question of whether a woman's actions were reasonable under the circumstances. See id. at 1421; Holly Maguigan, "Battered Women and Self-Defense: Myths and Misconceptions in Current Reform Proposals," 140 *U. Penn. L. Rev.* 379, 429–430 (1992).

154. See Maguigan, *supra* note 153, at 445.

155. Such redefinitions specific to a particular class of defendants are susceptible to narrow application by trial judges. See id. at 444–445; see, e.g., *State v Donna F. Williams,* 787 S.W.2d 308, 310 (Mo. Ct. App. 1990).

156. See Sharon Allard, "Rethinking Battered Woman Syndrome: A Black Feminist Perspective," 1 *UCLA Women's L.J.* 191 (1991); Bricker, *supra* note 153, at 1379.

157. How to think about the relationship of identity, experience, and behavior is a contested issue, fought on the terrain of identity politics. See Joan Scott, "Experience," in *Feminists Theorize the Political,* ed. Judith Butler and Joan Scott, 33 (1992).

158. Kimberle Crenshaw makes this point for "cultural defenses" attempted for African American men. See Crenshaw, "Whose Story Is It Anyway?" *supra* note 3, at 431.

159. See, e.g., Nilda Rimonte, "Domestic Violence Amongst Pacific Asians," in *Making Waves: An Anthology of Writings by and About Asian American Women,* ed. Asian Women of California United (1989). Id. at 328; Rimonte, *supra* note 20.

160. The dehumanization to which I refer is illustrated by descriptions of Asian communities as governed by "culture" when the behavior of the dominant community is described as explainable by "psychology" or political forces.

161. For example, immigrant women's difficulty in gaining access to the battered spouse waiver to the Marriage Fraud Amendments is not perceived as linked to the lack of translated materials or to the absence of laws that promote the interests of poor immigrant women. Rather, that lack of access is often explained as caused by a woman's "culture." See, e.g., Deeana Hodgin, "Mail-Order Brides Marry Pain to Get Green Cards," *Washington Times,* 16 April 1991, E1.

162. Gayatri Spivak has argued for strategic essentialism in a specific context. See Gayatri Spivak, "Subaltern Studies: Deconstructing Historiography," in *In Other Worlds,* 197, 205 (1988). Also, see Gayatri Spivak, "In a Word," 1 *Differences* 12 (1989).

163. This process is the essence of identity politics—naming and categorizing oneself as a means of identifying interests for purposes of empowerment. For a discussion of the relationship of identity politics, postmodernism, and antiessentialism, see Crenshaw, *supra* note 9, at 1296–1299.

164. 379 S.E.2d 701 (N.C. App. 1989). Also see Hyun Sook Kim, *supra* note 151, at 3–4.

165. One police officer described France as "sick," "crazed," and "hateful." Both investigating officers insisted that France must have staged the incident to look like an accident. She was provided with no interpreter, and the court reporter noted that her English was extremely difficult to understand. See Hyun Sook Kim, *supra* note 151, at 4.

166. See France, 379 S.E.2d at 704.

167. The petition circulated by the Free France Committee. New York Free France Committee, "Statement on Behalf of Chong Sun France" (1992) (on file with the *Harvard Women's Law Journal*).

168. See Mari J. Matsuda, "Public Response to Racist Speech: Considering the Victim's Story," 87 *Mich. L. Rev.* 2320, 2362 (1989).

169. See Mari J. Matsuda, "Beside My Sister, Facing the Enemy: Legal Theory Out of Coalition," 43 *Stan. L. Rev.* 1183, 1188–1189 (1991).

170. This is exemplified in the Wu case since it is also a story about the killing of a child by his parent.

171. See bell hooks, "marginality as a site of resistance," in *Out There: Marginalization and Contemporary Cultures,* ed. Russell Ferguson et al., 341 (1990); Hyun Sook Kim, *supra* note 151.

172. An example of how antisubordination must operate as a criterion for the decision about whether to present cultural information emerges in an article by Mark Kelman. See Mark Kelman, "Reasonable Evidence of Reasonableness," 17 *Critical Inquiry* 798 (1991).

173. See Stuart Hall, "Cultural Identity and Diaspora," in *Identity, Community, Culture, Difference,* ed. Jonathan Rutherford, 222, 225 (1990).

Theorizing Asian American Literature

HETEROGENEITY, HYBRIDITY, MULTIPLICITY

MARKING ASIAN AMERICAN DIFFERENCES

Lisa Lowe

In a poem by Janice Mirikitani, a Japanese American nisei woman describes her sansei daughter's rebellion. The daughter's denial of Japanese American culture and its particular notions of femininity reminds the nisei speaker that she, too, has denied her antecedents, rebelling against her own more traditional issei mother:[1]

> I want to break tradition – unlock this room
> where women dress in the dark.
> Discover the lies my mother told me.

The lies that we are small and powerless
that our possibilities must be compressed
to the size of pearls, displayed only as
passive chokers, charms around our neck.
Break Tradition.
　　I want to tell my daughter of this room
　　of myself
　　filled with tears of shakuhatchi,
　　. . . . .
　　poems about madness,
　　sounds shaken from barbed wire and
　　goodbyes and miracles of survival.
　　This room of open window where daring ones escape.
My daughter denies she is like me . . .
　　her pouting ruby lips, her skirts
　　swaying to salsa, teena marie and the stones,
　　her thighs displayed in carnivals of color.
　　I do not know the contents of her room.
She mirrors my aging.
She is breaking tradition.[2]

The nisei speaker repudiates the repressive confinements of her issei mother: the disciplining of the female body, the tedious practice of diminution, the silences of obedience. In turn, the crises that have shaped the nisei speaker—internment camps, sounds of threatening madness—are unknown to and unheard by her sansei teenage daughter. The three generations of women of Japanese descent in this poem are separated by their different histories and by different conceptions of what it means to be female and Japanese. The poet who writes "I do not know the contents of her room" registers these separations as "breaking tradition."

　　In another poem, by Lydia Lowe, Chinese women workers are also divided by generation but, even more powerfully, by class and language. The speaker is a young Chinese American who supervises an older Chinese woman in a textile factory.

The long bell blared,
and then the *lo-ban*
made me search all your bags
before you could leave.
Inside he sighed
about slow work, fast hands,
missing spools of thread—
and I said nothing.
I remember that day
you came in to show me
I added your tickets six zippers short.
It was just a mistake.

You squinted down
at the check in your hands
like an old village woman peers
at some magician's trick.
That afternoon
when you thrust me your bags
I couldn't look or raise my face.
Doi m-jyu.
Eyes on the ground,
I could only see
one shoe kicking against the other.[3]

This poem, too, invokes the breaking of tradition, although it thematizes another sort of stratification among Asian women: the structure of the factory places the English-speaking younger woman above the Cantonese-speaking older one. Economic relations in capitalist society force the young supervisor to discipline her elders, and she is acutely ashamed that her required behavior does not demonstrate the respect traditionally owed to parents and elders. Thus, both poems foreground commonly thematized topoi of immigrant cultures: the disruption and distortion of traditional cultural practices—like the practice of parental sacrifice and filial duty or the practice of respecting hierarchies of age—not only as a consequence of displacement to the United States but also as a part of entering a society with different class stratifications and different constructions of gender roles. Some Asian American discussions cast the disruption of tradition as loss, representing the loss in terms of regret and shame, as in the latter poem. Alternatively, the traditional practices of family continuity and hierarchy may be figured as oppressively confining, as in Mirikitani's poem, in which the two generations of daughters contest the more restrictive female roles of the preceding generations. In either case, many Asian American discussions portray immigration and relocation to the United States in terms of a loss of the "original" culture in exchange for the new "American" culture.

In many Asian American novels, the question of the loss or transmission of the "original" culture is frequently represented in a family narrative, figured as generational conflict between the Chinese-born first generation and the American-born second generation.[4] Louis Chu's 1961 novel *Eat a Bowl of Tea,* for example, allegorizes the differences between "native" Chinese values and the new "Westernized" culture of Chinese Americans in the conflicted relationship between father and son. Other novels have taken up this generational theme; one way to read Maxine Hong Kingston's *The Woman Warrior* (1975) or Amy Tan's *The Joy Luck Club* (1989) would be to understand them as versions of this generational model of culture, refigured in feminine terms, between mothers and daughters. In this chapter, however, I argue that interpreting Asian American culture exclusively in terms of the master narratives of generational conflict and filial relation essentializes Asian American culture, obscuring the particularities and incommensurabilities of class, gender, and national diversities among Asians. The reduction of the cultural politics of racialized ethnic groups, like Asian Americans, to first-generation/sec-

ond-generation struggles displaces social differences into a privatized familial opposition. Such reductions contribute to the aestheticizing commodification of Asian
American *cultural* differences, while denying the immigrant histories of material
exclusion and differentiation of the kind discussed in chapter 1 [of the volume in
which this chapter originally appeared—Ed.].

To avoid this homogenizing of Asian Americans as exclusively hierarchical and
familial, I would contextualize the "vertical" generational model of culture with
the more "horizontal" relationship represented in Diana Chang's "The Oriental
Contingent."[5] In Chang's short story, two young women avoid the discussion of
their Chinese backgrounds because each desperately fears that the other is "more
Chinese," more "authentically" tied to the original culture. The narrator, Connie,
is certain that her friend Lisa "never referred to her own background because it
was more Chinese than Connie's, and therefore of a higher order. She was tact
incarnate. All along, she had been going out of her way not to embarrass Connie.
Yes, yes. Her assurance was definitely uppercrust (perhaps her father had been in
the diplomatic service), and her offhand didacticness, her lack of self-doubt, was
indeed characteristically Chinese-Chinese" (173). Connie feels ashamed because
she assumes herself to be "a failed Chinese"; she fantasizes that Lisa was born
in China, visits there frequently, and privately disdains Chinese Americans. Her
assumptions about Lisa prove to be quite wrong, however; Lisa is even more critical
of herself for "not being genuine." For Lisa, as Connie eventually discovers, was
born in Buffalo and was adopted by American parents; lacking an immediate
connection to Chinese culture, Lisa projects on all Chinese the authority of being
"more Chinese." Lisa confesses to Connie at the end of the story: "The only time
I feel Chinese is when I'm embarrassed I'm not more Chinese—which is a totally
Chinese reflex I'd give anything to be rid of!" (176). Chang's story portrays two
women polarized by the degree to which they have each internalized a cultural
definition of "Chineseness" as pure and fixed, in which any deviation is constructed
as less, lower, and shameful. Rather than confirming a traditional anthropological
model of "culture" in which "ethnicity" is passed from generation to generation,
Chang's story explores the relationship between women of the same generation.
Lisa and Connie are ultimately able to reduce each other's guilt at not being
"Chinese enough"; in each other they are able to find a common frame of reference.
The story suggests that the making of Chinese American culture—the ways in which
it is imagined, practiced, and continued—is worked out as much "horizontally"
among communities as it is transmitted "vertically" in unchanging forms from one
generation to the next. Rather than considering "Asian American identity" as a
fixed, established, "given," perhaps we can consider instead "Asian American cultural practices" that produce identity; the processes that produce such identity are
never complete and are always constituted in relation to historical and material
differences. Stuart Hall has written that cultural identity

> is a matter of "becoming" as well as of "being." It belongs to the future as much as
> to the past. It is not something which already exists, transcending place, time, history
> and culture. Cultural identities come from somewhere, have histories. But, like every-
> thing which is historical, they undergo constant transformation. Far from being eter-

nally fixed in some essentialized past, they are subject to the continuous "play" of history, culture and power.[6]

Asian American discussions of ethnic culture and racial group formation are far from uniform or consistent. Rather, these discussions contain a spectrum of positions that includes, at one end, the desire for a cultural identity represented by a fixed profile of traits and, at the other, challenges to the notion of singularity and conceptions of *race* as the material *locus* of differences, intersections, and incommensurabilities. These latter efforts attempt to define Asian American identity in a manner that not only accounts for the critical inheritance of cultural definitions and traditions but also accounts for the *racial formation* produced in the negotiations between the state's regulation of racial groups and those groups' active contestation and construction of racial meanings.[7] In other words, these latter efforts suggest that the making of Asian American culture may be a much less stable process than unmediated vertical transmission of culture from one generation to another. The making of Asian American culture includes practices that are partly inherited, partly modified, as well as partly invented; Asian American culture also includes the practices that emerge in relation to the dominant representations that deny or subordinate Asian and Asian American cultures as "other."[8] As the narrator of *The Woman Warrior* suggests, perhaps one of the more important stories of Asian American experience is about the process of critically receiving and rearticulating cultural traditions in the face of a dominant national culture that exoticizes and "orientalizes" Asians. She asks: "Chinese-Americans, when you try to understand what things in you are Chinese, how do you separate what is peculiar to childhood, to poverty, insanities, one family, your mother who marked your growing with stories, from what is Chinese? What is Chinese tradition and what is the movies?"[9] Or the dilemma of cultural syncretism might be posed in an interrogative version of the uncle's impromptu proverb in Wayne Wang's film *Dim Sum*: "You can take the girl out of Chinatown, but can you take the Chinatown out of the girl?"[10] For rather than representing a fixed, discrete culture, "Chinatown" is itself the very emblem of shifting demographics, languages, and populations. The residents of the urban "bachelor society" Chinatowns of New York and San Francisco from the mid-nineteenth century to the 1950s, for example, were mostly male laborers—laundrymen, seamen, restaurant workers—from southern China, whereas today, immigrants from Taiwan, mainland China, and Hong Kong have dramatically reconfigured contemporary suburban Chinese settlements such as the one in Monterey Park, California.[11]

I begin with these particular examples drawn from Asian American cultural texts in order to observe that what is referred to as "Asian America" is clearly a heterogeneous entity. In relation to the state and the American national culture implied by that state, Asian Americans have certainly been constructed as different, and as other than, white Americans of European origin. But from the perspectives of Asian Americans, we are extremely different and diverse among ourselves: as men and women at different distances and generations from our "original" Asian cultures—cultures as different as Chinese, Japanese, Korean, Filipino, Indian, Vietnamese, Thai, or Cambodian—Asian Americans are born in the United States and born in Asia, of exclusively Asian parents and of mixed race, urban and rural, refugee and nonrefugee, fluent in English and non-English-speaking, professionally trained and working-class. As with other immigrant groups in the United States, the Asian-origin collectivity is unstable and changeable, with its cohesion complicated by intergenerationality, by various degrees of identification with and relation to a "homeland," and by different extents of assimilation to and distinction from "majority culture" in the United States. Further, the historical contexts of particular waves of immigration within single groups contrast one another; Japanese Americans who were interned during World War II encountered social and economic barriers quite different from those faced by individuals who arrive in southern California from Japan today. And the composition of different waves of immigrants varies in gender, class, and region. For example, in the case of the Chinese, the first groups of immigrants to the United States in the 1850s were from Canton province, male by a ratio of ten to one, and largely of peasant backgrounds, whereas the more recent Chinese immigrants are from Hong Kong, Taiwan, or the People's Republic (themselves quite heterogeneous and of discontinuous "origins") or from the Chinese diaspora in other parts of Asia, such as Malaysia or Singapore, and they have a heterogeneous profile that includes male and female assembly and service-sector workers as well as "middle-class" professionals and business elites.[12] Further, once arriving in the United States, very few Asian immigrant cultures remain discrete, impenetrable communities; the more recent groups mix, in varying degrees, with segments of the existing groups; Asian Americans may intermarry with other racialized ethnic groups, live in neighborhoods adjacent to them, or work in the same businesses and on the same factory assembly lines. The boundaries and definitions of Asian American culture are continually shifting and being contested by pressures both "inside" and "outside" the Asian-origin community.

I stress heterogeneity, hybridity, and multiplicity in the characterization of Asian American culture as part of a twofold argument about cultural politics, the ultimate aim of which is to disrupt the current hegemonic relationship between "dominant" and "minority" positions. Heterogeneity, hybridity, and multiplicity are not used here as rhetorical or literary terms, but are attempts at naming the material contradictions that characterize Asian American groups. Although these concepts appear to be synonymous in their relationship to that of "identity," they can be precisely distinguished. By "heterogeneity," I mean to indicate the existence of differences and differential relationships within a bounded category—that is, among Asian Americans, there are differences of Asian national origin, of generational relation to immigrant exclusion laws, of class backgrounds in Asia and economic conditions within the United States, and of gender. By "hybridity," I refer to the formation of cultural objects and practices that are produced by the histories of uneven and unsynthetic power relations; for example, the racial and linguistic mixings in the Philippines and among Filipinos in the United States are the material trace of the history of Spanish colonialism, U.S. colonization, and U.S. neocolonialism. Hybridity, in this sense, does not suggest the assimilation of Asian or immigrant practices to dominant forms, but instead marks the history of survival within relationships of unequal power and domination. Finally, we might understand "multiplicity" as designating the ways in which subjects located within social relations are determined by several different axes of power, are multiply determined by the contradictions of capitalism, patriarchy, and race relations, with, as Hall explains, particular contradictions surfacing in relation to the material conditions of a specific historical moment.[13] Thus, heterogeneity, hybridity, and multiplicity are concepts that assist us in critically understanding the material conditions of Asians in the United States, conditions that extend beyond the dominant, "orientalist" construction of Asian Americans. Although orientalism seeks to consolidate the coherence of the West as subject precisely through the representation of "oriental" objects as homogenous, fixed, and stable, contradictions in the production of Asians and in the noncorrespondence between the orientalist object and the Asian American subject ultimately express the limits of such fictions.

On the one hand, the observation that Asian Americans are heterogenous is part of a strategy to destabilize the dominant discursive construction and determination of Asian Americans as a homogeneous group. Throughout the late nineteenth and early twentieth centuries Asian populations in the United States were managed by exclusion acts, bars from citizenship, quotas, and internment, all of which made use of racialist constructions of Asian-origin groups as homogeneous. The "model minority" myth that constructs Asians as the most successfully assimilated minority group is a contemporary version of this homogenization of Asians. On the other hand, it is equally important to underscore Asian American heterogeneities—particularly class, gender, and national differences—to contribute to a dialogue within Asian American discourse, to point to the limitations inherent in a politics based on cultural, racial, or ethnic identity. In this sense, I argue for the need for Asian Americans to organize, resist, and theorize as Asian Americans, but at the same time I inscribe this necessity within a discussion of the risks of a cultural politics that relies on the construction of sameness and the exclusion of differences.

The first reason to emphasize the dynamic fluctuation and heterogeneity of Asian American culture is to release our understandings of either the "dominant" or the emergent "minority" cultures as discrete, fixed, or homogeneous and to arrive at a different conception of the terrain of culture. In California, for example, it has become commonplace for residents to consider themselves as part of a "multicultural" state, as embodying a new phenomenon of cultural adjacency and admixture; this "multiculturalism" is at once an index of the changing demographics and differences of community in California and a pluralist attempt at containment of those differences.[14] For if racialized minority immigrant cultures are perpetually changing—in their composition, configuration, and signifying practices, as well as in their relations to one another—it follows that the "majority" or "dominant" culture, with which minority cultures are in continual relation, is also unstable and unclosed. The understanding that the general cultural terrain is one social site in which "hegemony" is continually being both established and contested permits us to theorize about the roles racialized immigrant groups play in the making and unmaking of culture, and to explore the ways in which cross-race and cross-national projects may work to change the existing structure of power, the current hegemony. We remember that Antonio Gramsci writes about hegemony as not simply political or economic forms of rule but as the entire process of dissent and compromise through which a particular group is able to determine the political, cultural, and ideological character of a state.[15] Hegemony does not refer exclusively to the process by which a dominant group exercises its influence but refers equally to the process through which emergent groups organize and contest any specific hegemony.[16] The reality of any specific hegemony is that, although it may be for the moment dominant, it is never absolute or conclusive. Hegemony, in Gramsci's thought, is a concept that describes both the social processes through which a particular dominance is maintained, and the processes through which that dominance is challenged and new forces are articulated. When a hegemony representing the interests of a dominant group exists, it is always within the context of resistances from emerging groups.[17] We might say that hegemony is not only the political process by which a particular group constitutes itself as "the one" or "the majority" in relation to which "minorities" are defined and know themselves to be "other," but is equally the process by which various and incommensurable positions of otherness may ally and constitute a new majority, a "counterhegemony."[18]

Gramsci writes of "subaltern," prehegemonic, not unified groups "unrealized" by the State, whose histories are fragmented, episodic, and identifiable only from a point of historical hindsight. They may go through different phases when they are subject to the activity of ruling groups, may articulate their demands through existing parties, and then may themselves produce new parties. In "History of the Subaltern Classes" from his *Prison Notebooks,* Gramsci describes a final phase at which the "formations [of the subaltern classes] assert integral autonomy" (52). The definition of the subaltern groups includes some noteworthy observations for our understanding of the roles of racialized immigrant groups in the United States who have a history of being "aliens ineligible to citizenship." The assertion that the significant practices of the subaltern groups may not be understood as hegemonic until they are viewed with historical hindsight is interesting, for it suggests that some of the most powerful practices may not always be the explicitly oppositional ones, may not be understood by contemporaries, and may be less overt and recognizable than others. That the subaltern classes are by definition "not unified" is provocative, too—that is, these groups are not a fixed, unified force of a single character. Rather, the assertion of "integral autonomy" by "not unified" classes suggests a coordination of distinct, yet allied, positions, practices, and movements— class-identified and not class-identified, in parties and not, race-based and gender-based—each in its own, not necessarily equivalent manner transforming, disrupting, and destructuring the apparatuses of a specific hegemony. The independent forms and locations of challenge—cultural, as well as economic and political—constitute what Gramsci calls a "new historical bloc," a new set of relationships that together embody a different hegemony and a different balance of power. In this sense, we have in the instance of the growing and shifting racialized immigrant populations in California an active example of this new historical bloc; and in the negotiations between these groups and the existing "majority" over what interests constitute the "majority," we have an illustration of the concept of hegemony, not in the more commonly accepted sense of "hegemony maintenance," but in the often ignored sense of "hegemony creation."[19] The observation that the Asian American community and other racialized and immigrant communities are both incommensurate and heterogeneous lays the foundation for several political operations. First, by reconceiving "the social" so as to centralize the emergent racialized and immigrant groups who are constantly redefining social relations in ways that move beyond static oppositions such as "majority" and "minority," or the binary axis "black" and "white," we recast cultural politics so as to account for a multiplicity of various, nonequivalent racialized groups, one of which is Asian Americans. Second, the conception of racialized group formation as heterogeneous provides a position for Asian Americans that is both historically specific and yet simultaneously uneven and unclosed. Asian Americans can articulate distinct challenges and demands based on particular histories of exclusion and racialization, but the redefined lack of closure—which reveals rather than conceals differences—opens political lines of affiliation with other groups in the challenge to specific forms of domination insofar as they share common features.

The articulation of an "Asian American identity" as an organizing tool has provided a concept of political unity that enables diverse Asian groups to understand unequal circumstances and histories as being related. The building of "Asian American culture" is crucial to this effort, for it articulates and empowers the diverse Asian-origin community vis-à-vis the institutions and apparatuses that exclude and marginalize it. Yet to the extent that Asian American culture fixes Asian American identity and suppresses differences—of national origin, generation, gender, sexuality, class—it risks particular dangers: not only does it underestimate the differences and hybridities among Asians, but it may also inadvertently support the racist discourse that constructs Asians as a homogeneous group, that implies Asians are "all alike" and conform to "types." To the extent that Asian American culture dynamically expands to include both internal critical dialogues about difference and the interrogation of dominant interpellations, however, Asian American culture can likewise be a site in which the "horizontal" affiliations with other groups can be imagined and realized. In this respect, a politics based exclusively on racial or ethnic identity willingly accepts the terms of the dominant logic that organizes the heterogeneous picture of differences into a binary schema of "the one" and "the other." The essentializing of Asian American identity also reproduces oppositions that subsume other nondominant groups in the same way that Asians and other groups are marginalized by the dominant culture: to the degree that the discourse generalizes Asian American identity as male, women are rendered invisible; or to the extent that Chinese are presumed to be exemplary of all Asians, the importance of other Asian groups is ignored. In this sense, a politics based on racial, cultural, or ethnic identity facilitates the displacement of intercommunity differences—between men and women or between workers and managers—into a false opposition of "nationalism" and "assimilation." We have an example of this in recent debates where Asian American feminists who challenge Asian American sexism are cast as "assimilationist," as betraying Asian American "nationalism."

To the extent that Asian American discourse articulates an identity in reaction to the dominant culture's stereotype, even if to refute it, the discourse may remain bound to and overly determined by the logic of the dominant culture. In accepting the binary terms ("white" and "nonwhite" or "majority" and "minority") that structure institutional policies about race, we forget that these binary schemas are not neutral descriptions. Binary constructions of difference utilize a logic that prioritizes the first term and subordinates the second; whether the pair "difference" and "sameness" is figured as a binary synthesis that considers "difference" as always contained within the "same" or that conceives of the pair as an opposition in which "difference" structurally implies "sameness" as its complement, it is important to see each of these figurations as versions of the same binary logic. The materialist argument for heterogeneity seeks to challenge the conception of difference as exclusively structured by a binary opposition between two terms, by proposing instead another notion of "difference" that takes seriously the historically produced conditions of heterogeneity, multiplicity, and nonequivalence. The most exclusive construction of Asian American identity—one that presumes masculinity, American birth, and the speaking of English—is at odds with the formation of important political alliances and affiliations with other groups across racial and ethnic, gender, sexuality, and class lines. An exclusive "cultural identity" is an obstacle to Asian American women allying with other women of color, and it can discourage laboring Asian Americans from joining with workers of other colors. It can short-circuit potential alliances against the dominant structures of power in the name of subordinating "divisive" issues to *the* national question.

Some of the limits of "identity politics" are discussed most pointedly by Frantz Fanon in his books about the Algerian resistance to French colonialism. Before turning to some Asian American cultural texts to trace the ways in which the dialogues about identity and difference are represented within the discourse, I would like to consider one of Fanon's most important texts, *The Wretched of the Earth* (*Les damnés de la terre,* 1961). Although Fanon's treatise was cited in the 1960s as the manifesto for a nationalist politics of identity, on rereading it in the 1990s we ironically find his text to be the source of a serious critique of nationalism. Fanon argues that the challenge facing any movement that is dismantling colonialism (or a system in which one culture dominates another) is to provide for a new order that does not reproduce the social structure of the old system. This new order must avoid, he argues, the simple assimilation to the dominant culture's roles and positions by the emergent group, which would merely caricature the old colonialism, and it should be equally suspicious of an uncritical nativism or racialism that would appeal to essentialized notions of precolonial identity. Fanon suggests that another alternative is necessary, a new order, neither assimilationist nor nativist inversion, that breaks with the structures and practices of cultural domination, that continually and collectively criticizes the institutions of rule. One of the more remarkable turns in Fanon's argument occurs when he identifies both bourgeois assimilation and bourgeois nationalism as conforming to the same logic, as being responses to colonialism and reproducing the same structure of domination. It is in this sense that Fanon warns against the nationalism practiced by bourgeois postcolonial governments: the national bourgeoisie replaces the colonizer, yet the social and economic structure remains the same. Ironically, he points out, these separatisms, or "micronationalisms," are themselves legacies of colonialism: "By its very structure, colonialism is regionalist and separatist. Colonialism does not simply state the existence of tribes; it also reinforces and separates them."[20] That is, a politics of bourgeois cultural nationalism may be congruent with the divide-and-conquer logics of colonial domination. Fanon links the practices of the national bourgeoisie that has "assimilated" colonialist thought and practice with "nativist" practices that privilege one group or ethnicity over others; for Fanon, nativism and assimilationism are not opposites—they are similar logics that both enunciate the old order.

Fanon's analysis implies that an essentialized bourgeois construction of "nation" is a classification that excludes subaltern groups that could bring about substantive change in the social and economic relations, particularly those whose social marginalities are due to class: peasants, immigrant workers, transient populations. We can add to Fanon's criticism of nationalism that the category of "nation" often erases a consideration of women: the fact of difference between men and women and the conditions under which they live and work in situations of economic domination. This is why the concentration of women of color in domestic service or reproductive labor (child care, home care, nursing) in the contemporary United States is not adequately explained by a nation-based model of analysis.[21] It is also why the position of Asian and Latina immigrant female workers in the current global economy exceeds the terms offered by racial or national analyses. We can make more explicit—in light of feminist theory that has gone perhaps the furthest in theorizing multiple determinations and the importance of positionalities—that it may be difficult to act exclusively in terms of a single valence or political interest—such as race, ethnicity, or nation—because social subjects are the sites of a variety of differences. Trinh T. Minh-ha, Chela Sandoval, Angela Davis, and others have described the subject-positions of women of color as constructed across a multiplicity of social relations. Trinh writes:

> Many women of color feel obliged [to choose] between ethnicity and womanhood: how can they? You never have/are one without the other. The idea of two illusorily separated identities, one ethnic, the other woman (or more precisely female), partakes in the Euro-American system of dualistic reasoning and its age-old divide-and-conquer tactics. . . . The pitting of anti-racist and anti-sexist struggles against one another allows some vocal fighters to dismiss blatantly the existence of either racism or sexism within their lines of action, as if oppression only comes in separate, monolithic forms.[22]

In other words, the conceptualization of racism and sexism as if they were distinctly opposed discourses is a construction that serves the dominant formations; we cannot isolate "race" from "gender" without reproducing the logic of domination. To appreciate this interconnection of different, nonequivalent discourses of social stratification is not to argue against the strategic importance of Asian American identity or against the building of Asian American culture. Rather, it is to suggest that acknowledging class and gender differences among Asian Americans does not weaken the group. To the contrary, these differences represent greater opportunity to affiliate with other groups whose cohesions may be based on other valences of oppression rather than "identity." Angela Davis argues, for example, that we might conceive of "U.S. women of color" not as a "coalition" made up of separate groups organized around racial identities, but as a *political formation* that decides to work together on a particular issue or agenda. She states:

> A woman of color formation might decide to work around immigration issues. This political commitment is not based on the specific histories of racialized communities or its constituent members, but rather constructs an agenda agreed upon by all who are a part of it. In my opinion, the most exciting potential of women of color formations resides in the possibility of politicizing this identity—basing the identity on politics rather than the politics on identity.[23]

As we have already seen, within Asian American discourse there is a varied spectrum of discussion about the concepts of racialized group identity and culture. At one end are discussions in which cultural identity is essentialized as the cornerstone of a cultural nationalist politics. In these discussions the positions of "cultural nationalism" and of assimilation are represented in polar opposition: cultural nationalism's affirmation of the separate purity of its culture opposes assimilation of the standards of dominant society. Stories about the loss of a "native" Asian culture tend to express some form of this opposition. At the same time, there are criticisms of this cultural nationalist position, most often articulated by feminists who charge that Asian American nationalism prioritizes masculinity and does not account for women. Finally, at the other end, interventions exist that refuse static or binary conceptions of culture, replacing notions of "identity" with multiplicity and shifting the emphasis from cultural "essence" to material hybridity. Settling for neither nativism nor assimilation, these interventions expose the apparent opposition between the two as a constructed figure (as Fanon does when he observes that bourgeois assimilation and bourgeois nationalism often conform to the same colonialist logic). In tracing these different types of discussions about identity through Asian American cultural debates, literature, and film, I have chosen several texts because they are accessible, "popular," and commonly held. But I do not intend to limit "discourse" to only these particular forms. By "discourse" I intend a rather extended meaning—a network that includes not only texts and cultural documents but also social practices, formal and informal laws, policies of inclusion and exclusion, institutional forms of organization, and so forth, all of which constitute and regulate knowledge about its object, Asian America.

The terms of the debate about "nationalism" and "assimilation" become clearer if we look first at the discussion of Asian American identity in certain debates about the representation of culture. Readers of Asian American literature will be familiar with the attacks by Frank Chin, Ben Tong, and others on author Maxine Hong Kingston, attacks that have been cast as nationalist criticisms of Kingston's "assimilationist" works. Her novel/autobiography *The Woman Warrior* is the target of such criticism because it was virtually the first "canonized" piece of Asian American literature. In this sense, a critique of how and why this text became fetishized as the exemplary representation of Asian American culture is necessary and important. But Chin's critique reveals other kinds of notable tensions in Asian American culture: he does more than accuse Kingston of having exoticized Chinese American culture, arguing that she has "feminized" Asian American literature and undermined the power of Asian American men to combat the racist stereotypes of the dominant white culture. Kingston and other women novelists such as Amy Tan, Chin charges, misrepresent Chinese history to exaggerate its patriarchal structure; as a result, Chinese society is portrayed as being even more misogynistic than European society. While Chin and others have cast this conflict in terms of nationalism and assimilationism, perhaps it may be more productive to see this debate, as Elaine Kim does, as a symptom of the tensions between nationalist and feminist concerns in Asian American discourse.[24] I would add to Kim's analysis that the dialogue between nationalist and feminist concerns animates a debate about identity and difference, or identity and heterogeneity, rather than between nationalism and assimilationism. It is a debate in which Chin and others insist on a fixed masculinist identity, whereas Kingston, Tan, or such feminist literary critics as Shirley Lim or Amy Ling, with their representations of female differences and their critiques of sexism in Chinese culture, throw this notion of identity repeatedly into question. Just as Fanon points out that some forms of nationalism can obscure class, Asian American feminists point out that Asian American cultural nationalism—or the construction of a fixed, "native" Asian American subject—obscures gender. In other words, the struggle that is framed as a conflict between the apparent opposites of nativism and assimilation can mask what is more properly characterized as a struggle between the desire to essentialize ethnic identity and the condition of heterogeneous differences against which such a desire is spoken. The trope that opposes nativism and assimilationism can be itself a "colonialist" figure used to displace the challenges of heterogeneity, or subalternity, by casting them as assimilationist or anti-cultural nationalist.

The trope that opposes nativism and assimilation does not only organize the cultural debates of Asian American discourse but figures *in* Asian American literature as well. More often than not, however, this symbolic conflict between nativism and assimilation is figured in the topos with which I began, that of generational conflict. There are many versions of this topos; I will mention only a few so as to elucidate some of the most relevant cultural tensions. In one model, a conflict between generations is cast in strictly masculinist terms, between father and son; in this model, mothers are absent or unimportant, and female figures exist merely as peripheral objects to the side of the central drama of male conflict. Louis Chu's *Eat a Bowl of Tea* exemplifies this masculinist generational symbolism, in which a conflict between nativism and assimilation is allegorized in the relationship between the father Wah Gay and the son Ben Loy in the period when the predominantly Cantonese New York Chinatown community changes from a "bachelor society" to a "family society."[25] Wah Gay wishes Ben Loy to follow "Chinese" tradition and to submit to the father's authority, whereas the son balks at his father's "old ways" and wants to make his own choices. When Wah Gay arranges a marriage for Ben Loy, the son is forced to obey. Although the son had had no trouble leading an active sexual life before his marriage, once married, he finds himself to be impotent. In other words, Chu's novel figures the conflict of nativism and assimilation in terms of Ben Loy's sexuality: submitting to the father's authority, marrying the "nice Chinese girl" Mei Oi and having sons, is the so-called traditional Chinese male behavior; this path represents the nativist option. By contrast, Ben Loy's

former behaviors—carrying on with American prostitutes, gambling, and the like—
are coded as the American path of assimilation. At the "nativist" Chinese extreme,
Ben Loy is impotent and is denied access to erotic pleasure, and at the "assimilationist" American extreme, he has great access and sexual freedom. Rather than naming
the U.S. state as the "father," whose immigration laws determined the restricted
conditions of the "bachelor" society for the first Chinese immigrants, and the
repeal of which permitted the gradual establishment of a "family" society for the
later generations, Chu's novel allegorizes Ben Loy's cultural options in the "oedipal"
story of the son's sexuality. The novel suggests that a third "Chinese American"
alternative becomes available, in which Ben Loy is able to experience erotic pleasure
with his Chinese wife, when the couple moves to another state, away from his
father Wah Gay; Ben Loy's relocation to San Francisco Chinatown and the priority
of pleasure with Mei Oi over the begetting of a son (which they ultimately do
accomplish) both imply important breaks from his father's authority and the father's
representation of "Chinese" tradition. Following Fanon's observations about the
affinities between nativism and assimilation, we can consider Chu's 1961 novel as
an early masculinist rendering of culture as conflict between the apparent opposites
of nativism and assimilation, with an oedipal resolution in a Chinese American
male "identity." Only with hindsight can we propose that the opposition may itself
be a construction that allegorizes the dialectic between an articulation of a fixed
symbolic cultural identity and the context of heterogeneous differences.

Amy Tan's more recent *Joy Luck Club* refigures this topos of generational conflict
in a different social context, among first-and second-generation Mandarin Chinese
in San Francisco. Tan's book rearticulates the generational themes of *Eat a Bowl
of Tea* but deviates from the figuration of Asian American identity in a masculine
oedipal dilemma by refiguring it in terms of mothers and daughters. This shift to
the relationship between women alludes to the important changes after the repeal
acts of 1943–1952, which permitted Chinese women to immigrate to the United
States and eventually shifted the "bachelor" society depicted in Chu's novel to a
"family" society. Yet to an even greater degree than *Eat a Bowl of Tea, The Joy
Luck Club* risks being appropriated as a text that privatizes social conflicts and
contradictions, precisely by confining them to the "feminized" domestic sphere of
family relations. In *The Joy Luck Club,* both privatized generational conflict and the
"feminized" relations between mothers and daughters are made to figure the
broader social shifts of Chinese immigrant formation.[26]

The Joy Luck Club represents the first-person narratives of four sets of Chinese-
born mothers and their American-born daughters; the daughters attempt to come
to terms with their mothers' demands, while the mothers try to interpret their
daughters' deeds, the novel thus expressing a tension between the "Chinese" expectation of filial respect and the "American" inability to fulfill that expectation.
Although it was heralded and marketed as a novel about mother-daughter relations
in the Chinese American family (one cover review characterized it as a "story that
shows us China, Chinese American women and their families, and the mystery of
the mother-daughter bond in ways that we have not experienced before"), *The Joy
Luck Club* also betrays antagonisms that are not exclusively generational but due
as well to different conceptions of class and gender among Chinese Americans.

Toward the end of the novel, for example, Lindo and Waverly Jong reach a climax of misunderstanding, in a scene that takes place in a central site for the production of American femininity: the beauty parlor. After telling the stylist to give her mother a "soft wave," Waverly asks her mother, Lindo, if she is in agreement. The mother narrates: "I smile. I use my American face. That's the face Americans think is Chinese, the one they cannot understand. But inside I am becoming ashamed. I am ashamed she is ashamed. Because she is my daughter and I am proud of her, and I am her mother but she is not proud of me."[27] The American-born daughter believes she is treating her mother, rather magnanimously, to a day of pampering at a chic salon; the Chinese-born mother receives this gesture as an insult, clear evidence of a daughter ashamed of her mother's looks. The scene marks the separation of mother and daughter not only by generation but, perhaps more important, by class and cultural differences that lead to divergent interpretations of how "femininity" is understood and signified. On the one hand, the Chinese-born Lindo and the American-born Waverly have different class values and opportunities; the daughter's belief in the pleasure of a visit to an expensive San Francisco beauty parlor seems senselessly extravagant to the mother, whose rural family had escaped poverty only by marrying her to the son of a less humble family in their village. On the other hand, the mother and daughter also conflict over definitions of proper female behavior. Lindo assumes female identity is constituted in the practice of a daughter's deference to her elders, whereas for Waverly this identity is determined by a woman's financial independence from her parents and her financial equality with men, by her ability to speak her desires, and is cultivated and signified in the styles and shapes that represent middle-class feminine beauty. In this sense, it is possible to read *The Joy Luck Club* not as a novel that exclusively depicts "the mystery of the mother-daughter bond" among generations of Chinese American women, but rather as a text that thematizes how the trope of the mother-daughter relationship comes to symbolize Asian American culture. That is, we can read the novel as commenting on the national public's aestheticizing of mother-daughter relationships in its discourse about Asian Americans, by placing this construction within the context of the differences—of class and culturally specific definitions of gender—that are rendered invisible by the privileging of this trope.

Before concluding, I turn to a final text that not only restates the narrative that opposes nativism and assimilation but also articulates a critique of that narrative, calling the nativist/assimilationist dyad into question. If *The Joy Luck Club* can be said to pose the dichotomy of nativism and assimilation by multiplying the figure of generational conflict and thematizing the privatized trope of the mother-daughter relationship, then Peter Wang's film *A Great Wall* (1985)—both in its emplotment and in its medium of representation—offers yet another alternative.[28] Wang's film unsettles both poles of the antinomy of nativist essentialism and assimilation by performing a continual geographical juxtaposition and exchange between the national spaces of the People's Republic of China and the United States. *A Great Wall* portrays the visit of Leo Fang's Chinese American family to China and their month-long stay with Leo's sister's family, the Chaos, in Beijing. The film concentrates on the primary contrast between the habits, customs, and assumptions of the Chinese in China and the Chinese Americans in California by going back and forth between shots of Beijing and northern California, in a type of continual filmic "migration" between the two, as if to thematize in its very form the travel between cultural spaces. From the first scene, however, in the opposition between "native" and "assimilated" spaces, the film foregrounds that neither space begins as a pure, uncontaminated site or origin; and as the camera eye shuttles back and forth, both poles of the constructed opposition shift and are altered. (Indeed, the Great Wall of China, from which the film takes its title, is a monument to the historical condition that not even ancient China was "pure," but coexisted with "foreign barbarians" against which the Middle Kingdom erected such barriers.) In this regard, the film contains a number of emblematic images that call attention to the syncretic, composite quality of many cultural spaces, particularly in the era of transnational capital: the young Chinese Liu is given a Coca-Cola by his scholar-father when he finishes the college entrance exam; children crowd around the single village television to watch a Chinese opera singer imitate Pavarotti singing Italian opera; the Chinese student learning English recites the Gettysburg Address. Although the film concentrates on both illustrating and dissolving the apparent opposition between Chinese Chinese and American Chinese, a number of other contrasts are likewise explored: the differences between generations within both the Chao and the Fang families; differences between men and women (accentuated by two scenes, one in which Grace Fang and Mrs. Chao talk about their husbands and children, the other in which Chao and Leo get drunk together); and finally, the differences between capitalist and Communist societies (highlighted in a scene in which the Chaos and Fangs talk about their different attitudes toward "work"). The representations of these other contrasts complicate and diversify the ostensible focus on cultural differences between Chinese and Chinese Americans, as if to testify to the condition that there is never only one exclusive valence of difference but rather that cultural difference is always simultaneously bound up with gender, economics, age, and other distinctions. In other words, when Leo says to his wife that the Great Wall makes the city "just as difficult to leave as to get in," the wall at once signifies the construction of a variety of barriers—not only between Chinese and Americans but also between generations, men and women, capitalism and Communism—as well as the impossibility of ever remaining bounded and impenetrable, of resisting change, recomposition, and reinvention.

The film continues with a series of contrasts: the differences in their bodily comportments when the Chinese American Paul and the Chinese Liu play table tennis, between Leo's jogging and Mr. Chao's tai chi, between Grace Fang's and Mrs. Chao's ideas of what is fitting and fashionable for the female body. The two families have different senses of space and of the relation between family members. Ultimately, just as the Chaos are marked by the visit from their American relatives, by the time the Fang family returns home to California, each brings back a memento or practice from their Chinese trip, and they, too, are altered. In other words, rather than privileging either a nativist or an assimilationist view or even espousing a "Chinese American" resolution of differences, A Great Wall performs a filmic "migration" by shuttling between the two national cultural spaces. We are left, by the end of the film, with the sense of culture as dynamic and open material site.

In keeping with the example of *A Great Wall*, we might consider as a possible model for the ongoing construction of "identity" the migratory process suggested by Wang's filmic technique and emplotment, conceiving of the making and practice of Asian American culture as contested and unsettled, as taking place in the movement between sites and in the strategic occupation of heterogeneous and conflicting positions. This is not to suggest that "hybrid" cultural identities are occasioned only by voluntary mobility and literally by the privileges that guarantee such mobility; as Sau-ling Cynthia Wong has pointed out in *Reading Asian American Literature*, the American nation is founded on myths of mobility that disavow the histories of both the immobility of ghettoization and the forced dislocations of Asian Americans.[29] Rather, the materialist concept of hybridity conveys that the histories of forced labor migrations, racial segregation, economic displacement, and internment are left in the material traces of "hybrid" cultural identities; these hybridities are always in the process of, on the one hand, being appropriated and commodified by commercial culture and, on the other, of being rearticulated for the creation of oppositional "resistance cultures." Hybridization is not the "free" oscillation between or among chosen identities. It is the uneven process through which immigrant communities encounter the violences of the U.S. state, and the capital imperatives served by the United States and by the Asian states from which they come, and the process through which they survive those violences by living, inventing, and reproducing different cultural alternatives.

The grouping "Asian American" is not a natural or static category; it is a socially constructed unity, a situationally specific position, assumed for political reasons. It is "strategic" in Gayatri Chakravorty Spivak's sense of a "strategic use of a positive essentialism in a scrupulously visible political interest."[30] The concept of "strategic essentialism" suggests that it is possible to utilize specific signifiers of racialized ethnic identity, such as "Asian American," for the purpose of contesting and disrupting the discourses that exclude Asian Americans, while simultaneously revealing the internal contradictions and slippages of "Asian American" so as to insure that such essentialisms will not be reproduced and proliferated by the very apparatuses we seek to disempower. This is not to suggest that we can or should do away with the notion of Asian American identity, for to stress only differences would jeopardize the hard-earned unity that has been achieved in the last thirty years of Asian American politics. Just as the articulation of identity depends on the existence of a horizon of differences, the articulation of differences dialectically depends on a socially constructed and practiced notion of identity. As Stuart Hall suggests, cultural identity is "not an essence but a *positioning*. Hence, there is always a politics of identity, a politics of position, which has no absolute guarantee in an unproblematic, transcendental 'law of origin.'"[31] In the 1990s, we can afford to rethink the notion of racialized ethnic identity in terms of differences of national origin, class, gender, and sexuality rather than presuming similarities and making the erasure of particularity the basis of unity. In the 1990s, we can diversify our practices to include a more heterogeneous group and to enable crucial alliances—with other groups of color, class-based struggles, feminist coalitions, and sexuality-based efforts—in the ongoing work of transforming hegemony.

NOTES

1. *Issei, nisei,* and *sansei* are Japanese terms meaning first-generation, second-generation, and third-generation Japanese Americans.
2. Janice Mirikitani, "Breaking Tradition," *Ikon* 9, *Without Ceremony: A Special Issue by Asian Women United* (1988): 9.
3. Lydia Lowe, "Quitting Time," *Ikon* 9, *Without Ceremony: A Special Issue by Asian Women United* (1988): 29.
4. See Elaine Kim, *Asian American Literature: An Introduction to the Writings and Their Social Context* (Philadelphia: Temple University Press, 1982).
5. Diana Chang, "The Oriental Contingent," in *The Forbidden Stitch,* ed. Shirley Geok-lin Lim, Mayumi Tsutakawa, and Margarita Donnelly (Corvallis, Ore.: Calyx, 1989), 171–177.
6. Stuart Hall, "Cultural Identity and Diaspora," in *Identity: Community, Culture, Difference,* ed. Jonathan Rutherford (London: Lawrence and Wishart, 1990), 225.
7. See the discussion of Michael Omi and Howard Winant in this volume.
8. Recent anthropological discussions of cultures as syncretic systems echo some of these concerns of Asian American writers. See, for example, Michael M. J. Fischer, "Ethnicity and the Post-Modem Arts of Memory," in *Writing Culture,* ed. James Clifford and George Marcus (Berkeley: University of California Press, 1986); and James Clifford, *The Predicament of Culture: Twentieth-Century Ethnography, Literature, and Art* (Cambridge: Harvard University Press, 1988). For an anthropological study of Japanese American culture that troubles the paradigmatic construction of kinship and filial relations as the central figure in culture, see Sylvia Yanagisako's *Transforming the Past: Kinship and Tradition among Japanese Americans* (Stanford, Calif.: Stanford University Press, 1985).
9. Maxine Hong Kingston, *The Woman Warrior* (New York: Random, 1975), 6.
10. Wayne Wang, *Dim Sum* (1984).
11. See Peter Kwong, *Chinatown, N.Y.: Labor and Politics, 1930–1950* (New York: Monthly Review Press, 1979); and Victor G. Nee and Brett de Bary Nee, *Longtime Californ': A Documentary Study of an American Chinatown* (New York: Pantheon, 1972). Since the 1970s, the former Los Angeles "Chinatown" has been superseded demographically and economically by Monterey Park, the home of many Chinese Americans, as well as newly arrived Chinese from Hong Kong and Taiwan. On the social and political consequences of these changing demographics, see Timothy Fong, *The First Suburban Chinatown: The Remaking of Monterey Park, CA* (Philadelphia: Temple University Press, 1993); and Leland Saito, "Contrasting Patterns of Adaptation: Japanese Americans and Chinese Immigrants in Monterey Park," in *Bearing Dreams, Shaping Visions,* ed. Linda Revilla, Gail Nomura, Shawn Wong, and Shirley Hune (Pullman: Washington State University Press, 1993).
12. Sucheng Chan, *This Bittersweet Soil: The Chinese in California Agriculture, 1860–1910* (Berkeley: University of California Press, 1986); Paul Ong, Edna Bonacich, and Lucie Cheng, eds., *The New Asian Immigration in Los Angeles and Global Restructuring* (Philadelphia: Temple University Press, 1994).
13. See Stuart Hall, "Signification, Representation, Ideology: Althusser and the Post-Structuralist Debates," *Critical Studies in Mass Communication* 2, no. 2 (June 1985): 91–114.
14. While California's "multiculturalism" is often employed to further an ideological assertion of equal opportunity for California's different immigrant groups, I am here pursuing the ignored implications of this characterization: that is, despite the rhetoric about increasing numbers of racialized immigrants racing to enjoy California's opportunities, for racialized immigrants, there is not equality but uneven opportunity, regulation, and stratification.
15. See Antonio Gramsci, *Selections from the Prison Notebooks,* ed. and trans. Quinton Hoare and Geoffrey Nowell Smith (New York: International Publishers, 1971).
16. The notion of "the dominant"—defined by Raymond Williams in a chapter discussing the "dominant, residual, and emergent" as "a cultural process . . . seized as a cultural

system, with determinate dominant features: feudal culture or bourgeois culture or a transition from one to the other"—is often conflated in recent cultural theory with Gramsci's concept of "hegemony." Indeed, Williams writes in *Marxism and Literature* (Oxford: Oxford University Press, 1977), "We have certainly still to speak of the 'dominant' and the 'effective,' and in these senses of the hegemonic" (121), as if the "dominant" and the "hegemonic" are synonymous.

It is important to note, however, that in Gramsci's thought, "hegemony" refers equally to a specific hegemony (for example, bourgeois class hegemony), as it does to the process through which "emergent" groups challenging that specific hegemony assemble and contest the specific ruling hegemony.

17. See Antonio Gramsci, "History of the Subaltern Classes: Methodological Criteria," in *Prison Notebooks*, 52–60. Gramsci describes "subaltern" groups as by definition not unified, emergent, and always in relation to the dominant groups: "The history of subaltern social groups is necessarily fragmented and episodic. There undoubtedly does exist a tendency to (at least provisional stages of) unification in the historical activity of these groups, but this tendency is continually interrupted by the activity of the ruling groups; it therefore can only be demonstrated when an historical cycle is completed and this cycle culminates in a success. Subaltern groups are always subject to the activity of ruling groups, even when they rebel and rise up: only 'permanent' victory breaks their subordination, and that not immediately" (54).

18. "Hegemony" still remains a suggestive construct in Gramsci, however, rather than an explicitly interpreted set of relations. Within the current globalized political economy, it is even more important to specify which particular forms of challenge to an existing hegemony are significantly transformative and which forms may be neutralized or appropriated by that hegemony. We must go beyond Gramsci's notion of hegemony to observe that, in the present conjunction in which "modern" state forms intersect with "postmodern" movements of capital and labor, the social field is not a totality consisting exclusively of the dominant and the counterdominant; rather, "the social" is an open and uneven terrain of contesting antagonisms and signifying practices, some of which are neutralized, others of which can be linked together to build pressures against an existing hegemony. See Lisa Lowe, *Immigrant Acts: On Asian American Cultural Politics* (Durham, N.C.: Duke University Press, 1996), chapter 1.

19. Walter Adamson, *Hegemony and Revolution: A Study of Antonio Gramsci's Political and Cultural Theory* (Berkeley: University of California Press, 1980); Anne Showstack Sassoon, "Hegemony, War of Position, and Political Intervention," in *Approaches to Gramsci*, ed. Anne Showstack Sassoon (London: Writers and Readers, 1982). See Stuart Hall's reading of Gramsci, "Gramsci's Relevance for the Study of Race and Ethnicity," *Journal of Communication Inquiry* 10 (summer 1986).

20. Frantz Fanon, *The Wretched of the Earth*, trans. Constance Farrington (New York: Grove, 1968), 94.

21. The work of Evelyn Nakano Glenn is outstanding in this regard; see especially "Occupational Ghettoization: Japanese-American Women and Domestic Service, 1905–1970," *Ethnicity* 8, no. 4 (December 1981): 352–386, a study of the entrance into and continued specialization of Japanese American women in domestic service and the role of domestic service in the "processing" of immigrant women into the urban economy.

22. See Trinh T. Minh-ha, *Woman, Native, Other: Writing Postcoloniality and Feminism* (Bloomington: Indiana University Press, 1989), 105.

23. See Angela Davis, "Interview," in *Worlds Aligned: The Politics of Culture in the Shadow of Capital*, ed. David Lloyd and Lisa Lowe (forthcoming).

24. See Elaine Kim, "'Such Opposite Creatures': Men and Women in Asian American Literature," *Michigan Quarterly Review* (winter 1990): 68–93, for a comprehensive analysis of this debate between nationalism and feminism in Asian American discourse.

25. For an analysis of generational conflict in Chu's novel, see Ted Gong, "Approaching Cultural Change through Literature: From Chinese to Chinese American," *Amerasia* 7,

no. 1 (1980): 73–86. Gong asserts that "the father/son relationship represents the most critical juncture in the erosion of a traditional Chinese value system and the emergence of a Chinese American character. Change from Chinese to Chinese American begins here" (74–75).

26. Wayne Wang's film production of *The Joy Luck Club* has taken liberties with Tan's novel, the novel already being somewhat dehistoricized and fanciful. See, for example, Sau-ling Cynthia Wong, "Sugar Sisterhood: Situating the Amy Tan Phenomenon," in *The Ethnic Canon: Histories, Institutions, and Interventions*, ed. David Palumbo-Liu (Minneapolis: University of Minnesota Press, 1995). Unfortunately, Wang's film moves in this direction and tends to exemplify, rather than criticize, the privatization and aestheticizing of the Chinese mother-daughter relationship.

27. Amy Tan, *The Joy Luck Club* (New York: Putnam, 1989). The cover review cited is by Alice Walker.

28. Peter Wang, *A Great Wall*, 1985.

29. Sau-ling Cynthia Wong, *Reading Asian American Literature: From Necessity to Extravagance* (Princeton: Princeton University Press, 1993); see chapter 3, "The Politics of Mobility."

30. Gayatri Chakravorty Spivak, "Subaltern Studies: Deconstructing Historiography," in *In Other Worlds* (New York: Routledge, 1988), 205.

31. Hall, "Cultural Identity and Diaspora," 226.

In Search of Filipino Writing

Reclaiming Whose "America"?

E. San Juan Jr.

> *. . . Fertilizer . . . Filipinos. . . .*
>
> From a letter dated May 5, 1908, by H. hackfield and Company
> sent to George Wilcox of the Grove Farm Plantation, Hawai'i[1]

> *It must be realized that the Filipino is just the same as the manure that we put on the
> land—just the same.*
>
> From an interview of a secretary of an
> agricultural association in 1930[2]

Filipinos: Challenge and Enigma

Ever since the United States annexed the Philippine Islands in 1898, the discourse
of capital (as these opening quotations testify) has always been reductive, monologi-
cal, and utilitarian. Although luminaries such as Mark Twain, William James, and
William Dean Howells denounced the slaughter of the natives during the Filipino-
American War of 1899–1902, the Filipino presence was not registered in the public
sphere until their singular commodity, labor power, appeared in large numbers in
Hawai'i and on the West Coast from 1907 to 1935. Until 1946, when formal independence was granted, Filipinos in the metropolis (numbering around 150,000) occupied
the limbo of alterity and transitionality: neither slaves, nor wards, nor citizens. Carey
McWilliams believed that these "others" belonged to "the freemasonry of the ostra-
cized" (*Brothers,* 241). How should we address them, and in what language? Can they
speak for themselves? If not, who will represent them?

Called "little brown brothers," barbaric "yellow bellies," "scarcely more than
savages," and other derogatory epithets, Filipinos as subjects-in-revolt have refused
to conform to the totalizing logic of white supremacy and the knowledge of "the
Filipino" constructed by the Orientalizing methods of American scholarship. Intrac-

table and recalcitrant, Filipinos in the process of being subjugated have confounded U.S. disciplinary regimes of knowledge production and surveillance. They have challenged the asymmetrical cartography of metropolis and colony, core and periphery, in the official world system. Interpellated within the boundaries of empire, Filipinos continue to bear the marks of three centuries of anticolonial insurgency. Given this indigenous genealogy of resistance, which I have traced elsewhere (San Juan, *Racial Formations*), the Filipino writer has functioned not simply as *porte-parole* authorized by the imperium's center but more precisely as an organic intellectual (in Gramsci's sense) for a people whose repressed history and "political unconscious" remain crucial to the task of judging the worth of the American experiment in colonial "tutelage" and to the final settling of accounts with millions of its victims.

Up to now, however, despite the Philippines' formal independence, the texts of the Filipino interrogation of U.S. hegemony remain virtually unread and therefore unappreciated for their "fertilizing" critical force. Not demography, but a symptomatic reconnaissance of contested territory seems imperative. An inventory of the archive (by a partisan native, for a change) is needed as an initial step toward answering the questions I raised earlier. Foremost among these is why the Filipino intervention in the U.S. literary scene has been long ignored, silenced, or marginalized. Although the Filipino component of the Asian-Pacific Islander ethnic category of the U.S. Census Bureau has now become preponderant—1,255,725 persons as of 1989 (O'Hare and Felt, 2), and in the next decade will surpass the combined total of the Chinese and Japanese population-the import of this statistical figure so far has not been calculated in the existing Baedekers of U.S. High Culture.

Literary surveys drawn up in this era of canon revision ignore the Filipino contribution. In the 1982 MLA (Modern Language Association) survey of *Three American Literatures* edited by Houston Baker Jr., the Asian American section deals only with Chinese and Japanese authors. This omission is repeated in the 1990 MLA reference, *Redefining American Literary History*; no reference is made to Filipino writing except in a meager bibliographic list at the end under the rubric "Philippine American Literature" (Ruoff and Ward, 361–362). In this quite erroneous citation of ten authors' "Primary Works," three authors would not claim at all to be Filipino American: Stevan Javellana, Celso Carunungan, and Egmidio Alvarez.[3] Nor would Jose Garcia Villa, the now "disappeared" inventor of modern Filipino expression in English, who is a permanent U.S. resident but not a citizen. The classification "Philippine American" may appear as a harmless conjunction of equal and separate terms, but in fact it conceals subsumption of the former into the latter. In everyday life, the combinatory relay of American pragmatic tolerance easily converts the "Philippine" half into a routinized ethnic phenomenon, normalized and taken for granted. How, then, do we account for the absence, exclusion, and potential recuperability of Filipino writing in this society—at least that portion conceded recognition by institutional fiat?

EXPROPRIATING CARLOS BULOSAN'S WORLDLINESS

In general, the production, circulation, and reception of texts are necessarily, though not sufficiently, determined by the dynamics of class and race. Everyone agrees that in this system numbers do not really count unless the community exercises a measure of economic and political power. Filipinos in the United States remain an exploited and disadvantaged group, not at all a "model" minority. A 1980 study of income distribution among Filipinos found that young men (80 to 86 percent of whom are employed in the secondary sector in California) received only about two-thirds of the income of white males, while the older men get only half. Women, on the other hand, receive one-half the income of white men. Such income disparities persist despite comparable investments in human capital (education, work experience, etc.), which generate low returns "suggestive of race discrimination" (Cabezas and Kawaguchi, 99). Filipinos rank third among Asian Americans in median household income, behind Japanese and Asian Indians. Another survey (Nee and Sanders, 75–93) concludes that although Filipinos have a higher educational attainment than whites or recent Chinese immigrants, their average income is lower than Japanese Americans and Chinese Americans because they are confined to low-skilled, low-paying jobs.

Except in the last few years, Filipinos in the United States have not participated significantly in electoral politics (notwithstanding recent breakthroughs in California and Hawai'i), a fact attributed by mainstream sociologists to the inertia of "provincial allegiances and personality clashes" (Melendy, "Filipinos," 362). Collective praxis, however, is not a given but a sociohistorical construct. This implies that we have to reckon with the tenacious legacy of four centuries of Spanish and U.S. colonial domination to understand the Filipino habitus. What passes for indigenous music or architecture turns out to be a mimesis of Western styles; the refined skills of reading and writing needed for the production and distribution of the knowledge monopolized by the elite (compradors, landlords, bureaucrat capitalists) serve business interests. In brief, cultural literacy is geared to soliciting the recognition of American arbiters of taste and brokers of symbolic capital. We may have talented writers but certainly have had no sizable and responsive audience of readers and commentators up to now. And so this predicament of the community's powerlessness, together with its largely imitative and instrumentalized modality of cultural production/reception, may shed light on the invisibility of Filipino writing in the academy and in public consciousness. But its exclusion and/or marginalization cannot be grasped unless the irreducible historical specificity of the Philippines as a former colony, and at present as a virtual neocolony of the United States, and Filipinos as subjugated and conflicted subjects, are taken into full account.

This dialectical perspective explains the irrepressible centrality of Carlos Bulosan's oeuvre in the shaping of an emergent pan-Filipino literary tradition affiliating the U.S. scene of writing. What distinguishes Bulosan's role in this field of Filipino American intertextuality is his attempt to capture the inaugural experience of uprooting and bodily transport of Filipinos to Hawai'i and the North American continent. In Bulosan's life history, the itinerary of the peasant/worker-becoming-intellectual unfolds in the womb of the occupying power (the United States) a narrative of collective self-discovery: the traumatic primal scene of deracination is reenacted in the acts of participating in the multiracial workers' fight against U.S. monopoly capital and valorized in interludes of critical reflection (San Juan, *Carlos*

Bulosan, 119–143). This solidarity, forged in the popular-democratic crucible of struggling with whites and people of color against a common oppression, stages the condition of possibility for the Filipino writer in exile. In effect, writing becomes for the Filipino diaspora the transitional agency of self-recovery. It facilitates a mediation between the negated past of colonial dependency and a fantasied, even utopian, "America" where people of color exercise their right of self-determination and socialist justice prevails. Bulosan's historicizing imagination configures the genealogy of two generations of Filipinos bridging the revolutionary past and the compromised present, and maps out the passage from the tributary formation of the periphery to the West Coast's "factories in the fields" and canneries in *America Is in the Heart* (hereafter *America*), which cannot be found in the sentimental memoirs of his compatriots.

History for Bulosan is what is contemporary and prophetic. In "How My Stories Were Written," he evokes the childhood of Apo Lacay, the folk sage who inspired his vocation of allegorical remembering chosen during "the age of great distress and calamity in the land, when the fury of an invading race impaled their hearts in the tragic cross of slavery and ignorance" (*If You Want to Know What We Are,* 25). The allusion here is to the scorched-earth tactics of U.S. pacification forces during the Filipino-American War and the ruthless suppression of a nascent Filipino national identity—a foreign policy "aberration" in most textbooks, but recently vindicated by Stanley Karnow's apologia, *In Our Image* (1989). In stories like "Be American," in the quasi-autobiographical *America,* and in his novel, *The Power of the People,* Bulosan renders in symbolic forms of fabulation how the U.S. conquest exacerbated feudal injustice in the Philippines and accomplished on a global scale an iniquitous division of international labor that transformed the United States into a metropolis of industrial modernity and the Philippines into an underdeveloped dependency: a source of cheap raw materials and manual/mental labor with minimal exchange value.

Since it is impossible to ignore Bulosan's works in dealing with Filipino "ethnicity"—recall how his essay "Freedom from Want" (*Saturday Evening Post,* March 6, 1943), commissioned to illustrate President Roosevelt's "Four Freedoms" declaration, was subsequently displayed in the Federal Building in San Francisco—how does the Establishment handle the threat posed by their radical attack on capitalism? In other words, how is Bulosan sanitized and packaged to promote pluralist American nationalism? Instead of rehearsing all the possible ways, it will be sufficient here to give an example of a typical recuperative exercise from *The American Kaleidoscope* (1991) by Lawrence Fuchs:[4]

> The life of Bulosan, a Filipino-American, illustrates the process by which the political struggle against injustice and on behalf of equal rights often turned immigrants and their children into Americans. . . . Disillusioned, Bulosan considered becoming a Communist; at another time, he became a thief. But his principal passions were American politics and American literature, and these stimulated him to organize the Committee for the Protection of Filipino Rights, and to start a small school for migrant workers, where "I traced the growth of democracy in the United States" . . . recalling that his brother had told him "America is in the hearts of men." . . . When, after months of

illness and debility, he finished his autobiography, he called it *America Is in the Heart,* using words similar to those of President Roosevelt to Secretary of War Stimson, "Americanism is simply a matter of the mind and heart," and those of Justice Douglas, that "loyalty is a matter of the heart and mind."

 . . . Bulosan, the Filipino migrant worker, much more than Dillingham, the scion of an old New England family, had proved to be a prescient interpreter of American nationalism. Those who had been excluded longest from membership in the American civic culture had rushed to embrace it once the barriers were lifted. (237–238)

Earlier, Fuchs paternalistically ascribes to Bulosan the fortune blacks did not have of being befriended by a half dozen white women. Somehow Bulosan was also endowed with the exceptional gift of having access to a secret knowledge denied to other minorities: "When he spoke of the American dream he wrote of his migrant-worker students that 'their eyes glowed with a new faith . . . they nodded with deep reverence.' . . . Bulosan identified with the experience of the Euro-Americans who had come to this country as immigrants" (147–148). Shades of Andrew Carnegie, Horatio Alger, the Godfather? As if that were not enough, Bulosan is lined up with "Carl Schurz, Mary Antin, and tens of thousands of other self-consciously Americanizing immigrants" (357). Bulosan is thus appropriated by official discursive practice to hype a putative "civic culture" of "voluntary pluralism" by occluding the historical specificity of his anti-imperialist politics. Both his materialist outlook and his paramount commitment to genuine national sovereignty for the Philippines and to socialism are buried in the abstraction of a "political struggle against injustice." The strategy of containment here is one of tactical omission, calculated redeployment, selective emphasis, and, more precisely, decontextualization. Its mode of uprooting certain words and phrases from their historical habitat of political antagonisms recapitulates President McKinley's policy of "benevolent assimilation" and the duplicitous discourse of pacification from William Howard Taft to the latest scholarship on U.S.-Philippines relations. It can also be read as a textual analogue to the HSPA's (Hawai'ian Sugar Planters' Association) raid of peasant male bodies from occupied territory from 1906 to 1946. By such ruses of displacement and complicity, Bulosan is recruited by his enemies, the imperial patriots, who celebrate his romantic naïveté at the expense of his egalitarian principles and his repudiation of chauvinist-fascist apartheid founded on wars of conquest and the dehumanization of people of color.

We would expect a less distorting treatment of Bulosan from the revisionist anthology edited by Paul Lauter et al.: *The Heath Anthology of American Literature,* which was published in 1990. Unfortunately, this textbook disappoints us. Instead of using a more representative segment about migrant workers and socialist activism, the editors select one rather precious, introspective sketch that gives the impression that Bulosan is a neurotic existentialist from the tropics, a brown-skinned Wallace Stevens conjuring verbal fetishes from his head (1841–1843). Moreover, Amy Ling's prefatory note (1840–1841) compounds the problem by reproducing factual errors and misleading inferences derived from Elaine Kim's *Asian American Literature.* Kim might be chiefly responsible for the defusion of Bulosan's insurrectionary aesthetics, subscribing as she does to the immigrant paradigm of Euro-American success criticized long ago by Robert Blauner and others; for she claims that Bulosan "shares with the Asian goodwill ambassador writers a sustaining desire to win American acceptance" (57). (Because the term "America" denotes a complex overdetermined but not indeterminate relation of peoples and nationalities, I urge that its use should always be qualified, or replaced by other terms.) In spite of her good intentions, Kim's pedestrian conformism disables her from perceiving the deviancy of Bulosan's text. Like Fuchs, she fosters the instrumentalist prejudice that *America* is unilaterally "dedicated to the task of promoting cultural goodwill and understanding" (47), an opinion induced by her completely uncritical endorsement of the patronizing banalities of reviewers (46) and the damaged mentalities of her native informants (47). Indeed, Kim's prophylactic handling of Asian American authors for systemic recuperation and fetishism proceeds from the assumption that ethnic texts are produced by the minds of lonely, disturbed, and suffering immigrants, helpless and lost, but somehow gifted with inner resources capable of transcending their racial oppression and sundry adversities by way of hard work, genius, and luck. At best, in the spirit of a philanthropic liberalism shared by apologists of Anglo missionaries, Kim says that to become part of American society one can always rely on "the urge for good, for the ideal" which is "lodged permanently in the human heart" (51).

Reading (as Fuchs and his ilk practice it) turns out to be an act of violence in more ways than one. What all these reappropriations of Bulosan signify is the power and limits of the hegemonic consensus and its apparatuses to sustain its assimilative but ultimately apartheidlike project to absorb the Asian "Other" into the fold of the unitary hierarchical racial order. In the case of Filipinos settling in the United States, it forgets the original deed of conquest and elides the question, How did Filipinos come to find themselves in (as José Martí puts it) "the belly of the beast"? From a world-system point of view, it is the continuing reproduction of unequal power relations between the Philippines and the United States that is the matrix of the disintegrated Filipino whose subjectivity (more exactly, potential agency) is dispersed in the personae of migrant worker, expatriate intellectual (the major actant in Bienvenido Santos's fiction), cannery or service worker, U.S. Navy steward, and solitary exile. We should remind ourselves that Filipinos first appeared in large numbers in the landscape of an expansive military power not as fugitives (the "Manilamen" of the Louisiana bayous) from eighteenth-century Spanish galleons but as recruited laborers transported by the HSPA.[5] Reinscribed into this context of differential power relations, the Filipino imagination thus acquires its fated vocation of disrupting the economy of "humanist" incorporation by transgressing willy-nilly the boundaries of interdicted times and tabooed spaces.

WHO REPRESENTS WHOM?

What is at stake is nothing less than the question of Filipino self-representation, of its articulation beyond commodity reification, postmodern narcissism, and paranoia. In lieu of the usual atomistic and hypostatizing view, I submit this principle of world-system linkage (the colony integrally situated as the double of the imperial polity) as the fundamental premise for establishing the conditions of possibility for apprehending Filipino creative expression in the United States. Lacking this cognitive/reconstructive mapping, one succumbs to sectarian fallacies vulnerable to the "divide-and-rule" policy of laissez-faire liberalism.

An instructive case may be adduced here. In their foreword to the anthology *Aiiieeeee!,* Oscar Penaranda, Serafin Syquia, and Sam Tagatac fall prey to a separatist adventurism and thus inflict genocide on themselves: "No Filipino-American ('Flip'-born and/or raised in America) has ever published anything about the Filipino-American experience. . . . Only a Filipino-American can write adequately about the Filipino-American experience" (37–54). Writing in the early seventies, a time when Filipinos here born during or after World War II were undergoing the proverbial "identity crisis" in the wake of Third World conscientization movements that swept the whole country, our Flip authors contend that Santos and Bulosan, because of birth, carry "Filipino-oriented minds" whereas "the Filipino born and reared in America writes from an American perspective" (50). What exactly is "an American perspective"? Flawed by a crudely chauvinist empiricism, this position of identifying with the hegemonic order and its transcendent claims, which validates the "exclusively Filipino-American work," becomes supremacist when it dismisses Philippine literature produced in the former colony as inferior, lacking in "soul" (510).[6]

In contrast to this Flip manifesto, the singular virtue of the volume *Letters in Exile* (published two years later) lies in confirming the de-/reconstructive force of the premise of colonial subjugation I propose here. Its archival and countervailing function needs to be stressed. When the Philippine Islands became a U.S. colony at the turn of the century, its inhabitants succeeded the Africans, Mexicans, and American Indians as the "White Man's Burden," the object of "domestic racial imperialism" carried out through brutal pacification and cooptative patronage (Kolko, 41–43, 286–287). The first selection in *Letters in Exile,* "The First Vietnam—The Philippine-American War of 1899–1902," provides the required orientation for understanding the Filipino experience of U.S. racism culminating in the vigilante pogroms of the 1930s. Neither Chinese, nor Japanese, nor Korean history before World War II contains any comparable scene of such unrestrained unleashing of racial violence by the U.S. military (Vietnam later on exceeds all precedents). Without taking into account the dialogic contestation of American power (mediated in American English) by the Filipino imagination judging its exorbitance and "weak links," the critique of U.S. cultural hegemony worldwide remains incomplete.

Until 1934, when Filipinos legally became aliens as a result of the passage of the Tydings-McDuffie Independence Act, their status was anomalously akin to that of a "floating signifier" with all its dangerous connotations. Wallace Stegner described the breathing of their fatigued bodies at night as "the loneliness breathing like a tired wind over the land" (20). This index of otherness, difference incarnate in the sweat and pain of their labor, is the stigma Filipinos had to bear for a long time. Like it or not, we still signify "the stranger's" birthmark. Only in 1934 did the Filipino "immigrant" (at first limited to fifty) really come into existence; hence neither Bulosan nor Villa were immigrants. Nor were the laborers enraptured by dreams of success who were rigidly bound to contracts. In this context, the hyphenated hybrid called "Filipino-American" becomes quite problematic, concealing the priority of the second term (given the fact of colonial/racial subordination and its hallucinatory internalizations) in what appears as a binary opposition of equals. If the writings of Bulosan and Santos do not represent the authentic Filipino experience, as the Flips self-servingly charge, and such a privilege of "natural" representation belongs only to those born or raised in the U.S. mainland (which excludes territorial possessions), then this genetic legalism only confirms the Flips' delusions of exceptionality. It reinforces "the thoroughly racist and national chauvinist character of U.S. society" (Occeña, 35) by eradicating the rich protean history of Filipino resistance to U.S. aggression and thereby expropriating what little remains for Euro-American legitimation purposes.

By contrasting the polarity of ideological positions in the two texts cited, I intended to demonstrate concretely the dangers of systemic recuperation and the illusion of paranoid separatism. Even before our admission to the canon is granted, as Fuchs shows, the terms of surrender or compromise have already been drawn up for us to sign. Who, then, has the authority to represent the Filipino and her experience? Answers to this question and to the problem of how to define Filipino cultural autonomy and its vernacular idiom cannot be explored unless historical parameters and the totalizing constraints of the world system are acknowledged—that is, unless the specificity of U.S. imperial domination of the Philippines is foregrounded in the account. Since 1898, the production of knowledge of, and ethico-political judgments about, the Filipinos as a people different from others has been monopolized by Euro-American experts like W. Cameron Forbes, Dean Worcester, Joseph Hayden, and others. Consider, for example, H. Brett Melendy's discourse on "Filipinos" in the *Harvard Encyclopedia of American Ethnic Groups*, which offers the standard functional-empiricist explanation for Filipino workers' subservience to the Hawai'i plantation system due to their indoctrination "to submission by the barrio political system known as *caciquismo*" (358). Melendy claims that their kinship and alliance system inhibited social adaptation and "militated against their achieving success in American Politics" (362). Thus the Filipino becomes a "social problem." Not only does this expert blame the victims' culture, but he also acquits the U.S. state apparatus and its agents of responsibility for deepening class cleavages and instituting that peculiar dependency syndrome that has hitherto characterized U.S.-Philippines cultural exchange.[7]

FROM EXILE TO "WARM BODY" EXPORT

One of the first tasks of a decolonizing Filipino critical vernacular is to repudiate the putative rationality of this apologia and replace it with a materialist analysis. I have in mind exploratory inquiries like Bruce Occeña's synoptic overview "The Filipino Nationality in the U.S."[8] Except for patent economistic inadequacies, Occeña's attempt to delineate the historical, social, and political contours of the Filipino in the United States as a distinct nationality can be considered a salutary point of departure.[9] According to Occeña, two basic conditions have decisively affected the development of a unique Filipino nationality in the United States: first, the continuing oppression of the Filipino nation by U.S. imperialism; and second, the fact that as a group, "Filipinos have been integrated into U.S. society on the bases of *inequality* and subjected to discrimination due both to their race and nationality" (31).[10]

What follows is a broad outline of the sociopolitical tendencies of three waves of migration needed to clarify the heterogeneous character of the Filipino nationality. The first wave (1906–1946) covers 150,000 workers concentrated in Hawai'i and California, mostly bachelor sojourners—crippled "birds of passage"—forced by poverty, ill health, and so on, to settle permanently; the second (1946–64) comprises thirty thousand war veterans and their families, conservative in general because of relative privileges; and the third (about 630,000 from 1965 to 1984) encompasses the most numerous and complexly stratified group because of the fact that they have moved at a time when all sectors of Philippine society were undergoing cataclysmic changes. This latest influx harbors nationalist sentiments that help focus their consciousness on multifaceted struggles at home and keep alive their hope of returning when and if their life chances improve (although some will stay). Given the collapse of distances by the greater scope and frequency of modern communication and travel, linguistic, cultural, and social links of the Filipino diaspora to the islands have been considerably reinforced enough to influence the dynamics of community politics and culture here, a situation "quite different from the previous period when the Filipino community was in the process of evolving a conspicuously distinct sub-culture which was principally a reflection of their experiences in U.S. society and alien in many ways to the national culture of the Philippines itself" (Occeña, 38).[11] Contradictory networks of thought and feeling traverse this substantial segment of the community, problematizing the evolution of a monolithic "Filipino American" sensibility not fissured by ambivalence, opportunism, and schizoid loyalties. Recent immigrants are composed of (1) urban professional strata exhibiting a self-centered concern for mobility and status via consumerism, and (2) a progressive majority who occupy the lower echelons of the working class exposed to the worst forms of class, racial, and national oppression. Occeña posits the prospect that "the life options of many of these Filipino-Americans are grim—the 'poverty draft' will push them into the front lines of the U.S. war machine or the life of low paid service workers. Consequently, this emerging generation promises to be the most thoroughly proletarianized section of the third wave" (41) and thus ripe for mobilization.

Although I think the last inference is mechanical and does not allow for the impact of changing political alignments, ideological mutations, and other contingencies in the "New World Order" of late "disorganized" capitalism, Occeña's emphasis on the unifying pressure of racial and national marginalization serves to rectify the narcosis of identity politics that posits a mystifying "Filipino American" essence. In addition, a focus on the overlay and coalescence of the key sociological features of the three waves in the extended family networks should modify the schematic partitioning of this survey and intimate a more dynamic, hospitable milieu within which Filipino heterogeneity can be further enhanced and profiled.

It becomes clear now why, given these nomadic and deterritorializing circuits of exchange between the (in our reinterpretation) fertilizing margin and parasitic center, the use of the rubric "Filipino American" can be sectarian and thus susceptible to hegemonic disarticulation. Should we then bracket "American" (not reducible to heart or mind) in this moment of analysis, mimicking the antimiscegenation law of the thirties?

Oscar Campomanes has tried to resolve the predicament of the intractable nature of Filipino subjectivity (I hesitate to use "subject position" here because it may suggest a shifting monad, a disposable lifestyle unanchored to specific times and places) by postulating three historical moments: colonial generation, ethnic identity politics, and political expatriation. Given the global constellation of forces I have drawn earlier, Campomanes hopes to synthesize multiple literary productions by subsuming it in the phenomenology of exile:

> Motifs of departure, nostalgia, incompletion, rootlessness, leave-taking, and dispossession recur with such force in most writing produced by Filipinos in the U.S. and Filipino Americans, with the Philippines as always either the original or terminal reference point. Rather than the U.S. as the locus of claims or "the promised land" that Werner Sollors argues is the typological trope of "ethnic American writing" the Filipino case represents a reverse telos, an opposite movement. It is on this basis that I argue for a literature of exile and emergence rather than a literature of immigration and settlement whereby life in the U.S. serves as the space for displacement, suspension, and perspective. "Exile" becomes a necessary, if inescapable, state for Filipinos in the United States—at once susceptible to the vagaries of the (neo)colonial U.S.-Philippine relationship and redeemable only by its radical restructuring. (5)

This approach is provocative, inviting us on one hand to test the validity of Edward Said's conceptualization of exile as a reconstitution of national identity (359), and on the other to contextualize Julia Kristeva's psychoanalysis of every subject as estranged, the "improper" Other as our impossible "own and proper" (191–195). But how does this protect us from the internal colonialism at work in High Culture's idealizing of the worldwide division of mental/manual labor?

Although Campomanes does foreground the fact of dependency and its libidinal investment in an archetypal pattern of exile and redemptive return, he indiscriminately lumps together migrant workers, sojourners, expatriates, pseudo-exiles, refugees, émigrés, and opportunists at the expense of nuanced and creative tensions among them.[12] The hypothesis of exile is heuristic and catalyzing, but it fails to discriminate the gap between Bulosan's radical project of solidarity of people of color against capital and the integrationist "melting pot" tendencies that vitiate the works of N.V.M. Gonzalez, Bienvenido Santos, and Linda Ty-Casper. Subjugation of one's nationality cannot be divorced from subordination by racial and class stigmatizing; only Bulosan and some Flip writers are able to grapple with and sublate this complex dialectics of Filipino subalternity and bureaucratic closure. In a typical story, "The Long Harvest," Gonzalez easily cures the incipient anomie of his protagonist by making him recollect the primal scene of his mother suturing his narcissism with artisanal commodity production at home (28). As long as those sublimating images of an archaic economy survive, the petit bourgeois expatriate can always resort to a conciliatory, accommodationist therapy of mythmaking and need never worry about class exploitation, racism, and national oppression.[13]

This is the caveat I would interpose. Unless the paradigm of exile is articulated with the global division of labor under the diktat of U.S. finance capital (via IMF-World Bank, United Nations, private foundations), it simply becomes a mock-surrogate of the "lost generation" avant garde and a pretext for elite ethnocentrism. The intellectual of color can even wantonly indenture himself to the cult of exile à la Joyce or Nabokov. Bulosan also faced this tempting dilemma: stories like "Life and Death of a Filipino in the USA" and "Homecoming" (San Juan, *Bulosan*, 25–30, 105–111) refuse commodity fetishism by fantasizing a return to a healing home, a seductive catharsis indeed: "Everywhere I roam [in the United States] I listen for my native language with a crying heart because it means my roots in this faraway soil; it means my only communication with the living and those who died without a gift of expression" ("Writings," 153–154). But he counters this nostalgic detour, this cheap Proustian fix, by reminding himself of his vocation and its commitment to the return of symbolic capital expropriated from his people:

> I am sick again. I know I will be here [Firland Sanitarium, Seattle, Washington] for a long time. And the grass hut where I was born is gone, and the village of Mangusmana is gone, and my father and his one hectare of land are gone, too. And the palm-leaf house in Binalonan is gone, and two brothers and a sister are gone forever.
>
> But what does it matter to me? The question is—what impelled me to write? The answer is—my grand dream of equality among men and freedom for all. To give a literate voice to the voiceless one hundred thousand Filipinos in the United States, Hawai'i, and Alaska. Above all and ultimately, to translate the desires and aspirations of the whole Filipino people in the Philippines and abroad in terms relevant to contemporary history. Yes, I have taken unto myself this sole responsibility. (Kunitz, 145)

Bulosan's transplantation from the empire's hinterland to the agribusiness enclaves of the West Coast coincides with his transvaluative mapping of the future—not the "America" of corporate business—as the space of everyone's desire and emancipated but still embodied psyche (San Juan, *Toward a People's Literature*, 119–143; "Beyond Identity Politics," 556–558). When the patriarchal family disintegrates, the narrator of *America* (unlike Melendy's "Filipino") discovers connections with Chicano and Mexican workers, finds allies among white middle-class women, and taps the carnivalesque life energies of folklore in *The Laughter of My Father*, Bulosan's satire of a money-obsessed society. He encounters the submerged genius loci of anti-imperialist solidarity in gambling houses, cabarets, labor barracks—sites of loss, excess, and expenditure that found a new social bond; points of escape that circumscribe the power of the American "dream" of affluence. Bulosan's strategy of displacement anticipates the insight that "a society or any collective arrangement is defined first by its points or flows of deterritorialization" (Deleuze and Guattari, *A Thousand Plateaus*, 220), by jump cuts, syncopations, and scrambling of positions.

Borderlines, of course, include by excluding. It might be surmised that when the conclusion of *America* reaffirms the narrator's faith in "our unfinished dream"—an "America" diametrically opposed to the nightmares of history that make up the verisimilitude of quotidian existence—Bulosan suppresses history. One might suspect that he infiltrates into it a "jargon of authenticity" and forces art to fulfill a compensatory function of healing the divided subject. David Palumbo-Liu cogently puts the case against this kind of closure in ethnic textuality as capitulation to, and recapitalization of, the dominant ideology: "In ethnic narrative, the transcendence of the material via an identification with the fictional representation of lived life often suppresses the question of the political constitution of subjectivity, both within and without the literary text, opting instead for a kind of redemption that short-circuits such questions" (4). But, as Marilyn Alquizola has shown, a probing of *America*'s structure will disclose an ironic counterpointing of voices or masks, with numerous didactic passages and exempla, critical of the system undercutting the naive professions of faith so as to compel the reader to judge that "the totality of the book's contents contradict the protagonist's affirmation of America in the conclusion" (216). Beyond this formalist gloss, an oppositional reading would frame the logic of the narrator's structuring scheme with two influences: first, the routine practice of authors submitting to the publisher's market analysis of audience reception (wartime propaganda enhances a book's salability), and second, the convention of the romance genre in Philippine popular culture, which warrants such a formulaic closure. Further metacommentary on the subtext underlying *America*'s mix of naturalism and humanist rhetoric would elicit its Popular Front politics as well as its affinity with Bulosan's massive indictment of capital in "My Education," in the 1952 International Longshore and Warehousemen's Union *Yearbook* editorial, and in numerous letters, all of which belie his imputed role of servicing the behemoth of American nationalism. Ultimately, we are confronted once again with the masks of the bifurcated subject disseminated in the text, traces of his wandering through perilous contested terrain. Forgotten after his transitory success in 1944 with *The Laughter of My Father,* Bulosan remained virtually unknown until 1973 when the University of Washington Press, convinced of his marketability and impressed by the activism of Filipino American groups opposed to the "U.S.-Marcos dictatorship," reissued *America.* My current acquaintance with the Filipino community, however, confirms Bulosan's lapse into near oblivion and the unlikelihood of the Establishment's initiating a retrieval to shore up the ruins of the "model minority" myth. This immunity to canonization, notwithstanding the possibility that the fractured discourse of *America* can lend itself to normalization by disciplinary regimes, is absent in the works of Bienvenido Santos, whose narratives cultivate a more commodifiable topos: the charm and hubris of victimage.

Santos's imagination is attuned to an easy purchase on the hurts, alienation, and defeatism of *pensionados,* expatriated *ilustrados,* petit bourgeois mates marooned during World War II in the East Coast and Midwest, and other third-wave derelicts. His pervasive theme is the reconciliation of the Filipino psyche with the status quo.[14] Since I have commented elsewhere on Santos's achievement (*Toward a People's Literature,* 171–173; *Crisis in the Philippines,* 182–183), suffice it to note here its power of communicating the pathos of an obsolescent humanism such as that exemplified by David Hsin-Fu Wand's celebration of the universal appeal of ethnic writing, its rendering of "the human condition of the outsider, the marginal man, the pariah" (9) in his Introduction to *Asian American Heritage*. The patronage of the American New Critic Leonard Casper might be able to guarantee Santos's efficacy in recycling the ethnic myth of renewal, the born-again syndrome that is the foundational site of the hegemonic American identity. Casper's technique of assimilation differs from Fuchs's in its reactionary essentialism. Bewailing Filipino society's alleged loss of "agrarian ideals that guaranteed cultural uniformity and stability" (xiv), a loss that supposedly aggravates the traumatic impact of the "America of individualism" on poor tribal psyches, Casper superimposes his ante-bellum standard on his client: Santos is "offering an essentially timeless view of culture, which transcends history limited to the linear, the consecutive, and the one-dimensional" (xv). But read against the grain, Santos's *Scent of Apples,* and possibly his two novels set in San Francisco and Chicago, derive their value from being rooted in a distinctive historical epoch of Filipino dispossession. As symptomatic testimonies of the deracinated neocolonized subject, they function as arenas for ideological neutralization and compromise, presenting serious obstacles to any salvaging operation and any effort to thwart recuperation because they afford what Brecht calls "culinary" pleasure, a redaction of the native's exotic susceptibilities to tourist consumption and patronage.

So far we have seen how Fuchs's extortive neoliberalism can hijack the transgressive speech of Bulosan into the camp of "American nationalism"(!) and how Casper's paternalistic chauvinism can shepherd Santos up to the threshold of the Western manor of polite letters. Appropriated thus, our authors do not really pose any threat to the elite proprietorship of administered learning. Does that apply to Villa, the avant-garde heretic now *desaparecido,* who once scandalized the colony's philistines?

JOSE GARCIA VILLA: MASKS AND LEGERDEMAIN

When Villa arrived in the United States in 1930, he was already acclaimed as a modernist master by his contemporaries, a stature further reinforced when his two books of experimental and highly mannered poems, *Have Come Am Here* (1942) and *Volume Two* (1949), came out and earned praise from the leading mandarins in the Anglo-American literary establishment, among them Edith Sitwell, Marianne Moore, e.e. cummings, Richard Eberhart, and Mark Van Doren. His poems were then anthologized by Selden Rodman, Conrad Aiken, and W. H. Auden (though, as far as I know, no textbook of American literature has included Villa). He has received numerous prizes, including the American Academy of Arts and Letters Award and the Shelley Memorial Award; he was nominated for the Pulitzer Prize in 1943. Villa claims that he was denied a Bollingen Prize because he was not an American citizen. On June 12, 1973, the Marcos government bestowed on Villa its highest honor, "National Artist of the Philippines." After the publication of his *Selected Poems and New* in 1958, however, Villa immediately sank into obscurity—an enigmatic disappearance that can be plausibly explained (apart from rapid changes in taste and fashion) by the immense reifying and integrative power of mass consumer society to flatten out diverse or antithetical visions and philosophies.[15]

Villa had no problems being hailed as an "American" poet by the celebrities mentioned earlier, including the editor of *Twentieth Century Authors,* Stanley Kunitz. For this reference guide, Villa confessed the reason his poems were "abstract" and lacked feeling for detail and particularity:

> I am not at all interested in description or outward appearance, nor in the contemporary scene, but in *essence.* A single motive underlies all my work and defines my intention as a serious artist: The search for the metaphysical meaning of man's life in the Universe—the finding of man's selfhood and identity in the mystery of Creation. I use the term *metaphysical* to denote the ethic-philosophic force behind all essential living. The development and unification of the human personality I consider the highest achievement a man can do. (Kunitz, 1035–1036)

Thirty years later, Werner Sollors tries to smuggle Villa back into the limelight by focusing on the poet's reactive idiosyncrasy (not his metaphysical selfhood), which substantiates the myth of U.S. exceptionalism in which the languages of consent (to assimilation) and descent collaborate to Americanize almost any immigrant. Villa's indeterminate status in the United States motivated his fabrication of a new poetic language of "reversed consonance" (Sollors, 253–254). Positing the imperative of syncretic belonging, Sollors's pastiche of ethnic genealogy thoroughly cancels out Villa's descent. Meanwhile S. E. Solberg "naturalizes" Villa and so annuls Filipino collective self-determination, labeling the poet's spiritual quest a "personal and idiosyncratic fable, a protean version of the 'making of Americans'" (54).

   Elsewhere I have argued that Villa's poems can be properly appraised as "the subjective expression of a social antagonism," which constitutes the originality of the lyric genre (Adorno, 376; San Juan, *Reading the West*). What preoccupies Villa is the phenomenology of dispossession or lack in general, a malaise that translates into the double loss of the poet's traditional social function and audience when exile overtakes the Filipino artist. What is staged in Villa's texts are scenarios for overcoming the loss by the discovery and ratification of the imagination as a demiurgic logos expressing the poet's godhood, a process that also reciprocally evokes the forces of alienation and reification the poet is wrestling with; in short, both the reality-effect and the domination-effect (Balibar and Macherey, 91–97) are fused in the grammar of poetic enunciation. Such contradictions, pivoting around the themes of revolt against patriarchal power, psychomachia, negativity, and bodily uprooting, elude the neocolonizing maneuvers of Villa's critics and the parodic mimicry of his epigones.

   It is not too much, I think, to suggest that Villa has refused the "ethnic" trap by challenging imperial authority to recognize his authentic artist-self and so validate his equal standing with his white peers. But this also spelled his premature redundancy, since reconciliation via aestheticism is nothing but the hegemonic alternative of healing the split subject in a transcendental restoration of plenitude of meaning. We can observe this in the way the crisis of exile, rendered as metonymic displacement in "Wings and Blue Flame: A Trilogy" and "Young Writer in a New Country" (in *Footnote to Youth*), is dissolved by metaphoric sublimation: in his visionary representation of the primal loss (exile as castration; expulsion by the father), the antinomic discourses of place, body, inheritance, and need converge in the self-exiled native's being reborn in the desert of New Mexico, where the oedipal trauma (the loss of the mother's/patria's body) is exorcised by a transcendent trope of the imagination. Art, then, functions as the resolution of the conflict between solitary ego and community, unconscious drives and the fixated body, symbolic exchange and the imaginary fetish, between subjugated people and despotic conqueror.

In his sympathetic introduction to Villa's stories, Edward J. O'Brien intuits a "Filipino sense of race" or "race consciousness" embedded in the text, but this consciousness swiftly evaporates in the "severe and stark landscape of New Mexico" (Villa, 3). Such a gesture of alluding to difference acquires a portentous modality when Babette Deutsch, again with the best of intentions, apprehends something anomalous in Villa's situation only to normalize it as strange: "The fact that he is a native of the Philippines who comes to the English language as a stranger may have helped him to his unusual syntax" (56). But the stigmata of the alien are no hindrance to Villa's creation of "luminous and vibrant" poems "concerned with ultimate things," a sacrificial rite whose anti-utilitarian telos may not be so easily instrumentalized as Bulosan's idealism for the sake of vindicating the ethos of the pluralist market. Even if difference as plurality is granted, it is only at the expense of its subsumption in the sameness/identity of the artist, whose self-contained artifices, predicated on the organic reconciliation of ego and alter, transcend the exigencies of race, nationality, class, gender, and all other segmentations integral to profit accumulation in the planetary domain of the late bourgeoisie.

At this juncture, the quest for Filipino self-representation reaches an impasse. Villa's "abject" response to the world of commodities and the cash nexus combines both acquiescence and nausea, given our hypothesis that the lyric form harbors social antagonisms and yields both reality-and domination-effects. His work might be read as a highly mediated reflection of the vicissitudes of the conscienticized Filipino who is driven from the homeland by economic crisis, alternatively nostalgic and repelled, unable to accommodate himself to his new environment. Villa's "disappearance" is but one episode in the allegory of the Filipinos' pre-postcolonial ethnogenesis. The group's persistently reproduced subordination arises from its belief that it owes gratitude for being given an entry visa, and that by imitating the successful models of Asians and other immigrants who made their fortune, it will gradually be accepted as an equal; at the same time, it cherishes the belief that it originated from a distinct sovereign nation enjoying parity with the United States. To salvage Villa, we have to read his work symptomatically for those absent causes that constitute its condition of possibility, even as those very same ruptures and silences betray the manifold contradictions that define the "American civic" consensus. Villa's agenda is integration of the personality, ours the reinscription of our subject-ion in the revolutionary struggle to forge an independent, self-reliant Philippines and in the resistance of people of color everywhere to the violence of white supremacy.

FROM TOTEM WORSHIPERS TO DOGEATERS
AND OTHER NOMADS

In this emancipatory project to build the scaffolding of our cultural tradition, we can learn how to safeguard ourselves from the danger of reclamation by a strategy of retrospective mapping (performed in the preceding sections) and anticipatory critique. To advance the latter, I comment on two modes of narrating Filipino self-identification: Jessica Hagedorn's *Dogeaters* and Fred Cordova's *Filipinos: Forgotten Asian Americans.*

Conflating heresy and orthodoxy, Hagedorn's novel possesses the qualities of a canonical text in the making—for the multiculturati. It unfolds the crisis of U.S. hegemony in the Philippines through a collage of character types embodying the corruption of the Americanizing oligarchic elite (see San Juan, "Mapping the Boundaries," 125–126). In trying to extract some intelligible meaning out of the fragmentation of the comprador-patriarchal order that sacrifices everything to acquisitive lust, she resorts to pastiche, aleatory montage of diverse styles, clichés, ersatz rituals, hyperreal hallucinations—a parodic bricolage of Western high post-modernism—whose cumulative force blunts whatever satire or criticism is embedded in her character portrayals and authorial intrusions. This narrative machine converts the concluding prayer of exorcism and ressentiment into a gesture of stylized protest. Addressed mainly to a cosmopolitan audience, Hagedorn's trendy work is undermined by postmodern irony: it lends itself easily to consumer liberalism's drive to sublimate everything (dreams, eros, New People's Army, feminism, anarchist dissent) into an ensemble of self-gratifying spectacles. At best, *Dogeaters* measures the distance between the partisanship of Bulosan's peasants-become-organic intellectuals and the pseudo-yuppie lifestyles of recent arrivals. As a safe substitute for Bulosan and as one of the few practitioners of Third World/feminine "magic realism," Hagedorn may easily be the next season's pick for the Establishment celebration of its multicultural canon.[16]

Examining Cordova's photographic montage, we encounter again our otherness as "fertilizer" and "little brown brother." We discern here a symptom of the conflicted subaltern compensating for his lack by impressing the public with an overwhelming multiplicity of images of family/communal togetherness, simulacra of smiles and gestures that animate the rituals of the life cycle and whose repetition seems enough to generate illusions of successful adjustment and progress. Filipinos turn out to be "first" on many occasions. Despite the negative witness of parts of the commentary, the surface texture of those images serves to neutralize the stark evidence of a single photo (on p. 42) that captured stooping, faceless workers caught in the grid of a bleak imprisoning landscape. Nothing is mentioned of why or how these alien bodies were transported and smuggled in. What is suppressed here can be gleaned from a comparable though abbreviated photographic discourse, *Pearls* (Bock, 38–47). Its section "Pinoy" offers an apologetic history and the usual documentary exhibits of Filipinos adapting to their new habitat, but the inclusion of newspaper cutouts headlining anti-Filipino riots serves to demystify the ideology of adjustment and compromise that informs officially funded enterprises such as Cordova's.[17] *Pearls* records a vestigial trace, a lingering effect, of what

Letters in Exile strove to accomplish: a reconstruction of the historical conditions of possibility of the Filipino presence in the metropolis and their struggle to affirm their humanity by acts of refusal, solidarity, and remembering.[18]

The Marcos dictatorship interlude (1972–86) in Philippine history, which brought a flood of exiles and pseudorefugees to the United States at the same time that Washington amplified its military and economic aid to the national security state, has foregrounded again the reality of U.S. domination of the homeland that distinguishes the Filipino nationality from other minorities. Our neocolonial stigmata renew the signifiers of difference.[19] I reiterate my thesis that the creation of the vernacular résumé of the Filipino's experience of limits and possibilities here can only be theorized within the process of comprehending the concrete historical particularity of their incorporation in the U.S. empire and the ecology of this unequal exchange.

In the context of recent demography, Bulosan seems to be a "rural" misfit. The transplantation of recent Filipino immigrants to the urban wilderness of Los Angeles, San Francisco, Seattle, Chicago, and New York City has impelled young writers to conjecture the emergence of an "urbane" sensibility, adoptive and adaptive at the same time, born from the clash of cultures and memories. The trajectory of the proletarian imagination from Hawai'i's plantations to California's Imperial Valley to Washington's Yakima Valley no longer crosses the paths of "dogeaters" and "Flips." Recent subaltern anxiety, however, seeks legitimacy from the universal archetypes found in archaic folklore and myth—an ironic aporia, indeed. How can this recover from the "backwaters" the writings of Serafin Malay Syquia, for example? And how can it valorize the paradigm of the *sakada*'s redemptive agon in *Istorya ni Bonipasyo: Kasla Gloria Ti Hawai'i* for its lessons of inventing "history from below"?[20]

Only disconnect and recontextualize—that's our motto. What makes such disparate events as Fermin Tobera's killing in 1930 and the murder of Domingo and Viernes in 1981 the condensed turning points of the Filipino odyssey in the United States?[21] You have to conceive of both occurring in the space of the heterogeneous Other occupied by U.S. "civilizing" power. While the texts of the nationality's autochthonous tradition are interred in the imperial archive that cries for inventory and critique—I am thinking of the oral histories of the "Manongs"; interviews of veterans of union organizing; testimonies in letters and journals of immigrant passage; reportage and videofilms of various struggles, such as that over the International Hotel in San Francisco; and other nonverbal signifying practices—unfortunately there are few discerning and astute commentaries or informed reflections on these circumstantial texts. We need to disconnect them from the hegemonic episteme of Fuchs and Melendy, contextualize them in the resistance narrative of peasants and workers, and then reconfigure them in the punctual lived experiences of Filipinos today. Therefore I consider the production of transformative critical discourse a priority in the task of identifying, generating, and selecting the anticanon[22] of Filipino agency and praxis that in varying degrees have resisted co-optation and incorporation. Toward realizing this agenda of searching for our "representative" speech, I propose Bulosan's corpus of writings as central touchstone and researches like *Philip Vera Cruz: A Personal History of Filipino Immigration and the Farmworkers Movement* (Scharlin and Villanueva) as crucial linkages between popular memory and individualist dissidence. In this syllabus, we include Santos's and Gonzalez's fiction on the diaspora as loci for renegotiation, together with Villa's entire production as salvageable for counterhegemonic rearticulation in spite of his status as a legendary classic. Meanwhile, the prodigious creativity of a "third-wave" generation—among them Jessica Hagedorn, Marianne Villanueva, Michelle Cruz Skinner, the Flips, Peter Bacho, and many more who participated in the annual exodus from the Philippines in the last decade—remains a reservoir of practices for future hermeneutic appraisal and reader/writer empowerment.

To accomplish this project of discovery, rescue, and affirmation of Filipino agency against recolonizing strategies from above, we need a radical transformation of grassroots consciousness and practice, a goal addressed by Marina Feleo-Gonzalez's playbook, *A Song for Manong*. What is at stake here is a recovery of the inaugural scene of Filipino subject-ification and insurgency as a dialectical process. We find this event dramatized here when the script unfolds the figure of Pedro Calosa, a leader of the Tayug uprising in Pangasinan from whose milieu of sedition and dissidence Bulosan emerged, as one who learned the craft of resistance from the Hawai'i interethnic strikes of the twenties. Feleo-Gonzalez chooses to circumvent any easy return to a pristine homeland by concluding the performance with the solidarity-in-action of Euro-Americans and Third World peoples in the campaign to preserve the site of the International Hotel from corporate modernization.[23] Feleo-Gonzalez's intervention reawakens the community's conscience and redeems its "collective assemblage of enunciation" (to use Deleuze and Guattari's phrase) from the fate of recoding by the celebrated "melting pot" religion.

One such assemblage is Manuel Buaken's neglected book *I Have Lived with the American People*. Indeed, Buaken returns to haunt us with the lesson that no fable of dredging up a coherent and synchronized identity through memory alone, no privileging of the therapeutic power of art, no sacred ceremony of reminiscence by itself can cement together the fragments of our uprooting from the ravished homeland and repair the tragic disintegration of the nation's spirit. In the breakdown of Buaken's "goodwill autobiography" as a teleological fable, we find a counterpointing discourse: our quest for linkage and autonomy encounters the testimonies of such early migrants as Francisco Abra (117–120) and Felipe Cabellon (121–124) soliciting empathy and justice, interrupting our pursuit of wholeness. With the Filipino nationality in the United States still mind-manacled and the islands convulsed in the fire of people's war for liberation, the practice of writing by, of, and for Filipinos in the United States remains nomadic, transitional, hybrid, metamorphic, discordant, beleaguered, embattled, "always already" in abeyance. Such a genre of "minor" writing, which I define as a praxis of becoming-what-is-other-for-itself, is (to quote Deleuze and Guattari) "the revolutionary force for all literature."

NOTES

1. Takaki, *From Different Shores*, 4.
2. Takaki, *Strangers*, 324.

3. Eric Chock, another name listed by Amy Ling, identifies himself as a Hawai'ian writer and resident (Ruoff and Ward, 362). The Filipinos in Hawai'i, condemned to almost castelike conditions, constitute a community significantly different from Filipinos on the mainland. For a survey of the writing by Hawai'ian Ilocanos, see Somera.

4. Aside from having served as director of the Peace Corps in the Philippines (1961–63), Fuchs was executive director of the Select Commission on Immigration and Refugee Policy under President Carter. Another mode of recuperation is exemplified by Stanley, who insists on the "relatively libertarian character of U.S. rule" (4).

5. In 1946, six thousand Filipino workers were imported to Hawai'i to counter the industry-wide strike—proof once more that the Philippines is an "inside" factor in the U.S. imperial polity (Philippine Center, 6).

   To the early contingents of Filipino workers belongs the honor of spearheading the first and most resolute labor militancy in Hawai'i in modern U.S. history. According to Sucheng Chan, after the 1882 Chinese Exclusion Act and the Gentleman's Agreement of 1907 limiting the entry of Japanese labor, Filipinos became the predominant agricultural labor force in Hawai'i: "Not surprisingly, they became the main Asian immigrant group to engage in labor militancy. Moreover, as Beechert has noted, they did so in politically repressive environments with criminal syndicalist laws" (87). Although Bulosan does not claim to describe, for instance, the epic strikes of 1924 in Hawai'i's Hanapepe plantation and of 1937 in Puunene, the scenes of union organizing and strikes in America function as an allegorical emblem of all such instances of the sporadic or organized resistance of masses of people of color. Bulosan's life covers four major episodes in the Filipino workers' history: the action of the Agricultural Workers Industrial Union-Trade Union Unity League in 1930, the formation of the Filipino Labor Union in 1933, the affiliation of the Alaska Cannery Workers Union with the CIO in 1937, and the establishment of the Filipino Agricultural Workers Association in 1939.

   In the late thirties, 25 percent of Filipinos were service workers, 9 percent were in the salmon canneries, and 60 percent in agriculture (Takaki, *Strangers,* 316–318; Catholic Institute, 36).

6. Aside from Sam Tagatac's experimental "The New Anak" (Penaranda's "Dark Fiesta" deals with native rituals and folk beliefs in the Philippines), the Flips will only include the Flip poets—some of those in *Without Names* (Ancheta et al.) and some in Bruchac's collection. I will not repeat here the bibliographic data of Filipino American authors found in Cheung and Yogi's excellent reference guide.

   In fairness to the Flips, I should state here that Serafin Malay Syquia's poems and his essay "Politics and Poetry" (Navarro, 87–89) represent a crucial intervention that seeks to reclaim an "America" reconstituted by people of color. At a time when leaders of the community were rejecting Bulosan's socialist vision and the legacy of the Manongs, Syquia and his comrades were striving to reconnect via their ethnic rebellion with the insurgency in the neocolony—an emancipatory project of opening up the space prematurely closed by Santos's conciliatory acceptance of the status quo, Gonzalez's myths of restoration, and Villa's patrician withdrawal.

7. I take issue with the bias of functionalist, positivist social science in my book *Racial Formations/Critical Transformations.* The assimilationist doctrine of the ethnic paradigm, with its ahistorical empiricism, has vitiated practically most studies of the Filipino community in the United States. Typical is Pido's *Pilipinos in America,* littered with such blanket pronouncements as "Pilipinos fear alienation" (35). Far more insightful are articles such as Aurora Fernandez, "Pilipino Immigrants," *East Wind* (fall–winter 1982): 34–36, and Teresita Urian (written by Mila de Guzman), "Into the Light," *Katipunan* 4, no. 7 (October 1991): 10–11.

8. Occeña's pioneering effort can be supplemented and corrected by regional studies made by Barbara Posadas, Ruben Alcantara, Edwin Almirol, Antonio Pido, and original archival work now being done by Campomanes and others.

9. Although the term "Asian American" as an operational bureaucratic designation is

misleading because of the now widely disparate historical experiences of the groups concerned and tends to covertly privilege one or two of its elements (as in the Modern Language Association surveys cited earlier), Occeña points out that the self-recognition and societal recognition of the peoples involved stem from their integration into U.S. society "on the bases of inequality vis-à-vis whites; subjected to various forms of racial and national discrimination and constituted as an oppressed strata of U.S. society" (29). However, because the Asian and Pacific peoples, from their arrival up to the present, have not amalgamated to form one distinct nationality, it is best to discard the label "Asian American" and use the particular name of each nationality to forestall homogenizing ascriptions like "superminority."

10. Until 1946, Filipinos did not have the right to be naturalized. Nor could they marry whites in California until 1948, or own land until 1956 (Philippine Center, 8–9, 15–16).

11. This trend is discernible in the Flips' statement of identity politics. The Flips mainly descend from the relatively conservative formation of the second wave of Filipino immigrants (about thirty thousand), comprising war veterans enjoying some privileges (Catholic Institute, 41–42). Their code words registering anxiety toward "melting pot" miscegenation are found in phrases like "cathartic stage of ethnic awareness" and "maintaining ethnic awareness." But by juxtaposing inside/outside, they replicate what they want to negate: including the Same/excluding the Other.

12. Although Solberg is correct in pointing out the interdependence of Filipino American writing and indigenous Filipino writing in English, his ascription of a mythmaking function to Bulosan and others (which explains, for instance, Buaken's failure to produce a unified narrative out of his own fragmented life) is misleading since the myth's regime of truth turns out to be a discourse of co-optation as "the Filipino dream of independence fades into the American dream of equality and freedom" (56).

13. Gonzalez's subaltern mentality typically contrives an apologia for the Cordova volume (xi) when he cites the white master's endorsement of his servant: "My servant was a Manilla man." In this way the stereotype of Filipinos in the thirties as "wonderful servants" (Takaki, *Strangers,* 317) is repeated and reinforced.

14. To illumine the deceptive stoicism of Santos's closure in his stories "The Day the Dancers Came" or "Scent of Apples," it would be instructive to compare the ending of J. C. Dionisio's "Cannery Episode" (413), where the narrator captures the discipline and strength of the "Alaskeros" in the face of a horrible mutilation of one of their compatriots. We also find in Pete's character (reflected by the choric narrator) an embodiment of revolt against the inhumane system, a subject position typically absent in Santos's and Gonzalez's fiction.

15. Elaine Kim dismisses Villa as nonethnic (288). Bulosan's judgment of Villa reflects my own earlier polemical evaluation (*Toward a People's Literature,* 73–76). For Bulosan, Villa "is somewhat in line with Baudelaire and Rimbaud, for these two appeared when French poetry had already reached its vortex and was on the downgrade. Naturally they were great apostles of the poetry of decay. When we speak of literature as a continuous tradition, a growing cultural movement, Villa is out of place and time." Villa does not represent "the growth of our literature"; rather, he "expresses a declining culture after it has reached its height" ("Writings," 151).

16. Here I approximate the first mode of incorporation via commodity form that Hebdige outlines (94–96); the ideological mode of incorporation I exemplify in my remarks on Bulosan, Santos, and Villa.

17. Only two out of more than two hundred photos depict Filipinos on strike (pp. 76 and 81). Most are photos of families and relatives of the editor and the kin-related staff of the Demonstration Project. If one compares the text of the section "Alaska Canneries" with a contemporary account of the dismal conditions by Emeterio Cruz, one will notice the textual and iconographic techniques of neutralization and obfuscation deployed by Cordova's album, whose cutoff point is 1963, a revealing date that marks the initiation of radical activism in the Filipino community. In featuring Hilario Moncado (183),

Cordova commits an act of partiality and censorship—one of many—when he fails to mention Moncado's notorious opposition to Filipino workers' demands for justice (Chan, 76, 89).

Cordova's inadequacies include his false generalizations on religion (167) and his eulogy for one million Filipinos who died during World War II for the sake of "Americanism" (221). But these amateurish mistakes descend to unwitting racism when he lumps together inter alia Lincoln, the Lone Ranger, Superman, Charlie Chan, and Martin Luther King Jr. (230).

A similar reservation can be made regarding otherwise instructive documentaries like *In No One's Shadow,* where the cinematic sequence focuses on the normal adjustment of the Filipino immigrant despite all odds. This selective method of fetishizing individual success stories conceals the institutional structures and historical contingencies that qualified and limited such individual lives. The ideology of the image and its system of verisimilitude need to be elucidated and criticized as a determining apparatus producing a deformed Filipino subjectivity ripe for hegemonic reproduction.

18. A modest attempt has been made by the Philippine Center for Immigrant Rights in New York City to revive the example of *Letters in Exile* with the publication of its pamphlet *Filipinos in the USA.* But no major initiative has been taken to organize the Filipino community on the basis of its nationality and its unique response to continuing U.S. domination since the demise of various socialist formations with Filipino leadership in the 1980s.

19. Except for Puerto Ricans. In another essay I argue that the cultural history of the United States cannot be fully inventoried and assayed without registering the symptomatic absence in it of Filipinos and Puerto Ricans as colonized subjects. Operating in the field of American English, the Filipino interruption of U.S. monologism is unique insofar as it demarcates the limits of the imperial episteme, its canonical inscriptions, and its reflexive frame of reference.

20. A play directed by Behn Cervantes, who adapted materials from Virgilio Felipe's M.A. thesis, "What You Like to Know: An Oral History of Bonipasyo," presented in Hawai'i in late 1991. The assimilationist rationale for this event may be perceived from this statement in the program notes: "The Hawai'i [the chief protagonist] was lured to as 'paradise' seems harsh and full of hardships, but is compensated for by Bonipasyo's rightful pride in the conviction that his toil and sacrifice made Hawai'i." Whose Hawai'i?

21. Fermin Tobera, a twenty-two-year-old worker, was killed during the anti-Filipino riot in Watsonville, California, on January 22, 1930; his body was interred in the Philippines on February 2, marked as "National Humiliation Day" (Quinsaat, 55, 57; for a contemporary estimate of the Watsonville situation, see Buaken, 97–107). Silme Domingo and Gene Viernes were anti-Marcos union activists and officials of the International Longshore and Warehousemen's Union, Local 37, in Seattle, Washington, whose 1952 *Yearbook* Bulosan edited. They were slain on June 1, 1981, by killers hired by pro-Marcos elements and corrupt union operatives. Union sympathizers alleged that the FBI and the CIA were involved in this affair.

22. By "anticanon," I mean a mode of resisting standardization by the dominant Euro-American ideology and by the conservative aura of a comprador-bourgeois Filipino tradition. On the problematic of the canon, I have consulted Weimann, Guillory, and Scholes.

23. Berger inflects the theme of exile in this century of banishment by suggesting that "only worldwide solidarity can transcend modern homelessness" (67).

REFERENCES

Adorno, Theodor. "Lyric-Poetry and Society." *Telos* 20 (summer 1974): 56–71.
Alquizola, Marilyn. "The Fictive Narrator of *America Is in the Heart.*" In *Frontiers in Asian American Studies,* ed. Gail Nomura. Pullman: Washington State University Press, 1989.

Ancheta, Shirley, et al., eds. *Without Names.* San Francisco: Kearney Street Workshop, 1985.

Balibar, Etienne, and Pierre Macherey. "On Literature as Ideological Form." In *Untying the Text,* ed. Robert Young. New York: Routledge and Kegan Paul, 1981.

Berger, John. *And Our Faces, My Heart, Brief as Photos.* New York: Pantheon, 1984.

Bock, Deborah, ed. *Pearls.* Springfield, Va.: Educational Film Center, 1979.

Bruchac, Joseph, ed. *Breaking Silence: An Anthology of Contemporary Asian American Poets.* Greenfield Center, N.Y.: Greenfield Review Press, 1983.

Buaken, Manuel. *I Have Lived with the American People.* Caldwell, Idaho: Caxton Printers, 1948.

Bulosan, Carlos. *America Is in the Heart.* 1946. Seattle: University of Washington Press, 1973.

———. *If You Want to Know What We Are.* Minneapolis: West End Press, 1983.

———. *The Laughter of My Father.* New York: Harcourt, 1944.

———. *The Power of the People.* 1977. Manila: National Book Store, 1986.

———. "Writings of Carlos Bulosan." *Amerasia Journal* (special issue) 6, no. 1 (May 1979).

Cabezas, Amado, and Gary Kawaguchi. "Race, Gender and Class for Filipino Americans." In *A Look Beyond the Model Minority Image,* ed. Grace Yun. New York: Minority Rights Group, 1989.

Campomanes, Oscar. "Filipinos in the U.S.A. and Their Literature of Exile." In *Reading the Literatures of Asian America,* ed. S. Lim and A. Ling. Philadelphia: Temple University Press, 1992.

Casper, Leonard. "Introduction." In Bienvenido Santos, *Scent of Apples.* Seattle: University of Washington Press, 1979.

Catholic Institute for International Relations. *The Labor Trade.* London: CIIR, 1987.

Chan, Sucheng. *Asian Americans.* Boston: Twayne, 1991.

Cheung, King-kok, and Stan Yogi, eds. *Asian American Literature.* New York: Modern Language Association, 1988.

Constantino, Renato. "The Miseducation of the Filipino." In *The Filipinos in the Philippines and Other Essays.* Quezon City: Malaya Books, 1966. Also in *The Philippines Reader,* ed. D. B. Schirmer and Stephen Shalom. Boston: South End Press, 1987.

Cordova, Fred. *Filipinos: Forgotten Asian Americans.* Dubuque, Iowa: Kendall Hunt, 1983.

Cruz, Emeterio. "Filipino Life in the Alaskan Fish Canneries." *Philippine Magazine* 30 (June 1933): 25, 34–36.

Deleuze, Gilles, and Félix Guattari. *Kafka: Toward a Minor Literature.* Minneapolis: University of Minnesota Press, 1986.

———. *A Thousand Plateaus: Capitalism and Schizophrenia.* Minneapolis: University of Minnesota Press, 1987.

Deutsch, Babette. "Critical Essay." In *Poems 55,* by Jose Garcia Villa. Manila: Alberto Florentino, 1962.

Dionisio, J. C. "Cannery Episode." *Philippine Magazine,* August 1936, 397, 412–413.

Feleo-Gonzalez, Marina. *A Song For Manong.* Daly City, Calif.: Likha Promotions, 1988.

Fuchs, Lawrence H. *The American Kaleidoscope.* Hanover and London: University Press of New England, 1991.

Gonzalez, N.V.M. "The Long Harvest." *Midweek,* 23 May 1990, 25–26, 28.

Guillory, John. "Canon." In *Critical Terms for Literary Study,* ed. Frank Lentricchia and Thomas McLaughlin. Chicago: University of Chicago Press, 1990.

Hagedorn, Jessica. *Dogeaters.* New York: Pantheon, 1989.

Hebdige, Dick. *Subculture: The Meaning of Style.* London: Methuen, 1979.

Kim, Elaine. *Asian American Literature.* Philadelphia: Temple University, Press, 1982.

Kolko, Gabriel. *Main Currents in Modern American History.* New York: Pantheon, 1976.

Kristeva, Julia. *Strangers to Ourselves.* New York. Columbia University Press, 1991.

Kunitz, Stanley, ed. *Twentieth Century Authors.* New York: H. W. Wilson, 1955.

Lauter, Paul, et al., eds. *The Heath Anthology of American Literature.* Boston: D. C. Heath, 1990.

McWilliams, Carey. *Brothers under the Skin.* Boston: Little, Brown, 1964.

———. "Introduction. " In Carlos Bulosan, *America Is in the Heart.* Seattle: University of Washington Press, 1973. vii–xxiv.

Melendy, H. Brett. *Asians in America.* 1977. New York: Hippocrene Books, 1981.

———. "Filipinos." In *Harvard Encyclopedia of American Ethnic Groups.* Cambridge, Mass.: Harvard University Press, 1980. 354–362.

Navarro, Jovina, ed. *Diwang Pilipino.* Davis, Calif.: Asian American Studies, 1974.

Nee, Victor, and Jimy Sanders. "The Road to Parity: Determinants of the Socioeconomic Achievements of Asian Americans." *Ethnic and Racial Studies* 8, no. 1 (January 1985): 75–93.

O'Brien, Edward J. "Introduction." In Jose Garcia Villa, *Footnote to Youth.* New York: Scribner's, 1933.

Occeña, Bruce. "The Filipino Nationality in the U.S.: An Overview." *Line of March* (fall 1958): 29–41.

O'Hare, William P., and Judy C. Felt. *Asian Americans: America's Fastest Growing Minority Group.* Washington, D.C.: Population Reference Bureau, 1991.

Palumbo-Liu, David. "Model Minority Discourse and the Course of Healing." Forthcoming in *Minority Discourse: Ideological Containment and Utopian/Heterotopian Potential,* ed. Abdul JanMohamed.

Penaranda, Oscar, Serafin Syquia, and Sam Tagatac. "An Introduction to Filipino-American Literature." In *Aiiieeeee! An Anthology of Asian-American Writers,* ed. Frank Chin, Jeffery Paul Chan, Lawson Fusao Inada, and Shawn Wong. Washington, D.C.: Howard University Press, 1983.

Philippine Center for Immigrant Rights. *Filipinos in the USA.* New York: Philcir, 1985.

Pido, Antonio. *The Pilipinos in America.* New York: Center for Migration Studies, 1986.

Quinsaat, Jesse, ed. *Letters in Exile.* Los Angeles: UCLA Asian American Studies Center, 1976.

Ruoff, A. LaVonne Brown, and Jerry Ward Jr., eds. *Redefining American Literary History.* New York: Modern Language Association, 1990.

Said, Edward. "Reflections on Exile." In *Out There: Marginalization and Contemporary Culture,* ed. Russell Ferguson et al. New York: New Museum of Contemporary Art, 1990.

San Juan, E. "Beyond Identity Politics: The Predicament of the Asian American Writer in Late Capitalism." *American Literary History* 3, no. 3 (fall 1991): 542–565.

———. *Bulosan: An Introduction with Selections.* Manila: National Book Store, 1983.

———. *Carlos Bulosan and the Imagination of the Class Struggle.* New York: Oriole Editions, 1972.

———. *Crisis in the Philippines.* South Hadley, Mass.: Bergin & Garvey, 1986.

———. "Mapping the Boundaries: The Filipino Writer in the U.S.A." *Journal of Ethnic Studies* 19, no. 1 (spring 1991): 117–131.

———. *Racial Formations/Critical Transformations.* Atlantic Highlands, N.J.: Humanities Press, 1992.

———. *Reading the West/Writing the East.* New York: Peter Lang, 1992.

———. *Toward a People's Literature.* Quezon City: University of the Philippines Press, 1984.

Santos, Bienvenido. *Scent of Apples.* Seattle: University of Washington Press, 1979.

Scharlin, Craig, and Lilia Villanueva. *Philip Vera Cruz: A Personal History of Filipino Immigrants and the Farmworkers Movement.* Los Angeles: UCLA Asian American Center, 1992.

Scholes, Robert. "Canonicity and Textuality." In *Introduction to Scholarship in Modern Languages and Literatures,* ed. Joseph Gibaldi. New York: Modern Language Association, 1992.

Skinner, Michelle Cruz. *Balikbayan: A Filipino Homecoming.* Honolulu: Bess Press, 1988.

Solberg, S. E. "An Introduction to Filipino American Literature." In *Aiiieeeee! An Anthology of Asian-American Writers,* ed. Frank Chin, Jeffery Paul Chan, Lawson Fusao Inada, and Shawn Wong. Washington, D.C.: Howard University Press, 1983.

Sollors, Werner. *Beyond Ethnicity.* New York: Oxford University Press, 1986.

Somera, Rene. "Between Two Worlds: The Hawai'i Ilocano Immigrant Experience." *Diliman Review* (January–February 1982): 54–59.

Stanley, Peter. "The *Manongs* of California." *Philippine U.S. Free Press,* November 1985, 4,7–8, 45.

Stegner, Wallace. *One Nation.* Boston: Houghton Mifflin, 1945.

Takaki, Ronald, ed. *From Different Shores.* New York: Oxford University Press, 1987.

————. *Strangers from a Different Shore.* Boston: Little, Brown, 1989.

Villa, Jose Garcia. *Footnote to Youth.* New York: Scribner's, 1933.

Villanueva, Marianne. *Ginseng and Other Tales from Manila.* Corvallis, Ore.: Calyx Books, 1991.

Wand, David Hsin-Fu, ed. *Asian American Heritage.* New York: Washington Square Press, 1974.

Weimann, Robert. *Structure and Society in Literary History.* Baltimore: Johns Hopkins University Press, 1984.

THE FICTION OF
ASIAN AMERICAN LITERATURE

Susan Koshy

Epistemology is true as long as it accounts for the impossibility of its own beginning and lets itself be driven at every stage by its inadequacy to the things themselves. It is, however, untrue in the pretension that success is at hand and that states of affairs would ever simply correspond to its constructions and aporetic concepts.

THEODOR W. ADORNO

ASIAN AMERICAN LITERATURE: INSTITUTIONAL LEGACIES

The boundaries of what constitutes Asian American literature have been periodically interrogated and revised, but its validity as an ordering rubric has survived these debates and repeatedly been salvaged by pointing to some existing or imminent stage of ethnogenesis, in which its representational logic would be manifest. Inherent in more recent definitions of the term has been the practice of a strategic deferral—an invocation of the work of culture-building that the debates themselves perform, and through which Asian American identity and its concomitant literature would come into being. Unlike African American, Native American, or Chicano literature, Asian American literature inhabits the highly unstable temporality of the "about-to-be," its meanings continuously reinvented after the arrival of new groups of immigrants and the enactment of legislative changes.[1] However, the tactic of deferral in the interests of institutional consolidation has had its costs, and it is these costs that this essay will consider.

The affirmation of ethnic identity as a means of political and institutional space-claiming, and the very newness of the field (which originated in the late sixties), have deferred questions about its founding premises. But it is precisely this question, "How are we to conceptualize Asian American literature taking into account the radical disjunctions in the emergence of the field?" that it has now become historically and politically most urgent to ask, because of pressures both inside and outside the community. The radical demographic shifts produced within the Asian American community by the 1965 immigration laws have transformed the nature and locus of literary production, creating a highly stratified, uneven, and heterogeneous formation that cannot easily be contained within the models of essentialized or pluralized ethnic identity suggested by the rubric Asian American literature, or its updated postmodern avatar Asian American literatures.[2] Moreover, we have entered a transnational era where ethnicity is increasingly produced at multiple local and global sites rather than, as before, within the parameters of the nation-state. This dispersal of ethnic identity has been intensified, in the case of Americans of Asian origin, by dramatic geopolitical realignments under way in the Pacific, that have reshaped the political imaginaries of "Asia" and "America" and the conjunctions between these two entities. Asian American literary production takes place within and participates in this transformed political and cultural landscape. Asian American Studies is, however, only just beginning to undertake a theoretical investigation of these changes, rendering itself peripheral to the developments inside its constituent group. Instead of an engagement with the new critical forces shaping its interdisciplinary project, much of the scholarship in the field has either continued to rely on paradigms of ethnicity produced in the inaugural moment of the field, or has sought to incorporate the changes through the fashionable but derivative vocabulary of postmodernism, postcolonialism, or poststructuralism; formulaic invocations of "multiculturalism," "hybridity," "plural identities," or "border-crossing" are used promiscuously without any effort to link them to the material, cultural, or historical specificities of the various Asian American experiences. Although substantial historical scholarship has been produced, the field has been weak in theoretical work, especially when compared to Chicano, Native American, and African American Studies. The lack of significant theoretical work has affected its development and its capacity to address the stratifications and differences that constitute its distinctness within ethnic studies.

I will substantiate these arguments by reviewing the interpretive methods adopted thus far in delineating the boundaries of Asian American literature. I will do this by examining three paradigmatic attempts to discuss what constitutes Asian American literature, and analyzing the methodological problems and impasses revealed in these critical works: Frank Chin's Preface and Introduction to *Aiiieeeee! An Anthology of Asian-American Writers* (1974); Elaine Kim's full-length study *Asian American Literature: An Introduction to the Writings and Their Social Context* (1982), and her shorter essay on the subject, "Defining Asian American Realities Through Literature" (1987); and two essays by Shirley Geok-lin Lim: "Twelve Asian American Writers: In Search of Self-Definition" (1990), and "Assaying the Gold: Or, Contesting the Ground of Asian American Literature" (1993).[3] The methodological problems in these essays partake of larger historical/political and institutional legacies: the inadequacy of the pluralistic idiom of inclusion to confront the contradictions and heterogeneities within the field; the tensions between the formulation of a political identity and the critical task of situating the heterogeneity of ethnic literary production; the risks of archival recovery of ethnic texts without adequate theoretical and comparative work on the various literatures that constitute the field; and finally, the failure to come to terms with the scope and transformative impact of transnationalism on Asian American ethnicity. As an Asian American and a scholar in the field, I feel our most urgent task is to engage these problems theoretically and generate new conceptual frames that work in the interests of social change.

One of the major preoccupations in the field of Asian American literature has thus far been in documenting and compiling a rapidly expanding corpus, both through the recovery of older, neglected writers[4] and through the incorporation of new writers from the established and from the less-known immigrant groups from Korea, Southeast Asia, and South Asia. Since the official categorization of some of these groups under the designation "Asian American" is as recent as 1980 when, for instance, Asian Indians—classified since 1950 as "other white"—lobbied for and won reclassification in the census, the work of compilation is obviously one of urgency within the field. Moreover, the recognition ethnicity has recently accrued within an academy anxiously reconstituting its American canon has led to an increase in courses, job openings, and student interest in this emergent field. Hence the proliferation of anthologies and bibliographies within the field bringing together the range of primary source material in order to meet this recent surge in demand.[5] But if the expansion of the field proceeds at this pace, without a more substantial theoretical investigation of the premises and assumptions underlying our constructions of commonality and difference, we run the risk of unwittingly annexing the newer literary productions within older paradigms, overlooking radical disjunctions within more established formations like Chinese and Japanese American literature, and perpetuating hierarchies within the field.

The pluralism of inclusion, while appropriate for the task of building what Alastair Fowler has defined as the "potential canon" or "the entire written corpus, together with all surviving oral literature," can only fulfill a short-term, though crucial, purpose.[6] I share with John Guillory a suspicion of a "liberal consensus whose name is 'pluralism' and whose pedagogic agenda has been exhausted in the gesture of 'opening the canon.'"[7] Pluralism offers us a means of expanding the potential canon, certainly, but as Werner Sollors has noted, this expansion is undertaken in the name of the very categories through which exclusion formerly operated; the pluralist method thus always carries the danger of reifying the categories canonical change should work to transform.[8] Sollors offers some necessary cautions about the "mosaic procedure" that organizes many anthologies of ethnic literature: "The published results of this mosaic procedure are the readers and compendiums made up of diverse essays on groups of ethnic writers who may have little in common except so-called ethnic roots while, at the same time, obvious and important literary and cultural connections are obfuscated." The latest Asian American anthologies (even more so than the earlier ones) cannot even assume the existence of common ethnic roots, since they work to include the writings of as many of their different constituent groups as possible. Moreover, since the category Asian American is itself so novel, and has undergone such radical changes of meaning in a very short while, its value as an organizing framework for literary production is much more problematic than even Sollors's generalized critique would suggest. If the theoretical challenge posed by the nomenclature is met with the assertion of an outmoded identity politics, or the more recent trend toward the postulation of a nebulous pan-Asian American consciousness, we risk repressing important connections between Asian and Asian American literature and misconceiving the dynamic, nomadic, and dispersed nature of ethnogenesis in a transnational era, in the interests of recuperating a fictional notion of unity.

Although Shirley Lim has confidently asserted that "the pluralizing 's' which does not appear in discussions of Asian American literature is everywhere today assumed when critics discuss the emerging shape of Asian American literary studies" ("CGA," 162), I would argue, first, that such tacit acknowledgments do not relieve us of responsibility for theoretical articulations of the multiple, conflicted, and emergent formations that constitute Asian American literature, and second, that critical work which proceeds in the absence of such theoretical delineations avoids one of the major challenges facing the field today, namely, to examine the impact of the recent demographic and geopolitical changes on the reconstitution of ethnicity among all the Asian American groups. The pluralism Lim invokes merely offers an "additive approach," when what we need is a transformation of the paradigms ("CP," 276). Elaine Kim's *Asian American Literature: An Introduction to the Writings and Their Social Context,* which focuses on the writings of Chinese, Japanese, Filipino, and Korean Americans, was an invaluable contribution in its time, but now offers an obsolete mapping of the field. It remains, to date, the only book-length study that attempts to treat Asian American literature as a whole. Most other critical work offers thematic, sociohistorical, or rhetorical analyses of individual texts, authors, or ethnic groups focusing on generational narratives, assimilation, motifs of resistance or feminist emergence, or the challenge to stereotypes or cliches.

SHIFTING BOUNDARIES OF ASIAN AMERICAN ETHNICITY

What makes the category "Asian American" so complex is that it has undergone reconfiguration more rapidly and to a greater extent than any of the other ethnic categories have. A brief summary will help elucidate this. The following account provides merely an overview: it is not intended to delineate exhaustively the many shifts, nuances, and disjunctures in the historical constitution of Asian Americans. There are legitimate differences of interpretation over the content and significance of each pattern; however, such differences and debates are beyond the scope of my concerns here. Broadly speaking, then, one can chart five different historical patterns of ethnicity formation.

(1) From the mid-nineteenth century to World War II, ethnicity was shaped by policies of containment and exclusion that the various Asian national groups encountered on their arrival in the United States.[9] Economic competition and racist ideologies triggered the hostility of the white working class, particularly on the West Coast, leading to the passage of exclusionary immigration laws that were enacted first against the Chinese, then against the Japanese, Indians, and Filipinos, barring their entry into the country.[10] In the late nineteenth and early twentieth centuries, more than 600 pieces of anti-Asian legislation were passed limiting or denying Asians' access to housing, education, intermarriage, employment, and land ownership.[11] Immigration

laws limiting the entry of women, laws against miscegenation, and harsh, nomadic working conditions produced among Chinese, Indians, and Filipinos bachelor communities with such a skewed gender ratio that the communities were unable to reproduce themselves.[12]

The status of the various Asian national groups within the United States fluctuated historically, since it depended in part on the relations between the United States and the respective home governments. However, all the Asian groups posed the threat of economic competition domestically, and thus, as employers recruited new groups of Asians to fill the vacuum created by the exclusion of others, the hostility of nativist workers was redirected against the newcomers.

Legislative policies of exclusion and containment shaped the contours of the early Asian immigrant communities, as did the loyalties and allegiances of the various immigrant groups. Each of the groups identified itself by regional or national origin, and often occupied ethnic enclaves that reinforced these associations. Frequently, patterns of labor recruitment created narrow and cohesive subnational identities: most of the earliest Chinese immigrants were from Guangdong province, the Japanese laborers were primarily from four prefectures in Japan, and the Indian workers were predominantly from three districts in Punjab. Although the earliest Korean immigrants were more heterogeneous in origin, religious affinities did exist among them: 40 percent were Christian. Among Filipinos, 90 percent were Catholic (*SFD*, 31–62). Language barriers and the existence of strong national rivalries in their home countries often led the different Asian ethnic groups to actively dissociate from each other. Despite their sense of cultural distinctiveness, however, in the popular imagination Asians were commonly identified as "Orientals" or "Asiatics" and were seen as sharing physical and psychological attributes.

(2) The next historical shift in ethnic formation took place between World War II and the beginning of the protest movements of the sixties.[13] This period produced significant changes in the composition, status, and boundaries of Asian American communities. The alignments of the war redefined the relationships of the various Asian national groups to each other and to the United States. With World War II, Chinese and Filipino Americans found themselves viewed as favored allies; the enmity Korean Americans had long felt toward their colonizers, the Japanese, suddenly coincided with public sentiment; Asian Indians gained public consideration because of their country's strategic importance to Allied plans to block the Japanese advancement westward.[14] For Japanese Americans, however, Pearl Harbor was a wrenching, isolating, and harrowing experience: they were classified as "enemy aliens," interned, and their communities on the West Coast destroyed.

The war against Nazism overseas and the need to combat Japanese propaganda calling for a pan-Asian alliance to fight Euro-American racism made impossible the continuance of discriminatory practices and immigration laws. Consequently, the conditions of Asian Americans improved significantly. Restrictions on housing, employment, land ownership, naturalization, and miscegenation were gradually lifted. Furthermore, changes in immigration law allowed for the revitalization and augmentation of declining ethnic communities. Immigration from the Philippines, China, and India was re-opened, although severely restricted. However, loopholes in the law and the passage of the 1948 Displaced Persons Act and the 1953 Refugee Relief Act increased the number of immigrants. Most importantly, the War Brides Act, which allowed Asian wives and children of U.S. servicemen to enter on a non-quota basis, substantially increased the size of ethnic communities and created a more balanced gender ratio. Most immigrants entering at this time were women. The Chinese American community tripled in size between 1940 and 1960; for other groups the changes were less dramatic, but important. The Korean War also prompted a new wave of immigration from that country. Illegal immigration was prevalent among all groups, but most significant among Chinese Americans; in fact, the Border Patrol, now associated in the public consciousness with Mexican Americans, was established to combat illegal Chinese entries (*MRA,* 74).

While the 1940s focused public antagonism on Japanese Americans, the anti-Communist witch-hunts of the 1950s shifted attention to Chinese Americans. Raids, deportations, surveillance, and the implementation of a Confession Program (involving information gathering and loyalty tests) fractured and terrorized the Chinese American community. In Ronald Takaki's succinct formulation: "The new peril was seen as yellow in race and red in ideology" (*SFD,* 415).

(3) The identity category "Asian American" was a product of the struggles of the 1960s but has been used to organize and interpret this set of immigrant experiences retrospectively and prospectively. The struggles of the 1960s also led to the establishment of the academic discipline of Asian American Studies. The term "Asian American" emerged in the context of civil rights, Third World, and anti-Vietnam war movements and was self-consciously adopted (in preference to "Oriental" or "Yellow") primarily on university campuses where the Asian American Movement enjoyed the broadest support.[15] The opening up of higher education and the demographic changes of the postwar years made possible, for the first time, the presence of Japanese, Filipino, and Chinese American students in significant numbers on some university campuses. From these beginnings, the term "Asian American" has passed into academic and bureaucratic, and thence into popular usage.

The Asian American Movement was pivotal in creating a pan-Asian identity politics that represented their "unequal circumstances and histories as being related."[16] Asian American was a political subject position formulated to make visible a history of exclusion and discrimination against immigrants of Asian origin. This identity was then extended to represent the interests and circumstances of a very different group of Asian newcomers, who were entering the country with the change in immigration laws in 1965, and were destined to alter radically the demographic make-up of the constituency into which they were incorporated.

(4) The next pattern of ethnic formation emerged with the change in immigration laws in 1965 and extended to the end of the next decade. During the Cold War, the U.S. claim to world leadership in the name of democracy and justice created pressure for changes in immigration policies that would place Asians on an equal footing with Europeans. Simultaneously, the Civil Rights Movement intensified domestic and international awareness of and opposition to racial discrimination. The passage of the 1965 immigration laws was a result of these combined internal and external pressures. The new laws allowed for an annual quota of 20,000 from each Asian country and the reunification of immediate family members on a non-quota basis. As a result, Asian Americans, who were under 1 percent of the U.S. population in 1965, increased to 2.8 percent in 1990, and are projected at 10.1 percent by 2050, making them the fastest growing minority group in the country. Japanese Americans, who made up the largest group in 1960 representing 47 percent of the Asian American population, have declined rapidly to third position in the 1990 census (11.7 percent), barely ahead of Asian Indians (11.2 percent) and Korean Americans (10.9 percent). Chinese Americans make up the largest group in the 1990 Census (23 percent), closely followed by Filipino Americans (19 percent).[17] The influx of newer groups has further diversified the identity of Asian Americans. After 1975, large numbers of Vietnamese, Lao, Hmong, Mien, and Cambodians entered the United States as refugees. In the 1980 census, immigrants from India lobbied for and won reclassification from the "other white" category to Asian Indian.

The arrival of new immigrants after 1965 has transformed the group from a predominantly American-born constituency to a group that is 65 percent foreign-born.[18] The new immigrants carry strong homeland identifications, speak many different languages, practice various religions, and have a multiplicity of political affiliations. Some of the recent immigrants, especially Chinese and Indians, are part of "second phase migrations" arriving in the United States not from their countries of origin, but from Chinese diasporas in Singapore, Malaysia, and Cambodia or Indian diasporas in Uganda, Surinam, Fiji, or Trinidad. Even when joining older groups, the newer immigrants add layers of class difference: whereas many of the earlier Chinese, Filipino, and Indian immigrants were nonliterate laborers, the new arrivals from these groups include large numbers of middle-class professionals. The incorporation of such diverse groups within the notion of an Asian American identity has proved very difficult, since their arrival has profoundly destabilized the formation. Highlighting the ironies of the new immigration, B. O. Hing, an Asian American leader, observes: "The success of one thing that we have fought for, namely, fair and equal immigration policies, has institutionalized a system which keeps us in constant flux" (quoted in *AAP*, 95). Hing's comments overlook a further stratification in the constituency produced by the substantial number of Asians who are entering the country illegally, and are subsequently trapped within the most exploitative conditions of existence as workers in sweatshops, restaurants, and brothels. This destabilization of the Asian American constituency has been engaged within the discipline primarily through the rhetoric of pluralism. Once we include the experiences of all the constituent groups, it is reasoned, the representational logic of the rubric will become apparent. Furthermore, the conventional wisdom goes, the dissemination of a pan-Asian consciousness will eventually unify the various Asian groups.

(5) The fifth and latest historical pattern of ethnic identity formation has emerged in the last decade or so, and the scripts it has produced have further transformed the constituency we refer to as Asian America. This shift has been initiated by the reconfiguration of aspects of ethnicity within a transnational context. During this period, relations between the United States and Asia have undergone dramatic change and we have entered a transnational era that is remaking economic, political, and cultural relations in the Pacific. As a result, ethnicity can no longer be solely contextualized within the problematic of whether and how Asian Americans will be incorporated into the American body politic, but must also be read through the deterritorialization of ethnic identity. This transformation has begun to be engaged within the discipline, but is generally treated as a product or added feature of the fourth pattern, and addressed, if at all, through the overstrained and inadequate vocabulary of pluralism. The remaking of aspects of Asian American ethnicity during this period will be the subject of the last section of my essay. In historicizing these developments, I do not mean to imply that they are linear or progressive in their emergence; older formations often nest inside newer identity formations, or are unevenly developed across and within generations or ethnic groups. Certain patterns may be more significant in the experience of some groups than others. It is precisely because of the discontinuities and stratifications produced during these different periods that the concept of Asian American identity becomes such a complex one. The rhetoric and tropes that have been generated within the discipline to address or contain these differentiations, including the founding rubric of the discipline, are breaking under the strain of representing such heterogeneity. In the face of the staggering diversity of these emergent formations, interpellated by the transition from ethnicity to panethnicity, occupying differential positions in the vast imaginaries called "Asia," "America," and "Asian America," we face the theoretical challenge of constructing and examining our literatures and histories, without erasing our differences and conflicts.

D EFINING THE L ITERATURE: T HE A RITHMETIC OF I NCLUSION

In this section I will examine three paradigmatic discussions of Asian American literature. Each of them attempts to map the field of Asian American literary production, and the boundaries they draw reveal the political temper of their historical moment, as well as the defining forces within the field of Asian American Studies. It is, therefore, critical to examine these attempts as definitive moments in the development of the field. Despite the progressively greater "inclusiveness" that marks the efforts of these different critics, the practice of an additive approach leaves unresolved, and even obscures, fundamental theoretical questions about the rubric as an enunciatory and interpretive category. For Chin and Kim, Chinese American and Japanese American literature forms the core of the field, the source of the tropes, themes, and paradigms of ethnicity that constitute the literature. For all three critics, "other" Asian American literatures (Filipino, Korean, South Asian, Southeast Asian) are added on as auxiliary formations in deference to numerical ratios, the changing census classifications, or the critic's own ethnic affiliation; or incorporated through the free-floating idioms of postmodernism (multiplicity, hybridity) that lack any historical specificity or cultural thickness. To use numbers as a gauge of our ability to integrate various literary traditions is fundamentally fallacious; it offers the palliative of inclusion without requiring any serious theoretical engagement with analyzing the grounds of our commonality/ differences. The certainty and precision of numbers assume the power within critical discourse of signifying integration and coverage: note the rhetorical echoes in Shirley Lim's title "Twelve Asian American Writers: In Search of Self-Definition," or Jessica Hagedorn's insistence in her recent anthology, *Charlie Chan Is Dead*, that her inclusion of forty-eight different writers is an index of her commitment to the meanings of contemporary Asian American fiction.

In choosing these particular critical texts for analysis, I am attempting to investigate the modalities of primary definition. As a result, the concern of the essay is not to provide a comprehensive survey of all the participants in these debates, but to examine some of the influential ones. Furthermore, I am not suggesting that all these efforts were part of a self-conscious, individual, or collaborative effort to shape and authorize an Asian American literary canon. Canon-formation does not take place through a single referendum but is rather the product, as Barbara Herrnstein Smith's deft summary indicates, "of a series of continuous interactions among a variably constituted object, emergent conditions, and the mechanisms of cultural selection and transmission."[19] Within a new field like Asian American literary studies, certain emergent conditions and mechanisms of cultural transmission have exercised a critical influence over the definition of Asian American literature. Firstly, the pace of production of critical and theoretical statements about the writings has lagged well behind the prolific production of anthologies of Asian American literature. This is, in part, because significant scholarly energy has been directed toward editing and introducing the works of individual or groups of Asian American authors. This practice of what Wendell Harris has called "fortunate sponsorship" has almost become a cottage industry in the field (112). Certainly, some degree of effort in sponsoring the work of newer or unfamiliar writers is constructive in an emergent field, but it cannot assume a disproportionate importance, nor can the task be discharged through biographical summary or thematic observations on the texts, the favored modes in many introductions. One of the consequences of this prioritization of scholarly activity has been a theoretical weakness within the field.[20] When this problem is compounded by other conditions like the status of Asian American literature as an emergent field, and the enormous demand among readers and teachers of American literature for guidance in interpreting this literature, it becomes clearer why the influence of the few critical texts to undertake an analysis of the entire field has been so great. Thus, often inadvertently, these evaluations have assumed a canon-forming power. Moreover, it has become commonplace in the discipline for even leading scholars to refer to Chinese and Japanese American texts as the "canonical" Asian American texts and to refer to other Asian American texts as "marginal," "peripheral," or "emergent" Asian American literatures. It is thus not so much a canon, but a phantom canon that the analysis of the following works will reveal.

The category "Asian American literature" gained recognition with the publication of several anthologies in the 1970s, among which Frank Chin's offers the most polemical and influential elaboration of Asian American literature. Chin's anthology was published in the aftermath of the Asian American Movement of the 1960s and works from many of its ideological premises: that the separate circumstances of Asian ethnic groups are linked by a common history of exclusion and racism, that the myth of assimilation has been used to neutralize ethnic resistance and deny racial stratification, and that an assertive identity politics can be the basis of challenging Anglo hegemony. Chin's anthology works aggressively to enunciate and promote an Asian American identity that is independent of the determinations of white supremacy, and the search for autonomy leads him to formulate such authenticity in purist and separatist terms. He distinguishes between "real" Asian Americans who are "American born and raised, who got their China and Japan from the radio, off the silver screen, from television, out of comic books, from the pushers of white American culture" and "Americanized Asians," first-generation immigrants who maintain strong cultural ties to their countries of origin while fulfilling the subservient stereotype of the humble and passive Oriental (*AA*, vii). The authentic Asian American is here defined as a prototypical No-No Boy[21]: a political subject who says no to Asia, no to America, and is decidedly male.[22] Paradoxically, in order to claim an Asian American identity in defiance of hegemonic codifications, Chin is led to disclaim connections with Asia. He focuses on the domestic context of ethnic identity formation and on generational distance from Asia. Clearly, Chin's rejection of the Asian part of his identity is an effort to repudiate the prevailing stereotype of Asians as perpetual foreigners in America, and to affirm the experiences of the many Asians in America at this time, who are several generations removed from the homeland experience. But this formulation is vitiated by its obsession with the white gaze.

Chin's Introduction also put in place the idea of an essential Asian American identity, derived from the experiences and narratives of American-born Chinese and Japanese Americans, which he names "the Asian American sensibility" (*AA*, ix). This notion has long survived Chin's anthology and often functions as a founding assumption in other discussions in Asian American Studies, often despite critics' heated disagreement with Chin's other views. Recent discussions of Asian American Literature (including Kim's and Lim's) have taken issue with Chin's antifeminist and anti-immigrant postulations of Asian American literature; however, in their privileging of Chinese and Japanese American texts, and their inability to theorize the relationship between the newer and older formations, they inadvertently reproduce his framework. Even the current shift to the use of the plural *literatures* usually functions as a semantic cover for the continued reliance on essentialist paradigms through a token acknowledgment of the need for change. But the theorizing of this change is deferred—described as being beyond the scope of the current project, or reassuringly projected as being likely to be undertaken by others in the field. When such practices of deferral are accompanied by a tendency to group-specific research undertaken by "insiders" that eschews any comparative or theoretical work, the cumulative effect is a theoretical weakness in our conceptualization of the field as a whole.

Elaine Kim's discussion of Asian American literature increases the number of groups covered, by adding Korean American literature to Chin's list of Chinese, Japanese, and Filipino American texts, but this expansion of the field seems arbitrarily based on the accident of ethnic affiliation rather than on any critical or literary criteria. As Kim admits in a later retrospective evaluation of her exclusion of South and Southeast Asian literatures from her study:

> I admitted at the time that this definition was arbitrary, prompted by my own inability to read Asian languages and my own lack of access to South and Southeast Asian communities. But for these shortcomings, I wrote, I would have included in my introductory study works written in Asian languages and works written by writers from Vietnamese American, Indian American, and other communities. Nonetheless, it is true that I wanted to delineate and draw boundaries around *whatever I thought of as* Asian American identity and literature. (*CC,* viii; italics added)

The carte blanche Kim accorded her own decisions on defining Asian American literature is evidence of the degree of cultural authority that sometimes attaches to insiderism, and which, unchecked by vigilant scrutiny and challenge, can operate in powerfully exclusionary forms.[23]

The focus in Kim's analysis, as in Chin's, is on positing a literature that is expressive of the Asian American experience understood as sociologically distinct, separate from the mainstream, and shaped by settlement in the United States and the effects of American racism. But since Kim rejects Chin's central distinction between "real" and "fake" Asian American sensibilities—the crucial idea of authenticity that demarcates the boundaries of the Chin tradition—her definition of the literature incorporates the writings of first-generation immigrants and sojourners, which Chin had dismissed as the ventriloquist production of white racism. Instead of the notion of authenticity or "cultural integrity," Kim opts for an organizing framework that is chronological. Projecting the idea of a linear evolutionary pattern onto the emergence of Asian American identity allows her to claim a constitutive logic to the rubric "Asian American literature." Her projections of such a development are tentative but hopeful: "Distinctions among the various national groups sometimes do blur after a generation or two, when it is easier for us to see what we share as members of an American racial minority" (*AIW,* xii). Focusing on chronological emergence allows her to shift the emphasis from the internal stratifications and differences within Asian American literature to a unity-in-the-making. Moreover, such a formulation not only fails to recognize the differential and uneven insertion of the various national groups into America by locating them in the same progressive march toward greater unity, it also fails to account for the fact that the increasing racial diversity of Asian Americans disallows any easy assumption of a unifying racial identity.

In her later essay, Kim also argues that a broad thematic concern "claiming America" characterizes the writing ("DA," 88). Methodologically, the study seems to be straining to construct a notion of commonality. The purported commonality is so broad as to be inclusive of other ethnic literatures, even though it is described as unique to Asian American literature. Another effect of the thematic criteria she introduces is to suture the quite disparate productions of Filipino and Korean Americans to Asian American literature by repressing the historical contexts of colonization, exile, and postcolonial modernization that render their representation as local, American-based literatures much more problematic than in the case of earlier Chinese or Japanese American literature. The unique specificities of the colonial relationship between the United States and the Philippines, the topos of return that haunts Filipino American writing, and the continuities between Filipino and Filipino American writing create a distinctive literary formation that does not conform to prescriptions about Asian American writing derived from Japanese American and Chinese American literature.[24] Finally, much of the more recent writing, as I will show, is situated in a transnational context where America is not the exclusive locus of identification. While, on the one hand, Kim's delineation of Asian American literature is more inclusive than Chin's, her defining criteria work to reproduce the hegemony of the forms of Japanese and Chinese American literature by failing to reconfigure the field through the specificities of Korean and Filipino American writing.

Similarly, when Kim seeks to include Burmese American Wendy Law-Yone's *The Coffin Tree* within the same schema, she fails to distinguish between the refugee experience of forced dislocation, radical discontinuity, and political uncertainty, and the voluntary experience of migration, except by treating the former as a more extreme expression of the drive to "claim America" common to both. Kim's methods of incorporation are symptomatic of a larger problem. With a new self-consciousness in the field about the hegemony of Japanese and Chinese American literatures, essayists and anthologists seeking to include underrepresented Asian American groups often use one particular group to stand in for the rest. References to Filipino and Vietnamese American literature, in particular, have come to operate in this fashion in the field. While the task of creating new conceptual models is avoided, such annexing of newer formations has acquired the persuasive force of comprehensiveness now. What it institutionalizes is a perception of the transposability of the newer literatures and the foundational status of the established ones. One generic outcome of such scholarly procedures is that the critical essay breaks down into lists of thematic similarities that invoke a "tradition" through sheer numerical force and the power of proxies. Another result of the rush to incorporate the newer groups is that with the quantity of available materials quite low in many cases, an industry is emerging to produce materials to fill this demand. While on the one hand, the effort to encourage writers from less-known groups is commendable, publishing numerous hastily compiled, weakly conceived anthologies is, finally, counterproductive. Availability of texts cannot be an end in itself. Furthermore, since the newer material is frequently being made available through collaborative autobiographies and student writing, where the extent of mediation is very high (especially where translation complicates the process of transmission), we need to interrogate the structures that determine literary production. In the case of collaborative autobiographies, where the reconstitution of the absent figure of the underrepresented is caught up in the epistemic violence of a disciplinary emphasis on concrete experience and sovereign subjectivity, and where the place of the collaborator is marked by a singular transparency, we cannot proceed without a historical critique of the collaborating/editorial subject. Autobiographical voicing is a fraught project in this context. An uncritical recourse to productivity in order to facilitate inclusion might only create a disciplinary formation where some of the groups stand in quasi-ethnographical relation to others.

In Lim's earlier essay "Twelve Asian American Writers: In Search of Self-Definition," the number stands in for breadth of coverage although all the writers discussed as "Asian American" are either Japanese or Chinese American. What is most troubling about this kind of slippage is its institutional reproduction over several decades in the field, as we have seen in the criticism of Chin and Kim. Lim notes that Asian American writing is part of the macrocosm of American writing but also reveals "certain inextricably Asian psychological and philosophical perspectives. A strong Confucian patriarchal orientation is a dominant element and with that the corollary of female inferiority" (237). Not only is this statement incredibly reductive, but the collapsing of the distinctions between Asian and Confucian reveals what Gayatri Spivak has called a "sanctioned ignorance" about the cultural diversity of Asia that, interestingly enough, has its antecedents in American Orientalist writings, which have long centralized East Asian cultures because of a history of trade, military, and missionary contacts between these areas and the United States.[25]

This problem is compounded by the publication of Lim's essay in the MLA anthology *Redefining American Literary History* that undertakes as its project precisely what the essay most neglects to perform within the context of its own field. Moreover, the two other essays on Asian American literature included in the anthology focus on the work of Maxine Hong Kingston. The narrowness in the scope of what is covered as Asian American writing, and the complete absence of reference to this as an issue, suggest a kind of axiomatic force such an equivalence has gathered within the discipline, from which it is being disseminated amongst general readers of ethnic and American literature.

What is heartening are the significant critical shifts in the theoretical assumptions about Asian American literature between Lim's two essays. Shirley Lim's recent essay "Assaying the Gold" shows itself to be more aware of the dangers of an uncritical acceptance of the rubric Asian American literature, although the analytic methods and lexicon employed within the essay often finesse rather than confront the problems raised. Although she acknowledges, on the one hand, that "the rubric 'Asian American literature' . . . is both exceedingly contemporary, a newly invented epistemological tool, and already collapsing under the weight of its own contradictions," Lim avoids the implications of her own insight by settling for the nostalgic prediction that the increasing heterogeneity of the field will produce a greater pan-Asian consciousness among writers and readers. The evidence Lim summons to support this hope is rather slender and shifts between literary and sociological arenas. According to Lim, there are more signs of "biculturalism," "multicultur-alism," and "borderland" negotiations in recent Asian American literary texts. By way of sociological support for her position, Lim argues that a greater solidarity has emerged among Asian Americans in response to mainstream American discrim-ination and as a result of coalition building among Asian Americans. And these factors, we are told, augur well for the emergence of a new phase in Asian American writing: "The stage is set for the transformation of Asian American literature into Pan-Asian American readings, from the old singular ethnic body into a multiethnic body . . . and we are already reading the scripts" (164–165).

The major problem with Lim's critical assertions is that they make predictions about the growth of a sociohistorical, political, economic, and cultural phenomenon like pan-Asian consciousness by using evidence drawn from a limited arena. In this respect, Lim repeats an error often made by cultural critics who read in the changes effected in the academy seismic sociocultural transformations. Pan-Asian consciousness has enjoyed its greatest success on college campuses, as researchers of the Asian American movement have pointed out, but its political effectiveness and acceptance in the Asian American constituency as a whole have been much more uneven. Contrary to Lim's neat predictions, sociological research on the future of Asian American panethnicity is more mixed in its findings, indicating simultaneously the growth of pan-Asian organizations and increased conflicts among them.[26] Yen Le Espiritu has identified the ethnic and class inequality within the pan-Asian structure, the influx of post-1965 immigrants, and the reduction of public funding sources as causes of potential conflict among the various Asian ethnic groups (51). Moreover, contrary to the early hopes of activists, the institution-alization of Asian American Studies has had little effect on the various communities, and over time the gulf between the community and the academy has only widened. I will also argue in greater detail later that changes in the political distribution system are likely to further interrupt the growth of pan-Asian consciousness. The projection of a pan-Asian framework as encompassing the future direction of the literature is premature, unsubstantiated, and seeks to effect an emotional resolution to the problems of political identity raised by the very use of the term "Asian American." As in the work of Kim, the legitimacy of the rubric is finally salvaged as a signifier by pointing to a future in which it shall come to be. In the case of Kim and Lim, pluralism offers the avenue for that deferral: once everyone has been included, the representational truth of the rubric will be made manifest: "the next stage is for Asian Americans to become reflective of the multiple ethnicities that already compose their identity" ("CGA," 164).

Lim uses the terms "biculturalism," "multiculturalism," and "borderland" con-sciousness to represent some of the shifts discernible in the coding of ethnicity in contemporary Asian American literature, and then lists the work of writers who exemplify these new paradigms like Jessica Hagedorn, Bharati Mukherjee, and David Henry Hwang. Multiculturalism is a term so capacious that recognition of it as a textual feature signals a critic's self-positioning as progressive and up-to-date, rather than illuminating in any specific way the dynamics of the text. If it is a reference to an official policy that shapes the terms of social interaction and literary production, then a term like "multiculturalism" would mean something very different in the case of a Mukherjee novel like *Jasmine* than, say, in the case of a Hagedorn novel like *Dogeaters*.[27] But Lim makes no effort to differentiate between the usages; consequently, the terminology functions as a loose and free-floating signifier of Asian Americanness that lacks any cultural density. *Jasmine* begins in a Punjab enmeshed in religious conflict between Sikhs and Hindus—the postcolonial sequel to the fostering of ethnoreligious separatism, in the interests of political control, by the British colonial regime in India—an official multicultural policy that in colonialist and nationalist forms has had murderous consequences. Once she arrives in the United States, Jasmine enters into a different version of a multicultural imaginary, where her cultural difference as an Indian female (which lacks referential density in the United States) is reinscribed as exotic sexual power. In Hagedorn's text, the legacy of Spanish and American colonialism have created a society obsessed with colonial genealogies and infatuated with Hollywood films, caught in a modernity marked by political corruption and poverty, where sexual desire becomes the site for the inscription of the incoherence, exploitation, and violence that signify its experience of "multiculturalism." It could be argued that multiculturalism operates in so many different registers in these two texts that it differentiates them from each other rather than unifying them as Asian American texts. Finally, the use of multiculturalism as a unifying feature of contemporary Asian American texts leaves so many questions unanswered. Do Asian American texts operate in the category of multiculturalism any differently from other ethnic texts? Do they share more in common with each other in this respect than they do with "mainstream" texts? Since multiculturalism in its broadest sense has become a feature of most modern societies and texts, surely we need some more finely honed criteria if we are to argue for its common existence in these two and other Asian American texts. Critics of Asian American literature need to be particularly vigilant that their institutional location as interpreters of "Asian American literature" does not predispose them to recycle and accommodate disparate cultural products into the existing categories of their discipline, or into the convenient catch-all terms generated by pluralism. Instead, the expansion of the literature must be accompanied by the generation of new criteria on the basis of which our selections are made. Cultural production is a much messier process than the available categories of ethnicity allow for. It is therefore imperative, as Werner Sollors points out, "that the categorization of writers—and literary critics—as 'members' of ethnic groups is understood to be a very partial, temporary and insufficient categorization at best" (256). In the case of Asian Americans, who are categorized within the most novel and artificial of ethnic formations, the mutability and fictionality of membership is a much more intense experience, one that needs to be foregrounded and not dispelled in our theorizations of Asian American literature.

Before I turn to the last part of my argument, I would like to analyze briefly a recent heated exchange between Jessica Hagedorn, the editor of one of the latest anthologies of Asian American fiction, *Charlie Chan Is Dead*, and Sven Birkerts, who reviewed the anthology for *The New York Times Book Review*.[28] The exchange serves as a critical parable for the arguments I have made thus far about the axiomatic status of Asian American literature within the discipline, the theoretical weakness within the field, and the recourse to the affirmation of ethnic identity to defer addressing the challenges of its heterogeneity. My comments on the following exchange also prepare the way for the last part of my essay, in which I will discuss the effects of transnational forces on Asian American ethnicity, the failure of the discipline to take up this challenge in a significant way, and the incoherence that attaches to the term as a result of this failure.

The conflict between Hagedorn and Birkerts takes place over the ordering rubric for her collection—"Asian American fiction." For Birkerts, the problem with the anthology is its insufficiently formulated inclusiveness:

> To begin with, there are just too many different kinds of inclusions, everything from Indian-born Meena Alexander's aggressively hip "Manhattan Music" to "I Would Remember," a simple and powerful story by Carlos Bulosan, a Filipino born in 1913. "Asian American" has here become a term so hospitable that half the world's population can squeeze in under its banner. Generous and catholic, yes—but the mix is also jarring and too eclectic. The chaos is compounded—if chaos can be—by Ms. Hagedorn's reliance on an alphabetical ordering (effectively eliminating any impression of generational change) and by the unevenness of the contributions. First-rate work by authors like Joy Kogawa, David Wong Louie, Jose Garcia Villa, John Yau and Jocelyn Lieu must sit side by side with a number of less than distinguished stories from the post-modernist grab bag.

Hagedorn's acid retort to the reviewer directs his attention once again to the inclusiveness of the collection as its defining feature. But she explains neither the need for, nor the grounds of, such inclusiveness within the contemporary context of Asian American fiction:

> Rather than dealing with the literature presented in "Charlie Chan Is Dead: An Anthology of Contemporary Asian American Fiction" (Dec. 19), Sven Birkerts spends more than half of his review obsessing over the writers' bloodlines, and complaining that my inclusion of 48 writers as "Asian American" may have been too "hospitable." What exactly are his criteria for categorizing someone as Asian American? Since this is the first anthology of its kind, is this really the time to be narrow? . . .
>
> Is Mr. Birkerts an immigration official or a literary critic? Should we all send in our passports and green cards for verification? . . . What I hope from any reviewer of "Charlie Chan Is Dead" is that he or she treat seriously the form and substance of our literature.[29]

Birkerts's perplexity in confronting the staggering range of writings in the anthology is hardly surprising given the lack of an adequate theoretical or historical framework, a clear articulation of the criteria of selection, or in the absence of either, an explanation about the inability to provide such statements given the exceeding novelty of the field, the artificial conjunctions it effects, and the enormous transformations it has undergone within the last decades. Instead, both Elaine Kim, who has written a brief Preface, and Jessica Hagedorn, who provides an

Introduction, invoke the celebration of differences and the "international" as heady auguries of the new and liberating future that belongs to Asian American literature, and a sign of its break from the narrow cultural nationalism of its founding moment in the sixties. Hagedorn's page-length catalog that characterizes the "hipness" of her selections as "funky," "sassy," "sexy" substitutes affirmation for analysis. All too often the critical responsibilities that attend the task of introducing an inaugural volume ("the first anthology of Asian American fiction by a commercial publisher in this country") to a largely unfamiliar public are discharged by citing difference within a dizzying postmodern schema of montage and juxtaposition: "Some of these writers were originally poets, some still are. Others only write fiction. Some were born in the Philippines, some in Seattle. A few in Hawaii. Others in Toronto or London. . . . Seoul, Greeley, Colorado, India, Penang, Moscow, Idaho" (xxix–xxx). This technique has the effect of positing the arbitrariness of the category at the level of haphazard global positionings that emerge as signifiers of the unpredictable and the provocative, rather than as the product of specific historical conditions. The only gloss Hagedorn provides on the relationship between her category and the global list of place names is the following summation: "Asian American literature? Too confining a term, maybe. World literature? Absolutely" (xxx). Why, then, has the editor retained the first label when a clearly better one is at hand? Or, to quote the Michael Jackson song, what does it mean for Asian Americans to say "We are the World"? Both the Introduction and the Preface list (but do not explain or theorize) the dizzying array of differences but then move on to achieve closure by sounding the note of "celebration." The overwhelming need seems to be to reconstitute wholeness at the level of mood, so that identity can emerge at the level of emotion, when it cannot be created through theoretical or critical interpretation.

For his part, the conflation of the ethnic with the local/domestic is the grounding assumption in Birkerts's understanding of ethnic literature. His primary difficulty in reading the anthology and locating its rationale derives from his understanding of how "difference" operates as a signifier in literary production-as a category or categories of intelligibility that narrow the focus, producing a kind of "special interest subjectivity."[30] Contrary to his expectations, the Chan anthology "turns the funnel upside down" on the trend among anthologists to "narrow the focus, screening down by race, sex, ethnicity; sexual orientation, geography, age or topical criteria." In this anthology, the locus of the ethnic shifts to the global. The term "minority," which is popularly taken to signify the fractional, peripheral, tangential, seems to counter its own logic in assuming another aspect as overwhelming, or engulfing: "half the world's population can squeeze in under its banner." His consternation with the range of writings is imaged through the very geography that assumes the burden of imposing coherence on the notion of identity. The distance between the two perspectives that emerges in this encounter—between the Asian American writer-anthologist and the general reader—operating as it does as a site of charged accusations and defenses, points to the necessary theoretical work that needs to be undertaken in elucidating the fictionality of the rubric.

We have now entered an era in which the dispersion and reconfiguration of ethnic identity among Asian Americans will only accelerate, and it is to these new forces, which will recast aspects of ethnic formation, that I will now turn, in order to make some suggestions for the reorientation of theoretical investigations within the field.

RETHINKING AMERICAN LITERATURE AND THEORY

The emergence of pan-Asian ethnicity has been a vexed, conflicted, and incomplete process, especially in the recent past, and is further complicated by the fact that no readily available symbols or grounds of cultural commonality exist within such a heterogeneous formation. But Yen Le Espiritu argues that the problem of a lack of cultural commonalities, far from being unique to Asian Americans, is in fact typical, in various degrees, of the process of panethnicization in the United States: "culture has followed panethnic boundaries rather than defined them" because "panethnic groups in the United States are products of political and social processes, rather than of cultural bonds" (13). While Espiritu's statement has certainly been true of the historical experiences of African Americans and Native Americans, for groups like Latin Americans and Asian Americans who have a shorter, more internally uneven history of being shaped by American location, and whose panethnic formation is being continuously destabilized and transformed by fresh waves of immigration, the presumption of a progressive development of panethnicity is much less predictable.

Two structural factors will significantly interrupt the formation of panethnicity in patterns that were conceivable in the past: a more conservative political climate that is increasingly hostile to structuring access along ethnic lines, and changes in the global economy that will significantly have an impact on ethnic formation. I will analyze the transformative potential of both definitive shifts.

The 1994 elections have produced a transformed political landscape in which a more conservative agenda has defined discussions of welfare, affirmative action, and immigration. In addition, the recent recession, the temporization of the workforce, the numerous layoffs and decline in real wages, and the reduction in federal spending have created an embattled public that, mobilized by conservative rhetoric, has shown support for the curtailment of affirmative action and welfare programs and restrictions on immigration. The recent Supreme Court rulings that have mandated standards of "compelling federal interest" and "strict scrutiny" for affirmative action programs in education and federal contracts have reinforced this trend. What we see as a result of these changes that are already under way (and only likely to intensify) is that a polity that had structured access along ethnic lines since the civil rights era is slowly curtailing these policies. As social scientists have pointed out, the ascriptive force of the state is crucial to the production and consolidation of ethnicity. Joane Nagel notes that ethnic resurgences are strongest when the state uses the ethnic category as a unit in economic allocations and political representations (quoted in *AAP,* 10). When these identifications are reinforced over a period of time through the coincidence of political and economic interests, the emergence of panethnicity is encouraged despite lack of common cultural bonds. In other words, "shifts in ethnic boundaries are often a direct response to changes in the political distribution system" (*AAP,* 11). The recent structural changes in the political distribution system would seem to suggest that the state's increasing unwillingness to legitimize ethnic labels as determinants of access may lead to a weakening of panethnicity, especially among predominantly foreign-born Asian American populations.

To suggest that the panethnic rubric may not be as effective in producing the more stable formations of the past is not to argue that the alternative narrative of assimilation will define the orientation and identifications of Asians in the United States. Contrary to a long-standing tradition amongst critics that sets ethnicization in opposition to assimilation, I would argue that ethnicization will be influenced by a transnational context through polyethnic contacts across and within ethnic groups both inside and outside the country. It is here that I differ from Werner Sollors, who also challenges the ethnic identity versus assimilation opposition; however, Sollors undoes the opposition only to recuperate the transethnic within a narrowly domestic conception of American national identity.[31] For this reason, Sollors's formulations about ethnic literature are more successful in the analysis of aspects of the African American tradition or second-and third-generation writers from other groups, but are inadequate to addressing the patterns found in more recent immigrant writing. Americanization/assimilation, which was earlier associated with "Anglo conformity," will probably give way to a process of Americanization where most groups can, as Arjun Appadurai puts it, "renegotiate their links to their diasporic identities from their American vantage points."[32] It is precisely because the assimilationary process is losing its former power that presidential candidate Patrick Buchanan and conservative critic Peter Brimelow (author of *Alien Nation*) have issued alarmist calls for a "pause" in immigration similar to the one between 1924 and 1965; or for a restriction to European-only immigration to reinvigorate the absorptive process.[33] At present, entry into the United States entails an adjustment to American codes and practices (what we have called assimilation), but it also enables investments/remittances that reestablish links to the home country, return visits under a new status, and the entry of family members into the United States. Within this context, becoming American does not necessarily involve a loss of the home culture, or a choice between ethnicity and mainstreaming as in earlier patterns of immigration to this country.

The globalization of capital, the transnationalization of production, the migrations of diverse peoples, the varying trajectories of arrival, departure, and return (immigrants, exiles, refugees, temporary workers, intellectual exchange visitors), the creation of global information superhighways, and the electronic transfer of images and capital have seen an exponential increase in the sites, frequency, and variety of cross-cultural exchange. The shift from multinational corporations to transnational corporations with a global strategy has proliferated the points of exchange, transfer, and contact. The worldwide move away from socialist policies following the collapse of the Soviet Union, accompanied by the lowering of trade barriers and the spread of consumer culture, has encouraged this shift. Whereas multinationals maintained autonomous subsidiaries with separate strategies in various countries, transnational companies support a global strategy that is conceived and implemented in a worldwide setting. As a result, they create circuits of capital, personnel, and information that have multiple nodes, each more closely linked and dependent on the others than within the older multinational system.

The rapid economic growth of parts of Asia (Japan, Singapore, Taiwan, Korea, Hong Kong, and now China, Vietnam, Malaysia, Philippines, Indonesia, and India) over the last few decades has led to the proliferation of such transnational networks linking America and Asia, and as we move into what is being called the Pacific Century, these processes will only accelerate and proliferate. The emergence of the "borderless economy" has intensified linkages that defy containment within the nation-state. Plans are under way to establish a free trade zone modelled on NAFTA between the United States and Pacific Rim countries; Chinese government officials are establishing a Special Economic Zone linking the Yunan region to Laos and Vietnam; trade links within ASEAN and SAARC countries have increased and strengthened.[34] The effect of these changes on Asian Americans will be substantial. Asian Americans, who have historically disavowed their connections to Asia in order to challenge racist stereotypes as perpetual foreigners, will be able to renegotiate their links to Asia; mainstream Americans will reencounter Asia within changed geopolitical alignments, which will not allow the easy assumptions of patronage and wardship that stemmed from privileges of extraterritoriality and conquest in the nineteenth and early twentieth centuries.[35]

What we see appearing are global networks that do not conform to earlier models of departure from Asia and settlement in America that developed within a vastly different geopolitical economy. For instance, China's impending takeover of Hong Kong has led to the dispersal of capital and family connections across a number of sites in Canada, Britain, Australia, and the United States, with the possibility of return or realignment pending an uncertain political future. Furthermore, patterns of reverse migration are beginning to emerge among Taiwanese Americans and Korean Americans due to strengthened economic conditions and the increase in living standards in their home countries, and a decline in living standards in the United States. Over the last four years, the number of people who received immigration visas from South Korea to the United States has fallen by more than half, from 25,500 in 1990 to 10,800 in 1994; simultaneously, in each of these four years between 5,000 and 6,500 people have returned to Korea, compared to 800 in 1980.[36] Such reverse migrations may also take place amongst the other Asian American groups if the economic and political situations in their home countries improve.

Nor is migration exclusively a sign of "cosmopolitan" class privilege. Poverty and gender do not impede migration, but they inflect the forms it takes. Garment sweatshops in some of the major U.S. cities draw on immigrant female workers, most of whom are Asian and Latin American.[37] Owners of ethnic grocery stores, restaurants, or the ubiquitous 7–11 convenience stores employ impoverished workers from their home countries for low wages, sometimes using the prospective green card as a lure. Tony Chan's film *Combination Platter* provides a sympathetic view of the predicament of the restaurant owner of The Szechuan Inn, Mr. Lee, and the undocumented workers he employs, both of whom are under siege by the INS, while they purvey to oblivious New Yorkers one of the staples of their ethnic experience—Chinese take-out at cheap rates. The film cuts between the hectic, hot, and crowded male world of the kitchen workers and the leisurely, loquacious and self-absorbed world of the dining-room clientele, connected by commerce yet not in contact. Asian Americans inhabit both sides of the divide in this film, highlighting class differentiations within the group. The film follows Robert, who works as a waiter in the restaurant while he pursues, during his off-hours, his elusive quest for a green card, always under threat of exposure and deportation to Hong Kong.

Gender further defines the forms and trajectories of migration and the production of ethnicity in a transnational context. The international sex trade has connected Thailand and the Philippines to America, Japan and Europe through package flesh tours, prostitution smuggling rings, and mail-order bride catalogs (representations of these global networks appear in Jessica Hagedorn's *Dogeaters* and Wanwadee Larsen's *Confessions of a Mail Order Bride*).[38] The debt crisis in countries like Sri Lanka and the Philippines has created an enormous outflow of female migrant workers to the Middle East, Japan, Hong Kong, Singapore, the United States, and Europe, just as the entry of large numbers of middle-class women into the workforce in the West, and the increased prosperity of some Middle Eastern and Asian countries, has led to an enormous demand for such labor.[39] By March 1988, approximately 175,000 Filipinas were working overseas (about 81,000 as domestic workers) and sending home $60–$100 million in foreign exchange (*BBB*, 187–188). The recent protests in the Philippines against government indifference to the plight of its foreign workers—following the execution by the Singapore government of Flor Contemplacion, an overseas Filipina maid—highlight the growing symbolic importance of the migrant worker in the Filipino national consciousness.[40] The short story "Jasmine" from Bharati Mukherjee's collection *The Middleman and Other Stories* explores the layered ironies in the relationship between Lara, a white feminist who is a performance artist, and Jasmine, the young Indian woman from Trinidad she employs as a nanny or "day-mommy."[41] Lara's professionalism and feminism are enabled and subsidized by Jasmine's illegal status in the country, the underside to the successes of a liberal women's movement that argued from a platform of access, individual rights, and emancipation from domesticity.

The sites for the production of heterogeneous Asian ethnicities, therefore, defy easy containment within national boundaries. Ethnicity metamorphoses at multiple sites of transit, return, and arrival in the movement between and within nations; it can no longer be solely defined through the negotiation between origin and destination. It is imperative that Asian American Studies move beyond comforting affirmations of pluralism and the celebration of differences as the terms of their engagement with these transformative processes taking place.

The disjunctions and multiple migrations that deterritorialize ethnicity are the subject of many of the newer stories produced by Asian Americans. When ethnic identity is produced through multiple location, ethnic categories become destabilized and, consequently, open to misrecognition and reinscription. Once the narrator leaves Pakistan in Sara Suleri's *Meatless Days*, her family experience of the trauma of Partition and the genocidal divisiveness of the Bangladesh War render her loath to attach identity to place. The luminous and elliptical prose of the narrative refuses to name in the language of belonging the spaces through which she moves after her arrival in the United States.[42] Her discourse discreetly skirts the available American categories of identity, "ethnic" "minority" or "Asian American," locating itself instead in the transmogrifications to which identity is subject in the spaces opened up by death and displacement in her stories. The potential for reinscription of ethnic codings is taken up in a comic mode in Mira Nair's *Mississippi Masala*. Her story revises prototypical narratives of ethnic formation, and the rubric "Asian American" strains to contain the displacements through which ethnicity travels. The film moves between Africa and America, but the result is not a narrative of African America as we have come to think about it. Instead, the story is the unfamiliar one of displaced Indians moving across two continents. India as the space of "origin" never materializes as locale in the film; instead, India emerges in the Ugandan context as the boundary produced by British colonialism in the insertion of a middleman minority into an African colonial state, and then redrawn in post-Independence Idi Amin's Uganda, to reassert black nationhood through the expulsion of "foreign" elements. Within the racialized imagination of Mississippi, Ugandan "Indians" are an unfamiliar category misrecognized through older categories (Indian? American Indian—African? African American?). If the film unsettles our ideas about the category Asian American, it also ironizes the confidence with which we read the category African American by offering us another African American story set in Mississippi. The fictions of the putatively more stable Asian ethnic formations, like Chinese Americans and Japanese Americans, also show the effects of the diasporic renegotiation of identities as in Peter Wang's film *The Great Wall* or in David Mura's *Turning Japanese*, both stories of return to the country of origin.[43] The topos of return, which had appeared in earlier Asian American narratives as an imagined or actual endpoint to the action allowing for resolution to the dilemmas of identification, appears as one more nodal point in an ongoing action that highlights the perplexities and paradoxes of belonging. Many of these stories deliberately avoid closure, ending with their characters beginning a new journey, in transit, or on the road.

However, travel possesses a different valence in each story because of important political and material differences. Suleri enters the United States as a student, a voluntary migration enabled by her class status, although her decision to leave seems to be precipitated by the political crises that follow the Bangladesh War. In *Mississippi Masala*, once again, political turmoil prompts the journey, but this journey is a forced migration. Turned into political refugees, the Ugandan Indian extended family arrives in the United States with sufficient capital (that circulates through a diasporic ethnic network) to enter into a niche market at an opportune moment when the motel business is being abandoned by other Americans. The Chinese American family in *The Great Wall* is financially stable enough to afford an extended visit to China which, like Mura's, is a journey of cultural recovery. Mura himself is the beneficiary of a cultural exchange program that funds his one-year visit to Japan, and the cultural links that are sponsored by the two countries are underwritten by economic and political interests. The journeys undertaken from America are visits supported by a "strong" passport and a "hard" currency and involve an eventual return to a comfortable existence.

The earlier patterns of Asian immigrant experiences created more bounded immigrant communities where differentiations were experienced most keenly in separation from the dominant culture, from the home country, or across gender and generational divisions. The distance between Asia and America was more formidable at that time, the passages more dangerous, and the communications more tenuous, as the stories of Maxine Hong Kingston's *China Men* suggest.[44] The temporality of immigration as it emerges through the tropes of amnesia, exhaustion, and deferral mythifies the experience of Chinese laborers who made the journey to America fired by the ambition to make money and return, but were forced by harsh working conditions, poor salaries, or new attachments to delay or abandon the idea of return. But some of the newer fictions of Asian American writers show the emergence of different "chronotopes" of immigration that represent the production of ethnicity in passage through a smaller world where national borders are more porous.[45] Arjun Appadurai delineates the challenges the transnational poses for theorizations of American ethnicity:

> The formula of hyphenation (as in Italian-Americans, Asian-Americans, and African-Americans) is reaching the point of saturation, and the right-hand side of the hyphen can barely contain the unruliness of the left-hand side. . . . The politics of ethnic identity in the United States is inseparably linked to the global spread of originally local national identities. For every nation-state that has exported significant numbers of its populations to the United States as refugees, tourists, or students, there is now a delocalized *transnation*, which retains a special ideological link to a putative place of origin but is otherwise a thoroughly diasporic collectivity. No existing conception of Americanness can contain this large variety of transnations. (424)

Recently, critic Sau-ling Wong has coined a new term, "denationalization," to refer to some of the changes I have discussed in this essay.[46] It is necessary to address her criticisms in some detail since they have appeared at a crucial moment in the development of the field. While Wong acknowledges the significance of transnational influences on Asian American ethnicity, she cautions against a "trend" she sees as potentially depoliticizing: the loss of focus on "domestic" issues in a preoccupation with the "diasporic." However, the term "denationalization," which, according to the OED, means "to make (an institution, etc.) no longer national; to divest of its character as belonging to the whole nation, or to a particular nation" distorts the complexity, range, and effects of transnational perspectives on the field. It is important to recognize that the transnational is not antithetical to the national; it both reconstitutes the national, and exceeds it in crucial ways. Hence, Wong's conceptualization of these phenomena through the term "denationalization" is tendentious and fundamentally flawed. Moreover, the usage is vitiated by the associations of the term. The term "denationalized" is widely used in neoimperialist theory, where it refers to the indigenous elites who collaborate with transnational corporate interests, setting them in an exploitative relationship to, and severing them from the interests of, the people at large. Is Wong implying a parallel between transnational cultural critics and such elites? Since she does not indicate the source of her terminology, the prior associations of the term make her usage highly problematic. I would also argue that, in the politically contentious nineties, where the rhetoric against immigrants is so highly charged, a term like "denationalization" can be easily appropriated into right-wing arguments about the difficulty of incorporating Asians into American nationhood.

Many of the problems in her essay can be traced to the framing of false oppositions (between what she calls "domestic" and "diasporic" perspectives, and between politics and theory) from which conclusions are derived. In fact, a striking feature of the essay is the manner in which it attempts to resolve complex interrelated affiliations into neat sets of priorities in the name of *praxis*. The whole reason for employing perspectives for Asian American Studies that go beyond location in America is that it is often impossible fully to understand and respond to the local without a comprehension of global forces and institutions. Furthermore, diasporic loyalties do not necessarily prevent Asian Americans from mobilizing as Asian Americans: for example, Asian Americans organized in record numbers to oppose the recent proposed restrictions in immigration along with many Latin Americans. It is likely that the politics of Asian Americans will more and more be defined by issue-based strategic alliances with other groups as a way of responding to the political complexities of the nineties.

A further problem is the confusion at the descriptive and conceptual level of key terms like "transnational," "international," and "borderless economy" through which Wong advances her argument. For instance, she argues that the Third World linkages influencing the founding of Asian American Studies were "inherently transnational in outlook" (3). This is part of a defensive move to assert that the founding moment of the field was not far removed from current theoretical concerns. However, the "transnational" influences on the field today have few precedents in the "International" linkages and connections that shaped the originary moment of the field. It is patronizing, on the one hand, to seek to rehabilitate historically specific ethnic identifications by representing them in contemporary vocabulary, and misleading, on the other hand, to dismiss current concerns as a "trend."

Most disturbing are the conclusions the argument (which at times proceeds by implication, inferences from conversations, and speculations about interlocutors) draws. Wong asserts that the focus of the field must remain the originary one of "claiming the Americas" and "commitment to the place where one resides" (19). These, she claims, are the founding principles of Asian American Studies. It is baffling that such a simplistic formula is held to be adequate for dealing with the vastly changed and complex political realities of the nineties. When such formulas are then aligned with the issue of "commitment" we are on perilous ground indeed. After all, one usually hears the rhetoric of commitment in relation to Asian Americans from quite different sources. Moreover, the issue of "commitment" holds a particularly painful history for Asian Americans whose loyalty to America has been historically impugned by racist allegations (coded as "alienness" or "unassimilability"), most notably in the instance of the internment of Japanese Americans and the administering of a loyalty questionnaire. Certainly, doubts about the "commitment to the place one resides" have not been raised with respect to the politics of other diasporic groups like Irish Americans or Jewish Americans. If this is the route we are to take, how will we measure commitment, and who will serve as arbiter of these proceedings? The study of the influence of transnationalism in the field is not a "trend" that conforms to white expectations of theoretical sophistication, or the matter of a referendum among Asian American critics about the future development of the field. Wong's essay is problematic for the conservative tendency of its conclusions, the weakness of the evidence offered, the frequently distorting representation of the positions it challenges, and the preemptive nature of the intervention it makes on the development of the field in new directions.

It is clear from the foregoing analysis that the boundary marking of the field is caught up in a perception of competing needs: the tension between the need for political identity and the need to represent the conflicted and heterogeneous formation we call "Asian American." These needs are antagonistic to each other only if we work from the assumption that there is a "real" Asian American identity to which our vocabulary and procedures can be adequated. Hence the pluralist computation that the sum of the parts will give us the whole. I would contend that "Asian American" offers us a rubric that we cannot not use. But our usage of the term should rehearse the catachrestic status of the formation. I use the term "catachresis" to indicate that there is no literal referent for the rubric "Asian American," and, as such, the name is marked by the limits of its signifying power. It then becomes our responsibility to articulate the inner contradictions of the term and to enunciate its representational inconsistencies and dilemmas. For, as Adorno notes, "criticizing epistemology also means ... retaining it."[47] Asian American Studies is uniquely positioned to intervene in current theoretical discussions on ethnicity, representation, and writing not despite, but because of, the contested and contestatory nature of its formation.

NOTES

1. The newest group of Asian immigrants are Tibetans who had been living in exile in India and Nepal after the Chinese takeover of Tibet in 1959. The Tibetan-U.S. Resettlement Project has succeeded in bringing 1,000 refugees to the United States since 1990. The Tibetan provisions in the U.S. Immigration Act of 1990 refer to them as "displaced persons" and admit them to the United States as "immigrants," not "refugees," a reflection of the unwillingness of the government to jeopardize U.S.-China relations at this point in time. See Karma Gyatsho Zurkhang, "Strangers in a Strange Land," *Utne Reader,* March-April 1993, 94–97.

2. The first critical anthology that deals exclusively with Asian American literary studies was published under the title *Reading the Literatures of Asian America,* ed. Shirley Geoklin Lim and Amy Ling (Philadelphia: Temple University Press, 1992).

3. *Aiiieeeee! An Anthology of Asian-American Writers,* ed. Chin et al. (Washington, D.C.: Howard University Press, 1974), hereafter abbreviated *AA;* Kim, *Asian American Literature: An Introduction to the Writings and Their Social Context* (Philadelphia: Temple University Press, 1982), hereafter abbreviated *AIW;* Kim, "Defining Asian American Realities Through Literature," *Cultural Critique* 6/7 (1987): 87–111, hereafter abbreviated "DA"; Lim, "Twelve Asian American Writers: In Search of Self-Definition," in *Redefining American Literary History,* ed. A. LaVonne Brown Ruoff and Jerry W. Ward Jr. (New York: Modern Language Association of America, 1990), 237–250; and Lim, "Assaying the Gold: Or, Contesting the Ground of Asian American Literature," *New Literary History* 24 (1993): 147–169, hereafter abbreviated "CGA."

4. See *Island: Poetry and History of Chinese Americans on Angel Island, 1910–1940,* ed. Him

Mark Lai et al. (San Francisco, 1980); *Songs of Gold Mountain: Cantonese Rhymes from San Francisco Chinatown,* ed. and trans. Marlon K. Hom (Berkeley: University of California Press, 1987); Amy Ling, *Between Worlds: Women Writers of Chinese Ancestry* (New York: Pergamon Press, 1990); *Ayumi: A Japanese American Anthology,* ed. Janice Mirikitani (San Francisco, 1980). The University of Washington Press has played a very important role in reprinting the work of older writers like John Okada, Carlos Bulosan, Monica Sone, and many others.

5. Some of the important anthologies and bibliographies include *Asian-American Authors,* ed. Kai-yu Hsu and Helen Palubinskas (Boston, 1972); *Asian American Heritage: An Anthology of Prose and Poetry,* ed. David Hsin-Fu Wand (New York, 1974); *Breaking Silence: An Anthology of Contemporary Asian American Poets,* ed. Joseph Bruchac (New York, 1983); *Asian American Literature: An Annotated Bibliography,* ed. King-Kok Cheung and Stan Yogi (New York: Modern Language Association of America, 1988); *The Forbidden Stitch: An Asian American Women's Anthology,* ed. Shirley Geok-lin Lim and Mayumi Tsutakawa (Corvallis, Ore.: Calyx Books, 1989); *Making Waves,* ed. Asian Women United of California (Boston: Beacon Press, 1989); *Charlie Chan Is Dead: An Anthology of Contemporary Asian American Fiction,* ed. Jessica Hagedorn (New York: Penguin Books, 1993), hereafter abbreviated *CC.*

6. Quoted in Wendell V. Harris, "Canonicity," *PMLA* 106, no. 1 (1991): 112.

7. John Guillory, "Canon, Syllabus, List: A Note on the Pedagogic Imaginary," *Transition* 52 (1991): 39.

8. Werner Sollors, "A Critique of Pure Pluralism," in *Reconstructing American Literary History,* ed. Sacvan Bercovitch (Cambridge, Mass.: Harvard University Press, 1986), 255, hereafter abbreviated "CP."

9. For comprehensive accounts of Asian American history see Sucheng Chan, *Asian Americans: An Interpretive History* (Boston: Twayne, 1991), hereafter abbreviated *AAIH;* Ronald Takaki, *Strangers From a Different Shore* (Boston: Little, Brown, 1989), hereafter abbreviated *SFD;* and *Dictionary of Asian American History,* ed. Hyung-Chan Kim (New York: Greenwood Press, 1986).

10. See *Labor Immigration Under Capitalism: Asian Workers in the United States Before World War II,* ed. Lucie Cheng and Edna Bonacich (Berkeley: University of California Press, 1984); Joan M. Jensen, *Passage From India: Asian Indian Immigrants in North America* (New Haven: Yale University Press, 1988); H. Brett Melendy, *Asians in America: Filipinos, Koreans, and East Indians* (Boston: Twayne, 1977); Alexander Saxton, *The Indispensable Enemy: Labor and the Anti-Chinese Movement in California* (Berkeley: University of California Press, 1971); and Roger Daniels, *The Politics of Prejudice: The Anti-Japanese Movement in California and the Struggle for Japanese Exclusion* (New York: Atheneum, 1968).

11. Yen Le Espiritu, *Asian American Panethnicity: Bridging Institutions and Identities* (Philadelphia: Temple University Press, 1992), 135, hereafter abbreviated *AAP.*

12. The Japanese government encouraged the emigration of women to create more stable immigrant communities, and retained a loophole in the 1907 Gentlemen's Agreement that restricted the emigration of laborers, but allowed the parents, wives, and children of laborers already in America to enter (*SFD,* 46–47). As a result, 46 percent of Japanese in Hawai'i and 34.5 percent on the mainland by 1920 were women. Korean immigrant communities also had a higher ratio of women (21 percent by 1920). The women were drawn by the more attractive conditions for family life in Hawai'i; and many entered the United States as picture brides with Japanese passports issued to them as Japanese colonial subjects under the Gentlemen's Agreement (56). Numbers of Indian and Filipino men married Mexican women.

13. See Bill Ong Hing, *Making and Remaking Asian America Through Immigration Policy, 1850–1990* (Stanford, Calif.: Stanford University Press, 1993), especially 43–78, hereafter abbreviated as *MRA; SFD,* 357–420; *AAIH,* 121–144.

14. The War that "began" for other Americans with Pearl Harbor had long roused the passions and anxieties of Asian Americans whose home countries had been pulled into

it much earlier. The time lag in perception carried no small irony, since the entry of the United States into the war brought abrupt shifts in status for Asian Americans as well as opportunities long denied. These ironies are skillfully explored by the young Korean American narrator, Faye, in Kim Ronyoung's *Clay Walls* (Seattle: University of Washington Press, 1987).

15. For a detailed history of the Movement see William Wei, *The Asian American Movement* (Philadelphia: Temple University Press, 1993).

16. Lisa Lowe, "Heterogeneity, Hybridity, Multiplicity: Marking Asian American Differences," *Diaspora* 1, no. 1 (1991): 30, hereafter abbreviated "HH."

17. See *Statistical Record of Asian Americans,* ed. Susan B. Gall and Timothy L. Gall (Detroit: Gale Research, Inc., 1993): 569–693, hereafter abbreviated *SRAA.*

18. Among many of the groups, the percentage of foreign-born is even higher—81.9 percent for Koreans, 90.4 percent for Vietnamese, and 93.9 percent for Laotians (*SRAA,* 572).

19. Barbara Herrnstein Smith, "Contingencies of Value," in *Canons,* ed. Robert von Hallberg (Chicago: University of Chicago Press, 1984), 30.

20. The work of scholars like E. San Juan Jr., Lisa Lowe, David Palumbo-Liu, and Sau–ling C. Wong represents an important exception to this general trend.

21. The term "no-no boy" was used to describe Nisei (American-born, second generation Japanese American) men who refused to answer affirmatively the two "loyalty" questions on the Selective Service questionnaire issued by the War Department in 1943. The questions addressed their willingness to serve in the army and swear unqualified allegiance to the United States, and their willingness to forswear all allegiance to Japan. This political stance defines the main character Ichiro in John Okada's novel *No-No Boy* (Seattle, 1979), the double negative signifying the complete dislocation of Ichiro, who is no longer Japanese and can never be American within the discursive construction of Americanness produced through the questionnaire.

22. For feminist critiques of Chin's formulations of an Asian American tradition see King-Kok Cheung, "The Woman Warrior versus the Chinaman Pacific: Must a Chinese American Critic Choose Between Feminism and Heroism?" in *Conflicts in Feminism,* ed. Marianne Hirsch and Evelyn Fox Keller (New York: Routledge, 1990), 234–251; Elaine Kim, "'Such Opposite Creatures': Men and Women in Asian American Literature," *Michigan Quarterly Review* (1990): 68–93; "CGA," 154–155; "HH," 33–34.

23. Even as late as her essay on Asian American literature for the *Columbia Literary History of the United States* (1988), Kim continues to exclude writings by South Asians. "Asian American Literature," in *Columbia Literary History of the United States,* ed. Emory Elliott (New York: Columbia University Press, 1988), 811–821.

24. Oscar Campomanes, "Filipinos in the United States and Their Literature of Exile," in *Reading the Literatures of Asian America,* 49–78.

25. The problems with the use of the term are numerous. Fredric Wakeman and Peter Bol have indicated that the term "Confucian" is a modern coinage without an equivalent in premodern Chinese, and Lionel Jensen has traced its origins to the Jesuits in China. After "Confucianism" had waned, the Western term was picked up by Chinese intellectuals and used as a way to identify the Chinese elite. This narrow sense of the term was extended by others to include traditional Chinese culture as a whole, and subsequently to refer to the entire East Asian region in ways that are homogenizing and ahistorical. Quoted in Arif Dirlik, "Confucius in the Borderlands," *Boundary* 2, no. 22 (fall 1995): 261. According to Dirlik, the eighties have witnessed a revival of "Confucianism" as an explanatory framework that links the economic miracle of newly industrialized Asian countries with their cultural ethos: "The Confucian revival of the eighties is best understood as the articulation of two discourses—a discourse on Confucianism as a functional component of an emergent Global Capitalism, and a discourse on Confucianism (predating the former) as a problem in Chinese intellectuals' identity" (265). The circulation of the term within these discourses and its Orientalist genealogy reveal that its use as a descriptive is highly problematic.

26. See *AAP,* esp. ch. 3 and ch. 6.

27. Bharati Mukherjee, *Jasmine* (New York: Grove Weidenfeld, 1989); Jessica Hagedorn, *Dogeaters* (New York: Pantheon Books, 1990).

28. Sven Birkerts, "In Our House There Were No Chinese Things," *The New York Times Book Review,* 19 December 1993, 17.

29. Jessica Hagedorn, *The New York Times Book Review,* 23 January 1994, 27.

30. I am speaking specifically of the way the ethnic and mainstream are constructed as oppositions in popular perception, and am calling this assumption into question. The burden of referentiality is quite different in mainstream writing that assumes a "common knowledge" of its cultural matrices among readers, and are less pressed to establish such knowledge or to dismantle and reconstruct it. The historical and cultural contexts ethnic texts activate as they anticipate their multiple audiences have often led to the misperception that they are narrower or less "universal" than mainstream literature.

31. Werner Sollors, *Beyond Ethnicity: Consent and Descent in American Culture* (New York: Oxford University Press, 1986).

32. Arjun Appadurai, "Patriotism and Its Futures," *Public Culture* 5, no. 3 (1993): 424.

33. Peter Brimelow, *Alien Nation: Common Sense About America's Immigration Disaster* (New York: Random House, 1995).

34. Kenichi Ohmae, "Putting Global Logic First," *Harvard Business Review* (January-February 1995): 122.

35. For an account of changing American attitudes to China and India over the last two centuries, see Harold R. Isaacs, *Scratches on Our Minds: American Views of China and India* (White Plains, N.Y., 1958).

36. Pam Belluck, "Healthy Korean Economy Draws Immigrants Home," *New York Times,* 22 August 1995, A1, A12.

37. The illegal status of many of these women makes them even more vulnerable to exploitation in an industry caught in relentless global competition with companies that have located overseas where labor costs are 1/4 of U.S. costs. Moreover, as Gary Gereffi points out, technological innovations are making possible the performance of technology-intensive and high-value-added stages of apparel production within the United States, ensuring the increasing growth and resilience of the industry domestically and its continuing need for cheap labor. "Global Sourcing and Regional Divisions of Labor in the Pacific Rim," in Arif Dirlik, ed., *What's in a Rim? Critical Perspectives on the Pacific Region Idea* (Boulder, Colo.: Westview Press, 1993), 51–68.

38. Wanwadee Larsen, *Confessions of a Mail Order Bride: American Life Through Thai Eyes* (Far Hills, N.J., 1989).

39. Cynthia Enloe, *Bananas, Beaches & Bases: Making Feminist Sense of International Politics* (Berkeley, 1989), esp. 35–41 on sex-tourism, and 177–194 on domestic servants; hereafter abbreviated *BBB.*

40. This conflict between the Philippines and Singapore also exposes the economic contradictions within the myth of "Asian values" long propagated by the Lee Kuan Yew government as the sign of its successful assimilation of Western capitalism and its successful resistance to Western cultural influence. The invocation of a pan-Asian framework in Asia is frequently state-sponsored and covers over uneven development between and within various Asian nations.

41. Bharati Mukherjee, "Jasmine," in *The Middleman and Other Stories* (New York: Grove Press, 1988), 123–135.

42. Sara Suleri, *Meatless Days* (Chicago: University of Chicago Press, 1989).

43. David Mura, *Turning Japanese: Memoirs of a Sansei* (New York: Atlantic Monthly Press, 1991).

44 Maxine Hong Kingston, *China Men* (New York: Knopf, 1980).

45. M. M. Bakhtin, *The Dialogic Imagination,* ed. Michael Holquist and trans. Caryl Emerson and Michael Holquist (Austin: University of Texas Press, 1981). Bakhtin defines "chrono-

tope" as "the intrinsic connectedness of temporal and spatial relationships that are artistically expressed in literature" (84).

46. Sau-ling C. Wong, "Denationalization Reconsidered: Asian American Cultural Criticism at a Theoretical Crossroads," *Amerasia Journal* 211, no. 2 (1995): 1–27.

47. Theodor W. Adorno, *Against Epistemology–A Metacritique: Studies in Husserl and the Phenomenological Antinomie,* trans. Willis Domingo (Oxford: Basil Blackwell, 1982), 27.

Representations and Identities

32 CIPHERS

Ginu Kamani

The woman claiming the berth across from mine in the train compartment must have been my age, but she looked older, more self-important. She had the red mark of the auspicious married woman in her hair parting and three young children to prove her fertility. She stopped her children from sitting on the long hard seat, motioning them to wait.

"It's dirty," she scolded them in Gujarati, pointing to the dull green vinyl which had worn away in parts to reveal the coarse padding underneath. She reached into her oversized plastic shopping bag, pulling out a printed cotton bedspread that she snapped open with a quick flick of her wrists. She covered the seat and tucked the edges in. The woman nodded in satisfaction, patted her hair into place, then sat down and lifted the three children up beside her so they sat propped up against the seat back. The four of them sat squashed against each other in the middle of the seat, with ample room on either side.

The train whistle blew, and the tea and snack vendors who droned their wares by the windows suddenly switched into high gear, running from one window to the next, shouting out Hot tea! Hot tea . . . ! Fresh puri-bhaji . . . ! Hot samosas! Thin porters in bright red shirts raced by with tottering mounds of baggage balanced on their heads. I was sitting on an Indian train for the first time in a decade, but the scene was just as I remembered it from childhood. The big difference was that, this time, I was traveling alone.

The train slowly pulled out of the station. The woman across from me looked at me then for the first time. In her quick look, she took in my short hair, my knee-length dress and ringless third finger. Her evaluation made, she avoided my eyes. She looked over my head, through my feet, at the door and windows, but not into my eyes. Though her children were staring at me, through a series of subtle cues from their mother, they had understood that I was to be given the silent treatment.

I remembered being that young age, and staring at strangers in that same fascinated way, knowing that they were humans like us, but knowing that they were not from our family. If, by some chance, it was determined that these strangers were friends of friends, or hailed from our parents' natal villages, or were otherwise established as people of good family, then the ice would break quickly, and food would be offered from both sides, followed by the sharing of board games or card games or amusing pastimes like guessing the names of Hindi film songs. But until then, the adults sat stone-faced and the children stuck to their own.

The young mother across from me spoke to her children in a shrill Gujarati punctuated by such endearments as greedy, idiot, blackie and pig. The children were obviously used to these mocking asides and did not respond. But it had been years since I had heard those insults spoken with such fluency, and I was immediately flooded with memories of shouting matches when our group of young cousins would exhaust the usual English insults: You stupid! You idiot! Fool! Crackpot!, all of which had a peculiar weightiness that would quickly tire us out. But then we would switch to our reservoir of delicious Gujarati insults: Pig! Monkey! Cockroach! Elephant!, and somehow these abuses from our mother tongue were so much more raucous and full of abandon that they elevated us back into good humor and collaborative play.

Giggles rose up in me like bubbles as the woman chided her children. I stifled the first few, but I couldn't help but smile when the woman called her son a goat, and I finally had to guffaw and cough when she called her daughter a donkey. The woman looked up at me sharply and I pressed my twitching lips shut.

She opened her mouth to speak, but then turned and frowned at the window, unsure of whether to engage with me. After all, I was a stranger, and it was probably best not to get involved. But then as I snorted and cleared my throat again, she took a deep breath and sat forward.

"You are Christian?" she snapped. I shook my head apologetically. She looked pointedly at my dress, or frock, as she would have referred to it.

"You are Muslim from Delhi?" She was still cross.

"No," I replied politely.

"You are Madrasi," she sneered.

"No. I've never been to Madras."

"Then you must be Punjabi," she taunted.

I smiled faintly. She was bent on pinning me down.

"Where you are from?" she rasped.

"From right here in Bombay," I said sweetly. She nodded and waved her hand.

"Now I know. You are Malayali." She looked away, signaling that the discussion was over. But from the corner of her eye she saw me shake my head.

"Maharashtrian," she continued emphatically. She straightened the pleats of her sari.

I stared at her. I was suddenly aware of feeling hurt. If she weren't so prejudiced by my short hair and Western dress, and the quickly made assumption that I was unmarried and childless, she would surely have seen right away that I was Gujarati. I opened my book and began reading to signal that the conversation really was over.

"I know a girl from Goa who looks just like you."

I turned the page and crossed my legs, settling into my stance.

"But naturally you are Bengali." She turned to her children and nodded sagely

Suddenly I tired of her game and decided to burst her bubble. I reached into my purse and pulled out a package of Gluco biscuits. I tore the wrapper slowly, to make sure that I had the attention of all three children. They looked at me hungrily.

"Biscuit aapu?" I asked in Gujarati and held out the pack to the older boy.

The woman gasped in horror and slapped down her son's outstretched hand.

"You're Gujarati!" she howled in rage. She was so offended by this realization that she instinctively reached back and covered her head with her sari for protection.

"Yes, auntie," I said in wide-eyed sing-song. "I am a pukka Gujarati."

All three children were staring at me slack-jawed. Their mother slapped each one quickly across the mouth. She shouted at them. "How many times have I told you not to take things from strangers, huh? Have you no shame? Sit up straight and keep your hands to yourselves!"

I put down my book and looked at the woman fumbling for her handkerchief with shaking hands.

"Are you also Gujarati?" I asked with a smile.

She pursed her lips and looked out of the window. Her fingers twisted the handkerchief into a tense rope.

"We are the real Gujaratis, from *Gujarat*!" she spat.

"My family is from Saurashtra," I said gently. "We are Jains."

Her face turned pale and her brow knitted furiously.

"These days anybody can say they come from anywhere," she muttered in exasperation. "I'm not so stupid that I will believe everything!"

She pushed her children out of the way and stretched out on the seat. She crossed her arms tightly over her chest and pressed her lips shut. She stared pointedly at the miniature ceiling fan. The three youngsters re-seated themselves timidly by the window, looking at each other nervously. Their mother was now in a bad mood, and any disturbance was likely to result in a hard slap across the head. Even though I was Gujarati, I was obviously a troublemaker if I had caused their mother to reach this state.

The first time I realized that there were others besides Gujaratis in the world was when my oldest cousin married a Punjabi woman. My cousin had returned from studying "abroad" and announced to the family that he was now a married man. The adults were shocked to hear that *she* was Punjabi. That made her completely different! There was much grumbling among the women of the family about having to cope with *her* on top of all their countless chores.

We children could tell she was completely different because she laughed a lot and gave us lots of sweets and kisses every time we went to her room to visit her. Her kisses left big red splotches on our faces which we gigglingly rubbed off each other. She dressed in chiffon saris printed with dazzling sunflowers, roses, hibiscus. She let the saris fall carelessly across her bosom instead of securing them at the shoulder with pins. She wore tight blouses that were always on the verge of bursting, and didn't mind in the least if we barged in on her while she was dressing. She wore her hair short, with an enormous red bindi moistly spreading between her eyebrows. And to top it all, she had the most daring collection of sunglasses we had ever seen.

This woman was *not* Gujarati, most especially with her given name of Lajinder. My grandmother, matriarch of the household, quite firmly changed Lajinder's name to Lakshmi, after the goddess of wealth and prosperity. After all Lakshmi bhabhi hailed from a very wealthy family and should bring a considerable dowry to her husband's home, even if the newlyweds had joined in a "love marriage." For many months there was an angry stand-off in the house between my grandmother and Lakshmi, as Lakshmi refused to negotiate any dowry from her family. During those early months, every morning Lakshmi would perform the young wife's duty of massaging my grandmother's feet, but she did it wearing the lowest-cut blouses, the tightest dresses and the flimsiest nightgowns, kneeling dutifully at my grandmother's feet so that the old woman was forced to look at Lakshmi's bouncing breasts, or hold her head high and look away. One morning my grandmother had had enough and she burst into tears, wailing to god to release her from the torments of her life. From then on, all talk of the dowry ceased, and Lakshmi dressed far more modestly in our family home.

For all the ease with which Lakshmi bhabhi picked up the Gujarati language and followed every Gujarati custom concerning food, cleanliness, and finances set up by our family, she was never ever considered Gujarati. She was always referred to as "that Punjabi." There was an invisible line that she was not allowed to cross, even after she had become one of the most powerful women in our family. For me, the very fact that she would never turn into a Gujarati made her my favorite female relative. I couldn't really explain why.

I sat on the train wondering about my clothes. I was wearing a printed rayon dress and closed shoes. I wore no jewelry other than my silver hoop earrings and my nondescript watch. I had eyeliner around my eyes and a little petroleum jelly on my lips. Would I have gone unnoticed in a sari or salwar-khameez?

I walked out of the compartment into the swaying corridor of the train. I slowly walked past all the compartments in the ladies' section, looking at how the women were dressed. Rich, poor, thin, fat, none of them resembled me. It wasn't just that none of them wore a dress, but that all of them looked at me with burning eyes, without recognition. I walked back to my berth and sat by the window. I watched my reflection in the dusty window pane, superimposed on the dazzling green fields that stretched out to the horizon.

I thought about how and where I directed my gaze when evaluating an unknown woman. Whenever possible, I always looked directly at the eyes and mouth first, then at the rest of the face, and only then would I attempt to integrate the woman's clothing with what was expressed in her face. My guess was that even in a sari, or other traditional Indian clothes, something in my eyes, and the set of my mouth, would give me away, would mark me as other, outsider, oblique.

The second non-Gujarati whom I remember being aware of was my Maharashtrian ayah, or bai. She was most certainly different, because she wore her sari in the traditional Maharashtrian manner, the long material pulled through her legs and out the other side and tucked in at the back of the waist in such a way that her buttocks were perfectly outlined. This way of wearing the sari was similar to how Indian men wear the traditional dhoti, but somehow the material stretching taut between the legs of the men never outlined anything quite as interesting as my bai's wonderful hips. As a young girl I never thought about her body consciously, but every time she walked by me, I was drawn to look at her shapely quivering flesh.

Neither the Gujarati style nor the North Indian style of wearing the sari allowed for the outlining of any sensuous shapes below the waist. Thus, in my childish imagination, it was only Maharashtrian women servants who had buttocks. As I visited the houses of my Gujarati friends, most of whom also had bais working for them, I came to have an appreciation for the various kinds of sari-wrapped buttocks that jiggled and sweated on the hips of our bais. Eventually my friends and I realized that we could do our bai-watching in the park, where dozens of these women came during the evening, bringing their young charges to play on the swings and slides.

These bais were definitely not Gujarati. They were too different! No matter that in some Gujarati households the Maharashtrian bais had worked there for decades and spoke only Gujarati, ate only Gujarati food and regaled their gods with only Gujarati bhajans. Wearing their saris the way they did, there was no question of these bais ever becoming one of us.

After all my years in America, my being Gujarati had lost its potency. In the West, I was Indian. Nothing further. In India, we had never been *Indian*. Though the word India was used everywhere all the time, "Indian" was used so rarely in my early years that the American term cowboys and Indians entered our vocabulary unchallenged. The only uses of Indian I can remember from my early years were from the radio reports of the steadily advancing Indian Army during the 1971 war with Pakistan, and from the title of the English-language newspaper, *The Indian Express.*

Sitting on the train, watching the Gujarati woman carefully avoiding me, I wondered if my retort to her angry attempt at pinning me down should simply have been, *I'm Indian!* She would have looked at me blankly. On top of everything, the woman might have wondered, is this insolent girl so stupid as to imagine that I can't see that she is from this country? My dark skin, hair and eyes made me visibly Indian. On the other hand, if I had been lightskinned, there might have been some doubt about my identity, and consequently, less of a need to judge me harshly.

That reminded me of where else the term Indian had come up in my youth. It was to describe yet another non-Gujarati, a Kashmiri girl, who was appraised by my mother as being so fairskinned that she definitely did not look Indian. This was my friend Radha, who looked exactly like a doll, with her curly brown hair and eerie hazel eyes. Her eyebrows were sparse golden arcs, unlike my black ones that almost met in the center of my forehead; her lips were light pink, unlike my dark purple ones. I didn't see any of this until my mother pointed it out. To me, Radha was exactly like a doll, a foreign doll. I wanted nothing more than to play with her.

Radha had the most benevolent nature of any child I knew. She was always mentally alert but quiet, always ready for action but motionless. She would do anything I wanted her to do. She would lift up her dress for me, higher and higher, until her entire gleaming white torso was revealed, right up to the sloping pink nipples. I would shout, "Simon Says, keep your hands in the air!" and she would stand rigid for minutes on end with her face hidden behind her upturned dress.

I would walk up to her and lightly dig my finger into her bellybutton. She would sigh, but not laugh. Then I would walk behind her and wedge her hand-sewn white panties in between her buttocks. She would clench the muscles as I touched her, then relax them. Then I would order, "Simon Says, hold your dress up with one hand and pull your chuddis off with the other!" And Radha would willingly oblige by pushing her panties down with one hand and squirming and kicking out of them. Then I would kneel down and tense my forearm and push Radha's thighs apart. Radha would slide onto my arm. She was so small, I could stand up and lift her into the air, where she balanced gracefully on my limb, her naked legs tautly extended like those of a tiptoeing ballerina, her head lost in the flying flounces of her tutu.

Radha was not Gujarati. She did not even have to be Indian if she didn't want. All around her were adults and children who would help her take on any fantasy identity she wanted. When Radha did occasionally speak, she made it clear that when she grew up she was going to be a famous actress in Hollywood. The adults loved this vision of Radha as performer. Such a light-skinned girl should definitely be put on show. I wasn't quite sure how Radha the doll would grow into Radha the Hollywood film star, but when at a private film screening in Bombay I saw an American actress in the nude for the first time, I noticed immediately the small pink nipples that glowed on her breasts, and realized that Radha would fit right in.

The rocking and rumbling of the train has put the three children to sleep. The woman is now sitting up, reading a Gujarati paperback. She looks at me occasionally with long frowning stares, then returns to her book. When I return her look, it is many long seconds before she looks away. She has steeled herself against both my strangeness and my familiarity. She acknowledges my presence, but there is nothing about me that she wants to know. The persistent unabashed flood of questions that is the mark of curious Indians will not pass her lips. So we sit in amicable silence in the cramped quarters of the train. We can finish our long journey in peace.

I could have told the Gujarati woman that I was Brazilian, Mexican, or even Ethiopian, just a few of the identities commonly ascribed to me by hopeful strangers in the United States. I could have claimed to be Israeli, Egyptian or Turkish; even Italian, Spanish, Portuguese. That is the beauty of being Gujarati. The ports of Gujarat have been active centers of trade for millennia, and have attracted not only Arabs, Turks, Mongols, Persians, Greeks, Romans, and Africans, but then later also the English, Spanish, French, and Portuguese, all of whose genes have mingled over centuries with the original inhabitants of Gujarat so that even we Gujaratis are fooled by each other.

I want to take the face of the woman between my hands and tell her gently, so as not to scare her: Don't you know that there are Gujaratis in every country on earth now? Don't you know that our culture has caused subtle shifts in every community, and in turn, every community is subtly shifting the Gujaratis?

I intensify my stare and try to blaze a telepathic message into her frowning brow: It doesn't matter anymore what identity I was born into.

She melts a little under my stare, her face softening into concern. I lean forward and breathe deeply as I imagine conveying the ultimate: What matters is that I am *sexual.*

She puts her book down and looks at me languidly through drooping lashes. I frame the last of my message, wishing she would read me like her book: Being sexual has reshaped my knowledge, my feelings, my very breath. *That* is what fools you; that is what you turn away from in *yourself* when you turn away from me.

The Gujarati woman remains unmoved by my secrets. She leans forward and slides shut the compartment door. Then she reaches behind her and quickly undoes the tightly coiled bun at the nape of her neck. She shakes free her long hair and runs her fingers slowly down the length of it, head bowed to one side.

I am shocked, as I always am to see how sensuality abruptly descends on the sternest of Indian women when they loosen their thick dark hair. With her hair down, this smug judgmental mother of three is suddenly so breathtakingly beautiful that I want to cry. She looks at me slyly, conspiratorially, savoring the feel of her long tresses between her fingers.

"Why don't you grow your hair," she murmurs. "Long hair looks so good on us, don't you think?"

She pushes up her window as high as it will go. The wind lifts her hair around her like a lone hawk suspended on a bank of air. Her hair spreads out, shading her, like the flat top of a solitary baobab tree. If only I could climb into those silken branches. . . .

An old familiar longing rushes into my throat, hammering at my vocal chords, drying me out with desire. I know this woman. I know her well. She is part of my recurring dream of coming home to India to be greeted by thousands of women running down a hill with their long hair swooping behind them like black garlands of welcome, like black birds released from captivity to honor my return.

I feel the slow uncoiling in my groin as the heat of my many tightly held selves burns through me. Resistance I'm not aware of holding suddenly snaps, and the train compartment, the woman, her sleeping children, the rusted ceiling fan, the tracks, the fields, the hazy sky, spin me so fiercely that I have to lean back and let it all rock through me. The brooding, dreaming girl I had been ten years earlier, wanting to be embraced and ensnared and embodied by these ciphers of women that surrounded me, has become a brooding, dreaming adult, still aching to decipher, derange, delight. I need to start over: I require once again a pliant will, a chameleon identity, and the reconfigured time of cycles and sieves that runs me aground again and again in a rut of meaningless circumstances, but then suddenly drops me right down the trap door of surface and superfice into the rushing female river below.

I feel the hair on my head jumping and growing and the hem of my dress lengthening and unfolding, drawing me closer to home.

TALE OF APRICOT

Minh Duc Nguyen

I wake up this morning and feel no different than when I went to sleep. For hours, I lie here and observe the branches of the apricot tree that I slept under. I have recently made a promise not to sleep under any tree more than once. This third tree, so far, has the most complicated structure to remember.

I get up and wander around the apricot orchard. These days I have a lot of free time. And I don't have any friends left. They either died or disappeared some time ago. But I'm too old to need friends. The only face that I can remember anyway is that of Chu Que. At times, I look at my hands like they are the young faces of me and him, and I watch them speak to each other. At other times, I just laugh with the crickets and roll around on the wild grass, and I hug the yellow sand by the creek and sleep with the fallen apricots. And slowly, I feel more and more like, what if, I am a ghost.

I can't help but walk toward the apricot cannery. From where I am, the cannery appears as a gray umbrella, shielding the workers inside from the harsh sun of Fresno. Beneath that faded roof, each family, mainly of mother and daughters, gathers around a long wooden table, slicing apricots in halves. They peel out the large brown seed inside the apricot and assemble the halves on a tray as large as the table. They stack one full tray on top of another. And at the end of each day, Mr. and Mrs. Best, the owners of this plantation, would give them two-fifty cash for each tray. Time is money, as people say, so they cut fast.

Inside the warehouse, I walk from one family to another. It is something that I have done for the past two days. I eavesdrop on their conversation but I keep my distance. I hear all kind of languages: Spanish, Chinese, Cambodian, Vietnamese, and more, but rarely English. The only time these workers would make an effort to speak English is when Mr. Best is around. But his tall frame is nowhere to be seen today. His wife, a small but attractive Chinese woman in her late thirties, is now chatting freely in her dialect among the Chinese families. Mrs. Best lets her dog, a black mutt with a stubby tail, skip around from one table to the next. The dumb dog jumps on everyone it sees and leaves prints of its dirty paws on their shirts.

"No, Vita! No!" Mrs. Best yells at her dog.

Briefly still, Vita stares back at its owner, confused. Then it runs away and resumes its bad manners.

I move toward the right wing of the cannery where all the Vietnamese families are concentrated, and I find the spot where I can be in the center of all of them. I hear that Mrs. Tan is giving Mrs. Anh tips on how to cook bun bo Hue without using MSG—just stew the beef back and tail bones in a large pot for three days to maximize the richness of the broth. Mrs. Nga is telling her daughter Linh not to go out with her boyfriend Minh any longer since he's not going to college. Mrs. Bich, probably the youngest mother there, is pregnant again. She wants a boy this time. Mrs. Thi, who stands in the corner, still hasn't said a word since I first saw her, but rumors tell me that her husband has left her for another woman. Mrs. Ha, a recent immigrant, complains that there aren't any good Vietnamese restaurants in Fresno, how the dishes that they make here are so plain, more like for the American healthy taste, and how the chicken meat here is too tender. She longs for egg noodles from Da Lat, fresh nuoc mam from Phu Quoc, longans from My Tho.

I stand here and listen to the Vietnamese that these families speak. Their words dance in my mind and it doesn't take many beats before I am back in Saigon.

I was three and was already wandering around the main streets day after day with Chu Que, my one-legged uncle, begging for spare change. Chu Que was not my blood relative but it didn't really matter because he was the only one who took care of me, and I didn't know how I came into existence anyway. He said he found me one night in a garbage can located in the back of a dog-meat restaurant. It was dark at the time he picked up my arm and thought that it was a dog bone with some skin left on it. I started to cry when he bit me, and Chu Que then thought that I was a dog with some horrible disease that the chef didn't want to cook and threw away half-killed. But when he saw my fingers grabbing tightly on his crutch, he knew right away that I was someone who had come into his life to fill in as his missing right leg. He lifted me out of the garbage can and into this world, and he bandaged my bleeding arm with a banana leaf. He found a rope and tightened one end around my neck and the other end on his crutch. And Chu Que called me Cho Con, his little dog, until he died.

I was lucky, Chu Que told me. My life could have been much worse. I could have been found by other beggars, perhaps a leper who would pass me his disease, and my hands and feet would have deteriorated when I reached ten, and I would have had to push my body around on a four-wheeled cart, or I could have been found by a desperate beggar who would have twisted my arms and legs and turned me into a freak—a showcase of pity to get more spare change. I asked Chu Que if that was what happened to him, that perhaps some beggars had kidnapped him from his family and broke off one of his legs. But Chu Que didn't say anything. To this day, I still don't know how he'd lost half of his right leg. Well anyway, at least with Chu Que, I still had all my body parts and grew up somewhat normally in the place I knew best. At least with him, I turned out somewhat a human being, or partly.

And standing here in the apricot cannery and in the middle of these families who speak my language, I am not asking for their pity. I am not asking for their spare change. I only seek their recognition that I have the same body parts as them, that I am a human being like them. I want them to see me, if not all of me, then parts of me.

Standing very close to me is little Trang. She has a dirty face even though the morning is still young. Her hands and slingshot are tucked deeply in her pant pockets. The rubber bands on the slingshot hang loose outside. She is standing around with nothing to do, so she decides to try her luck again.

"Ma," says Trang. "Can I help, please?"

Mrs. Ly and her oldest daughter Ngoc are busy with the apricots in their hands. The left hand holds the apricot with three fingers. The right hand holds the small knife with a short curve blade. The right thumb presses the sharp blade deep into the apricot. The three fingers on the left hand rotate the fruit, allowing the blade to slit along the groove that nature imprints on every apricot.

"I can do it, Ma. Let me show you." Little Trang sneaks her hand into Mrs. Ly's blouse pocket where she keeps the extra knife.

"Go away." Mrs. Ly pushes Trang's hand away. "You don't know how."

"Ma, I know how. It's like cutting apple."

"How many times have I told you that this is not an apple? This is an apricot, like a small peach. There's a large seed inside. You have to cut around it, and you have to cut right to get two equal halves. Otherwise, the lady boss will yell, understand? You don't know how. Now, go go, so I can work!"

Sister Ngoc feels pity for her much younger sister, so she says, "Trang, you can help me peel out the seed."

"I don't want to peel seed. I want to cut. Why don't you peel seed and I cut?"

Sister Ngoc smiles. "All right. Let me see if you can cut." And she is about to hand little Trang her knife, but Mrs. Ly stops her.

"No. I said she's too young to know how to cut. She'll cut her fingers instead. Girls with scars are ugly." Mrs. Ly rumbles on to explain that a girl's hands should be soft and white like steamed rice. The fingers should be long and somewhat fat where they meet the knuckles and pointed at the tips. But most importantly, the hands should be free of scars. If a hardworking girl has beautiful hands, it is a sign that she is *kheo leo,* clever, and she will know how to keep her house together when she has a family of her own. It's strange how Mrs. Ly's hands are nothing like what she described. Her frail hands appear used and dry around the finger tips. Red marks rest on her palms and long veins emerge through the brown skin. Perhaps they were once white and soft.

"Why don't you go play with the other kids?" Sister Ngoc tells little Trang, who is still staring at the knife. "Go go and come back later for lunch."

Finally, little Trang trots away toward the apricot orchard, kicking her feet high. She raises her hands and gazes at them. Her fingers clench into tight fists. I don't think she realizes how small her hands are.

I follow her. The poor girl must not think of herself as useless. I have a feeling she will do something of great importance for me.

I wish I could stop little Trang at this moment and talk to her and teach her the art of begging. All she had to do was to look deeply at her mother's hands with her light brown eyes and say, "Ma, you have beautiful hands." And I'm sure Mrs. Ly would soften and wrap her daughter's hands inside her own and they would cut together.

I knew all there was to know about begging. Chu Que taught me all the tricks, and I formulated some myself. The secret was to look like a beggar but talk like a poet.

"Cho Con, don't beg and they will give," said Chu Que. He often used breakfast as an example to show his point.

"It's early morning, and you are hungry and you want to eat breakfast. A man walks by. He's neither rich nor poor. Cho Con, what would you do?"

"Chu Que, I'd say, 'Chu a Chu, I'm hungry. Would you be kind and spare me some change?'"

"Well, that's not bad, Cho Con. You asked politely. And you look like a cute little girl, although very dirty. The man will pity you and give you two dong. With that, you can buy one Chinese donut for breakfast. But suppose you want more. Suppose you want a bowl of porridge with stuffed pork intestines to go with your donut. How do you convince this man to give you five more dong?"

"Hmmm? . . . I'll say that you are my father . . . and you are very sick . . . and . . . that I need money to go buy you medicine."

"Oh, Cho Con, you lie. That's very good. You're learning every day. But there's no need to lie unless it's a matter of life and death. And besides, what if I'm not with you? Who would be your father?"

"Chu Que, what would you do?"

"Now, listen. You're a little girl. People like little girls. It's early morning, a man walks by, you're hungry and want to eat breakfast. If you wave your hand at him, look him straight in the eyes, and greet him with a smile, just this much I'll guarantee you that most of the time the man will already give two dong so you can buy a Chinese donut. But now you want a bowl of porridge, so it's a little trickier. You'll have to play a game with the man. Nothing is for free, understand? You play a game with him and he'll pay you for it."

"What game, Chu Que?"

"A game of words. Man likes to play games to test his wit. It's his stupid nature. So you ask him a silly question that makes him think but he cannot answer . . . like . . . like 'Chu a Chu, do you know how big the moon is?' Hah, see? The man probably stops, thinks about it for a few seconds, and says, 'I really don't know. Why do you ask, little girl?' Now, this is when what you say counts the most! How much more the man will give you depends on how smart your answer is. You'd say something like this, 'Chu a Chu, last night I was so hungry that I couldn't sleep. So I laid here on the street awake all night and I watched the moon. The moon was so beautiful. It was bright, round and large, as large as your face! But I think the moon is probably much bigger than that. Chu a Chu, am I right?' What can he say now? Nothing! The man will nod his head in defeat. He'll pat you on the head and give you the extra five dong for your bowl of porridge, and he'll walk away smiling at his own kindness."

By the time I was seven, I had mastered this game of wit, which was played differently with a rich man or a poor man, young man or old man, a man or woman, tourists or local people. I rarely had to say "please" or even "spare change." But things became worse as I got older. I was no longer a cute little girl. I had to readjust and that was a new lesson. When I came to America, I encountered several beggars in San Francisco. They either sat in their corners and shook their paper cups with a few coins inside, or they just said, "Spare change?" And I laughed so hard at them.

Little Trang runs as fast as she can across the apricot orchard. She is anxious to meet the other children at the wild blackberry shrubs by the creek. But at halfway, her right foot steps into a squirrel's hole, and she falls down hard and scratches her left elbow on a sharp stone. Slowly, little Trang sits up. She holds her bleeding elbow close to her face and observes her wound carefully, with admiration. Then, with her fingertips, she rubs saliva off her tongue and cleans her wound. The touch of saliva on her injury must have created a burning pain, for her left cheek twitches continuously. But she remains still and quiet. The blood on the round scrape, which seems redder than a Tet good luck money envelope, soon clots in the dry summer heat. In a week, she'll have a new scar, and she'll have to hide it from her mother. The girl stands up on her feet. She kicks the dirt off her pants. As if she's forgotten about her fall, she races toward the creek, as fast as she can, like a wild mustang.

I run after her.

She stops to rest under an apricot tree with a few fruits left. She pulls down a drooping branch, shaking it vigorously until an apricot falls. She bends down and picks up the overripe fruit. With her long thumbnail, she stabs through the yellowish pink skin. Golden juice rushes out, racing down her thumb and wrist, cooling the pores of her skin along the way. She slides her sharp nail around the apricot and tears it apart into two messy halves. The large seed on one half stares at her.

"It's not that hard," she mumbles. "I can cut anything."

A large, black creature runs toward her and dives on her back. Little Trang falls, face down, but eases her crash with her hands. The apricot's halves crush in her palms.

"Uneducated dog! I'll teach you a lesson!" she curses.

Dumb Vita licks her ear and then quickly runs away. Little Trang pushes herself up. She pulls out her slingshot from her pocket. She takes the wet apricot seed in her hand and shoots it at Vita. But she misses badly. Vita barks and disappears behind some bushes.

Trang swallows her anger and continues down until she reaches the narrow creek curving behind the apricot orchard. She finds the blackberry shrubs but sees no one. Usually the children gather here and play hide-and-seek, or they hunt for squirrels and birds with their slingshots or fish for crawdads in the muddy creek with the raw chicken parts that they brought from home. She walks further down along the creek. Tall pines embed both sides of the creek now. Perhaps the children have hiked deep down the creek to find a perfect tree that extends its large branches from one side of the creek to the other, and the boys can climb up and tie a long rope on that branch so they can swing like monkeys from one side to the other.

After a long while, I become more and more reluctant to follow the little girl. I recognize this path, and I know what secret lies ahead. And suddenly, I feel weak, and I don't want to follow her any longer. But she's going down there no matter what, with or without me. Why can't a secret be a secret? But nothing can be a secret if it isn't discovered. Sometimes it is better to leave something unknown.

Chu Que always treated me like I was his pupil. But when I was old enough, I realized that he was only about fifteen years older than me, so I told him to cut that act out. And he did. He had to. I was a young woman now, and I could easily live on my own any day. In a way, Chu Que was relieved to be rid of the fatherly responsibility of all those years.

We became friends, friends in the way that we could swear at each other freely, and run away from each other for a few days, until we crawled back in the same corner and shared our cup again. Our difference in age didn't matter anymore. In a way, we were immortal.

"We're angels on the streets," Chu Que described us.

"But angels are the slaves of God," I contradicted him. "They are worse off than beggars."

Chu Que was very handsome. A brave soldier dressed in a new uniform couldn't be as handsome. He was neither tall nor did he carry himself well, especially with his limp. But he had the saddest face in Saigon. Every time I looked at him I felt very fortunate for my own life. His eyes, which were long and deep as the creek here, could see through any soul. Every day, we sat around and observed people on the streets. And randomly as he chose, Chu Que would point his finger at any person and tell me about him or her like he had known that person for years.

So I began to love. I don't know how or exactly when or what for, but I did, like I can't help but dream when I sleep. And everybody has to sleep, even if they live outside on the streets, and it's raining. And in Saigon, did it rain. It was late that August when the monsoon had come down hard for eight straight days and still wouldn't quit. Standing on the sidewalk, the flood had risen to our knees. That night I lost my sandals as we waded for many blocks to find a high step on some house or building. But with Chu Que's leg, we moved slowly, so all the dry spots were occupied by other beggars. We searched for miles with no luck.

"We're going to drown tonight," I said to him.

"Don't be silly. There must be a dry place somewhere in this damn city." He cried.

I could hardly hear him. The storm pounded hard against metal sheet rooftops, and water gushed down the sidewalks. The wind shoved violently, snapping tree branches and knocking over parked cyclos and scooters. Our streets became a river of floating trash. Wind and rain, earth and heaven, there must be a dry spot somewhere. We stared real hard, into the corners of brick walls, the pits of long alleys, under iron balconies and behind trash cans. And slowly, from these darkest places, round eyes, many of them, began to light up like stars, gazing out at us. We looked down with shame. We could not see our feet.

Then Chu Que said, "Follow me."

He held my hand and led me to a motel nearby. He pulled me inside the office room where the owner of the motel was leaning at the front counter. He was sipping hot tea. His wife and children were eating rice in the back.

"No," I said. "They would never—"

But Chu Que motioned me to say no more.

"How much for a room?" Chu Que asked the owner.

The owner didn't bother to answer. But his wife, she noticed how serious Chu Que seemed. So she replied, "Four hundred dong."

Chu Que slowly bent his back. He untied the knot on the short leg of his trouser. A tightly-wrapped plastic bag fell out, and Chu Que caught it. He took off the rubber band and unwrapped the plastic bag. Inside was a roll of money, a big roll of small bills. He counted the money in front of the owner and his wife.

"Here's the four hundred," Chu Que said. "And there are twenty-three left. I will throw that in also if you make us a pot of hot tea like that and give us your leftover rice."

Astonished, the owner nodded. His wife took the money.

The owner showed us our room. A short while later, the wife served us hot tea and rice with salted fish and sour cabbage.

Chu Que and I both removed our soaked clothes, and we wrapped ourselves with the blankets that the room provided. We ate our rice and drank our tea. It was our best meal together.

After that, we crawled onto the bed and laid next to each other, like we always did on the street anyway. Only this time we were naked. I asked him about the money since I was as surprised as the motel owner. Chu Que shook his head in regret. He said he had been saving it to buy me a sweater. I inched closer to him. I told him that I already had him to keep me warm. Then his hand crawled slowly beneath the blankets and found its place on my small breast and covered my cold nipple. And just like that, we discovered ourselves all over again. And after an hour or so, we held tightly to each other and rolled down to the floor because we weren't used to lying on a soft mattress. I remember we giggled like little kids.

After that night, our lives changed completely. We still begged and dragged ourselves on the streets as usual. But I mean the invisible changes that you can't see. Whatever it was, it was comforting to know that someone would always be there for me, even though he was there since the beginning.

But nothing lasts. Money has to be spent, and food has to be eaten or it will spoil. Why discover something when one cannot hold on to it forever?

The night Chu Que died, we were sitting on Le Loi Boulevard, near Ben Thanh Market. Many things had changed. For one thing, Saigon was now Ho Chi Minh City, but we beggars couldn't care less. I was only worried about Chu Que's health. He was in constant pain. At night, he couldn't sleep in peace, always tossing and turning inside our blanket, ending up crouching like a fetus that tucks its hands in front of its stomach. I held him still as much as I could with one hand, and with the other hand, I massaged his head since it helped to ease his pain a little. I took him to the hospital, but it was no use. The doctor told us that he would require surgery, and there were other poor sick people with worse cases waiting.

"What are we supposed to do?" I asked the doctor. "Just wait to die on the street?"

The doctor said nothing.

"Let's go," Chu Que told me. "It's not his fault."

That night we sat in our corner. I was too tired to beg so I leaned back against the wall. The apartment's balcony above cast a shadow over my body. Chu Que, skinny and weak, crawled out to the sidewalk to be visible under the streetlights. It was nice to see him from a distance. He was indeed a poet in the degradation of time and mass. Sitting by myself, I watched him play his last game of words.

A man with black boots walked by.

"Chu a Chu, do you know what time it is?" asked Chu Que before he looked up and saw that the man's green hat glittered with a red metal star.

"It's ten after nine." The man's metal watchband and the large buttons on his khaki uniform shined at us. "Why do you ask? Does it matter to you what time it is?"

"No. I guess not. But a long time ago, I used to have a nice watch and I always knew what time it was . . . and . . . and I used to wear leather shoes that warmed my feet . . . and I used to live in a large house that had a tall ceiling to shield my head from the rain . . . like your beautiful hat there. No. I guess I don't need to know what time it is. It's just an old habit of this . . . poor . . . bum." And then Chu Que coughed abruptly.

The tall man stared at Chu Que for a while before, finally, he pulled out a hundred dong bill and dropped it in Chu Que's bowl.

"And did you used to have two legs, too?" asked the man.

"Huh? Two legs, one leg, what's the difference, dong chi?" Chu Que acknowledged him as Comrade.

"It's obvious."

"No, it's not. I'm almost blind, so why don't you tell me the difference between two legs and one leg."

The man shook his head and was about to leave.

"Tell me, or you don't know, dong chi!"

"All right, since you want to know so bad. I walk, you skip. I run, you crawl."

"You forget that you work and I beg, you give and I take!"

"You're right." The man laughed and dropped the second hundred dong bill. As the man turned away, Chu Que suddenly coughed out in a fury.

"Let me tell you what's the difference between two legs and one leg. Listen up. There's no difference! You and I are stuck together like a kite with a tail and a head, understand? Without my tail, you can't fly straight with your big head. Without a beggar like me, you'd have no one to show off your wealth to. Without me, you're nothing!"

The man in black boots laughed even louder. He walked away in long strides.

Chu Que died that night, in defeat at his own game, leaving his Cho Con by herself in this world. Before he passed away, he gasped by my neck, "Leave this place."

I wrapped his body and crutch inside two blankets, his and mine, and tightened them with the same rope that he once used to put around my neck. I paid a cyclo to take us to the border of the Saigon River. There, I slid his body into the black water. I was hoping that his body would flow out to reach the South China Sea and then to the Pacific Ocean. But instead, Chu Que's body just sank and vanished, carrying all the weight of his pain with him.

I knew that I couldn't play the game of wit any longer. It wasn't a game anymore. It was begging now. Chu Que and I had lied to ourselves. In truth, we weren't poets. We were bums on the streets who begged for a living. We begged for meals. We begged for cigarettes. We begged for clothes. We begged for shelter. And after Chu Que died, I begged my way to America.

I took the bus from Ho Chi Minh City to Vung Tau, the peninsula where the Bay of Boats was located. In the daytime, I went to the restaurants, the villas, and the cafes that lined the resort's beach, and I begged. But at night, I walked to the Bay of Boats, and I sat and waited. I waited for weeks before one night I saw people creeping out like spiders from the darkest corners. I knew it was the moment, and I quickly changed into a clean outfit that I had saved. I crawled quietly from behind and slowly, I rose and joined them. No one noticed that I was an outsider. We waited, at least fifty of us, by the shore with our heads low, until these small boats that looked like coffins became visible in front of us. We waded out quietly and climbed on. The small boats rowed out in an hour between water and blackness. We reached a much larger fishing boat that had been waiting for us, and we crawled over quickly. The fishing boat sailed out for hours before daring to turn on its motor. The boat people crouched on deck, leaning on each other, seasick, like spiders entangled in their own web.

We reached Malaysia in seven days. No one knew I cheated. They were too happy to care. I spent seventeen months at a refugee camp before I was sponsored to America by a Catholic church in Fresno.

For many years, I worked as a custodian in an elementary school. I swept and mopped and days dried by. I sorted the papers, pencils, and crayons that were dropped on the floor, and I tried to piece my life together. But most of the time, I picked up little pieces of trash and threw them in a large garbage can, and I dumped the loose fragments of my life in with them. Eventually, I had nothing left of myself to throw away.

And now I stare at the muddy water in this creek, and I wonder if this water carries any trace of Chu Que. It must. A body of water merges into other bodies of water, no matter how different they are in volume, in salt concentration, or in geography. Water from a river in one country flows out to join a sea, then meets an ocean, then travels a long distance to meet another sea, then joins a river in a new country, and ends up in a little creek. What do I know anyway? One leg or two legs, on boat or not, it still takes one to the same place. There's no difference.

I see no more need to follow little Trang. Obviously, she would never see me, and even if she could, she doesn't need my teaching. In this land, no one wants to beg, even if one is a beggar, and no one wants to play a game of wit, and definitely one would not pay for it. One just gives what one feels like, and one takes more than one can carry.

I jump into the creek and let the water carry me. It's something that I wanted to do three days ago but never had a chance. The water encloses my body, merges into me and stretches me. If I stay in this water long enough, gradually, I'll become the creek.

The water carries me, and I flow past little Trang who is still trotting anxiously further down the creek. The water takes me by many pines before it brings me back to the pathetic woman sitting by the creek with her bare feet in the water. Her back leans against a large trunk, but her head tilts toward the ground like she is about to fall down. She has one skinny hand clutching at her neck. Her eyes, pale yellow and barely open, gaze down at the water.

What are you staring at, you miserable woman? Why are you sitting there by yourself at a place like this? How did you end up here, Cho Con?

I grab her feet and pull myself out of the water. I sit next to her. I ask her many questions, but she does not respond. I wave my hand in front of her eyes, but she does not blink. I poke and tickle her feet but she does not move. At one point, I try to creep inside of her.

Damn you, you're worthless, useless, nothing but a heavy bag of rice.

Soon little Trang walks by, and she sees the woman sitting by the creek with her bare feet in the water. She stops before the woman and asks, "Aunty, have you seen any boys and girls walking by here?"

Forget it little girl. She won't answer you. She can't. She's dead.

"I've been looking for them, but I can't find them anywhere. We were supposed to meet and play down there." She points to the direction where she came from. Then she grins, showing off her little teeth. "Have you seen them, Aunty? They're small, like me."

The woman has a black bag open on her lap. A strong breeze flies by and knocks the bag off her lap. Green bills of ones, fives, and tens roll out of the bag and hang loose at its mouth.

"Aunty, there's your money. You better put them back inside your bag, or they're going to fly into the water and get all wet."

Take the money, little girl. There are twenty-four dollars and some coins there. This woman does not need money any longer. She has begged all her life, and now she has a chance to give some back. Please take her money, little girl. Don't you want to help your mother? Take the money and give it to her. Take the spare change, little girl, and return this woman a favor.

A stronger wind rushes by. The bills flap loose, but little Trang quickly kneels down and grabs them. She puts the bills on the ground and rolls them into a tight bundle. Then she tucks the money back inside the bag. As she does this, she sees several apricots resting inside.

"My mother thinks I cannot cut apricots. I can, I know I can, if only she gives me a chance. What's so hard about cutting apricots?" asks little Trang. "There you go, Aunty. I put your money back inside your bag. Be careful now."

You old fool. You didn't think this would happen to you, right? You thought that on the anniversary of Chu Que's death, you would walk across the broad apricot orchard near where you live, pick a few apricots, and hike to the little creek here. You thought that at this creek, you could take off your shoes and cool your feet in the water. And you thought that you would have time to share a few apricots with Chu Que. You thought you would have time to do all that before you'd drown yourself so you could join him in the creek here. But what do you know? You died before you could do much. You died as you choked on an apricot's seed.

"What's in your hand? What are you hiding?" asks little Trang. "My sister plays a guessing game with me all the time. She hides a coin in one hand and makes me guess."

Little girl, would you do me a favor and push my body into the water. As long as it sits here, I cannot rest in peace. As long as it stays there, I'll never join him.

Little Trang bends down and holds up the tight left fist of the woman. She peels out one finger at a time. Resting inside the white palm is the other rotten half of the apricot, the half without the large brown seed.

Loud barking suddenly echoes through the pines. Little Trang turns around. Black Vita is charging toward her. She drops the woman's hand to pull out her slingshot. She picks up several pebbles from the ground. And quickly, she races toward Vita, head to head. She aims at its nose. The dog sees the slingshot and retreats. But little Trang chases after it.

"I'll get you this time, you dumb dog! I'll get you this time!"

Please don't go.

But little Trang has disappeared after Vita.

I lean back on the pine and stare at the profile of the dead woman. She's there and I'm not, like an apricot without the seed inside. I pity her, love her more. I think I will sleep under this tree tonight.

THREE STORIES

R. Zamora Linmark

LIPS

Exotica is a woman trapped in a foreigner's body. Like Jodie Foster trapped in her mother's body in *Freaky Friday,* except Exotica is a man from the waist down.

"I keep it neatly packed in a nylon stocking and pull it out in case of emergencies," Exotica tells Edgar and me. "It is such a nuisance, honey. It feels like a huge mole."

She draws out a blusher from her makeup bag and accentuates her cheekbones until they look as if they're ready to pop. Then, "I'm just waiting for D-Day to come when the doctors cut it off so I can finally straighten out my act. In the meantime, I'm contented with my adopted twins," she says, petting her breasts.

"If ever I had one pair," says Edgar, "I like 'em be full as yours, Exotica, but they gotta be petal-shaped and bloomin'." He breaks out into an Arnold Horshack laugh.

"Do the men you go out with ever know what you really are?" I ask.

"I try to be discreet about it," Exotica says, spilling the contents of her makeup bag onto the vanity. "It's such a bother—I have to spend hours and hours just wrapping it up and tucking it tight between my legs."

She picks up a black kohl eyeliner and paints her eyes Egyptianesque like Elizabeth Taylor's in *Cleopatra.*

"Have you always wanted to be a woman?" I ask, watching Edgar stretch out his shirt to examine his chest.

"Since the day I saw the light," Exotica says. "I even have my own theory on why I am the way I am."

"What is it?" I ask.

"Well, I always knew deep inside me that I was made to follow in Sister Eve's footsteps, but my mother hated apples. In fact, she was allergic to them, especially mountain apples. That's why I came out a boy instead of a princess," Exotica says, giving them her revised version of Creation.

"Although to be honest with you, honey, I don't know why I had to be one of the chosen few." She pauses to grab the mascara. "I don't know what forces impel me to be this way, and I'm not just talking about putting on a dress and makeup, or deceiving men either."

She twists the cap open and begins the task of combing and lengthening her lashes until they spread out like spider's legs.

"It's got to do with feelings, honey, *feelings*," she continues. "At first I went through my guilt-trip episodes, but those were a centuries-old program, if you know what I mean."

"How did you finally accept yourself?" I ask, staring at Exotica's reflection in the mirror.

"I woke up one morning and realized I was pretending to be something I could never be—a man. Honey, let me tell you, it was the worst acting stint I'd ever done in my whole entire life. It made me feel so uncomfortable and cheap, I get goosebumps just thinking about it."

She catches me staring at her and throws a smile through the gilded, oval mirror. "Anyway, to make a long drama short, I finally had to choose between being miserable for the rest of my life, or beautiful. God knows where I'd be right now if I'd continued pretending."

"Probably the same sanitarium as me," answers Edgar.

"You're probably right." Exotica picks up a lipstick and stretches her mouth into an oblong shape. Edgar and I watch the reflection delicately paint red arcs.

"Exotica," Edgar says, interrupting her concentration, "you think you can make my eyes look like Liza Minnelli's in *Cabaret*?"

"Why?" she asks, snatching a tissue and pressing it between her painted lips.

"So I can come famous," answers Edgar.

"It's the lips that make a person famous, honey," she says. She turns to us and holds up the tissue as if she were displaying the Shroud of Turin.

"Not the nose, cheeks, ears, tits, legs, nor eyes," she says. "They say eyes speak a thousand languages, but the lips, honey, the lips hold a million secrets—and it's the secrets that attract attention."

"Is that how you get men to go home with you?" I ask.

"No, honey. I wait for them to stumble out of the bars. Once they start log-rolling on the pavement, that's when I take off my pumps, lug one over my shoulder, and whistle for a cab."

"You think my lips hide a million secrets?" asks Edgar.

Exotica examines Edgar's lips the way a fortune-teller reads cards. "Your lips aren't full enough to carry the heavy weight of enigma. But you have a beautiful pout—a princess pout."

"What's that?" Edgar asks.

"Very ambitious, manipulative, and powerful," Exotica replies, her eyes fixed on Edgar's lips as if there are more traits to foretell. "In short, honey, you come from a kingdom full of excitement and danger."

"Cuz I get one princess p—"

"A king never wants his daughter to possess too much power," she interrupts him. "But he also doesn't want to make her unhappy because once he does, all she has to do is unwind her long, braided hair and use it as a rope to climb down the tower and escape. In the end, he's left with no choice but to grant his daughter's wishes."

Taking pride in his newly discovered asset, Edgar tightens his pout until the lines around his mouth show.

"That's a no-no, honey," warns Exotica. "Pout like that and everyone, including the king, will mistake you for a wicked stepmother, or a plebeian's daughter with a monkey overbite."

"What about my lips?" I ask, drawing them closer together until they're shaped into a small O. "Are they full enough to carry mysteries?" Exotica studies my lips.

"He get famous lips, yeah?" Edgar asks.

"The definite curves mean eternity," Exotica says, as if hypnotized. "The redness for birth—"

"Like in 'children'?" interrupts Edgar, puzzled.

"No, not children, but creativity," she replies.

"What else?" I ask.

"The fullness for . . . " She raises her eyebrows.

"For danger and excitement?" Edgar suggests, prodding her for an answer.

I look at Exotica's eyes, spellbound and watery. I know she's discovered the secret I'm trying to hide. I want to rip the lips off my mouth so she can say it's all a mistake and has to start again. But I feel my lips caving in, my teeth digging into flesh.

"The fullness for what, Exotica?" badgers Edgar.

"For a kiss that means beauty and sadness," she says. She snaps out from under the spell.

"What does that mean?" he asks.

Exotica turns to me. I want to run far away from her and Edgar, but my legs feel like rubber.

"What does that mean?" Edgar asks again.

"It's nothing important," Exotica says. She turns her back, looks at me through the mirror, and winks. "You have a beautiful smile," she says, "so quit biting your lips."

"I will," I say. "I will."

Encore

In the Philippines, Vicente De Los Reyes was Christopher De Leon and his sister Jing was Nora Aunor, the country's best actor and actress. This year Jing retired from their faux show business. She said she was getting too old for that kind of stuff. Too busy, too actively involved with the Key Club, the Fil-Am Club. Plus she's a JV cheerleader. Plus this. Plus that. So Vicente replaced her with an ensemble which includes Edgar, Katrina, Loata, Florante, and Mai-Lan.

The stage is a low, thick stone wall that separates Mr. Batongbacal's house from Mrs. Freitas's. Two or three times a week, they climb up the wall to perform sold-out concerts like *Bee Gees: Live In Kalihi,* or scenes from box-office hits like *Grease* and television shows like *Charlie's Angels* and *The Facts of Life.*

The main audience includes: Vicente's brother Bino; Bino's friend Rowena; Mr.

Batongbacal, Vicente's landlord, who watches from behind the kitchen curtains; Mrs. Freitas, who watches Mr. Batongbacal from behind her living room curtains; and Roberto, Mrs. Freitas's son, who watches from the garage while he waxes his yellow Plymouth between guzzles of beer.

This past week was a replay of the Grand Prix finals of *Dance Fever*. Starring Edgar Ramirez as Deney Terrio, Loata Faalele as the video disc jockey Freeman King, and Katherine Katrina-Trina Cruz and Vicente De Los Reyes as Dianne and Toni, otherwise known as The Motions. The special musical guest was Grace Jones (Edgar) who sang "Do Or Die." The three special judges were . . .

First, one of the hottest young TV actors working today. We all know him as the handsome older brother of Arnold Drummond from the hit show *Diff'rent Strokes*. Please give a warm welcome to Todd Bridges (Florante);

Next, the actor who could write a book on cross-dressing in the military. He makes us laugh every Friday night as he plays Corporal Maxwell Klinger in the Emmy Award-winning series *M*A*S*H*. Give a round of applause to our second judge for the evening—Jamie Farr (Bino);

Our third and final judge is the main reason why teenage boys want to spend their Friday nights sitting at home with their mothers. Everyone across America knows her as the feisty Lucy Ewing from the hit soap *Dallas*. Please welcome the sexy, the vivacious, the Princess of Prime-time Soaps, Ms. Charlene Tilton (Rowena).

The first finalists were a couple (Edgar and Katrina) from Flint, Michigan, who danced to Dan Hartman's "Instant Replay." The next finalists were a husband-wife team (Edgar and Vicente) from the heart of the Big Apple. They touch-danced and dipped each other to "Bridge Over Troubled Water" by Linda Clifford. The third finalists were twin brothers Shawn and Shane (Edgar and Edgar) from Fire Island, New York, who wowed and won the crowd with their (his) dramatic disco interpretation of Donna Summer's "MacArthur Park."

While they wait for Edgar to make his appearance from around the corner where he is squatting behind Mrs. Freitas's plants, Vicente catches Roberto's eyes darting at him as he waxes his car. Vicente looks away, pretends he doesn't see Roberto's eyebrows go up to form thick lines across his forehead; instead, he turns to Bino and Rowena who sit cross-legged on the lawn, reading *Madeline* books.

"Edgar," Katrina shouts towards Mrs. Freitas's house, "come out of the bushes already cuz we turnin' into fungus over here."

No answer, though she knows he'll pop up from the potted plants as he always does. He once told Katrina that he has to stall for time and must always be the last one to show up because he is *the lead* star and *the lead* star never shows up early or on time.

Edgar makes his dramatic entrance as Venus surrounded by bougainvilleas, with his arm around a boom box and a duffel bag on his shoulder. He wears an ear-to-ear smile and his favorite Angel Flights bell-bottoms, Famolare shoes, and a T-shirt. Sprawled across his chest is an iron-on sticker of Andy Gibb.

He throws one hand in the air, the signal for Katrina and the others to scream and pretend they just spotted their favorite idol incognito. He hurries towards them and rests the boom box and his duffel bag on the stone wall.

"You guys never goin' believe this," Edgar says.

"What?" Vicente asks.

"Yesterday, I went to the dentist for a check-up," Edgar says.

"So?" Katrina says.

"So the whole time I was there, I was forced to listen to elevator music," Edgar says, referring to KUMU, the all easy-listening station, twenty-four hours a day.

"So?" Katrina repeats.

"So no get wise before I punch your face," Edgar says. "Anyways, you guys never goin' believe the kind songs I was hearin'."

"Like?" Loata asks.

"Like the instrumental version of 'More Than A Woman,' 'I Love The Nightlife,' 'Got To Be Real,' 'Boogie Wonderland.'"

"Nah," Loata interrupts.

"For real," Edgar says. "I no could believe myself. Anyways, when I got home I called up KUMU and requested all these songs."

He unzips his duffel bag and pulls out a tape. "I spent the whole night listenin' and recordin' all the songs I wen' ask the DJ for play," he says. "Except for 'Love to Love You Baby.' That one he never had, but he had all the others."

"Like?" Vicente asks.

"Like 'Makin' It,'" he says.

Katrina screams. It's hers and her babe Erwin's theme song.

"And 'On The Radio,'" Edgar continues.

Mai-Lan gasps.

Edgar turns to Florante. "And," he pauses, "I also got 'Do That To Me One More Time,' Florante's favorite Captain and Tennille song."

"What else?" Vicente asks.

"And 'Enough Is Enough.'"

"No way," Vicente says.

"First song on this tape, brah," Edgar brags. "And this goin' be the first thing we goin' sing and dance to. And cuz I so so nice, I goin' sing the Barbra Streisand part and let you sing the Donna Summer part even though I sound just like her."

"But I don't know all the lyrics," Vicente says.

"No worry," Edgar says, producing two *Song Hits* magazines from his bag.

"What about the words to 'Makin' It'?" Katrina asks.

"I get 'em, too," he says. He turns the bag upside down. A beaver dam of *Song Hits* piles up on the stone wall.

He hands Vicente a magazine. Vicente pages to the table of contents. "Enough is enough is enough is enough," he starts singing.

"Wait," Edgar says, "I not ready. And you not ready either."

"Why?" Vicente asks.

"Cuz you not on the stage, dummy," he says, handing the tape over to Katrina.

They haul themselves to the top of the wall. Edgar gestures to those below him, reminding them to applaud once the song begins.

Silence.

Silence.

"Katrina, start the freakin' song, dumbass," Edgar shouts.

Katrina obeys.

Silence then static.

"Dolby," Edgar hisses. "Put it on Dolby."

The music starts: Piano, violins, flutes, harps.

"Shit, Edgar," Vicente says. "When you said instrumental, you didn't tell us it was going to be the forest version."

Edgar walks over to the cassette recorder and turns it off.

"What you expected, stupidhead?" Edgar shouts. "The Studio 54 mix? We talkin' KUMU here, not KIKI or KKUA. You so ingrateful sometimes."

"Yeah," Katrina seconds. "Just shut up and sing. At least Edgar's idea beats lip-synching. Besides, now we can really positively know for sure if you get one choirboy voice like you always brag about. Plus you should be thankful he makin' you sing the Donna Summer part."

"Okay, I get the message," Vicente says.

Edgar rewinds the tape and once again reminds the audience to please applaud.

The song begins with a piano prelude (Florante, Loata, and Mai-Lan applaud), violins (Katrina screams), flutes (Rowena tears up). Opening lines are Edgar's. He hums to Rowena and Bino then tells them that it's raining, pouring, and his love life is boring him to tears.

He turns to Vicente, who's sweating cats and dogs as he tries to resurrect a voice dormant for almost a year. "No sunshine, no moonlight, no stardust, no sign of romance, no nothing," Vicente quivers.

"Use your imagination, Donna," Edgar lip-tells Vicente, then pauses when he catches Roberto's eyes fixed on them. Edgar turns to Roberto and flies him a kiss. Roberto flashes a grin as his hands continue to wax. Edgar flies him another kiss. Roberto throws the rag aside, leans against the trunk, crosses his arms, and listens to Edgar recount to him that he once dreamt he had found the perfect lover but he turned out to be like every other man.

Vicente leans over to ask him why is the beat not picking up. Edgar half-closes his eyes, begins gyrating, then tells Vicente again to use his imagination.

Vicente joins him, echoes that it's raining, pouring once again, and that they're not going to hang around waiting to shed another tear. He closes his eyes and imagines singing to the original disco version he dances to at America discotheque and not the one that will accompany him to the cemetery.

He imagines that Edgar, Katrina, Loata, Florante, Mai-Lan, Bino, and Rowena are not there. No Roberto's eyes. No Mr. Batongbacal or Mrs. Freitas behind their curtains. He shakes his hips, lets loose his choirboy voice. "Enough is enough is enough is enough is I've had it."

Surprised by Vicente's rich voice, Edgar tells him, "Sing it, Donna."

Altoing loud and clear, Vicente imagines strong hands kneading his neck, his shoulders. He stretches his neck to the right, to the left, then back, then forward, the way one does when being massaged by someone like Richard Hatch or Jan-Michael Vincent. He opens his lips and offers his song to the sky.

Katrina sees Vicente's father's car driving into Mr. Batongbacal's driveway. "Edgar," Katrina says, pulling his pants.

Eyes closed, Edgar, who's imagining that he's just been betrayed by Scott Baio, shouts to Katrina: "I want him out I want him out the door now goodbye Mister."

"Edgar," Katrina says, shaking his legs.

Edgar opens his eyes to Mr. De Los Reyes's face heating up like a volcano about to erupt. He vaults down from the stone wall, shoves the *Song Hits* into his duffel bag, turns off the music, and walks away with his boom box and bag. Katrina and the rest follow him, except for Bino. Roberto, who's gone back to waxing his car, starts whistling.

With eyes still closed and imagination wide open, Vicente sings to his father. "I can't go on no longer because enough is enough is enough is I gotta listen close to my heart. Wooooo-wooo-wo."

Mr. De Los Reyes climbs up on the wall and grips his son's neck, wrenching it until Vicente snaps free of his imagination. Then he pushes him off the wall. Bino rushes to Vicente, who's fallen on his hands and knees. But Mr. De Los Reyes has jumped down from the wall and is pulling Vicente up by the hair, shoving him away from the stone wall and the curtain of eyes trailing after them.

KALIHI IS IN THE HEART

The #7 green bus that rattles in and out of Kalihi Valley looks as if it's been salvaged from a junkyard with its rusty sides, hard seats, and tightly shut windows that could only be opened by the muscles of an Arnold Schwarzenegger.

"Ridin' that bus make me feel like I re-livin' the freakin' plantation days," Katrina says. "All I need when I in that bus is one cane knife and the picture goin' be perfect."

"I know, yeah, so hot in there, I feel like I in one sauna," Edgar says. "Only thing missin' for make my bus ride picture come perfect is Scott sweatin' beside me."

When the doors of the green bus squeak open to invite Edgar for a hot ride, he makes sure that he's brought his First Aid Kit: his blue duffel bag carrying two T-shirts, a bottle of ice-cold water, a face towel, magazines, Jordache sunglasses, magic markers, and Bain de Soleil.

While the others roast on wooden seats, Edgar gives himself a Portuguese sponge bath, which lasts for ninety seconds, before he applies the suntan lotion. To maintain freshness, he fans his face with back issues of *Boys' Life* or *GQ*; to keep himself breathing, Vicks Inhaler; and to preoccupy and prevent himself from fainting, he flips through *Tiger Beat* or *Dynamite* magazines, or he magic markers the seats to tell the rest of Kalihi that E&S WUZ HEA. E for Edgar, and S for Scott, as in Scott Baio.

For only a dime—twenty-five cents for high school graduates and over—the #7 green bus offers a passenger an hour's tour around Kalihi: Kam Shopping Center, the open market between Kalakaua Intermediate and Kalihi-Kai, Libby's Manapua Shop, Asagi Hatchery, Puuhale School, Dillingham Prison, Puuhale Market, Warren's Store, the Purple Man's house on Gulick, and the projects named after Hawaiian kings and princes, like King Kamehameha Housing, King Kamehameha IV Housing, and Prince Kuhio Park Terrace.

One afternoon, a deaf-and-dumb couple visiting from Orange County, California was on their way to pay tribute to the drowned souls of the USS *Arizona*. By accident, they got off on Dillingham Street and transferred to the unventilated green bus, clutching their bags.

The bus was jammed with passengers, mostly students and hotel workers in their hotel uniforms. After three bus stops, the woman signed to her husband to tell him she was having an asthma attack: Worse: Than: Pago: Pago. She signed off before the paramedics arrived. Her husband fainted then DOA'd at Queen's Hospital.

The tragedy reached their son, a very powerful and conservative Republican who served in the Nixon Administration. He sent a telegram to Bob Matayoshi, the Councilman for the Kalihi district, who was busy preparing for his '78 Wanna-Job-Vote-For-Bob gubernatorial speech. The telegram read: Will be there . . . Be prepared . . . Your ass . . . Grass. An hour later, Councilman Matayoshi was rushed to Kuakini hospital with uncontrollable palpitations. He had an angina the size of a fist, then RIP'd at the age of thirty-nine.

It's only the green bus that makes its home in Kalihi, not the yellow, air-conditioned one that is striped with orange-and-black and has leather-upholstered seats. The yellow bus is for tourists wearing Noxzema on their Rudolphs, Polaroid shades, and plastic colored visors, and shouldering complimentary airline bags packed with films, flyers for discount meals, and group tickets to see the SOS band perform at the Outrigger Showroom. Dinner includes two complimentary drinks, but not the latest SOS cassette tape that comes with a free autographed poster of the band known for its versatility and sequins.

Like a spaceship on wheels, the yellow bus flies from Waikiki and Ala Moana to: (1) the USS *Arizona* that looks like MacArthur's dentures floating in Pearl Harbor; (2) the long stretches of pineapple fields in Whitmore Village, Wahiawa; (3) the sugar plantation in Waialua; or (4) Sea Life Park where Flipper's understudies live.

Except for the Bishop Museum and the Planetarium, Kalihi is not listed in *Places To Visit In Oahu.*

"Every time I pass by all those tourists waitin' for go inside Bishop Museum," Katrina says, "I like break their line and tell 'em, 'Eh, you guys blind or what? When come to old and dead stuffs, your eyes bulge out, but when come to me, you guys pretend for be blind.'"

"Cuz to them, you invisible," Edgar says. "But to you, they not."

"I no catch, Edgar," Loata says.

"Dumbass, close your eyes and pretend you one tourist in Kalihi. What you see?"

Eyes closed, Loata begins to map out Kalihi. "Get Kam Shopping Center, the open market, Higa's store, Boulevard Saimin, Fujiya's Ink, Sato's Shave Ice Store, the Purple Man's house, Pohaku's Bar. . . . "

"Dumbass, that's all local places you seein', not tourist traps," Edgar interrupts.

"What else he supposed to see, smartass?" Katrina jumps in.

"You guys not gettin' the whole picture," Edgar says. "What's right next to Bishop Museum and the Planetarium?"

"Kalihi-Palama Library and the freeway," Loata says.

"Edgar, I not blind," Katrina says. "I pass the museum and cross that manini overpass every day when I go Farrington High for meet Erwin."

"If you not blind, then tell me what you see," Edgar says.

Katrina shuts her eyes and taps her fingers on her temples. "Get the museum, the planetarium, the library, the freeway, then Farrington High. . . . "

"Hurry up, Trina, I no more all day," Edgar says.

"Wait, it's comin'," she says.

Lightbulb opens her eyes. She grins at Edgar. "Ohhhhh, I get it."

"What?" Loata says.

Edgar clears his throat, then signals Loata to applaud. "Welcome back to the 25th Annual Ms. Kalihi Universe 1979. I'm your host, Bob Barker," he says, holding an invisible microphone to his mouth. "And now I'm going to ask our tenth and final contestant Ms. Cruz to please come on down."

Katrina sashays to Edgar.

"Ms. Katherine Katrina-Trina Cruz, if you are to become Ms. Kalihi 1979, what is the first thing you are going to change in Kalihi?" Edgar asks.

Katrina takes the invisible microphone from Edgar's hand. "If I'm chosen Ms. Kalihi 1979, the first thing I'm going to do is move the freakin' freeway away from the Bishop Museum and the Planetarium so the tourists no can make one quick getaway to Waikiki, thank you," Katrina says, smiling wide.

"Why?" Loata interrupts, still confused.

"Dumbass, you think the tourists goin' like go wanderin' around Kalihi?" Katrina snaps.

"They no gotta go wanderin' around," Loata says. "They can just walk to Kam Shopping Center from Bishop Museum."

"And what? Freak out when they run into Tutu Mail or the Purple Man?" Katrina asks.

"You no remember what wen' happen to the Orange County couple or what?" Katrina asks.

"Yeah, I do," Loata says. "The wife wen' have one heart attack and the husband wen' die right after that, but that's cuz they was ridin' the green bus and they no could breathe."

"For your information, Loata, she never had one heart attack. She had one attack of Asthmatic Claustrophobia," Edgar says.

"Asthmatic what?" Loata says.

"Not Asthmatic Claustrophobia, Edgar, but Asthmatic Otraphobia," Katrina says.

"What's that?" Loata asks.

"That's this newly diagnosed mental disorder that give foreigners asthma when they come across locals. That's what wen' happen to the Orange County woman. She had one asthma attack cuz she no could handle being surrounded by all the locals on the green bus."

CHANG

Sigrid Nunez

The first time I ever heard my father speak Chinese was at Coney Island. I don't remember how old I was then, but I must have been very young. This was in the early days, when we still went on family outings. We were walking along the boardwalk when we ran into the four Chinese men. My mother told the story often, as if she thought we'd forgotten. "You kids didn't know them and neither did I. They were friends of your father's, from Chinatown. You'd never heard Chinese before. You didn't know what was up. You stood there with your mouths hanging open—I had to laugh. 'Why are they singing? Why is Daddy singing?'"

One of the men gave each of my sisters and me a dollar bill. I cashed mine into dimes and set out to win a goldfish. A dime bought you three chances to toss a Ping-Pong ball into one of many small fishbowls, each holding a quivering tangerine-colored fish. Overexcited, I threw recklessly, again and again. When all the dimes were gone I ran back to the grown-ups in tears. The man who had given me the dollar tried to give me another, but my parents wouldn't allow it. He pressed the bag of peanuts he had been eating into my hands and said I could have them all.

I never saw any of those men again or heard anything about them. They were the only friends of my father's that I would ever meet. I would hear him speak Chinese again, but very seldom. In Chinese restaurants, occasionally on the telephone, once or twice in his sleep, and in the hospital when he was dying.

So it was true, then. He really was Chinese. Up until that day I had not quite believed it.

My mother always said that he had sailed to America on a boat. He took a slow boat from China, was what she used to say, laughing. I wasn't sure whether she was serious, and if she was, why coming from China was such a funny thing.

A slow boat from China. In time I learned that he was born not in China but in Panama. No wonder I only half-believed he was Chinese. He was only half-Chinese.

The facts I know about his life are unbearably few. Although we shared the same house for eighteen years, we had little else in common. We had no culture in common. It is only a slight exaggeration to say that we had no language in common. By the time I was born my father had lived almost thirty years in America, but to hear him speak you would not have believed this. About his failure to master English there always seemed to me something willful. Except for her accent—as thick as but so different from his—my mother had no such trouble.

"He never would talk about himself much, you know. That was his way. He never really had much to say, in general. Silence was golden. It was a cultural thing, I think." (My mother.)

By the time I was old enough to understand this, my father had pretty much stopped talking.

Taciturnity: They say that is an Oriental trait. But I don't believe my father was always the silent, withdrawn man I knew. Think of that day at Coney Island, when he was talking a Chinese blue streak.

Almost everything I know about him came from my mother, and there was much she herself never knew, much she had forgotten or was unsure of, and much she would never tell.

I am six, seven, eight years old, a schoolgirl with deplorable posture and constantly cracked lips, chafing in the dollish Old World clothes handmade by my mother; a bossy, fretful, sly, cowardly child given to fits of temper and weeping. In school, or in the playground, or perhaps watching television, I hear something about the Chinese—something odd, improbable. I will ask my father. He will know whether it is true, say, that the Chinese eat with sticks.

He shrugs. He pretends not to understand. Or he scowls and says, "Chinese just like everybody else."

("He thought you were making fun of him. He always thought everyone was making fun of him. He had a chip on his shoulder. The way he acted, you'd've thought he was colored!")

Actually, he said "evvybody."

Is it true the Chinese write backwards?

Chinese just like evvybody else.

Is it true they eat dog?

Chinese just like evvybody else.

Are they really all Communists?

Chinese just like evvybody else.

What is Chinese water torture? What is foot-binding? What is a mandarin?

Chinese just like evvybody else.

He was not like everybody else.

The unbearably few facts are these. He was born in Colón, Panama, in 1911. His father came from Shanghai. From what I have been able to gather, Grandfather Chang was a merchant engaged in the trade of tobacco and tea. This business, which he ran with one of his brothers, kept him traveling often between Shanghai and Colón. He had two wives, one in each city, and, as if out of a passion for symmetry, two sons by each wife. Soon after my father, Carlos, was born, his father took him to Shanghai, to be raised by the Chinese wife. Ten years later my father was sent back to Colón. I never understood the reason for this. The way the story was told to me, I got the impression that my father was being sent away from some danger. This was, of course, a time of upheaval in China, the decade following the birth of the Republic, the era of the warlords. If the date is correct, my father would have left Shanghai the year the Chinese Communist party was founded there. It remains uncertain, though, whether political events had anything at all to do with his leaving China.

One year after my father returned to Colón his mother was dead. I remember hearing as a child that she had died of a stroke. Years later this would seem to me odd, when I figured out that she would have been only twenty-six. Odder still, to think of that reunion between the long-parted mother and son; there's a good chance they did not speak the same language. The other half-Panamanian son, Alfonso, was either sent back with my father or had never left Colón. After their mother's death the two boys came into the care of their father's brother and business partner, Uncle Mee, who apparently lived in Colón and had a large family of his own.

Grandfather Chang, his Chinese wife, and their two sons remained in Shanghai. All were said to have been killed by the Japanese. That must have been during the Sino-Japanese War. My father would have been between his late twenties and early thirties by then, but whether he ever saw any of those Shanghai relations again before they died, I don't know.

At twelve or thirteen my father sailed to America with Uncle Mee. I believe it was just the two of them who came, leaving the rest of the family in Colón. Sometime in the next year or so my father was enrolled in a public school in Brooklyn. I remember coming across a notebook that had belonged to him in those days and being jolted by the name written on the cover: Charles Cipriano Chang. That was neither my father's first nor his last name, as far as I knew, and I'd never heard of the middle name. (Hard to believe that my father spent his boyhood in Shanghai being called Carlos, a name he could not even pronounce with the proper Spanish accent. So he must have had a Chinese name as well. And although our family never knew this name, perhaps among Chinese people he used it.)

Twenty years passed. All I know about this part of my father's life is that it was lived illegally in New York, mostly in Chinatown, where he worked in various restaurants. Then came the Second World War and he was drafted. It was while he was in the army that he finally became an American citizen. He was no longer calling himself Charles but Carlos again, and now, upon becoming a citizen, he dropped his father's family name and took his mother's. Why a man who thought of himself as Chinese, who had always lived among Chinese, who spoke little Spanish, and who had barely known his mother would have made such a decision in the middle of his life is one of many mysteries surrounding my father.

My mother had an explanation. "You see, Alfonso was a Panamanian citizen, and *he* had taken his mother's name" (which would, of course, be in keeping with Spanish cultural tradition). "He was the only member of his family your father had left—the others were all dead. Your father wanted to have the same last name as his brother. Also, he thought he'd get along better in this country with a Spanish name." This makes no sense to me. He'd been a Chinatown Chang for twenty years. Now all of a sudden he wished to pass for Hispanic?

In another version of this story, the idea of getting rid of the Chinese name was attributed to the citizenship official handling my father's papers. This is plausible, given that immigration restrictions for Chinese were still in effect at that time. But I have not ruled out the possibility that the change of names was the result of a misunderstanding between my father and this official. My father was an easily fuddled man, especially when dealing with authority, and he always had trouble understanding and making himself understood in English. And I can imagine him not only befuddled enough to make such a mistake but also too timid afterward to try to fix it.

Whatever really happened I'm sure I'll never know. I do know that having a Spanish name brought much confusion into my father's life and have always wondered in what way my own life might have been different had he kept the name Chang.

From this point on the story becomes somewhat clearer. With the Hundredth Infantry Division my father goes to war, fights in France and Germany, and, after V-E Day, is stationed in the small southern German town where he will meet my mother. He is thirty-four and she has just turned eighteen. She is soon pregnant.

Here is rich food for speculation: how did they communicate? She had had a little English in school. He learned a bit of German. They must have misunderstood far more than they understood of each other. Perhaps this helps to explain why my eldest sister was already two and my other sister on the way before my parents got married. (My sisters and I did not learn about this until we were in our twenties.)

By the time I was three they would already have had two long separations.

"I should have married Rudolf!" (My mother.)

Nineteen forty-eight. My father returns to the States with his wife and first daughter. Now everything is drastically changed. A different America this: the America of the citizen, the legal worker, the family man. No more drinking and gambling till all hours in Chinatown. No more drifting from job to job, living hand to mouth, sleeping on the floor of a friend's room or on a shelf in the restaurant kitchen. There are new, undreamed-of expenses: household money, layettes, taxes, insurance, a special bank account for the children's education. He does the best he can. He rents an apartment in the Fort Greene housing project, a short walk from the Cantonese restaurant on Fulton Street where he works as a waiter. Some nights after closing, after all the tables have been cleared and the dishes done, he stays for the gambling. He weaves home to a wide-awake wife who sniffs the whiskey on his breath and doesn't care whether he has lost or won. So little money—to gamble with any of it is a sin. Her English is getting better ("no thanks to him!"), but for what she has to say she needs little vocabulary. She is miserable. She hates America. She dreams incessantly about going home. There is something peculiar about the three-year-old: she rarely smiles; she claws at the pages of magazines, like a cat. The one-year-old is prone to colic. To her horror my mother learns that she is pregnant again. She attempts an abortion, which fails. I am born. About that attempt, was my father consulted? Most likely not. Had he been I think I know what he would have said. He would have said: No, this time it will be a boy. Like most men he would have wanted a son. (All girls—a house full of females—a Chinese man's nightmare!) Perhaps with a son he would have been more open. Perhaps a son he would have taught Chinese.

He gets another job, as a dishwasher in the kitchen of a large public health service hospital. He will work there until he retires, eventually being promoted to kitchen supervisor.

He moves his family to another housing project, outside the city, newly built, cleaner, safer.

He works all the time. On weekends, when he is off from the hospital, he waits on tables in one or another Chinese restaurant. He works most holidays and takes no vacation. On his rare day off he outrages my mother by going to the racetrack. But he is not self-indulgent. A little gambling, a quart of Budweiser with his supper— eaten alone, an hour or so after the rest of us (he always worked late)—now and then a glass of Scotch, cigarettes—these were his only pleasures. While the children are still small there are occasional outings. To Coney Island, Chinatown, the zoo. On Sundays sometimes he takes us to the children's matinee, and once a year to Radio City, for the Christmas or Easter show. But he and my mother never go out alone together, just the two of them—never.

Her English keeps getting better, making his seem worse and worse.

He is hardly home, yet my memory is of constant fighting.

Not much vocabulary needed to wound.

"Stupid woman. Crazy lady. Talk, talk, talk, talk—never say nothing!"

"I should have married Rudolf!"

Once, she spat in his face. Another time, she picked up a bread knife and he had to struggle to get it away from her.

They slept in separate beds.

Every few months she announced to the children that it was over: we were going "home." (And she did go back with us to Germany once, when I was two. We stayed six months. About this episode she was always vague. In years to come, whenever we asked her why we did not stay in Germany, she would say, "You children wanted your father." But I think that is untrue. More likely she realized that there was no life for her back there. She had never gotten on well with her family. By this time I believe Rudolf had married another.)

Even working the two jobs, my father did not make much money. He would never make enough to buy a house. Yet it seemed the burden of being poor weighed heavier on my mother. Being poor meant you could never relax, meant eternal attention to appearances. Just because you had no money didn't mean you were squalid. Come into the house: see how clean and tidy everything is. Look at the children: spotless. And people did comment to my mother—on the shininess of her floors and how she kept her children—and she was gratified by this. Still, being poor was exhausting.

One day a woman waist-deep in children knocked at the door. When my mother answered, the woman apologized. "I thought—from the name on the mailbox I thought you were Spanish too. My kids needed to use the toilet." My mother could not hide her displeasure. She was proud of being German, and in those postwar years she was also bitterly defensive. When people called us names—spicks and chinks—she said, "You see how it is in this country. For all they say how bad we Germans are, no one ever calls you names for being German."

She had no patience with my father's quirks. The involuntary twitching of a muscle meant that someone had given him the evil eye. Drinking a glass of boiled water while it was still hot cured the flu. He saved back issues of *Reader's Digest* and silver dollars from certain years, believing that one day they'd be worth a lot of money. What sort of backward creature had she married? His English drove her mad. Whenever he didn't catch something that was said to him (and this happened all the time), instead of saying "What?" he said "Who?" "Who? Who?" she screeched back at him. "What are you, an owl?"

Constant bickering and fighting.

We children dreamed of growing up, going to college, getting married, getting away.

And what about Alfonso and Uncle Mee? What happened to them?

"I never met either of them, but we heard from Mee all the time those first years—it was awful. By then he was back in Panama. He was a terrible gambler, and so were his sons. They had debts up to here—and who should they turn to but your father. Uncle What-About-Mee, I called him. 'Think of all I've done for you. You owe me.'" (And though she had never heard it she mimicked his voice.) "Well, your father had managed to save a couple of thousand dollars and he sent it all to Mee. I could have died. I never forgave him. I was pregnant then, and I had one maternity dress—one. Mee no sooner got that money than he wrote back for more. I told your father if he sent him another dime I was leaving."

Somehow the quarrel extended to include Alfonso, who seems to have sided with Mee. My father broke with them both. Several years after we left Brooklyn, an ad appeared in the Chinatown newspaper. Alfonso and Mee were trying to track my father down. He never answered the ad, my father said. He never spoke to either man again. (Perhaps he lied. Perhaps he was always in touch with them, secretly. I believe much of his life was a secret from us.)

I have never seen a photograph of my father that was taken before he was in the army. I have no idea what he looked like as a child or as a young man. I have never seen any photographs of his parents or his brothers, or of Uncle Mee, or of any other relations, or of the houses he lived in in Colón or Shanghai. If my father had any possessions that had belonged to his parents, any family keepsakes or mementos of his youth, I never saw them. About his youth he had nothing to tell. A single anecdote he shared with me. In Shanghai he had a dog. When my father sailed to Panama, the dog was brought along to the dock to see him off. My father boarded the boat and the dog began howling. He never forgot that: the boat pulling away from the dock and the dog howling. "Dog no fool. He know I never be back."

In our house there were no Chinese things. No objects made of bamboo or jade. No lacquer boxes. No painted scrolls or fans. No calligraphy. No embroidered silks. No Buddhas. No chopsticks among the silverware, no rice bowls or tea sets. No Chinese tea, no ginseng or soy sauce in the cupboards. My father was the only Chinese thing, sitting like a Buddha himself among the Hummels and cuckoo clocks and pictures of Alpine landscapes. My mother thought of the house as hers, spoke of *her* curtains, *her* floors (often in warning: "Don't scuff up my floors!"). The daughters were hers too. To each of them she gave a Nordic name, impossible for him to pronounce. ("*What* does your father call you?" That question—an agony to me—rang through my childhood.) It was part of her abiding nostalgia that she wanted to raise her children as Germans. She sewed dirndls for them and even for their dolls. She braided their hair, then wound the braids tightly around their ears, like hair earmuffs, in the German style. They would open their presents on Christmas Eve rather than Christmas morning. They would not celebrate Thanksgiving. Of course they would not celebrate any Chinese holiday. No dragon and firecrackers on Chinese New Year's. For Christmas there was red cabbage and sauerbraten. Imagine my father saying *sauerbraten*.

Now and then he brought home food from Chinatown: fiery red sausage with specks of fat like embedded teeth, dried fish, buns filled with bean paste that he cracked us up by calling *Chinese pee-nus butter*. My mother would not touch any of it. ("God knows what it really is.") We kids clamored for a taste and when we didn't like it my father got angry. ("You know how he was with that chip on his shoulder. He took it personally. He was insulted.") Whenever we ate at one of the restaurants where he worked, he was always careful to order for us the same Americanized dishes served to most of the white customers.

An early memory: I am four, five, six years old, in a silly mood, mugging in my mother's bureau mirror. My father is in the room with me but I forget he is there. I place my forefingers at the corners of my eyes and pull the lids taut. Then I catch him watching me. His is a look of pure hate.

"He thought you were making fun."

A later memory: "Panama is an isthmus." Grade-school geography. My father looks up from his paper, alert, suspicious. "Merry Isthmus!" "Isthmus be the place!" My sisters and I shriek with laughter. My father shakes his head. "Not nice, making fun of place where people born!"

"Ach, he had no sense of humor—he never did. He never got the point of a joke."

It is true I hardly ever heard him laugh. (Unlike my mother, who, despite her chronic unhappiness, seemed always to be laughing—at him, at us, at the neighbors. A great tease she was, sly, malicious, often witty.)

Chinese inscrutability. Chinese sufferance. Chinese reserve. Yes, I recognize my father in the clichés. But what about his Panamanian side? What are Latins said to be? Hot-blooded, mercurial, soulful, macho, convivial, romantic, rash. No, he was none of these.

"He always wanted to go back. He always missed China."

But he was only ten years old when he left.

"Yes, but that's what counts—where you spent those first years, and your first language. That's who you are."

I had a children's book about Sun Yat Sen, the Man Who Changed China. There were drawings of Sun as a boy. I tried to picture my father like that, a Chinese boy who wore pajamas outdoors and a coolie hat and a pigtail down his back. (Though of course in those days after Sun's revolution he isn't likely to have worn a pigtail.) I pictured my father against those landscapes of peaks and pagodas, with a dog like Old Yeller at his heels. What was it like, this boyhood in Shanghai? How did the Chinese wife treat the second wife's son? (My father and Alfonso would not have had the same status as the official wife's sons, I don't think.) How did the Chinese brothers treat him? When he went to school—did he go to school?—was he accepted by the other children as one of them? Is there a Chinese word for half-breed, and was he called that name as we would be? Surely many times in his life he must have wished that he were all Chinese. My mother wished that her children were all German. I wanted to be an all-American girl with a name like Sue Brown.

He always wanted to go back.

He never forgot that dog howling on the dock.

In our house there were not many books. My mother's romances and historical novels, books about Germany (mostly about the Nazi era), a volume of Shakespeare, tales from Andersen and Grimm, the *Nibelungenlied,* Edith Hamilton's *Mythology,* works of Goethe and Heine, *Struwwelpeter,* the drawings of Wilhelm Busch. It was my mother who gave me that book about Sun Yat Sen and, when I was a little older, one of her own favorites, *The Good Earth,* a children's story for adults. Pearl Buck was a missionary who lived in China for many years. (Missionaries supposedly converted the Changs to Christianity. From what? Buddhism? Taoism? My father's mother was almost certainly Roman Catholic. He himself belonged to no church.) Pearl Buck wrote eighty-four books, founded a shelter for Asian-American children, and won the Nobel Prize.

The Good Earth. China a land of famine and plagues—endless childbirth among them. The births of daughters seen as evil omens. "It is only a slave this time—not worth mentioning." Little girls sold as a matter of course. Growing up to be concubines with names like Lotus and Cuckoo and Pear Blossom. Women with feet like little deer hooves. Abject wives, shuffling six paces behind their men. All this filled me with anxiety. In our house the husband was the meek and browbeaten one.

I never saw my father read, except for the newspaper. He did not read the *Reader's Digest*s that he saved. He would not have been able to read *The Good Earth.* I am sure he could not write with fluency in any tongue. The older I grew the more I thought of him as illiterate. Hard for me to accept the fact that he did not read books. Say I grew up to be a writer. He would not read what I wrote.

He had his own separate closet, in the front hall. Every night when he came home from work he undressed as soon as he walked in, out there in the hall. He took off his suit and put on his bathrobe. He always wore a suit to work, but at the hospital he changed into whites and at the restaurant into dark pants, white jacket, and black bow tie. In the few photographs of him that exist he is often wearing a uniform—his soldier's or hospital worker's or waiter's.

Though not at all vain, he was particular about his appearance. He bought his suits in a men's fine clothing store on Fifth Avenue, and he took meticulous care of them. He had a horror of cheap cloth and imitation leather, and an equal horror of slovenliness. His closet was the picture of order. On the top shelf, where he kept his hats, was a large assortment—a lifetime's supply, it seemed to me—of chewing gum, cough drops, and mints. On that shelf he kept also his cigarettes and cigars. The closet smelled much as he did—of tobacco and spearmint and the rosewater-glycerin cream he used on his dry skin. A not unpleasant smell.

He was small. At fourteen I was already as tall as he, and eventually I would outweigh him. A trim sprig of a man, dainty but not puny, fastidious but not effeminate. I used to marvel at the cleanliness of his nails, and at his good teeth, which never needed any fillings. By the time I was born he had lost most of his top hair, which made his domed forehead look even larger, his moon face rounder. It may have been the copper-red cast of his skin that led some people to take him for an American Indian—people who'd never seen one, probably.

He could be cruel. I once saw him blow pepper in the cat's face. He loathed that cat, a surly, untrainable tom found in the street. But he was very fond of another creature we took in, an orphaned nestling sparrow. Against expectations, the bird survived and learned to fly. But, afraid that it would not know how to fend for itself outdoors, we decided to keep it. My father sometimes sat by its cage, watching the bird and cooing to it in Chinese. My mother was amused. "You see: he has more to say to that bird than to us!" The emperor and his nightingale, she called them. "The Chinese have always loved their birds." (What none of us knew: at that very moment in China keeping pet birds had been prohibited as a bourgeois affectation, and sparrows were being exterminated as pests.)

It was true that my father had less and less to say to us. He was drifting further and further out of our lives. These were my teenage years. I did not see clearly what was happening then, and for long afterward, whenever I tried to look back, a panic would come over me, so that I couldn't see at all.

At sixteen, I had stopped thinking about becoming a writer. I wanted to dance. Every day after school I went into the city for class. I would be home by eight-thirty, about the same time as my father, and so for this period he and I would eat dinner together. And much later, looking back, I realized that was when I had—and lost—my chance. Alone with my father every night, I could have gotten to know him. I could have asked him all those questions that I now have to live without answers to. Of course he would have resisted talking about himself. But with patience I might have drawn him out.

Or maybe not. As I recall, the person sitting across the kitchen table from me was like a figure in a glass case. That was not the face of someone thinking, feeling, or even daydreaming. It was the clay face, still waiting to receive the breath of life.

If it ever occurred to me that my father was getting old, that he was exhausted, that his health was failing, I don't remember it.

He was still working seven days a week. Sometimes he missed having dinner with me because the dishwasher broke and he had to stay late at the hospital. For a time, on Saturdays, he worked double shifts and did not come home till we were all asleep.

After dinner, he stayed at the kitchen table, smoking and finishing his beer. He never joined the rest of us in the living room in front of the television. He sat alone at the table, staring at the wall. He hardly noticed if someone came into the kitchen for something. His inobservance was the family's biggest joke. My mother would give herself or one of us a new hairdo and say, "Now watch: your father won't even notice," and she was right.

My sisters and I bemoaned his stubborn avoidance of the living room. Once a year he yielded and joined us around the Christmas tree, but only very reluctantly; we had to beg him.

I knew vaguely that he continued to have some sort of social life outside the house, a life centered in Chinatown.

He still played the horses.

By this time family outings had ceased. We never did anything together as a family.

But every Sunday my father came home with ice cream for everyone.

He and my mother fought less and less—seldom now in the old vicious way—but this did not mean there was peace. Never any word or gesture of affection between them, not even, "for the sake of the children," pretense of affection.

(Television: the prime-time family shows. During the inevitable scenes when family love and loyalty were affirmed, the discomfort in the living room was palpable. I think we were all ashamed of how far below the ideal our family fell.)

Working and saving to send his children to college, he took no interest in their school life. He did, however, reward good report cards with cash. He did not attend school events to which parents were invited; he always had to work.

He never saw me dance.

He intrigued my friends, who angered me by regarding him as if he were a figure in a glass case. Doesn't he ever come out of the kitchen? Doesn't he ever talk? I was angry at him too, for what he seemed to be doing: *willing* himself into stereotype—inscrutable, self-effacing, funny little Chinaman.

And why couldn't he learn to speak English?

He developed the tight wheezing cough that would never leave him. The doctor blamed cigarettes, so my father tried sticking to cigars. The cough was particularly bad at night. It kept my mother up, and she started sleeping on the living-room couch.

I was the only one who went to college, and I got a scholarship. My father gave the money he had saved to my mother, who bought a brand-new Mercedes, the family's first car.

He was not like everybody else. In fact, he was not like anyone I had ever met. But I thought of my father when I first encountered the "little man" of Russian literature. I thought of him a lot when I read the stories of Chekhov and Gogol.

Reading "Grief," I remembered my father and the sparrow, and a new possibility presented itself: my father not as one who would not speak but as one to whom no one would listen.

And he was like a character in a story also in the sense that he needed to be invented.

The silver dollars saved in a cigar box. The *Reader's Digest*s going back to before I was born. The uniforms. The tobacco-mint-rosewater smell. I cannot invent a father out of these.

I waited too long. By the time I started gathering material for his story, whatever there had been in the way of private documents or papers (and there must have been some) had disappeared. (It was never clear whether my father himself destroyed them or whether my mother later lost or got rid of them, between moves, or in one of her zealous spring cleanings.)

The Sunday-night ice cream. The Budweiser bottle sweating on the kitchen table. The five-, ten-, or twenty-dollar bill he pulled from his wallet after squinting at your report card. "Who? Who?"

We must have seemed as alien to him as he seemed to us. To him we must always have been "others." Females. Demons. No different from other demons, who could not tell one Asian from another, who thought Chinese food meant chop suey and Chinese customs were matter for joking. I would have to live a lot longer and he would have to die before the full horror of this would sink in. And then it would sink in deeply, agonizingly, like an arrow that has found its mark.

Dusk in the city. Dozens of Chinese men bicycle through the streets, bearing cartons of fried dumplings, Ten Ingredients Lo Mein, and sweet-and-sour pork. I am on my way to the drugstore when one of them hails me. "Miss! Wait, miss!" Not a man, I see, but a boy, eighteen at most, with a lovely, oval, fresh-skinned face. "You—you Chinese!" It is not the first time in my life this has happened. In as few words as possible, I explain. The boy turns out to have arrived just weeks ago, from Hong Kong. His English is incomprehensible. He is flustered when he finds I cannot speak Chinese. He says, "Can I. Your father. Now." It takes me a moment to figure this out. Alas, he is asking to meet my father. Unable to bring myself to tell him my father is dead, I say that he does not live in the city. The boy persists. "But sometime come see. And then I now?" His imploring manner puzzles me. Is it that he wants to meet Chinese people? Doesn't he work in a Chinese restaurant? Doesn't he know about Chinatown? I feel a surge of anxiety. He is so earnest and intent. I am missing something. In another minute I have promised that when my father comes to town he will go to the restaurant where the boy works and seek him out. The boy rides off looking pleased, and I continue on to the store. I am picking out toothpaste when he appears at my side. He hands me a folded piece of paper. Two telephone numbers and a message in Chinese characters. "For father."

He was sixty when he retired from the hospital, but his working days were not done. He took a part-time job as a messenger for a bank. That Christmas when I came home from school I found him in bad shape. His smoker's cough was much worse, and he had pains in his legs and in his back, recently diagnosed as arthritis.

But it was not smoker's cough, and it was not arthritis.

A month later, he left work early one day because he was in such pain. He made it to the station, but when he tried to board the train he could not get up the steps. Two conductors had to carry him on. At home he went straight to bed and in the middle of the night he woke up coughing as usual, and this time there was blood.

His decline was so swift that by the time I arrived at the hospital he barely knew me. Over the next week we were able to chart the backward journey on which he was embarked by his occasional murmurings. ("I got to get back to the base—they'll think I'm AWOL!") Though I was not there to hear it, I am told that he cursed my mother and accused her of never having cared. By the end of the week, when he spoke it was only in Chinese.

One morning a priest arrived. No one had sent for him. He had doubtless assumed from the name that this patient was Hispanic and Catholic, and had taken it upon himself to administer Extreme Unction. None of us had the will to stop him, and so we were witness to a final mystery: my father, who as far as we knew had no religion, feebly crossing himself.

The fragments of Chinese stopped. There was only panting then, broken by sharp gasps such as a person makes when reminded of some important thing he has forgotten. To the end his hands were restless. He kept repeating the same gesture: cupping his hands together and drawing them to his chest, as though gathering something to him.

Now let others speak.

"After the war was a terrible time. We were all scared to death, we didn't know what was going to happen to us. Some of those soldiers were really enjoying it, they wanted nothing better than to see us grovel. The victors! Oh, they were scum, a lot of them. But your father felt sorry for us. He tried to help. And not just our family but the neighbors too. He gave us money. His wallet was always out. And he was always bringing stuff from the base, like coffee and chocolate—things you could never get. And even after he went back to the States he sent packages. Not just to us but to all the people he got to know here. Frau Meyer. The Schweitzers. They still talk about that." (My grandmother.)

"We know the cancer started in the right lung but by the time we saw him it had spread. It was in both lungs, it was in his liver and in his bones. He was a very sick man, and he'd been sick for a long time. I'd say that tumor in the right lung had been growing for at least five years." (The doctor.)

"He drank a lot in those days, and your mother didn't like that. But he was funny. He loved that singer—the cowboy—what was his name? I forget. Anyway, he put on the music and he sang along. Your mother would cover her ears." (My grandmother.)

"I didn't like the way he looked. He wouldn't say anything but I knew he was hurting. I said to myself, this isn't arthritis—no way. I wanted him to see my own doctor but he wouldn't. I was just about to order him to." (My father's boss at the bank.)

"He hated cats, and the cat knew it and she was always jumping in his lap. Every time he sat down the cat jumped in his lap and we laughed. But you could tell it really bothered him. He said cats were bad luck. When the cat jumped in your lap it was a bad omen." (My mother's younger brother Karl.)

"He couldn't dance at all—or he wouldn't—but he clapped and sang along to the records. He liked to drink and he liked gambling. Your mother worried about that." (Frau Meyer.)

"Before the occupation no one in this town had ever seen an Oriental or a Negro." (My grandmother.)

"He never ate much, he didn't want you to cook for him, but he liked German beer. He brought cigarettes for everyone. We gave him schnapps. He played us the cowboy songs." (Frau Schweitzer.)

"Ain't you people dying to know what he's saying?" (The patient in the bed next to my father's.)

"When he wasn't drinking he was very shy. He just sat there next to your mother without speaking. He sat there staring and staring at her." (Frau Meyer.)

"He liked blonds. He loved that blond hair." (Karl.)

"There was absolutely nothing we could do for him. The amazing thing is that he was working right up till the day he came into the hospital. I don't know how he did that." (The doctor.)

"The singing was a way of talking to us, because he didn't know German at all." (My grandmother.)

"Yes, of course I remember. It was Hank Williams. He played those records over and over. Hillbilly music. I thought I'd go mad." (My mother.)

Here are the names of some Hank Williams songs:

Honky Tonkin'. Ramblin' Man. Hey, Good Lookin'. Lovesick Blues. Why Don't You Love Me Like You Used To Do. Your Cheatin' Heart. (I heard that) Lonesome Whistle. Why Don't You Mind Your Own Business. I'm So Lonesome I Could Cry. The Blues Come Around. Cold, Cold Heart. I'll Never Get Out of This World Alive. I Can't Help It If I'm Still in Love With You.

About the Contributors

Sucheng Chan is professor emerita of history at the University of California at Santa Barbara. She is the author of *This Bittersweet Soil: The Chinese in California Agriculture, 1860–1910* and *Asian Americans: An Interpretive History.*

Robert Chang is assistant professor of law at Loyola College of Law in Los Angeles. He is the author of several law journal articles and also of *Disoriented* (forthcoming).

King-Kok Cheung is associate professor of English and Asian American studies at the University of California at Los Angeles. She is the author of *Articulate Silences: Hisaye Yamamoto, Maxine Hong Kingston, Joy Kogawa* and editor of *An Interethnic Companion to Asian American Literature.*

Shamita Das Dasgupta is assistant professor of psychology at Rutgers University. She is a founding member of Manavi, an organization that focuses on violence against South Asian immigrant women, author of *In Visible Terms: Domestic Violence in the Asian Indian Context,* and editor of *A Patchwork Shawl: Chronicles of South Asian Women in America.*

Sayantani DasGupta has just completed a M.D./M.P.J. program at Johns Hopkins University and is the coauthor, with her mother, of *The Demon Slayers and Other Stories: Bengali Folk Tales.* She has also authored articles that have appeared in *Ms., Z,* and *A. Magazine.*

Yen Le Espiritu is associate professor of ethnic studies at the University of California at San Diego. She is the author of *Asian American Panethnicity: Bridging Institutions and Identities, Filipino American Lives* and *Asian American Women and Men.*

Richard Fung is an independent filmmaker currently residing in Toronto. He is the director of "Dirty Laundry."

Neil Gotanda is professor of constitutional law at Western State University College of Law in Fullerton, California. He has written and lectured extensively on issues of race and legal ideology.

Ginu Kamani is the author of *Junglee Girl,* a book of short stories, and has contributed her work to *On A Bed of Rice: An Asian American Erotic Feast, Traveler's Tales: A Taste of the Road,* and *au Juice: the journal of eastin drink and screwin around, Dick for a Day,* and *Herotica 5.*

Nazli Kibria is assistant professor of sociology and director of the women's studies program at Boston University. She is the author of *Family Tightrope: The Changing Lives of Vietnamese Americans.*

Elaine H. Kim is professor of Asian American studies at the University of California at Berkeley. She has written, edited, and coedited many books and articles, including *Writing Self/Writing Nation, East to America: Korean American Life Stories, Dangerous Women: Gender and Korean Nationalism,* and *Asian American Literature: An Introduction to Their Writings and Their Social Contexts.*

Susan Koshy is assistant professor of English at the University of California at Santa Barbara. She is currently working on a project that examines the problematic emergence of Western feminism as a new universalism through the agency of organizations like the United Nations in the post-cold war era.

Peter Kwong is director of the Asian American Studies Program at Hunter College and professor of sociology at the Graduate Center of the City University of New York. He is the author of *Forbidden Workers: Chinese Illegal Immigrants and American Labor* and *The New Chinatown and Chinatown, New York: Labor and Politics 1930–1950.* He is a regular contributor to *The Nation* and *The Village Voice,* a member of the Board of Directors of Downtown Community T.V., the International Center for Migration, Ethnicity and Citizenship, and the New Press. He is also a video documentary filmmaker, and recipient of CINE Golden Eagle Awards as one of the co-producers of the PBS program on immigration.

R. Zamora Linmark has lived in Manila, London, Madrid, and Honolulu, and presently makes his home in San Francisco. His first novel, *Rolling the R's,* was published in 1995. He is the recipient of a Fulbright Fellowship. His work has appeared in *Charlie Chan Is Dead: An Anthology of Asian American Contemporary Fiction,* edited by Jessica Hagedorn.

Lisa Lowe is professor of comparative literature at the University of California at San Diego. She is the author of *Critical Terrains: French and British Orientalism* and *Immigrant Acts: On Asian American Cultural Politics.*

Masao Miyoshi is professor of comparative literature at the University of California at San Diego. He is the author of *Off-Center* and coeditor of *Global/Local* and *The Cultures of Globalization.*

Minh Duc Nguyen is a graduate film student at the University of Southern California. He is currently at work on several screenplays.

Sigrid Nunez is the author of the novels *A Feather on the Breath of God* and *Naked Sleeper.*

Gary Okihiro is professor of history at Columbia University. He is the author of *Margins and Mainstream: Asians in American History.*

Glenn Omatsu teaches Asian American studies at UCLA, California State University, Northridge, and Pasadena City College. He serves as associate editor of *Amerasia Journal,* the nation's oldest interdisciplinary publication of Asian American studies. He is active in community movement, labor struggles, and international solidarity.

Michael Omi is associate professor of ethnic studies and chair of the Asian American Studies Program at the University of California at Berkeley. He writes about racial theory and politics, and is the coauthor, with Howard Winant, of *Racial Formation in the United States: From the 1960s to the 1990s* (2nd edition).

E. San Juan Jr. is professor and chair of comparative American cultures at Washington State University at Pullman.

Bienvenido Santos was born in the Philippines and came to the United States in 1941. Since then, he has lived intermittently in both countries and is the author of six volumes of writings. *Scent of Apples* is the first collection of his work to appear in the United States.

Jane Singh is professor of South Asian studies at the University of California at Berkeley.

Paul Spickard is professor of history at the University of California at Santa Barbara. He is the author of *Mixed Blood: Intermarriage and Ethnic Identity in Twentieth-Century America.*

Sui Sin Far is the pen name of Edith Maude Eaton, born in Macclesfield, England, in 1865 to a Chinese missionary worker and the son of English silk traders. She and her family moved to the United States when she was very young and then to

Montreal, where she spent the bulk of her life. In her early thirties, she traveled to Jamaica for a year to work as a reporter, then moved on to Seattle, San Francisco, and Boston, before passing away in Montreal in 1914. She wrote newspapers articles, short stories, and autobiographical essays, and is the author of *Mrs. Spring Fragrance*, now a widely recognized cornerstone of Asian American literature.

Dana Y. Takagi is associate professor of sociology at the University of California at Santa Cruz and is the author of *The Retreat from Race: Asian American Admissions and Racial Politics*.

Ronald Takaki is professor of ethnic studies at the University of California at Berkeley. He is the author of *Pau Hana, Iron Cages: Race and Culture in Nineteenth-Century America, Strangers from a Different Shore: A History of Asian Americans, Hiroshima: Why America Dropped the Bomb*, and *A Different Mirror: A Multicultural History of America*.

Jinhua Emma Teng is assistant professor of Chinese, history, and women's studies at the Massachusetts Institute of Technology. She is the author of numerous articles on Asian American literature, history, and culture, as well as essays on Chinese literature.

Linda Trinh Võ is assistant professor of sociology at Washington State University in Pullman, Washington.

Leti Volpp is assistant professor of law at Washington School of Law, American University, and author of numerous articles on immigration, cultural defense cases, and garment workers' rights.

Howard Winant is professor of sociology at Temple University. He is coauthor, with Michael Omi, of *Racial Formations in the United States*, and author of *Racial Conditions*.

K. Scott Wong is associate professor of history at Williams College. He has published several articles on Asian American history, and has coedited *Claiming America: Constructing Chinese American Identities during the Exclusion Era*.

Hisaye Yamamoto was born in 1921 in Redondo Beach, California. From 1942 to 1945, she and her family were interned in the concentration camp in Poston, Arizona. She has been writing for publication since she was fourteen and is the author of *Seventeen Syllables and Other Stories*.

Copyrights and Permissions

Index

About the Editors

Jean Yu-wen Shen Wu is senior lecturer in the American Studies Program at Tufts University. She teaches race studies and Asian American studies.

Min Song is assistant professor of Asian American literature at Boston College. He is the author of several essays on issues related to ethnic studies, and is currently at work on a book about representations of the Chinese in American realism.